HISTORY OF VATICAN II

HISTORY OF VATICAN II

General Editor

GIUSEPPE ALBERIGO
Istituto per le Scienze Religiose, Bologna

Editorial Board

History of Vatican II

Vol. III
The Mature Council
Second Period and Intersession
September 1963 - September 1964

edited by
Giuseppe Alberigo

English version edited by
Joseph A. Komonchak

2000

ORBIS | PEETERS
Maryknoll | Leuven

Acknowledgment:

The Menil Foundation, Houston TX
The Rothko Chapel, Houston TX

Library of Congress Cataloging-in-Publication Data

A record for this book is available from the Library of Congress

ISBN 1-57075-153-6

CIP Royal Library Albert I, Brussels

History of Vatican II. — Vol. III
edited by G. Alberigo and J.A. Komonchak. — Leuven: Peeters, 2000

No part of this book may be used or reproduced
in any form by print, photo print, microfilm or any other means
without written permission from the publisher.

ISBN 90-429-0848-3 (PEETERS)
ISBN 1-57075-153-6 (ORBIS)
D 2000/0602/53

ORBIS BOOKS
PO Box 308
Maryknoll, NY 10545-0308

© PEETERS
Bondgenotenlaan 153
B-3000 Leuven
BELGIUM

TABLE OF CONTENTS

II. BISHOPS AND DIOCESES AND THE COMMUNICATIONS MEDIA (NOVEMBER 5-25, 1963) [JOSEPH FAMERÉE]

PREFACE

With this third volume the *History of Vatican II* moves beyond the half-way mark of a journey begun ten years ago. It describes how, beginning with the last months of the summer of 1963 and on through its second period of work, Vatican II unfolded under the pontificate of Paul VI, who was both a son and a father of the Council. (Unfortunately, despite all efforts, it has not been possible to gain access to Pope Montini's personal documents on the Council, except in a fragmentary degree, unlike what the project was granted for the comparable documents on Pope Roncalli.)

The international team for the *History of Vatican II* project has continued and intensified its commitment to providing an adequate knowledge of the composition of a collective phenomenon of quite unusual proportions. As in the preceding volume on the first period of the Council, it has been thought proper above all to sort out the experience of the assembly by closely following its daily unfolding, even in its undeniable meandering, rather than to attempt a thematic reconstruction, which, while more straightforward, would also be less respectful of the concrete reality of the event.

For this volume, too, we have continued a broad and fruitful international scholarly collaboration both during the preparatory research and discussions of the subject (Colloquies of Moscow and São Paulo in 1995, Québec and Bologna in 1996) and in the construction of the narrative, for which we regret that no English-language collaborator was available. The contributors to this volume have gathered at special meetings to deepen their understanding of the critical points of the second conciliar period and the subsequent intersession. The differences in the viewpoints of the contributors have been respected, since they constitute one of the values of a work in which we have committed ourselves to the ambitious project of a work by several hands that provides a continuous and organized reconstruction and not simply a collection of essays.

We have continued to acquire unpublished documents on the course of the Council from many participants (fathers, experts, and observers); this documentation has been brought together and classified at the Istituto per le scienze religiose in Bologna. At the same time, inventories have been published of the various collections of documents (Leuven, Louvain-la-Neuve, Montréal, Notre Dame (U.S.A.), Paris, and others), while Msgr. V. Carbone's gigantic undertaking of editing the official sources on the work of the general congregations and on the functioning of the Council's directive bodies is being completed.

By making use of these new sources we have been able to move beyond a mere chronicle and to provide a hitherto impossible multidimensional understanding of the Council that takes into account the many levels of the event itself: the general congregations, the commissions, the informal groups, the effect on and also of public opinion. Only in this way has it been possible to follow developments at the Council step by step, to weigh the influences that determined its course, and to take into account the great importance of the work done during the ten-month suspension of the intersession. We have come to realize that the "invisible council" going on in the pauses between the assembly's periods of work had an importance too often unrecognized or underestimated. In this respect Vatican II differed from both Vatican I, which did not have any such pauses, and Trent, whose work was completely suspended during its lengthy interruptions.

In addition, our knowledge of the Council's work has been considerably enriched, above all in regard to some critical moments that till now were known only as elements of a chronicle. Thus, only now has the development of the complicated and tortuous preparation for the straw votes on the schema on the Church taken on October 30, 1963, been reconstructed in a critically satisfactory way and in all its phases and dimensions. The same is to be said of the so-called Döpfner Plan to reduce the number of subjects that the Council was to treat so that it might end with the third period of 1964. It has been possible to throw light on the origin and various versions of this plan and on its gradual fading as the result of a complex strategic skirmish. New light has also been thrown on the attitude of Paul VI to Vatican II, especially as regards his inspiration of the plan put forward by Cardinal Döpfner and the modifications he suggested during the intersession for the chapter on episcopal collegiality in the schema on the Church.

During the preparation of this volume two of the leaders at Vatican II have died, Cardinal Léon-Joseph Suenens and Professor Don Giuseppe Dossetti, both of whom had a lively interest in this *History* and repeatedly assisted it. We take this occasion to express publicly our deep gratitude to them, not only for the exceptional contribution they made to the Council but for the witness of their fidelity to its teaching.

The successive chapters were written by Alberto Melloni, Rome-Bologna; Joseph Famerée, Louvain-la-Neuve; Reiner Kaczynski, Munich; Claude Soetens, Louvain-la-Neuve; Evangelista Vilanova, Montserrat; and G. Alberigo, who also supervised the overall coordination of the work.

The work is being published in six parallel editions: Italian, ed. A. Melloni (Il Mulino, Bologna); English, ed. J. A. Komonchak (Peeters, Leuven, and Orbis Books, Maryknoll, New York); Portuguese, ed. O. Beozzo (Vózes, Petrépolis); German, ed. K. Wittstadt (Grünewald, Mainz); French, ed. E. Fouilloux (Cerf, Paris); Spanish, ed. E. Vilanova (Sígueme, Salamanca). Peeters of Leuven is coordinating all the editions. The reception given the work by the press and scholarly periodicals in the various cultural and linguistic areas has thus far been very cordial and encouraging.

As in the case of the preceding volume, the Rothko Chapel and the Menil Foundation of Houston, Texas, have contributed generously to the costs of research.

Giuseppe Alberigo   Bologna, October 11, 1997

For this English edition I must also express gratitude not only to the translator, Matthew J. O'Connell, but also to William R. Burrows, managing editor of Orbis Books, and to Joan Laflamme and Patrick Hayes, who provided invaluable editorial assistance.

Joseph A. Komonchak   Washington, D.C., November 14, 1999

ABBREVIATIONS

AAS	*Acta Apostolicae Sedis*, Vatican City
ACO	Archives du Conseil Oecuménique des Eglises, Geneva
ACUA	Archives of the Catholic University of America, Washington, D.C.
ADA	*Acta et Documenta Concilio oecumenico Vaticano II apparando: Series prima (antepraeparatoria)*. Typis Polyglottis Vaticanis, 1960-1961.
ADP	*Acta et Documenta Concilio oecumenico Vaticano II apparando: Series secunda (praeparatoria)*. Typis Polyglottis Vaticanis, 1964-1995.
Agende	A.G. Roncalli. *Agende 1936-1963*, unpublished
AS	*Acta Synodalia Sacrosancti Concilii Vaticani II*. Typis Polyglottis Vaticanis, 1970-
Attese	*Il Vaticano II fra attese e celebrazione*, ed. G. Alberigo. Bologna 1995.
AV2	Archives of the Second Vatican Council, Vatican City
Beitrag	*Der Beitrag der deutschsprachigen und osteuropäischen Länder zum zweiten Vatikanischen Konzil*, ed. K. Wittstadt and W. Verschooten. Leuven 1996
Belgique	*Vatican II et la Belgique*, ed. Claude Soetens. Ottignies, 1996
BPR	Biblioteca de Pesquisa Religiosa CSSR, São Paolo do Brasil
Caprile	G. Caprile, *Il Concilio Vaticano*, 4 vols. Rome, 1966-68
CCV	Centrum voor Concilestudie Vaticanum II, Faculteit der Godgeleerdheid. Katholieke Universiteit te Leuven.
CivCatt	*La Civiltà Cattolica*, Rome
CLG	Centre "Lumen Gentium" de Théologie, Université Catholique de Louvain. Louvain-La-Neuve
CNPL	Centre National de Pastoral Liturgique, Paris

COD	*Conciliorum Oecumenicorum Decreta*, ed. Istituto per le Scienze Religiose. Bologna, 1973
Commentary	*Commentary on the Documents of Vatican II*, ed. H. Vorgrimler, 5 vols. New York 1968
Commissions	*Les commissions conciliaires à Vatican II*, ed. M. Lamberigts *et al.*. Leuven, 1996
CrSt	*Cristianesimo nella Storia*, Bologna
DBetti	Diary of U. Betti, published in *La "Dei verbum" trent'anni dopo: Miscellanea in onore di Padre Umberto Betti, o.f.m.*, ed. N. Ciola (Rome 1995) 299-373
DC	*Documentation Catholique*, Paris
DChenu	M.-D. Chenu, *Notes quotidiennes au Concile: Journal de Vatican II*, ed. A. Melloni (Paris 1995)
DDevoto	Diary of Alberto Devoto
Deuxième	*Le deuxième Concile du Vatican (1959-1965)*. Rome 1989
DFenton	Diary of Joseph Clifford Fenton, Washington
DFlorit	Diary of E. Florit, Bologna
"Dinamiche"	G. Alberigo, "Dinamiche e procedure nel Vaticano II: Verso la revisione del Regolamento del Concilio (1962-1963), in *Cristianesimo nella Storia* 13 (1992) 115-164
DMC	*Discorsi Messaggi Colloqui del S. Padre Giovanni XXIII*, 6 vols. Vatican City 1960-67
DNAlberigo	Diary of Angelina Nicora Alberigo, ISR, Bologna
DOlivier	Diary of Bernard Olivier, partially published in *Vatican II et la Belgique*, ed. C. Soetens (Louvain-la Neuve 1996) 197-209
DOttaviani	Diary of A. Ottaviani, edited in E. Cavaterra, *Il prefetto del S. Offizio. Le opere e i giorni del card. Ottaviani*. Milano 1990.
DSiri	Diary of G. Siri, edited in B. Lai, *Il papa non eletto. G. Siri cardinal di S. Romana Chiesa*. Rome/Bari 1993, pp. 301-403
DTucci	Diary of R. Tucci, Rome
DUrbani	Diary of G. Urbani, Venice
DZazpe	Diary of V. Zazpe
Evento	*L'evento et le decisioni: Studi sulle dinamiche del concilio Vaticano II*, ed. M.T. Fattori and

	A. Melloni. Bologna, 1997
Experience	*Experience, Organizations and Bodies at Vatican II*. Leuven, 1999
History	*History of Vatican II*. Vols. I and II. Leuven/Maryknoll, 1995, 1997
HK	*Herder Korrespondenz*
Horton	*Vatican Diary*
ICI	*Informations Catholiques Internationales*. Paris
Igreia	*A Igreia latino-americana às vésperas do concilio. História do Concilio Ecumênico Vaticano I*, ed. J.O. Beozzo. São Paolo 1993
Indelicato	A. Indelicato, *Difendere la dottrina o annunciare l'evangelo. Il dibattito nella Commissione centrale preparatoria del Vaticano II*. Genoa 1992
Insegnamenti	*Insegnamenti di Paolo VI*. 16 volumes. Vatican City, 1964-1978
ISR	Istituto per le Scienze Religiose di Bologna
JCongar	Journal of Y.M.-J. Congar, Paris
JDupont	Journal of J. Dupont, Louvain-La-Neuve
JEdelby	Journal of N. Edelby, Aleppo, published as *Il Vaticano II nel diario di un vescovo arabo*, ed. R. Cannelli. Cinisello Balsamo, 1996
JLabourdette	Journal of M.M. Labourdette, Toulouse
JPrignon	Journal of A. Prignon, CLG, Louvain-la-Neuve
JS	Pope John XXIII, *Journal of a Soul*, revised edition. London, 1980.
Laurentin	R. Laurentin, *L'enjeu du Concile: Belan de la deuxième session 29 septembre-4 dicembre 1963*. Paris, 1964
Lettere	G. Lercaro, *Lettere dal Concilio, 1962-1965*. Bologna, 1980
Mansi	*Sacrorum Conciliorum amplissima collectio*. 32 vols.
NChenu	M.-D. Chenu, *Notes quotidiennes au Concile*, ed. A. Melloni. Paris, 1995
OssRom	*L'Osservatore Romano*, Rome
Primauté	*Primauté et collegialité: Le dossier de Gérard Philips sur la Nota Explicativa Praevia (Lumen gentium cap. III)*, ed. J. Grootaers. Leuven, 1986
"Procedure"	A. Melloni, "Procedure e coscienza conciliare al

	Vaticano II: I voti del 30 ottobre 1963," in *Cristianesimo nella Storia: Saggi in onore di Giuseppe Alberigo*, ed. A. Melloni et al. (Bologna, 1996) 313-96
Protagonisti	J. Grootaers, *I protagonisti del Vaticano II*. Cinisello Balsamo, 1994
RT	S. Tromp, [Relationes secretarii commissionis conciliaris] De doctrina fidei et morum. Typescript in fourteen fascicles
Rynne	X. Rynne, *The Second Session*. New York, 1964
S. Paulo	*O Concilio vaticano II: as contribuições das Conferências Episcopais latino- americanos e caribenhas às quatro sessões (1962-1965) e momentos decisivos da III sessão do Concilio*, volume 3 of *Cristianismo na America Latina: História, Debates, Perspectivas*. Petropolis 1996
TJungmann	Diary of J. Jungmann, Institut für Liturgiewissenschaft, University of Innsbruck
TSemmelroth	Diary of O. Semmelroth, Frankfurt am Main
Vatican II commence	*Vatican II commence... Approches francophones*, ed. E. Fouilloux. Leuven, 1993
Vatican II Revisited	*Vatican II Revisited By Those Who Were There*, ed. A. Stacpoole. Minneapolis 1985
VCND	Vatican II Collection. Theodore M. Hesburgh Library. University of Notre Dame, Notre Dame.
Vatican II à Moscou	*Vatican II à Moscou. Actes du colloque de Moscou, 1995*. Moscwa-Leuven, 1996
Veille	*À la veille du Concile Vatican II. Vota et réactions en Europe et dans le Catholicisme oriental*, ed. M. Lamberigts and C. Soetens. Leuven, 1992
Verso il Concilio	*Verso il concilio Vaticano II (1960-1962). Passaggi e problemi della preparazione conciliare*, ed. G. Alberigo and A. Melloni. Genoa, 1993
Vìsperas	*Cristianismo e iglesias de América Latina en vìsperas del Vaticano II*, ed. J. O. Beozzo. Costa Rica 1992
Wenger	A. Wenger, *Vatican II. Chronique de la deuxième session*. Paris, 1964
Wiltgen	R. Wiltgen, *The Rhine Flows into the Tiber: A History of Vatican II*. New York, 1967

SOURCES AND ARCHIVES

In the course of research on the history of Vatican II, access has been requested and granted to many private collections of people who participated in the Council in various ways. These papers integrate and complete the documents of the Archives of Vatican II which, under the careful direction of Msgr. Vincenzo Carbone, Pope Paul VI wished to remain distinct from the secret Vatican Archives and to be open to scholars. Systematic use of such collections has been made in numerous studies, in monographs, and in the colloquia which have prepared and complete these volumes of the *History of Vatican II*. Three recent analytical reviews of these publications have been published: Joseph Famerée, "Vers une histoire du Concile Vatican II," *Revue d'Histoire Ecclésiastique* 89 (1994) 638- 41; A. Greiler, "Ein internationales Forschungsprojekt zur Geschichte des Zweitens Vatikanums," in *Zeugnis und Dialog: Die katholische Kirche in der neuzeitlichen Welt und das II. Vatikanische Konzil. Klaus Wittstadt zum 60. Geburstag*, ed. W. Weiss (Würzburg 1996), 571-78; and G. Routhier, "Recherches et publications récentes autour de Vatican II," *Laval Théologique et Philosophique* 53 (1997) 435-54.

The authors of this volume have made use of documents (original or copied) collected in the archives of various research-centers: Istituto per le Scienze Religiose di Bologna; Biblioteca de Pesquisa Religiosa CSSR, São Paolo do Brasil; Centre "Lumen Gentium" de Théologie, Université Catholique de Louvain, Louvain-la-Neuve; Centruum voor Concilestudie Vaticanum II, Faculteit der Godgeleerdheid, Katholieke Universiteit Leuven; Vatican II Collection, Archives of the Catholic University of America, Washington, D.C.; Vatican II Collection, Theodore M. Hesburgh Library at the University of Notre Dame, Indiana.

In addition, many dioceses, libraries, religious houses, and families have given access, under various restrictions, to particularly valuable documentation: the Archdioceses of Chicago, Florence, Mainz, New York, and Paris; the Archives of the Jesuit Province of France, Vanves; the Berchmanskolleg, Munich; Bibliothèque du Saulchoir, Paris; Civiltà Cattolica, Rome; Couvent St. Jacques, Paris; Domarchiv, Cologne; Institut Catholique, Paris; Institut für

Liturgiewissenschaft, Innsbruck; Pontificio Collegio Angelicum, Rome; Pontificium Consilium pro Laicis, Rome; Sankt Georgen Haus, Frankfurt a.M.

Many diaries have also been made available; on their use see A. Melloni, "I diari nella storia dei concili," in M.-D. Chenu, *Note quotidiane al Concilio: Diario del Vaticano II, 1962-1963* (Bologna 1996). Other diaries of conciliar fathers and experts consulted are those of: J.C. Fenton, Washington; E. Florit, Florence; G. Siri, edited in B. Lai, *Il papa non eletto: Giuseppe Siri cardinale di Santa Romana Chiesa* (Rome-Bari, 1993); R. Tucci, Rome; Y.M.-J. Congar, Paris; M.M. Labourdette, Toulouse; J. Jungmann, Innsbruck; N. Edelby, edited in Italian translation in N. Edelby, *Il Vaticano II nel diario di un vescovo arabo*, ed. R. Cannelli (Cinisello B., 1996).

A list of the location of sources cited may be found in the appendix to *Verso il Concilio Vaticano II: Passaggi e problemi della preparazione conciliare*, ed. G. Alberigo and A. Melloni (Bologna, 1993). An updated list, prepared by G. Turbanti, now available for scholars to consult at the Istituto per le Scienze Religiose in Bologna, is being prepared for publication.

CHAPTER I

THE BEGINNING OF THE SECOND PERIOD: THE GREAT DEBATE ON THE CHURCH

ALBERTO MELLONI

I. TOWARD A NEW BEGINNING WITH A NEW POPE

What did Paul VI expect of the Council? What did he hope or fear? How far and in what direction would the great assembly go, which his predecessor had finally succeeded in starting? These questions formed the background against which advance indicators of the second conciliar period sorted themselves out during the summer of 1963. Events since the death of John XXIII basically had taken the expected course.

Neither those disappointed nor those enthusiastic had any reason to be surprised by the election to the papacy of the Archbishop of Milan, Giovanni Battista Montini, at the June conclave. Roncalli's dependence on this former assistant in the Secretariat of State, who had been "in exile" in Milan, had given him the role of the *papabile* par excellence, a role for which he had already seemed destined in the waning days of Pius XII's pontificate. In addition to giving him the purple without delay and thus admitting him to the next conclave, John XXIII had offered the Cardinal of Milan various signs of esteem (a residence in the Vatican during the work of the Council; presiding at the liturgy on November 4, 1962), which, given the atmosphere of the papal court, were interpreted as a kind of nomination.

Nor was there anything surprising about the statements in which the newly elected Paul VI showed his profound veneration for Roncalli's magisterium by announcing his intention to continue the Council. Despite all the limitations put on the Council by the nature of the preparation, by the pressure that the quarrelsome Roman schools exerted on the commissions and their theologians, and by the unnatural supremacy of a Doctrinal Commission that was a faithful mirror of the organizational chart of the Curia, John XXIII's decision to go ahead with the Council had imposed the hopes, insights, and expectations of the episcopate upon the college of cardinals. Those who wanted a break with the Roncallian past had the opportunity to make their voices heard during the nine days' mourning, in the sermons on electing a pope, and in the press.[1] But if these meant anything, it was simply that there were some in the Roman Curia who feared the "return" of Montini in the guise of an avenging continuator. To those who observed this papal transition with a minimum of detachment and experience, for example, the diplomats accredited to the Holy See, it was obvious that there was no possibility of a cardinal being able to win the votes of fifty-eight cardinals who would at the same time announce to 2,500 bishops that Vatican II would not be continued. In addresses given before the opening of the Council Montini had stated that he agreed with Roncalli's choices and with his Council, and this enabled him to withstand the distrust of some politicians[2] and to win the support of the embryonic majority that had emerged during the first period of Vatican II.[3] It was therefore somewhat

[1] See the report on the conclave and on Montini's chances by James W. Spain, the former United States ambassador to Pakistan, May 13, 1963 (Central Intelligence Agency, n. 27-63). P. Hebblethwaite relies too much on this report in his *John XXIII, Pope of the Council* (London, 1984), 491-95; see my remarks in "Pope John XXIII: Open Questions for a Biography," *Catholic Historical Review* 72 (1986), 51-67.

[2] This was true, for example, of German Chancellor Adenauer, who thought of urging the candidacy of Cardinal Testa as a way of limiting the damage John XXIII had already done to relations with the communist world, which, in Adenauer's judgment, would be worsened by the election of Montini. The chancellor said as much to French ambassador Margerie at a luncheon on May 27, 1963; see the secret telegram sent by Margerie from Bonn to Paris on May 28, 1963, n. 3786/88, QO, EU-30/24. Adenauer did not assess the chances of Bea, whose candidacy, regarded as "highly improbable" by the French, might unite those who "wanted a conclusion to the Council that would be entirely in harmony with the wishes of the majority;" see QO, EU-30/24, telegram from Ambassador La Tournelle N. 169-77, Rome, June 2, 1963. The chancellor, who clearly had been disconcerted by *Pacem in terris*, feared that a Montini pontificate would carry still further the tendencies of the pontificate of John XXIII, tendencies "dangerous both for the West and the future of Christendom;" see QO, EU-30/24, telegram from Ambassador Margerie, n. 101-3, Bonn, May 27, 1963. The same was true of the president of the Italian Republic, who, through Luigi Gedda, made known the opposition of the Christian Democratic right to the election of a man regarded as too much in agreement with the attempts of the secretariat of the Christian Democratic Party to establish a stable majority of the center-left; see QO, EU-30/24, telegram of Ambassador La Tournelle, 207-8, Rome, June 17, 1963: "The President of the Republic has had M. Gedda make a series of interventions with the Italian cardinals and some cardinals from abroad. The former president of Catholic Action told these prelates of M. Segni's fear that if Cardinal Montini emerged victorious from the conclave, he would commit the Church to the opening to the left."

[3] Vain attempts were made that were connected with or reflected the hostility to Montini's candidacy on the part of many Italians and/or members of the Curia. The French tried to gauge this hostility at a meeting in the embassy on June 12. According to the French embassy to the Holy See, the choice would be between two candidates, Siri and Montini, with secondary candidates on both sides: Antoniutti or Marella, on the one hand, Urbani on the other. According to the ambassador, the French cardinals had unanimous and complete confidence in Montini, see ET-30/24, telegram of ambassador La Tournelle, n. 201-4, Rome, June 13, 1963.

ironic that the Italian cardinals, inside and outside the Curia, who were opposed to Montini's candidacy and were looking for a suitable countermove, should threaten that, if they had no other alternative, they would vote for Giacomo Lercaro, who, in the debate on the *De ecclesia* in December 1962, had taken a stronger and more innovative position than that defended by Montini!

Some readings of the conclave claim that in the Sistine Chapel Cardinal Frings kept any opposition between Lercaro and Montini from benefiting wedge moderates such as Antoniutti.[4] The fact is, however, that the majority which emerged in the fourth and fifth balloting wanted Vatican II to continue.[5] La Tournelle, the French ambassador, was able to say truthfully, "The Council has made the conclave."[6] But what kind of council would the pope who emerged from the conclave hold?

A. THE FIRST STEPS OF PAUL VI

As early as the rite of "obedience" of the cardinals to the newly elected pope, Paul VI gave concrete form to his commitment by announcing that the Council would continue.[7] But in these very first hours Paul VI had already made the two choices that were essential for his role in the control of the Council. He confirmed as Secretary of State Amleto Cicognani, who as president of the Coordinating Commission (CC) had assumed a supremacy that the Regulations of the Council in

---

[4] An informal but explicit agreement was reached between the cardinals and whoever would be elected — and, to some extent, between Lercaro and Montini — on the continuation of Vatican II (and on defending the *aggiornamento*); on this see Lercaro, *Lettere*, 37. In *Epoca*, in the days after the election, Agasso accepted the hypothesis of a Spellman-Montini meeting that gave the votes of the conservatives to the Cardinal of Milan.

[5] The pope-elect, too, bet his election on the scenario of a continued Council and the directions it had begun to take, if the rumor is true that after Montini had received fifty-three votes in the fourth balloting, a fifth vote (somewhat comparable to the *accessus* of antiquity) was taken that was meant to strengthen a majority and a program that had more to do with a desire for unanimity in the Council than with the electoral procedures of the conclave.

[6] QO, EU-30/24, coded telegram of Ambassador La Tournelle, n. 231-34, Rome, June 24, 1963.

[7] *Insegnamenti* (1963), 1:4: "The continuation of the Second Ecumenical Vatican Council claims priority among the tasks of the pope." During the greetings he told the bishops that he promised to embrace them "during another session of the ecumenical council" (ibid., 7). Nothing was said about the date for the continuation. but some, Giuseppe Dossetti, for example, were being at least unrealistic when, a few weeks later, they hoped that the intersession might be extended for some months to make possible a meditative reading of the schemas; see Alberigo, "Dinamiche," 139.

1962 had not been intended to give him; and the pope told Cardinal Suenens of his desire to appoint one or possibly more legates to the Council.[8] These were the two levers with which — admittedly along with various contributions and important shifts of balance — Paul VI was to act
in the course of the Council, never defining their reciprocal relations and
always reserving to himself the balance between them.

No source available today tells us whether the pope understood the
consequences of this early choice to give free rein to competition
between one person (the Secretary of State), who mediated the will of
the pope for the work of the assembly but did so as an instrument of the
Curia, and others (the delegates/moderators) who, for their part, received
from Paul VI himself the duty of representing the hall to him and of
directing its debates. Nothing in any case was made public about the balance between those two, or about the content,[9] plans, and schedule for
the work.[10] Subtle attempts to probe the papal intentions, like those of
the Belgian ambassador at the reception for the diplomatic corps,
received in answer a polite silence.[11]

[8] Testimony of Suenens, given first in *HK* 34 (1980), 176, then repeated in *Giovanni
Battista Montini Arcivescovo di Milano e il Concilio Ecumenico Vaticano II.
Preparazione et primo periodo* (Brescia, 1985), 186, and finally, with some variants, in
his *Souvenirs et espérances* (Paris, 1991), 110.

[9] The date for the convocation of the opening public session of a second conciliar
period was initially planned for the middle of September but then was put back two
weeks. Now that the date was certain, it provided the framework for a series of addresses
in which Paul VI made public his thinking about the Council. Nothing was said about the
Council at the meeting with the Roman clergy on June 24, and even in response to the
greeting of the diplomatic corps (which had suggested to the pope that "the Council was
the cradle of his election in the bosom of the conclave"), Paul VI gave no information
about the Council. On the other hand, at his meeting with the journalists on June 29, he
did devote a lengthy paragraph to "the proximate resumption of the ecumenical Council"
and promised to improve services for information and interpretation of the event; *Insegnamenti* (1963), 1:46.

[10] In his address at his coronation, June 30, in which the pope formally repeated that
"we shall resume the celebration of the Council," there is a singular citation from the
preparatory schema on the Church regarding the role of the successor of Peter ("having
been raised to the *top of the hierarchical ladder of powers at work in the militant Church*,
we regard ourselves as at the same time put in the lowest office as servant of the servants
of God," *Insegnamenti* [1963], 1:26), and there is also a resolve ("We shall defend Holy
Church from errors in doctrine and morals") that could have been found in the schema on
the deposit of faith that had been removed from the conciliar agenda.

[11] See *OssRom*; the greeting was read by Ferdinand Poswick, ambassador from Belgium and dean of the diplomatic corps, and a person well known to both John XXIII and
Paul VI; it would be his responsibility to take back the Message to the Governments at
the end of the Council.

But even the several cardinals to whom the pope listened in order to get information or suggestions remained ignorant of the limits, the possibilities, the framework within which the pope would use their proposals.[12] Thus the pope asked Cardinal Döpfner of Munich for a note on the possibility of reducing the schemas to be submitted to the Council;[13] he asked Cardinal Lercaro of Bologna and his Bolognese associates connected with Dossetti for suggestions on the expected modification of the Regulations; he asked Suenens, as has already been said, to be ready to play the part of a legate; he asked others (Guitton, Bevilacqua) to collaborate on the encyclical on the Church that he wanted to write and publish as the official announcement of his assumption of the Petrine office.[14] As for his requests concerning other aspects of his governmental action,[15] in areas in which the relationship between pope and Council was most sensitive (both in itself and because of a concept of papal authority as "solitary" that was familiar to Paul VI and on which he composed an eloquent meditation in July 1963[16]), they also did not clarify what the pope wanted.[17]

[12] See Alberigo, "Dinamiche," for the variations in Dossetti's proposal and for contacts with Jedin.

[13] K. Wittstadt, "Vorschläge von Julius Kardinal Döpfner an Papst Paul VI: Zur Fortführung der Konzilsarbeiten (Juli 1963)," in *Julius Kardinal Döpfner 1913-1976*, ed. K. Wittstadt (Würzburg, 1996), 135-56.

[14] See G. Colombo, "Genesi, storia e significato dell'enciclica *Ecclesiam suam*," in *"Ecclesiam suam" première lettre encyclique de Paul VI. Colloque internationale (Rome, October 24-26, 1980,* 131-60 (Brescia, 1982), 136.

[15] References in the Léger Archive; Congar learned of a papal audience with Lebret, concerning which see G. Turbanti, *La chiesa nel mondo,* a doctoral dissertation mentored by G. Alberigo, University of Turin, 1996/97, p. 96. Indications in memoirs point to similar contacts with others (e.g., Suenens, Daniélou, Frings, Guitton, De Luca).

[16] On retreat the pope reflected on the meaning and dramatic character of his mission: "Like a statue on a pinnacle, so does a person in my position live... I must emphasize this loneliness; I must not be afraid, I must not look for external support that excuses me from my duty of willing, of deciding, of accepting every responsibility, of guiding others even if this seems illogical and perhaps absurd. And I must suffer alone. Consoling confidences can only be rare and discreet; the depths of my spirit must remain with me. I and God"; note transcribed by P. Macchi, "Commemorazione di Paolo VI," *Istituto Paolo VI — Notiziario* (1979), no. 1, p. 53. In these spiritual meditations, so clear in their understanding of the meaning of the Petrine function, the Council for practical purposes does not exist and, in any case, does not condition the sketch of the papacy. It is as if Paul VI — despite being the man who had "studied being pope" at great length — was unable to visualize the difficulty already experienced by John XXIII during the first period, that is, of finding a balance in his relationship with a free and sitting Council. In January 1963 Pope Roncalli reproached himself for having remained overly passive during the debates in the Council and seemed to criticize himself for his behavior during the work, in which he had "responded," point by point, to requests from the hall, but had never anticipated them. See A. Melloni, "Giovanni XXIII e l'avvio del Vaticano II,"

Did Paul VI want to speed up the work? The request made to Döpfner suggests as much. The need to lighten the conciliar agenda had been strongly felt for a year. After the "pruning" done first by the Central Preparatory Commission (CPC) and then by the Secretariat for Extraordinary Affairs, which had reduced the schemas to twenty,[18] the CC provided only for minor consolidations that reduced the total number of schemas on the agenda to seventeen, obviously still too many for a council that hoped to finish its work in three (if not two) periods of work. Who, then, was to reorganize the agenda? The Council itself? Or, instead, its organs and, first and foremost, its natural president, the pope? The request that Döpfner, who both in the CPC and in the CC had been rather eloquent on the need to reduce the number of schemas, draw up a "plan" for reduction presupposed the idea of a council whose petitions were to be accepted and rendered operative by papal authority.

Did Paul VI want to give the assembly the ability to express itself by breaking from the tutelage exercised by the curially controlled commissions that John XXIII had left him as a heritage?[19] This seems to be the significance of the degree of openness shown to Lercaro and then to Dossetti, who for some months had been advocating such a move. Dossetti had maintained that the set of rules designed for a council that was expected to approve the prepared schemas by acclamation was inadequate to the completely different situation that had arisen since the beginning of Vatican II.[20] The goal that Dossetti set for himself — to give the assembly effective and functioning tools for self-government — interested Paul VI, who was, however, also being pressed by a different demand from within the Roman Curia.[21]

---

in *Vatican II commence*, 75-104. Six months later and in the middle of his novitiate as pope, Pope Montini had no direct experience against which to measure himself.

[17] This remained a question for not a few bishops even after the beginning of the second period, at least until October 30, 1963; see (*History*, 2:9-10, and A. Melloni, "Procedure e coscienza conciliare al Vaticano II: I voti del 30 ottobre 1963," in *Cristianesimo nella Storia: Saggi in onore di Giuseppe Alberigo*, ed. A. Melloni et al. (Bologna, 1996) 313-96 (hereafter cited as Melloni, "Procedure").

[18] *History*, 1:339-50.

[19] G. Alberigo, "La preparazione del regolamento del Concilio Vaticano II," in *Vatican II commence*, 54-74.

[20] See the explanation in *NChenu*, October 11, 1962.

[21] Montini knew Dossetti's past, especially as a member of the constituent assembly of the Christian Democratic Party and its political leader before he decided to abandon Roman political life in order to establish a study center and a monastic community in Bologna, the diocese in which he had been a priest since 1959. See A. Melloni, "Un discepolo nella storia. Per gli studi su Giuseppe Dossetti," *Rivista di storia della chiesa in Italia* 51 (1997) (in press).

As for the new CC, established in January 1963 as a body linking the Secretariat of State and the Council, did Paul VI want it to continue the coordinating functions that it had been exercising in a by-no-means-regrettable manner?[22]

Did the pope want to set limits to the subject matter of the debates? The fact that he was hastening to make notes for an encyclical was not known to the public in the summer of 1963, but it is interesting that the preliminary collection for what would be the encyclical *Ecclesiam suam*, published on the Feast of the Transfiguration, 1964, contained forty-five pages on dialogue, twenty-two on the self-awareness of the Church, and four on the subject of "reform or renewal."[23] The plan to publish a programmatic encyclical on the Church that would forestall the mature discussion by the Council of the utterly crucial subject of the Church suggests that at least some circles especially close to the pope could suppose in him a prior readiness to limit the Council's agenda.[24]

B. THE COUNCIL APPROACHES: PREPARATIONS, INVITATIONS, LETTERS

Uncertainties *about* the pope? Uncertainties *of* the pope? In any case, a surprising degree of disorder marked the close of the second preparation for the Council, which had been under way between the end of winter and the beginning of spring 1963.

1. The Regulations for the Council (Ordo Concilii)

In regard to these Regulations everything is said when we know that the revision, which the CC had been discussing from January to its meeting of July 3-4 inclusive, was a subject that Paul VI reserved to himself.[25] Carlo Colombo informed Dossetti of this so that the latter, by

---

[22] Alberigo, "Dinamiche." See *JOlivier* (in *Evento*, 337 and 353) on the problem of the pope's "dissatisfaction," and Felici's general report, July 20, in *AS* VI/2, 212-18.

[23] Colombo, "Genesi," 136.

[24] John XXIII had already done the same in two different circumstances. In February 1962 he signed the Apostolic Constitution *Veterum sapientia* on Latin in the Church (see A. Melloni, "Tensioni e timori nella preparazione del Vatican II: La *Veterum sapientia* di Giovanni XXIII (22 febbraio 1962)," *CrSt* 11 [1990], 275-307) and on Easter 1963, in his encyclical *Pacem in terris*, he adopted a series of positions on problems of the modern world that objectively gave direction to the debate on drafting a new schema on relations between the Church and the world.

[25] Alberigo, "Dinamiche," 135. The letters of the Commission for the Regulations are in *ADP* II/4, 1.

way of Lercaro, might make suitable suggestions to the pope that would integrate those sent in a note of March which Paul VI had already seen.[26] But Dossetti, who for months had been trying to convey some of his ideas about freeing the commissions from their enslavement to the Holy Office, had been very cautious,[27] even entertaining the possibility of "not changing the *Ordo concilii* in any substantial way for the moment,"[28] in order not to have too troubled a second period and thereby prejudice the results to be obtained in the third period of the Council, which most thought would be the last one. The "possibility and opportuneness of appointing papal legates to the Council," for which he had argued in a previous memorandum,[29] remained bracketed until the middle of August.

Before Colombo brought Paul VI the new proposals for appointing a new body with legatine powers (August 16), Dossetti contacted Suenens, the primary candidate for this role. But on August 20 Felici was already convoking a meeting of the CC, with an extended membership,[30] for August 31. At this meeting Cicognani informed those present that the pope would soon appoint "a new body of three or four cardinals, chosen from the CC or from the council of presidents, that was to guide the discussion."[31]

It is odd that Cicognani introduced a short but lively discussion of the character of this body, which he wanted to be a subordinate voice of the CC itself, but which, according to Felici (who was better informed on the number of members), was to have the function of representing the

---

[26] The pope told Lercaro that these seemed to him "moderate and concrete"; see Alberigo, "Dinamiche," 136.

[27] When Lercaro was about to attend an audience on July 19, Dossetti urged a new prudence, suggesting that Lercaro "not take positions which, though fundamentally correct, were not in keeping, either in language or in form, with the pope's views, but that, at the same time, he be able to make the pope realize that behind an explanation that was for the moment very simple and reasonable there lie very substantial and long-meditated arguments which ought to be known and assessed before making decisions, however innovative;" ISR, Dossetti Archive, 107; see Alberigo, "Dinamiche," 135.

[28] Ibid., 137.

[29] Dossetti Archive, 570; see Alberigo, "Dinamiche," 136. The text maintains — and this was perhaps the weak point in the entire plan for revising the rules of the Council — that a body giving unified direction to the assembly could and ought to free the Council from the control of the Curia, and in particular of the Holy Office, which was mediated through the General Secretariat. Was it not realized, then, what a potential source of imbalance would be created by stabilizing the functions of the CC and its president, the Secretary of State?

[30] The appointment of moderators who were not already members of the CC (Lercaro and Agagianian) was officially dated August 21, 1963.

[31] *AS* V/1, 646-50.

pope.[32] The pope had chosen but had not decided, and the uncertainty about procedure lasted more than a week. Various drafts of the new *Ordo* were hammered out on September 3, 5, and 7. In the meantime, Lercaro sent Cicognani a note with three suggestions about the new body, calling for the appointment of legates or, secondarily, of vice-presidents, but advising against the creation of a college of "moderators" without "clearly defined functions and sufficient authority."[33] On September 9, the Secretary of State sent a letter to Agagianian,[34] Döpfner, Lercaro, and Suenens, informing them that the pope had appointed them "delegates or moderators of the Council, with the task of directing the meetings of the Council by executive mandate." The same formula would be used in the letter *Quod apostolici*, which the pope addressed to Cardinal Dean Tisserant on September 12 and in which he reviewed the innovations made with an eye to the opening of the second period.[35]

---

[32] Felici claimed that on August 29 he suggested to the pope the appointment of four "moderators" (V. Carbone, "L'azione direttiva di Paolo VI nei periodi II e III del Concilio Ecumenico Vaticano II," in *Paolo VI e i problemi ecclesiologici al Concilio* [Brescia, 1989] 60 and 64); there had also been thought of making Cardinal Dean E. Tisserant president of this body (Lercaro to Dossetti, October 3, 1963, Dossetti Archive, 548).

[33] *ADP* IV/1, 420-30; see Alberigo, "Dinamiche," 141-43.

[34] According to some, Agagianian was appointed in addition to the other three at the request of Cicognani; see Ph. Levillain, *La mécanique politique de Vatican II. La majorité et l'unanimité dans un Concile* (Paris, 1974), 309.

[35] The nominating formula, with its distinction between the direction of the work in the hall and the role of *tutor legis*, which was reserved to the Council of Presidents, is repeated in the letter *Quod apostolici*, dated September 12 and addressed to Tisserant. Paul VI says that he is "unequal" to the task left him by his predecessor and "prostrated" by "anxiety" about carrying out the work of the Council. The way he points out is that of simplifying and shortening decisions: "keep in mind, above all, the most general principles and leave aside questions of detail," everything being viewed in light of the principle of the Council's pastoral character. The pope therefore approved the list of seventeen schemas and announced six innovations: (1) a new press office, assigned to a bishop, Martin J. O'Connor; (2) admission to the council hall of some Catholic lay men and representatives of international organizations; (3) a renewed invitation to the observers, and the announcement of the establishment of a Secretariat for Non-Christians; (4) the abolition of the Secretariat for Extraordinary Affairs and the appointment to the Council of Presidents of members of that Secretariat who had not belonged to this Council before; (5) the election of "some cardinals as delegates or moderators," in accordance with the description in the letter sent to those already chosen; (6) the determination of breaks to be taken, and the announcement of four solemn celebrations to take place in St. Peter's (beatifications, consecration of missionary bishops, commemoration of John XXIII, and celebration of the fourth centenary of Trent); *AS* II/1, 9-13.

Was this to be the letter that would specify powers?[36] When Dossetti was summoned to an audience with the pope, he was brought up to date on the state of the work by Angelo Dell'Acqua. As late as September 21, Dossetti still had no assurances (not even the modest one of being appointed a peritus of the Council).[37] As for the college of moderators, Lercaro saw "difficulties" beginning with the very first meeting of the new group.[38] Dossetti, who "was supposed to be" the secretary of the four, was satisfied with the energy with which Suenens and Lercaro asserted the role of future legates that the pope had "promised" them in July.[39] Msgr. Prignon, rector of the Belgian College, learned from Suenens that the papal audience on September 25 had not eliminated possible interference by the Council of Presidents and the CC.[40] At the joint meeting of the Council of Presidents, the CC, and the moderators on September 26, tasks were distributed in a

[36] See *JPrignon* (A), October 30, 1963: "S. D. L. [Suenens, Döpfner, Lercaro] have drafted a text asserting their role in the ideological direction of the council....The cardinal tells me that this text reflects the views expressed by Paul VI at last week's audience....For myself, I told Cardinal Suenens that I found the text 'too strong' as it stands and giving too many powers to the moderators. They are falling back into what they want to avoid."

[37] Dossetti told Angelina Nicora Alberigo that the meeting "had been rather sibylline": after having received him unexpectedly, "he [the pope] did not invite him to the Council and showed himself dissatisfied with the term 'delegates' for the four cardinals. 'Whose delegates? The pope's? No!' He says that they must be like prompters in a box." At the meeting he was told that the typesetting had not been done in time to print the revised rules; Dossetti offered "to stay in Rome, but they were quick to tell him to return to Bologna. He went but would return to Rome during the Council"; see *DNAlberigo*, September 21, 1963.

[38] Lercaro, *Lettere*, 155, letter of September 25, 1963.

[39] In her "Diary of the last week of September," A. Nicora Alberigo notes that Dossetti "was called to Rome on Wednesday evening [September 25], at the same time as Suenens and our cardinal [Lercaro], as a result of independent initiatives. Meeting at the Belgian College, Thursday the 26th at 1.00 p.m." Dossetti found both men "very determined to carry out the role which the pope had explicitly promised them at the audience in July: he had told both that they would be made legates. Suenens said this in so many words," whereas Lercaro implied this when "still in July, he said that the Holy Spirit was at work." Döpfner is more cautious, and Suenens says Döpfner is practicing the virtue of prudence. Agagianian is completely outside what is going on; in fact the other three contemplate holding meetings of just the three of them at which they would decide what to do, and only then hold meetings of the four. Don Giuseppe [Dossetti] is supposed to be the secretary of the 'moderators,' if not 'the one to provide the inspirations.'" It was the moderators, according to *JPrignon*, who chose Dossetti as their "secretary" on September 26; Dossetti was not a conciliar expert and had had no entree to the hall.

[40] *JPrignon*, September 25, 1963: "After the audience of the four moderators with the Holy Father: an in-depth discussion of the role of these moderators. Ambiguity in relation to the presidency of the Council. The pope asked Card. Suenens to submit a report and suggestions."

way that made Frings, one of the presidents, say: "We have been retired."[41] But the question was not really closed.

The minutes of the very first meetings, which were kept by Dossetti,[42] show how the subject raised concerns and questions. On September 27, he notes, first, the problem raised for the "three" (Döpfner, Lercaro, and Suenens) by the "internal norms (text of the Holy Father)"; in a note of that same day for Lercaro alone, he maintains that the question should be raised of an "udienza di tabella" for the moderators and that a formula should be composed attributing to them the delegated powers necessary to run the assembly.[43] All the other proposals were comparatively secondary — to set up a group of experts specifically for the college of moderators (Lanne, Pannikar, Küng, and Colombo); to establish direct links with some major continental organizations of bishops; to engage with Siri's Italian Episcopal Conference; to circulate in L'Avvenire d'Italia some clarifications of points in theology; to define the dogmatic scope of the decrees.

When the Regulations, which resulted from interventions carried on without interruption for weeks, were distributed to the fathers on September 30, they caused some puzzlement, and Paul VI told Suenens that the text did not "completely" reflect his thinking.[44] The Bologna group, which more than any other had been pressing the procedural problems, was wavering between a general satisfaction with the system of regulations and a more considered concern about the relevance of the few suggestions that had been discarded. In fact, the revised Regulations now contained the norm for giving stability to the CC (by suppression of the

[41] JPrignon (A), September 26, 1963.

[42] JPrignon (A), September 27, 1963: "Morning: Meeting of the four moderators. They chose Dossetti as secretary." On this occasion it was decided that the "four" would meet in the library of the Secretariat of State, and Browne was heard on the presentation of the schema on the Church.

[43] "And we grant you all the faculties necessary and appropriate for carrying out so important a task in a way that is fruitful in the Lord"; see G. Alberigo, "Concilio acefalo? L'evoluzione degli organi direttivi del Vaticano II," in Attese, 230.

[44] But Suenens did not immediately share with his colleagues what Paul VI had told him in private; he only instructed Prignon to get in touch with Dossetti, whose idea of extending the authority of the moderators seemed dangerous to the rector of the Belgian College, given the possibility (perceived as real? feared without ground?) that this "power" might tomorrow pass into other hands; see JPrignon, September 25, 1963: "The Regulations as published do not correspond to the views of the Holy Father. Felice [sic!] will be called tomorrow. I am asked to summon Dossetti (whose plan — for the authority of the moderator — I find exaggerated, imprudent, and very dangerous should others be given that post) and prepare a preliminary plan for submission to the Holy Father."

Secretariat for Extraordinary Affairs), for reducing to a ceremonial role the function of the Council of Presidents, and for introducing the new office of the moderators. In addition, the organization of the debates foresaw the possibility of reports from both the majority and the minority in the hall, but the role of the commissions and their subordination to the hall were not yet assured. Relations among pope, Secretary of State, and moderators were not organized, and the composition and direction of the commissions did not provide procedures for replacing members.[45] In the space of a month Paul VI had been subjected to enormous pressures, which had remained invisible to the majority, but he had not cut the knot of the self-awareness of the assembly: the "cup" of the conflicting explanations of roles had not passed.[46]

---

[45] The genesis of the office of moderator was summed up on October 1 in *DNAlberigo*: the first reading of the Regulations on September 26 (?) gave rise to "a certain sense of euphoria" because it seemed to Dossetti that "all the changes in the Regulations that he had proposed in July have been accepted"; he was satisfied that there was no longer "the possibility of a minority report from the commission at a G[eneral] C[ongregation], or the possibility of continuing a discussion even if the majority had voted for closure. In the new scheme of things the moderators have been given the place of the council of presidents. The term 'moderator' has replaced the term 'president.'" But Dossetti voiced "two uncertainties: that this was really not the will of the pope, and that relations with the CC, the president of which was still the Secretary of State and which still seemed to have the final say on the new schemas presented, remained unknown. His doubts were further increased when, that afternoon, after a careful rereading, he realized that included were all the changes suggested in July, which the pope had received while still at Castelgandolfo and which he had personally studied, whereas none of those presented in the early days of September and having to do with the legates was included."

[46] According to *DNAlberigo*, October 1, Dossetti believed that the pope — as Paul VI told him at an audience — had not read the most recent proposals for change but had "passed them on, pages uncut, to the cardinal Secretary of State, something we had all feared, since among the proposals it was said in so many words that the Secretary of State ought not to have any authority at the Council and that the whole point of the office of moderator was to give the Council a center of authority distinct from the Curia." It was this "naiveté" that explains how the pope "did not know that it was explicitly [in the proposals] that it would be better not to appoint legates than to appoint them without power" and thus "the lack of clarity in ideas on the subject. In July he [the pope] has talked about legates with Suenens, Lercaro, and Don Giuseppe [Dossetti], as being people who should be the prompters in the box; to the four, whom he received, if I am not mistaken, on Wednesday, September 25, he showed that he did not know and did not like what Lercaro told him was written in the Regulations about the position of at least formal pre-eminence of the four. How, then, a pope could see a set of rules be issued that were not according to his wishes, was impossible to understand. But (as the pope told Don Giuseppe) to explain the last-minute publication, the Curia said that the printery did not have time, and, what was worse, the pope even seems to believe this."

2. *The Exhortations to the Bishops and the Comforting of the Curia*

The surface of the swell of Council members returning to flood the Roman scene was ruffled by some actions of the pope. On September 14, Paul VI addressed "twin" letters to the bishops: one having to do also with the faithful,[47] the other of a personal nature.[48] The exhortations, divided into two letters for reasons not easily explicable except by the hypothesis that there were two versions regarded as "alternatives," conveyed messages that were not especially relevant and seemed to have been written out of a sense of duty; perhaps they were meant to be a simple repetition of what had been done in 1962.

A good deal more telling, on the other hand, was a second action that was unexpected and marked by a certain solemnity. While all were awaiting clarifications of the revised Regulations and of the tasks of the moderators, September 21 saw the pope delivering the significant address to the Curia that had been announced to the CC three weeks earlier.[49] In these pages, read to a gathering of 800 people, which included all the members of the Roman congregations in full force and a number of Council fathers who had already returned to Rome, Paul VI made a series of statements and offered some reassurances. For those in the Curia who feared that the enmities of which Msgr. Montini had been victim would become an agenda for revenge or for reform, the address on September 21 removed all anxieties.[50] Paul VI showed that during his exile in Milan he had not been planning the destruction of the machine that had cast him out, but that he remained convinced of the need of the curial structure for the exercise of papal government. For many this was no small reassurance.

---

[47] *AS* II/1, 13-17. The letter *Cum proximis* repeats the exhortations to prayer and penance which John XXIII had given at the opening of the Council; it recommended the practice of fasting to both people and priests as a way of asking for divine help; and it insisted again on some characteristics of the Council, the responsibility for which would make the pope feel "a certain reserve, were it not the manifest will of God."

[48] *AS* II/1, 17-19. The second letter, *Horum temporum*, addressed directly to the bishops, had almost unconditioned praise for Roncalli; it expressed the conviction that he had "merited the abundance of heavenly graces"; at the same time, it described the nature and purpose of Vatican II in a "reassuring" selection of expressions that Roncalli had used in his addresses. Paul's references to the "deposit to be preserved in its purity" and to the Petrine chair, at the expense of passages on mercy and peace, provides a key for understanding this selection.

[49] *AS* V/1, 646. Only Lercaro was opposed to the address, regarding it as coming too close to the beginning of the Council's work.

[50] *AS* II/1, 49-56. At the ceremony of obedience on June 22, 1963, the pope had greeted the Curia as a powerful helper, "especially in preparing for the Second Ecumenical Vatican Council, to be celebrated with the other bishops of the Catholic Church."

But Paul VI was responding to two different categories of churchmen. He addressed those who saw the Council as a sharp, polished tool with which to reform the very structure of the Curia, which was accused, in the tactful ecclesiastical language used in the past in the *vota* and in private conversations during the Council, of abusing its office and oppressing the bishops. The pope also responded, not least, to those who feared that the leaders of the conciliar majority, the men who had elected him, were now in a position to condition his guidance of and attitude toward the work of the assembly. Although nuanced in the Montini manner, the message to these two "currents" was perfectly legible.

Without leaving room for negotiation, the pope made it known that residential bishops were to have an active and constant role in the work of the curial congregations, and he clearly and forcefully demanded the Curia's acceptance of the Council. At the same time, however, he consoled the Curia for the sharp defeat it had suffered in the hall in the first period of Vatican II when in the discussions of the liturgy and the Church, the Curia, "more than any other sector of the Church, learned the extraordinarily complex dimensions [of these subjects]."[51] Pope Montini was aware of and indulgent toward the fact that the Curia had "allowed something of its astonishment and something of its apprehension to show through," but in the future he demanded "an identity of views" and "a conformity of minds with what the pope commands or desires."[52]

In contrast with this preliminary alignment, Paul VI offered his audience, as a concession, something which many, although not the bishops, regarded as an acquired right; namely, that the Curia itself should retain the right to formulate and *promulgate* the reforms applying to it. This, however, would not exclude the Council from asking "to see...some representatives of the episcopate, in particular from among prelates in charge of a diocese, associated with the supreme head of the Church itself." On this subject (all the more so when expressed by the nuanced term *associated*) it was not, said the pope, the Curia that would raise objections.[53]

[51] *Insegnamenti* (1963), 1:144.

[52] Ibid., 1:145.

[53] Semmelroth placed in his diary a clipping of an article that appeared in the *Frankfurter Allgemeine Zeitung*, September 23, 1963, 5, under the headline: "The pope announces a radical reform of the Curia. Solidarity in the work of Church renewal called for. Report of our Roman correspondent."

This papal address, delivered eight days before the allocution that opened the second period of the Council, found a modest echo in the diaries of the fathers preparing to return to Rome. Prignon refers only to "rumors of the Curial reactions of opposition to the pope's address."[54] There is a reference to the Curia in the diary of Neophytos Edelby, a Melkite bishop who happened to be in Rome but who, though invited, decided to skip the audience. Despite his absence, echoes of Montini's address reached him through Pierre Duprey, of the Secretariat for Unity, who visited the Melkite metropolitan at noon on that September 21. Duprey was enthusiastic because, he said, the pope had announced "the reform of the Curia." It was typical of Edelby that he spent some hours on his own careful and cautious reading of the discourse, and his analysis of it led him to decide that the point of Montini's prudent "wording" was that "the Curia should desire the reforms which Paul VI wanted to impose on it." Still Edelby did share Duprey's impression that Montini had announced a reform of the structure of curial authority. Although as a Melkite and a theologian he was an expert on synodality, the climate of confidentiality kept the metropolitan from desiring anything more radical; much less did he or others seem to realize that while the address may have announced a possible future reform of the Curia, it also clearly revealed the pope's intention to remove, by a papal act, such an important question from the agenda of Vatican II.[55]

Similarly, Jedin's memoirs give very little space to the papal address,[56] although it had elicited an indirect comment from him in a letter to Klostermann regarding the first chapter of the schema on the bishops. "In my view," he wrote, "an internationalization of the curial bureaucracy brings us from the frying pan into the fire, because experience shows that Romanized foreigners are more intolerant than the

---

[54] *JPrignon*, September 24, 1963.

[55] *JEdelby*, September 21, 1963, 141-44. Edelby notes that he had discussed with Duprey the question of the seating of the patriarchs. It was typical of the climate at the Council that on September 24, while in the dark about agreements made, Prignon should note: "With Thils: proposal to give the eastern patriarchs special seats, or, in any case seats distinct from those of the other archbishops and bishops"; *JPrignon* (A), September 24, 1963.

[56] According to Jedin's memoirs, it was the clash between Frings and Ottaviani on November 8 that explains why Paul VI decided to ask Jedin, Ratzinger, and Onclin for some views on reform of the Curia. While waiting for the diary to be made available, see H. Jedin, *Lebensbericht*, ed. K. Repgen (Mainz, 1984), 212-13, and J. Ratzinger, *Theological Highlights of Vatican II* (New York, 1966), 33-35.

Italians. I do see an opportunity here in a wider distribution of consultors, who hitherto have been almost exclusively recruited from among Roman religious."[57]

C. THE COUNCIL OF PAUL VI

The delicacy of the transition from pontificate to reopened Council could obviously not be eliminated simply by promises of continuity. Despite his familiarity with the workings of papal government, managing the reopening of the Council was for Paul VI a novitiate within a novitiate. Elected pope in the presence of a Council convened by another, he could not seek guidance in precedents any closer than the Council of Trent, the last council of the Latin world that saw a change of pontificate while it was in session. Having to build up new points of reference for himself, he looked for collaborators outside the Curia (Döpfner, Lercaro, Suenens), while at the same time carrying on a dialogue with the Curia in order to win its loyalty; he considered, sketched out, and then delayed an encyclical on ecclesiology; he appointed *his* moderators in order to ensure the efficiency of the conciliar procedure; he voiced his full acceptance of the pastoral character of the *aggiornamento* and, at the same time, went back again to the classic sources of the mysticism of papal authority.[58]

By comparison with the first period, the lack of attunement between assembly and pope was reversed in Paul VI's council. Roncalli had set the conciliar machine going from a standstill and was familiar with its entire course from within; his decision to play no part in the preparation until the opening discourse had left the Council with a door open upon an abyss of condemnations. Paul VI, on the other hand, had to "leap onto a moving train"; if its movement was not yet frenetic, it certainly added to the difficulty of being a pope in the Church the extraordinary task of being a "pope in a council." While the assembly had already been able to examine and experience itself at least at a very elementary level of discourse, the pope had to invent for himself a role which, by definition and by circumstance, could be anything but a repetition of the Roncallian non-paradigm.

[57] Jedin to Klostermann, September 23, 1963 (Jedin Archive, G5 a 21). It escaped Jedin that he was echoing the Lutheran thesis that "the Church needs reformation," on which see G. Cereti, *Riforma della chiesa e unità dei cristiani nell'insegnamento del Concilio Vaticano II* (Verona, 1985).

[58] See above, note 16.

II. Preparation for the Assembly

While questions focused predominantly on the person of the pope, expectations, hopes, and some doubts had to do with matters of substance and with the schemas on which the Council would be called to deliberate. During the summer the fathers and perhaps also the observers had received the schemas on the Church and on revelation; on September 16 they also learned from Felici the five subjects that the CC had decided would be discussed during the coming period.[59] Many of the fathers had received commentaries and interpretations on the texts, asked for explanatory notes, read many articles circulated in the specialized press, and accumulated remarks made in ecumenical circles and sometimes even in political circles.[60] One general observation holds for all the fathers: the deadlines imposed by the conciliar bodies for the submission of observations overlooked one element that affected the timing, that is, the widespread desire to understand, to comment, and to correct. In addition, the experience of collaboration within and among the various episcopates had led to ways of proceeding that twelve months before would have been unthinkable.

A. Meetings of Bishops

More notable as a sign of openness than for the importance of the discussions was the initiative taken by some Italian bishops, who until this point had been distinguished rather by their lack of any tendency in this direction and who had had no experience whatever of international collaboration.[61] Florit invited a small delegation to a meeting of Italian and French bishops in Florence, September 26-27.[62] It was not simply a

---

[59] For the sending see *History,* 2:493-95. For the coming period, the sequence of Church, Blessed Virgin, bishops, lay apostolate, and ecumenism was decided by the CC on August 31 (*AS* V/1, 651-52).

[60] See the various essays in *Experience*; for press reactions as part of public opinion see Appendix I in *Paolo VI e i problemi ecclesiologici,* 431-560.

[61] Only in August 1963 did Castelli, secretary of the Italian Episcopal Conference (CEI), appoint a theological commission of bishops — Calabria (president), Carraro, Florit, Carli, Castellano, Compagnone, Fares, and Nicodemo — to examine closely the schemas and the observations to be passed to all the Italian fathers; see F. Sportelli, "La conferenza episcopale italiana al Vaticano II," in *Experience.*

[62] The meeting in Florence gave the lie to facile but automatic and anachronistic reactions; if it certainly was not a meeting of the "majority," whose real leaders were not present, neither was it governed by the logic of opposition to the "anti-Roman feeling" that pervaded some episcopates; see *DBetti,* for this date.

meeting of friends but an important step in the effort to coordinate two
episcopates, or at least parts of them, which during the first period and
the intersession had seemed rather to diverge in their tendencies. That it
was indeed an important meeting can be seen both from the level of the
participants (more numerous on the French side — Lefebvre, Garrone,
Marty, Veuillot, Ancel, and Etchegaray — than on the Italian — Florit,
Baldassari, Carli, and Calabria, who brought Betti[63]) and from the
agenda, central to which was the problem of the fate of the schema on
revelation.

The French episcopate had held meetings and produced works of
information and analysis.[64] Among these was a quite sharply critical
note from Father Yves Congar in July. He regarded the schema from the
mixed commission as unacceptable because of the confused definition of
revelation at the beginning of the schema; the concept was still more
weighted in favor of a view of revelation as a "content" than as an "act"
of God's self-communication, and this would have a negative effect on
the entire subsequent treatment (relation to tradition, limits of exegesis,
and so on).[65] Father Betti, too, passed a negative judgment on the
schema and takes credit for having persuaded everyone at the Florence
meeting to agree to scuttle the schema from the mixed commission.[66]

Other episcopates held preparatory meetings, but these were in continuity with what they were used to doing.[67] As usual the joint meeting of
the German bishops played a decisive role; there they laid the foundations for the major interventions to be made at the general congregations

[63] Lercaro, Motolese, Carraro, and Piazza were invited but not present; Lercaro had
turned down the invitation, fearing a reaction from Siri (*Lettere*, 160), but a joint meeting
of the CC, the Council of Presidents, and the moderators was also being held on that same
day.

[64] At Angers, on June 25-27, the Episcopal Conference of Western France had approved
a set of observations on the revelation schema, now published in *AS* III/3, 901-3.

[65] Congar's remarks on the schema appeared on July 11 in *Études et Documents*, no.
14, 1-8 (Florit Archive, 365); his remarks on "Les deux premières chapitres du schéma
De ecclesia" were in *Études et Documents*, pp. 1-7 (ISR, Gagnebet Archive, I, 20, 7).

[66] *DBetti*, September 27 (p. 307).

[67] The Argentineans met on August 6-10 (see L. Zanatta, "L'episcopato argentino
durante il Vaticano II," in *Experience* and *AS* III/3, 894-96). On August 9-10 the episcopate of the Flaminian region met, on August 10-12 the episcopate of Lombardy-Veneto,
and on August 27-28 the entire Italian Conference (Dossetti Archive, 257; Lercaro
Archive, 769). The bishops of Uruguay met on August 12-14 (see P. Dabezies, "Los obispos de Uruguay en el concilio," in *Experience*). For the Canadian Conference and the
recurring difficulties between Cardinal Léger and the bishops, see J.-M. R. Tillard,
"L'épiscopat francophone au Concile," in *L'Eglise canadienne et Vatican II* (Québec,
1997), 291-301.

in the name of the entire German-speaking group;[68] Rahner's notes on the schemas on the Church, revelation, and the Blessed Virgin, sent on July 4, were mimeographed and distributed for this meeting.[69] The German bishops were also familiar with notes on the schema on the bishops that Jedin had sent to Döpfner in the spring; although commenting on an earlier draft of the text, they retained their value. The bishops also heard a report from Schäufele.[70] Brouwers, secretary of the Dutch Conference, exchanged with the bishops and theologians some preparatory notes and commentaries on various points of the agenda, especially on collegiality and the episcopate.[71]

Some conferences, such as the Brazilian, had booklets of notes on the schemas prepared by various experts and had them sent also to fathers of other countries.[72] At the meeting of the Spanish Conference on May 14, the bishops ordered various groups of experts to draft observations and notes on various schemas; and canonists, spirituality experts, and mariologists held several meetings during the summer that led to notes and points of information which were given to the bishops, not at their meeting of September 9-11,[73] but at their plenary meeting in Rome on September 29.[74]

The Spanish Conference was not, however, the only one to maintain contacts that would give rise to a pattern of rapid work, but only after the bishops had taken up residence in Rome once again. Among the subjects that caused anxiety among the bishops of the United States, who met in Chicago on August 6-7 for a first examination of the texts, was the fate of the schema on religious freedom, which might appear as a fifth chapter of

[68] At the Fulda meeting on August 26-27 the observations on the schemas were approved (for those on revelation see *AS* III/3, 905-13). Döpfner had already tried at the beginning of the year to distinguish among the subjects on the agenda with a view to reducing their number; the idea then was to refer problems of detail to a commission for the revision of the Code of Canon Law, which, in an interesting parallel with the secret commission on birth control, was expected to be established in March. Döpfner was basically maintaining and adapting the German "thesis" that the schemas of 1962 should be thrown out and a central core be decided upon.

[69] See H. Vorgrimler, *Understanding Karl Rahner: An Introduction to His Life and Thought* (New York, 1986), 173.

[70] Jedin Archive, G5 a 7 and 19; Schäufele Archive, 154/20.25.

[71] E.g., letter of August 10 from Brouwers to Schillebeeckx, in Onclin Archive, 128.

[72] Houtart Archive, 226, a document of 147 pages. See O. Beozzo, "A conferencia episcopal brasileira," in *Experience*.

[73] *Actas de las Conferencias de Metropolitanos Españoles (1921-1965)*, ed. V. C. Orti (Madrid, 1994), 625-36.

[74] *Dicionario de historia eclesiastica de España*, ed. Q. A. Vaquero, T. M. Martinez, and J. V. Gatell, I (A-C) (Madrid, 1972), 523.

the schema on ecumenism but whose printing and distribution to the fathers, despite the pleas of Bea, would not be ordered.[75] Before the beginning of the work a meeting of the conference, or at least of its top officers, considered sending a letter to the pope requesting that this text be printed and distributed, since American Catholics regarded it as necessary for the development of their presence in society. The question was left in abeyance (at least until the first meeting of the conference in Rome) and would be placed on the agenda again with Spellman's petition, of which I shall speak shortly.[76]

The bishops from countries under communist control had very little information and devoted their cautious mutual contacts to evaluating the possibilities they had been granted to take part in the work. Among the Poles, for example, Wyszynski set up worthwhile meetings after his arrival in Rome.[77] Other "anomalous" bishops were the Algerians, who settled, after independence, at the Retraite, a convent on the Janiculum, and were struggling with the difficult problem of finding a place in the African episcopate.[78]

On September 5, the financial committee told the episcopates that for the sake of maintaining contacts it would be a good idea for them to bring the secretaries of the conferences to Rome — at their own expense.[79]

B. Problems, Comments, and Positions of Non-Catholics

On the eve of the second period the Orthodox world was rent by mutual distrust: the lack of coordination between Moscow and Constantinople for the sending of observers in 1962 was still an open wound, and the steps taken in Rome during the summer had not yet overcome

[75] See V. Carbone, "Il ruolo di Paolo VI nell'evoluzione e nella redazione della dichiarazione *Dignitatis humanae*," in *Paolo VI e il rapporto chiesa-mondo al Concilio* (Rome, 1991), 126-75, esp. 129-30.

[76] See Rynne, 192-93.

[77] See P. Raina, *Kardynal Wyszynski. Czasy Prymaskaie 1962-1963* (Warsaw, 1994), 4:150-65.

[78] Gouet, secretary of the French conference, wrote to Duval on September 2, 1963, telling him that he had telephoned Annecy to find out whether Duval was still a Savoyard; Archive of the Archiepisopate of Paris, cited by M. Impagliazzo, "I vescovi nordafricani al concilio," in *Experience*, note 6.

[79] See Caprile, III, 18: the same committee made it known that group journeys, at the expense of the Holy See, would be organized through the pontifical representatives and the nunciatures.

Athenagoras's doubts. Meanwhile, the change of pontificate had been anything but painless: Athenagoras sent neither greetings at the election of John XXIII's successor nor a representative to the papal coronation. Paul VI, for his part, had included in his coronation address some sentences on the primacy and on the achievement of Catholic unity that were certainly not sensitive to his non-Catholic counterparts.[80]

The signal given by Athenagoras was a serious one and implied that the throne of Constantinople would not compromise its high place by sending useless spectators to Rome. A summer mission of Willebrands and Duprey to Istanbul was meant to respond to these doubts and concerns.[81] Rome, they said again, was asking not for "spectators" at the Council but for "observers" with a part to play. While the procedures for accrediting the observers from other Churches went off without difficulties, even on the Soviet side, whose spokesman, Nikodim, Paul VI received at an audience in mid-September, the decision of the Phanar was still awaited. Montini tried to remedy the situation, but the outcome was disappointing. The letter that the pope, in a courageous and innovative step, personally addressed to the Patriarch was without effect; the sending of observers was made dependent on the Panorthodox Conference, which would not begin until September 26 in Rhodes,[82] and there the powerful objections of the Greeks proved decisive and barred the way.

Meanwhile the confessional federations and organizations prepared to approve their representative delegations;[83] and they found it easier to return than to start initially. The World Council of Churches (WCC) continued to act as a meeting place for views on questions of substance. Thus the Faith and Order Colloquium on "Tradition and Traditions," held in Montreal, July 12-26, 1963, went to the heart of one of the key debates during the coming period of the Council. The presence of observers from the Secretariat for Christian Unity, the warm welcome given to the participants by Cardinal Léger, the fact that for the first time a Catholic (R. Brown) gave a report — all this gave the meeting an element of greater "reciprocity" and so of advance with regard to the

---

[80] *Insegnamenti* (1963), 1:23-31.

[81] M. Velati, *Una difficile transizione. Il cattolicesimo tra unionismo ed ecumenismo* (Bologna, 1996), 372-83; idem, "Gli osservatori del Consiglio ecumenico delle chiese al Vaticano II," in *Evento*, 189-257.

[82] Chrysostomos of Athens sought to have the government bar this meeting in Greek territory; see V. Martano, *Athenagoras il patriarca (1886-1972). Un cristiano fra crisi della coabitazione ed utopia ecumenica* (Bologna, 1996), 460.

[83] See Velati, "Gli osservatori," 189-257.

non-Catholic presence at Vatican II. The reports and discussions there showed clearly how fortunate it was that the schema "On the Sources of Revelation" had been withdrawn during the first period; ecumenical circles regarded the way in which the relationship of scripture to tradition would be treated at the Council as decisive for grasping the truer and more lasting tendencies of the Roman Catholic Church.[84]

C. THE WORK OF THE COMMISSIONS

The activity of the commissions had basically come to a halt with the death of John XXIII and in some cases even earlier. The wait for the new pope and for decisions by the CC left the initiatives begun in the spring of 1963 in a state of suspense.

1. The Commissions for the Liturgy, Seminaries, and Missions

The waiting was, however, marked by different attitudes in different commissions. Some, like the Commission for the Liturgy, were preparing for the final discussion of their work in a spirit essentially of confidence.[85] Others (Commission for Religious, Commission for Seminaries) were afraid that the demand for the reduction of the schemas might handicap their work of revision, which for that reason seemed useless. Still others were becalmed. The schema of the Commission for Missions was in a state of suspension, buried under criticisms from the CC, which asked for a definition of mission, greater juridical exactitude, and a plan for restructuring the Congregation for the Propagation of the Faith. Though its numbers were filled up, after the death of Msgr. Platero, by the papal appointment of the first German in the group (Bolte, Bishop of

---

[84] The documents are in *Foi et constitution*, ed. L. Vischer (Neuchâtel, 1968), 160-217; the context is described in R. Burigana, "Scripture, Tradition and Traditions: Examples of Dialogue among Christians. Vatican II and the Fourth Conference on Faith and Order (Montreal, 12-26 July 1963)," in *L'Eglise canadienne et Vatican II* (Montreal, 1997), 373-96. Among the conclusions was the need for a "universal ecumenical catechism" that would promote the Bible as a meeting ground. On the climate of the intersession see O. Cullmann and L. Vischer, *Zwischen zwei Konzilssessionen* (Zurich, 1963). See also L. Vischer, "*Storia del concilio Vaticano II*. Reactions and Comments by an Observer at the Council," *Ecumenical Review* 49 (July 1997), 348-53.

[85] See A.-G. Martimort, "Où en est le schéma *De sacra liturgia*?" *Études et Documents*, no. 19 (September 2, 1963), 1-8 (Florit Archive, 960). On the evolution of the text see M. Paiano, *Sacrosanctum Concilium. La costituzione sulla liturgia nella preparazione e nello svolgimento del Vaticano II. Continuità o rottura?*, a doctoral dissertation, directed by G. Alberigo and D. Menozzi, University of Bologna, 1995/95.

Fulda), this commission would not hold any meetings. In fact, facing the possibility that the blockage might prove definitive, Agagianian would even have some theologians of the old preparatory commission draft a chapter for possible insertion into the schema on the Church.[86]

2. The Commission for Bishops

The commission responsible for the schema on bishops and the care of souls was formally summoned to meet on October 1,[87] but during the summer the various members had corresponded about the reactions the schema was eliciting. There were groups, such as the one titled "The Bishop of Vatican II,"[88] which made their demands known with a view to the coming work. So great was the mass of observations received or published that on September 12 five commissions were set up "to sort, coordinate, and weigh the observations submitted in writing by the fathers on the two schemas."[89] On October 7 Carli gave a report to the commission and asserted the need to link this schema with the schema on the Church, but without rewriting it. According to Carli, however, it would be necessary that, while providing a role for the bishops in the Roman Curia, the schema not play down the pope's right to decide entirely on his own how to reform the central governmental bodies.[90]

---

[86] E. Louchez, "La commission De missionibus," in Commissions, 263.

[87] Marella to the members, July, 1, 1963; Veuillot Archive, 71.

[88] This was the self-description given by A. Muñoz Duque, F. N. Adam, L. de Cour-reges, A. de Moura, J. A. Dammeert, F. Gonzalez, M. Maziers, M. Vial, and B. Pineda in a letter of early July in which they announced that at the beginning of the second period there would be international research "seminars" to prepare some interventions (two-paged typed notes in Florit Archive, F 459).

[89] Eldarov Archive, III.12-15 and Onclin Archive, 172. The subcommissions were given a working method (ratio procedendi) that took into account the structure of the sub-commissions and showed how to handle requests for changes. The members of the sub-commissions were (1) (On bishops and the government of dioceses): reporter: L. Carli; secretary: A. Sabattani; subsecretary: P. Fernandez; experts: E. Cibardi, G. D'Ercole, E. Eid, J. Gouet, H. Hoffmann, H. Jedin, G. Mariani, and G. Pasquazi; (2) (Care of souls: Ch. 1: Pastoral Office of Bishops): reporter: E. M. Guerry; secretary: A. Piovesana; experts: F. Boulard, V. Carbone, G. Ceriani, P. Cremin, and A. Ramselaar; (3) (Care of souls: Ch. 2: Pastoral Office of Pastors): reporter: H. Schäufele; secretary: C. Berutti; experts: R. Bandas, V. Che-Chen-Tao, A. Deskur, F. Klostermann, P. Pavan, and J. Quinn; (4) (Care of souls: Ch. 3: Relations between Bishops and Religious, especially in Apostolic Works): reporter: N. Jubany Arnau; secretary: G. Stano; experts: P. Abellan, G. Eldarov, G. Michiels, W. Onclin, J. Rousseau, and P. Whitty; (5) (Care of souls: Ch. 4: Pastoral Care of Special Groups of the Faithful): reporter: J. Gargitter; secretary: G. Arrighi; experts: A. Deskur, D. Grasso, D. Herlihy, and L. Ligutti.

[90] Veuillot Archive, 92.

3. The Commission for the Lay Apostolate

The themes treated by the commission for the laity were in danger of being absorbed into the chapter of the same name in the schema on the Church and into the parts dealing with the temporal order in Schema XVII. The commission was not holding any meetings at the time when Suenens proposed the division of chapter III of the schema on the Church into two parts, one on the People of God in general, to be placed before the chapter on the hierarchy, and the other on the laity, to be made the fourth chapter, after the treatment of the hierarchy. Suenens's motion was proposed to the CC on July 4;[91] it would be approved by Paul VI on September 1, communicated to the Council of Presidents on September 16, but made known to the fathers only after the beginning of the debate in the hall, even though this proposal had been put forward within the Commission for the Lay Apostolate while it had been examining the ecclesiological schema in order to evaluate the possibilities of overlap.[92] A small group (Sabattani, Klostermann, Papali, Tucci, and Cento) worked during the summer on a first draft of a directory on lay activity. It was only in September that the experts already in Rome were asked to begin examining the observations sent in by the fathers. However, as the rector of the Belgian College, who was called upon for this work, summed matters up: "General impression: impossible to do serious work before the study of the *De ecclesia*. In-depth discussion of the definition of the laity and of the lay apostolate."[93] Cardinal Cento's commission, then, was waiting. It does not seem that at this point it had inspired or even seen the list of invited lay men, although this represented the answer to a desire expressed by that commission.[94]

---

[91] *AS* V/1, 594. On August 3 Philips wrote to Colombo that "Cardinal Suenens is asking for a small working team that will change somewhat the order of the schema in order to insert a special chapter on 'the People of God.' We will probably be working on it at the beginning of September, together with the Louvain professors, Father Congar, Father K. Rahner, and so on. The idea is to shift into this chapter the scattered points already made in the schema on the People of God, as well as, among other things, no. 24 of the chapter on the laity, and perhaps also no. 23 on the equality and inequality of the members of the Church. If you have any suggestion to make on this matter, I urgently ask you to keep me in mind" (Colombo Archive, C-XXII).

[92] For Klostermann's authorship of the proposal, see M. T. Fattori, "La commisione *De fidelium apostolatu* e la redazione del decreto sull'apostolato dei laici (settembre 1962 — maggio 1964)," in *Experience*.

[93] The overall impression is that the group had not made progress on its basic theme — not an inch in three years; see *JPrignon*, September 23, 1963.

[94] At the end of June, Paul VI had greeted with pleasure the possibility of having women (but only religious women) present; see G. Turbanti, "La presenza e il contributo

4. The Commission for the Oriental Churches

This commission was summoned to a belated meeting on September 20, at which Edelby complained that no meeting of the commission had been called throughout the long intersession, but these pertinent remarks received no satisfaction. The reworking of the texts was put off until the following Monday. On that day Edelby saw his fear confirmed of an aggressively Latin attitude on the part of the majority of the commission, against which he had "to struggle, but reluctantly." The Melkite bishop's unyielding attitude caused some softening of the other position, and the text would include the emendations proposed in the name of his patriarch and repeated, to some extent, in a more comprehensive set of observations from the patriarchal synod of that Church.[95]

Edelby's diary (the "synodal" diary, as it has been called) also reports the attitudes and positions of Patriarch Maximos, in whose name Edelby was speaking. It relates that Maximos himself, who in 1962 had in protest refused to take part in the inaugural liturgy of the Council, took part on September 27, 1963, in the meeting of the Oriental Commission, at which both relations with the Secretariat for Christian Unity and the pressure toward Latinization were discussed. Edelby points out that Maximos IV was of one mind with the Maronite and Armenian patriarchs. Would the conciliar commission, so niggardly in its results, foster an alignment of the Orientals on common positions?[96]

5. The Commission for Religious

The Commission for Religious met three times before the Council reopened.[97] Cardinal Antoniutti placed on its agenda the extensive observations which the fathers had sent in during the summer on the schema on the states of perfection. The commission acted decisively, dividing itself into four subcommissions, thus revealing its determination to

del laici al Concilio Vaticano II," in *Vittorio Veronese dal dopoguerra al Concilio: un laico nella chiesa e nel mondo* (Rome, 1994), 184. In an interview on Radio Popular, printed in the newspapers on September 14, 1964, Morcillo announced that there might be lay "auditors, not observers" during the second period; Caprile, III, 15-16.

[95] Mimeographed by the Little Sisters of Tre Fontane on September 24, 1963; see *JEdelby* for that date, 140-41). The file would be handed in on September 28.

[96] *JEdelby,* September 27, 148-50 (Italian ed.). The Commission on the Oriental Churches would be the scene of a turbulent meeting in the early days of October, as Moeller told the rector of the Belgian College; *JPrignon* (A), October 10, 1963, 4.

[97] On September 23, 25, and 27; there would be another plenary meeting on October 7. After July 31 the French episcopate circulated a booklet by J. Daniélou, "Le chapitre IV du schéma *de Ecclesia*," *Études et Documents,* no. 18.

obtain, *before* the beginning of the debate on the Church, a revised text
that could, if necessary, be incorporated into that constitution.[98]

6. The Doctrinal Commission

The Doctrinal Commission was, of course, overwhelmed by written
observations on the schemas for which it, either alone or in mixed commissions, was responsible. We have no exhaustive information on the
state of mind with which the commission received the notes sent in by
fathers or episcopates before the reopening, but there was a clear gap
between the members and consultors who had taken part in the preparatory work and those who represented the assembly.

The reactions of the fathers and episcopates to the schema on revelation were numerous, but in the end of no use. The decision to postpone
discussion of the mixed commission's revised schema, with the expectation that it would be either suppressed, incorporated into the schema on
the Church, or reshaped, had made irrelevant both the criticisms and the
praises of the schema that had come in between July and September.[99]
While individual bishops proposed limited corrections, mostly accompanied by praises suited to the occasion, the episcopates, for their part,
asked for extensive changes in the text. The French episcopate was
known to have reservations, and it was foreseeable that the German
Conference would identify all the compromise solutions adopted. On the
other hand, the fact that the Canadian experts, the Argentinean bishops,
and even more, the Mexican bishops and those of Emilia and Romagna
would take the initiative and criticize the schema (as only a few —
Schillebeekx, Rahner, Ratzinger — had dared to do in the summer of
1962) says something about the atmosphere in which the bishops were
packing their bags to return to Rome.

There was, however, a much broader agreement on the schema on the
Church; while the conferences and many bishops sent comments and
requests for changes, they agreed in their appreciation of the great step
forward taken in the new schema.[100]

---

[98] See J. Schmiedl, "Erneuerung im Widerstreit. Das Ringen der *Commissio de Religiosis* und der *Commissio de Concilii laboribus coordinandis* um das Dekret zur Zeit-
gemässen Erneuerung des Ordenslebens," in *Commissions*, 293-303. Caprile, II, 26,
reprints the information from *Kipa* for September 24, 1963.

[99] In these circumstances one sector of the commission saw a revenge for the failure
of the 1962 schema on the sources, while another saw proof that dealing with the
"Romans" had proved useless; see R. Burigana, *La Bibbia nel concilio: La redazione
della costituzione "Dei verbum" del Vaticano II* (Bologna, 1998), 228-45.

[100] The observations were mimeographed; see RT; *AS* II/1, 282-336 and 605-801.

III. THE NEW BEGINNING: THE RETURN OF THE COUNCIL

The assembly was the point at which the two "vigils" studied so far came together and interacted. The two main streams of the summer — that which carried the pope through his breaking-in period and that which carried the bishops along with their confident hopes — came together in St. Peter's.

A. JOURNEYS AND ARRIVALS

The reassembling of the conciliar "anthill," with its 2500 bishops, their experts, the observers, the newly admitted laymen, the escorts, and the hundred of journalists, brought both repetition and novelty. Behind it were dealings with nuncios and governments to pay for the costly journeys to Rome.[101] Most of the fathers returned to the lodgings of the previous year. Rome was no longer as unknown to them as it had been the year before: everyone now knew the religious houses and centers where lectures were given; they knew the bookstores; and they had also become acquainted with the chaotic traffic, the restaurants, and the little social life of the embassies.

1. The Bishops

The bishops who traveled again to Rome and their Roman apartments in September 1963 were more at ease. Typical was the tone in which Bergonzini told of his arrival, his worries about another absence from home (Volterra!), his effort to spiritualize the sacrifice of being far from his sister ("Let us leave it to Jesus"), but also his sense of returning as a man changed by his experience in 1962, due to which he feels "more open-minded" in Rome.[102]

This conviction supported once again the labor of keeping a diary, an effort that a number of bishops found impossible to keep up in 1963. Among the Italians in 1963, Florit's diary was kept with increasing infrequency; Siri's was interrupted; even a vitriolic portrait-painter like Msgr. Borromeo from the Marches gave up the satisfaction of putting

---

[101] On the Brazilian government, which was falling victim to a coup, see J. O. Beozzo, "A conferencia episcopal brasileira," in *Experience*; on the attitude toward the African bishops, see the extract from the *DOlivier*, 197-98.

[102] *Diario del concilio*, ed. E. Leonelli (Modena 1993).

his gibes at his colleagues down on paper, something which he had duti-
fully done the year before. There was more here than a simple loss of
fervor; in fact, many bishops faced the beginning of the second period
with less emotion, without the puerile enthusiasm that makes one note
down things of beauty and changes of weather and without the naive
enthusiasm that in 1962 had sustained the great number of fathers who
still had little realization of the commitment that the great questions
being discussed would require of them.[103]

2. The Laity

The Commission for the Lay Apostolate and the Permanent Committee for International Congresses of the Apostolate of the Laity (COPE-
CIAL) won their great victory with the appointment of a little force of
lay men, who, from October 2 on, were admitted to St. Peter's, where
they were given a special place in the tribune of St. Andrew.[104] Jean
Guitton, who had been invited to the first period as a guest, had sat with
the observers — a somewhat anomalous position for a Catholic, even
though it brought out the ecclesiological status of those members of Vatican II who did not have a full right to be there. For the second period,
however, a group of thirteen lay men were appointed, who were now
distinct by location from the observers.

The list, which seems to have been revised and may have been drawn
up by Paul VI himself, included, in addition to Guitton, two other
Frenchmen, Jean Larnaud, secretary of the CCC in UNESCO, and Henri
Rollet, president of The International Federation of Catholic Action for
Men. Also invited were three Italians: Silvio Golzio of COPECIAL;
Raimondo Manzini, editor-in-chief of L'Osservatore Romano; and
Francesco Vito, rector of the Catholic University of Milan. There were
six others from various countries: Auguste Vanistendael, a Belgian,

---

[103] About 400 bishops were present during the second period who had not been present for the first. Some were the "justifiably absent" of the first period (mostly diplomats
and the elderly); some had only recently been consecrated. Four were prelates who had
been prevented from coming in 1962 by communist governments but in 1963 had
obtained permission to take part. Journalistic sources supposed that attempts had been
made particularly to get the People's Republic of China to allow the Chinese bishops,
prevented from leaving the country, to take part; see Wei Tsing-Sing, La Saint- Siège et
la Chine (Rouen, 1971), 286-88, and A. Lazzarotto, "I vescovi cinesi al concilio," in
Experience.

[104] The decision had been endorsed by the CC on August 31, at which meeting Felici
made it known that Paul VI had a list (see Fattori, "La commissione De fidelium apostolatu"), but the pope's request of July 11 did not include one; AS VI/2, 206 and 271-72.

secretary general of the International Federation of Catholic Workers' Movements;[105] Ramon Sungranyes de Franch, a Spaniard, president of Pax Romana; James J. Norris, from the United States, president of the International Catholic Migration Commission; Mieczyslav de Habitch, a Pole, secretary of the International Conference of Catholic Organizations; Vittorino Veronese, a delegate to Unesco and director of Italian Catholic Action and of COPECIAL; and Juan Vazquez, an Argentinean, director of Young Catholic Action. Vito alone was not only appointed but also assigned to a commission (the Commission for Studies); for the others, the range of possible interventions in the commissions, allowed by the Regulations, was not spelled out. After October 4 Guitton's status would be clarified and Vittorino Veronese and Emilio Inglessis would be named.

To Bishop Guano, a member of the Commission for the Lay Apostolate, was entrusted the role of "assessor" of the group, whose activity at meetings for the study of schemas was modeled on that of the observers.[106]

3. The Observers

The observers received a new invitation on the morrow of the election of Paul VI, who also ordered Cardinal Bea to reformulate the invitation to be sent to the Throne of Constantinople asking that the ecumenical patriarchate be represented during the new period of the Council.[107] Among the delegations that came were those of five churches that had not been present in 1962 but had been invited to send delegates for the second period. Three of these were from the Indian subcontinent (the

[105] This appointment caused some discontent within the federation; the French section feared that the appointment might confirm the conviction that the federation was "dependent" on the Vatican; see the report of G. N. McKelvey to the Department of State from Brussels, November 13, 1963, A-461, Central Archives, Washington, D.C., CFPF, SC-Religion, Vatican, b. 4223.

[106] Guano would also raise the question of reimbursing the lay men for their expenses; see Fattori, "La commissione De fidelium apostolatu." Later appointments are given in AS VI/2, 335-37, 342-42, 351.

[107] Bea wrote on July 8; see M. Brun, "La documentazione della partecipazione ortodossa al Concilio," in Evento 259-93, and Martano, Athenagoras, 459. See JEdelby, October 4, 1963, 159, for the conversations of both König and Maximos IV with Georges Ollenbach, Great Referendary of the ecumenical patriarchate. This prelate (an Orthodox with Lutheran training) gave assurances, via Maximos IV, that the ecumenical patriarch wanted to come to Rome and exchange permanent delegates with Rome, but that this exchange could take place after Constantinople had sent an observer to the Secretariat for Christian Unity.

Syro-Orthodox Church, the Church of Mar Thomas of Malabar, and the
Church of South India), and two were subject to Soviet authority (the
Armenian Apostolic Church of Etchmiadzin, and the Orthodox Church
of Georgia, which, however, was forced to accept as observer Proto-
priest Vitaly Borovoy, who was also a delegate of the Patriarchate of
Moscow).

In the end, Constantinople stayed away. Fear of being trapped in an
unacceptable position as a satellite in relation to the Catholic council and
the need to take its own stand over and against the decision of the Rus-
sians convinced the synod to put off any form of official participation in
Vatican II. Orthodoxy, it was felt, should not be a spectator or accept
invitations; instead, as Athenagoras said when opening the Second
Panorthodox Assembly in Rhodes, it "should take the role of one who
acts and calls."[108] At Vatican II the young Rumanian Archimandrite
Andrey Scrima would continue to play a profitable informal role; he did
not officially represent anyone, but he had a direct relationship with the
Patriarch, which made him a valuable and respected intermediary for
requests and messages.

4. The Theologians

A marginalized theologian such as Chenu could only jot down the
fact of his arrival at the Salesian fathers, with no mention of the
renewal of contacts that marks the diaries of others.[109] In contrast,
Fenton, an American and a prominent person in the group of confi-
dants of the secretary of the Holy Office, found on his arrival a welcoming and sympathetic atmosphere. Having suffered a heart attack in
May, he was rather concerned about his health and fully absorbed by
the imminent discussion of the paragraph in the *De ecclesia* that
defined the Church as a sacrament, an expression he detested and had
fought for years.[110]

---

[108] See Martano, *Athenagoras*, 461.
[109] *NChenu*, October 1, 1963: "Here since Thursday, September 26. Opening ceremony, Sunday the 29th."
[110] Fenton stayed initially in the Salvator Mundi clinic, but was preparing to move
elsewhere: "Now I am leaving for the Grand Hotel to stay with the bishop. Ed Hanahoe
gave me two books on Modernism. In one of them I found evidence that the teaching in
the first chapter of the new schema on the Church and the language are those of Tyrrell.
May God preserve His Church from that chapter. If it passes, it will be a great evil. I must
pray and act" (*DFenton*, September 24, 1963).

5. The Journalists

The presence of journalists at the Council was impressive, pervasive, and difficult to evaluate.[111] The great slowness of procedures and debates; the systematic refusal of all efforts to gain simultaneous translation of the discussions; the inability of the Regulations to provide a more flexible method of participation than the mere exercise of the right to vote and the preparation of an intervention in the hall — all this did not lessen the bishops' and the public's desire to know what was going on, a desire as deep as was their dissatisfaction. The press and the journalists served, therefore, as multipliers of news, circulators of sensations and judgments, and collectors of notes that the fathers exchanged with one another. The choice of a bishop such as Martin O'Connor as head of the press office[112] gave journalists the hope that they might be able to obtain more information and, if we judge by the tone of his letter of September 19, to learn in greater detail who supported this or that thesis in the hall.[113]

It is not surprising, therefore, that a man like O. Semmelroth, a theologian who was always sensitive to the external reception of doctrinal movements, should fill the first pages of his diary for the new period with newspaper articles.[114] Above all, in some areas the collaboration

[111] There are few subjects on which the difference between testimonies and official sources is so great. On the one hand, testimonies insist, often in emphatic tones, on the "role" of headlines and journalists; on the other hand, in the reconstruction of the debates and in the official sources it is difficult to find precise evidence of such an impact. In various instances, the profession of journalist meant some risks for the individuals concerned, since they were viewed as enemies in Roman circles. Typical of this phenomenon was Redemptorist F. X. Murphy, who collaborated with *The New Yorker* magazine to produce "Letters from Vatican City," but under the pseudonym "Xavier Rynne," while telling his own General that he was not the writer of the articles. An indicator of the way the press was listened to in the hall was the hundreds of letters that the editor of *Avvenire* received from the fathers when they were leaving Rome at the end of the second period; see the La Valle Archive at the ISR.

[112] *History*, 2:555-56.

[113] See *ADP* II/1, 434: When organizing the *Notiziario*, O'Connor asked Cicognani "whether or not it was appropriate…to publish, along with the names of the individual speakers, a summary of their statements." The answer (unpublished or oral) was negative, but the tone of the *Notiziari* and then of the chronicle in *Avvenire d'Italia* very quickly allowed journalists to identify the author of each intervention.

[114] According to the Fenton Diary, however, everything was still a matter of personal sympathies and antipathies: "This morning, the 25th, they were wonderful to me at Santa Susanna. I met Murphy (Xavier Rynne), and he gave me his usual toothy and vacuous smile." In *TSemmelroth* for September 26, 1963: "I flew to Rome today on a pleasant flight. The second period of the Council is to begin next Sunday, the feast of St. Michael. I am again well housed at the Germanicum. Father Garbolino, with whom I became acquainted in Oberjoch, drove me from the airport. Father Haspecker, who at the moment is staying in Rome at the Biblicum, was also with him. Around six o'clock I went to the

with journalists by bishops such as Hurley and theologians such as Tillard had considerable weight.[115] Nor was it by chance that one of the first actions of Lercaro as "moderator" was to ask and obtain from the Secretary of State that *L'Avvenire d'Italia*, the Bologna daily edited by Raniero La Valle, be sent to all the fathers, subscriptions being paid by the Vatican for the entire period.[116]

B. The Opening: September 19, 1963

The feelings experienced at the opening ceremony of the second period were different from those of 1962, when those present were moved chiefly by the triumphalistic and completely hierarchical self-manifestation of the Church. At the beginning of the second period there was, on the contrary, a mood of disenchantment[117] and also a felt need of comfort that is typical of routinized events,[118] despite the fact that for many this was their first chance to see Paul VI, who had been pope for 100 days but was now appearing for the first time before the body of bishops. The question of the seats for the patriarchs, which had, the year before, shown the gap between Melkite sensibilities and Latin rudeness, had this year been raised again on the eve of the ceremonies[119] and would have happy results. Edelby thought he even saw the pope stop and greet the patriarchs "with especially warm gestures"—but, after all, Maximos IV was the only "novice" when it came to session openings.[120]

press conference given by Father Hirschmann for the German-speaking journalists; Auxiliary Bishop Kampe arranged it, as he did the one last year. Generally speaking, the mood is incomparably more positive than at the beginning of the first period last year. What has been worked out and achieved in the interim gives grounds for a certain confidence. In addition, there is a great deal of trust in the new pope." This is followed by an article from the *Frankfurter Allgemeine Zeitung* for September 26, 1963 on "Reform of the Curia."

[115] See A. Henriques, "Vatican II in the Southern Cross," *Bulletin for Contextual Theology in Southern Africa & Africa* 4 (1997), 31-39, and *L'Eglise canadienne et Vatican II*.

[116] See Lercaro, *Lettere*, 162.

[117] The fathers did not process across the square but down into the loggia of the basilica: *JEdelby*, September 29, 1963, 151-52.

[118] Fenton, who was "pleased" with the papal address, listened to it on TV (*DFenton*, September 30) in the hotel, as did Olivier (*DOlivier*, 198).

[119] *JPrignon*, September 25, 1963: "I asked the cardinal to intervene on behalf of a special place for the patriarchs; he agreed in principle." On September 24 Prignon had already noted that he had made "with Thils, a proposal to give the Oriental patriarchs special seats, seats in any case separate from those of the other archbishops and bishops" (*JPrignon* [A], September 24, 1963). However, the matter had already been discussed a few days before by Duprey and Edelby: see *JEdelby*, September 21, 1963, 141-44.

[120] *JEdelby*, 152.

Some bishops, like Argentinean Zazpe, was impressed by the greater sobriety of the ceremony.[121] The bishops were allowed to choose whether to come down directly into the basilica and sit on the first available seats or to enter in a procession ahead of Paul VI, but not across the square; those entering in procession would likewise take any seat without heed to the order of their consecration.[122] The desired simplification of the ceremony was crowned, so to speak, by the fact that the pope was not carried in but made his entrance on foot up the central nave of St. Peter's.[123] But others — a minority if the sources available are representative of the average — found the "spectacle" as beautiful and interesting as the year before.[124]

There were also those like Father Congar, who made a severe analysis of the ecclesiology implicit in the ceremonial. Paul VI's entrance into the hall on foot, meant as a gesture of respect to the bishops, did not impress him; the courtly pomp that still surrounded the person of the pope (the guards, the halberds, the sixteenth-century costumes, the fans, and above all the applause) scandalized him, although this time he managed to stay to the end of the rite.[125] Congar indulged in some over-interpretation; measuring the intensity of the applause in the several areas of the basilica, he was mistaken in thinking that the pope was applauded more by the archbishops than by the bishops, for he did not

[121] This had been the explicit wish of the Secretary of State; see *AS* V/1, 651. *DZazpe* for September 29 says: "Here I am at the opening of the Council....It was not as solemn as the opening last year....Paul VI....A noble figure whose gestures are measured....Address. A composition full of thought, a little long....Four points: (a) belief of the Church; (b) episcopate; (c) ecumenism; (d) dialogue with the world....I took a siesta and had a conversation with Trusso. He has financial difficulties."

[122] *DDevoto*, September 29: "9 — public session for the reopening of Vatican Council II.—Free choice of seats in the Council hall, next to Msgr. Aguirre — *Veni Creator* — Pontifical Mass celebrated by Cardinal Tisserant — Pope's oath — Obedience of the Council fathers — Papal address: (1) Idea of the Church; (2) Renewal of the Church; (3) The Church and non-Catholics; (4) The Church and the world — Rest — Mass at the hotel (for the people) — Rest." Note the private mass, on the eve of the voting on the liturgy!

[123] Thus the Press Department of the American episcopate; now in *Council Daybook — Vatican II, Session 1–Session 2*, ed. F. Anderson (Washington, D.C., 1964), 141.

[124] Thus Bergonzoni, September 29, 1963.

[125] *JCongar*, September 29, 1963: "Towards 10 a.m., you can hear, first far off, then drawing nearer, the chanting of the Sistine Choir. The pope is making his entrance. Ahead of him, his court: the Swiss guards and their halberds, cardinals in priestly (or diaconal) vestments, wearing very tall miters, prelates in purple and in red, chamberlains in sixteenth-century dress, the insignia (the pope's tiara and miter), and finally the pope, accompanied by a deacon and subdeacon carrying fans. The pope wears the precious miter. He enters on foot; as he advances up the nave, the people in the rows he passes applaud, which greatly scandalizes me."

take into account that the fathers were seated in haphazard fashion.[126] Similarly, he gives an ecclesiological value, which others did not sense, to the singing of the *Veni Creator* by all the fathers (and the laity), who until that point had been mute spectators of the pontifical pomp.[127]

1. The Address of Paul VI

The pope's address was a sketch of what was to have been his programmatic encyclical, but which had been delayed for a time. Paul VI tells us as much in the opening greeting,[128] which he extends both to his "brothers in the episcopate" who have been called to the Council, and to those invited "that you may be with us" during this new period of the

---

[126] "Rather thin applause from the rows of the young bishops, much more abundant from the rows of the archbishops. I cannot but give an ecclesiological interpretation of the very structure of the ceremony: between two hedges of mute episcopal spectators, the pontifical court passes, dressed as in the sixteenth century, preceding a pope who appears as at once a temporal sovereign and a hierarch *above*, only above. The Sistine Choir bills and coos, the fathers join in one or two stanzas of the *Ave Maris Stella*. Is *this* the face the Church will retain? *This* the visibility it will have? Will it continue for a long time yet to give *this kind* of sign? It seems to me at this moment that the gospel *is* in the Church, but a captive."

[127] "Paul VI intones the *Veni Creator*. The Church recovers its voice, a sound of mighty waters, in order to pray. When, then, the pope alternates the verses with the choir of bishops, it is Peter praying with the Twelve. It is no longer the temporal prince of the sixteenth century. The bishops asked to sing the Ordinary of the Mass. The Sistine choir warbles a *Kyrie* and warbles an *Agnus Dei*, while displaying some splendid voices, but the bishops chant the *Gloria*, the *Credo*, the *Sanctus*. People sing along with them with all their heart, at least according to their strength. Thus, in the chants as in the entire ceremony, the truth of the *Ecclesia* alternates with the ways of the Renaissance. Cardinal Tisserant celebrates, poorly and without unction. After the Mass, the pope makes his profession of faith: the Creed and the profession of faith of the Council of Trent. Once again, it is Peter who appears and confesses Christ. After him, each order, in the person of one of its representatives, and then Msgr. Felici slowly read the same texts on behalf of those who might not yet have made their profession of faith. Then the pope, wearing a miter and seated on a throne between a deacon (Cardinal Ottaviani) and a subdeacon, reads his address. The bishops too are wearing their miters."

[128] The address, in *Insegnamenti* (1963), 1:166-85 and *AS* II/1, 183-200, makes this clear: "Our intention, following the tradition, was to present you with Our first encyclical letter. But, We asked ourselves, why communicate in writing what We might communicate to you orally in your presence on such a unique and very favorable occasion, namely, the ecumenical council? We cannot now set forth everything We have in mind; some subjects are more easily discussed in writing. But We think that this address can serve as introduction both to this council and to Our pontificate" (167-68). There are some remarks in Colombo, "Genesi," 138, on the parallel sequence of subjects in the address and in chapters of the encyclical. See also G. Colombo, "I discorsi di Paolo VI in apertura e chiusura dei periodi conciliari," in *Paolo VI e il rapporto chiesa-mondo al Concilio*, 253-63, based on documents at the Istituto Paulo VI, access to which is barred to scholars.

Council, which brilliantly displays the marks of the Church "by which we proclaim it to be one and catholic." The assembly, "like another upper room," brings together the successor of Peter and the bishops, to whom Paul VI gives a title significant in terms of the agenda of the coming days: "You, venerable brothers, are yourselves apostles; you have your origin in the apostolic college and are its authentic heirs."[129]

The pope assures everyone that he is not motivated by a quest for human domination or by a concern for his own authority, and he assures the bishops of his veneration, esteem, confidence, and love. The greeting is followed by two short introductory sections. The first consists of praise of John XXIII[130] and repeats some points from *Gaudet Mater Ecclesia* — the passage on the safeguarding of doctrine and its proposal in forms required by the modern age, which ends with the reference to the pastoral character of the Council. Pope John, according to his successor, had thereby opened up a providential path along which the Council must now advance. The second introductory section is devoted to describing Christ as the source, way, and purpose of the Council:[131] there is no light, there is no truth except Christ, who must shine forth in the deliberations of the Council; the fathers must therefore fix their eyes on only one object: "The whole Christ, of whom we read in St. Augustine and who pervades the entire teaching of the Church, will show more clearly the main purposes of the Council."[132] The allocution now gets to the heart of the matter as it points out how the Council is to adhere to this christological principle in its discussion of the doctrine on the Church and the Church's self-consciousness, matters on which Cardinal Montini had already touched in his address to the Council ten months earlier.[133]

The first of the four parts into which the address is divided specifies as the Council's task a full definition of the idea or consciousness of the Church. Paul VI lists a number of images describing the Church (the plurality of images had inspired the effort at revision during the intersession), but he suggests that the fuller definition of the Church for which Pius XII had asked in his *Mystici Corporis* requires an investigation of the *nature*, the *definition*, and the *constitution* of the Church (a list that gave support to the ecclesiological positions defeated during the first

[129] *Insegnamenti* (1963), 1:167.
[130] Ibid., 1:168-70.
[131] Ibid., 1:170-72.
[132] Ibid., 1:172.
[133] See *History*, 2:344-45.

period). The statement that a deeper understanding of the doctrine of the episcopate could be a way of helping and supporting the pope's ministry was interpreted by some, in the optimism of the moment, as a reference to some form of institutionalized collegiality.[134]

The second section has to do with the renewal of the Catholic Church. This renewal is necessary not because the Church has departed from the plan of its founder in any essential way, but because it will make it possible to drop transitory and outdated forms of a tradition which remains valid and enduring in its core.[135] An example of this effort at renewal is the Constitution on the Sacred Liturgy, which the pope hopes to see approved during the period now beginning.

In the third section the pope takes up the conciliar goal of the restoration of unity.[136] This is the strongest part of the address; in it Paul VI utters some sentences of great weight and impact, which, however, are really not homogeneous with the other parts of the address. The pope defends an ecumenism that combines unity and variety, and he addresses to the other Churches, by way of the observers, a request for forgiveness for faults committed by the Catholic Church, while he in turn forgives injuries done to the Catholic Church.[137]

Finally, Paul VI says that the key for relating to the present age is dialogue.[138] This is the most substantial anticipation of the programmatic encyclical and the key to Pope Montini's thinking, and its tone is more personal. Referring back to the "Message to the World" of the first period,[139] which was testimony to the impulse of charity by which the Church desired to be motivated, Paul VI asks that the Council be able to look at the great dramatic needs of the world: poverty and cultures, workers and governors, the young and seekers after justice, and finally, those who "preserve the awareness and idea of God, as one, the creator, provident, supreme, and transcending

[134] *Insegnamenti* (1963), 1:172-75. On the reaction of the secretaries of the episcopal conferences, see below (61-62).

[135] Ibid., 1:175-77.

[136] Ibid., 1:177-80.

[137] Throughout the second period Lukas Vischer will see this passage as a decisive key for interpreting the beginning of the pontificate. Visser't Hooft would maintain that "the value of words of repentance depends on their spontaneity." See Velati, "Gli osservatori," notes 61-63.

[138] *Insegnamenti* (1963), 1:180-84. The edition of the discourse that is being cited here conveys an insidious rejection in its title, which should be not *collocatio* (the *lectio facilior?*) but *collocutio*, which is correctly given in *AS* II/1, 195.

[139] *History*, 2:50-54.

nature."[140] The Church wants to engage all in a dialogue that conveys the gospel, but it does not forget the situations of conflict in which the Church meets opposition and which account for the "many places which the pope sees empty in the hall."[141] The address ended, after sixty-four minutes,[142] with a greeting in Greek and Russian to the Oriental communities.

Journalists greeted Montini's address with satisfaction. Xavier Rynne interpreted it as a bridge of continuity between the "Johannine" Council and the "Pauline" Council;[143] Raniero La Valle singled out the call for dialogue;[144] Antoine Wenger noted the more pessimistic tone of Montini's address.[145] The reports of the ambassadors accredited to Rome or to the Holy See added nothing new, nor did they mention the negative judgments that were circulating.[146]

The papal discourse had echoes even in private diaries and letters. Lercaro thought Paul VI had delivered a "truly great" address.[147] The editor-in-chief of *Civiltà Cattolica*, R. Tucci, who published an edition of the address, noted in his diary some points on the recurrent problem of "last minute editing" of the text, concerning which he brings together

---

[140] *Insegnamenti* (1963), 1:183-84. The quoted words are the formula Pius XI derived from the study of primitive monotheism.

[141] As in the first period, the entire episcopates of China, North Vietnam, and North Korea were missing from the Council. In the communist countries of Europe circumstances had changed somewhat: of the seventeen Hungarian bishops with the right to attend (two of whom had come in 1962), five were given permission to come to the Council in 1963; from Czechoslovakia four bishops (but none of the eight released from prison between the election of Paul and the beginning of the period) came to the second period, as against three the year before; all the bishops in Soviet territory, except for Slipyi, an exile, were prevented from coming, as were three Rumanians and one of the two Bulgarians. The Yugoslav episcopate came in its entirety, as in 1962, while of the seventy Polish bishops, who had requested forty-five exit permits, only twenty-five were able to leave for Rome. On this subject see H.-J. Stehle, *Geheimdiplomatie im Vatikan. Die Päpste und die Kommunisten* (Zurich, 1993). An account of the activities undertaken by Cardinal König and Msgr. A. Casaroli was given in *La Croix* and is now available in Wenger, 19-22.

[142] See the chronicle in *The New Yorker*, now in Rynne, 34.

[143] Rynne, 36-37.

[144] This editor's articles were collected in R. La Valle, *Coraggio del Concilio* (Rome, 1964).

[145] Wenger, 18.

[146] G. Richard-Molard judged the address harshly, describing it as "cold, dense, at times triumphalist, at times paternalist in tone" (*L'hiver de Vatican II. Un pasteur au Concile* [Paris, 1965], 25).

[147] Lercaro, *Lettere*, 164.

valuable details.[148] Bartoletti, one of the Italian bishops who had waxed
lyrical on October 11, commented on the main lines of the address, on
the first page of his diary for the second period, having jotted them down
as it was being delivered (something he had become accustomed to do
during the long mornings of discussion in 1962).[149] Bergonzoni, too,
praised the address as "beautiful and important" in that the pope had
dictated the program "for the entire period, even, one may say, for the
entire Council."[150] The need to understand what the pope wants is a
requirement, if not an instinct, of the body of Latin bishops. Congar was
among the few who could see the lack of symmetry between the Coun-
cil-as-light of John XXIII (for whom the otherness of church and world
is overcome by the gift of grace) and the Council-as-dialogue of Paul VI
(which builds a bridge, but in doing do acknowledges the gap).[151]

[148] "I asked Manzini about the original text of the papal discourse on September 29.
He assured me that the Italian text published in *L'Osservatore Romano* is the one which
they 'received' and which was also adopted by the Secretariat of State. It is therefore the
'official' text, to use Manzini's word. This even though there was the strange case of
Msgr. Tondini correcting the Italian text at a point where it did not correspond to the
Latin translation!!! I think, therefore, that in our periodical it is better not to touch anything and not to call it 'our translation.' I don't remember who told us that the fathers of
our General Curia worked hard on translations of the document into the various languages
and that at the last moment the brothers who did the typing had a lot of work to do
recopying many pages, because corrections and changes were made from On High at
eight different points"; *DTucci*, 162.

[149] "Though the address of the Holy Father did not have the spontaneity of Pope John,
it seemed to me nonetheless important and decisive in relation to the work of the Council. He pinned down its subject, pointed out its spirit, and traced its itinerary without possibility of *further* [italics added] ambiguities. The ceremony was rather untidy. The lack
of novelty has chilled the warmth that was so keenly perceptible at the opening of the first
period"; see the extract from the diary of Msgr. Enrico Bartoletti, in M. Toschi, "Enrico
Bartoletti e il suo diario al concilio," in *Cristianesimo nella storia. Saggi in onore di
Giuseppe Alberigo*, ed. A. Melloni *et al.* (Bologna1996), 421.

[150] *DBergonzini*, September 29, 1963, 57.

[151] Congar's analysis of the entire text, rather than mentally reconstructing the text (a
rather useless piece of work, since he, like everyone else, knew that at midday they would
have the text in their hands), stressed the points read by the pope with greater warmth, as
well as those little statements (either directed at the bishops or in his explanation of why
the encyclical had not come out) that could be important in discerning moves that might
immediately become part of a program. "A very long, very structured address, read at
some moments with lively and eloquent feeling. The pope clearly underscores the role of
the bishops, whom he calls 'brothers in the episcopate,' and says that they are heirs of the
apostolic college. He says that he wants to pray, study, and discuss *with them* during the
Council. He will publish an encyclical only later on; his present address sketches its program. He refers to the address of John XXIII last October 8. For quite a while he
addresses John XXIII directly, thus making him present. He emphasizes the usefulness of
the council, something that some were a short while ago doubting, as if papal authority
were enough! He also emphasizes the *pastoral* character of the present Council. There is
no question of simply *preserving*. What path is to be taken? What is to be the starting

2. The Complementary Audiences

The dominant themes of the allocution were repeated in the addresses that completed the opening ceremonies. Unlike his predecessor the year before, Paul VI did not give audiences to the politico-diplomatic delegations that were present; even the meeting with the observers was postponed to October 17 in the vain expectation that delegates would arrive from Constantinople.[152] As a result, the first audience given to a conciliar group was to the journalists on October 1. Paul VI bade them not to be fooled by the fact that the Council "resembles in certain respects" parliamentary and international assemblies, and he urged them not to concentrate on these appearances; in fact, the bishops "try to avoid giving any foundation for these differences" in orientation or origin, in order to let themselves be guided by the "objective divine truth" that they profess.[153]

Only on October 17 would there be the meeting with the observers, but the delay was amply compensated for by the atmosphere of exceptional

point? Where are we to go? There is only one answer to these key questions: Jesus Christ. It is he who is our source, our way, our goal. The pope says as much and develops the thought with a great deal of power and emotional intensity. Christ the source of all. The pope recalls the mosaic in St. Paul's Outside the Walls in which Honorius III has himself represented as a very small figure, prostrated before Christ....Christ the goal. This ought to shed light on the goal of the Council, which is (1) to define the idea of the Church: What does she say of herself? The pope, who develops rather at length and very energetically each of his four points emphasizes here mystical body and society. (2) The renewal of the Church, whose necessary relationship with Christ the pope takes up here: as a historical and human reality, the Church is never completely what Christ requires her to be. (3) The reunification of all Christians. Paul VI speaks here both forcefully, specifically, and with feeling. His expressions are carefully chosen. The phrase 'the venerable Christian communities' occurs several times as a description of the other Churches....He admits that the other Churches have sometimes successfully developed what they have accepted of Christianity. If there has been any fault on our part, he asks forgiveness of it; we, too, forgive. (4) Dialogue with the world. Paul VI recalls the "Message to the World," in which he sees a witness to the Church's prophetic role....He places the relationship of the Church with the world — those who are near and those who are far off — under the sign of *Christ's universal love*. It is in this section that he says a little about the martyrs in countries in which persecution is alive. A very strong, very structured address which gives precise guidelines for the work of the Council. The address ended at 1:00 p.m." (*JCongar*, September 29, 1963).

[152] That this address was originally intended to be read shortly after the opening address is still clear from the second section, which speaks of this audience as "a renewal, in a more intimate atmosphere, of the occasion with which the Council provided us *just the other day*."

[153] *Insegnamenti* (1963), 1:186-88.

fraternal feeling.[154] Kristen E. Skydsgaard read a greeting,[155] after that of Bea,[156] and the pope responded to both in French and in a spirit of openness even "more than John XXIII," as Congar remarked when analyzing his remarks.[157] The pope assured the observers of his friendship and respect and suggested an encounter of the Churches that would rise above the temptation of looking to the past. The group of observers had a positive view of the meeting; the fact that they had entered the papal apartment with a sense of irony rather than of scandal ("It does not look like the house of a carpenter from Nazareth," said one person on entering; "No, he has greatly improved it," was the response[158]) bore witness to a certain confidence in situations that a few years before would have been intolerable.[159]

IV. THE PROBLEM OF THE SCHEMA ON THE CHURCH: FIRST STEPS

Quickly putting the opening ceremony behind them, the fathers prepared to return to work; bishops, journalists, and experts resumed their several series of meetings. Knowing that the discussion of the schema on the Church would begin the next day, the theologians were immediately

[154] Ibid., 1:229-35. On October 17 the moderators would find the pope quite satisfied; see Lercaro, *Lettere*, 190.

[155] Skydsgaard began by recalling the person of John XXIII and thanking Bea for having encouraged the observers to state their views freely on the schemas; the Danish theologian signaled the importance, in the ecclesiological debate now going on, of Catholics and non-Catholics together facing up to the difficulties of the subject, and hoped that the conciliar ecclesiology would be rooted in the Bible; in closing he thanked Paul VI for having continued in the line of his predecessor by linking openness to ecumenical dialogue to openness to the world in service. The text of the address is in *Insegnamenti* (1963), 1:234-35.

[156] *Insegnamenti* (1963), 1:233-34. On October 2 Bea had been appointed a member of the plenary assembly of the Holy Office; see S. Schmidt, *Augustine Bea: The Cardinal of Unity*, trans. L. Wearne (New Rochelle, N.Y.: New City Press, 1992) 536-70.

[157] *JCongar*, October 17, 1963. The event was regarded as a historic dialogue by H. M. Féret, "La théologie concrète et historique et son importance pastorale présente," in *Le service théologique dans l'église. Mélanges offerts au Père Yves Congar* (Paris, 1974), 193-247.

[158] Horton, 72.

[159] A rather mutual diffidence emerged, as Congar joined Nissiotis in defending the role of the Taizé Brothers; *JCongar*, October 17, 1963: "Finally, regarding the Taizé Brothers, they find that they 'exaggerate': in one respect, by their excessively clerical appearance (their slippage toward St. Peter), in another, by their systematic policy of contacting as many bishops as possible. They see here a hint of indiscretion or professionalism (sic). But I stress the point that within its very human limits Taizé is a real miracle, a work of God, and as such cannot be measured in the usual way!"

faced with the problem of the order among the chapters and the possible integration of other schemas into this one.[160]

Various episcopates set up meetings among themselves and with theologians that would became regular or quasi-regular affairs.[161] The Pan-African group, which would be very active in the coming weeks, gave birth to "a committee of theologians for all of Africa."[162] The "strategy workshop," a French-speaking group that would hold meetings on Wednesdays, also got under way during these early days.[163] The best-organized conferences (the French, the German-speaking, the Dutch, the Polish, the Canadian, and others) had calendars of meetings to listen to views on the work they were resuming.

The debate continued on what should be in the schema on the Church, and various proposals were made to *add* other sections and themes to this schema, to which the pope had assigned a central role in the work of Vatican II. The possibility of incorporating other schemas into the schema on the Church was part of the discussion for several weeks, as though everyone shared the impression that only the constitution on the Church could "save" the other schemas from being annulled, an outcome that would have been an implicit humiliation for the various circles that had promoted their composition.

Even for relations with the non-Christian religions and for the controverted schema on the Jews, some thought that the best solution would be to introduce a chapter into the schema on the Church, if for no other reason than to ensure a careful and binding *dogmatic* statement on relations with Israel.[164] But if this bunch of subjects, which at bottom represented an embryonic revision of a course *De Deo revelante*, could be incorporated, could not the entire schema on revelation also be made part of the

---

[160] Some prepared for the work by taking a break: "In the morning I received a call telling me that Bishop Volk had gotten me a ticket of admission to St. Peter's. So I went there....in the afternoon Father Garbolino came, and we took a ride to Tivoli, where we viewed the gardens of the Villa d'Este with their wonderful water displays. It was a very nice excursion. But the last few days were too stressful for my body. I have probably taken on too much. In any case, I feel quite poor physically. But I hope that with more rest I will feel better" (*TSemmelroth*, September 29, 1963).

[161] The Congolese met at 4 p.m. on September 29, 1963; see *DOlivier*, 199.

[162] See the testimony of Bernard Olivier, an expert for the Congolese bishops; *DOlivier*, 199. Of limited value (but with a good outline of the interventions of the African bishops, both missionary and native) is G. Conus, *L'Eglise d'Afrique au Concile Vatican II* (Immensee, 1975).

[163] *JCongar*, September 29, 1963.

[164] *JCongar*, October 2, 1963.

De ecclesia,[165] as Elchinger wanted?[166] Could not the *De traditione*, which Garrone considered decisive? The group that revised the schema on the states of perfection were obviously ready to argue the need for a chapter on vowed consecration (and the pace of their work in September showed that they wanted to be ready); as for the laity, should it have a separate schema? It was also known that some were thinking also of incorporating the schema on the missions into the *De ecclesia*.[167]

---

[165] Congar took part in a meeting on the incorporation of the *De revelatione* into the *De ecclesia*, the first hint of a lively and lasting debate: "I learned today, at the meeting of the French bishops, that they have decided (1) who can take part in the Wednesday meetings: *not* the theologians, unless they are invited as lecturers; (2) to establish a commission that will organize and moderate the work of the bishops; it is made up of Msgrs. Marty, Gouyon, Ancel, Guyot, Maziers, de Provenchères, Elchinger, and Le Cordier; (3) to appoint a bishop for relations with each of the other episcopates; (4) before the Council, there was a meeting in Florence of some French bishops (Cardinal Lefebvre, Msgrs. Garrone, Marty...) and five Italian bishops (in fact, only four), *who were delegated by the conference of Italian bishops*. They sent a paper to this effect to the presidents of the Council. — On the other hand, Abbé Haubtmann told me that the French bishops are very largely in agreement that, along with the *De revelatione*, the *De Beata Virgine Maria* should also be incorporated into the *De Ecclesia*. It was only at 4.30 p.m. that Father Féret took me to the Angelicum, together with my baggage. I can hardly stand up. Father Gagnebet told me that by the pope's decision the *De revelatione* will not be taken up at this session. The program has been set: they will study five schemes, *De ecclesia*, *De Beata Virgine Maria*, *De oecumenismo*, *De Apostolatu laicorum*, *De regimine Dioecesium*" (*JCongar*, September 29, 1963).

[166] "Around 7.30 p.m. I took my three friends from Vietnam to St. Thomas of Villanova in order (1) to see Father Féret, make his acquaintance, and get from him a text of his remarks; (2) to see Msgr. Elchinger, who, as a member of the commission that is organizing the work of the French bishops, can set us on the right track. Our visit was in fact very productive. We saw not only Féret and Msgr. Elchinger, but Father Liégé as well. We found them in the midst of the work. In fact, this little group is planning a *De Ecclesia* that puts everything together according to the progress of the economy or the history of salvation. I agree with the ideas, but I am less sure that this is the real question, or even that it is concretely possible. On the other hand, I very much agree with Msgr. Elchinger, who intends to intervene tomorrow and who read us the text of a planned intervention that emphasizes the difficulties against voting immediately on the schema as a whole and then immediately beginning the discussion of the prologue and chapter I. In fact, on the one side, there are still too many unanswered questions about the content of *De Ecclesia*. A number of people speak of incorporating into it the *De Revelatione* or the *De Beata* or a chapter on the eschatological Church or a chapter *De missione*....This raises the question of the overall conception and plan, on which there is no clarity. The schema reflects its origins. It was never conceived as a *De Ecclesia*; in fact, it was never 'conceived' as a unity at all. As a result, people are proposing to add this or that chapter...following a certain order that would in itself have doctrinal value. Otherwise they will keep making additions, and the thing will not really be a whole!" (*JCongar*, September 30, 1963).

[167] *JCongar*, October 1, 1963. The development of this schema would be blocked by the contrary vote of the Doctrinal Commission on October 23, 1963.

Finally, there was the question of the schema on the Blessed Virgin. There had already been a discussion of Balić's schema, which in comparison with that of the year before had changed only the second part of the title, from "Mother of God and Humanity" to "Mother of the Church"; a choice had also been made regarding its place in the "system" of schemas drawn up during the preparatory period.[168] But the request to incorporate the subject into the *De ecclesia* had acquired a different meaning: the mariologists claimed that not to devote a schema to the Blessed Virgin would be a culpable reduction, while the ecumenists feared that mariology would be used in a way that would cause difficulties for dialogue.

A. THE BEGINNING OF THE DEBATE

The debate began on September 30, 1963. At the end of the long nave of the basilica the new table provided for the moderators was a physical sign of the simplified organization represented by the new body. Some of the announcements of the General Secretary, as well as of his undersecretaries who served as translators, seemed to point in the same direction. Msgr. Felici announced the beginning of the discussion and recalled some of the new regulatory norms urging bishops to make collective statements so as to avoid repetition; he also announced that no new experts would be appointed. The rule requiring bishops to submit a summary to the secretariat three days in advance served to dissuade aspiring orators; since precedence in speaking in the hall was determined by ecclesiastical rank, this meant that an individual bishop had little chance of saying something at the right moment about a question. The reassertion of the law of secrecy "always and everywhere" was not very comforting.[169]

The debate began at the point where it had broken off the year before: with the schema on the Church. The new schema was presented by the same protagonists, Cardinals Ottaviani and Browne, president and vice-president of the Doctrinal Commission.[170] And yet a great deal had

---

[168] The schema had become independent of the *De ecclesia* on June 2, 1962; see *History*, 2:480-81, and C. M. Antonelli, "Le rôle de Mgr Gérard Philips dans la rédaction du Chapitre VIII de *Lumen gentium*," *Marianum. Ephemerides Mariologicae* 55 (1993), 17-97; Indelicato, 307-11.

[169] *AS* II/1, 205-13.

[170] The presentation (*AS* II/1, 337-42) was deliberately and exceptionally sober; see U. Betti, *La dottrina sull'episcopato del Concilio Vaticano II. Il capitolo III della costituzione dommatica Lumen gentium* (Rome, 1984), 118.

changed. The spirit of the bishops was different, for they had become used to saying No calmly and without fear; the Council was different, since it had instrumentalities and a self-consciousness it did not have when it first opened; the pope was different and held that the Council's work should have an all-embracing focus — precisely this one, the Church. Two general congregations (37-38) and the first interventions, twenty of them, on the schema in general were all it took to show that a real and fruitful change had taken place.

Once again, in this period, Frings was one of the first speakers, presenting requests in his own name and in the name of sixty-five German and Scandinavian fathers. While approving the schema, he asked for a more explicit emphasis on the Church as sacrament;[171] an emphasis on poverty; greater detailing of the key points of disciplinary reform; the inclusion of the schema on the Virgin (to which Agagianian replied aloud that it was "being studied").[172] Siri spoke next, followed by the non- cardinals.[173]

At the end of the morning Giuseppe Gargitter, Bishop of Bolzano-Bressanone, an Italian by nationality who in Rome took part in meetings of the German Episcopal Conference, made a proposal that was to have great weight in the final arrangement of the schema. The division of the chapter on the laity into two parts (on the People of God in general, and on the laity in particular) had already been proposed by Suenens in July in the CC, where a different ordering of the chapters had been suggested so as to place these two sections in two different places in the schema (one before and one after the chapter on the hierarchy). But it was only *after* the Bishop of Bolzano (who always maintained that he had not spoken with others[174]) made his intervention in St. Peter's that this proposal, rich in systematic value and doctrinal importance, was put on the agenda again and became a reality.

The second day of the general discussion, October 1, also saw some important interventions. Chilean Cardinal Silva Henriquez, who early in 1963 had directed the composition of a well-organized schema on the

---

[171] The use of this category embodied one of the basic theological petitions of German circles, as Ratzinger explained in his *Theological Highlights*, 48-49. During the second period some major contributions were made by the group of German experts (Rahner, Semmelroth, Mörsdorf, and Hirschmann, who were joined by Küng, Ratzinger, and Jedin), the list of whom is given in Vorgrimler, *Understanding Karl Rahner*, 175-76. Jedin wrote: "The hour of the dogmaticians had come" (*Lebensbericht*, 211).

[172] *AS* II/1, 343-47.

[173] The very short statement of Siri, almost a declaration of his vote, is in *AS* II/1, 347.

[174] This in a letter of September 9, 1985, to G. Colombo (copy at the ISR).

Church, asked that more space be given to two leading ideas: *koinonia* and the integration of the many images of the Church with the trinitarian dimension, of which the commission's schema had not taken much account.[175] Again, like others,[176] he took the occasion to plead that the schema on the Virgin Mary be incorporated into the Constitution on the Church, a proposal that was aimed at reducing the danger of anti-ecumenical use of mariology. But while the first proposal on the structure of the constitution (putting the chapter on the People of God first) produced only agreement and praise, this second motion prompted greater uncertainties and would be resolved only at the end of the month.[177]

While the interventions were taking place, an announcement was made that a vote would be taken on the acceptability of the schema as a whole. This vote, the first of the second period, seemed to be a plebiscite on what had until this point been the "Philips schema," although filled out and revised by various bodies, but now would become the base text (or "*textus receptus,*" in conciliar Latin): of 2301 fathers present, there were 27 invalid votes, 43 against, and 2231 in favor.[178] The text accepted was thus the four-part one sent out in the spring: chapter I, on the mystery of the Church in the light of the economy of salvation, from the Father's plan to the Son's earthly pilgrimage; chapter II, on the hierarchical structure of the Church and on its bishops, who are called to govern the Church in accordance with a responsibility imposed by communion (collegiality) and using the gifts that the sacrament of their consecration bestows on them; chapter III, on the People of God and the laity, leading to an acknowledgment of the part to be played by all the baptized in the mission of the Church; and chapter IV, on the call to holiness of the entire Church, which is both the instrument and the fruit of grace.

The text, however, was already being modified: the division of the chapter on the laity and the setting up of a new chapter II on the People of God had already taken form; the structuring of a special chapter on religious had already been entrusted during the summer to Bishops

[175] *AS* II/1, 366-68. *JPrignon* (A), September 30, 1963: "I cannot forget that I tried for three months during the commission meetings to have the trinitarian schema brought in and that in doing so I had to overcome the resistance of Msgr. Charue himself."

[176] *AS* II/1, 374-75 (Garrone); 378-80 (Elchinger); 385-87 (Mendez Arceo).

[177] Congar notes that Laurentin wrote "his own" schema on the Virgin (*JCongar*, October 1963 [f. 10]).

[178] *AS* II/1, 111 and 391: the counting of the ballots, for which punch cards were used, took less than an hour (10:59 to 11:51 a.m.).

Charue and McGrath, with the assistance of some experts.[179] Still the "general" vote provided for by the Regulations was a decisive and irreversible transition for Vatican II and its principal constitution. Although immense possibilities remained for correcting the text, the order of chapters, the balance of the formulas, and the doctrinal solutions, in fact this schema on the Church had now burned its bridges behind it — even without the question yet having been raised of its dogmatic status, regarding which the moderators had, the evening before, proposed a three-level plan to the pope.[180]

On the one hand, the vote on October 1 had forever buried the preparatory schema, and it would be impossible now to turn back. Vatican II, the vote said, would write neither a treatise on the nature of the Church nor one of those scholastic reviews that the preparatory schema contained; the only things that would remain in the schema were the things that Philips had taken over from the theses of Lattanzi and Gagnebet. On the other hand, the vote accepted the "new" schema as the measure of what was possible; and after this vote the many remarks written or sent in during the summer, which had shown a desire for rather radical changes, would have to follow patiently the path of intervention and emendation. While Philips's cautious and politically astute work of weaving together the new schema had broken down the prejudice (invoked to defend the preparatory schema) that no change could be made, his work also still bore the mark of the original schema in its uncertainties, ambiguities, compromises, and juxtapositions.[181] With the approval of this schema, efforts to rethink the questions of the schema

[179] Tromp, *RT*, 32-40; the experts were Gagnebet, Häring, Philips, Medina, Thils, and Labourdette.

[180] On September 30, 1963, Dossetti had informed Colombo that he had sent the moderators a note on the dogmatic qualification of the schemas. His statement would be discussed by the Doctrinal Commission on September 15 and would be the subject of a written *observatio* from Tromp at the meeting on September 30 (Colombo Archive, XXI).

[181] On Philips's fears that his text would be withdrawn, see *JPrignon*. The desire to consolidate the result achieved had already been voiced by Philips in a letter to Colombo of August 8, 1963: "For my part, I hope that the attractiveness of the schema *De Ecclesia* will not be changed; otherwise we could be endlessly beginning anew. Some editorial adaptations will obviously be needed. It is desirable that the new session of the Council should immediately finish the schema on the liturgy, then take up the *De Revelatione* and the *De Ecclesia*, that is, the parts that are most awaited and undoubtedly the most important. It would perhaps be useful if the Holy Father were to make it known that the text of the Theological Commission, with the transpositions suggested by Cardinal Suenens, is to serve as the basis for the Council's deliberations. Changes could always be proposed. But if we allow entirely new versions to be discussed, we will never end. I leave these thoughts for your enlightened judgment" (Colombo Archive, C-XXII).

on the Church that had come to light during 1963 were barred; only by abandoning their distinct synthetic visions, which is what gave them their value, would the French schema or the Chilean schema be able to influence the constitution. Everything that followed an internal law of doctrinal development (for example, the chapter on communion in the Chilean document) would have to be reduced to an amendment, which meant in practice that it would be lost in the thicket of small corrections.

In any case, the result of the vote showed that the Council wanted and was able to move forward.[182] The letter that the moderators sent to Paul VI asking for an audience on the following Thursday, along with the documents enclosed with it,[183] showed that Suenens, Döpfner, Lercaro, and to some extent even Agagianian (undoubtedly a spokesman for a minority curial wing at the Council, who now, at the beginning of the moderators' work, chose passive collaboration) saw clearly the point of the new phase of the Council, namely, the agreement of the commissions with the intentions voiced in the hall.[184]

At their first Tuesday meeting of this period, it became clear that the text to be discussed and the way in which it was being studied also satisfied the non-Catholic delegates. The requests for corrections (on the eucharistic dimension and pneumatological aspect of the Church) were not remarks on details concealing definitive criticisms; rather they offered real and proper emendations by means of which the observers, their Churches, and the bodies they represented made a direct contribution to the development of the text.[185]

B. THE INTERVENTIONS ON THE MYSTERY OF THE CHURCH (CHAPTER I)

With the general approval of the schema, the discussion could begin with the introduction and chapter I, which were debated October 1-4. The Introduction reworked the earlier material with both novelty and variation. The novelty was not only that the Church no longer gave itself priority over the truth to be proclaimed, as in the preparatory schema,

---

[182] This explains Congar's remark about the weight exerted by assembly procedure, which, in itself, could be accepted as necessary for reaching any result in a deliberative assembly; see *JCongar*, September 30, 1963, cited in note 165, above.

[183] See Alberigo, "Concilio acefalo," 231-33.

[184] See ibid. Dossetti's minutes of the moderators' meetings on October 2, 3, and 7.

[185] E.g., Cullmann enthusiastically endorsed the proposal to bring in the People of God before the hierarchy; there is a lively account of the meeting in Horton, 23-25.

nor any longer described itself as "light of the nations" (as the Germans proposed); instead it gave this position and this description to Christ. The variation had to do with the theme of the Church's character as a sacrament. Borrowing from the notes of the German theologians, the schema proposed to say that the Church is a sacrament of the unity of the human race. The text given to the fathers introduced a brief explanation ("sacrament," that is,"sign and instrument"), which was meant to make more acceptable the extension of the term *sacrament* to other aspects and realities, thus moving beyond the Tridentine limitation of the term to those seven sacraments ("neither more nor fewer") by which that Council wanted to differentiate between Catholicism and Protestantism.

Chapter I (seven pages of text, and seven of notes, for ten paragraphs) reworked the preparatory material on the *nature* of the Church in a new setting, that of the *mystery* of the Church. Here the trinitarian economy becomes the source of the Church's life; the salvation-history model is accepted (this was the strong point in the French schema, which bore Congar's stamp). Thus the Church is born of the one and triune God, so that it has its ground in "the primordial dogma of Christianity."[186] The consequences of this statement, however, are expressed rather uncertainly. The "Church since Abel" (*ecclesia ab Abel*) is prefigured in God's people of the promise and lives in the communion of grace that comes from the Incarnation. At the same time, however (no. 3), the German perspective on the Church as the place in which the unity of the human race in Christ is made manifest reopens the door to a description of the structural reality of the Church in its juridical framework.

This bipartite aspect is completed by the reference (of Chilean origin) to the action of the Spirit, who establishes the connection between the ministries and is protagonist in the sacramental life and who is forcibly introduced here in order to take account of the various "alternative" perspectives to the preparatory schema. A citation in which Cyprian speaks of the Church made one "in the unity of the Father, the Son, and the Holy Spirit" introduces the section on the images of the Church.[187]

---

[186] *Commentarius*, in *Constitutio dogmatica De ecclesia*, a booklet distributed to the fathers: part I, p. 20

[187] The summer commentary just cited specified that the Church "is not only the People of God but the very Body of Christ" (20). In the Central Preparatory Commission, Hurley, Bishop of Durban, had courageously fought against the way the schema was organized; now, during the Council's work, he served as an anonymous correspondent for *The Southern Cross*. He saw the theme of ecclesial images as the real turning point: "The Second Vatican Council finds the Church in the throes of a transition from a theology of

There is a significant advance here beyond the preparatory schema in which the mystical body was offered as the first and essential image of this hierarchical society. The relation between Church and the Kingdom of God is still referred to in terms of a germination.

Number 7 takes up the visibility of the Church while a pilgrim on earth and repeats from *Mystici Corporis* and from the preparatory schema the strong assertion of the unity of the visible Church and the mystical reality of the Church. Unlike the line taken in the French schema, however, the assertion that the Church is a *means* of sanctification (an idea intended to reduce the dangers of a triumphalistic ecclesiolatry) does not prevent the statement being made in this context that the Church of Christ *is* the Catholic Church.

The schema also loses its innovative character in the section on "members," which had led people to judge that the proposals of the preparatory commission were incompatible with the ecumenical expectations aroused by the Council. The new text included neither the tripartite division of catechumens, baptized non-Catholics, and "people of good will," which had been in Philips's proposal of the year before, nor Vagaggini's formula, which distinguished between the intention of complete and visible membership, and the action of grace, which "by its power" makes members even of those outside the institutional boundaries of Roman Catholicism. Schauf's thesis, borrowed from Tromp, had been victorious,[188] even though the concluding sections try to show how Catholics, Christians in general, and non-Christians are related to the hierarchical structure of the Church.

The discussion, which lasted through three general congregations with forty-six oral and six written interventions, had to do chiefly with the description of the Church as sacrament of the unity of the human race.[189] This question, which had been debated in the preparatory phase, had an emblematic importance. It was on this point that Cardinal Ruffini made

---

concept to a theology of image. The concept was fine for defensive purposes but it is no good for progressive pastoral strategy. In shifting to the image, the Church finds itself in a 'back-to-the-Bible' campaign." See Ph. Denis, "Archbishop Hurley's Contribution to the Second Vatican Council," *Bulletin for Contextual Theology in Southern Africa and Africa* 4/1 (1997), 11.

[188] See H. Schauf, "Zur Frage der Kirchengliedschaft," *Theologische Revue* 58 (1962), 217-24.

[189] See Antonio Acerbi, *Due ecclesiologie: Ecclesiologia giuridica ed ecclesiologia di comunione nella "Lumen Gentium"* (Bologna, 1975) 261-67.

the first of his many interventions,[190] setting forth in bitter language his conviction that the definition of the Church as sacrament came from George Tyrrell and was therefore to be rejected as modernist! Only when the time came to vote on chapter I were Ruffini and his fellows made to realize that their image of a council of naive people seduced by ruffians was false. The paternalism with which the cardinals tied to the Roman schools threw their purple onto the scales of the debate accomplished nothing; the bishops listened, reasoned, gained information, linked up with others, and exchanged views.

However, the fact that the themes needed to be adequately digested became clear when Alfrink responded to Ruffini's objections. The latter had attacked the passage which said that the Church had as its foundation "Peter *and* the apostles," because, according to the Archbishop of Palermo, this suggested an unacceptable equality between the prince of the apostles and the others. The Dutch cardinal, who considered a clear assertion of collegiality to be necessary, allowed that the conjunction "and" might be changed and that it might be better to say "Petrus *ceterique* apostoli."[191] At the same time, other remarks were made that only the more attentive experts were in a position to grasp. The suggestion of Abbot Butler to distinguish between the Kingdom of God and the Kingdom of Christ seemed "very interesting" to Congar but remained a dead letter for others.[192] Even Bea's statement challenging the non-rigorous use of biblical citations, because of its lengthy written proposals, was on a level most could not reach.[193]

In contrast, it was changes in long-accepted theological viewpoints that kept the hall tense. When the moment came to abandon the dominance of the image of the mystical body, bishops and cardinals such as Ritter, Malanczuk, Dalmais, Lercaro, Enciso Viana, Volk, and Garrone asked that the schema might accept the germinal character of the

---

[190] *AS* II/1, 392-94. Unlike Siri, Ruffini was one of those who supported organizing a group opposed to innovations in ecclesiology. The fathers behind this undertaking (Sigaud, Lefebvre, Prou) and their experts (Berto and Frénaud) were not worried about the liturgy; they wrote that "the decrees on the liturgy are ready; they add only a few things to past practice" (cited by L. Perrin, "Il 'Coetus Internationalis Patrum' e la minoranza," in *Evento*, 173-87).

[191] Alfrink was thus ready to bring in a distinction (lacking in the NT source!) between Peter and the apostles (see *AS* II/1, 428-30); his comment was admired in *JEdelby*, October 2, 155-56.

[192] *AS* II/1, 428-651. Congar's comment in *JCongar*, October 2, 1963. On that same day Liénart told Congar he had heard the pope praise him as a theologian.

[193] *AS* II/1, 20-32.

Church, which is a sign of the Kingdom of God, and renounce hierarchic triumphalism. From various quarters and levels came complaints that the changes made were insufficient. Silva Henriquez criticized the weak emphasis on *koinonia* as the bond between Christians but also between Churches; he had suggested this at the end of the first period, but no heed had been taken of it.[194] A large number of fathers considered statements made in the discussion of the liturgical schema to be cues for correcting the schema on the Church.[195] Lercaro, for example, asked that the presence of Christ in the Church be described in terms of the sign and logic of the Eucharist; but other bishops, too, and many collective interventions, asked for references to the liturgy and to the hearing and keeping of the word of God.[196]

During the debate other groups urged their demands in the form of very general remarks about the spirit of the text.[197] Thus Rugambwa wanted a presentation of the Church that did not focus on its static existence but showed the dynamics of its progress, a view that Congar would explain to the African episcopate at one of the lectures promoted by Father Greco. Himmer asked that room be made for the idea of the *ecclesia pauperum* (the Church of the Poor), something which the group of the same name, to which he belonged, regarded as essential.[198] Finally, the core group of what was to become the *Coetus Internationalis Patrum* (International Group of Fathers), namely, Gerardo Proença Sigaud and Marcel Lefebvre, proposed an alternative schema, composed by Frénaud, the Abbot of Solesmes, and Berto, which sketched an image of the Church that was very much top-down and hierarchical, in opposition to

[194] *AS* II/1, 366-69 and 786-89. *JPrignon* (2), September 30, 1963, refers to a brusque contact between the Latin American cardinal and Suenens, whom he asked to make a statement on the text and who urged him instead to make his own speech in the hall.

[195] See, in particular, the statement of Van der Burgt, bishop from Indonesia, on October 3 (*AS* II/2, 59-61). On the same day Martin of Rheims made similar statements (ibid., 61-63).

[196] Lercaro, *AS* II/2, 9-13, and Volk, 45-47; on the redaction of the text see *TSemmelroth*, October 4, 1963. Whereas in the first period there had been few interventions by conferences, in this new period they multiplied and gave support to the request that would be made by the African episcopates that the conciliar week be divided in two: one half for work in the hall, and one half for work in the conferences. The interventions by groups and conferences of African, French, Argentinean, Uruguayan, Indonesian, and Dutch bishops are in *AS* II/1, 749-86 and 796-802.

[197] On October 3 there was a meeting exclusively of the observers that raised some difficulties about their acting and taking positions as a conciliar "group"; see Horton, 31-32.

[198] *JPrignon* (A), October 45, 1963, notes in Italian that Himmer spoke "from the heart" (*con cuore*). For the two interventions see *AS* II/1, 368-70, and II/1, 79-81.

the emphases on communion that were present in the second schema on the Church.[199]

Meanwhile, the results of working meetings remained in the background. Philips asked and obtained from the Belgian, Dutch, and German bishops the acceptance of his push for the reincorporation of the schema on the Virgin as the final chapter of the Constitution on the Church.[200] Some experts were meeting elsewhere with Ancel, Garrone, Maziers, and Elchinger. In short, the fact was that "the bishops themselves have organized their work. Instead of being led about to some extent by experts, they are breaking up into small groups and calling on the experts to assist them. They seem to be more in their element and more active than last year. They are entering into the Council seriously."[201]

C. THEMATIC AND PROCEDURAL INTERSECTIONS: GROUPS AND DEBATES

As the debate on the Church unfolded, the work of the commissions resumed. Unlike during the intersession, these were now working with an increasingly full membership and in a close, even if in some cases implicit, relationship with the debate in the hall.

1. Slow Resumptions: The Commissions for Missions and Religious, for Seminaries and Clergy, for Oriental Churches, and for Bishops

Some commissions were slow to reposition themselves. The Commission for the Liturgy had by now packed up its results and needed only to manage the final phase of the work; the Commission for Bishops saw that the discussion of its schema was coming up on the agenda; the Commission for Missions would meet for the first time only on October 23,[202] and with the prospect of a document that would simply lay down principles. If very little is known of the commissions that were to offer documents on religious, on seminaries, and on the clergy, that is because there was little to be known, since they were for the present excluded

---

[199] AS II/2, 34-36; the "schema" is the one Acerbi speaks of in his *Due ecclesiologie*, 267, and Perrin in his "Il 'Coetus Internationalis Patrum.'"

[200] See *DMoeller*, October 4, 1963, in Antonelli, "Le rôle," 30-31; the proposal was explained in a letter of Prignon to Suenens, October 4, 1963 (Prignon Archive, 514).

[201] *JCongar*, October 3, 1963.

[202] It would hold its final meeting on December 3; see Louchez, "La commission *De missionibus*."

from the agenda and placed in a procedural limbo from which they did not know whether, or how, they would emerge.[203]

On October 7 there was a meeting of the Commission for Bishops, one of the commissions whose subject was destined to be taken up in the hall. Luigi Carli, Bishop of Segni, was appointed as reporter.[204] This stern opponent of episcopal collegiality would act in such a manner that Veuillot and others decided, as early as October 29, to appeal to Tisserant. The cardinal dean of the Council of Presidents, the body charged with being "protector of the law" (*tutor legis*), had an obligation, according to the petitioners, to see to it that Carli took into account the view of the majority on the commission, which had not been called upon to discuss the outline of a report, as would have been desirable.

2. The Commission for Schema XVII

The so-called "Malines Schema," the result of a summer's work on Church-world relations, remained in abeyance during the entire month of October. This schema, which was heavily indebted conceptually to two successive reworkings inspired by Congar,[205] had two basic parts (tell Christians what the world asks of them, and tell the world what the Christian faith thinks on the most serious questions) and a conception of presence in the world based on the sequence *koinonia-diakonia- martyria*. Philips, who did the actual writing, suggested a simplification for teaching purposes, and at the end of the work in Malines his suggestion led to the emergence of an *Adumbratio* (Outline) containing three chapters. The first was "The Proper Mission of the Church," this being in turn divided into "The Evangelization of the World" and "The Influence of the Church on the Secular Order"; the second was on "Building up the World," subdivided into "The Autonomy of the World," "The Unification of the World," and a short section entitled "Overcoming a Threefold Ambiguity"; and the third was "The Duties of the Church toward the World," subdivided into "The Duty of Bearing Witness" and "The Service of Love and Communion."[206]

[203] See *Commissions, passim*.

[204] *JCongar*, October 8, 1963.

[205] See "Propositions en vue de la révision du Schema XVII," in Prignon Archive, 238. At the end of July the French episcopate had circulated the notes of P. Delhaye, "Premier chapitre du schema XVII. De admirabili vocatione hominis," in *Études et Documents*, no. 16 (July 24, 1963), 1-8, and in Gagnebet Archive, III, 7, 4.

[206] G. Turbanti, "La commissione mista per lo schema XVII-XIII," in *Commissions*, 227-28. The meetings were held on September 7 and 27.

By order of the CC this outline was sent to the presidents of the mixed commission at the end of September, but it also circulated in informal ways. Prignon sent it to Philips on September 22, to Glorieux on the 25th, and to Tromp on the 27th, probably under the impression that it could be examined at least by the Doctrinal Commission.[207] In fact, however, the debate on the Church put a stop to other work of the Doctrinal Commission, as also of the Commission for the Lay Apostolate,[208] and no one took the initiative to activate the procedures for evaluating and correcting the text. It was only the frenzy roused by the announcement on November 12 that the third and presumably last period of the Council would occur in May 1964 that brought movement again to a schema whose "invisibility" would motivate various interventions in the debate on the Church.

3. The Commission for the Lay Apostolate

Because its schema was one of those on the agenda for the end of the period, the Commission for the Lay Apostolate resumed its work on October 3.[209] Movements within the commission in favor of a complete reconsideration of the text were countered by a directive from the General Secretariat to the effect that the commission was to await the outcome of the debate in the hall on the chapter on the laity in the Constitution on the Church.[210] At its first meeting, at which the lay auditors now began to be present and active, it elected Hengsbach to be its reporter.[211] It had immediately to face a long-suppressed dilemma about the direction of its work: Should it continue reducing the document to a minimal size or even to a short declaration on the obligation of an apostolate in society? Or should it simply keep the present document while awaiting the views of the fathers? Or should it even expand the schema, giving it a unified perspective that would locate the laity within a renewed ecclesiology?

The dispute, which was apparently on the length of the schema, among three views represented by De Vet, Civardi, and Castellano, was not settled. Instead, the commission broke up into two working

---

[207] Turbanti, "La commissione mista," 228.

[208] Glorieux thought that Suenens had given the schema to Browne and Cento; see ibid., 229.

[209] It would hold sixteen meetings during the second period, seven of them in October.

[210] See Fattori, "La commissione De fidelium apostolatu," note 97.

[211] Hengsbach was elected on the second ballot by 13 votes to 8 for Castellano.

subcommissions[212] that commented further on the chapter on the laity in the schema on the Church, studied the report to be given in the hall, and evaluated the proposed changes in the schema that had come in from the fathers during the summer. The discussions were rather repetitive. Only Pavan, in the second subcommission, raised clearly the question of the contradiction between the ecclesiology of the mystical body and that of the People of God. Apart from this there were dragged-out discussions of the usual question, "What is a lay person?," and of some practical proposals for once again augmenting the number of auditors;[213] but this was all discussed in the perspective proper to this commission, which was to give a voice not to the "Christian people" but to international organizations of the laity.

In fact, the prolonged debates on the Church would postpone the schema on the lay apostolate well beyond the date for which the commission had been preparing; while on October 15 it had discussed and modified the report drawn up by Hengsbach, on November 9 the moderators decided that the schema on the lay apostolate would be discussed after the schema on ecumenism.[214]

4. The Commission for the Liturgy

Meanwhile, preparations were being made for the report and the voting in the hall on the revised liturgical schema. The text surviving from the preparatory period had undergone some changes but was now in its semi-definitive form. Moreover, the fact that the reporter on the schema in the hall was a moderator, Cardinal Lercaro,[215] strengthened the will of a large majority, which in the voting that began on October 7 and ended on October 15 produced close to a two-thirds unconditional agreement on all chapters of the schema with requests for only minor changes.[216]

[212] See Fattori, "La commission De fidelium apostolatu," notes 102ff. and 107.

[213] Petit proposed to reimburse them and to expand their tasks.

[214] AS V/3, 710.

[215] Lercaro, Lettere, 165; the report is in AS II/1, 276-79. On the dispensation given to Lercaro from the prohibition against combining the functions of a moderator in the hall with those of a member of a commission, see G. Alberigo, "L'esperienza conciliare di un vescovo," in Per la forza dello Spirito: Discorsi conciliari del card. Giacomo Lercaro (Bologna, 1984), 25.

[216] In the final vote on October 13 (AS II/1, 125) 2242 votes were cast: 1495 placet and 781 placet iuxta modum, against 36 non placet and 8 invalid ballots. Even the disappointment that the schema had once again to pass through the commission for the weighing of the 781 changes requested in the final vote on October 13 had at least some positive effect: the chapters that came back to the hall had been significantly improved in various areas. On the procedure, see below, 192-202.

In addition, the liturgical experience of the Council itself supported
and strengthened the decisions made in more than one area. On the one
hand, the succession of liturgies in the various rites was for many bishops a seminar on variety that proved very helpful in getting them away
from the inherited idea of "the unity of the Roman Rite." On the other,
the experience of celebrating privately in the morning, then assisting at
the mass of another, and finally attending mass in St. Peter's confirmed
the need to do something about a practice whose limitations all could
see. Finally, the possibility of seeing some reforms in action proved
especially fruitful. The concelebration on October 3 seemed like a miracle to proponents of the liturgical movement,[217] but no less important
was the permission requested and granted that the lay auditors receive
communion at the morning mass (October 11, 1963).[218]

The repetition of votes brought the assembly alive and helped it to
realize that the renewal of the liturgy now had been legitimated and was
favored by a majority in the Church and that, as would be seen in the
second half of October, this renewal had ecclesiological implications,
which some fathers would ask be applied in the schema on the
Church.[219]

5. The Secretariat for Christian Unity and Its Proposals

If Pope John had left behind an orphan, it was Cardinal Bea's Secretariat for Christian Unity. After having been Roncalli's executor and
source of inspiration, the cardinal now had to find a role for himself and
to do this at the very moment when it was announced that the schema on
ecumenism would be coming to the hall. What Bea did is therefore
understandable: he remained out of the line of fire, prepared for the
debate, and looked after the observers present.[220] The vain wait for
Athenagoras's delegates did not detract from his commitment to seeing to it that the delegates from the non-Catholic Churches should be

[217] See *TJungmann*, and R. Pacick, "Das Konzilstagebuch von Josef Andreas Jungmann, S.J.," in *Experience*.

[218] *AS* II/1, 123 (summary minutes). Since the bishops celebrated mass in private early
in the morning, the lay auditors were the only ones needing to receive communion; the
decision was therefore important and was reinforced by their desire to receive communion *during* the mass and not outside of it, as a kind of private devotion.

[219] The development of the ecclesiological debate would be influenced in some passages by the fundamental relationship of Eucharist to Church that the liturgical constitution had established.

[220] See Velati, *Una difficile transizione*, 365-66.

participants in the debates and not mere spectators. As can be seen from the reports of the participants, the Tuesday meetings were very successful.[221]

There were, however, no interventions of the secretariat as such on the ecclesiology schema. Instead, there was patient activity geared to sending for discussion a schema on ecumenism that not only explained the principles of Catholic ecumenism but also took up the two questions that during the next two years would arouse the greatest opposition. The first was the question of chapter V, on the freedom of the religious conscience. On October 9 Bea once more asked the moderators and then Cicognani that the chapter on religious freedom be again made part of the schema, as had been agreed (in vain) after the meeting of the CC in July.[222] Felici defended himself, saying that the sketch for the chapter had never been passed by either the CC or the General Secretariat, and that only at this moment had he received a very elementary text on the rights of a right conscience. Shortly afterward (October 22), the petition of 240 United States bishops, submitted by Spellman, would be received by Cicognani and passed on to the Doctrinal Commission for a judgment on its merits.[223]

No less ticklish was the attempt to introduce a decree on the Jews into the same text on ecumenism. Paul VI had assured Willebrands that the authority to produce a chapter on Israel belonged, and would belong, to the Secretariat for Christian Unity,[224] but there was persistent opposition,

---

[221] The meeting on October 1 was introduced by Thils, and the one on October 8 by Philips. The meetings of the observers on October 15, 22, and 29 took up the aspects of the episcopate that were to be voted on and on which there was to be conflict. On L. Vischer's reports to the WCC, see Velati, "Gli osservatori," and Brun, "La documentazione," in *Evento*, 259-93.

[222] See "Notes sur le Schéma 'De libertate religosa' présenté par le Secrétariat pour l'unité," September 30, 1963 (Dossetti Archive, 33b). Bea's letter to the moderators, which is cited in Carbone, "Il ruolo di Paolo VI," 130, is also to be found in Suenens Archive, *IIa sessio, De ecclesia, De oecumenismo*. On October 1, Willebrands,"following a suggestion of the Holy Father," had paid a visit to Lercaro in order to consult with him on the subject of religious freedom; see Lercaro, *Lettere*, 167-68. On this subject there had also been a bit of propaganda at the opening, when a seven- page pamphlet entitled *Pro sanctae matris Ecclesiae libertate* and signed by 367 Basque priests (with an eye on the Franco regime?), was distributed (copy in De Smedt Archive, 17.4).

[223] On November 7 a *Relatio adnotationis sub-commissionis...ad schema "De libertate religiosa" examinandum* would come to the Doctrinal Commission (Gagnebet Archive, 1.12.80). Its author was Bishop J. Wright, reporter for the subcommission. Spellman's note on religious freedom was composed by J. C. Murray; see D. E. Pelotte, *John Courtney Murray: Theologian in Conflict* (New York, 1975), 82.

[224] *JCongar*, October 1, 1963.

which came, for political reasons, from the Arab countries, from an anti-
semitic culture, and from the Churches of the Middle East.[225]

6. The Doctrinal Commission

As the debate on the Church went on in the hall, the Doctrinal Commission pursued its work, at times responding to the debate, as in particular with regard to the orienting or straw votes, at times succeeding in
anticipating developments. From its very first meeting on October 2 the
commission decided to get ready to deal with the emendations the
fathers would request in the schema on the Church. A subcommission on
emendations, which began its work on October 4, was made up of Florit,
Garrone, Charue, Spanedda, and Browne (president) and was aided by a
group of experts headed by Philips.[226] The procedure devised by Tromp
and Ottaviani for the work of this group was to "disassemble" the interventions of the fathers and to transform them into emendations on index
cards; these cards, duplicated in several copies,[227] were to provide the
material on the basis of which the experts could supply the commission
with suggested corrections.[228] The meeting of this subcommission on
October 7 showed a plan at work:

> Msgr. Philips told me yesterday that the subcommission met to sort out the
> amendments. It was a painful experience; he had to face the same mentality

[225] For the opposition of Maximos IV, see *JCongar*, October 4, 1963, and *TSemmelroth* on the same date: "The story is that this morning Patriarch Maximos was supposed
to have spoken, but shortly before the session he was told that he might not speak except
in Latin. As a result, he was unable to speak. This caused a general indignation, and the
bishops registered an official complaint with the moderators."

[226] *JPrignon* (A), October 4, 1963: "'Election' of a subcommission by Ottaviani himself, for sorting out the emendations." See also S. Tromp, *Relatio secretarii de textu
revisendo secundum observationes Patrum*, October 15, 1963 (Philips Archive,
P.052.06). The experts were Gagnebet, Schauf, Medina, and Philips; see *Relatio de
labore Subcommissionis Centralis [CD/Dec]*, December 4, 1963 (Philips Archive,
P.052.08).

[227] On October 15 Tromp announced that the commission now had a duplicating
machine for this purpose.

[228] The machinery set up by Tromp would have made it possible to bring everything
up for constant discussion; in his *Relatio* of October 15 the Dutch theologian gave a significant example: "For example, with regard to the diaconate they [the experts] ought
carefully to define the various views as well as the arguments pro and con from sacred
scripture, tradition, the practice of the Church, present-day needs, and so on. Because this
kind of technical work would be excessive, each expert on the subcommission should
choose an assistant. Only if this technical work is done carefully and with the greatest
possible objectivity can the main work of the Commission itself begin, that is, to pass
judgment on the objective value of the various remarks, emendations, omissions, additions, transpositions and arguments pro and con."

and the same obstructiveness from those on the other side. Tromp dominated and came in talking about the stupid things being heard in the hall. This will be my Siege of Saragossa: line by line and word by word![229]

The plenary meeting of the commission on October 9 came to a vote on the two points under greatest discussion at the moment: whether the chapter on the People of God (with this or some other title) should come before or after the chapter on the hierarchy, and whether the schema on the Blessed Virgin should or should not be incorporated into the schema on the Church.[230] The results of the votes were clear enough: the commission approved the title "The People of God" with fifteen votes in its favor (seven votes favored "Christ's Faithful" and one "The Equality and Inequality of the Members").

On the problem raised by the schema on Mary, Ottaviani suggested a procedure that would have an effect in the hall: hear two fathers and two experts of the commission whose views were opposed. The debate, begun by Franić and Balić in favor of the autonomy of the Marian schema and continued by Garrone and Philips in favor of its incorporation into the schema on the Church, ended with a vote by the commission. There were 9 votes in favor of an autonomous schema on the Virgin, 12 in favor of incorporating it into the schema on the Church, and 2 abstentions. It was decided unanimously that this chapter should be placed at the end of the constitution, as proposed by Philips.[231] No one mentioned that by these actions the commission was presenting as if its own the suggestion on voting that the pope had already given to Suenens. At an audience prior to October 6 Paul VI had told the Belgian primate that he "does not wish to impose anything. He wants the assembly to decide... It has been decided to take up two questions on the *De beata*.

---

[229] *JCongar*, October 7, 1963. The meetings were also occasion for confrontations; at this one Rahner asked that Wolf, an expert on religious, be called in; see Vorgrimler, *Understanding Karl Rahner*, 176.

[230] The moderators had requested this vote, although at that meeting Ottaviani had objected that the CC had no authority to impose changes in the order of subjects as decided by the commission. The purpose of the vote was in fact to limit the autonomy of the commissions (and especially of the Doctrinal Commission) in relation to the Council and its directive bodies. The autonomy of the commissions, however, also had a quite different purpose, being claimed also by commissions (e.g., those for religious and for the laity) whose subject areas were being "invaded" by the Doctrinal Commission's desire for control; see Tromp, *Relationes*, May 15 and 31, pp. 10-13, and *JCongar*, 245-46, and October 9, 1963.

[231] Antonelli, "Le rôle," 29-30. The decision was made known to Suenens in Prignon's note reporting what was done on October 9 (Suenens Archive, *IIa sessio, De ecclesia, generalia*).

Two bishops or two periti will be asked to present the two viewpoints. The two would be Balić for giving Mary her own place and Philips for incorporation into the *De Ecclesia.*"[232]

The commission met again on October 15.[233] Ottaviani had obtained a letter from Agagianian, in which the cardinal moderator accepted the vote of October 9 on "The People of God" as a sufficient basis for proceeding.[234] But, in accordance with the still secret desire of the pope, Agagianian came to a different decision regarding the schema on the Virgin. Given the weak majority in the commission, he asked that the latter prepare to submit the question of the placement of the Marian schema directly to the conciliar assembly, along with an explanation in the hall of the two opposed positions; the commission obediently appointed Santos and König. In addition, still at the request of the moderators, it appointed a small committee (Parente, Schröffer, Fernandez) to draft a note on the theological qualification of the schemas.

As a result, the commission began its study of the new chapter on the People of God, starting with the role of the Church in the forgiveness of sins;[235] it continued on October 18 with the reports on the Bible and theology by Moeller and Congar.[236] At the meeting on October 23, from which Ottaviani and all the Italians were absent and the first at which Volk was present, taking the place left vacant by the death of Peruzzo, the atmosphere was dominated by the question of votes on the propositions being considered for the chapter on the hierarchy. Tromp announced that subcommissions would be set up for evaluating changes suggested by the fathers in their interventions. At this meeting there was question only of small details of procedure; but at the next meeting, on October 28, Léger and Garonne would see signs of catastrophe in the fact that the questions on the third chapter delivered to them differed from those of the moderators.[237]

---

[232] *JMoeller*, October 6, 1963, in Antonelli, "Le rôle," 31.

[233] It was also necessary to bring in a new member after the death of Peruzzo. In Suenen's name Moeller collected suggestions in the hall. Congar suggested an Oriental (Edelby, Zoghby, or Hermaniuk) or a black from Africa (*JCongar*, October 11, 1963), but the choice fell to Volk.

[234] Ottaviani said in the commission that Paul VI had told him that he preferred to have the chapter on the hierarchy come before that on the People of God. Philips challenged the motives of the commission and announced he was sending a note to persuade the pope; see *JCongar*, October 15, 1963.

[235] Congar's idea of an exposition based on the salvation-history of the People of God was not accepted (*JCongar*, October 15, 1963).

[236] *JCongar*, October 18, 1963.

[237] Ibid.

Faced with the unknown, that is, a breakdown of the *modi* into a myriad of fragmentary and conflicting proposals, and still ignorant of the result of the votes on key points in the schema on the Church, the Doctrinal Commission was experiencing the possibility of a dramatic shift. Did what was happening indicate that a change in the presidency of the commissions was near, something which some considered necessary?[238] Or was it the beginning of a new attempt to dodge or nullify the assembly's ability to choose its own direction, an ability which, however limited, had so greatly helped the Council?

7. Informal Groups

In addition to the commissions, the activities of and pressures from various informal groups played a part in the debates. To some extent these working groups were simply carrying forward undertakings already at work during the first period; but in 1963 the groups reached a new level of maturity. We have seen how the activism of the Church of the Poor Group made sure it was represented in the interventions in the hall[239] and how the nucleus of what would become the anticonciliar fraction that was the International Group of Fathers took some public initiatives.[240]

The Domus Mariae Group, which brought together representatives of many episcopal conferences, resumed its work on October 4, under the aegis of the statements of Paul VI to the Curia and in his opening address for the second period.[241] Under the prudent rubric of "the internationalization of the commissions" its members discussed the possibility of a renewal, if not a re-election, of the conciliar commissions. The African group came to the meeting on October 25 with two *vota* that called for a re-election, alteration, or supplementary election for all the commissions: a president who was not the head of the corresponding curial congregation and the direct election of vice-presidents and secretaries.[242] Also proposed, by both the Africans and the Germans, was a

[238] Thus Küng to Congar, *JCongar*, October 12, 1963. The African episcopates sent the moderators a proposal for a comprehensive re-election of the commissions and their respective presidents; Dossetti wrote a note on this for the use of the four moderators (Dossetti Archive, 120 and 131).

[239] A summary of the interventions that were the fruit of the group's activity is given in P. Gauthier, *La chiesa dei poveri e il concilio* (Florence, 1965), 215-32.

[240] See Perrin, "Il 'Coetus Internationalis Patrum,'" 173-87.

[241] See P. Noël, "Gli incontri delle conferenze episcopali durante il Concilio: il 'Gruppo della Domus Mariae,'" in *Evento*, 95-133.

[242] Baudoux Archive, in Noël, "Gli incontri," note 38.

reorganization of the conciliar week: that on two or three days there be no general congregation, so as to leave time for discussion within the episcopal conferences, the latter being understood as exercising an intermediate role after the manner of the old *nationes* at councils in medieval Christianity. These ideas were not formally passed on to the moderators,[243] but Etchegaray did convey them to Dell'Acqua, substitute at the Secretariat of State, as early as October 28.[244]

The group planned a series of lectures to prepare for the discussion of the schemas on the Church (which contained a single reference to such groups) and on the bishops. While the planned hearing of the secretaries of the German and Indian conferences and of CELAM was postponed indefinitely, on October 18 the Canadian conference did hear Baudoux, who maintained that the decisions of episcopal conferences were binding on the individual members; but in fact his description was really begging the question, since relations between the Canadian conference and its primate, Cardinal Léger, were certainly not good.[245]

As the Domus Mariae Group, so also other groups labored through the long afternoons as the Council came to life. The group known as Conciliar Strategies, which Elchinger brought together, was not new as far as its members went.[246] Volk (and his auxiliary), Musty, Guano, Garrone, Butler, Philips, Rahner, Féret, Häring, Liégé, Grillmeier, Martelet, Smulders, Martimort, Laurentin, Ratzinger, Semmelroth, Daniélou, Congar, and some others formed a team that had already been active the year before in preparing opinions contrary to the preparatory schemas. In the second period, however, they moved with greater ease, having mastered some aspects of the assembly's work (the importance of the first interventions in a debate; the difficulty caused by the presence of *modi* in votes; the need to make sure that there were conciliar interventions on various subjects). Because of German opposition, this group gave up the idea of incorporating the schema on revelation and even a schema on tradition into the Constitution on the Church, although Congar tried to prepare such an incorporation.[247]

---

[243] The moderators received them directly from the conferences before being given them by the pope; see Felici to Veuillot, November 11, 1963, in Etchegaray Archive, mentioned by Noël, "Gli incontri," note 42.

[244] Ibid., notes 40-41.

[245] Léger did not sign the interventions of the conference at the Council; see J.-M. Tillard, "Souvenirs d'un expert canadienne à Vatican II," in *L'Eglise canadienne et Vatican II*, 291-302.

[246] According to *JCongar* it met on Fridays at the Redemptorists'.

[247] *JCongar*, October 4 and 5, 1963.

Among the journalists more accurate information was being circulated, enabling not only readers far from Rome to stay abreast of things, but also the fathers themselves, who because of the babel of Latin pronunciations still understood little, and that poorly. An incredible rumor spread that simultaneous translations would begin on November 4.[248]

The non-Catholic observers and the lay auditors formed two other collegial groups for circulating ideas and approaches, the former being bound together by an experience that had matured during the previous year, the latter being already familiar with common strategies from their participation in groups that represent the various lay movements.

Theological literature was also making its solemn entrance into the Council. It would be difficult to exaggerate the importance of Philips's article in the *Nouvelle Revue Théologique* on two tendencies in contemporary theology and the ecclesiologies resulting from them,[249] for it gave a way of interpreting the passage from the old to the new schema on the Church. Works that a year later were to change the horizon of historical theology — such as the monograph which Giuseppe Alberigo wrote, on the advice and at the request of Dossetti, "Lo sviluppo della dottrine sui poteri nella chiesa universale" (The Development of the Teaching on Powers in the Universal Church)—were anticipated in the form of chapters intended to document and support the idea that the Council was retrieving age-old and venerable traditions.[250] It was also during these weeks that the idea was conceived of starting a periodical on the conciliar renewal; *Concilium* would begin to be published about a year later.[251]

Among the opponents of collegiality there was on the whole a different sense of danger. Fenton's complaints about the use of *sacramentum*

---

[248] *JPrignon* (A). On October 12 Prignon was told that with the consent of Dell'Acqua work would begin on the 14th to set up the simultaneous translation system that the moderators had requested of the pope on the 10th. On October 18 Prignon told Congar that beginning on November 4 there would be simultaneous translation in five languages, initially for 800 fathers; see *JCongar*, October 12, 1963. Horton, 59, had also heard the rumor. Its basis remained unknown, but there was no follow-up. On the question of Latin accents see, simply as an example, Horton's satisfaction when "presently one bishop was introduced whose name I did not catch, but whose voice seemed familiar so that I listened intently. Sure enough, it was our own Bishop Primeau of Manchester, New Hampshire. It was refreshing to hear good rugged American Latin" (27).

[249] "Deux tendances dans la théologie contemporaine," *NRT* 85 (1963), 225-38.

[250] One chapter of Alberigo's work was duplicated and given out to some fathers. The work was published a year later and elicited strong reactions from the Roman canonists; see Acerbi, *Due ecclesiologie*, 242-44.

[251] For the meeting on *Concilium*, see *JCongar*, October 19, 1963.

were geared to the preparation of an authoritative intervention that he thought could eliminate all ambiguity. Gagnebet would publish his essay "La primauté pontificale et la collégialité de l'épiscopat" only after the end of the debates on the ecclesiology schema.[252] Pretty much isolated was the work of Heribert Schauf, whose articles defended the primacy "against" collegiality.[253]

Finally, the individual episcopal conferences played a decisive role, and again on a higher qualitative level than in 1962. The key event then had been the unblocking of things achieved by the preparation of lists of candidates for the conciliar commissions; now the conferences were communicating understanding, shaping opinions, guiding votes, and stimulating work. A proposal such as that of the Africans on renewing the commissions testifies to a sense of responsibility that would have been unthinkable four hundred days earlier.

V. THE DEBATE ON COLLEGIALITY (CHAPTER II)

October 4 brought the beginning of the crucial debate on the schema on the Church: the debate on the hierarchical constitution of the Church, that is, on the episcopate and collegiality. After an introduction, the schema developed the following themes in ten brief paragraphs: the appointment of the twelve apostles; the bishops as their successors; episcopal consecration as a sacrament; priests and deacons as the bishops' helpers (11-15); the episcopal college and its head (16); and relations between bishops and their three ministries of teaching, sanctifying, and governing (17-21). The fathers discussed these 360 lines of texts in nine general congregations, with 119 addresses and 56 written interventions.[254] While it

---

[252] In *La France catholique*, November 15, 1963.

[253] It should be noted that the greater part of the academic debate against collegiality, which Acerbi reviews in his *Due ecclesiologie*, 242-60, occurred from 1964 on.

[254] *AS* II/2, 82-124 and 222-914. At the beginning of this period there occurred an incident revelatory of the climate, both in what happened and in the way it was interpreted. On October 4 Maximos IV was denied the right to speak, officially because he had prepared his address in French; see *JEdelby* (October 4), 158-59. *JPrignon* (A), October 7, reports that according to Suenens "the question of language was mainly a pretext to hide the real reason for the refusal: the very aggressive content of the text, especially against the Holy Office." On October 5 Rahner lodged a protest with Döpfner, and the French, too, organized against this kind of mistreatment; see Vorgrimler, *Understanding Karl Rahner*, 176. On the denial by subsecretaries of the fathers' right to speak Congar, too, reports some expressions of discontent (*JCongar*, October 4, 1963); he knows that Volk and Blanchet were unable to speak on the dogmatic qualification of teachings on the ground that this question had been left to the pope.

had been known for a year that collegiality was the crucial issue, the liveliness of the disagreements was due not to the schema itself (the formulas of Philips and Gagnebet did not differ that much) but to the presence of the Council. What some were afraid of was not a formula but an experience.

In its treatment, in fact, the chapter still had quite a few limitations, embodying as it did the outline for which Philips had won a large degree of consensus the year before and which he himself had defended in the essay already mentioned on the two "tendencies" (the juridicizing tendency, opposed but also complementary to the communion tendency). Anticipating the treatment of the function of the episcopal college, the chapter avoided describing the role and activities of bishops as though they were isolated monarchs. But it still showed the weight of the preparatory schema when it began by reasserting the papal prerogatives established by Vatican I. The result provoked contradictory reactions: if for some this repetition of Vatican I sounded superfluous, for those who would have liked it to be the sole content of a schema on the hierarchy, it was certainly inadequate. Moreover, the development of the doctrine on ministry as "for the good of the body" was still not homogeneous with a treatise on residential bishops.

The point that showed a doctrinal development was the statement that the Church was founded on Peter and the apostles and that all these in solidarity make up a college, although not in a "juridical" sense. The uncertainties of the draft left undecided the question of who succeeded to that original college (the retention of the title "on residential bishops" became a source of serious ambiguity). Similarly, there were no solid connections between the rest of the chapter and no. 13, which, while asserting the sacramentality of the episcopate and the significance of consecration as the aggregation of a new member to an *ordo* (and not simply the transfer of a power), did not succeed in linking this datum to the exercise of episcopal powers and functions; in fact, only the power to sanctify was left as certainly bestowed in consecration.

Number 16, at the center of the chapter, did not try to harmonize the powers of the pope and the powers of the college; it defined them by juxtaposition and related them to each another on the basis of the fact that in exercising its authority the college had to take into account the supremacy of its head. The lack of a canonical way of regulating the two powers compelled the schema to recall at this point "the non-canonical nature of the hierarchic structure"[255] in order to explain the balance

---

[255] Acerbi, *Due ecclesiologie*, 208.

between the two. The schema courageously provided for the possibility of hitherto unknown ways of exercising the powers of the college, but it found no connection between this and the innovative idea of the *communio ecclesiarum*, expressed in no. 17 but relegated to a conceptual corner of a chapter in which the very assertion of the college was, as it were, swallowed up by the question of the relations between pope and episcopate. Not by chance, then, the functions of the bishops, their relations with presbyters and deacons, and their shared but distinct rootedness in orders continued to be heavily influenced by the functional minimalism of the 1962 schema.

Following the principle of precedence, the debate, which went on from October 4 to 16, opened with the addresses of Spellman, Ruffini, and Bacci, who were opposed to collegiality and to the diaconate.[256] The address of Guerry, who in the name of the French episcopate spoke in favor of sacramentality, remained an isolated event.[257] These words did not fall into a void, because, as we shall see increasingly in the days that followed, the activity of the journalists and the attention of the press restored balance and comprehensibility to a discussion that was carried on in the usual and often indecipherable Latin that after 10:30 a.m., the time when the two Council bars opened, drove many prelates to the side aisles. With the aid of the not always "disinterested" reports of the journalists from *L'Avvenire d'Italia*, *Le Monde*, *Il Tempo*, and *La Croix*, they were better able to grasp differences, understand answers and objections to preceding interventions, reflect anew on questions, and plan clarifying statements.

The debate on collegiality and the diaconate resumed on Monday, October 7, and the impressions given on the first day of the discussion were turned upside down. Even Siri and Florit accepted that collegiality "exists," but they were concerned that it not be interpreted in a way that would diminish the primacy.[258] In particular, Léger, König, Döpfner,

---

[256] *AS* II/2, 82-89. Rahner drafted Döpfner's intervention on the diaconate and on October 7 asked that his friend Hannes Kramer, founder of the *Diakonatszentrum* in Freiburg a. M., be informed of it; see Vorgrimler, *Understanding Karl Rahner*, 175-76. As for collegiality, it may be noted that Jedin, *Lebensbericht*, 212, expresses his puzzlement at this "new and strange" term.

[257] *AS* II/2, 89-90. It was the subsecretaries who collected the requests to intervene and drew up the lists of permissions to speak.

[258] *AS* II/2, 222-23. According to Siri there existed a nonreciprocal relationship between Peter and the college of the apostles and between the pope and the college of bishops: Peter "exists" without the college; the college does not exist without Peter, so that, if there is a college, this is by reason of the Petrine mandate. Florit expressed a more wavering position and asked for clarifications on the relationship not between college and pope but between the powers of the college and the primacy of the Roman pontiff; *AS* II/2, 259-63.

Meyer, Alfrink, Lefebvre, Rugambwa, and Maximos IV ("a long line of 'big guns'"[259]), and then Bishops De Smedt, Beck, and van Dodewaard took the stage with a series of sharp and timely proposals.[260] A Yugoslav bishop, Zazinović, asked that as an expression of collegiality the pope establish "an institution something like a council of bishops, to be invited periodically from all countries," whose advice "would count more than all the dicasteries of the Holy See and serve him as a helping hand in the more important business of the Church."[261]

On the next day, Liénart, speaking in the name of the entire French episcopate, and Richaud supported collegiality and the diaconate, but opposition was also voiced (Šeper, Sigaud, Franić).[262] The use of the term *college,* applied to the body of bishops with the pope and referring to the organ that exercises authority in the church established by Jesus Christ in the persons of the Twelve, elicited two kinds of objection. Some voiced their fear of a vision of relations between bishops and pope that did not begin by isolating the powers and prerogatives of the pontiff; others maintained that the powers of the college were not and could not be delegated;[263] and still others were really uncertain, not ready to judge.[264]

The series of addresses tended to become more rapid but also more inscrutable, and they often were in contradiction to the votes being taken at the same time on the liturgical schema. If in the addresses the call for

---

[259] G. Vallquist, *Das Zweite Vatikanische Konzil* (Zurich, 1966), 119.

[260] *AS* II/2, 223-38, 263-66, 268-70, 270-72. Father Chenu had written to van Dodewaard on September 30, 1963, asking him to intervene on the chapter "De Populo": "In speaking of the foundations of this priesthood, and in order to define the place of the laity, it would perhaps be appropriate to state explicitly the 'messianic' role of Christ, which the Christian people carry on through history as a sign of the coming of God's kingdom. We ought not leave to temporal messianisms, which are at once seductive and perverted, the benefit of a truth that is basic to the Christian economy. What disturbing experiences we have in a matter that should be a toothing-stone of grace! Messianism is a truth that is part of the definition of the relationship between Church and world" (Schillebeeckx Archive, Leuven).

[261] *AS* II/2, 268. This would also be requested by Ghattas on October 10 (see *JEdelby* [in the Italian ed.], 169); Heenan and Beck told one of the observers of their opinion that such a council could be one of the "new structures" to be formed (Horton, 41).

[262] *AS* II/2. 342-45, for the one side; and 358-60 and 366-70, for the other.

[263] With van Dodewaard as its spokesman, the Dutch conference maintained that the power of the college could not be delegated; this, they said (partly on the basis of canon 227 of the Code of Canon Law), was of divine law and ought to be defined as such (*AS* II/2, 270-72).

[264] On October 7 Rahner voiced a pessimistic suspicion: everything was moving toward the making of "little, well-intentioned improvements which don't change much" (Vorgrimler, *Understanding Karl Rahner*, 176).

renewal seemed very widely prevalent, in the votes objections and
strong warnings kept cropping up. For example, Cento accepted the diaconate but only if celibate; Nicodemo feared the lack of "juridical" precision in the text.[265] When Slipyi, the Ukrainian metropolitan who, in
response to a wish of John XXIII, had been freed from the gulag a year
earlier, asked that the infallibilist positions be strengthened, he was not
convincing but he certainly made himself heard, speaking for twenty
minutes without anyone daring to interrupt.[266] When a young auxiliary
bishop of Bologna, Luigi Bettazzi, read his statement against those
"innovators" who reject collegiality and cited against them Roman writers of the eighteenth and nineteenth centuries, he roused Chenu to
delighted mirth and persuaded a few but important fathers, among them
Pietro Parente, but it could not be said that he cut a still tight knot or
clarified an uncertain situation.[267]

It was not only innovative aspects but also older questions that
remained open, among them the problem of gaining an adequate perspective on the schema's repetition of the *ex sese* of Vatican I.[268] At their
meeting on October 8 the observers challenged the way in which the
Philips schema spoke of the powers of the bishops as "concessions":

> Schmemann: There is a certain pluralism in the structure of the Church, but
> there is nothing about it here; there are other primacies…and on the *ex
> sese*. The document seems consistently to treat the episcopate as a conces-
> sion, while every unqualified affirmation is on the side of the pope. Every
> statement about the episcopate is referred to the pope and his authority.[269]

Another repeated request had to do with a glaring lacuna: the schema
on the Church that the bishops had before them devoted only a page and

---

[265] Cento spoke at the 45th general congregation on October 10 (*AS* II/2, 393-94), and
Nicodemo at the 46th on October 11 (ibid., 459-61).

[266] *AS* II/2, 442-46; see also Wenger, 47. Marcel Lefebvre elicited a degree of comment when he spoke on October 11 of the danger represented by the collegiality of the
episcopal conferences: *AS* II/2, 471-72.

[267] *AS* II/2, 484; see *DChenu*, October 11, 1963.

[268] The question was raised, in relation to no. 9, by Bishop Saboia Bandeira de Mello
of Palmas, (see *AS* II/2, 114-23). Congar drafted an interpretation of it on October 7 (see
JCongar for that day), apparently on his own initiative; the next day he offered his note
as an intervention for Martin, who received it on October 9.

[269] *JCongar*, October 8, 1963. See also Horton, 45-46. It was Philips who introduced
the Council's work at this meeting, During the discussion Cullmann maintained that it is
not possible to speak of "succession" in a strict sense when dealing with a role that is due
to the experience of encountering the risen Christ. *JPrignon* (A), October 8, remarks that
Cullmann was impressed by comments against the possibility of combining collegiality
and primacy, and that Philips "answered."

a half to the presbyterate and said nothing about problems that had been agitating priests for almost twenty years: from their work to their role in society; from celibacy to formation; from relations with the bishops to relations with one another. While this choice of emphasis may have been explicable in terms of the systematic approach taken in the preparatory schema, it had now become unintelligible, and not only to the bishops.[270]

It became even more unintelligible when one considers the fact that the schema opened up the question of restoring the diaconate as a permanent degree of sacred orders, with or without celibacy. For this reason the debate saw a great many interventions on the subject of the diaconate by those who saw it as a Trojan horse introduced into the precincts of priestly celibacy, by those who saw it as a necessary solution to the lack of clergy, and by those who thought it a gesture showing the desire to bring the Roman Catholic Church back to an apostolic tradition that, with some exceptions had generally permitted married deacons. On the diaconate there was a closing of ranks by the major leaders, first among them Döpfner, who read a statement drafted by Rahner and the team of writers at the German College.[271] In particular, the possibility set down in no. 15 of the schema, according to which "it is for the heads of the Church to decide whether such deacons are or are not to be bound by the sacred law of celibacy," led to the expression of repeated uncertainties.

The debate seemed to swing back and forth between the pros and the cons. Was this due to the management of it by subsecretaries who controlled the scheduling of the interventions and announced who was to speak? Was there a real lack of clarity? In order to assess the extent of the agreements and disagreements and to limit the uncertainty that was being produced, the possibility was raised as early as October 8 that the assembly itself be asked to provide some direction on the subject. This was what Suenens suggested during his address in the hall on the

---

[270] This was the question which L. Vischer raised at the meeting of the observers on October 8; see Velati, "Gli osservatori." The same was said by Añoveros Ataún in the hall on October 9; AS II/2, 348-51.

[271] See above n. 256. The question was discussed from varying perspectives by different groups. Some saw in the diaconate a solution to the lack of clergy. Others saw it as giving an impulse to the reform of the presbyterate as well, and possibly a solution for the problems of a celibate ministry, which in the years before the Council had already been experiencing great difficulties. The discussions on this subject lacked cogent historical precedents but nevertheless opened the way to more original thinking. Linked in a special way to the indigenization of a sector of the clergy was the favorable position taken by forty bishops who were Chinese either by birth or by missionary vocation and who passed a motion of Yü Pin; see Lazzarotto, "I vescovi cinesi."

restoration of the diaconate as a permanent order to be conferred on both celibate and married men.[272] At a press conference that afternoon the Belgian cardinal again asked that the hall take a separate vote on the subject.[273] For some weeks the fathers remained in the dark about what happened to the Belgian moderator's stimulating proposal; this was true even of the seventy-seven Latin American fathers who on that same October 8 had sent the moderators a proposal of their own: that in the hall, on "questions of greater importance,"

> (such as, in chapter II of the schema on the Church: episcopal collegiality, the sacramental nature of consecration, and the restoration of the dia-conate), after these have been discussed, they be set forth in a brief and clear manner so that they may be the subject of a provisional vote before the competent commission begins its study of the emendations. There are two reasons in particular for such a vote: a) lest, after a long period, i.e., of several months, the fathers reach the point of voting when the arguments given in the hall have to some extent already been forgotten; b) lest the commissions waste their time drafting texts on questions which the major-ity of the council fathers may perhaps maintain should be eliminated.[274]

A. Partial or Straw Votes

On October 10 the four moderators had their usual audience with the pope: a triumphal audience, "collegiality in practice." The pope shared the material on his work table with the moderators and elicited their emphatic comments: "The Holy Spirit is blowing up a storm!" said Suenens; and Lercaro stated: "This is a historic day." The pope gave

---

[272] Suenens distanced himself from the text, which proposed to make temporary the obligation of celibacy imposed on the ordained, and he asked instead for a diaconate to be bestowed on celibates under the same conditions as the temporary diaconate, and a dia-conate for the married.

[273] See the text of the address in the hall (AS II/2, 317-20) and the variations taken from the memorandum that Dossetti prepared for Suenens, in Per la forza, 313-20, and what Suenens himself says in his Souvenirs et espérances, 113. For the press conference see, among other sources, the chronicle in L'Avvenire d'Italia for October 9, 1963. The Dossetti Archive, 381, for October 7, 1963, has this on a page in Dossetti's handwriting: "Suenens: propose two texts, one for the majority, one for the minority." The French text is in Suenens Archive, IIa sessio, De ecclesia, De diaconatu.

[274] R. Silva Henriquez to the moderators, October 8, 1963, with the signatures of sev-enty-seven fathers from the following countries: Colombia (27 fathers), Chile (17), Argentina (7), Uruguay (6), Costa Rica, Honduras, Mexico, Panama (2 each), Cuba, El Salvador, Guatemala, Paraguay, Venezuela (1 each), and 7 other Spanish-speaking bish-ops from various countries; copy attached to the follow-up letter from Silva Henriquez to the pope on October 22, now in Moeller Archive, 311.

the moderators the task of receiving and managing the lay members, approved the initiatives dealing with poverty, and was not entirely closed to the possibility of using the vernaculars in the debates.[275]

Dossetti's sheet of notes was more meager. He had been acting for two weeks as secretary of the new body and had prepared the list of subjects to be discussed at the audience: (1) the report on the week; (2) the problem of the theological note to be given to the decrees; (3) the meeting with the president and vice-president of the Doctrinal Commission; (4) the vote on chapter II of the Constitution on the Sacred Liturgy. At the bottom of the page, Dossetti's hand-written notes state what "the Holy Father approved":

- Votes in the Council, binding on the commissions, on very serious questions (e.g., diaconate; sacramentality [of the] episcopate).
- "Separate law" on immediately implementing the liturgical Constitution.
- Commission on questions of women and religious [life].[276]

Nothing was said about how to consult the assembly, but the examples given — sacramentality and, above all, the diaconate — speak for themselves; they are the issues on which, two days before, Silva Henriquez privately and Suenens publicly had asked for a provisional vote in order to see what the Council wanted. pope and moderators were thus in agreement on proceeding quickly to such "very serious" votes and on thereby obliging the commission to accept the principles set down by the hall.[277]

The audience dealt with other subjects as well — the pope had asked that the approved liturgical reforms be immediately implemented and that the requests from the Church of the Poor Group be granted[278] — but the agreement on that main point seems finally to have clarified the relations between the will of the hall and the will of the commissions. The next day, at their regular meeting, the moderators studied the

---

[275] *JPrignon* (A), October 10, 1963. The moderators had been granted an audience of the kind known in curial jargon as an "udienza di tabella," that is, regularly scheduled for a set day and time, as for the heads of the congregations.

[276] The question of women was one of the wealth of subjects for the *De ecclesia* that Montini had already pointed out in his letter to Cicognani on October 18, 1962. See letter of A. Nicora Alberigo to Dossetti on October 15, 1963 (Dossetti Archive, III, 167).

[277] There is also a reference to the "customary audience" in Lercaro, *Lettere*, 176-77. According to Congar (who learned of it at the Belgian College, where he was staying), the moderators had seen the pope three times "*before proposing* the five questions" (italics added; see *JCongar*, November 8-9, 1963; typescript, 36).

[278] Lercaro, *Lettere*, 177, October 10, 1963. During dinner at the Secretariat of State Lercaro heard praise of *L'Avvenire d'Italia* for the help it was rendering to the conciliar debates.

details. Lercaro was in favor of a straw vote, of the kind which a year before had opened the way for the principles of liturgical reform to travel their course.[279] Agagianian not only agreed[280] but even maintained the "the best formula" was the one "in the schema."[281]

By the next day various members of the Council had become aware of this "separate" vote. Karl Rahner spoke of it to Congar.[282] Cavagna wrote to the pope asking for a vote that would "not be on the schema as a whole."[283] In fact, what the moderators had proposed and the pope had already endorsed was not simply a series of votes aimed at determining the degree of consensus and, perhaps, dissent, but also a maieutic act of a quite different significance.

On that same Saturday, October 12, at Monteveglio near Bologna, Dossetti wrote a first draft of proposals — not queries — to be submitted to the assembly and to be agreed on in advance with Carlo Colombo, his old friend and now not only a qualified expert but, more important, a trusted collaborator of Paul VI on theological questions under discussion at the Council. Dossetti defined the object of the vote as "propositions to be submitted for votes of the general congregation." He did not intend, therefore, to replace the vote on the schema or to split the approval into segments, but to obtain from the assembly sure guidelines for the commission's examination of emendations.[284]

---

[279] See Lercaro, *Lettere*, 115-16, on the vote of November 14, 1962; see also *History*, 2:158-66.

[280] See Lercaro, *Lettere*, 180: the cardinals had gone to the Basilica of St. Mary Major where Paul VI was presiding at a celebration of the anniversary of the Council's opening.

[281] Dossetti Archive, 378a, ms. of Dossetti dated October 11, 1963, "A S. M. Maggiore"; see Melloni, "Procedure," 325-26.

[282] See *JCongar*, October 12, typescript, 316: "[Rahner] told me that the moderators were going to have separate votes on episcopal collegiality / sacramentality of episcopal consecration / diaconate."

[283] Prignon Archive, 459. In the Suenens Archive, *IIa sessio, De ecclesia, 5 propositiones*, there is a letter of Castellano to the moderators on October 11 asking for "separate and clear votes."

[284] A synopsis of the successive redactions may be found in Melloni, "Procedure," 388-96. Dossetti Archive, 110, at the bottom of the typescript. The expression *suffragia interlocutoria*, which according to C. Troisfontaines, "A propos de quelques interventions de Paul VI," in *Paolo VI e i problemi ecclesiologici al Concilio* (Brescia, 1989), 135, reflects the original description by Dossetti, was in fact the description proposed by Silva Henriquez to the moderators and would be taken over by Dossetti only in his sketch of an introduction to the votes (Dossetti Archive, 177-78, cited below), but which a handwritten note of Prignon on his copy (Prignon Archive, 576) dates to October 18. On Friday, October 11, the Belgians had discussed the need of "carefully" balanced formulations, "neither too much nor too little" (*JPrignon* [A], October 12, 1963).

The five points brought up were not strictly connected conceptually among themselves but instead singled out crucial themes in the debate. The first theme had to do with episcopal consecration and its consequences in relation to the conferral of the *tria munera* (Questions I, II.1, and II.2);[285] the second had to do with the episcopal college as a subject, by divine right, of full and supreme power over the universal Church (Questions III, IV.1, and IV.2);[286] the third raised the question of the diaconate (Question V), which seems to have been the subject that had given rise to the idea of straw votes and on which what was asked, as Agagianian had suggested, was the freezing of a formula in the schema.[287]

Dossetti worked on his text as on a canvas whose forms were flexible; the suggestions given by Don Colombo on October 13 led to a second version that was better structured and more complex.[288] Colombo asked and obtained a better linking of episcopal consecration, apostolic succession, and collegiality. He proposed that the exercise of a bishop's actual jurisdiction not come about *per collationem* or, as Dossetti had proposed, in ways to be defined, but only (*non acquiritur nisi*) through a *collatio* or according to already tested *consuetudo*. In addition, to the description of the pope as "head and source of the unity" of the college of bishops, he added and underscored "their head," which was grammatically superfluous but expressed a line of thought aimed at preserving this dimension to the bitter end. Finally, he toned down the sentence

[285] These questions had an internal unity, and Dossetti and Colombo considered replacing them with a single question that simply repeated the text of the schema.

[286] On Mörsdorf's contribution to clarification of this point there is no evidence except some allusions in the Rahner Archive (Würzburg).

[287] Following the request of Agagianian on October 11 the restoration of the diaconate was proposed "according to the words of the schema, page 26, lines 36-41."

[288] Dossetti Archive, 110, Dossetti manuscript with corrections by Colombo at Monteveglio on October 13; a handwritten note on the text reads: "At Monteveglio–10/13, 1963 / Corrections / proposed by D. Carlo [Colombo]." Tucci was aware of the Milanese theologian's involvement, as can be seen from a note in *DTucci* for January 17, 1964, p. 168: "As for the 5 points of October 30, [Suenens] told me that they were prepared by Msgr. Carlo Colombo, with the help of Dossetti, and that he had only had them reviewed and touched up a bit by Msgr. Philips and Canon Moeller." On Sunday, October 13, Dossetti returned to Rome with a text that would ensure that "the theological commission would have a straw vote on the problems of collegiality, relations between college and primacy, and I no longer remember whether on the diaconate as well. The proposals announced in the Council have not yet been voted on as of today. Pippo [= Dossetti] had revised them and toned them down, along with Don Carlo [Colombo]; Döpfner toned them down even further" (*DNAlberigo*, October 21, 1963); see Melloni, "Procedure," 330-31.

on the diaconate by proposing not that the fathers approve the formula in the schema but that they grant the freedom to restore the diaconate as provided in the schema.

The proposal was now ready; the next day Colombo saw a version with the corrections agreed to and with some more slight variants.[289] In fact, a new section V had been introduced that repeated (who was it that thought this necessary?) the primatial and vicarial titles of the pope and the prerogatives connected with these. In addition, the version reserved to the pope the role of judging the "opportuneness" of collegial action; in the following days this theme would be developed in a section of the *Nota bene* on the third question.

B. The Announcement of the Straw Votes

Meanwhile, what was being said in the hall gave rise to some excessive hopes. After the replacement of Tromp by Philips, of Lio by Häring and Hirschmann, and of Balić by Butler, Hans Küng anticipated that Ottaviani would be replaced as head of the Doctrinal Commission. If on Monday, October 14, Parente, despite wanting Peter's role as rock to be differentiated from that of the other apostles, defended the sacramentality of the episcopate and the thesis that episcopal collegiality is of divine law, was it not time to speed things up? If, as Philips told Congar, Ottaviani had not succeeded in getting the pope to reverse the new order of the chapters on the People of God and on the hierarchy, must one not conclude that the conflict could be waged to the end, "to the point when Cardinal Ottaviani would be led to resign the presidency of the theological commission"?[290]

The first two days of the week thus passed in an atmosphere of expectation. Some important addresses (Höffner on the structuring of the *tria munera*) passed unnoticed,[291] while an effort was being made to think of

---

[289] A new version in Colombo Archive, 13. 7, October 14, 1963; he notes there: "14-X-1963, Dossetti, Cardinal Moderators." See Melloni, "Procedure," 330-31.

[290] *JCongar*, October 15. A note by Philips, "sent to the Holy Father to explain the importance of the inversion," was dated October 15 (Suenens Archive, *IIa sessio, De ecclesia, Caput III*).

[291] *AS* II/2, 522-24; The problem was a favorite of one of the canonists who, according to various sources (*TJedin*), was collaborating on the composition of the addresses of the German bishops and who would rehash the whole problem; see N. Mörsdorf, "Munus regendi et potestas iurisdictionis," in *Conventus Canonistarum*, 199-211, and G. Vallquist, *Das Zweite Vatikanische Konzil* (Zurich, 1966), 131-34.

some solution that would blunt the fears of those who, like the prudent Bishop of Verona,[292] had again become open to a permanent diaconate, as long as it was celibate.[293]

The solution given by the moderators was, however, not explanatory but maieutic. On October 15, the day of attacks by Siri, Wyszynski, Jubany, and Browne,[294] the vote to close debate on the chapter was finally taken, and the moderators announced the straw vote to the Council. After closing the discussion of the chapter on the hierarchic Constitution of the Church in the ecclesiological schema and after all had been assured that the rights guaranteed by the Regulations remained intact,[295] it was announced that the next day a ballot of questions on four key issues would be distributed and that these would be voted on the following Thursday, *before* the chapter as a whole was put to a final vote.[296] At the moment of the announcement the ballot had already gone to the printer, Lercaro having sent it to Felici and Felici to the printer.[297]

---

[292] *AS* II/2, 524-30.

[293] Prignon received a note from Congar, asking that the moderators have Philips explain to the hall the precise bearing of the formulas (*JCongar*, October 14, 1963).

[294] *AS* II/2, 572-74, 574-77, 580-86.

[295] Article 56 §6 established that after a debate had been declared "closed" cardinals and bishops could still intervene if they were speaking in the name of at least five others. The minority that had voted against the end of the debate could still appoint three speakers who had a half hour to explain their theses in the hall. This was the only room left by the Regulations for interventions by bishops who were not reporters for commissions.

[296] "On the following day, here in the hall, you will receive a sheet containing four propositions put to you: these are intended to give the Theological Commission guidelines or directive norms for the further development of the schema, so that the work of the commission may proceed more easily and with greater clarity. The text of the propositions will be given to you tomorrow, but the vote on them will be taken only on Thursday" (*AS* II/2, 597). According to Caprile, II, 97, Döpfner was the moderator who announced that a vote would be taken on the questions "instead of on the chapter as a whole," a point not found in the minutes in the *AS*; this information on a substitute (and not an additional) vote was, however, to be found in press communiqué no. 12/1963, p. 7 (provisional draft in Lercaro Archive, 117). But from the communiqué it also emerged that the moderator whose turn it was that day was Suenens; nothing in the communiqué suggests that the "cardinal moderator" who at the end of the morning told of the straw votes had changed in the meantime. The announcement is also attributed to Suenens by R. Aubert, "Lo svolgimento del concilio," in *La chiesa del Vaticano II (1958-1978)*, ed. M. Guasco, E. Guerriero, and F. Traniello (Cinisello B., 1994), 260; Aubert is followed in this by Troisfontaines, "A propos," 104. Suenens himself claims to have made the announcement (*Souvenirs et espérances*, 116) but with details that do not fit in with the entirety of the documentation now available.

[297] A witness stated that when Lercaro found it difficult to read a handwritten note, he called Dossetti, the one who incorporated it, to decipher the sentence: in the copy of the typescript in the official Vatican II Archives, the handwritten sentence inserted into the text also appears, in a different hand, at the bottom of page 1. These might have been corrections that Döpfner wanted at the last moment; on this see above.

The ballot sheet had undergone some changes. In form, the statements became questions; in content, there was a development of the insight of Colombo, who, before describing the characteristics and tasks of the college, asked whether one entered it by episcopal consecration. The emphasis on the superiority of bishops over priests and the repetition of the title of Vicar of Christ for the pope had both been dropped. Instead, an explicit but general homage was paid to the decrees of Vatican I. Finally, what was said of the diaconate was expanded in the form of three different propositions: in addition to what was said in the schema it was proposed to open the diaconate to married men and to bestow the diaconate even on those who had chosen celibacy only as a temporary state.[298] This explains, as Lercaro wrote, the change in the number of questions.[299]

On the morning of October 15, then, the impression was that the decision to take straw votes on the questions was now settled and that everyone was simply waiting for the executive body — the General Secretariat, which was responsible for the printing — to produce the means of voting.[300] A victory in the hall, even if risky, would not greatly affect the contents of the schema, but it would lessen the highhandedness of the commissions and especially of the Doctrinal Commission. But for men like Felici, the link that from the antepreparatory phase onward had bound the commissions to the Roman congregations was the expression of papal control of the Council; therefore, in principle, the subordination of the commissions to the will of the assembly was prejudicial to papal authority, although in fact it only limited the discretionary power of the heads of the congregations.

This conflict of views makes it credible that Felici informed Cicognani, on whom Felici thought the General Secretariat should depend, and involved him in the proposed move and the meaning of the straw votes. Cicognani had the right and authority to consult the pope and ask that Paul VI, who had shown himself, or was considered to be, ignorant of

[298] This would be a contribution from Suenens. On Moeller's notes and on the copy of the typescript without notes in Prignon Archive, 466, see Melloni, "Procedure." The list, with the corrections from the copy in the Vatican II Archives, is in AS V/1, 698.

[299] Writing to the children who were his friends and guests at the archiepiscopal residence, Lercaro said of the questions that "from four they have become five" (Lercaro, Lettere, 198, October 29, 1963).

[300] At the afternoon meeting of the observers the matter was also taken as now certain. At the meeting Cullmann asked for a more careful use of biblical texts in the ecclesiological schema, a point that Bea would bring into his intervention in the aula, which is discussed below; see Horton, 62-65.

the vote announced for the morrow, should block it.[301] On the evening of October 15, by mandate of the pope, Cicognani telephoned an order to destroy the ballots, and he informed the moderators that the voting had been suspended *sine die*.[302] The halt was not secret,[303] but the information given to the assembly was quite vague.

1. The Crisis of October 16

October 16 was supposed to mark the transition from discussion of the chapter on the hierarchy to that on the People of God and especially on the laity.[304] It was also to have seen the taking of the votes announced on the criteria for studying the emendations to the previous chapter. Ignorant of the bonfire lit in the night, the front page of *L'Avvenire d'italia* that day announced: "The Council called upon to vote on collegiality and the diaconate. The vote to be taken on four questions asked by the 'moderators' is to take place tomorrow." With an accuracy deriving from circles close to Dossetti, who was a friend of editor-in-chief Raniero La Valle, the newspaper announced:

> It is believed that the fathers will be called upon to take a stand on four matters that have been the main subjects of discussion and are the key points of the second chapter: the episcopate as a sacrament; membership of bishops in the episcopal college in virtue of their consecration; the powers of the college in relation to papal primacy; the diaconate, with or without celibacy.[305]

The newspaper's mistake could only strengthen the feeling of alarm of men like Cicognani and Felici. Did not the vote that had been "thwarted" by authority suggest that the time had come to start a "barrage against

---

[301] Thus *AS* V/1, 608, note. According to Prignon, the pope said that he "had never seen them"; see *JCongar*, February 2, 1965.

[302] Testimony of V. Carbone, "L'azione direttiva di Paolo VI," 80-82. According to Prignon, at 7 a.m. Cicognani had telephoned only Agagianian; see *JCongar*, February 2, 1965.

[303] Dossetti's letter of October 15 against "watering down" suggests at least fear of an impending blockage.

[304] There were still interventions on chapter II by fathers who spoke in the name of a group; then the assembly moved on to discussion of chapter III, which would occupy seven general congregations, until October 24.

[305] *L'Avvenire d'Italia*, October 16, 1963. The official press communiqué said simply that "tomorrow four questions will be given to the fathers on chapter two of the *De Ecclesia*, their intention being to define precisely the four main subjects. A vote will be taken on them Thursday, instead of a vote on the chapter as a whole" (duplicated communiqué no. 12, October 15, 1963, copy in Lercaro Archive, 117).

Dossetti"?[306] In St. Peter's, the news traveled at varying speeds. After a lengthy murmured conversation during the mass between Cicognani and Agagianian, moderator for that day, who was soon joined by his other three colleagues,[307] the Armenian Cardinal told the assembly that the vote announced the day before was being put off to a date to be determined. Those who knew that the ballots had been burned realized that this was more than Felici's jealousy of Dossetti.[308]

That some authoritative, qualified person, capable of persuading Paul VI to change his mind about a text that had been examined and analyzed by Colombo himself, must have intervened is also attested by a "note" containing objections against the straw votes, which the pope received at about the moment when he was rethinking his position.[309] This note contained seven theses against the plan of the moderators and challenged the value and signification of the procedure.[310] An attack of this kind from the circle of the pope's institutional collaborators left him "puzzled and embarrassed," as Suenens maintains in a passage of his memoirs.[311]

---

[306] Wenger got this from Villot; see A. Wenger, *Les Trois Rome* (Paris, 1991), 138. At the same time, Moeller, Daniélou, and Laurentin told Congar that the suspension of the voting was due to Ottaviani's rebellion against the moderators, who had exceeded their powers (*JCongar*, October 17, 1963, typescript, 328).

[307] See *JCongar*, October 16, 1963, typescript, 323: "During Mass, Cardinal Cicognani, Secretary of State, looked for Cardinal Agagianian and took him aside to speak with him. The other moderators soon joined in the conversation. They seemed very worried. The game was repeated *three times*, with the Cardinal Secretary of State going away and then returning a while later. Those who saw it from close up and reported it to me thought that it had to do with the disagreement that had arisen regarding the question of the 3 [4] votes which the moderators wanted to submit to the Council."

[308] See Melloni, "Procedure," 335-38. It is easy to infer not only from the way things went during the following days but also from a memorandum to the pope on October 16 that Tisserant was not an opponent of the moderators. See the recently published letter from Dell'Acqua to Felici, October 23, 1963, with which the substitute sent along a note given to the pope from Tisserant during the audience on October 16, in which he raises no objection (*AS* V/3, 695).

[309] A note of October 30 for the use of the moderators cited fragments of that note, making it possible to identify a document by an unknown author in Dossetti Archive, 112. In the note to the moderators some expressions of it are cited (on "confusions" and "misunderstandings"; on "distinguishing the dogmatic side of the problem from the juridical and pastoral"). As regards the authorship, Haubtmann's suggestion is far from unrealistic, namely, that it was Ottaviani who was leading a "determined opposition" (Lercaro Archive, 122, November 15, 1963, mimeographed sheet from the Secrétariat national de l'Information religieuse). Semmelroth regarded the pope's choice to be the decisive question: "What influence is the pope exerting on the Council? Is it true that General Secretary Felici has for days now been opposing the moderators and working against the anticipated vote on the text?" (*TSemmelroth*, October 21, 1963).

[310] See Melloni, "Procedure," 338-40.

[311] Suenens, *Souvenirs et espérances*, 116.

What were the moderators to do now? Obey? Or react with firmness on the doctrinal content, as Dossetti asked Lercaro and Suenens to do on this same day, October 15?[312]

There were, however, some who did not yet know of the crisis that had arisen. On that very afternoon there was a meeting of experts who discussed the method of proceeding on the schema on the Virgin and the possibility of correcting the text by replacing it, not with the Butler schema (distributed around October 10[313]) but with the Chilean schema.[314] Martimort, Medina, Laurentin, Martelet, Butler, and the others present continued their routine work without having gotten wind of the serious clash that had begun. A short distance away, in the Spanish College, there was another meeting (Morcillo, Guerry, Rahner, Dupuy, Salaverri, Féret, Dournes, Urresti, Lopez Gallego, Congar, and others), at which the members discussed the chapter on the People of God once again, without knowing what had happened.[315] The French working group of Lefebvre and Garrone continued its own work on the People of God.[316] The bewilderment of those who had no information on what had happened and on the immediate future found an outlet in private conversations; it took some time before table conversations, the newspapers, and the meeting places of the episcopal conferences permitted the news to spread.

---

[312] Dossetti Archive, 38. Notation on the manuscript "15.X.63, to Lercaro, to Suenens": "Your Eminence, forgive me for allowing myself to plead with you insistently that the text to be voted on not be changed in such a way as to attenuate it. In fact, it is perhaps already too weak. Even a word less can leave everything very uncertain. It seems to me that this is the most serious action we can take during this session. To say anything less on behalf of the episcopate would not be *true*; it would not be in line with the wishes of the majority, and, *above all, it would have very serious ecumenical repercussions, especially in relations with the Orientals* at this very moment (think of the Rhodes Conference). I will soon give you a report on this last aspect, the work of one of the Secretariat's experts. Finally, I can say in good conscience that the Holy Father too is certainly in agreement with these propositions. If we were to say anything less, it would be better to leave everything undecided and not even to raise the question of the episcopate at this Council."

[313] See *JCongar*, October 11, 1963. Congar read the text and considered it "a fine text."

[314] See the note in Moeller Archive, 00373.

[315] *JCongar*, October 16, 1963: "We talk about the *De populo Dei*; the deaf one wants to locate the whole thing in the framework of a definition taken from rational sociology; the same for the idea of royal priesthood. Rahner, as usual, monopolizes the dialogue....The Spaniards would have liked us to compose a text that would have been signed by a number of episcopates; they want to get out of their isolation, build bridges, and that is why, despite my unbelievable workload, I decided to answer their call. But Rahner very justly observes that we are already taken up with work for our respective bishops and must not create a new moral person. In our respective groups we will echo what is done in these meetings, without it giving rise to a special activity in relation to the Council."

[316] *JCongar*, October 17, 1963.

2. The Debate Continues (People of God and Laity)

In the hall, too, where the chapter on the People of God and the laity had been reached, the debate continued but was marked from the beginning by a consensus on making the People of God the subject of chapter II and giving it a place before the chapters on the hierarchy and the laity.[317]

What was still at this point chapter III was the child of an initial revision of the chapter on the laity from the preparatory phase and had kept almost everything from that chapter, which Philips himself had written. Gagnebet had strongly criticized the stance taken by Philips, who, according to Gagnebet, from the time when he first wrote his substitute schema, had protected this chapter. The superficial revision had been followed by some more decisive interventions, due mostly to the forceful protest of Léger, who did not want a treatment of clergy and laity in terms of subordination. For this reason the chapter had been given a spacious introduction on the People of God as a whole; during the summer it was then proposed to locate the chapter between that on the mystery and that on the hierarchy, so as to make of it not simply an "image" but a framework for the subsequent treatment of clergy, laity, and religious.

The chapter began with a strong emphasis on the equality of the members of the Church by reason of their ultimate vocation, their participation in the gift of salvation, and their call to holiness. With regard to priesthood, too, thanks to some German suggestions, the schema clearly described the unity of the priestly vocation of all the baptized and the distinction between ministerial and universal roles, all of these, however, being ordered to the one plan of salvation.[318] But the emphasis on the *sensus fidei* of the community was not at that time harmoniously connected with the chapter on the laity, this being still in thrall to a theology of the laity that various ideas in the schema had already largely left behind. As a result, the chapter on the laity, which in 1962 had represented one element of theological "modernity" in a Scholastic production, came a year later to represent a residue of questions mostly left behind: What is a "lay person"? What is his or her place in the Church and the world? What does the sanctification of temporal realities mean?

The discussion in the hall, which occupied eight general congregations and saw ninety fathers rise to speak (with thirty-three written interventions as well), clearly took place on two different levels. On the one

---

[317] See above, 59.

[318] In the debate on the chapter on the hierarchy there had been an especially forceful intervention by Beck on October 7, 1963; *AS* II/2, 268-70.

hand, there were interventions that supported or opposed shifting the chapter on the People of God and placing it before that on the hierarchy.[319] In this context there were heated addresses by the fathers who had supported the renewal in ecclesiology of which the *Lumen gentium* schema of 1963 had been the pledge rather than the realization. The conceptual link created by the shift was not perceived in the same way by all. Thus Jaeger of Paderborn praised the idea because this new arrangement would make clear the continuation of Christ's work and life in the Church, this being expressed precisely by the unity of various roles and tasks within the one people. Wojtyla of Cracow also spoke, but he maintained that the establishment of a people by God was a necessary premise for the definition of the hierarchy that was to guide and serve that people.[320] Larraìn and Silva Henriquez, making use of the plentiful material in the Chilean schema on the Church, once again took the most advanced positions, asking not only that the chapter on the People of God be placed first but also that *koinonia* be highlighted as an essential characteristic and not just an effect of the People of God and that there be an outline of the threefold mission of Christ, which would then be repeated and explained again in the chapters on the hierarchy and the laity.[321]

Siri and Ruffini spoke against this position by calling for a more definite distinction between the priesthood of the people and the hierarchical priesthood.[322] These two speakers, and others even more strongly, stressed the point that the connection between people and hierarchy can only be expressed by giving priority to authority, within which the people find their unity. These men showed a real inability to grasp the way in which the others were putting the question; it was symptomatic that Bacci understood "priesthood of the faithful" to mean a "priesthood of the laity."[323]

[319] Léger himself complained of this duplication as an attempt of Suenens "to impose his thinking" on the Council (*JCongar*, October 3, 1963). See also H. Denis, "Réflexions sur le *De laicis* du Schéma sur l'Eglise," *Études et Documents*, no. 22 (October 22, 1962). (Suenens Archive, *IIa sessio, De ecclesia, Caput III*); see also C. Soetens, "La Squadra belga et la majorité à Vatican II," in *Evento*, 143-72.

[320] *AS* II/3, 92-95 and 154-57.

[321] Larraìn, *AS* II/3, 223-26; Silva Henriquez (*AS* II/3, 399-417) also added a lengthy extract from the Chilean schema.

[322] Ruffini, *AS* II/2, 627-32; Siri, *AS* II/3, 278-80. In the Doctrinal Commission, Father Fernandez had raised the alarm against an "exaggerated democratism" (*JCongar*, October 2, 1963).

[323] Bacci, *AS* II/2, 637-38; Seper, *AS* II/3, 201-3. No less strong was the Melkite-Maronite reaction to a lecture by Congar: "In the evening at the Botticelli Hotel, where the Vietnamese bishops, some Melkite bishops, some Maronite bishops (Msgr. Doumith) are staying. After dinner, a lecture on the *De laicis* and the *De populo Dei*. Then questions and dialogue. I realize that the bishops (30 to 35) are rather ill at ease with the texts

On a less innovative level, but one gladly listened to by many fathers, there were addresses that tackled the "definition," the "tasks," the "characteristics" of the laity. These were questions typical of a theology of the laity that had arisen within the narrow limits of a Pacellian ecclesiology, and of which Civardi appointed himself spokesman in the hall.[324] This was the most complicated part of the debate, the part that was weighed down by the indecisiveness which, in another setting, had hindered the work of the Commission for the Lay Apostolate. Not by accident it was Ménager, a member of that commission, who in a lengthy address proposed a solution that played down the elements defining the laity in favor of those that were descriptive.[325] Here the clash of opinions had to do with the relative emphases on authority and roles. Some, who had not adopted the explicit communion-perspective of the Chileans, asked that the schema sanction the principle of subsidiarity even for the life of the Church.[326]

Other problems of a more general kind also came up in the addresses given during these days. The question of the obedience of the laity elicited new interventions on the *sensus fidei* of the community; the French and German fathers who had discussed the theme of the unity of the human race in connection with the introduction to the schema raised it again during these discussions;[327] Suenens's address on the charisms in the Church made a deep impression on the observers;[328] other speeches discussed the conversion of the Church[329] and the need to hear from some experts on present conditions in the world, as requested in a report from the lay auditors.[330] On October 20 the Abbot of the Premonstratensians summed up a general reaction:

> I have the impression, and I am not the only one, that for the last four or five days the gears have been grinding because the brakes lack fluid, and

and discussions *De Ecclesia*. They tell me as much, even in rather strong terms. They can't make sense of them. They have a tradition of thought, categories, concerns which are not those of the texts and discussions. It's too bad. I realize once again how much the Catholic Church is Latin, how much it deceives itself, in good faith, in thinking itself 'catholic.' It isn't. Romanism, Italianism, Latinism, Scholasticism, the analytical mind have permeated everything and have almost been elevated to the status of dogma. What a job remains to be done!" (*JCongar*, October 17, 1963).

[324] *AS* II/3, 35-36.
[325] Ibid., 208-10.
[326] Lázló's written intervention asked for a chapter on "the validity of the principle of subsidiarity in the Church"; *AS* II/2, 496-502.
[327] Dubois, but also Jaeger and Garrone, *AS* II/3, 24-27, 92-95, 465-67.
[328] Ibid., 174-79; see Horton, 82-83.
[329] Jaeger, *AS* II/3, 92-95, but also Meyer, ibid., 146-48.
[330] *JCongar*, October 18, 1963.

those who are pushing to make the wheels turn are tiring themselves and getting nowhere. The cardinal moderators are trying to clear the way but the back wheels are slipping. The boldest are coming to the rescue, but they are racing the engine instead of getting it to turn over. They want to change speed and get the car rolling without clutching.[331]

3. The Crisis Is Resolved: The Supercommission (October 23)

While the debate was unfolding in the hall, the struggle over the propositions was being discussed by the moderators and the pope at the audience on October 19. For four days pressures had been building up around Paul VI from those who had remained on the periphery of this undertaking,[332] that is, from the Council of Presidents, the CC, the General Secretariat, and even the Doctrinal Commission, or, in other words, Tisserant, Urbani, Wyszynski, Cicognani, Felici, Ottaviani. None of them could now claim the agreement of the pope against the moderators, but neither did any of them give the impression that they had found Paul VI deaf to criticisms of the men who for three weeks now had been directing Vatican II on his behalf.[333]

The pope now asked the moderators to explain the straw votes and gain approval of them from a "supercommission" formed of the moderators themselves, the entire General Secretariat, the Council of Presidents, and the CC.[334] The meeting was called in the name of Cicognani, president of the CC, in a document signed by Felici on October 19.[335]

---

[331] N. Calmels, La vie au Concile (Forcalquier, 1966), 110-11. Only on October 20 would the moderators meet with the lay auditors; see Lercaro, Lettere, 190.

[332] The audience on October 19 seems to have been the decisive one. DNAlberigo, October 21, 1963, notes that "at the audience for the moderators (I don't know whether it was on Thursday [17th] or on Friday [18th] morning) it was discovered that the pope had not seen the proposals and now saw them for the first time, and had no objection to them." The source of her information was Dossetti who also told her that he had voluntarily given up the role of secretary to the entire group of moderators on October 14.

[333] On Friday, October 18, the moderators met with the CC (AS V/1, 18-19). Some months later, Prignon sent Congar a dramatic picture of the day: at Döpfner's urging, Felici wanted to postpone the meeting with the CC to Wednesday, October 23; Suenens bounced back and forth between Cicognani and Felici and won a meeting on Saturday, which was then put off to Monday, October 21, but extended to include the Council of Presidents (JCongar, February 2, 1965, typescript, 416).

[334] At the press conference given by subsecretary Krol on October 30, the failure to consult the Council of Presidents would be alleged as one reason for the postponement; news of this conference was carried by the NCWC News Service on October 31 and is cited in Caprile, II, 168.

[335] There is a lengthy handwritten note of Dossetti for Lercaro (Dossetti Archive, 126) in preparation for the meeting of the supercommission; see Melloni, "Procedure," 342-43. The lawyer from Bologna argues in ten theses that the pope appointed the moderators in order to give the Council "a special body, quite homogeneous in its makeup, authori-

On that same day Döpfner sent a new version of the propositions to the Secretary General in order that it might be included with the call to the meeting; whether it would be included or not remained a question.[336] This version showed some variations in the structure of the propositions; these variations can be traced back to a larger working group to which Colombo seemingly no longer belonged and in which the role of Dossetti had been reduced and, instead, Philips, Moeller, and Prignon had become the principal actors.[337] Along with some preventive measures for exercising control,[338] a note of Dossetti's suggested to the moderators some technico-procedural ideas for use against objections that could arise at the expanded meeting.[339]

---

tative, free from other duties, and devoted solely to advancing the Council in a direction conformed to its purpose," and that therefore the conflict should be settled in the light of that principle. In Dossetti's view, the subjection of the commissions to the conciliar majority was "the primary problem of Vatican Council II since its beginning," a problem made clear by the "very stubborn resistance" with which the commissions have responded to the directives of the hall when these "were not conformed to the direction given by the Congregations [i.e., the Curia]." According to Dossetti, the need was "to demand that all submit to the will of the majority, which is to be consulted in the form of provisional, clear, and binding votes, and to prescribe that the commissions be free to work in conformity therewith and not be obliged to submit to the will of their presidents or secretaries. In particular, article 64. 4, which allows the fathers to be heard by the commissions, and the regulation on [submitting] alternative proposals to the congregation, will vastly facilitate things. Instead of having one text rather than another imposed by the presidents, two alternative texts expressing two different main tendencies will allow the Council to get its bearings and choose clearly and quickly."

[336] *AS* V/1, 699-700.

[337] Although this last-named, who was rector and director of the Belgian College, supported the version of October 19, "which was drafted by Msgr. Philips with the aid of Msgr. Moeller and myself," it must be said that the changes in the text were modest both in importance and in weight. The authors are given in Prignon Archive, 463, in a handwritten note. The changes for the most part were mitigating: to tone down the difference between *corpus* and *(seu) collegium*; to introduce protection of the *ius primatiale*; to explain in an N.B. the question of the "never rejected" ways in which the pope exercises collegiality, and to moderate the expression of these; to guarantee that a collegial act can take place only at the invitation of the pope himself or by his free acceptance of it; and finally, to refer to needed future theological investigations, to which the Council does not commit itself, in regard to the "practical means" of implementing collegiality. With regard to the diaconate, the propositions excluded the possibility previously proposed of a temporary celibacy and introduced a direct authority of the episcopal conferences. For the detailed development of the versions, see Melloni, "Procedure."

[338] At Dossetti's residence in Rome, there was some thought of using a young priest, Pierre Riches, to deliver to Tisserant the note that the canonist of Bologna had drafted for the moderators; see *DNAlberigo*, October 21, 1963.

[339] Dossetti Archive, 124: the note points out that the CC was being involved for the first time, that the moderators had legitimately put an end to the assembly's debate, and that a straw vote did not require a quorum of two-thirds of the membership; it criticized Urbani's proposal; it asked for a more systematic adoption of the regulatory norms on the

At 5:00 p.m. on October 23, in the apartment of Cicognani, Secretary of State, the members of the so-called supercommission met to discuss the changes in the Regulations and "the proposal of a directive vote on the second chapter of the schema on the Church."[340] The only person absent was the elderly Tappouni, which brought the number of cardinals present to eighteen.[341]

By reason of his ecclesiastical rank, Cardinal Dean Tisserant was given the job of leading the meeting. Without letting himself be influenced either by the Secretary of State or, much less, the Secretary General, he led the discussion with surprising efficiency and control. He had the moderators explain the first point on the page they had prepared, and he accepted it as approved. On the second and third questions he forced Cicognani to emerge from the shadows and explain his objections. It seemed somewhat like a return to the rapid but superficial pace of the Central Preparatory Commission; even Siri showed some approval. The dean of the Council of Presidents (the body that claimed to have been

choice between alternative texts; it urged a meeting of the moderators with Bea, Willebrands, and the other authorities of the Secretariat for Christian Unity. Lercaro regarded the crisis as "a matter of procedure," "against" which "some conciliar bodies have rebelled" (*Lettere*, October 21, 1963, [191]). As was often the case, Dossetti was worried and pessimistic: "On Saturday evening [October 19] he asked: 'Will we succeed in saving the Council?'...The danger is great: 'The Council is like a stutterer who cannot put together connected words and sentences'" (*DNAlberigo*, October 21, 1963). The meeting of the observers on October 22 did not touch on the procedural problem but confined itself to reacting to Moeller's report (Horton, 85-86).

[340] The proposed changes had to do with articles 39 §2 and 60 §3; the lengthy minutes are in *AS* V/1, 701-35. Willebrands' intervention allayed the fears of the observers from the WCC about the celebration of mass in the Rumanian Uniate rite in remembrance of the Union of 1698 and the suppression of the Church in 1948 (see WCC Archive, 6.38).

[341] The meeting of the Italian Episcopal Conference, set for the same time, was postponed in order to spare many Italians (especially Siri, Lercaro, and Urbani) the embarrassment of having to make a choice. The previous afternoon, October 22, at via del sant'Uffizio, 22, Siri had attended the first meeting of the International Group of Fathers, the coordinating body for the traditionalist fathers, which had been called by M. Lefebvre and G. de Proença Sigaud. Siri would not thereafter take part in these meetings, which would be held on subsequent Tuesdays (see B. Lai, *Il papa non* eletto (Rome/Bari, 1993), 200-201, who relies on the diary of Don Barabino). The two opponents, Bea and Ottaviani, who embodied the polarized positions on many subjects, were missing from the meeting of the supercommission because they did not belong to any of the bodies represented there. The absence of Ottaviani, in particular, shows how specious and flimsy was the accusation leveled at the moderators, that in proposing the votes on the 15th they had violated the legitimate rights of the Doctrinal Commission, of which no one on the supercommission took the least account. Nor did Silva Henriquez take part in the meeting. On October 8 he had presented his own proposal to the moderators and then, on October 22, had sent it directly to the pope; no reference was made to this proposal.

wronged by the decision of the moderators) said he was in favor of the procedure and sent a message—"I do not know the reasons why the voting was suspended"—that was very embarrassing to the Secretary of State, who had set in motion the tremendous effort to put on the brakes. The alternative to a vote was to proceed (as in mariology) by way of opposing reports — a prospect that frightened some.

On the question of whether to speak of the "body" or of the "college" of bishops Tisserant proposed removing the word "college,"[342] but not all the moderators were persuaded. The other objections (that the fathers' responses were conditioned by the questions; that there was no knowing precisely what a yes vote was approving) called for answers and led to interventions. Surprisingly, Suenens asked that Siri, author of an obstinate intervention (the only one given in Latin!) against collegiality, should take responsibility for a better formula.[343] But it was on the diaconate that Tisserant, former prefect of the Oriental Congregation, expanded; the suppression of the diaconate was a Latin invention in the 1917 Code of Canon Law, and the restoration of the older state of things could only be good.[344] Felici, who was taking the minutes, was in difficulties ("no one here has understood anything"); Caggiano thought the meeting was over and left. In this atmosphere a vote was taken by show of hands on whether the three questions on the diaconate could be put forward. Felici counted and announced that the motion was rejected; but Liénart[345] or one of the assistants or Felici himself realized that there had

[342] In a lengthy note to Lercaro, Dossetti had also supported this solution; see Melloni, "Procedure," as well as Ratzinger, *Theological Highlights*, 48-52.

[343] Prignon explained to Congar that "Siri is against Suenens" and that the acceptance of the role of mediator was given with the idea of submitting to the hall two formulas to vote on (*JCongar*, February 2, 1965, typescript, 415). The day was an especially busy one for Siri. In the morning, Segni, president of the Italian Republic, had been received by Paul VI, the crisis of the Leone government had begun, and the way had been opened again for what would be the first Center-Left government, led by Aldo Moro. Siri and the Italian Episcopal Conference had launched very harsh attacks against these possibilities (which were shipwrecked by June). These attacks, in their connections with the conciliar event, were neatly gathered together by the author of an anonymous little book attacking Montini that appeared under the nom de plume Michel Serafian, *The Pilgrim* (New York, 1964). According to Murphy/Rynne, the pseudonym Serafian belonged to Malachi Martin, an Irish Jesuit in Rome at the time.

[344] In polemical tones Tisserant told Cicognani that he would have "gladly" spoken "in the hall if I had been able to examine how the composition of canon 873 had been arrived at, but unfortunately the Vatican Secret Archive does not have the documents on the preparation of the Code; they are in the special archive of the Sacred Congregation for Extraordinary Affairs. I asked Msgr. Giusti to request them of the archivist of that Congregation, but they were not found."

[345] Thus Haubtmann, according to *JCongar*, October 18, 1964.

been a mistake, and in a heated atmosphere it was put in the minutes that the questions were to go to the hall (it would be said later that Spellman's vote was mistakenly counted as favorable).[346]

The meeting ended while Wyszynski and Tisserant continued their disagreement. No discussion was made of Frings's proposals for another revision of the conciliar Regulations in order to reduce the number of schemas to six.[347] This was not an unwarranted suggestion; after less than a month the Regulations had already been criticized by the pope (who, as noted above, told some persons that he had signed them without realizing that they did not correspond to his thinking), by Buckley, who had presented an alternative proposal, by the African episcopate, which wanted radical changes both in the carrying on of the work and in the role of the episcopal conferences, as well as by those circles, including Dossetti's first and foremost, which had been seeking a change in the Regulations during the intersession.[348]

---

[346] Felici's minutes did not take account of the fact that Tisserant had been openly opposed to the moderators' delegating Siri to compose the third question; nor did he consider the president to have a deciding vote when there was a tie vote on the question of the diaconate. Felici's summary was as follows: "Responses: to the first, affirmative; to the second, affirmative without the word 'college'; to the third, let the text be emended by the moderators and ambiguities removed so that the meaning of the word 'college' will be clear; in addition, let His Eminence Cardinal Siri compose another text, to be submitted again to a vote of the fathers; to the fourth, affirmative for the restoration of the diaconate, but nothing is decided about married deacons (since the fathers voted nine for and nine against)." In this way Felici settled the dispute that arose on the voting on the diaconate, which, according to a witness who was present, involved a very sharp verbal dispute between Felici and his recorders, on the one hand, and the subsecretaries, on the other. This squabble does not appear, however, in Suenens's version, *Souvenirs et espérances*, 17, according to which a distracted Spellman voted in favor of the diaconate (Suenens advised Villot, who became aware of the mistake, to let it go). The minutes do not differ from this version when they report that Cardinals Agagianian, Döpfner, Lercaro, Suenens, Tisserant, Confalonieri, Liénart, Alfrink, Frings, and Gilroy voted yes and that Cicognani, Secretary of State, Meyer, Roberti, Ruffini, Spellman, Urbani, Siri, and Wyszynski voted against. On the specific question of a married diaconate, Gilroy switched to the opponents, but the question was approved by the vote of the president.

[347] *JPrignon* (B), 4.

[348] The proposals for change began on October 12 with a request from Carli, followed on the 15th by Urbani and on the 17th by Gauci. Buckley submitted a voluminous memorandum with twelve articles on October 18. The African proposal was presented by Zoa on October 23. Frings repeated his proposals at the general congregation on the 24th, and on that same day Lefebvre called for an extension of the *iuxta modum*. On the 25th other proposals for individual changes were handed in by A. Dupont and Mabathoana. On the 28th Villot sent the pope the proposals of twenty secretaries of episcopal conferences (see above). On the next day Maccarrone submitted his proposals for ensuring that the Council would "judge" and not "discuss," as if it were a parliament. On November 6 Mason asked that the experts explain the texts in the hall and that the debate be shortened. On that same day Šeper, then Morris on the 9th, Alfrink on the 11th, C. P. Greco on November 21, and

If the results of the meeting reveal that the central question during this phase of Vatican II was not the Regulations but the assembly's self-awareness,[349] it remained difficult to determine what that outcome was. Yes, there would be a vote in the hall, as the moderators wanted; but now, after three weeks of conciliar work, they were having to defend, on their own and with some serious confusion within their group,[350] the role the pope had assigned them. What would have happened, had it not been for the self-confident and energetic leadership of Tisserant? The knotty points could indeed come up for discussion, but it was feared that the victory would be Pyrrhic if doctrinally crippling limitations were accepted. According to Moeller, section (a) of the *Nota bene* was disastrous: "What they have just said — conceded — at the theoretical and dogmatic level...will seem disastrous to the Easterners, and *in fact* it paralyzes the scope of the dogmatic statement."[351]

The text would be revised as Siri and perhaps Cicognani wanted, but the opposition of Tisserant and Liénart to Siri's meddling in matters proper to the moderators did not help the adversaries of the propositions. And since Felici composed minutes that reinterpreted the meeting according to the desires of the Secretary of State, it was clear that the enemies of the moderators did not have the power it was supposed they might have.

Everyone, then, had something with which to find fault: if Caggiani had not departed before the first vote...if the subsecretaries and not Felici's clerks had composed the minutes...if the role of Ottaviani had

---

Frings again on December 2, asked for simplifications in the work of the intersession and in the debates of the third period. All these documents are in *AD* II/4. 1, 443-76. The remarks drafted for the moderators by their secretaries until October 23 are in Dossetti Archive; on that day Suenens drafted a note titled "To Gain Time" ("Pour gagner du temps"), which was connected with the proposals being circulated (Suenens Archive, *IIa sessio, De Ecclesia, Ordo Concilii*).

[349] In the already cited document duplicated by the Secrétariat national de l'Information religieuse, November 15, 1963 (Lercaro Archive, 122), Haubtmann says that "on the morning of the 24th we learned that the atmosphere had been 'heavy,' 'burdensome.'" Lercaro, *Lettere*, p. 194, October 23, 1963, speaks of a "far from easy meeting."

[350] In the discussion it was not Agagianian but Suenens (on the third question) and Döpfner (on the fourth) who distanced themselves from the text being proposed. Lercaro had waxed ironic about the fact that the moderators, like the gospels, comprised three synoptics and a fourth and different one, represented by Agagianian, with Dossetti representing the Acts of the Apostles, as an appendage to Luke (Lercaro); see Lercaro, *Lettere*, September 28, 1963, 162. Emphasis on the anti-conservative role and character of Dossetti's contribution was also seen in the article, "Clima teso al concilio giunto a un punto critico," in *Corriere della sera*, October 24, 1963 (copy in Prignon Archive, 472).

[351] Moeller Archive, 318, handwritten note.

been more strongly defended.[352] By the next day, however, it was difficult to come up with a realistic recollection of the events, and the suspicion of conspiracy was widespread. Nabaa, one of the subsecretaries
present, talked of "a real sabotage: the Italians (eleven of them!)
together with men like Spellman and even Tisserant! The Italians are
relentlessly *against* collegiality, and the very *word* has been left out of
the second question." Congar, who reports this outburst, heard from
Arrighi a confirmation of its diagnosis of catastrophe, a "sinking into
the sand."[353] And while Nabaa was convinced that not even the dogmatic Constitution on the Church would be promulgated, Congar was
not much more optimistic, convinced as he was that the maneuvering
had caused the favorable moment to pass and that it would not return.
Even Paul VI was afraid that things were entering into an irreversible
impasse, for that very day he decided to send a note of his own, via
Felici, to the Doctrinal Commission urging it to pursue its work and
activities.[354] The handwritten note read: "It would be a serious matter if
the session were to end without having taken a stand on some of the
principal points in the schema on the Church. Consider how the work
may be speeded up. One meeting a week is not enough." While the
note was telegraphic in style, was not the reference to the "principal
points" an invitation to the commission to play a constructive and not
merely an obstructionist role?

In circles around the moderators the atmosphere was less pessimistic
or at least more combative.[355] Still on the 24th, Dossetti sent a new
proposal to Lercaro "after the points made at the united commissions."
He was attempting, perhaps in common with the Belgian College, to

---

[352] The personal documents of the clerks of the time, Carbone and Fagiolo, as well as
the letters of the subsecretaries would all be especially enlightening on these points, but
at present they are inaccessible.

[353] *JCongar*, October 24, 1963.

[354] Sent by Felici to Ottaviani on Saturday, October 26, 1963: *AS* V/2, 12. The note
perhaps reflected also the harsh judgment that Suenens expressed to the pope at the point
when the moderators felt abandoned by him: "He raised with the pope the question of the
authority of the moderators....If the pope yields on this point, the newspapers will soon
display the headline: 'Paul VI has betrayed John XXIII'" (reported by Prignon to Congar, *JCongar*, February 2, 1965).

[355] Even Edelby, who in his diary for October 23, 1963, noted the pessimism of Nabaa
and his own discouragement after the meeting of the Commission for the Oriental
Churches that same afternoon, had this reaction: "But let us have confidence in the Holy
Spirit who is guiding his Church. When the right moment comes he will reverse these
positions" (*JEdelby*, 185).

produce a balanced revision.[356] But, with a view to a final examination
of them by the pope,[357] the propositions themselves would be further
corrected by Dossetti, who sent with them a series of remarks (all in the
first person) that justified the choice of words to Lercaro and the other
moderators.[358]

On October 25, at Suenens's invitation, and in ignorance of the
objections of Tisserant and Liénart, Siri sent the Belgian cardinal the
text he proposed for submission to the hall as question III. Suenens
probably did not know that Tromp, too, and perhaps some members of
the Doctrinal Commission (as we shall see in a moment) had worked on
the formula.[359]

In proposing his own version to replace that of the moderators, Siri
respected the agreements made at the meeting of the united commissions.[360] He proposed, however, a version "provocative" in its substance
by a skillful shifting of words that drastically altered the meaning of the
proposition. The reference to the college of bishops disappeared, thereby
turning the surrender of the word "college" in the second question,
effected so that there would be a graduated series of requests, into a
complete abandonment of it. As for the existence of aspects of the college of bishops that were irreformable by divine right, Siri proposed to
declare that these aspects boiled down to apostolic succession. Finally,
the full and supreme power of bishops over the Church was to come into

---

[356] But the new text (Lercaro Archive, 784) left out the possibility that collegial acts
might take forms "not rejected" by the papacy. This version spoke only of "approved"
forms (which did not exclude future approbations, but was certainly weaker). Prignon
(but only several months later) told Congar of this phase of revision and listed among the
collaborators Philips, himself (not Moeller), and Rahner, but there is no check on this (see
JCongar, February 2, 1965).

[357] See, in Dossetti Archive, 113, "Mia proposta al card. Lercaro il 24.10 dopo i refer-
imenti delle commissioni riunite." This version repeated the formula: "Actuale exerci-
tium potestatis Corporis Episcoporum regitur ordinationibus a Romano Pontifice adpro-
batis (vel saltem secundum consuetudines ab eo non reprobatas)" (according to Prignon,
this was with the express verbal authorization given by Paul VI to Suenens).

[358] Melloni, "Procedure," 366-68.

[359] At the Belgian College, Prignon maintained that Siri's intervention at the supercommission had been composed by Calabria (*JCongar*, February 2, 1965). On the rector's own copy in Prignon Archive, 471, a handwritten note says "brought back by Calabria." See Melloni, "Procedure," 368.

[360] Thus Troisfontaines, "A propos," 137, who says that the text was rejected by Suenens on that same October 25 because it was not possible to submit it as an alternative
votum. Suenens (but Felici, too, in the minutes of the October 23 meeting, cited above)
had understood that this was what Tisserant wanted when he asked for separate votes on
"two different questions: fact and right," *AS* V/1, 719. But Tisserant (followed in this by
Siri) meant following the system of a series of votes with graded content.

play only on condition of legitimacy, but this legitimacy would exist only when the pope freely willed to leave a "decision" to the college; this would automatically limit any collegial act to being a variant of the pope's personal exercise of his authority.

But by the time Siri's proposal came in, the pope had already approved the "restored" version of the moderators' proposals, as we know from the already cited note of Dossetti.[361] All in all, during these final hours of frantic corrections, there was in a sense a "return" to version "a" of October 24 and really to the very first corrections made by Colombo. Restored, for example, was Philips's phrase "acceptante vel libere invitante" in the *Nota bene*;[362] above all, the "legitimating" equivalence of *corpus seu collegium*, so dear to Moeller among the Belgians, was defended. As for the diaconate, the proposition retained the possibility of a choice by the episcopal conferences, a choice to which Döpfner had also objected.[363]

C. THE CRISSCROSSING OF THE DEBATES

The Council, however, was not marking time; rhetorical and procedural weapons were being sharpened for the three "banner" questions: religious, Pope John, and the Madonna.

1. The Debate on Religious

The beginning of the debate on religious mobilized the sector of the assembly that regarded itself as "represented" by this chapter.[364] The underestimation of the importance of the "regular" episcopate, that is, bishops belonging to an order or congregation, was certainly one significant factor in the composition of the schema on ecclesiology.[365] On the

[361] Dossetti Archive, 114.

[362] Moeller Archive, 318, dates it to the 26th; according to Prignon, it was the moderators who, at the audience with the pope and "with his agreement...restored the words suppressed by Siri: 'vel saltem libere recipiat'" (*JCongar*, February 2, 1965, typescript, 416). The temporary restoration of the "non reprobatas" modality in the exercise of collegial power (on this see above, note 114) thus signaled a convergence of Dossetti and Philips.

[363] See Melloni, "Procedure," 371.

[364] The debate would occupy October 25, 29-31, and November 7; see J. Schmiedl, *Das Konzil und die Orden: Krise und Erneuerung des gottgeweihten Lebens* (Vallendar-Schönstatt, 1999), 437- 46.

[365] The hall was impressed by the reminder of Father Schütte, Superior of the Divine Word Fathers, that 1050 Council fathers were members of religious orders (see Wenger, 120).

other hand, as Laurentin had written prophetically, the loud complaint of bishops about the problems caused by the exemption system would embitter minds, "as had already happened in the Middle Ages."[366]

In fact, in the original intention of those who had revised the preparatory schema, chapter IV on religious was meant to be an element in an unbroken continuity. Transformed at Suenens's insistence into a chapter on holiness in the Church, it provided an important preface before the repetition of the ideas in the old preparatory chapter. The chapter asserted the common call of all Christians to a holiness that was understood, however, in primarily ethical terms and to be lived out in many different forms (nos. 29-30). The evangelical counsels would then be simply means to the ultimate goal, which is charity.[367] All this had little impact on the second part of the chapter, the one on the states of perfection. The idea of a chaste, poor, and obedient life as an "eschatological sign" was perhaps the one that would lend itself best to a renewal of religious life in Roman Catholicism.

The debate took place in somewhat fragmented form, the early and later interventions being interrupted by a gap of some days. A series of requests typical of the entire month were made, that is, requests for the harmonization of the final chapters with the guiding principles set down in the first chapter. It was as if the process of formation of the Philips schema in the first period of the Council had put a drag on the degree of development of the entire new ecclesiological schema of 1963. A year earlier the Belgian team had attached to a plan marked by renewal a conjectural first chapter, in the making of which many theses, corrections, and improvements had been voiced and weighed. The entire 1963 schema, on the other hand, and especially chapter IV, still knew nothing of that new step.

As a result, many fathers reacted against a text that described holiness as an individual ethical effort. Coderre of Canada asked for a clear statement that the communion, the enjoyment of which is anticipated by the Church, is "holiness itself."[368] This desire to stress the charismatic[369] and communion-dimension of the Church's holiness converged with the call, already made by Larraona, for a chapter on the "communion of

---

[366] In *Le Figaro*, October 26-27, 1963.

[367] See Acerbi, *Due ecclesiologie*, 223-24.

[368] *AS* II/4, 134-35, presented in writing. On Coderre himself, see D. Robillard, "Mgr Coderre à Vatican II," in *L'Eglise canadienne et Vatican II*, 265-76.

[369] Silva Henriquez, *AS* II/3, 369-72; see also Suenens's written intervention, *AS* II/4, 90-92.

saints"[370] or at least for bringing out this eschatological dimension of holiness.[371]

The point of conflict, however, lay elsewhere and had to do with the nature of religious profession and the privileges connected with it, first among them the troubling question of the exemption of monasteries and convents from episcopal jurisdiction. Silva Henriquez's attempt to set forth the brilliant Chilean solution (exemption, according to the Cardinal, could be seen as a "concrete realization of collegiality" in act) went to the commission among the written interventions but did not compete in the hall.[372] The more effective positions were the clearly conservative ones (which simply wanted to keep exemption) and those that openly attacked this privilege.[373] Prominent among the latter was Léger, Cardinal of Montreal and himself a religious, who spoke in the light of a very rough personal experience with the religious of his vast diocese.[374] The course of the debate on the religious state caused the German-speaking episcopate to take two different tacks (one of Leiprecht and the other of Döpfner[375]). These show how clear the division was between those who wanted privileges to be located in the new ecclesiological context and those who asked instead that the present rethinking of the episcopate be carried out to its ultimate conclusions, which could perhaps not be reached without a reflection on the local Church and eucharistic communion that had never reached critical mass.

2. The Commemoration of John XXIII

Meanwhile, on October 28, the assembly celebrated the fifth anniversary of the election of John XXIII. The decision to hold the celebration had required the personal endorsement of Paul VI who had already announced it in the official calendar communicated to the Cardinal Dean in September.[376] There was something anomalous about a celebration of the election of a dead pope, but it had its explanation in a setting in

---

[370] Larraona handed in a written statement, AS II/4, 81-85.

[371] De Provenchères, AS II/4, 157-60.

[372] After October 31 the discussion was intermingled with preparation for, and the beginning of, the debate on the schema on the bishops, in which the same problem came up again in a different perspective; see below.

[373] De Barros Camara, AS II/3, 592-95; Gúrpide Beope, AS II/4, 197-200 (written).

[374] AS II/3, 632-35; see D. Robillard, *Paul-Emile Léger. Evolution de sa pensée 1950-1967* (Quebec, 1993) and *L'Eglise canadienne et Vatican II*.

[375] AS II/4, 41-42, and AS II/3, 603-16, with the proposal of an alternative chapter.

[376] *Quod apostolici*, September 14, 1963, in AS II/1, 9-13; see above.

which the problem still existed of managing a heritage of consensus and of the lines for the development of the Council. The preacher on the occasion was Suenens, a major elector of Paul VI at the recent conclave, but also previously a trusted adviser to John XXIII.

While it is of interest to note that, in Suenens's view, the lengthy applause with which the Catholic episcopate and the observers greeted his discourse had an effect on the decision of Paul VI to allow the vote on the five guideline questions on the *De ecclesia*, questions that marked one of the high points in the Council's self-consciousness,[377] there is reason today to believe that this was not the case. For the observers, the discourse remedied the unfortunate remarks of the pope on the day before, when, in beatifying the Passionist Dominic of the Mother of God, he had extolled the latter's role in the "conversion" of John Henry Newman from Anglicanism to Catholicism. As for the fathers of the Council, the reference to the pope who had called them together in council elicited a perhaps superficial yet strong approval. It remains a fact, nonetheless, that the memory of the Belgian prelate could make him regard the assembly's reaction to the "name" of John XXIII as part of a procedural "miracle."[378] The funeral eulogy of October 28 attributed some marks of holiness to the activity of John XXIII but did not go into the question of the recognition of these qualities. Not did it pass unremarked that here was praise of a dead pope in the presence of his successor, given by a cardinal and not in Latin.[379]

What led a skillful assembly leader like Suenens to a prudent reference in the council hall led, outside the hall, to more muddled and ambiguous steps. In the diocese of Roncalli's birth a petition was circulated asking Paul VI to beatify his predecessor; it bore 50,000 signatures and was entrusted to the bishop.[380] The move echoed a lasting interest in the Catholic popular press[381] and was a symptom of a desire — for the canonization of John XXIII at the Council — of which only a seeker of

---

[377] This was the belief of some reporters and publications; e.g., D. Fisher, *The Catholic Herald*, November 8, 1963, as well as J. Grootaers, "Een sessie met gemengde gevoelens," *De Maand* 6, no. 10 (1963), 590, on which Troisfontaines relies in his "A propos," 137.

[378] See A. Melloni, "La causa Roncalli: origini di un processo canonico," *CrSt* 18 (1997), 607-36.

[379] See *JEdelby* for this date.

[380] K. L. Woodward, *Making Saints* (New York, 1990), 282. It is not clear whether this petition was brought to the Council.

[381] *Famiglia Cristiana*, May 21, 1964, no. 21, tells a reader who asks "for medals of Pope John XXIII, along with a relic" that he "can ask for them at Post Office Box 5023, Rome," and it gives the cost: 400 lire for plain metal, 450 for gilded.

the impossible such as Helder Câmara could say that some unknown "they" are working on it.[382]

3. The Marian Question

Of all the banner questions that accompanied the rewriting of and voting on the propositions on collegiality, the most passionate had to do with the location and content of the schema on the Blessed Virgin, which in its new version included the title "Mother of the Church."[383] As we have seen, the question had arisen even before the beginning of the period, then in the first remarks during the debate on the Church, and finally in the Doctrinal Commission, but without finding anywhere sufficient consensus or authority to decide and end the disagreement between those who thought a special document on Mary was needed if the Council were not to abandon an essential element of Roman Catholicism and those who thought it more profitable, and a sign of ecumenical awareness, to make mariology a chapter of or appendix to the schema on the Church. As was said a little earlier, the pope in private and the moderators in public had given the commission the mandate to arrange a debate between two bishops in the hall, so that the assembly might proceed to a decisive and fully informed vote.

The composition of the two addresses given by Cardinals König and Santos, who had been chosen by the Doctrinal Commission, took several days, during which real propagandizing went on. Pamphlets, duplicated materials, and appeals, primarily from groups that wanted the Marian constitution, which not even Pius IX had issued, to be circulated among the fathers, touched an already sensitive spot in the higher Catholic clergy. Finally, at the 55th general congregation, the two sides were allowed to explain the opposed theses that had already been debated in the Doctrinal Commission on October 9.

Santos gave ten arguments in favor of a separate schema that would better bring out the preeminent place of Mary in the Church, whereas the incorporation of the treatise into the schema on the Church would give rise to an incomplete explanation or, worse, to one that would be dangerously prolix when compared to the section on the Trinity. Furthermore,

---

[382] See Circular 2, made available to me by L. C. Marques, who edited it.

[383] On October 20 Congar observed that this title, "launched" by Balić, had already had an intrusive effect on the discussion. It was during these same days that the question of religious freedom, the schema on which had not yet gone to the fathers, was attracting more and more attention; Spellman, with the signatures of 240 American fathers in his pocket, asked the pope that the schema be distributed (*JCongar*, October 23, 1963).

Mary belongs to the People of God by a title different from that of the laity and the hierarchy, and her call to holiness was such as to forbid its being dealt with in the chapter on this subject. According to Santos, the incorporation of Mary into the schema on the Church would be interpreted by the faithful as a reduction and a loss; the entirety of Catholic doctrine and its dogmas ought to be explained without reservations to the faithful and to the separated Christians; not to do so would give the appearance of preferring a mariology that is "ecclesio-typical" rather than, as it ought to be, "Christo-typical," and this would only intensify debate. Finally, the incorporation of the schema on Mary would demand radical revisions in the constitution, since the latter dealt only with the pilgrim Church, whereas a revision of the schema on Mary in the form of a constitution would make possible the necessary harmonizations.[384]

König, for his part, expounded four kinds of reasons why the schema on Mary should be incorporated into the schema on the Church.[385] The first was theological; namely, that the treatment of Mary in the Constitution on the Church would avoid the objections against an excessively institutional conception of the Church, which is in fact the community of the saved, on pilgrimage indeed but looking forward to an eschatological fulfillment prefigured by Mary. König stressed the point that the failure to adhere to this theological principle would lead people to think that the Council intended to create new Marian dogmas, something excluded by the conciliar agenda, or wanted to encourage false and baseless exaggerations. The incorporation of the one schema into the other did not imply any lessening of veneration of the Virgin or any concealment of teaching about her, but rather an explanation of her place that would be consistent with the purposes of Vatican II.

The historical reasons for this incorporation were numerous, beginning with the fact that attention to Mary had reached the doctrinal level due to the meditation of Mother Church; two important reminders, one of the teaching of Paul VI (in the address on October 11) and the other

---

[384] *AS* II/3, 338-42.

[385] *AS* II/3, 342-45. Philips had prepared a note for König on the four reasons for placing the material on Mary at the end of the *De ecclesia* (Moeller Archive, 00384). Philips suggested giving first a concrete reason, namely, the usefulness of treating Mary in the key document of the Council; then a theological reason, namely, the biblical basis of an ecclesio-typical exposition of mariology; then a pastoral reason, namely, the need of directing the piety of the people toward essentials; finally, an ecumenical reason, that is, enabling the Orientals and the Protestants to accept a presentation of Mary that adhered more closely to the ancient tradition. König's address would maintain the division into different motivations, although he would alter the titles, order, and content.

of the Marian Congress at Lourdes in 1958 ("Mary and the Church") confirmed the idea that the incorporation did not mean reticence about Mary but rather represented a position. The pastoral reason König cited was that the faithful were being encouraged to purify their devotion to Mary and to focus on what was essential to it. Finally, the ecumenical reason was that an ecclesio-typical mariology made possible a convergence with both the Oriental and the Protestant traditions.[386]

The two addresses were printed and distributed in the hall and were quickly accompanied by widespread distribution of propaganda-booklets in support of the opposing positions. On October 25 some bishops of the Oriental rite circulated a position paper maintaining that precisely for the sake of ecumenism and of the Orient a separate schema was necessary. In opposition, Abbot Butler distributed a well-balanced note in which he distinguished between the useless repetition of solemnly defined doctrines and a joint study of the figure and roles of Mary in the scriptures, but as a result he had to endure insults from the conservative Roman press.[387] Suenens's request to Dhanis and others for an outline of a mariological schema received no response.[388]

Some among the experts viewed these bouts with optimism; according to Moeller, König was "more precise, more nuanced. More prolonged applause."[389] Rahner, on the other hand, would justify his own pessimism — he thought he would be the one who would have to "pay" for König's eventual defeat — with regard to activities he regarded as libelous: "A Ukrainian bishop distributed pamphlets in front of the Aula; the Spaniards distributed printed leaflets everywhere; Roschini produced a brochure; people were talking of a battle for and against the Madonna; Balić distributed a lengthy booklet printed by the Vatican

[386] "While Cardinal König was speaking, I looked over at Brother Max Thurian, who was opposite me. His whole being was engrossed as he leaned over the banister of the tribune toward the speaker. What Cardinal König was saying about Protestant Mariology corresponded exactly to the thought of Brother Thurian, as expressed in his book, *Marie. mère du Seigneur, figure de l'Eglise* (Taizé Press, 1962)" (Wenger, 125).

[387] He was violently attacked in the conservative daily *Il Tempo*, October 27, 28, and 29, 1963. Balić attacked Congar in a talk to the Croatian bishops. There is a Latin letter of scornful response to an accusation calling into question the honesty of Congar as a Catholic, in *JCongar*, October 20, 1963.

[388] The document, *De mysterio Mariae in Ecclesia*, which Dhanis sent in on September 18, must therefore have been commissioned well before the debates in the hall, although it became known only belatedly; see, e.g., *JCongar*, October 25, 1963. See also D. Aračić, *La dottrina mariologica negli scritti di Carlo Balić* (Rome, 1980), 106-19.

[389] Moeller Archive, 0016, 36; on October 14, Moeller had been appointed substitute reporter of the subcommission for the emendations of the *De ecclesia*.

Press in the form of a schema."[390] Philips, too, was afraid that the idea
had spread that "if one votes for incorporation into the *De ecclesia*, one
is voting against the Virgin," but Suenens was reassuring: "Tomorrow
they will see that neither vote is against the Virgin."[391]

Finally, on October 29, the vote was taken that Paul VI had recommended twenty-three days before. Of the 2193 voting, 1114 voted for
the unification of the schemas on the Blessed Virgin and on the Church,
while 1074 voted for the composition of two schemas. Thus the very
small gap between the two sides that had been seen in the Doctrinal
Commission appeared again in the hall. Although there was no shadow
on the vote from a procedural standpoint,[392] it gave the impression that
the Council was split in half not only on the question of Mary but on the
whole formulation of the ongoing reform in ecclesiology.[393] What would
happen when the Blessed Virgin was left aside, and the assembly moved
on to collegiality, the sacramentality of the episcopate, and the diaconate? How would a weak majority respond to propositions much more
subtle and important than the mere, simple placement of a short
schema? Even the optimists of the day before were shivering: "Today's
vote deeply divides the assembly at the doctrinal level. It is united at the
pastoral level but deeply divided at the doctrinal level. If we have the
same weak majority tomorrow and therefore the same division, there is
nothing left for us but to pack our bags."[394]

D. The Meeting of the Doctrinal Commission on October 29

The text of the five questions on collegiality and the diaconate that the
moderators had sent to Felici on October 28 was now settled. It was
unaffected by the belated activity of the Doctrinal Commission, which at
its meeting on the 29th made a last attempt to prevent the vote.
Colombo's notes summed up the situation schematically:

[390] Vorgrimler, *Understanding Karl Rahner*, 177-78.

[391] Moeller Archive, 0016, 97, in Antonelli, "Le rôle," 37.

[392] Rahner (in Vorgrimler, *Understanding Karl Rahner*, 177-78) recalled that Parente
had protested against a choice made by a simple majority; but it should be remembered
that even if a decision had been made, contrary to the Regulations, to require a two-thirds
majority, the situation in November 1962 in regard to the *De Fontibus* would have been
repeated.

[393] The work of revising Balić's schema would begin on November 8 in a subcommission on Mary that was made up of König, Santos, Doumith, and Théas; see Antonelli,
"Le rôle," 38-58.

[394] Moeller Archive, 0016, pp. 90-91, cited in Antonelli, "Le rôle," 37.

B. *Points dealing with the "De Ecclesia"*
a. Points prepared by Msgr. Parente;
b. Charue:
a. The moderators have already announced the votes on the "points"
b. Ottaviani claims the Commission's authority over the "points."[395]

Tromp's summary of the discussion in his *Relatio de schemate de Ecclesia denuo reformato* (1 October 1963 — 1 April 1964) was a little less terse:

On the next day, October 29, at the sixth plenary meeting of the Commission, the new formula for dogmatic qualification was definitively approved by 17 out of 24 votes. Action was also taken on the five doctrinal propositions soon to be set before the fathers in Council. Finally, standards were established for the special commissions for revision, in order that these might proceed in a uniform manner under the direction and revisory activity of the central subcommission for revision.[396]

The real climate, however, was the one displayed in the morning in the bickering between Ottaviani and Suenens:

This morning Ottaviani spoke to Suenens. He told him: "You have no right to do what you are doing. Why are you constantly going to the pope?" Suenens's answer: "Because you too go to the pope. Furthermore, I am a member of the presidential council, the CC, and the moderators." Ottaviani went away furious. Philips comments: "Ottaviani wants from the Commission a vote declaring that the moderators have exceeded their authority. If a secret vote is called for, the Commission declares itself opposed to Ottaviani; if the vote is public, the Commission will not dare vote against him."[397]

At the meeting, at which Philips played the card of the vote on the subcommissions for revision, two different documents were studied.[398] One of them contained six propositions, duplicated by the commission, of unknown authorship, but in the tenor of an "extreme Sirianist.."[399] The propositions were born of the suspicion voiced at the meeting of the

---

[395] Colombo Archive, *Note Comm. Doctr.*, manuscript.
[396] Tromp, *Relatio de schemate de Ecclesia.*
[397] Moeller Archive, 0016, 36, in Antonelli, "Le rôle," 36-37.
[398] A note says that these were discussed on the 28th, which seems to me have been simply a slip in typing. On Philips's strategy of patience, see *JPrignon* (B), 2-3: when the alternative questions are finally dropped, "they can proceed to the establishment of the famous subcommissions, the plan for which was made at the [Belgian] college by Msgr. Philips, Moeller, and myself [Prignon]."
[399] Thus *JPrignon* (B), 2. A note of Colombo's suggests Parente as author; this is possibly an impression strengthened by the fact that Parente asked for an intermission, given that the vote "has been delayed." Charue, however, protested: "I know that it is coming quickly." Apart from confirming Parente's already known position in favor of collegiality, there is no special contribution here in the nonetheless praiseworthy work of M. Di Ruberto, *Bibliografia del cardinale Pietro Parente*, with a preface by J. Ratzinger (Vatican City, 1991).

cardinals on October 23; namely, that the votes would ipso facto "attract" consensuses. This was but the extreme version of the prejudice that had sustained the vast and useless preparatory machinery: the bishops do not think, the bishops will approve. Following this logic, the leaders of the Doctrinal Commission would want to ask the hall to vote (I) on a definition of the Church (which omitted the elements of both mystery and sacrament)[400] and on five other propositions: (II) on the episcopate as the highest degree of orders;[401] (III) on the power of the college which succeeds "to the apostles" (and not to the college of the apostles);[402] (IV) on episcopal consecration, by which there is communicated a power (*potestas*) to be exercised with the approval of the pope, but not jurisdiction;[403] (V) on the restoration of the celibate diaconate (saving exceptions, among which is marriage *after* ordination);[404] and (VI) on placing a higher value on the priesthood of the lay faithful as collaborators with the hierarchy in the sanctification of the world.[405]

---

[400] P.052.12, titled "De Ecclesia / VI propositiones" and listed as "CFM, De Eccl. Vota 2." The first proposition read as follows: "I (definition of the Church). In order to continue his saving work to the end of time, Christ the Redeemer established his Church as his mystical body. She reproduces in herself the mystery of the incarnate Word; she is equipped with a hierarchical structure and enriched with supernatural life so that by means of the sacraments, the teaching office, and the discipline of laws she may labor for the salvation of souls and advance the kingdom of God in the world so as to form and ceaselessly augment a people that glorifies God."

[401] "II. The holy synod teaches that the episcopate is the highest degree of the sacrament of orders with its own character."

[402] "III. While maintaining undisturbed and safe the teaching on the primacy and infallibility of the Roman Pontiff as solemnly defined by Vatican Council I, we teach that the body or college of bishops, which succeeds to the apostles in the office of teaching, governing, and sanctifying, together with the Roman Pontiff, its head, and subject to his approval, has power over the universal Church, but that the exercise of this power always depends directly or indirectly on the approval of the Roman Pontiff."

[403] "IV. The holy synod likewise holds and teaches that individual bishops, in virtue of their legitimate consecration, are incorporated into the episcopal college and are thereby a suitable subject of the power of the Church, which, as was said above, can be exercised only in communion with and by the approval of the Roman Pontiff."

[404] "V. The holy synod decrees that, following very ancient practice, the permanent diaconate can be restored according to the conditions and needs of regions, but with the provision that individual deacons normally remain subject to the law of celibacy. Exceptions can be made, especially if there is a question of a married man seeking the diaconate, according to the judgment of the episcopal conferences, which, however, are subordinate to the judgment of the Holy See."

[405] "VI. The lay faithful of Christ, who are in a way configured to Christ the Priest by the sacramental characters of baptism and confirmation, so that they share in a certain universal priesthood, have an honorable place and function in the Church of Christ, both in collaborating with the hierarchy and in working by their own decision and on their own responsibility for the sanctification of the world, with the aid both of ordinary grace and of special charisms that God may bestow."

The other document (dated October 28, at 4:30 p.m.) that was discussed and approved proposed only three questions and a formula, all of which were composed "by some members of the Commission."[406] These questions were sent out by Ottaviani before the meeting;[407] once approved, they were delivered to Felici, but only after he had received the propositions of the moderators.[408] The text of the concluding formula was none other than its immediate antecedent, the formula proposed by Siri to Suenens the previous Friday.[409] It accepted the definition of the power of the college over the universal Church as being *full* and *supreme*, but it also introduced an important alteration, when it limited the exercise of the college's power to the *customary* ways.[410]

The three accompanying questions were important because through at least two of them the commission was seeking to obtain (or thought it could obtain) from the hall an endorsement for retrieving elements of the preparatory schema that had been dropped at the beginning of the year.[411] Thus a first proposal asked whether the fathers willed "to declare that they wanted the definition" of the coherence between the visible and social and the mystical and invisible dimensions of the

[406] *AS* V/1, 739 (also found in the Philips Archive, P.052.14). According to Colombo's Bloc notes, the author was Parente (Colombo Archive).

[407] *AS* V/1, 738: "Today...some formulas were studied that were composed by some members of the Commission itself." Ottaviani also noted that "the Holy Father has been informed beforehand of this." But it is not clear whether he means that the pope was informed of the activity of the commission, or of the meeting, or of the commission's desire to have its competence recognized when it came to the formulation of texts.

[408] On that same October 29 Felici assured Ottaviani that "at this evening's meeting, if the opportunity arises, I will communicate Your Eminence's request to their Eminences, the fathers of the presidential council, and the moderators of the Council."

[409] *AS* V/1, 739: "Formula: Whether it pleases the fathers to declare that the body of bishops, who by divine right are the successors of the apostles in the office of evangelizing, sanctifying, and governing the Lord's flock, when together with their head, the Roman Pontiff (and never without this Head, whose power over all [*and each*] of the pastors and faithful remains untouched), agree together under the legitimate *and usual* conditions [*or when in some other way a matter is entrusted to them for decision by the Roman Pontiff*], possess full and supreme power over the universal Church." Usually, the duplicated materials from the commission, like the *AS*, use italics within square brackets to indicate changes introduced during the debate. Therefore the working text of the Commission's formula would have preceded Siri's formula.

[410] Perhaps this was a movement away from Tromp's corrections, the consistency of which was perhaps known only to the editor of the *AS*. Thus the note in *AS* V/1, 736 n.1 (V. Carbone).

[411] *AS* V/1, 739.

[412] "On the Church I (votum): I. Whether it pleases the fathers to declare it their desire that a definition or description of the Church be given in which it is clear how the social and visible and the mystical and invisible aspects of the Church are harmoniously connected by its divine constitution?"

Church.[412] A second proposal, using two different questions, asked for the definition of the Church as a society established so as to form the mystical body.[413] The third question represented a further diminished version of the formula on collegiality, describing this as a supreme (but not full) power activated solely by the pope's invitation to a collegial act which he would then be able to approve or disapprove.[414]

E. THE CHOICE AND THE VOTES

Finally, on October 28, thirteen days after they were first announced, two versions of the proposed questions were sent to Felici. The one from the moderators with corrections by the pope arrived at 10:30 a.m.; the one from Ottaviani arrived after it. The latter was set aside, apparently by the Secretary General himself.[415] Felici had those of the moderators printed because they displayed "the approval of the Supreme Pontiff," given in definitive form on the evening of the 27th.[416]

On the afternoon of the 29th there was another meeting of the super-commission, that is, the Council of Presidents, the moderators, and the General Secretariat; once again it was held in the apartment of the Secretary of State.[417] As he had promised Ottaviani, Felici informed the meeting of the Doctrinal Commission's requests, but since there had been the delay in sending in Ottaviani's proposals and since the moderators showed a duplicated page with the pope's handwritten notes (and therefore his unequivocal approval), Felici altered the tenor of the

---

[413] "On the Church II (Vota): II. Whether it pleases the fathers to declare that the Church is a society of the baptized faithful, instituted by Christ the Lord in order to sanctify human beings, endowed by him with sacred power, and constituting his mystical body?"

[414] "III. Whether it pleases the fathers to declare that the college of bishops, under the Roman Pontiff and in union with him, enjoys supreme power in the Church whenever he invites them to perform a collegial act which he may freely approve?" This was the kind of collegiality to which the now current norms for the synod of bishops were adapted; on this see the contributions to the conference on *Paolo VI e la Collegialità episcopale: Colloquio internazionale di studio, Brescia 25- 26-27 settembre 1992* (Brescia, 1995).

[415] *AS* V/1, 739.

[416] See Lercaro, *Lettere*, October 28, 1963, 196: "Yesterday evening...the four had another meeting with the Holy Father and the famous questions were definitively approved."

[417] Tapouni and Lercaro were absent.

demand made by the Cardinal of the Holy Office[418] and asked simply that the vote be further "delayed."[419]

Tisserant, who once again had the Council of Presidents solidly with him, asked the moderators whether they intended to proceed to the voting. Döpfner and Suenens immediately answered yes, but Confalonieri also spoke up and gave his consent, "since confusions must be avoided, and these would arise from delaying the vote. Therefore His Eminence Ottaviani should accept the decision taken." The interventions of Ruffini, Roberti, and Siri did not budge the majority; these three, backed by Cicognani, Spellman, and Wyszynski, voted for delaying, but all the others approved putting the questions to a vote.[420]

The little card distributed to the fathers the next day finally brought into public view a text that had for two weeks remained beneath the surface of the Council waters.[421] On the 29th, while this text was being distributed to the fathers for a vote, *Il Quotidiano*, a newspaper close to Ottaviani, published a long article by Msgr. Dino Staffa, which made a radical attack on positions in favor of collegiality and sounded like a statement of curial ecclesiology made in view of the next day's vote. It was a skillful move and had a great impact, because as far as the concepts involved in collegiality were concerned the bishops and even the pope were novices. Who could say that the "cram course" and crises of October had not persuaded the bishops to judge the subject not ripe for a vote? Who could say that the votes, put off for two weeks, might not prove to be a great boomerang and, as Dossetti feared on the evening of the 15th, "prejudice," negatively, the doctrinal developments?[422]

But Colombo intervened against Staffa in a lengthy and courageous mimeographed note of four pages, which, according to a handwritten note of Dossetti on his copy, went from "Don C. Colombo to the pope."[423] The Milanese theologian, who, after taking part in the first inspection of Dossetti's draft, had remained somewhat on the edge of the swirling series of formulations of the questions, refuted three key points

[418] Which had made known the formulation of the already cited new questions, *AS* V/1, 738.

[419] *AS* V/2, 14-15.

[420] Agagianian, Döpfner, Suenens, then Tisserant, Confalonieri, Alfrink, Frings, Caggiano, Gilroy, and Urbani.

[421] *AS* II/2, 573-77.

[422] Even Edelby, who on October 8 anticipated a "unanimous" approval of collegiality, had some fears on the morning of the 30th; see *JEdelby* for the 30th (in the Italian ed.), 191-92.

[423] Dossetti Archive, 126c.

in the article and offered a fourth digression on Kleutgen's schema on the Church at Vatican I. First of all, Colombo questioned whether it was possible to conceive both the college and the body of bishops "in strictly juridical categories derived from secular positive law; rather, since we are dealing with a divine positive institution, its characteristics are to be taken from revelation in the Bible and tradition." Furthermore, Colombo denied the possibility of setting college and pontiff over against each other, and thirdly, he showed how in asserting a power that is at once supreme and delegated, Staffa forgets the possibility of distinguishing between the origin of a power and the ways of exercising it. "It is completely conceivable that the Roman Pontiff should decide on the conditions for the exercise of the power, but that the power itself should be of divine origin (analogously to what happens in determining the conditions for the validity of the sacraments by the Roman Pontiff)."[424]

The second part of the note challenged Staffa's reading of Kleutgen's schema for the never discussed "Constitution on the Church" of Vatican I. As Colombo shows, Kleutgen uses "college of apostles" and "body of bishops" in parallel and denies that the latter can exercise an authority in the Church "except *in union with* and at the *determination* of the Roman Pontiff." But in his explanatory report Kleutgen states that conciliar practice shows it to be "a most certain dogma of faith" that the bishops share "in the government and instruction of the universal Church."[425]

The conciliar papers of Carlo Colombo do not say if the note was requested by Paul VI or if its purpose was to prevent second thoughts at the last minute.[426] The vote in the hall on October 29 on whether or not to place the schema on the Virgin in the schema on the Church had been an agonizing moment and certainly had not given the impression of a solid and tranquil majority. The possibility that there was no such majority was present for at least a week in the minds of the moderators. They had wanted it to be clear that a two-thirds agreement was not required for the approval of these guidelines and that a simple majority sufficed. Staffa's objections, as the place of publication showed, had for their purpose a reappraisal of the consensus that the moderators were preparing to gain. Colombo's responses, on the other hand, confirmed the fact that

---

[424] Ibid., 247.

[425] On this subject there was in circulation a mimeographed synthesis of G. Alberigo's monograph *Lo sviluppo della dottrina sui poteri nella chiesa universale. Momenti essenziali tra il XVI ed il XIX secolo* (Rome, 1964).

[426] The notes on Colombo's audience with Paul have not yet been placed in the Colombo Archive.

within the group that had composed the questions, even though they were shaken by the attacks, there was unanimity on the need to respond to the questions on their merits.

On the 30th, when it was Lercaro's turn to serve as moderator, the votes on the questions were collected and counted.[427] Here are the results:

> On I: the episcopacy as the highest level of the sacrament of orders, 2,123 (98.42%) *placet*, 34 (1.58%) *non placet;*
> on II: episcopal consecration, 2,049 (95.13%) *placet*, 104 (4.83%) *non placet* (1 null);
> on III: succession to the apostolic college: 1,808 (84.17%) *placet*, 336 (15.64) *non placet* (4 null);
> on IV: divine right: 1,717 (80.31%) *placet*, 408 (19.08%) *non placet* (13 null);
> on V: the diaconate: 1,588 (74.91) *placet*, 525 (24.76%) *non placet* (7 null).

It will be seen that the number of positive votes was very great, fluctuating between 98 percent and 74 percent of the total votes. The fathers voted point by point and avoided the danger raised by the logic connecting the questions. The point that a full and supreme power (III) could only be of divine right (IV) showed a difference of 72 negative votes. The question on the diaconate, which was proposed in a form more restrictive than that of the Doctrinal Commission (where, the reader will remember, temporary celibacy was retained by way of an exception) was the one that met with a stronger resistance, although the negative votes fell 540 short of the number needed to reject the restoration of the third degree of orders.[428]

VI. AND NOW WHAT? LATENT APPREHENSIONS

The shift to discussion of the schema on bishops and to the final votes on the liturgical schema did not erase the sense that Vatican II had

---

[427] When the vote was about to be taken, Cardinal Bacci approached the moderators' table to ask that he might announce a correction of the text: *ius primatus* and not *primatiale*, as the page on which to vote had it; he was not allowed to speak; see Caprile, II, 169.

[428] At the moment it is not possible to analyze the fluctuations in the votes, but it might provide interesting surprises. We know, for example, from the *Bolletino diocesano di Segni* for November 1963, that Carli, one of those who would remain a determined opponent of the decisions on collegiality, voted in favor on questions I, II, and V, while voting against on questions III and IV; see Caprile, II, 264.

passed through a dramatic and vitally important transition. When the
pope received the moderators and greeted them with "We have won!"
he was not using a simple plural of majesty.[429] The idea cultivated during the summer of freeing the Council by supporting the majority, leaving it indeed time to mature but not giving it time to crumple, proved not
only victorious but solidly victorious. If we compare the vote on the
location of the schema on the Virgin with the votes on the propositions
outlined by Dossetti, we see how the debate had increased awareness
and choices. Although not understanding much, relying more on the
official papers and afternoon conversations, and depending on the chronicles of journalists, the Council fathers grew in their convictions and
awareness during that October of discussions and exchanges. They
understood themselves not as a majority on the basis of power, but as in
agreement on the matters at issue and gave the moderators the investi-
ture that the pope had hesitated to formalize in September.

Paul VI's proposal during the summer to withdraw into his lonely
position of power was now likewise only a memory. The pope did not
remain "on a pinnacle" but was at the center of the Council and caught
up in the tensions of a new tri-polar relationship (Council/moderators,
Curia/Secretariat of State, pope) of which no one had had any experience. John XXIII had kept himself apart from the conciliar scene, had
placed the assembly and its freedom at the center of things, and, at the
other extreme, had left the commissions room to act. Paul VI, on the
contrary, had firmly taken the central place on the stage by making himself a filter, as it were, between the hall and the commissions. No one
knew yet whether this was also a cushioning role that could become very
burdensome. Those wanting to disparage Paul VI said that in taking this
role the pope was afraid of letting the conciliar machine run its
course;[430] in the absence of firsthand documentary material it is impossible to say whether a "Pyrrhic syndrome" can be excluded.

Contacts during the summer and proposals heard and collected during
the fall were aimed at speeding up the Council's work by manipulating
its agenda; this was still the solution adopted by the CC when it effected
a first reduction of the schemas. The ecclesiological development of
October and the votes on October 30 showed that the problem was rather

[429] *JChenu*, 144.
[430] The anonymous controversialist Serafian, *The Pilgrim*, who seems to have had a
good understanding of Montini's personality, described October 1963 as the decisive, and
regressive, transition of his pontificate.

that the Council should express itself, the commissions should do their work, and the product of their work should be subordinated to the choices of the majority in the assembly, a majority that could reach unambiguous levels if and when it was in a position to make itself known. It was here that Montini's new and special difficulty and that of his management of the Council arose: he not only had to decide, but to decide without letting himself by moved by the noisiest parties in the case.

It is beyond the limits of historical reconstruction to say how and in what way the theological character of the transition that took place influenced the development of the Council, and yet the ecclesiological meaning of the votes was not without verifiable effect. In fact, from the doctrinal viewpoint, the votes meant the acquisition of some of the key points in the dogmatic Constitution on the Church, which was now beginning to take its complete form. In part, the question was of choices that were important but also less disruptive. The problems present in the first, general questions, which had to do with the individual bishop, in the end acknowledged the soundness of a tradition that was once again becoming a conscious element in the Catholic heritage, even though there was no transition to a consideration of the local Church. The diaconate was being restored in a perspective that was still shapeless and in which disparate needs and ideas were intermingled; the vote on it was valuable above all for the choice made to entrust to the episcopal conferences the management not only of liturgical adaptations but also of the institutional procedures of pastoral government.

The problem of collegiality was different. The vote meant the acquisition of a category whose decisive character it acknowledged. Other sections of the constitution (on the Church of Christ and the Catholic Church; on the *sensus fidei* and the Spirit) were and would become increasingly more important, but the vote on a full and supreme power, which because it is of divine right cannot be suppressed for any reason, had an extraordinary effect on the constitution and the Council. The wager of John XXIII that the Council would be a Pentecost, the place where the pastoral nature of Christian truth would find expression, had often seemed risky or naive. The agreement of the bishops on asserting collegiality finally gave a meaning to the road traveled, for the Council acquired a new "word" with which to express a fundamental dimension of the Church's experience, so fundamental that some, like Congar, would not hesitate to put it on the same level as the "discoveries" of the great councils of the past, such as consubstantiality, the title *Theotokos*, and transubstantiation.

At the same time, and differently from Vatican I, there was no question of the victory of a lobby able to have its own obsession approved. Instead, the very experience of synodal action showed the bishops that such action was part of the essence of the Church; not only, therefore, was there a communion in the magisterium, but a magisterium of communion to which the very large majority of the episcopate wanted to listen. While not knowing how to articulate this realization, the bishops gave their *placet* to a kind of existence whose developments they did not know but whose "truth" they recognized. It was this — was it the "pastoral character"? — that rendered some sectors of the Council so sensitive to this problem, which in the end might be limited in its effects, as indeed happened when the Synod of Bishops was established.

Collegiality was not, in fact, the enemy of the preparatory schema on the Church. Anyone trying to guess the points of disagreement between the supporters of that schema and *Lumen gentium* would be led to believe, if he prescinded from the conciliar event, that the priority given to the chapter on the People of God, the definition of the Church as sacrament, and the sections on the magisterium were the ones that should have drawn opposition. The lengthy and wearisome procedure with regard to the propositions created, understandably, a conciliar consciousness and the corresponding allergic reactions. After October 30 collegiality and Vatican II were synonymous, and a challenge to the former was simply a case in point for boycotting the latter.

VII. THE SUBCOMMISSIONS FOR THE SCHEMA ON THE CHURCH

After the debate ended, there began the lengthy task of reworking the schema on the Church. A first phase of this work occupied the time between October and the early days of December. On December 2 the Doctrinal Commission (which in the meantime had taken in as new members A. Ancel, J. Heuschen, Ch. Butler, and L. Henríquez Jiménes, all elected by the fathers, and A. Poma, appointed by the pope[431]) was authorized to elect a second vice-president and a second secretary to join Browne and Tromp, who had been appointed to their respective roles during the preparatory phase. Charue, Bishop of Namur, was chosen as second vice-president, and Philips as second secretary. The latter's role

---

[431] Caprile, III, 317-19. See *Commissioni conciliari*, 3d ed., 23-25.

would eventually became a purely formal one, but only after he had played an exceptionally important role, especially during the work of revision.[432]

Once the vote had been taken on October 1 to accept the Philips schema as a working basis, an ad hoc subcommission was set up, which as early as October 2 began its study of the requests for changes that the assembly was voicing during the debate. At the meeting of the Doctrinal Commission on October 23 the prudent mediation of Philips, who was arbiter on the subcommission for the schema on the Church, won approval to have the very numerous requests of the fathers sifted by special subcommittees of "his" subcommission. This tool guaranteed that, amid the uncertainty of the fate of the five propositions on episcopal collegiality and the diaconate, possible defeats would not become catastrophes.[433]

A first phase of this revision by sections occupied the month of November and the first days of December; next came a close examination by the central subcommission for revision at its meetings on November 13 and 30, 1963, and then on January 31, 1964. From there the recommendations went to the plenary commission and finally to examination by the CC; they were then sent to the fathers with a view to new discussion in the hall.

In the subcommittees, all of which worked *after* the votes on October 30, tasks were further subdivided and entrusted first of all to individual experts or very small groups of experts, with some fluctuation in the carrying out of the various tasks; Philips served as active supervisor of all the groups.

The introduction and chapter I (on the mystery of the Church) were revised without too many problems. Charue, who was in charge of this subcommittee, provided it with a little group of experts headed by Cerfaux. Charue arranged that the study of remarks on the phrase "foundation on the Apostles" be examined by Garofalo; Rigaux studied questions on poverty; Cerfaux, as well as Rigaux and Castellino, examined

---

[432] See J. Grootaers, "Le rôle de Mgr. G.Philips à Vatican II," in *Ecclesia a Spiritu Sancto edocta: Mélanges théologiques. Hommage à Mgr. Gérard Philips* (Gembloux, 1970) 343-80.

[433] On October 25 the subcommission on the Church (called, in the sources, the "central subcommission for revision") drew up a proposal for a division into seven special subcommittees; this was approved at the plenary meeting of the Doctrinal Commission on the 28th. Various experts were then assigned to these subcommittees, and, after the vote on the 29th, an eighth group was added that would concern itself with the chapter on the Blessed Virgin (Tromp, *Relationes*, October 1, 1963 to April 1, 1964, 3).

the paragraph on the Kingdom of God and the images of the Church; Fenton was given the question of the Church as sacrament, which bothered him so much, and Castellino the chapter on mystery. Only during this phase was a study made also of the *vota* sent in by the bishops after the opening of the second period, which had not been considered before.[434]

In addition to the members, others, too, worked on the formulation of some critical passages; thus the minutes tell us that Garofalo's formula, speaking of the Church as founded "on Peter and on the twelve apostles," passed with the explicit approval of Philips, who took part in the work; they record a contribution of Daniélou on the relationship of the Church to the Kingdom of God, one which broke up the exaggerated connection suggested by *Mystici Corporis*. A section on poverty, which was to make room for the recommendations of Lercaro, Ancel, and Hammer, was presented to the subcommission by Rigaux, although it was really written by Dupont.[435] Fenton's predictable worries about the definition of the Church as a sacrament were being blunted by a series of interventions in the subcommittee by Philips himself.[436]

Eighteen pages of corrected text and of a report on the emendations were passed on to the subcommission for revision (and made available to the Doctrinal Commission), which approved the results achieved at meetings on November 18, 25, and 26, 1963. A fuller report of thirty-one pages by B. Rigaux would accompany the text to the Doctrinal Commission, in the form of an *expensio modorum*.

The editing of the chapter on the People of God was entrusted to the second subcommittee.[437] Sauras and Witte drew up an extensive forty-page report, which was sent on through the usual channels at the end of November. This new chapter was intended to take up primarily the priesthood of the faithful, the *sensus fidei* of the entire Church, the charisms, union with non-Catholics, and the missionary nature of the Christian community. The text was to result from the consolidation of

[434] Charue Archive, *Subcommissio theologica I, sessio I*, 1-2. The members of this subcommission, which met five times in November, were Charue, Pelletier, van Dodewaard, and then Heuschen (fathers), with Cerfaux, Fenton, Garofalo, Castellino, and Rigaux as experts.

[435] Ibid., *sessio IV*, for the minutes.

[436] A report of two short pages by Castellino explained the meaning and limits of the term *sacrament*.

[437] This was composed of R. Santos, G. Garrone, J. Dearden, and J. Griffiths (fathers), assisted by experts Congar, Kerrigan, Naud (and Lafortune?), Reuter, Sauras, and Witte. It met eight times in November and once in December.

no. 24 of chapter IV, which contained material both on the laity and on the People of God in general, with nos. 8, 9, and 10 of chapter I of the second schema, as well as of some proposals of Suenens. This subcommittee held a series of meetings in November and the beginning of December 1963, and then resumed its work at the end of January and the beginning of February 1964.

There were two points of greater importance. On the one hand, the chapter on the People of God made it possible to look at the Church as a whole and to set forth the mission of pastors in the ministry of the means of grace for the faithful.[438] On the other hand, in regard to the common priesthood (no. 10), the existence of the universal priesthood was affirmed against some petitions seeking to abolish or substantially modify this assertion. Some fathers had insisted on retaining the expression "they [the two priesthoods] differ in essence and not only in degree" and specifying that this essential difference consisted in the "power," attributed to the ministerial priesthood, to form and guide the priestly people.[439]

In addition, the chapter on the People of God made it possible to introduce the salvation-history perspective that seemed necessary after decades during which the sociology of the mystical body as a social reality had dominated. During this phase the effect such a chapter would have on the systematic structure of *Lumen gentium* was not felt as a ticklish matter. Ticklish indeed, however, was the analysis of no. 12, "The *sensus fidei* and the charisms of the Christian people." In fact, it became clear that this chapter was a crucial one in the schema as a whole, because it made the indefectibility of the Church an attribute of the entire people when there was a universal consent among them. The decision to retain the text was not made without objections, and the subcommittee introduced a reference to the role of the magisterium that was much more nuanced than the one which those interested in restoring the preparatory schema wanted: there, indefectibility had been described as a passivity guided by the magisterium; here, the people were an active subject "under the leadership of the magisterium."

But it was the chapter on the hierarchy, which now became the third instead of the second chapter, on which the minority concentrated its attack, making it, especially in relation to the subject of collegiality, the banner for its own direction in ecclesiology and its own vision of the

---

[438] Congar wrote of this explicitly during those days: *"Ecclesia Mater,"* La vie spirituelle (March 1964), 324-35.

[439] *AS* II/1, 331, nos. 28-29.

Council. But in getting the revision of this chapter under way, Philips was already proceeding with great caution, and he entrusted the study of the emendations for the sections on sacramentality, the presbyterate, and the diaconate to three different groups. The course of the work had three different phases: first, the work of the subcommittees, which between November 1963 and January 1964, formulated the text and presented it to the Doctrinal Commission; second, at its meeting on March 6-11 the Doctrinal Commission discussed and approved the texts of the subcommissions; finally, at the meeting of the Doctrinal Commission on June 5-6, 1964, the chapter already approved was studied once again, following an intervention of the pope, who had offered thirteen "suggestions" for the text.[440]

During six meetings in November the third subcommittee completed the revisions of the numbers dealing with the institution of the apostles, the bishops as their successors, and the sacramentality of the episcopate.[441] When the intersession began, then, the text reworked by this subcommittee was ready.

The fourth subcommittee, which was in charge of the numbers on presbyters and deacons, finished its work at eight meetings in October and November.[442] The main innovation consisted in a greater development of the teaching on presbyters. The subcommittee again raised the question of the arrangement of the material. Its wish was, in fact, that the two lower degrees of the hierarchy be placed at the end of the chapter, but independently, instead of being treated in the doctrinal context of the episcopate. This subcommittee, too, finished its work before the intersession.

Finally, the very crowded fifth subcommittee was given the task of revising the numbers dealing with the episcopal college and the three episcopal roles of teaching, sanctifying, and governing; it held ten rather lively meetings.[443] The work of theological development was divided

---

[440] See U. Betti, *La dottrina sull'episcopato nel capitolo III della Costituzione dommatica "Lumen gentium"* (Rome, 1968), 190-210; and especially J. Grootaers, *Primauté et Collégialité. Le dossier de Gérard Philips sur la Nota Explicativa Praevia ("Lumen gentium," chap. III)* (Leuven, 1986).

[441] The members of the third subcommission were F. König, F. Barbado, and M. Doumith (fathers), with experts Ciappi, D'Ercole, Lécuyer, Xiberta, and Turrado.

[442] The members of the fourth subcommission were A. Scherer, M. Roy, and F. Franić (fathers), with experts Grillmeier, Trapè, Kloppenburg, Lambert, Rodhain, and Smulders.

[443] The members of the fifth subcommission were P. Parente, E. Florit, J. Schroeffer, L. Henríquez Jiménez, J. Heuschen (fathers), and Salaverri, Betti, Rahner, Ratzinger, Colombo, Dhanis, Thils, Maccarrone, Gagnebet, D'Ercole, Lambruschini, Moeller, Schauf, and Smulders again (experts).

into several areas: Salaverri, Maccarrone, Rahner, and Ratzinger worked on the specific question of collegiality, while Thils and Dhanis studied the more general problems raised by the fathers; Semmelroth (with D'Ercole) took up the interventions on the ministries and functions (*munera*) of a bishop; and Betti and Colombo studied the paragraphs on the magisterium and its infallibility.

The storminess of the theological debate had as a result that only three meetings of the entire committee (fathers and experts) were held in November and December and that the final phase of the re-examination was reduced to the period January 20-25, 1964. Yet the material produced, and brought together by Betti, the reporter, added up to over 150 pages!

The four theologians of the first group divided the material on collegiality into eight different problems, a sorting out that was reached by compromises that were not always decisive. On the use of the word *college* Maccarrone was compelled to admit that there were no serious objections from the hall, but the others agreed to recommend to the Doctrinal Commission the expression "episcopal order" (*ordo episcopalis*), as being a "classic expression" in the sources "of the entire Middle Ages" [*sic!*]. Ratzinger drew up a report on what was required in order to be part of college; in it he acknowledged that the majority at the Council and the foundation of the liturgical tradition made preferable the formula that a man becomes part of the college "in virtue of his consecration and his communion with the head" (*vi consecrationis et communionis cum capite*).

On the other hand, no agreement was reached on the need to repeat the formula of Vatican I on the primacy of the pope. Salaverri and Maccarrone wanted it incorporated into the section on relations between pope and college, but Rahner and Ratzinger did not agree. Rahner composed the report on the problem of the conditions required for a collegial act as an act that the pope must "at least freely accept" (*saltem libere recipere*); the idea was accepted by all, although the proposal was made to say that papal reception of an act of the college needs to be clearly verifiable (*vel de eius libera acceptatione certe constat*). On the action of the college when scattered (outside a council), Rahner suggested that the schema be kept as it was; all agreed. On the nature and right (*ius*) of the college, the last subject discussed, there were attempts (by Salaverri in one case, by Salaverri and Maccarrone in another) to introduce serious limitations on the argument of the text; only the firmness of Rahner and Ratzinger in explaining and maintaining the arguments of the fathers in favor of the schema prevented a series of small mutilations.

In the second theological group Dhanis and Thils prepared a short examination of the emendations in order to explain the necessity of nos. 16 and 17 in the structure of the schema. The two reports went the rounds. Schauf drew up a *votum* asking that the reports of Maccarrone-Ratzinger-Rahner-Salaverri be corrected and be made to propose not keeping the text as it was but correcting it so that it would limit to residential bishops in communion with Rome the title of members of the college, deny a juridically effective character to the acts of the college, and deny the possibility of a collegial act outside a council. The other reports were rather in favor of the text. In addition, Betti drew up a reply to the interventions of those fathers who worried that the statements on collegiality would endanger the personal prerogatives of the Roman pontiff, and he showed the collegial character of infallibility. Colombo, whose views were always interesting both in themselves and in light of his closeness of Paul VI, limited himself to taking up some of the requests of Cantero and other bishops; not once did he ask for a change in the character of the schema.

The fathers of this fifth subcommittee introduced into the section on collegiality the two requisites, indispensable in different degrees, for becoming a member of the episcopal college, namely, sacramental consecration and communion with the head and other members of the college. They stated with greater clarity the equality of the power exercised by the Roman pontiff alone and of the power exercised by all the bishops together with him, in order to eliminate the slightest suggestion that, as critics alleged against the text, papal power was inferior to that of the college as a whole or that he could not exercise this power independently of the action of the other bishops. They also supplied the biblical foundation for the grant of such power by Christ.

At the end of the section on relations among the bishops, reference was made to relations organized in the form of the patriarchates in the East and in the form of episcopal conferences in the West. The paragraph on the teaching office carefully set forth the distinctions between ordinary and extraordinary magisterium and between the non-infallible and infallible magisterium; an attempt was also made to explain the definition of the Roman pontiff's personal infallibility in the context of the infallibility of the entire Church. The local Churches were mentioned in connection with the episcopal duty of sanctifying, but in a reductive way as "communities that celebrate the Eucharist."

The sixth subcommittee undertook the revision of chapter III (which had become chapter IV in the new version), namely, on the People of

God and in particular on the laity.[444] It began its work toward the end of November 1963 and ended it in Zurich at the beginning of February 1964, on the eve of the meeting on schema XIII, in which the same individuals were involved. Since the section dealing with the People of God in general had been transferred to the new chapter II, the group now completed the teaching on the laity with two new numbers on the participation of the laity in the universal priesthood and in the prophetic role of Christ. Chapter IV on the laity, accompanied by reports from Häring, Delhaye, and Hirschmann, was approved without difficulty at meetings on March 10, 11, and 12.

The seventh subcommittee, which was charged with the revision of chapter IV, on the call to holiness, held a preliminary meeting on December 3, 1963, and was able to begin its real work on January 27, 1964, and end it in February.[445] On January 17-18 the subcommittee held an important meeting at Leuven, with the abbot primate of the Benedictines presiding; the participants were Msgr. Šeper, Archbishop of Zagreb; Abbot Butler of Downside; Father A. Fernández, General of the Dominicans; and experts Thils, Laurentin, Bouyer, Franciscan P. Lio, and Dominicans Philippon and Labourdette, as well as some other expert individuals.[446] The experts had to study the request that the call to holiness be separated from the chapter on vowed religious. This was a request strongly backed by a large number of religious among the experts and the bishops, but it was also supported by those who, like Daniélou, held the distinction to be needed in order to make it clear that the structure of the Church gave a place to those who professed vows, not by reason of that act but only in the framework of their response to their baptismal call.[447]

---

[444] This was a mixed subcommittee that included members from the Commission for the Lay Apostolate. It comprised J. Wright (president), A. Ancel, J. Schroeffer, and M. McGrath from the Doctrinal Commission, and E. Guano, J. Blomjous, F. Hengsbach, and J. Ménager from the Commission for the Lay Apostolate. The experts were Delhaye, Häring, Hirschmann, Klostermann, Lafortune, Medina, Moeller, van Riedmatten, Tucci, and three laymen (Habicht, Sugranyes de Franch, and Vázquez).

[445] This too was a mixed subcommittee. The Doctrinal Commission was represented by M. Browne, A. Charue, F. Seper, B. Gut, Ch. Butler, and A. Fernández, while the Commission on Religious was represented by E. Compagnone, C. Sipovic, B. Stein, S. Kleiner, and A. Sépinski; the group was assisted by twelve experts.

[446] The reports and the final version of the schema (written by Dom Dupont), as well as the connected correspondence, are in the archive of the CLG at Louvain-la-Neuve (nos. 446-90).

[447] See J. Daniélou, "La place des religieux dans la structure de l'Eglise," *Etudes* 320 (January- June 1964), 147-55.

CHAPTER II

BISHOPS AND DIOCESES
AND THE COMMUNICATIONS MEDIA
(NOVEMBER 5-25, 1963)

JOSEPH FAMERÉE

INTRODUCTION

The unusual course taken by the schema on bishops and the government of dioceses during the intersession was not calculated to make it very acceptable when it was presented in the conciliar assembly by Cardinal Paolo Marella on November 4, 1963. The conciliar Commission for Bishops did not hold a single plenary meeting between December 1962 and November 1963; each of the several times such a meeting was announced, it was canceled. The commission itself was therefore never able to amend or approve the schema before the debate proper, with the result that even members of the commission voiced serious dissatisfaction in the hall.[1] In the interest of saving time and because of the difficulty foreign bishops had in coming to Rome, Marella had appointed a small subcommission made up of some members who resided nearby and some experts from the commission. It was, in fact, Msgr. Luigi Carli, Bishop of Segni and one of

---

[1] Here is the composition of the commission during the second period of the Council: Cardinal P. Marella (Curia), president; Cardinals J. F. McIntyre (Los Angeles) and J. Bueno y Monreal (Seville), vice-presidents; members: Cardinal P. Doi Tatsuo (Tokyo), Bishops L. Mathias (Madras and Mylapore, India), E. Guerry (Cambrai, France), L. Binz (St. Paul, Minnesota, USA), K. Alter (Cincinnati), F. Carpino (Titular Archbishop of Sardica, Italy), G. Gawlina (Titular Archbishop of Ladito, Italy; a new member), M.-J. Lemieux (Ottawa), L. Del Rosario (Zamboanga, Philippines; also new); H. Schäufele (Freiburg, Germany), D. Hayek (Aleppo, Syria), A. Fernandes (Titular Archbishop of Neopatras, coadjutor of Delhi, India), J. Rakotomalala (Tananarive, Madagascar). A. Castelli (Titular Archbishop of Rusio, Italy), P. Veuillot (Titular Archbishop of Constance, Thrace, coadjutor of Paris), M. Browne (Galway and Kilmacduagh, Ireland), G. Gargitter (Bressanone, Italy), A. N. Jubany (Titular Bishop of Ortosia in Phoenicia, aux. of Barcelona), L. P. Correa (Cúcuta, Colombia), R. Primatesta (San Rafael, Argentina), L. Carli (Segni, Italy), and G. Dwyer (Leeds, England); Msgr. L. Governatori, secretary; C. Berutti, assistant secretary; G. Pedretti, writer-archivist. See *Commissioni conciliari*, ed. General Secretariat of the Council (Vatican Polyglot Press, November 30, 1962), 15-16 (2d. ed., November 4, 1963), 29-31.

the most obdurate representatives of the minority at the Council, who oversaw the revision of the text within this "rump commission," to use the expression Jan Grootaers borrowed from K. Mörsdorf.[2] The amended schema was passed on to the Coordinating Commission, which approved it in principle in March, 1963. Neither the schema nor Carli's official introductory report were submitted to the Commission for Bishops before they were presented to the conciliar fathers.[3]

The debate on bishops and the government of dioceses began in the hall right after the end of the month-long discussion of the schema on the Church. On October 29 the vote had been taken on the insertion of the section on the Blessed Virgin into the schema on the Church. On the 30th, after the pope's approval on the 27th, the five questions on the direction to be taken with regard to collegiality and the diaconate had finally been submitted to the conciliar assembly for its vote. It was in this atmosphere of the "point-by-point defeat" of the minority[4] that on November 5, 1963, at the 60th general congregation, Marella and Carli gave their introductory reports on the new schema on bishops and the government of dioceses.

The schema, which had been sent to the fathers during the intersession, contained thirty-seven paragraphs. After an introductory paragraph, the decree was divided into five chapters. Chapter I was devoted to relations between the bishops and the Roman congregations (nos. 2-5: I. The faculties of bishops; II. The practice of the sacred congregations in dealing with bishops). Coadjutor and auxiliary bishops were the subject of chapter II (nos. 6-16). Chapter III dealt with the national assembly or conference of bishops (nos. 17-25: I. The establishment of a conference; II. The leadership of a conference; III. The decisions of a conference; IV. Relations among episcopal conferences of different countries). Chapter IV had to do with the suitable limits of dioceses and ecclesiastical provinces (nos. 26-32). Lastly, chapter V dealt with the erection and boundaries of parishes (nos. 33-37). Two appendices followed: one listed the specific episcopal faculties to be acknowledged, while the

---

[2] For the whole story of *De episcopis* during the intersession, see *History*, 2:446-55.

[3] See the typewritten letter of Msgr. Veuillot to Cardinal Tisserant, head of the conciliar Council of Presidents, October 19, 1963 (*Fonds Veuillot*, Diocesan Archives of Paris, doc. 70; *History*, 2:452 n.231).

[4] But nothing had yet been settled, because the points in question would have to be discussed in the hall.

other took up some points regarding relations between bishops and the Roman dicasteries.[5]

The earlier schema, composed during the preparatory period, had never been distributed to the fathers.[6] It had the same title as the revised draft, contained fifty-two paragraphs in addition to a preface, and was divided into six chapters. Chapter I was devoted to relations between the bishops and the congregations of the Roman Curia (nos. 1-8: I. The faculties of bishops; II. The practice of the sacred congregations in dealing with bishops). The special faculties of residential bishops in particular were listed at length (no. 3); in the new draft they were relegated to an appendix. Chapter II was entitled "Coadjutor and Auxiliary Bishops, as well as the 'Resignation' (*cessatione*) by Bishops from their Pastoral Office" (nos. 9-21: I. Coadjutor and auxiliary bishops; II. Resignation by bishops from their pastoral office). The new schema included an additional paragraph on relations between the coadjutor and the vicar general (no. 10), and the section on the resignation was reduced to a single number (no. 16).

---

[5] See *Schema Decreti de episcopis ac de diocesium regimine*, AS II/4, 364-92. At the beginning of the 60th general congregation the fathers also received a booklet containing the written amendments on that schema which had been submitted during the intersession; see *Emendationes a Concilii Patribus scripto exhibitae super schema Decreti de episcopis ac de diocesium regimine*, AS II/4, 393-435 and 827-923). For the whole of the debate on this schema during the second period see Caprile, III, 187-98, 205-17, 245-58, and 261-75; AS II/4, 363-748; II/5, 1-401 and 409-11; for a short summary one may also see R. Aubert, "Lo svolgimento del Concilio," in *Storia della Chiesa* 35/1 (Cinisello Balsamo, 1994), 263-66. This debate went on through nine general congregations (60-68), November 5-15 and involved 149 oral interventions and 219 written observations.

[6] See AS II/4, 364 n.2. The text of this preparatory schema is in *Sacrosanctum Concilium Vaticanum Secundum. Schemata constitutionum et decretorum ex quibus argumenta in Concilio disceptanda seligentur. Series tertia* (Vatican Polyglot Press, 1962), 67-90. According to Msgr. Carli's report (see the next note), the five preparatory schemas were studied by the CPC in February and May 1962; they were then sent back to the preparatory Commission for Bishops to be reviewed in light of the observations and wishes of the CPC. The schemas were revised and submitted for examination by the subcommission for mixed subjects. The latter studied them carefully and rewrote them as a single decree, which it sent on to the General Secretariat of the Council on December 6, 1962, with a double request: that the decree be discussed after the debate on the Church and that notes be added to explain each chapter and to provide an in-depth study of the new material being proposed. This work was done by the conciliar Commission for Bishops beginning on December 12, 1962. After receiving the remarks of the CC in January 1963, the Commission for Bishops sent back to the latter a new draft in March. This was the present form of the schema, and it was decided on April 22, 1963, to send it to the fathers. See A. Indelicato, *Difendere la dottrina o annunciare l'evangelo* (Genoa, 1992), 147-57.

The national assembly or conference of bishops was the subject of
Chapter III (nos. 22-33: I. Establishment and nature [of the assembly];
II. Leadership of the assembly; III. The force of its decisions; IV. Relations among episcopal conferences of different nations). While in this
original draft the decisions of the conference never had juridical force,
the new text introduced the rule that they became obligatory by a vote of
two-thirds of the members (no. 24). Chapter IV dealt with the division of
dioceses (nos. 34-44). Chapter V, finally, dealt with the erection of
parishes and their boundaries (nos. 45-52). The differences between the
two documents were thus chiefly formal: an abridgment and reorganization of the body of the text.

After the very general introduction by Cardinal Marella, who
emphasized the purely pastoral and juridical character of the decree,
Bishop Carli of Segni reviewed the history of the schema and described its contents, with special attention, given the circumstances, to the
first chapter.[7] Particularly noteworthy is the way in which the reporter
explained the first and fundamental principle on which the drafting of
the schema on the bishops was based (no. 3): on the one hand, the
schema had deliberately avoided theological questions that were still to
be taken up in the schema on the Church (an allusion, among other
things, to episcopal collegiality); on the other hand, Carli insisted,
with a reference to Pius VI, that it was schismatic, or at least erroneous, to assert, as had been done at the Synod of Pistoia, that a bishop
receives from Christ all the rights he needs for the good government of
his diocese or that these rights cannot be changed or hindered by the
pope.[8] As the ensuing discussion would reveal, this implicit comparison with schismatics of those in favor of collegiality and of reasserting
the value of the episcopal ministry would not be well received by the
conciliar majority.

---

[7] For this double introduction see *Relatio super schema Decreti de episcopis ac de
diocesium regimine, AS* II/4, 435-44). We may doubt the objectivity of certain points in
Msgr. Carli's historical review, especially when he claims that the CC at its session on
March 26, 1963, heaped praise on the schema and said that it was not necessary to wait
for discussion of the schema by the Commission for Bishops, planned for April 30, but
that the draft of the decree should be printed immediately (440). See *History*, 2:451.

[8] See *AS* II/4, 442.

I. The Schema on the Bishops:
A Reflection of the Conservative Minority

At the request of the moderator, Cardinal Suenens,[9] the initial discussion was to be limited to the schema as a whole and was to end the next day (the 61st general congregation) with a vote on whether to accept the text in principle and as a basis for a chapter-by-chapter discussion. Thirty fathers spoke. Most of them regretted that the approach to the episcopal office was overly juridical or theoretical and insufficiently pastoral.[10] They called, therefore, for a rewriting of the schema that would take as its basis the sacramentality and collegiality of the episcopate as these had been formulated just days before in connection with the schema on the Church: the powers of bishops are not granted by the Holy See, and episcopal conferences are a way of exercising collegiality.[11] Along the same line, the desire was several times expressed that bishops might be more fully associated with the government of the universal Church through an internationalization of the Curia or the creation of an international group of bishops who would collaborate directly with the pope.[12]

These two proposals were more or less explicitly related to the openness to greater episcopal collaboration that Paul VI had manifested in his addresses to the Curia on September 21 and to the Council on September 29.[13] While, in the view of Paul VI, the Council was not charged with conceiving and deciding how to renew the Roman dicasteries (this was, in effect, the first question being "reserved" to the pope), he did speak in the first address of a more international recruitment of Curia members and of a decentralization of some curial powers to the advantage of the

---

[9] In a concern for continuity the moderators no longer took turns at successive general congregations; instead, each took charge of a part of the schema. Thus Suenens was to lead the discussion of the schema in general, Agagianian, the discussion of chapter I, Lercaro of chapter II, Döpfner of chapter III, and Suenens again of chapter V.

[10] See AS II/4, 456-59 (N. Jubany), 460-62 (L. de Bazelaire), 462-64 (P. Correa), 465-66 (G. Garrone), 488-91 (F. Gomes dos Santos), 493-5 (C. Bandeira de Mello), 505-8 (R. Gonzalez Moralejo), 509-12 (A. Fernandez).

[11] See AS II/4, 445-46 (A. Liénart). 450-52 (P. Richaud), 453-55 (G. Gargitter), 456-59 (N. Jubany), 460-62 (L. de Bazelaire), 462-64 (P. Correa), 467-69 (F. Marty). 469-71 (M. Baudoux). 478-79 (F. König). 479-81 (B. Alfrink), 481-85 (A. Bea), 487-88 (P. Veuillot), 488-91 (F. Gomes dos Santos), 495-97 (H. Schäufele), 497-99 (A. Olalia), 499-501 (F. Simons), 503-5 (J. Hodges), 505-8 (R. Gonzalez Moralejo), 512-16 (M. Hermaniuk).

[12] See AS II/4, 450-52 (P. Richaud), 453-55 (G. Gargitter), 478-79 (F. König), 481-85 (A. Bea), 495-97 (H. Schäufele), 497-99 (A. Olalia), 513-16 (M. Hermaniuk).

[13] See Insegnamenti, 1:142-50 (especially 150) and 166-85 (especially 174-75).

local episcopate. The pope also spoke of representatives of the residential bishops being in some measure associated with himself, should the Council request it, in his responsibilities for the government of the Church. The second address likewise mentioned the increased help, in ways still to be determined, which the bishops could bring to the exercise of the pope's universal office.

Considering the maneuvering that had gone on in the intersession, it is of interest to note that on the first two days of the debate six members of the Commission for Bishops asked to speak, in most cases in order to criticize the schema for not conforming to the doctrine in the schema on the Church.[14] Thus Gargitter called for a real and effective decentralization. In his view the present text actually favored a greater centralization and gave even greater importance to the main organs of the Curia; the real issue was nothing more nor less than concretely applying the doctrinal principles in the schema on the Church.[15] Jubany, Veuillot, and Schäufele also asked that the text be revised on the basis of those same principles.[16] Veuillot even thought it premature to discuss the schema on bishops until the teaching on the episcopate had been clarified.[17] Schäufele in one passage of his address formally rejected Carli's accusation concerning the faculties of bishops: the Synod of Pistoia had denied the pope any right to reserve privileges; this was essentially different from the principle that residential bishops have inherent rights.[18] Finally, Correa began by complaining explicitly of the infringements of the conciliar regulations that had occurred between the first and second periods: "More than half of us who belonged to this conciliar Commission for Bishops and the Government of Dioceses were not heard in connection

[14] In the chronological order of their interventions the six were J. McIntyre, G. Gargitter, N. Jubany, P. Correa, P. Veuillot, and H. Schäufele.

[15] See AS II/4, 453-55.

[16] See AS II/4, 456-59 (Jubany), 487-88 (Veuillot), 495-97 (Schäufele).

[17] We know how much this bishop, along with other French colleagues, resented having been systematically excluded from the work of the Commission for Bishops during the intersession; see History, 2:451 n.228.

[18] Msgr. E. Schick, auxiliary of Fulda, saw in Schäufele's speech an attempt to remove from the new schema the last traces of the former text; see his letter to Cardinal Frings, November 6, 1963, 2 verso (Frings Archive, in the Diocesan Archives of Cologne, De episcopis ac de diocesium regimine 181/8). In this connection, I warmly thank Alessandro Chiesa (Istituto per le scienze religiose, Bologna), for having allowed me to consult his material on the various archival collections having to do with the schema (the collections of Onclin, Dwyer, Browne, Veuillot, Boulard, Schäufele, Frings, and Jedin, deposited at the ISR in Bologna). See B. Ulianich, "Il Sinodo di Pistoia," L'Avvenire d'Italia, November 17, 1963, now in R. La Valle, Coraggio del concilio (Brescia, 1964), 319-21.

with the drafting of the schema that is now submitted for examination by all the fathers"; the Bishop of Cúcuta deplored even more that, contrary to the conciliar prescriptions, the mind of the commission had not been sought with regard to the report Carli gave on November 5.[19]

In this context it is also not without interest to note the reaction of two certified members of the conciliar minority, Cardinals Ernesto Ruffini and Michael Browne, on November 6.[20] As was to be expected, the former came to the defense of the schema, which had thus far been very roughly handled. In his view the reproaches were not justified. On the one hand, the doctrine of collegiality was far from being clearly established, and the vote on October 30 did not prejudge the outcome of the debate; on the other hand, for Ruffini, who referred explicitly to the "very prudent" address of Cardinal McIntyre, vice-president of the Commission for Bishops, to give the episcopal conference more than consultative authority would lead to numerous evils and, in particular, would imperil the pontifical primacy of jurisdiction.[21] These were the typical arguments of the minority.

The Dominican Cardinal Browne also thought that it was not legitimate to criticize the schema for not taking sufficient account of collegiality, since the latter was still being studied by the Doctrinal Commission, of which he was, of course, the vice-president.[22] This last assertion was a serious one and symptomatic of the curialist tendency. For the first time the very validity of the vote on October 30 was being openly chal-

---

[19] AS II/4, 462-64.

[20] Ruffini was a typical representative of Italian Catholic intransigency with its centralist and papalist conception of the Church; see F. Stabile, "Il Cardinal Ruffini e il Vaticano II," CrSt 11/1 (1990), 83-176; and Protagonisti, 486-94.

[21] See AS II/4, 476-78.

[22] See AS II/4, 486. On the day before, November 5, during the first meeting of the Doctrinal Commission after the vote on the five questions, Cardinal Ottaviani had sharply criticized these questions, going so far as to describe them as illegal in principle, because they had not been drafted by the Doctrinal Commission, as was clear from the errors they contained (see Wenger, 80; in his manuscript notes on the Doctrinal Commission meeting of November 5, peritus A. Prignon says that at this point he was distracted by Y. Congar, who was speaking to him, so that he could not understand what Ottaviani was saying; he caught only these words: "a vote that was almost without notice and hasty"; see Prignon Archive, CLG, no. 481). Ottaviani would repeat this accusation in the council hall on November 8 and in an interview on November 13 (see below). According to Tromp, "The subject was the five propositions accepted in the council hall on October 30, and in what way the Doctrinal Commission would be bound by them" (Relatio, October 1, 1963 — April 1, 1964, 5); and Congar notes, "They wasted time" (see JCongar for that date).

lenged.[23] The conservative group that still controlled the Doctrinal Commission regarded it as in fact superior to the Council; it was not only the authority of the moderators that was thus being questioned but the very development of the Council and its freedom of action. Appearances were deceptive, then, in the early fall of 1963: the minority had not laid down its arms and the confrontation of the previous year was continuing.[24] Other interventions in the course of the debate would confirm this, especially those of Cardinal Ottaviani and Msgr. Lefevbre, who two days later repeated the same challenge to the conciliar vote; nor should we forget Carli's speech on November 13.

At the end of the first two mornings of discussion, of the 2100 fathers who voted, 1610 agreed to continue the discussion of the schema, despite the criticisms made of it, while 477 voted against continuing, and 13 turned in an invalid ballot.[25]

II. THE ROMAN CURIA UNDER FIRE

A. A SUPREME, PERMANENT COUNCIL OF THE UNIVERSAL CHURCH?

Before the results of the vote were announced, a first and important intervention on the first chapter of the schema on bishops had already occurred, that of His Beatitude Maximos IV Saigh, Antiochene Patriarch of the Melkites; it was made in French (he was the only one who flouted the rule of using Latin).[26] The collegial responsibility of the episcopate

---

[23] *DC*, December 15, 1963, no. 1414, col. 1677 n.2, repeats accurately the information given by A. Wenger in *La Croix* for November 8 and comments as follows on Browne's intervention: "Without saying so, Cardinal Browne alluded to a meeting of the theological commission that took place on the evening of November 5 and in the course of which Cardinal Ottaviani challenged the theological significance of the vote taken by the fathers"; see above, note 22.

[24] See *Protagonisti*, 478.

[25] See *AS* II/4, 527. Father J. Dupont, O.S.B., a "private theologian" at the Council, gave the following interpretation of this favorable vote in his manuscript review of the second period, which he wrote shortly after its close: "The fathers apparently preferred to use a poor text for tackling the problems they regarded as important rather than to send the text back and risk never again seeing a text that would allow them to tackle those problems. In discussing this text, the Council found itself once again faced with the problem of collegiality" (Dupont Archive, CLG, no. 1759, 4 and 4a).

[26] Maximos IV Saigh was the great representative of the Oriental tradition at the Council; a defender of the local Churches and a firm opponent of Roman centralism, he was one of the most respected personages in the conciliar majority; see O. Rousseau, "Une des grandes figures du concile. Le Patriarche Maximos IV (1878-1967)," *Revue Nouvelle* 47 (1968), 64-70; *Protagonisti*, 460-68.

for the Church, he said, is not adequately exercised when the Roman Curia alone embodies the collaboration of the Catholic episcopate in the central government of the Church. The patriarch therefore offered a new solution: since all the bishops of the world cannot be continuously gathered in a council, a limited group of them, representing their colleagues, should have the concrete responsibility for assisting the pope in the general government of the Church as an "authentic *Sacred College* of the universal Church"; it would be composed of the residential and apostolic patriarchs, the residential cardinal-archbishops or bishops, and bishops chosen in the episcopal conferences of each country. Some members of this Sacred College would take turns in being at the side of the pope, who always has the final say; this would be the permanent, supreme, executive, and decision-making council of the Church, to which all the Roman offices would be subject as to a center that is by definition open to the entire world and not closed in on itself in order to run the whole show. With the help of the new Sacred College, the Asiatic and African bishops would enjoy a greater cultural autonomy than the Mediterranean countries, while maintaining the necessary bond with the See of Peter.[27]

The next two days (62nd and 63rd general congregations) were devoted to this first chapter on relations between bishops and the Roman congregations. Many of the interventions rejected the idea of faculties granted to bishops on the grounds that bishops by divine right have all the powers needed to govern their dioceses.[28] A number of the fathers also urged the establishment of a new body for the exercise of collegiality, a permanent body of bishops from the entire world, somewhat along the lines of that proposed by Maximos IV.[29] Msgr. Florit, Archbishop of Florence and a member of the Doctrinal Commission, advocated a much more moderate solution: a new general Sacred Congregation, likewise composed of residential bishops, would resolve problems submitted to it by the pope; a central congregation of this kind would be "both the concrete application and the legitimate development of episcopal collegiality."[30]

[27] See *AS* II/4, 516-19.
[28] See *AS* II/4, 556-57 (J. Ritter), 571-73 (P. Kalwa), 574-76 (F. García), 578-60 (Bishop M. Browne), 580-84 (A. Ferreira), 584-91 (S. Méndez). 595-96, (I. Ziadé), 629-31 (A. Granados), 639-41 (J. Schoiswohl), 641-43 (E. Martínez), 636-38 (E. D'Souza).
[29] See *AS* II/4, 568-70 (P. Gouyon), 571-73 (P. Kalwa), 576-77 (O. McCann), 578-80 (Bishop M. Browne), 580-84 (A. Ferreira), 592-94 (H. Van der Burgt), 612-15 (J. de Barros Câmara), 618-21 (G. Lercaro), 621-23 (L. Rugambwa), 636-38 (E. D'Souza).
[30] See *AS* II/4, 559-61: the Archbishop of Florence also criticized the appeal to episcopal collegiality in the strict sense, which had not yet been approved by the Council and, in his view, could not be; he also criticized any argument based on the vote of October 30, which was simply a straw ballot.

B. DEFENSE OF CENTRALISM

Three other speakers on November 7 made an outright defense of the Curia, although this had thus far not been directly attacked, the question having been rather of its updating or internationalization. The three were His Beatitude Ignace Pierre XVI Batanian, Patriarch of Cilicia of the Armenians (Lebanon); Msgr. Del Pino Gómez, Bishop of Lerida (Spain); and Msgr. Mason, Apostolic Vicar of El Obeid (Sudan).

It was surprising to find an Oriental patriarch displaying a radical ultramontanism:[31] "This power of jurisdiction of the Roman Pontiff is not subject to any human restriction, either de jure or de facto"; in observations on the present way in which the Church is centrally administered, it is necessary "to take into account the merits of the Sovereign Pontiff's collaborators and the obligation to avoid scandal," while also being careful lest "the criticism wound the Head himself."[32] For the Bishop of Lerida, too — though this was less surprising[33] — the Roman Curia deserved very high praise, and inappropriate criticisms of the Curia to some degree touch the Roman pontiff himself; the Church is founded on Peter, but collegiality has no scriptural basis.[34] The Apostolic Vicar of El Obeid, for his part, insisted on reminding everyone that the Curia "should be listened to by all, as being the voice of the Supreme Shepherd" and that it is "not merely a useful instrument but one that is altogether necessary for the government of the Church," especially in an age of continental and worldwide associations.[35] The common point in this triple defense of the Roman congregations was thus the quasi-identification of these with the pope, as well as the exaltation of pontifical jurisdiction.

But the real attack on the Curia came the next day. It was to come from Cardinal Frings of Cologne and drew a sharp reply from Cardinal Ottaviani, followed by other members of the minority, who were

[31] But it becomes less surprising when we know that the future patriarch had done his theological studies in Rome and had been a student of Ernesto Ruffini, at that time professor of sacred scripture at the Pontifical Atheneum of the Roman Seminary and at the Lateran University; see Ruffini's address in the hall on November 8 and his open congratulations to the Armenian Patriarch for his intervention the day before; AS II/4, 651-53; *Protagonisti,* 486-87 n.1.

[32] See AS II/4, 558-59.

[33] See E. Vilanova, "Los 'vota' de los obispos españoles después del anuncio del concilio Vaticano II," in *Veille,* 53-82.

[34] See AS II/4, 596-99.

[35] See AS II/4, 606-7.

likewise listed to speak on November 8. Meanwhile, Cardinal Lercaro of Bologna gave a more moderate and conciliatory address.

C. FRINGS VS. OTTAVIANI: A MAJORITY-MINORITY DUEL AT THE SUMMIT

The German archbishop's intervention was plain and incisive.[36] First of all, he set the record straight about the functioning of the Council: even if the vote of October 30 on the college of bishops was only a straw ballot, could anyone for that reason completely disregard the almost unanimous vote of the fathers? He was surprised therefore by Cardinal Ruffini's address on November; Frings was of the view that the conciliar commissions were instruments of the general congregations and of the thought and will of the fathers, and not the other way around. Second, he asked for a list of the powers reserved to the pope rather than a list of faculties to be granted to bishops. The very content of the regulations governing the procedure of the Roman congregations should have a place in the text of the schema on the bishops. These regulations, especially those on the clear distinction between the administrative and the judicial spheres, should be extended to all the congregations, including the Holy Office, "whose procedure in many respects is no longer suited to our age, harms the Church, and is scandalous to many." Applause broke out in the hall. Frings went on to demand that even in the Holy Office no one be condemned before having been heard and having the opportunity to correct himself.[37] Third, the number of bishops residing in the Curia should be lessened: the episcopate is not an honorific title. The same for priests: many curial offices could just as well be filled by lay people.

We may easily imagine the stir caused by such a speech both at the Council and in the Catholic world, especially because the archbishop had dared to say in plain language, on the platform of the Council, what many of the fathers (to say nothing of numerous Christians) thought and expressed behind the scenes regarding the procedures of the Holy

---

[36] See AS II/4, 616-18.

[37] These thoughts had often been expressed, as late as the eve of the second period, by Catholic authors and journals in France, Germany, the Netherlands, and the United States. The incident caused by the withdrawal of Hans Küng's book, *Kirche im Konzil* (Freiburg, 1963) (English translation: *The Council in Action: Theological Reflections on the Second Vatican Council*, trans. C. Hastings [New York, 1963]) and some other works from Catholic libraries in Rome at the beginning of the second period was undoubtedly connected with this passage in Frings's address (see Wenger, 147 n.1).

Office.[38] To gauge its impact, one need only look at the newspapers of the time and the space they gave to this speech, as well as to the reply of Cardinal Ottaviani, secretary of the tribunal under attack.[39]

After the scheduled interventions of Cardinals Lercaro and Rugambwa, to which I shall come back, it was the turn of the Secretary of the Supreme Congregation.[40] According to the commentators of the time,[41] Ottaviani's intervention was especially awaited, and it was with strong feeling and even with a sob in his voice that he gave an improvised response to the accusation made by the Cardinal of Cologne before returning to his prepared remarks.[42] He issued a "very indignant protest in answer to the words spoken against the Supreme Congregation of the Holy Office, whose president is the Supreme Pontiff." Applause came

[38] Later in the morning, despite the passionate protest of Ottaviani, Msgr. E. D'Souza, Archbishop of Bhopal (India), did not hesitate to call the Curia into question once again as being a "centralized power" that is ill-adapted to the present time; he also called for a well-defined restriction of the Curia's powers and for giving bishops all the faculties that belong to them by common and divine law; he even ad-libbed: "Aren't the bishops yet old enough [to settle the questions that arise in their region]?" Like Frings, he flatly supported "the clear vote of 85% of the Fathers": "To say that no account of this vote should be taken in the discussion" seems a "mockery of the Council"; see *AS* II/4, 636-38. This intervention was applauded at length, according to Wiltgen, 117-18.

[39] On Frings's address see *OssRom*, *La Croix*, *Le Figaro*, *Quotidiano*, and *Daily American* for November 9; *Le Monde* for November 10-11, Kipa Agency (November 10); *ICI*, December 1, no. 205, p. 2, col. 1 (Congar) and p. 8, cols. 1-2; *DC*, December 15, no. 1414, col. 1686. On Ottaviani's intervention see the dailies for November 9 and 10; *Le Figaro*, November 11; *ICI*, December 1, no. 205, p. 8, cols. 2-3; *DC*, December 15, no. 1414, cols. 1687-89. See also the many interviews given by Ottaviani in which he defended the Holy Office: *France catholique* November 22; *La Croix*, December 1-2 (see Wenger, 149-53); French television, "Cinq colonnes à la une," on Friday, December 6; *ICI*, December 15, no. 206, p. 17, col. 3 to p. 18, col. 2. See also the statement of Maximos IV on the Holy Office to French television. Finally, one should mention the press conference given by Msgr. Th. Roberts (Great Britian; Titular Archbishop of Sugdea), reported by *Le Monde*, October 24, and *ICI*, November 15, no. 204, p. 13, col. 1: "The members of the Holy Office use methods that would immediately bring them before English courts if they were used in Great Britain," and the article of Msgr. Garrone in *Semaine catholique de Toulouse*, November 24, cited by *La Croix*, November 28-29, p. 4, col. 6: "The Holy Office...carries on its difficult work under the cloak of a secrecy which we may legitimately think to be an anachronism" (see Laurentin, 120ff. and 287-89 nn.8-10, 11-12, and 14). Frings himself mentions in his memoirs the unexpected impact of his address and the general welcome it received: "This address had an entirely unexpected and almost eerie echo....And when I appeared in the bar around 11 o'clock, I was congratulated from all sides" (J. Frings, *Für die Menschen bestellt. Erinnerungen* [Cologne, 1973], 274). See the commentary of R. La Valle in *L'Avvenire d'Italia*, November 9, 1963, now in idem, *Coraggio del concilio*, 279-84.

[40] On his personality see *Protagonisti,* 474-80.

[41] See Wenger, 148; Rynne, 184; Laurentin, 121; Y. Congar, *Le Concile au jour le jour. Deuxième session* (Paris, 1964), 130.

[42] See *AS* II/4, 624-26.

from the seats of the Italian and curial group.[43] These words, he continued, sprang from ignorance, to use a no more offensive description, of
the procedure followed by the Holy Office.

As for chapter I of the schema on the bishops, the cardinal was obliged to remind everyone that collegiality had not yet been defined; the
vote on it was "only a straw vote." It was the Doctrinal Commission,
elected by the fathers, that would decide. As for the vote, he himself
regretted that the questions had not first been submitted for study by the
Doctrinal Commission, which could have eliminated equivocal expressions. Finally, in his view, the collegiality of the apostles cannot be derived from the scriptures. Furthermore, he was surprised that all those who
were so insistent on collegiality should have deduced from it a lessening
(to say the least) of papal primacy. "Anyone desiring to be a sheep of
Christ must be shepherded by Peter, and it is not for the sheep to lead
Peter, but for Peter to govern the sheep."

The private diaries of several persons active at the Council reveal how
this "crossfire" between Frings and Ottaviani was viewed. Edelby's
journal allows us to understand better the attitude of this father and,
more broadly, of the Melkite group toward the Curia.[44] He describes
Frings's criticism of the Holy Office as "very strong and accurate;" the
applause following the discourse of the German father is said to have
been "frenzied;" Lercaro's address calling for a "council superior to the
Supreme Congregation of the Holy Office" is also regarded as "courageous." Edelby found Ottaviani's address "so harsh that even his parti-
sans did not dare applaud."[45] Clearly, Maximos IV's adviser belonged to
the conciliar majority.

Y. Congar's attitude is no less clear, even though he could offer only
a second-hand testimony and commentary because he had missed this
"great moment." In his opinion, Ottaviani, as a result of his anger, "is
rather discredited in the minds of many." Congar defends the moderators, at whom the secretary of the Holy Office had taken aim, by writing
that "they *too* are representatives of the pope (they had consulted him
three times before proposing the questions)." As far as the rest of the
general congregation was concerned, Congar appreciates Lercaro's
address because "he proposes things that are *possible* and yet go a long

---

[43] See Laurentin, 121; Rynne, 184.

[44] See *JEdelby*, 230.

[45] This last remark does not correspond fully to other testimonies, which speak of
applause from the seats of the Italian and curial group, at least at the beginning of Ottaviani's protest.

way." As for Msgr. Lefebvre's intervention, Congar very firmly takes the opposite theological and historical view (on the powers of the pope and those of the bishops).[46] Congar's thinking was already well known, of course, but here we see more clearly how this theologian responds concretely, one by one, to the addresses of the fathers in the hall, without either neglecting or being indulgent toward what was said there.

Thanks to C. Moeller, general impressions of the "row between Ottaviani and Frings and Ottaviani and the moderators" take on individual names and faces: it is Prignon who tells Moeller that "Ottaviani has hereby lost some of his prestige"; it is doubtless J. C. Murray who reports to Moeller what two bishops (perhaps Americans) said to him ("such a man *cannot* any longer be president of the theological commission"); further, it is the Belgian bishops (more especially Van Zuylen, Schoenmaeckers, and Daem) who express their indignation at Ottaviani's intervention in the hall, while Suenens "takes the matter more lightly" and asks the commission to continue its work.[47]

For his part, A. Prignon reports an alleged consequence of the incident on November 8, a rumor according to which Ottaviani, Antoniutti, and Siri "demanded a public apology in the hall for Frings's attack on the Curia; otherwise they would leave the Council." Here is an opportunity for the historian to see how someone involved at the time prudently assesses this rumor; Prignon writes: "I told the cardinal that there was probably an element of truth in this story, but it was possible that people had exaggerated what happened." We also learn of Suenens's spontaneous private reaction, which took the form of a very meaningful quip: "If they could go away, so much the better; things would go more easily."[48]

J. Dupont tells of the on-the-spot reaction of Dom Butler as he was leaving the Basilica: he was "shocked" by Ottaviani's answer, which, by identifying the pope and the Holy Office, made "the pope responsible for methods that are against the natural law." Dupont also gives his own impression of what he saw in St. Peter's Square: "Everyone seems very excited by the outbursts that occurred this morning."[49] In B. Olivier's comments one finds a general feeling: "Ottaviani's attack on the authority of the moderators was deeply resented by many of the fathers. They must respond if they do not want to see their authority held up to ridicule."[50]

[46] See *JCongar*, typescript, 1:361-63.

[47] Moeller Archive (CLG), C.00017, pp. 4-5.

[48] See Prignon Archive, no. 512 bis, pp. 7-8 (typscript).

[49] See the manuscript journal of Father Dupont, Dupont Archive, no. 1728 (November 1963), 118-19.

[50] See Olivier Archive (CLG), typescript, no. 169, 21.

Cardinal Frings's own memoirs speak of an angry and threatening address of Ottaviani against him; he denies having intended to attack the Roman cardinal or the pope; he also minimizes the disagreement by reporting what Ottaviani said to him the next day, after embracing him: "After all, we both want the same thing!"[51]

Whatever the judgments of individuals may have been, this confrontation of two cardinals at the top, while certainly dramatically played up by the media and the press because of its emotional overtones, was nonetheless illustrative, once again, of the serious difference between the majority and the minority on the subject of collegiality and of relations among bishops, pope, and the Roman congregations.[52] In the view of the majority, collegiality was, as it were, already defined, and its consequences had to be drawn regarding the participation of the bishops in the papal government of the universal Church.[53] In the view of the minority nothing had yet been settled, and therefore it was not possible to act as if collegiality had been already defined; it was even necessary to delay a definitive vote on the subject as long as possible and to take all the

---

[51] Frings, *Für die Menschen bestellt*, 274.

[52] Wenger wrote at the time: "We had the impression that a fissure had opened" (149). And here is how C. Moeller, an expert of the Doctrinal Commission, interpreted the events, this time in a letter to his mother on November 11 (Moeller Archive, no. 12888): "The struggle has resumed: Ottaviani refuses to take account of the votes on October 30. You already know from the newspapers of the commotion that took place last Friday between Frings and Ottaviani; what the press did not say so much about is that Ottaviani appeared, in the eyes of all, to be also attacking the moderators. He has thereby greatly diminished his credit. Everyone is speaking openly of the change needed in the commissions, which can no longer do their work properly, being paralyzed by the leadership; this is extremely catastrophic in our view. Otherwise, the work of the subcommissions is advancing rapidly; they will perhaps be able by the end of the session to present chapter I of the schema on the Church. Yesterday, after two hours of discussion, there was a vote in favor of the schema on religious freedom: 18 for, 5 against, 1 blank ballot. That is a struggle won: the schema can now go over to the Council. The subject is one of the most important. We expect to be done with the schema on the bishops Thursday or Friday, and move on then to the schema on ecumenism, of which the schema on religious freedom forms chapter V. In short, Ottaviani is defeated each time, but after a very hard and wearying battle."
Along the same line, in connection with Frings's address of November 8, it should be mentioned that, on that very evening, the pope asked him to draw up proposals for a reform of the Holy Office; on November 12, during a conversation with the cardinal and Ratzinger and Jedin, Onclin undertook the composition of a memorandum that Frings then submitted to Paul VI; see H. Jedin, *Lebensbericht* (Mainz: Grünewald, 1984), 212.

[53] Within the majority, some, like Maximos IV, were maximalists and called for an effective and deliberative involvement in the pope's decisions for the entire Church. Others were satisfied with a consultative participation or saw in collegiality not a real dogmatic question but a practical question concerning greater pastoral effectiveness. See J. Grootaers, "Een Sessie met gemengde gevoelens," *De Maand* 6 (1963), 596, col. 2.

time needed for studying the subject in order to eliminate any ambiguity that might seem to water down the supreme and absolute plenitude of the papal power of jurisdiction; only one thing was sure: it was on Peter alone that Christ founded his Church.

During the rest of the morning several advocates of this current of thought, "minimalist" in regard to collegiality, gave more or less direct support to the position of the secretary of the Holy Office. Curial Cardinal Browne warned that the right of the college to "co-govern" the entire Church along with the pope lessens the pontifical power of governing and contradicts the definition of the plenitude of power at Vatican I.[54] According to Msgr. de Castro Mayer, Bishop of Campos (Brazil), "the establishment of the college of bishops as subject of a full and supreme power to be exercised habitually over the entire Church does not seem to have been sufficiently demonstrated or sufficiently explored for it to be able to be the basis of a conciliar decree.[55] The intervention of Msgr. Lefebvre, Titular Archbishop of Synnada in Phrygia and Superior General of the Spiritans, provided a kind of synthesis of the minority thesis on relations among pope, Curia, and bishops: the full power of the pope should not be touched in any way, and his freedom to exercise this power should be completely safeguarded when it comes to choosing the members of the Roman dicasteries; harking back to Cardinal Browne, the French archbishop gave it as his judgment that the principle of juridical collegiality could not be proved; falling back on an emotional argument, he warned that the solemn affirmation of that principle would amount to acknowledging that the Church had been in error for many centuries; everyone accepts a moral collegiality, but this gives rise only to moral relations.[56]

D. THE "REASONED" ADDRESS OF A MODERATOR

We may here return to the important intervention of Cardinal Lercaro, one of the four moderators and doubtless the greatest moral and religious authority in the assembly.[57] It was one of the most critical moments in the

---

[54] *AS* II/4, 626-27.

[55] Ibid.

[56] *AS* II/4, 643-44.

[57] *AS* II/4, 618-21; for the original Italian text, see G. Lercaro, *Per la forza dello Spirito: Discorsi conciliari del card. Giacomo Lercaro* (Bologna 1984), 197-205. For a better understanding of the many-sided personality of the Archbishop of Bologna, see A. Alberigo, ed., *Giacomo Lercaro. Vescovo dell chiesa di Dio (1891-1976)*, Testi e ricerche di Scienze religiose 6 (Genoa 1991); *Protagonisti*, 451-59.

whole Council. The opposition between conciliar majority and minority was troubling and seemed to be endangering the normal course of the Council. Two days earlier Cardinal Browne had said that the position taken by the Council on the five questions was subject to study by the Doctrinal Commission, thus continuing the earlier opposition to that vote and indirectly challenging once again the authority of the moderators, to say nothing of the authority of the Council itself. At that very time Frings had given a firm response, to which Ottaviani had quickly and vigorously replied. A number of fathers had called for the reform of the Curia and the creation of a central organ of episcopal collegiality to help the pope in his government of the Church, but they had perhaps given the impression that they wanted to limit the papal primacy.

In this setting, so tricky and so dangerous for the proper execution of the Council's work, the Archbishop of Bologna, "a modest and reserved, but also a determined and shrewd man,"[58] would endeavor to ease minds and balance somewhat the various points of view. To this end, he reminded his hearers that "all of us can without hesitation agree" on certain points: the Roman pontiff has supreme and full jurisdiction; he can exercise this jurisdiction independently of the body of bishops; he can use the help of executive bodies he has freely chosen; the body of bishops in union with the pope has a full and supreme (therefore not delegated) authority over the universal Church, but only in ways ordained by the pope; nothing prevents the pope from making the exercise of this power of the episcopal body more frequent and more habitual, at least through the mediation of a new body that faithfully represents the body of bishops. The final decision on the opportuneness of such an institution must belong to the pope; even after its establishment, he must remain free to follow some other procedure; but if this institution is not in fact intended as the habitual way of dealing with and settling major matters, it seems suitable and advisable not to introduce it at all.

Such a body assisting the pope in his government of the universal Church is lacking today. In order to ensure a regular participation of the bishops in the care of the entire Church, it is not enough to internationalize the Curia or to establish a new congregation "more supreme than the supreme Congregation of the Holy Office." The various problems involved in the renewal of the Curia are so closely interconnected that they are beyond the scope of the decree on bishops, but also, to a certain

---

[58] Congar, *Le Concile au jour le jour*, 2:134.

degree, beyond the competence of the Council. The question so directly touches on the personal competence of the pope that the fathers could not have discussed it if the sovereign pontiff had not in a way entrusted it to the Council, as if to learn how it was leaning.

The cardinal therefore suggested removing from the decree everything having to do with the participation of the bishops in the government of the universal Church; instead of a normative text on that subject, the fathers should prepare a message that in response to the wish of the pope, would present "some desires of the Council regarding the general renewal of the offices of the Roman Curia and the appropriate participation of the bishops in the supreme government of the Church." Because such wishes touched on "centuries-old questions of the highest importance," they could emerge only after adequate study and careful development by a special conciliar commission to be appointed before the end of the second period. It should be noted that the expression by the Council of "some wishes" regarding the association of the episcopate in the government of the universal Church was entirely in keeping with the address of Paul VI on the preceding September 21.[59]

At the time, many thought that Lercaro's attempt at clarification represented the thinking and wishes of the pope;[60] "it was so nuanced that some claimed it was inspired by the pope himself."[61] In fact, the address seems to have been decided on by agreement of the four moderators with Paul VI the previous evening (November 7).[62] But the proposed commission was never established;[63] the pope chose instead to

[59] See *Insegnamenti*, 1:150 in particular.

[60] See Congar, *Le Concile au jour le jour*, 134.

[61] Wenger, 145. J. Dupont likewise wrote as he looked back on the second period "[The] intervention of Cardinal Lercaro, which gave rise to numerous commentaries,...captured attention because in the manner of its presentation it seemed hardly in keeping with some ideas of Cardinal Lercaro. Many saw it as an address written to order, in which the cardinal was simply passing on the thinking of the pope" (Dupont Archive, no. 1759, 4b verso).

[62] See *Lettere*, 208 and 212 n.5.

[63] The proposal, which Lercaro would mention again in a letter of November 11, 1963 (see *Lettere*, 217), was also repeated in the next intervention, that of Cardinal Rugambwa, speaking in the name of the episcopates of Africa and Madagascar (*AS* II/4, 621-23; see the draft in *Per la forza*, 331-36), by the Venezuelan episcopate (ibid., 702-3), and in a written observation of some French bishops (ibid., 547-48). On November 13, at the Pan-African meeting of the presidents of the episcopal conferences of Africa and Madagascar, the sending of two letters to the moderators was on the agenda. The first was about "preparing for the appointment of the future commission which, according to the addresses of Cardinal Rugambwa and Lercaro, would bring together persons capable of helping the Holy Father in the establishment of the body which the pope himself wants for the sake of a better government of the universal Church"; the second was "to ask

ask Cardinal Marella to draw up in haste the draft of the Motu Proprio that, in September 1965, established the Synod of Bishops, a body far removed from the one proposed by the Cardinal of Bologna and from the expectations of the conciliar majority.[64]

In this famous compromise statement of November 8 the Archbishop of Bologna adopted a realistic outlook, whereas usually he made no concessions but defended positions of principle; here the question was to reach an agreement with Paul VI himself and to dispel his uneasiness, which had increased since the beginning of the discussion of the schema on the bishops. Therefore Lercaro did not hesitate to call to mind the papal prerogatives, using the language of Vatican I, and to maintain, to the surprise of the conciliar majority, that the assembly should limit itself to formulating proposals for the pope; according to Lercaro it was necessary at once to avoid any tension between the competencies of the pope and of the Council and to avoid a complete exclusion of the Council from the desired reform of the central organs of the Church.[65]

This 63rd general congregation was undoubtedly the most difficult one, and one of the most important during the Council.[66] The repercussions of the duel between Frings and Ottaviani (or Council and Doctrinal Commission, the latter still controlled by the conservative group) would be felt at the end of November, when Paul VI announced the inclusion of new members in the conciliar commissions in order to make them more representative. Furthermore, in addition to the concern voiced in the hall by the cardinal of Cologne, a memorandum on the conciliar commissions, addressed to the pope personally, immediately after November 8, attacked quite straightforwardly the attitude of the president of the Doctrinal Commission: he was working directly against the commission of which he was president; according to him, the Doctrinal Commission was above the Council

what follow-up might be expected on the letter written several weeks ago with a view to a better organization of the Council's work and especially of the commissions" (the letter in question was perhaps anticipatory, but in any case it shared a concern common to a number of episcopates; see below, note 68). The same meeting of the "Pan-Af" also discussed texts "offered, for the possible signatures of bishops, on the future constitution of the pope's senate and on the reform of the Curia" and which "come from the Chilean group" (see note 67, below); see the report of this meeting, in Olivier Archive, no. 159, 1 and 3.

[64] On the address of November 8 see *Protagonisti*, 456-59; on its exact meaning, see *Per la forza*, 197-205.

[65] See G. Alberigo, "L'evento conciliare," in Alberigo, *Giacomo Lercaro*, 126-27.

[66] Laurentin, 132; *Protagonisti*, 478.

itself. The document concluded that the president of the Doctrinal Commission was no longer qualified to preside over a commission on which the success or failure of the Council so greatly depended, for the Doctrinal Commission should be an expression of the Council and not of a single individual.[67] Such a conclusion fully reflected the seriousness of a situation that not only might paralyze the Council but challenged its very reason for being.[68]

III. SHOULD A BISHOP RECEIVE AN ASSISTANT OR RESIGN AT A CERTAIN AGE?

Before the end of the 63rd general congregation, the assembly moved on to the examination of chapter III of the schema on bishops. After Msgr. Carli's report there were interventions by Cardinal Ruffini and Archbishop Garibi y Rivera of Guadalajara, Mexico. Another thirty-one fathers would speak on this chapter on November 11, 12, and 13.

A. BISHOP CARLI'S REPORT

The reporter described the eleven articles of this chapter (nos. 6-16) that dealt with coadjutor bishops and auxiliary bishops; both of them might be given to a residential bishop, the former with right of succession,

---

[67] See Philips Archive (CCV) P.049.01. This anonymous memorandum in French, of Chilean origin (perhaps by J. Medina Estevez whose name is handwritten on a Latin document along the same lines: no. 545 of the Prignon Archive), can be dated between November 10 and 15; in all likelihood it was a bit earlier than the redaction of the petition addressed to the pope during the second half of November. In this petition Cardinal Silva Henriquez of Santiago de Chile took the initiative; he was, it appears, backed by the signatures of 500 bishops; see J. Grootaers, "Une forme de concertation épiscopale au concile Vatican II: la 'Conférence des Vingt-deux' (1962-1963)," *RHE* 91 (1996), 66- 111, especially 89). Note that the same outlook in the letter of Ch. Moeller to his mother, November 11, 1963, which says that the view seemed to be widespread at the Council (see above, note 52). See also the earlier *desiderata* of the commission of representatives of the episcopal conferences (meeting of October 1963 at the Domus Mariae) that were sent by Msgr. Veuillot to Msgr. Dell'Acqua on October 28 (Lercaro Archive, no. 23, 1963; and *Per la Forza*, 273-75 n.6; Archive of the "Conférence des Vingt-deux," II 6 and 7 A-C). See Grootaers, "Une forme de concertation," 89-90 and 107: the existence of this confidential episcopal memorandum began to be known to the general public on November 8; it was mentioned by Desmond Fisher in the weekly *Catholic Herald* for November 8, 1963.

[68] See *Protagonisti*, 478-79.

the latter without it. Their juridical status was specified, as well as their faculties and their relations with the residential bishop. The final article had to do with the voluntary resignation of the residential bishop.

The Bishop of Segni described the difficulties raised on this last point and the answers given in the preparatory commission: (a) according to tradition, a bishop is, as it were, married to his diocese until his death; but this comparison should not be forced, and in the course of time this irremovability had undergone a major development; (b) in case of his resignation, a bishop should not be put on the same level as a civil official; the latter claims retirement as a right for his own benefit, but a bishop, on the contrary, must think of it as a meritorious sacrifice for the good of souls; (c) it is enough that in particular cases the Apostolic See either urge resignation or appoint a coadjutor or an auxiliary; but experience tells of the difficulty of securing a spontaneous resignation, while the appointment of a coadjutor or an auxiliary raises new problems; (d) the choice of age sixty-five is arbitrary, but at a certain age many bishops can no longer govern their dioceses, and it is appropriate that a legal directive offer them an honorable reason to retire. However, after several interventions by higher commissions, the juridical clause was softened and took the form of an urgent invitation, as in the present text.[69]

B. Ruffini against Maximos IV?

The address given late in the morning of this November 8 by the Archbishop of Palermo, Cardinal Ruffini, caused a stir. This was not so much due to his insistence on the unity of government in a diocese and the problematic coexistence of two pastors, one the residential bishop, the other a coadjutor; it was not due to his opposition to voluntary resignation by reason or age or health; nor finally was it due to his criticism of putting on the same footing (something he thought promoted division) the Apostolic See and the competent authority in the East (in connection with the distinction between the Latin Church and the churches of the Oriental rites). The stir was due particularly to his mention of the "bitter and distressing speech" recently directed against the Roman Curia and the Latin Church, but happily atoned for by some fathers, primarily His Beatitude Ignace Pierre XVI Batanian, "formerly

---

[69] See *AS* II/4, 647-50.

my very dear student and now the honor of the Church, whom I thank also in the name of His Eminence Cardinal Siri, President of the Italian Episcopal Conference."[70]

Many saw this as a hardly veiled allusion to the intervention by Maximos IV on November 6. This certainly is how the latter, absent that day from the hall, took the remarks. On this very day Maximos sent a telegram to the Council of Presidents and the moderators, protesting the words of Ruffini, who he said was "using the council hall to attack anyone not sharing his views" and also expressing astonishment at the silence of Cardinal Agagianian, moderator of the meeting; he also expected some reparation. Made aware of the situation, Ruffini immediately wrote to Maximos, regretting the latter's absence and protesting his respect for the Oriental Churches. The Patriarch, however, did not accept the cardinal's right to praise Ignace Pierre XVI Batanian publicly for having been his student, as if this were a stamp of good theology in comparison with others.[71]

[70] *AS* II/4, 651-53. Does the surprising reference to the president of the Italian Episcopal Conference implicitly point to a shared conviction that the Curia was de facto an exclusively Italian firm? See Rynne, 186. More broadly, the reference to Siri points to an understanding between him and Ruffini; see B. Lai, *Il Papa non eletto. Giuseppe Siri, cardinale di Santa Romana Ecclesia* (Rome-Bari: Laterza, 1993), 212-13. Lai also cites a letter of November 8, 1963, from Siri to Ottaviani (Siri Archives, Archbishopric of Genoa), in which he assures the latter of his solidarity and opines that Frings's attack had gone beyond what he intended.

[71] See Wenger, 153-54 (private remark of Maximos IV, November 12, 1963); Rynne, 185-86. Msgr. Edelby did not fail to remark on Ruffini's address: it was "rather conservative in tone" and made an "allusion to the address of our Patriarch" (it spoke of "a certain father who, two days ago, attacked the Latin Church"). Ruffini "heaps praise on 'His Beatitude Patriarch Batanian....Let him please accept my thanks for his fine words, in my name and in the name of Cardinal Siri.'" Here, according to Edelby, "the game was shown for what it was: Batanian's address was delivered with the agreement of Cardinals Ruffini and Siri. Moreover, Batanian was discredited not only for having lent himself to their machinations but for having linked his own thinking henceforth with the most reactionary elements of the Council." As a result of this "unveiled" attack on the Patriarch, says the Archbishop of Edessa, a telegram of protest had been sent that very day to the cardinal-presidents, the cardinal moderators, the Cardinal Secretary of State, and the secretariat of the Council ("to be kept among the Acts of the Council," he notes). He then cites the text of the telegram asking for reparation, signed by the Patriarch and the other Melkite fathers (*JEdelby*, 162-63). Two later reactions should be mentioned: an exculpatory letter from Ruffini, saying that "he had by no means intended to offend (Maximos IV)"; and a less known but perhaps more surprising response from Tisserant, giving it as his opinion "that if Cardinal Ruffini ought to have been stopped, the diatribe of the Patriarch on the previous day should have been stopped."

C. A "SELF-INTERESTED" DEBATE?

Two days before the conciliar assembly met again on November 11, the moderators had met to make some important decisions and, in particular, to get the Council out of its present impasse.[72] Furthermore, the homily the pope preached on Sunday, November 10, on the occasion of "taking possession" of his cathedral, the Lateran Basilica, certainly did not point in the direction of an "extreme papalism," which might have appeared to support Ottaviani; quite the contrary.[73] On the morning of this November 11, when the discussion of coadjutor and auxiliary bishops resumed, it was not sure that the conciliar "storm" had died down; everyone was still thinking of the "historic" and lively meeting of the previous Friday.

Chapter II of the schema on the bishops dealt with particular problems that, because they closely affected the members of the assembly, gave rise to a sustained interest. Many bishops had themselves begun by being auxiliary or coadjutor bishops, and all saw the day coming when age or illness would raise the question of a collaborator or of possible resignation. The debate on this twofold remedy for aging bishops was "at times marked by a remarkable frankness and a slightly macabre humor"[74] and would often display "a personal or self-interested aspect,"[75] as elderly bishops appealed to more or less theological arguments against an age limit, while the coadjutor and auxiliary bishops were almost unanimous in complaining about their lot.

Positions on the coadjutors varied: some wanted them given more powers so that they could act;[76] others, on the contrary, were afraid of a "diarchy" or "bicephalous regime" that would be harmful to the head of the diocese;[77] still others advocated a radical solution, to do away with coadjutors.[78]

---

[72] "First the 'Synoptics'" (Döpfner, Lercaro, and Suenens), without Agagianian, a member of the Curia, "and then all the moderators with the secretariat," says Lercaro (*Lettere*, 214); on the "official" meeting (of the four moderators with Felici, Villot, Fagiolo, and Carbone), see *AS* V/3, 700-710.

[73] Rynne, 189-90. For the complete text of the homily see *OssRom*, November 11-12, 1963, 1-2 (in the homily the pope stressed his own littleness and claimed no merit "except the indisputable one of having been canonically elected Bishop of Rome").

[74] Laurentin, 135.

[75] Wenger, 157.

[76] *AS* II/4, 709-10 (C. Confalonieri); II/5, 10-12 (L. Suenens), 20-21 (F. Zak).

[77] *AS* II/4, 651-53 (E. Ruffini), 744-46 (E. Gavazzi); II/5, 27-28 (T. Cahill).

[78] *AS* II/4, 724-28 (A. Añoveros Ataún); II/5, 14-20 (J. Hervás y Benet).

It became apparent that, with regard to resignation at a fixed age, a majority favored the innovation planned in the schema, although a number of fathers were formally opposed to an obligatory resignation.[79] This age limit found an especially effective defender in Suenens in his intervention on November 12.[80] In the beginning, said this moderator, almost all the members of the preparatory commission had been opposed to an order of this kind, but at the end of the discussion by far the greater number of the bishops were in favor of it. While the question might touch on the theology of the episcopate, it was necessary to avoid unilaterally invoking certain principles (fatherhood is perpetual; indissolubility of the marriage between a bishop and his people).

The real question, in Suenens's view, was: What does the salvation of souls require here? From this point of view some regulation seemed necessary, because the increased pastoral responsibility of today's bishop requires a greater aptitude as well. The accelerated social evolution of the modern world, he went on, also demands a youthfulness of mind and body, to say nothing of the example a bishop ought to give to the aging pastor whose resignation he requests for the good of the parish; in the same way, bishops would give the faithful a sign of their own sincere desire of the pastoral renewal willed by the Council. Suenens ended by saying that even if the Council did not come to the point of making a bishop's retirement obligatory at the age of sixty-five, a coadjutor should always be given him at that age, with the coadjutor gradually taking the single government of the entire diocese into his hands.

Many other problems were likewise touched on in the course of this debate: the juridical fiction of sees given to titular bishops; the "honorary" episcopate; the status of auxiliary bishops; the means of ensuring bishops a decent retirement. In his intervention on November 11 Msgr. Caillot, coadjutor of Evreux (France), urged doing away with the practice of making nonresidential bishops titulars of ancient churches that no longer exist: theologically, episcopal ordination is enough for full incorporation into the episcopal college; pastorally, such a bishop's title should at least match the diocese in which he is actually exercising his pastoral responsibilities; from the ecumenical point of view, it seems

[79] Among the opponents of the measure: *AS* II/4, 651-53 (E. Ruffini), 653-54 (J. Garibi y Rivera), 717-19 (M. Gonzi), 721-23 (A. de Vito), 728-32 (E. Nowicki), 736-38 (B. Reetz), 742-44 (C. Saboia Bandeira de Mello); II/5, 27-28 (T. Cahill), 28-32 (J. Slipyj).

[80] *AS* II/5, 10-12. On the influence exerted on the Council by the Primate of Belgium see *Protagonisti*, 494-504.

strange to link Latin-rite bishops with the names of former sees in the East.[81] Along the same line, on November 12 Msgr. Zak, Bishop of Sankt Pölten (Austria), made his own the desire expressed by the coadjutor of Evreux; in his written text he specified that the episcopate can never be conferred simply as an honorific, since the evangelization of the entire world is at stake; for this reason, one could also ask whether the episcopate is compatible with the carrying out of purely administrative tasks.[82] Many fathers also asked for a reduction in the number of auxiliary and especially of titular bishops.[83]

The testimony of Msgr. Le Cordier, an auxiliary of Paris, captured attention by its originality. He was in fact a "resident" (*residens*) auxiliary. This experiment in a vast urban area had been going on for seven years in the Diocese of Paris; the auxiliary bishops had a "fixed domicile" in the suburbs of Paris and had received "all the faculties necessary and appropriate for governing the people living in that part of the diocese." The experiment had been undertaken for two reasons: to ensure the closeness of the bishops to the Christian people and for unity of pastoral action or evangelization. Against this background Le Cordier asked for the development of a "new juridical kind" of bishop alongside the "simple auxiliary."[84]

Msgr. Reuss, auxiliary of Mainz, called for some revaluation of auxiliary bishops. The "status of the auxiliary" should be defined primarily in light of the divine institution of the episcopate, and his faculties should be determined much less in the light of juridical or administrative considerations. All bishops, by reason of the same episcopal consecration, become members of the college of bishops and share in the same "responsibilities and powers, at least those that are fundamental." It was therefore fitting that ecclesiastical law covering auxiliaries be more adapted to divine law: an auxiliary should always be assigned to a see and not to a person; he should also be the vicar of the residential bishop when the latter is hindered or absent; an auxiliary should be directly subject to the residential bishop and not to the vicar general; finally, an auxiliary should always possess the ordinary power that is due him and suitable for him.[85] Other fathers likewise expressed the wish that a

---

[81] *AS* II/4, 738-40.
[82] *AS* II/5, 20-21.
[83] *AS* II/4, 711-15 (J. Döpfner); II/5, 22-24 (H. Volk); 24-25 (R. Tchidimbo), 60-61 (J. Busimba).
[84] *AS* II/5, 25-26.
[85] *AS* II/5, 32-34.

bishop give his auxiliary appropriate faculties for the entire diocese, so that the latter may effectively carry out his pastoral responsibilities there.[86]

On the subject of a decent retirement, Cardinal Cento proposed the creation of an episcopal solidarity fund for bishops who have resigned.[87] Msgr. A. Fernandes, coadjutor of Delhi (India), suggested in addition the establishment of houses to which bishops might retire and "in which appropriate care might be provided for their bodily needs and their souls' salvation."[88]

D. AN AUTHORITATIVE REPLY TO THE ATTACKS OF THE MINORITY

Before we leave the debate on chapter II, it will be profitable to turn back to the address of Cardinal Döpfner, Archbishop of Munich and Freising and one of the four moderators,[89] in order to appreciate the atmosphere that still prevailed on this November 11, two weeks after the vote on the five questions and three days after the incidents described earlier. In his intervention Döpfner called for a better understanding of the dignity of auxiliary bishops by reason of the sacramentality of episcopal ordination and of their resultant regular membership in the college of bishops; he also called for a reduction in their number of the name of diocesan unity, which has its basis solely in the residential bishop.

Döpfner also thought it appropriate to make some parenthetical remarks on the straw vote of October 30; this meant that in his view and that of his fellow moderators the question did not yet seem settled. For, "during these recent days the impression has perhaps been given in the council hall that while the Holy Spirit was busy elsewhere, an enemy had sown in the field of the Council these votes on questions proposed by the moderators and on the responses of the fathers." The moderator tried to show what had really happened: it was the competent body of the Council, namely the moderators, who according to the conciliar regulations were directors of the Council's work, who after lengthy reflection had proposed the questions to the fathers. The terms of the

---

[86] *AS* II/4, 733-34 (J. Pohlschneider); II/5, 20-21 (F. Zak).
[87] *AS* II/4, 710-11.
[88] *AS* II/5, 58-60.
[89] For a portrait of the Cardinal of Munich, see *Protagonisti*, 418-25.

questions, it was to be noted, had been taken either verbatim or at least according to sense from the schema offered by the competent commission (the concept of "apostolic college," for example, had not been introduced "by stealth" into the questions but was to be found at several places in the schema). While not definitive, the vote nonetheless did point the way to the commission whose task, in the service of the general congregation, was to organize, coordinate, and evaluate the amendments. The cardinal also wanted to reassure the fathers regarding trends at the Council. The vote had been provisional, in the sense of "looking ahead" (*providendi*). "Let us not obscure what is already sufficiently clear."[90]

Three days after the crisis on November 8, then, and two days after a meeting of the pope and the moderators, the confrontation between majority and minority could not be left unresolved after the strong counteroffensive of the minority; the future of the Council was at stake. For this reason, right at the beginning of the next general congregation, Döpfner judged it necessary to give this authoritative and very plain clarification. He was not wrong about its urgency. Two days later Ottaviani was to give an interview against the votes of October 30[91] and Carli would criticize them in the hall.[92] The minority was not yet ready to lay down its arms.

IV. EPISCOPAL ASSEMBLIES WITHOUT JURIDICAL POWERS?

Before taking up the Council's discussion of episcopal assemblies, we must recall that during the intersession, and even during the first period, bishops had learned to work together as national conferences and the latter to collaborate among themselves. The actual experience of episcopal conferences thus preceded and accompanied the debate over them.[93]

---

[90] *AS* II/4, 711-15.

[91] Interview on Wednesday, November 13, to the *Divine Word News Service* (see Rynne, 198- 99); it is also worth noting that on the very evening of Döpfner's statement Ottaviani expressed his uneasiness to R. Wiltgen: "I have just come from a meeting of the Theological Commission and things look very bad; the French and the Germans have united everyone against us" (Wiltgen, 118).

[92] *AS* II/5, 72-75.

[93] One will think especially of the group of twenty-two representatives of episcopal conferences. See J. Brouwers, "Vatican II, derniers préparatifs et première session: Activités conciliaires en coulisses," in *Vatican II commence*, 365-68; J. Grootaers, "Une forme de concertation épiscopale" (note 68, above); P. Noël, "Les regroupements de Conférences épiscopales durant le Concile. Le groupe de la *Domus Mariae*," in *Evento*, 95-133.

By a vote of 2025 for and 141 against, it was decided on November 12 to end the discussion of chapter I and to move on immediately to a study of chapter III.[94] The discussion of this chapter was to last from November 12 to November 15 and was to elicit thirty-two oral interventions.

A. A "PURELY PASTORAL" BASIS?

Carli began his report with the juridical novelty of what was being proposed by this chapter: the national assembly or conference of bishops; this made it necessary to provide at least in outline their juridical character which was described in the nine articles of the chapter (nos. 17-27). The introduction (17) stated the "essentially pastoral" origin of the new institution: modern times require, for the good of souls and no longer simply for the good of the state, that the bishops, at least those of a single nation, have some way of taking common action in the carrying out of their pastoral responsibility. The obligation of setting up national conferences was thus established (18 §1); the possibility of setting up international conferences was also foreseen (18 §3). Very little was decided, however, about the "direction" of a conference: each national conference could develop its particular statutes, adapted to its own situation, with the approval of the Holy See. Juridical inclusion in the national conference, by a deliberative vote, was granted to all local ordinaries, of whatever rite, vicars general being excluded but coadjutors being included because of their right of succession (19 §1).

According to Msgr. Carli, the third part of the chapter, which had to do with the decisions of the conference (22-24), was very important. In this area the commission had followed three principles: (a) a national conference is not the same as a plenary or provincial council and does not make the latter useless; quite the contrary; (b) a residential bishop possesses a real, ordinary, and immediate authority over his faithful; this authority is, by divine law, subordinate only to that of the pope (22); (c) however, the common good of the souls of a nation, which redounds ultimately to the good of each diocese, requires a unity of pastoral action among all the bishops of the nation. In almost all areas this requirement is only moral, with each bishop remaining free to act according to his conscience for reasons whose seriousness he must weigh in the presence of God (22-23).

[94] *AS* II/5, 34.

But it seemed to the commission that in some carefully defined areas (24) a purely moral obligation was not enough and that a juridical obligation needed to be imposed by reason both of the seriousness of these matters and of the harmful consequences caused by bishops acting in opposed way. In such cases the monarchical power of the bishops was nevertheless protected by the following, proportionately serious provisions: (a) the list of cases (infrequent by their nature) is strict and complete: major statements, relations with the state, serious matters; (b) the decisions of the conference require at least a two-thirds majority; (c) they must be confirmed (*recognosci*) by the Holy See; (d) finally, each bishop has the right to appeal to the Holy See, but only "as a last resort" in order not to empty the statute of its substance. Thus this statute was less reductive of the ordinary power of each bishop than were the statutes of plenary or provincial councils.[95]

This report made quite clear the two key questions raised by the chapter: whether the foundation of episcopal conferences was theological or "purely pastoral," and, correlatively, whether their decisions were juridically or morally binding. The report also betrayed the rather restrictive or minimalist positions of the commission (at least of those members who had met during the intersession to rework the text). This "rump commission" clearly opted for a nontheological, "purely pastoral" basis for the new institution; so too, the requirement that each bishop accept the pastoral decisions of the conference was purely moral; and, as Carli was careful to emphasize, even in the very limited instances in which decisions were juridically binding on all the bishops, the monarchical power of each bishop was protected to the maximum (obligatory confirmation by the Holy See, and possible recourse to the Holy See in case of disagreement with the conference).

B. DIVISION WITHIN THE MAJORITY

The subject was an important one, because the episcopal conferences would be responsible for the implementation of the conciliar decrees and for taking account of regional differences in the implementation. The question most discussed during the debate was precisely the legislative power of the conferences. Was this authority to be strengthened by making obligatory all decisions taken by a two-thirds majority? Or was

[95] *AS* II/5, 35-36.

this authority on the contrary to be lessened by restricting the cases, by requiring an even greater majority, or even by excluding all legislative power? The majority, which had thus far agreed on collegiality despite the very aggressive minority, now found itself divided on the basis for conferences and especially on their authority.

If we may believe Msgr. A. Bontems, the French were generally in favor of a strict legislative power for territorial assemblies of bishops.[96] But it is to be noted that the only Frenchmen who intervened orally in the hall, while they linked episcopal conferences to collegiality or the universal mission, did not formally come out in favor of a "strict juridical power" for the conferences and, instead, made the point that the latter could not be defined solely in juridical terms[97] and even that it would necessary to be on guard not to multiply juridically binding decisions.[98]

The German Episcopate, for its part, at least if it was well represented by its sole intervention, that of Cardinal Frings,[99] was not very much in favor of juridical decisions by episcopal conferences. The Archbishop of Cologne spoke from the long experience of the German national conference since 1847: its decisions did not have juridical force, and each bishop governed his diocese according to his own conscience and the norms of law; the conference had only a president and a secretary who composed the minutes. This rather free manner of operating had not

---

[96] "We French would have liked to see an affirmation of the authority of the conferences, that is, the obligatory force of their decisions when these are taken by a sufficient majority. We feel this to be necessary pastorally. That is why you could see six French bishops intervening on the same day and taking the same line. We regretted, however, not finding at our side those who a year ago were walking with us, especially the German episcopate. This is understandable: different countries, different points of view, different reactions" (Msgr. Bontems, in *Bulletin religieuse du diocèse de Tarentaise*, December 1, 1963, cited in *DC* [December 5, 1963], col. 1671 n.4).

[97] *AS* II/5, 75-78 (A. Ancel), 80-82 (E. Guerry), 90-92 (G. Riobé), 231-33 (J. Lefebvre: "collegiality" cannot be a univocal term). A Peruvian bishop, J. Dammert Bellido, also spoke in favor of a theological basis for conferences, defining these as a "communion of local Churches" (*communio Ecclesiarum localium*) (*AS* II/5, 82-85).

[98] *AS* II/5, 75-78 (A. Ancel).

[99] *AS* II/5, 66-69. It is doubtful, in fact, whether his position was representative of the German Episcopate. In a report of A. Prignon that was made at the same time as the events (the tape to which the Belgian expert confided his daily recollections could not always be understood by his typist), we read the following: "On the subject of episcopal conferences Döpfner was not in agreement with Frings; he took the view that Frings's intervention in the hall that day or the day before had been due chiefly to the fact that Frings was all-powerful in Germany and that he was head of the episcopal conference and had no intention of seeing a change in the system, because that would lessen his prerogatives, his authority, or whatever. In any case, Döpfner thought that Frings's intervention was, unconsciously, due more to personal reasons than to a thorough study of the question" (Prignon Archive, no. 512bis; typewritten report on events beginning on October 27, 10-11).

prevented the conference from performing important "humanitarian" and missionary works. The important thing was not to have written statutes but "the spirit of freedom, voluntariness, and fraternal charity." Expressing his agreement with what had been said by Cardinal Spellman, who had spoken just before him on November 13, Frings stated his desire that binding decisions be reduced to a minimum.[100]

The Americans, for their part, were divided. With emphases that differed, Cardinals McIntyre, Meyer, and especially Spellman were opposed to legislative powers for the conferences,[101] but Cardinal Ritter was clearly in favor of them: such conferences "will be a strong force promoting decentralization."[102]

In fact, the juridical powers of episcopal conferences were caught between two fires: the "centralizing" and the "individualist" tendencies, although the two were perhaps less opposed than they seemed to be. The advocates of centralization were afraid that national or regional — or even international — legislation would thwart what they regarded as the sole source of law: the pope and, more broadly, the Roman dicasteries. Others, at the local level, were afraid of no longer being masters in their

---

[100] The applause that punctuated this address was doubtless for the Fulda conference's generosity in money and men, rather than for Frings's restrictive view of the powers of episcopal conferences, and perhaps even more for Frings personally because of his courageous intervention on November 8 and the insulting remarks he had thereby elicited and for which he did not seek an apology. See Laurentin, 290.

[101] McIntyre saw in these powers an attack on the government of the Curia (AS II/5, 37-38); Meyer, in the name of over 120 United States bishops, feared "undue interference in the government of a diocese that has been entrusted to a residential bishop" and "a new, overly broad and complicated centralization" (ibid., 41-43); Spellman opposed a binding juridical power for conferences in the name of the complete freedom each bishop ought to have in governing his own diocese (ibid., 65-66). For others who opposed such powers, see AS II/5, 38-40 (V. Gracias), 45-48 (J. Landázuri Ricketts, who wanted a four-fifths majority for the very rare binding decisions), 69-70 (M. Olaechea Loizaga), 78-80 (A. Pildáin y Zapiáin), 87-90 (L. Alonso Muñoyerro), 92-94 (L. Bianchi), 209-10 (A. Santin). Cardinal Siri, in the name of the "almost unanimous" Italian Episcopal Conference, opposed introducing too many details regarding the structure of a conference and the value of its decisions: bishops should retain their legitimate freedom; and conferences are based on purely ecclesiastical law (ibid., 193). Cardinal Wyszynski was in favor of a moral rather than juridical obligation for decisions of the conferences (ibid., 193-95). F. Franić was opposed to an excessive broadening of the powers of conferences (ibid., 203-6),

[102] AS II/5, 44-45. Others likewise spoke in favor of such powers: 48-53 (M. Klepacz asked for a clearer determination of cases of obligation), 195-97 (B. Alfrink, who saw the conferences as bringing a degree of centralization that was desirable for pastoral practice; he also answered Carli that the fathers did not want a juridical definition of the word "college" but a decision on the power which all the bishops, including the pope, had over the Church), 200-2 (J. Gardner), 236-37 (E. Zoghby), 237-38 (M. Ntuyahaga, who wanted such juridical power for the sake of a real decentralization in matters liturgical and in impediments to marriage).

own houses and of seeing their monarchical power being eaten away by a bureaucracy or a dominating national collectivist spirit.

Looking through the gamut of interventions we see also a warning against describing conferences as national, and this for various reasons: "individualist" (freedom of each bishop), "regionalist" (within a country), "antinationalist" or even "universalist" (papal point of view, regard for the entire Church).[103] Taking the nation as the standard ran the danger of politicization and suppression of infranational differences; it was also urgently important to surmount "the isolation rising from national particularisms" and to reach a supranational level.[104]

Other addresses were notable for calling attention to the operation of the Oriental Catholic Churches. French Bishop G. Amadouni (titular bishop of Amathusius in Cyprus) pointed out a fundamental disparity between episcopal conferences and patriarchates (the latter have a permanent synod with a supraepiscopal jurisdiction defined by law), and he regarded the concept of particular Churches as indispensable for understanding the mystery of ecclesial communion.[105] Msgr. Coderre, Bishop of S. Jean de Québec (Canada), speaking in the name of forty-five Canadian colleagues, regretted that the schema did not bring out with sufficient clarity the administrative structure of the Oriental Churches but represented a one-sidedly Latin viewpoint, as if the Oriental Churches did not have a completely rightful place within the universal Church.[106]

Finally, Msgr. Zoghby, Patriarchal Vicar of the Melkites of Egypt, placed his very clear and courageous intervention under the sign of ecumenism. If Vatican Council II wanted to advance the ecumenical dialogue with the Orthodox, it could only set up for itself a synodal system, that is, episcopal conferences having a true juridical authority. In the Catholic Church of the Oriental rite, he said, the synods or episcopal conferences have been stripped of all real power of jurisdiction by the Congregation for the Oriental Churches. If the episcopate does not have a collective authority, it certainly cannot organize the lay apostolate at either the national or the world level. Nor should there any longer be a fear that "nationalism" will take over the episcopal conference, for nowadays nationalism is rather a source of enrichment for the whole of human society.[107]

---

[103] *AS* II/5, 69-70 (M. Olaechea Loizaga). 78-80 (A. Pildáin y Zapiáin), 198-99 (E. Peiris), 203-6 (F. Franić), 206-8 (B. Reetz).

[104] Laurentin, 140-41.

[105] *AS* II/5, 85-87.

[106] *AS* II/5, 197-98

[107] *AS* II/5, 236-37.

C. A New Attack on Collegiality

Special mention must be made of the November 13 intervention of the Bishop of Segni,[108] who was speaking, he claimed, in the name of thirty bishops of various countries whose signatures appeared on the list.[109] Carli wished first to justify his election as official reporter of the commission: he had been legitimately appointed by the conciliar Commission for Bishops by more than two-thirds of the secret ballots; he had explained to the Commission, in a general way, in what "spirit" he intended to explain the schema in the hall, and no one had objected. In his opinion, then, Article 65 §5 of the conciliar regulations had been "scrupulously" observed.

One might grant the reporter that the regulations had been observed "materially," according to their letter; but that their spirit had also been respected may be doubted when we know that during the intersession the commission had never held a plenary meeting or even one with a majority present, as Carli (in his report on November 5) had admitted[110] and as a member of the commission, Msgr. Correa, had complained in the hall that same day when he criticized above all the commission's failure to consult about the report.[111] Thus, even at this late date, Msgr. Carli did not really answer the criticisms that had been voiced regarding the commission's functioning between the first and second periods.[112]

The reporter then endeavored to explain the reference he had made to Pius VI's Bull *Auctorem fidei* in his report of November 5: it had not

---

[108] *AS* II/5, 72-75.

[109] When the list was checked (*AS* II/5, 75), it contained only nine signatures: one residential archbishop, three residential bishops, two titular bishops (if Msgr. Lefebvre, Superior General of the Spiritans, is counted), one prelate *nullius*, and two religious (but if the bishops and prelate, who were religious, are counted here, there were five religious). In the order of signatures: G. de Proença Sigaud, Archbishop of Diamantina (Brazil); M. Lefebvre, Superior General of the Spiritans; J. Nepote-Fus, Titular Bishop of Elo (Brazil); Ioannes (= J. Pereira Venâncio), Bishop of Leiria (Portugal); Fray L. Rubio, Prior General of the Hermits of St. Augustine; Frère J. Prou, Superior General of the Benedictine Congregation of France; Fray G. Grotti, Prelate *nullius* of Acre and Purús (Brazil); A. de Castro Mayer, Bishop of Campos (Brazil); C. Saboia Bandeira de Mello, O.F.M., Bishop of Palmas (Brazil).

[110] The composition of the schema on the bishops had been the work of a special subcommission made up of some "Romans," bishops and experts ("commission experts living in Rome were quickly chosen"; "it was made up of nearby members of our commission and some experts"); see *AS* II/4, 440.

[111] *AS* II/4, 462-64.

[112] See also the grievances addressed by Msgr. Veuillot to Cardinal Tisserant, president of the Council of Presidents, in his letter of October 29, 1963 (see note 3, above).

been intended to "offend";[113] it meant that the preparatory commission had not considered the granting of faculties to the bishops as the restitution of something unjustly taken away, for that would have been insulting to the pope.

After this twofold explanation "in order to establish the real situation," Carli spoke from that point on as a private father of the Council, while at the same time speaking in the name of thirty bishops of various nations. He wanted to set the record straight on just one point: the institution of national episcopal conferences should not be based on the supposed principle that "episcopal collegiality is of divine right," contrary to what certain speakers had claimed. Citing by name Cardinals Ruffini, Browne, and Ottaviani and Msgr. Florit, he then once more attacked the legitimacy of the call for a vote on October 30. To the substantial reasons already given by those men, he wished to add a formal reason: in his judgment the validity of the vote was doubtful because it had been taken suddenly and without a preceding twofold report, read or written, and, above all, without the fathers having had enough time to take counsel or reach a mature judgment of a matter of such importance and in connection with such an equivocal text.

Second, even if the "alleged" collegiality were defined to be of divine right by the pope with the approval of the Council, it could never constitute the legitimate basis of episcopal conferences, and this for three reasons. First, theologically, the episcopal conferences do not show the three elements that seem essential to this collegiality, namely, the entire "body"of all the bishops; the formal "authoritative" participation of the head of the college; and matters that concern the entire Church. Next, juridically, the "monarchical" authority of each bishop over his diocese would then be limited by divine law not only by the pope (which is as it should be) but also by the other bishops of the same nation — something no bishop is ready to allow in his diocese. Finally, historically, in the composition of the schema on the conferences no member of the commission even thought of a divine-right collegiality as the foundation; more important, no popes had ever spoken of such a basis when they recommended national conferences; they always limited themselves to reasons of a pastoral or moral but never a jurisdictional kind. Furthermore, in the earliest

---

[113] As noted earlier, this implicit assimilation of the defenders of collegiality and a revitalization of the episcopate to the Jansenists of Pistoia had elicited, the very next day, a very strong statement from Schäufele, who spoke in the name of the German-speaking fathers and of the Scandinavian Episcopal Conference; AS II/4, 495-97.

practice of the Church there was question of a "horizontal" collegiality (between bishops, especially of the same province) and never of a "vertical" collegiality (with the visible head of the Church), and that collegiality was based solely on the bonds of unity and mutual harmony and not on a juridical bond.

This new attack on the vote of October 30 and on episcopal collegiality as being of divine right created a sensation at the Council; it was once again a frontal attack not only on the moderators in regard to the five questions but also on the majority of the fathers and their conception of collegiality. The attack proved, if proof was still needed, the active and unwearying tenacity of the minority. It also had repercussions outside the council hall. The *L'Avvenire d'Italia* for November 14 reported the event as follows:

> Msgr. Carli's intervention did not fail to provoke deep feelings at the Council. He is, as a matter of fact, one of Cardinal Ottaviani's immediate collaborators on the theological commission; his criticism of the moderators for their questions and of the vote of October 30 on collegiality seemed even sharper than that delivered in the hall by the secretary of the Holy Office. Furthermore, Msgr. Carli, who yesterday, as reporter, had explained the text of this chapter of the schema, today, acting as an individual, attacked the very same text. Finally, he likened the positions taken by a large majority of the fathers to those of the Jansenists of Pistoia, who were condemned in the eighteenth century by the Bull *Auctorem fidei* of Pius VI.

This extract from the press makes clear the atmosphere at the Council, but it also shows how the commentaries and rumors that circulated about the event often distorted it, consciously or not, in accordance with the views of the journalist or the newspaper. Carli, paragon of the "anti-collegialists" and the conservative wing, was spontaneously associated with Ottaviani as one of his collaborators; he had spoken as an individual against the text of the schema that — as the reporter — he had defended the day before; and he had likened the fathers of the majority to the Pistoians condemned by Pius VI. But, as we have seen, the reality was somewhat different from this account. For one thing, Carli mentioned the Bull *Auctorem fidei* simply in order to explain the uncontroversial meaning that, he maintained, the citation had had in his report on November 5; for another, he could not be accused of denigrating chapter III of the schema on the bishops, since he was trying, on the contrary, to show the precise meaning of a text in which there was never any question of collegiality. Indeed, at the end of his address he declared himself in favor of adopting the text in substance.

The Bologna daily made some corrections in its issue of November 21:

Above all, [Msgr. Carli] is not a member of theological commission, as we wrote in error, but of the Commission for Bishops and the Government of Dioceses....With regard, next, to the reference which Msgr. Carli made in his address to the Bull *Auctorem fidei* of Pius VI, which condemned the theses of the Jansenist synod of Pistoia, we have now been able to see the complete text of his intervention and are therefore in a position to give an accurate account of the passage in question, the meaning of which seems to be different than that reported earlier.[114]

If we add the interview that Ottaviani gave that same day on the same subject (the vote of October 30), it is clear that the atmosphere at the Council was not very serene at the time the chapter on episcopal conferences was being discussed. A struggle was still going on, and its outcome was not yet certain.

V. "DIOCESES NEITHER TOO SMALL NOR TOO LARGE"

During the second half of the morning of November 14, at the request of the moderators the fathers agreed to close the debate on chapter III.[115] After Msgr. Carli gave his report on chapter IV, six other fathers gave their views; twelve others spoke on the subject the next day, and one more on November 18.

A. A MINOR, PRAGMATIC CHAPTER

Carli's report began by observing that chapter IV, "on the suitable boundaries of dioceses and ecclesiastical provinces" (nos. 26-32), was meant to offer a remedy to bishops who had trouble governing their dioceses because their territory (or the number of its inhabitants) was too small or too big. The main issue was the division or combination of dioceses and the alteration of their boundaries. Since the problem was not felt everywhere in the same way, the schema avoided overly detailed considerations, the Apostolic See being in a better position to provide for individual cases.

The pastoral importance of the chapter came through clearly in the introduction (26), in which general cautions and criteria were set down. "Supported" by the desires of "a great many" fathers, the preparatory commission thought that the Council should tackle the question and provide at

---

[114] For these two extracts in the original Italian, see Caprile, III, 263 n.4.
[115] *AS* II/5, 211-12.

least a general solution so that the ecclesiastical authorities could be vigilant in adapting institutions to developing realities and so that the faithful and clergy would be able to face the problem with greater tranquility. The entire matter is entrusted to the national conferences, who are thought to be able to give advice based on a better knowledge of the facts, but approval and the implementation are reserved to the Apostolic See, which is in a better position to deal with this difficult matter, which entails the resignations and appointments of bishops and diplomatic agreements with states.

With regard to ecclesiastical provinces and their grouping into regions, a new and "essentially" pastoral criterion was introduced into the law, namely, similarity in human and spiritual conditions and in dangers and remedies. The schema proposed the abolition of "immediate subjection" to the Holy See (27 §3) on the grounds that nowadays the common good of souls urges the gathering of all the bishops in the same part of a national territory into provinces and regions. Finally, no. 31 provided for the erection of personal dioceses based on rite; this was intended both for the Oriental rites in the West and the Latin rites in the East.[116]

Even a superficial reading of this report shows the minor and pragmatic nature of chapter IV. Dioceses should be neither too small or too large; this, in substance, is the harmless generalization made (see 27 §1). Admittedly, the introduction to the chapter (26) does tackle the pastoral problem behind the subject: to be viable a diocese should be human in scale so that the bishop may personally gain a good knowledge of each priest and each parish and have at his disposal the human and material resources necessary for the administration of the diocese. But the differences between dioceses are considerable. At that time, Italy, for example, had 288 dioceses, whereas Germany had only 22. Alongside sprawling dioceses were others no larger than a good-size parish. Thus the Diocese of Bosa (Italy) had, at that time, 30,800 inhabitants, 19 parishes, 28 diocesan priests, and 3 seminarians, while the Diocese of Trier had 1,775,836 Catholics, 941 parishes, 1,288 priests, and 259 seminarians.[117]

[116] *AS* II/5, 212-13.
[117] See Laurentin, 141-42, for these examples.

B. A Debate More "Pastoral" Than Theological

In the various interventions the bishops' personal experiences played a larger role than theological considerations. In fact, pastoral care cropped up regularly as the supreme criterion, whether for the erection of personal dioceses or the demarcation of territorial dioceses.[118] The address of Msgr. Renard, Bishop of Versailles (France), was of interest because it tried precisely to establish criteria by which a diocese could achieve its proper end: the salvation of souls and the good of the Church. Two questions, he said, could be asked regarding a diocese: Is it an effective local presence of the universal Church in its diversity? Is it viable in terms of personnel, institutions, and material resources? Two questions will likewise be asked regarding the bishop: Has he the means of carrying out his mission as pastor and meeting each of his priests individually? Is the diocese too large for the bishop to exercise his responsibility as successor of the apostles, visit all the parishes of the diocese in the course of a few years, and administer confirmation in each parish properly so called?[119]

When some fathers suggested the subdivision of the great cities into new dioceses,[120] and others the combination of small dioceses,[121] they generally did so with an eye to episcopal collaboration and a better distribution of apostolic resources.[122] It is worth while here to single out Msgr. Sorrentino's address in favor of regrouping small dioceses, for it came from an Italian bishop who was himself head of a small see, that

[118] *AS* II/5, 214-15 (M. Feltin), 215-17 (A. Renard), 217-20 (F. Peralta y Ballabriga), 220-22 (F. Jop), 222-24 (A. Sorrentino), 224-27 (S. Soares de Resende), 249-50 (J. Urtasun), 262-64 (F. Romo Gutiérrez).

[119] *AS* II/5, 215-17.

[120] *AS* II/5, 217-20 (F. Peralta y Ballabriga), 246-48 (B. Stein, who commended this division only when the collaboration of auxiliaries proved insufficient).

[121] *AS* II/5, 222-24 (A. Sorrentino), 249-50 (J. Urtasun, who for the sake of greater apostolic effectiveness, asked that overly small dioceses, however venerable, disappear; the Church was not a museum). Others did not share this last argument, being moved by the antiquity of some Churches (*AS* II/5, 220-22 [F. Jop]) or by the viability of certain small dioceses (*AS* II/5, 249-50 [R. Massimiliani]).

[122] See also *AS* II/5, 239-41 (S. Lázló), 256-58 (M. Gonzalez Martin). For the sake of a better distribution of activities and personnel in the dioceses, Msgr. Peralta y Ballabriga wanted some principle laid down for the organization and rationalization of pastoral work, especially that of priests (*AS* II/5, 217-20); Msgr. Urtasun, while desiring the establishment in each region of an episcopal commission for the regrouping of dioceses (see no. 32 of the schema), reminded his hearers that this regrouping could not ignore the studies of experts in religious sociology (*AS* II/5, 249-50; see also, Msgr. Renard's conclusion, 217).

of Bova, mentioned earlier. In Italy, he said, there were almost 300 dioceses, many of which were too small, with 10 to 30 parishes, and a total of only 10,000 to 30,000 faithful. A reappraisal was urgently necessary, often called for by the faithful themselves, acknowledged by the priests, and desired by the majority of bishops. The boundaries of the Italian dioceses went back to the year 1000; today, he said, they are anti-historical, anti-geographical, and anti-pastoral. There is need of a general rearrangement, undertaken for the sake of the common good. This discussion at the Council, he added, can already be regarded as a good psychological preparation of the faithful.[123]

Here again, the Oriental bishops were anxious to express their viewpoint at an almost exclusively Latin council. Thus, with regard to personal dioceses some bishops of the East, of the Oriental, and even of the Latin rite, raised the problem of the coexistence of different rites in the same locale. Speaking in the name of very many of his confreres in northern and southern India, Msgr. Athaide, Bishop of Agra, pleaded for unity of jurisdiction: a single bishop for a diocese, whatever the plurality of rites within it; an Oriental ordinary in a territory entrusted to Oriental missionaries, an ordinary of the Latin rite in a territory entrusted to a Latin bishop.[124] In like manner Msgr. Scandar, Bishop of Assiut (Egypt), advocated a single jurisdiction for all the Catholics of the same territory, whatever their rite (in Egypt, Syria, or Lebanon, for example), and he did so with an appeal to the ancient ecclesiastical tradition of a single bishop for each place.[125]

Motivated by a concern for the equality of rites, Msgr. Khoreiche, Bishop of Saïda of the Maronites (Lebanon), made the same plea, but he added the possibility that, within one and the same territory, there might be personal jurisdictions for all rites having a sufficient number of faithful. He also recommended that every episcopal jurisdiction depend on a higher authority of the same rite (for the Orientals, on the patriarch), and finally, that territories proper to each rite be recognized.[126] On the other hand, Msgr. Valloppilly, Bishop of Tellicherry, speaking in the name of the entire Oriental Indian hierarchy (Syro-Malabar and Syro-Malankar), was opposed to jurisdictional unicity, because in practice it worked against the equality of rites. In his view unity of jurisdiction was acceptable only when in a given territory there were few faithful belonging to

---

[123] *AS* II/5, 222-24.
[124] *AS* II/5, 250-53.
[125] *AS* II/5, 264-65.
[126] *AS* II/5, 265-66.

a rite different from that of the ordinary. In other cases, "territorial-personal" dioceses should be erected.[127]

In less than two sessions the father finished with this rather organizational and practical chapter and thus with the schema. On November 12 chapter V (on the erection and boundaries of parishes), which was even less fundamental, had already been simply and without qualification sent back to the commission for the revision of the Code of Canon Law (2025 for, 141 against).[128]

At the end of the morning of November 15, Cardinal Marella, president of the Commission for Bishops and the Government of Dioceses, was able to thank the fathers and assure them that all their observations would be taken into account in the revision of the schema. He did not realize what he was promising, since he did not know that on November 21 the pope would decide to expand the commissions to thirty members[129] and that a small commission, mandated by the enlarged Commission for Bishops, would in January 1964 begin composing a new schema under conditions quite different from those of the preceding intersession.[130]

C. AN ASSESSMENT OF LIGHTS AND SHADOWS

The debate on the schema on bishops and the government of dioceses was a lively one, filled with sudden reversals but also with constructive suggestions. It may be remarked, however, that the manner of choosing

---

[127] *AS* II/5, 409-11.

[128] *AS* II/5, 9-10 and 34.

[129] An increase of five members, four elected by the conciliar assembly and one appointed by the pope; see the *Notificatio* from Felici, Secretary General of the Council, dated October 21, 1963 (Delhaye Archive (CLG), no. 339; Rynne, 246; *AS* II/1, 78-79; II/5, 634-36, and II/6, 206-7). The thoughts of an observer on this subject show how completely the non-Catholics present were involved in the conciliar event and with the majority of the fathers: "The five new members will certainly strengthen the position of the majority, but it will still not be possible to eliminate the opposition of the conservative group. Why did the pope not take more courageous steps?...It is very rare that in Rome something existing is simply abolished and replaced" (photocopy of letter of L. Vischer to W. Visser't Hooft, November 22, 1963 [ISR], Aco 6).

[130] The reference is to the "first subcommission," dircted by Msgr. Veuillot, coadjutor of Paris (reporter), and Prof. W. Onclin, canonist of Louvain (secretary); see *History*, 2:454 and note 238. This subcommission would be entrusted with the introduction and the schema as a whole; its other members were Guerry, Rakotomalala, Castelli, and Primatesta, while its experts were Arrighi, Stano, Pavan, D'Ercole, Carbone, Mörsdorf, and Quinn; see the Onclin Archive (CCV) C.D. 3.

bishops, which conditioned many questions of the schema (resignation, episcopal conferences, and so on), was not discussed as such. The problem of episcopal nomination, which at that time was in the purview of the Consistorial Congregation, aided by the nuncios, would have given rise in turn to the question of the difficult relations between "periphery" and "center," between bishops (and their respective Christian peoples) and the Curia, and, more basic still, between collegiality and primacy.[131]

It was clearly against the background of these problems and of the vote on October 30 that the entire discussion on bishops unfolded. In this respect the debate ended with a general feeling of discomfort. On many points the interventions expressed opposed views, but it was not clear which side had the majority. Should the institution of coadjutors be kept or eliminated? Should an age limit be binding or merely suggested? Should episcopal conferences be given powers that would be juridically binding on all of their members? Should the boundaries of dioceses be revised? The uncertainty was even increased following the challenge of Browne, Ottaviani, Lefebvre, and especially Carli to the legitimacy of the October 30 vote. What was the authority of decisions taken by that kind of vote? By implication, what authority did the moderators have to initiate and direct? Did they have the right to decide on taking a straw vote in order to clarify a discussion?[132] What was the real role of the commissions, and especially of the Doctrinal

---

[131] Congar writes, "[In the minority and majority] two positions clashed at a level which, in my opinion, is where the Council faces its most serious issue as far as ecclesiological structures are concerned. It is not a matter of challenging the dogma of 1870, but of deciding whether, at the doctrinal level, the Council is to make a serious effort to complete that dogma with the dogma of the episcopate, and whether, at the level of the Church's manner of life, we shall move away from a papal monarchy and give the Church a form that reflects the relative duality, which the New Testament asserts, between the authority of Peter and the authority of the Twelve. The stakes are sizeable and powerfully affect the chances of ecumenism." What is at stake, the French theologian goes on to say, is "the harmony between primacy and collegiality" (Congar, *Le Concile au jour le jour*, 2:141).

[132] On November 11, forty-six Spanish-speaking Latin American bishops had again, but vainly, approached the moderators with a written suggestion along these lines. They expressed their wish that at the end of the discussion of the schema on bishops and the government of dioceses, three questions be put to a vote: the first was whether a bishop had, by his office, all the powers needed for exercising his pastoral responsibility to feed the flock entrusted to him, except for such powers as the pope reserved to himself in virtue of his rights as primate; the second had to do with the correction of the schema, though this would not be definitive as long as the doctrine on the hierarchy of the Church had not been promulgated; the third had to do with combining the schemas on the bishops, the care of souls, and clerics (Thils Archive (CLG), no. 1256).

Commission, in relation to the conciliar assembly?[133] Despite a number
of very strong attempts to set the record straight by members of the
majority, this continual questioning of what had been gained during the
preceding month depressed the assembly and instilled new doubts in
some.[134] On November 15 the Council seemed to be back in the atmosphere at the end of October, although a debate on another sensitive subject, ecumenism, was to begin three days later.[135]

D. A PROGRAMMATIC REPORT

When the pope realized the restlessness of a number of Council
fathers at the slowness of the debates and the confusing differences in
the interpretation of the famous vote, he called a plenary meeting of the
directing bodies of the Council: the Council of Presidents, the Coodina-
tiing Commission, and the moderators. With the pope himself presiding,
the meeting was held at 6:15 p.m. on November 15 in the hall of the
"congregations" on the third floor of the Apostolic Palace.[136] The members of the General Secretariat of the Council were also present. Most of

[133] Two days after the end of the debate on bishops, "Helveticus," whom the conservative party regarded as an authority, took up this question in his commentary in *Il Tempo*
(November 17). If the regulations are vague (he wrote), they should be very quickly
changed in order to state accurately the competence of the commissions. Let the question
be submitted to the pope or a petition be voted on in the hall to ask him for new elections!
It is impossible to continue on the present course without danger of shipwreck. "The theological commission, the most important of all of them, cannot be permitted to continue
working in an atmosphere of suspicions and opposition," he added, with his eye on certain
newspapers, especially French ones, and their attacks on the Curia. See Wenger, 84-85.

[134] B. Olivier remarks: "One senses a hardening, by all possible means, of the conservative wing. Msgr. Carli, speaking in the hall, returned once again to the straw
vote....His words were greeted by a murmur of hostility in the hall. One must record the
fact that despite the very clear explanation by Cardinal Döpfner, one of the moderators,
the opposition has not laid down its weapons. It seems that this very stubborn hostility is
bearing fruit and that some fathers are beginning to ask whether it is worth speaking of
collegiality. For myself, I ask the opposite question: whether the ungenerous means used
by this opposition are not causing the fathers of the majority to speak out only to thwart
these maneuvers, without much reliance on a strong conviction. It is natural for each
group to stand up for its convictions, but the bitterness of the conservative party, which is
clearly in the minority, makes a painful impression" (Olivier Archive, "Chronique du
Concile. IIe Session," no. 169, 24).

[135] For this assessment see Laurentin, 142-44.

[136] The date of this joint meeting, intended for assessing the work of the Council, had
been suggested to the pope by the moderators after their own meeting on November 9 (*AS*
V/3, 709-10); on the morning of November 15 Cardinal Lercaro had obtained an audience with the pope (*Lettere*, 221-22).

the meeting was devoted to Cardinal Lercaro's report on the work of the Council during the second period;[137] the cardinals and bishops present then offered their comments, and the report was generally approved.[138] At the request of Paul VI the text was to be distributed to the fathers in a Latin translation on the following December 2; extensive extracts would also be published in the Bolognese daily. *L'Avvenire d'Italia* on that same date. Yet this important document would be more or less ignored by the world press, even though its intention was to make public an entire program of action for the coming intersession and the continuation of the Council.[139]

Lercaro was essentially positive in estimating the progress made on the schemas that were on the agenda during the second period and in his quantitative assessment of the work accomplished to this point, but he did not hide problems. It did not seem possible to improve, either quantitatively or qualitatively, the pace of the work done at the general congregations. On the other hand, progress did seem possible at the level of the commissions, some of which had too much material to deal with. We may see here a rather clear allusion to the Doctrinal Commission, which its president, Cardinal Ottaviani, considered to be the supreme conciliar commission, superior even to the Council itself. Lercaro then suggested that there be a really fluid relationship between the general congregations and the commissions, since, he pointed out, the latter were bodies at work in the service of the former. He mentioned also the use, which he said was desired by many episcopates, of the kind of straw vote already used for chapter II of the schema on the Church. What was needed was to perfect it by concentrating the debate on major questions and, as far as the moderators were concerned, to formulate questions that would recapitulate and point the way.

In the second part of his report, a qualitative assessment addressed perhaps more directly to Paul VI, Lercaro spoke with strong conviction of the catholic spirit of the conciliar majority. This spirit was continually intensifying, as almost all the fathers endeavored to look beyond their

---

[137] This action, the most solemn of Lercaro during the second period, was due to his being the oldest of the moderators. For the original Italian text of this report, see *Per la forza*, 265-75; for the Latin translation, see *AS* II/1, 101-105, and V/2, 29-33.

[138] In the Lercaro Archive at the ISR in Bologna (no. 23, undated) are the handwritten notes of Lercaro on the short discussion that followed his report; the minutes of the discussion are now published in *AS* V/2, 25-29. See also *Lettere*, 222 (see *Per la forza*, 33 and note 57).

[139] For these various points of information, see Rynne, 201-4; *Per la forza*, 30-33; and G. Alberigo, "L'evento conciliare," 127-28.

particular problems and open themselves to a more universal vision in which every human being would allow himself to be permeated by the leaven of the gospel in all aspects of his humanity. Finally, he continued, the entire episcopate shows itself to be very strong and unanimous in its consciousness of unity and of submission to the Roman pontiff; there is no longer any real opening for the anti-Roman currents of Gallicanism and Jansenism, whether transalpine or Italian. This assertion was a new and authoritative response to the more or less veiled accusations of the minority, and especially of Msgr. Carli, who were hoping thereby to win the pope to their cause. The moderator ended by speaking of the universal mission for the service of which the bishops intended to make themselves entirely available, in union with and in dependence upon the successor of Peter.

This report would have a calming effect on the conciliar gathering by dispelling part of the uneasiness; it would reaffirm the authority of the moderators and would underscore a special convergence of thought between Lercaro and Paul VI. The following November 21 would bring the announcement of the pope's acceptance of the expansion of the commissions.[140]

---

[140] See *Per la forza*, 33, and above, note 131. We may read on this same subject the contrasting impressions of Moeller in another letter to his mother, dated November 20 (Moeller Archive, no. 02887): "Here is some news from the Council. After All Saints, a clear need of recourse to the pope. The anticipated votes on the 'powers' bishops have by their office, on the formation of a commission that would try, between this and the next session, to present the pope with proposals regarding the establishment of a central episcopal body to help him in his major decisions — these votes were abandoned. No renewal of the commissions. In recent days the pope has once again taken some big steps in the direction of the moderators: a plan will be proposed for a partial renewal of the commissions (highly secret). The central body is studying the matter; the pope has five plans on his desk, which he will study, then discuss, doubtless with the moderators (secret). The majority is for having only one more session, approximately from September 8 to November 20, 1964. A minority, but an active and well-advised one, is working to have a further session in 1965 (to discuss, among other things, the reform of seminaries and universities, since in the final analysis theological formation is crucial). The discussion of ecumenism is filling the tribunes — a sign of the times. On the whole, a very good discussion. It is unbelievable that people are talking of 'religious freedom' in the terms used by de Smedt. This is an enormous advance in relation to Rome; but in relation to reality, it is still very little. There is talk of prolonging this session until December 20. That is a fantasy, in my opinion. Since the pope wants the first chapter of the Constitution on the Church to be promulgated before the end of the session, we are working on it day and night. It is possible that we shall make it, but we are killing ourselves with the work. We are seeing nothing of Rome. No time. The fate of the Council depends on the setting up of episcopal conferences and especially of a central body....I am very tired, but happy."

VI. NUMEROUS MEETINGS ON THE FRINGES OF THE ASSEMBLY

Ideally, one would have to speak, first of all, of the many contacts made during the debates: at the edges of the conciliar assembly itself, in the side aisles or back of St. Peter's, and in the two annexes of the basilica that served as bars.[141] Unfortunately, we have only very infrequent allusions in personal diaries and a few oral or written testimonies to the chance encounters that occurred in such places where also small circles voiced their reactions in the heat of the moment, both during the course of the assembly and at moments of striking interventions, all this contributing not a little to the strengthening of a common mind among many in both the majority and the minority.[142]

Alongside these private conversations in the walkways of the assembly, numerous meetings were held in Rome: from informal contacts among fathers, experts, and journalists[143] to the most official meetings of the conciliar commissions; from lectures to the general public to very closely argued discussions between experts and bishops on the teaching of this or that schema and on the tactic to be adopted: whether to propose an "ideal" text or one capable of winning a broad agreement among the fathers?).[144]

---

[141] The refreshment rooms were given pious nicknames: Bar-Jonah and Bar-Abbas.

[142] There are, for example, the few notes of an "ordinary" auxiliary bishop, Msgr. Musty (of Namur); see his *Notes sur le Concile oecuménique Vatican II* (photocopies at CLG). See also the testimony of expert B. Olivier, O.P., on the second period: "Around 10:30, especially if the speakers are repeating one another, there is the beginning of a movement toward the side naves and the bars. Two bars have been set up in the annexes of the basilica. Coffee (espresso, capuccino) is served there, as are tea, Coca-Cola, orangeade, as well as an assortment of cakes, crackers, and sweets. These bars are rather narrow passageways, and around 11:00 there is a crush there. It is the place for private conversations, quick meetings. The air is thick with smoke; one has to protect one's cup from the movements of the crowd, but people comment and discuss. Chiefly the Council, but also the revolution in Vietnam, Kennedy's death" (Olivier Archive, no. 168, "Une journée au Concile," 7).

[143] We may think here also of the "private" notes of experts (e.g., Prignon Archive, nos. 493-95: an anonymous note on the schema on the bishops, and two others of L. Anné on episcopal conferences and on "Father Féret's annotations"). Then too there were various more or less informal "pressure groups or study groups," such as the one called The Bishop of Vatican II; this group, due to the initiative of Canon F. Boulard, in cooperation with Bishops A Muñoz Duque and L. de Courrèges, met twice a month at Saint-Louis des Français and brought together about fifteen bishops. In the list of those invited on November 5, 1963, we find the names of members of the Commission for Bishops — P. Correa León, J. Gargitter, N. Jubany Arrau, and J. Teusch — but also R. Etchegaray, C. Colombo. P.-A. Liégé, F. Houtart, J. Medina, and K. Wojtyla (see Boulard Archive, Diocesan Archives of Paris, no. 4 A 1, 24b, 25, and 26, a note dated October 30, 1963).

[144] See, e.g., the lecture given by Msgr. Bonet, an auditor of the Sacred Roman Rota, to the bishops of Africa on the schema on the bishops, in which the lecturer examined it

A. TUESDAY MEETINGS WITH THE OBSERVERS

Among these meetings those held on Tuesdays between the non-Catholic observers and the Secretariat for Christian Unity stood out. They were privileged moments during which the other Christian Churches could gain a better understanding of the direction in which the conciliar debates were moving and during which, most important, they could by way of the members of the secretariat make their voices more directly heard at Vatican II and even exert a more or less significant influence on the schemas being composed.

During the period that concerns us here, on November 5, the day on which the discussion of the schema on the bishops began and on which the conciliar majority was under the somewhat euphoric influence of the five questions, the traditional Tuesday meeting took up chapter IV of the schema on the Church. It is of interest to note the approval and the constructive criticisms of the observers, who in this case were Protestants.[145] On the one hand, they appreciated the fact that this chapter of the schema on the Church voiced an undifferentiated and universal call to holiness, without two kinds of "ethic," one for ordinary Christians, the other for truly committed Christians. This could mean the burial of an ancient controversy between Catholics and Protestants. On the other hand, they regretted — as also, they noted, did many of the Council

in the light of episcopal collegiality (Prignon Archive, no. 490). The lecture was given shortly after the presentation of the schema to the Council (see p. 1) and, it seems, even before its acceptance as a basis for discussion (see p. 19); it must therefore be dated November 5, rather than the 7th, as in the handwritten notation in the Prignon papers, since the schema was accepted on the 6th. On November 5 Prof. K. Mörsdorf gave a talk on the episcopate and collegiality to the weekly meeting of the German Episcopal Conference at the Collegio Santa Maria dell'Anima; we can read the "agitated" reactions of Msgr. E. Schick, auxiliary of Fulda, to Mörsdorf's very restrictive vision of an auxiliary bishop, as well as his thoughts on the debate then going on in the Council, in his handwritten letter of November 6, 1963, to Frings (Frings Archive, "De episcopis ac de Diocesium regimine," 181/8). For the number of lectures that a well-known theologian such as Y. Congar was led to deliver, just between November 1 and November 15, 1963, see *JCongar*.

[145] See Moeller Archive, no.00430: "Remarks of the observers on the schema *De Ecclesia*. Meeting of Nov. 5, 1963" (the interveners, in the order in which they appear in the minutes were P. Lalande, Dr. R. McAfee Brown, Prof. K. E. Skydsgaard, Msgr. Höfer, Msgr. Willebrands, Prof. Miguez-Bonino, P. Baum, P. Ahern, and Dr. L. Vischer). See also the letter of L. Vischer to W. Visser't Hooft, November 8, 1963, which touches on the remarks on the ecumenism-schema that Msgr. Willebrands had asked from the observers and on the agreement that seemed to be emerging among the latter on the "German" text, as well as an initial, rather positive assessment of *De catholicorum habitudine ad non christianos et maxime ad Iudaeos* (ISR, Bologna, Aco 6, photocopy).

fathers — the excessively moralistic and inadequately christological and biblical character of the chapter; sanctification seemed to be too much a work accomplished by human beings and not sufficiently the unmerited justification offered by God to the sinner. This was a somewhat impoverished note on which to end a schema on the Church in today's world. In addition, some passages seemed to suggest that religious are closer to God than other people are, thus establishing a "ladder" of holiness and contradicting the universal call to holiness. The problem was that this universal call was being discussed in function of the religious life. One observer shrewdly remarked that the doctrine of the exemption of religious seemed to have been formulated without taking into account the collegiality of the bishops as taught in chapter II. From all this we can see how a certain collaboration developed between the observers and the Council fathers and how the pertinent suggestions of the former could influence the active agents of Vatican II and the composition of some texts.

The next meeting took place on November 12 and focused on the schema on ecumenism. Chapter IV of this document ("On the Relationship of Catholics to Non-Christians and Especially to the Jews") had been distributed to the fathers on November 8 at the sixty-third general congregation, which was devoted to a discussion of chapters I and II of the schema on bishops.[146] There do not seem to have been any direct echoes of that sometimes lively discussion at the meeting on November 12, which wholly centered on the ecumenism schema.[147] On this occasion too the observers had stimulating remarks on the Council.[148]

---

[146] *AS* II/4, 612.

[147] In private, at least, the observers and the Catholics traded reactions to events in the hall. For example, in his intervention on November 8 Cardinal Ottaviani had claimed, with an appeal to a well-known New Testament exegete, that the apostles had not acted collegially. Danish Lutheran K. E. Skydsgaard tells of speaking about this with a Catholic priest, who at the moment remained silent, but a short time later handed him a small image of the Crucified, on the back of which he had written in German: "The apostles acted collegially in the Garden of Gethsemane, where all of them left the Lord in the lurch." Skydsgaard observed that behind the witticism was a profound truth: without this dimension of rejection, the fall, and the cross, but also of resurrection, being graced, and the bottomless love of God we cannot understand the mystery of the Church; see Moeller Archive, no. 00437 (K. E. Skydsgaard, *Die zweite Sitzungsperiode des Vatikanischen Konzils in den Augen eines Beobachters* [Deutsches Konzilszentrum, C.C.C.C., Via S. Uffizio, 25], November 27, 1963). This is but one example of fruitful interactions between observers and Catholics concerning the Council. Still in connection with the schema on bishops, I note a further example of attentive presence at the conciliar debates, as seen in the letters of German Lutheran G. Maron in his *Evangelischer Bericht vom Konzil. Zweite Session* (Bensheimer Hefte 23; Göttingen, 1964), 34-42.

[148] Moeller Archive, no. 00431: "Meeting of the Observers, Tuesday, November 12, 1963" (interveners according to the order in the minutes were Prof. Cullmann, Pastor

In general, the observers regarded the current schema on ecumenism as an immense step forward in comparison with the texts presented during the previous year, and they credited the secretariat with this progress. As it stood, the document could serve as a good starting point. On the other hand, it also elicited numerous reactions and reservations from the non-Catholics. They saw a problem in the way it referred to non-Catholics (*Church* used only of the Orthodox, while *communities* was always used of the Protestants) and presented the relationship between the unity and apostolicity of the Church (were Peter and his successors alone capable of ensuring perfect unity in faith?) and the ideas of catholicity and fullness (was "fullness" in fact to be identified with the Roman Church?). Furthermore, the inclusion of the chapter on relations between Catholics and non-Christians and especially between Catholics and Jews was questionable, since ecumenism had to do only with Christians; the addition of this chapter could give non-Catholics the impression that they were being located among the other religions. Another intervener, L. Vischer, made the point, however, that the relationship of the Church to the people of the Old Testament was an essential element in ecumenism.

B. THE CHURCH OF THE POOR GROUP

This special group, which was intent upon having the Council take seriously the poor and poverty, became more closely knit during the second period of the Council. In addition to a meeting of the committee in charge (October 10), six general meetings were held at the Belgian College (26 via del Quirinale), one each week (October 18 and 25; November 8, 15, 22, and 29).[149] Various bishops and experts attended these meetings, which were under the patronage of Cardinals Lercaro and Gerlier (Lyons), as well as of Patriarch Maximos IV. The group was energized above all by Bishops C. Himmer (Tournai) and G. Hakim (Galilee), as well as by Father P. Gauthier (Nazareth). Ten or so other

H. Roux, Prof. Mathew, and Dr. L. Vischer). See also L. Vischer's letter to W. Visser't Hooft, November 17, 1963, in which he speaks of some differences among the observers. Vischer shows himself more reserved than Canon P. Pawley, an Anglican, who wanted to promise "the enthusiastic cooperation of the Anglican communion in every respect" (ISR, Bologna, Aco 6, photocopy).

[149] For all this information, see the Himmer Archive (Centre Lumen Gentium, Louvain-la-Neuve), nos. 41-61 ("Second session").

Council fathers from various continents were members of the committee in charge.[150]

The group felt the need to base its efforts on doctrine in order to deepen and extend its influence at the Council. To this end three study teams were set up (dogma, pastoral, sociology), each consisting of a group of bishops and theologians;[151] lectures were to be given to all interested bishops;[152] there were also to be interventions in the hall, and texts or ideas were to be introduced into various schemas still being developed (on the Church, on ecumenism, but above all schema XVII).[153] The episcopates ought to be more fully informed about the activities of the group; but, according to Msgr. Himmer at the November 22 meeting, since the group did not have an official secretariat, it was likely to remain peripheral to the Council.

Also on November 22 the group sent a petition to the pope. It was disturbed that the second conciliar period was ending "without a single word having been said about the serious social problems that distress the people of our time." To make up for this disappointment, the Council should announce, before the intersession, that it will examine schema XVII on "the effective presence of the Church to the modern world" at the very beginning of the next period; the eucharistic congress to be held in Bombay (November 28, 1964) should also be a social congress.[154] The petition also asked the pope to intervene "with all his authority to exhort."

[150] Bishops A. Ancel (auxiliary of Lyons, France), J. Angerhausen (auxiliary of Essen, Germany), J. Blomjous (Mwanza, Tanganyika), H. Câmara (auxiliary of Rio de Janeiro, Brazil), G.-M. Coderre (St. Jean de Québec, Canada), P. Nguyen-Kim-Dien (Can-Tho, Vietnam), R. Gonzalez Moralejo (auxiliary of Valencia, Spain). M. Larraín (Talca, Chile). G. Mercier (Laghouat, Sahara), G. Riobé (Orleans, France), and B. Tago (Abidjan, Ivory Coast).

[151] The following names may be noted: Bishops Fauvel (Quimper, France), Van Melckebeke (Ningsia, China), Leuliet (Amiens, France), Frani_ (Split-Makarska, Yugoslavia), and Mercier, for the pastoral side; Msgr. Blomjous, and Fathers Dalé (Brazil), Diez Allegria (Gregorian University), and Chenu (France), for the "spirituality of development"; Bishops Ancel, Himmer, Gonzalez Moralejo, and Martin (New Caledonia), and Fathers Congar, Dupuy, Le Guillou, Tillard, and Villain (France), for dogma.

[152] For example, that of Joseph Folliet, "Vers une économie de la sainte pauvreté," at 4:30 p.m., November 21, at 21 via Santo Ufficio; or that of Abbé F. Houtart, "Ecclésiologie et sociologie," at 5:00 p.m., November 25, at the Angelicum (1, Salita del Grillo).

[153] In this perspective there would be an ecumenical contact made with Pastor H. Roux on the way in which the different Churches viewed the relationship between Christ and the poor, and on their own situation in the face of this mystery.

[154] It was Msgr. Mercier who at the general meeting of November 15 had expressed his anxiety about the coming eucharistic congress; he feared a display of wealth that would scandalize the poor populations of India, and he hoped that the congress would deal with social issues.

All these activities translated into practice the intention to have a direct impact on what was going on both in the Council and outside it; they showed the energies at work in one episcopal "circle" among many.[155]

C. THE CONCILIAR COMMISSIONS

The official conciliar commissions also met on afternoons after the general congregations. I shall mention only those that met between November 5 and 15, 1963. There was, of course, the Liturgical Commission,[156] whose schema was to be voted on shortly.[157] On November 7, 1963, while the debate on the bishops was in full swing, the commission for that schema planned a plenary meeting, the first since the preceding conciliar period. On the agenda were the establishment of subcommissions for the emendations and for the study of the interventions of the fathers; election of members of the subcommissions; appointment of reporters; coopting of experts for the subcommissions; and various other matters.[158] The Doctrinal Commission likewise held

[155] The number of activities and meetings of the Church of the Poor group during this second period was remarkable when we know how full any bishop's schedule was at the time: general congregations, commission meetings, working groups; see the testimony of a member of the group, Msgr. P. Puech, (Carcassonne, France) in a letter to Himmer, November 28, 1963: "Since I am unable once again to take part tomorrow in the meeting on 'The Church and the poor,' I venture to send you this short account. Overly absorbed by other meetings or 'work groups.... Many bishops (about fifteen) have taken a great interest in this project....Unfortunately, other questions being debated at the Council were so important that they led to setting up many working groups, with the result that it has become difficult to find time for meetings during crowded weeks" (Himmer Archive, no. 55).

[156] Meetings took place on November 6, at 5:30 p.m., in the rooms of the Sacred Congregation for Rites (study of the report of the subcommission for chapter III, on sacraments and sacramentals), on November 13 (study of the *modi* for chapter I), and on November 14 (study of the *modi* for chapter II).

[157] On November 14, during the 68th general congregation, Msgr. Felici, the Secretary General, announced that new votes on the liturgical schema would begin on the following Monday, November 18. The liturgical schema had already obtained the necessary majority, except for chapters II and III; nevertheless, the introduction and chapter I were distributed along with the response of the commission to the *modi* for these two sections already approved; see *AS* II/5, 245-46. The route traversed by the schema will be discussed later in the present volume.

[158] See the Veuillot Archive, Diocesan Archives of Paris, doc. 52, a typewritten letter from Marella to Veuillot, November 2, 1963 (agenda for the full session on the following November 7). On the subcommissions set up, the members elected, the reporters appointed, and the experts coopted see Onclin Archive, C.D. 3: "Subcommissiones pro emendando et recognoscendo schemate Decreti 'De episcopis ad de diocesium

regular meetings,[159] which up to this time had usually been weekly.[160] The Secretariat for Christian Unity also met regularly.[161]

The four subcommissions of the Commission for the Discipline of the Clergy and the Christian People set to work between October 15 and

regimine.'" On November 20, at a meeting of the presidents and secretaries of the five established subcommissions, the cardinal president of the commission would provide guidelines for the revision to be done: the schema should be completely reworked and a new outline drawn up in view of the criticisms made during the preceding debate and of the wish of some fathers that a number of pastoral directives contained in the schema on the care of souls be incorporated into the schema on the bishops. Before the end of the second period the first subcommission, which was to see to the new organization of the schema, would meet (on November 25 and 28) to decide on the program of the work and the method to be followed. On December 3 the limited group of reporters and secretaries of the subcommissions would be called together to respond to the directives of the CC given on November 29, which ordered the revision of the schema in the light of the desires of the fathers. On this further history of the commission see W. Onclin, "La genèse du décret, le titre et la structure du décret," in *La charge pastorale des évêques. Decret "Christus Dominus"* (Paris, 1969), 76.

[159] November 5, on the schemas on the Blessed Virgin and on religious freedom (see Prignon Archive, no. 481); November 6, subcommission on the people of God; November 7, subcommission for study of the religious freedom schema (Prignon Archive, no. 498, report of the meeting); November 11, J. Courtney Murray explained the religious freedom schema to the Doctrinal Commission (a meeting from which Ottaviani returned somewhat depressed; see above, note 92; see also Moeller's letter of November 11 to his mother, note 52 above; Prignon Archive, no. 482); November 14, subcommission on the people of God (subcommission II, no. 15 [previously no. 9] of chapter I of the *De ecclesia*; see Prignon Archive, no. 361); and November 15, subcommission 1 (Prignon Archive, no. 379). On these various meetings see also *JCongar*, typescript, I, 355-69. We know also of the dissatisfaction of the majority with the functioning of this commission, which was still under the control of the minority before the increase in its membership and the election of a new vice-president (Charue) and of an adjunct secretary (Philips) on the following December 2; see Prignon Archive, no. 488. The result of this situation, meanwhile, was the petitions to the pope; on these see note 67, above.

[160] But on October 24, 1963, in a *monitum* to the Doctrinal Commission, the pope had just expressed his desire that the Council should reach some important conclusion before the end of the second period and issue some important decisions regarding the schema on the Church; it was therefore necessary to try to speed up the work; a weekly meeting was not enough. See *AS* V/2, 12-13.

[161] In October a systematic analysis of the observations from the fathers had begun with the appointment of six subcommissions (see Thils Archive, no. 1317/A: "Subcommission on Ecumenism," October 10, 1963). On November 7 the secretariat worked up internal norms for the revision of the ecumenism schema (Thils Archive, no. 1317/A: "Method to Be Followed in Working on the Written Observations of the Fathers on the Schema on Ecumenism," November 7, 1963). For example, subcommission V (dealing with improvements of chapter II, section I) met on November 15 (Thils Archive, no. 1317/A). Beginning on November 18 the secretariat was to be in readiness to rework the schema in light of the conciliar debate (on this, see below). The work of the subcommissions continued during the conciliar debate and after it: November 18, 20, 26, 27, and 29, and December 2 (see the minutes in Thils Archive, no. 1317/A). On this activity of the secretariat see M. Velati, *Una difficile transizione. Il cattolicesimo tra unionismo ed ecumenismo (1952-1954)* (Bologna: Il Mulino, 1996), 378-80.

November 10, 1963. The new draft of its schema, now entitled "On Priests," would be corrected and adopted by the commission between November 17 and 27.[162] The Commission for Religious did not meet between November 5 and 15, 1963, but it had just held several meetings from September 23 to October 7, with a later, single meeting on December 3.[163] The Commission for the Missions held ten meetings between October 23 and December 23, three of them during the period that concerns us here (November 5, 11, and 14). Among other things the discussions dealt with the text to be included in the schema on the Church and with the composition of a new schema, "The Missionary Activity of the Church", which, thanks to the intense labors of four subcommissions, was sent to Cardinal Cicognani on December 5.[164]

Special note must be taken of the Coordinating Commission, the real location of the "strategic" organization of the Council's labors. During the period of time that concerns us here, this commission held only one meeting, its ninth, on November 15.[165] This was the joint meeting with the presidents and moderators mentioned above in connection with Lercaro's report.[166] In addition to a report on the second period of the Council, the agenda included three other points: information on the public session; proposals for the work to be done between the second and third periods; and suggestions for the third period. A number of fathers wanted a public session before the end of the second period, at which the liturgical constitution would be approved and promulgated, along with

---

[162] See J. Frisque, "Le Décret *Presbyterorum Ordinis*. Histoire et commentaire," in *Les prêtres. Décrets "Presbyterorum Ordinis" and "Optatam totius"* (Paris: Cerf, 1968), 124.

[163] Four subcommissions were set up to evaluate the material hitherto introduced for insertion into four schemas: the fourth chapter of the schema on the Church ("The Call to Holiness"); the third chapter of the schema on the bishops ("Relations between Bishops and Religious"); the schema on the states for the attainment of perfection; and the schema on the missions. See J. Schmiedel, "Erneuerung im Widerstreit. Das Ringen der *Commissio de Religiosis* und der *Commissio de Concilii laboribus coordinandis* um das Dekret zur zeitgemässigen Erneurung des Ordenslebens," in *Commissions*, 293-94 and 315.

[164] See S. Paventi, "Le cheminement laborieux de notre schéma," *Rythmes du Monde*, new ser., 15 (1967), 118; E. Louchez, "La commission *De Missionibus*," in *Commissions*, 263-64. See especially the paper read by E. Louchez at the Colloque de Bologne (December 12-15, 1996), in *Experience*, where, drawing on the archives of G. Eldarov, the author summarized the minutes of the commission's meetings as edited by this expert, who was one of the secretaries.

[165] The eighth meeting had been held on October 29, the eve of the famous vote, and the tenth would be held on November 29, two days after the presentation of the schema on ecumenism to the conciliar assembly; see *AS* V/2, 7-58.

[166] *AS* V/2, 21-33.

the decree on the means of social communication, and even some part of the schema on the Church, because the world was anxious to learn of the Council's decisions. The pope ought also decide on the formula for the approval and promulgation of the decrees.

While approving Lercaro's report and even suggesting that it be distributed to the fathers, Ruffini thought it unwise to "hasten decisions on serious matters and questions of principle, as had already happened in the past." In his opinion no decree had reached the point where it was ready for the public meeting. With regard to the intersession, many called for a lessening of the numbers of schemas or the reduction of their content by leaving certain subjects for the revision of the Code of Canon Law. They also recommended giving a pastoral character to the norms that would be set forth and they called for adaptations of the Regulations. During the third period, which some wanted to be the final one, it would be necessary to continue examining schemas of the second period and, most especially, to begin the examination of schema XVII. It is also worth noting that Cardinal Spellman and Secretary General Felici criticized "leaks" to the press about controversies within the Council; they described these as "irresponsible" and called for better control of news.[167]

The diversity of views within this commission, whether or not it extended to other directive bodies of the Council, reflected to some degree the divergence in the hall. In decisions determining the future of the Council the majority and minority currents within the assembly itself were reflected, although in a more mitigated fashion.[168]

[167] Some (e.g., Spellman and Felici) did not look kindly on the more open relations established between the press and the Council during the second period; see below in connection with the schema on the means of social communication.

[168] With regard to this point I mention the impressions Suenens conveyed to Prignon about the expanded meeting of November 15: "The cardinal also told me, however, that, generally speaking, the left and the right did not line up against each other at that meeting; everyone said what he thought; some showed a great deal of good sense, Confalonieri for example, although he was somewhat longwinded....Except on the part of Siri and the Secretary of the Council, there was no real left-right opposition" (Prignon Archive, no. 512bis: typewritten report on events beginning October 27, 18).

VII. The *Coetus Internationalis Patrum*

A. Catalyst of the Minority

In comparison with many other groups of bishops (national or continental conferences, for example), the International Group of Fathers was set apart by being "intercontinental," like the Conference of the Twenty-two, but with an entirely different mind-set. The International Group was certainly the most important and effective of all the conservative-minded groups.[169] It was made up of formally enrolled members[170] but remained permanently open to sympathizers, who were much more numerous.[171] Because they shared the same convictions, the members and the sympathizers displayed great discipline in response to orders issuing from the directors. The International Group was especially attentive to questions of procedure (especially when it came to blocking the approval of texts it considered ambiguous) and can be regarded as a "global ideology" group whose hard and fast conservatism was displayed in all the subjects discussed by the Council: an a-historical

---

[169] In order to describe the global context within which this group developed I begin by repeating some of its major traits, well described by H. Raguer in *History*, 2:195-200. On this "anticonciliar bloc" that was to give rise to the *Romana Colloquia* (*ROC*) as a conservative counterweight to the Dutch Documentation Center (Do-C), see the weekly *Katholiek Archief* 20, nos. 44-45 (October 29 and November 5, 1965), cols 1147-48.

[170] In addition to the three main leaders (de Proença Sigaud, Lefebvre, and Carli), the first to enroll were A. de Castro Mayer (Campos, Brazil) and P. de La Chanonie (Clermont, France). Later members included L. G. da Cunha Marelim (Caxias de Maranhão, Brazil), L. Pereira Venancio (Leiria, Portugal), C. E. Saboia Bandeira de Mello, O.F.M. (Palmas, Brazil), J. Rupp (Monaco), X. Morilleau (Titular Bishop of Cappadocia; France), J. Nepote-Fus, of the Consolata Missionaries (Titular Bishop of Elo; Brazil), G. M. Grotti, a Servite (prelate nullius of Acre y Purús, Brazil), A. Grimault, a Spiritan (Titular Bishop of Maximianopolis in Palestine, a native of Canada, living in France), J. Prou (abbot of Solesmes, Superior General of the Benedictine Congregation of France), and L. Rubio (Superior General of the Hermits of St. Augustine). A majority of the members were thus Brazilian and French, and several were religious; to these must be added some experts and some members of the Curia. See S. Gómez de Arteche y Catalina, *Grupos "extra aulam" en el II Concilio Vaticano y su influencia* 3 vols. (doctoral dissertation, Biblioteca de la Facultad de Derecho de la Universidad de Valladolid), the source par excellence on our subject; see II/3, 240-65 and especially 250-51 n.20.

[171] Sympathizers came from, among others, those opposed to collegiality, to the melding of the schema on the Blessed Virgin and the schema on the Church, and to religious freedom. This last, for example, was opposed in a critical analysis of the schema on religious freedom that was produced at the end of the 1965 intersession by the "Comitatus Episcopalis internationalis seu Coetus Internationalis Patrum" and entitled *Animadversiones criticae in textum reemendatum (28-V-65) schematis Declarationis de Libertate Religiosa*; it was specified as "reserved to the fathers of the Council" (Dupont Archive, no. 1516). See also Wiltgen, 94-95, 148, 231, 235ff., 247ff.

approach to the truths of faith; Roman Catholic triumphalism; distrust of change; and apprehensiveness in the presence of ecumenical openness.[172]

Msgr. G. de Proença Sigaud, Archbishop of Diamantina (Brazil), was the founder and guiding light of the group. He was not a "reactionary" solely in matters ecclesiastical; he had an "antirevolutionary" obsession, as well as a passionate opposition to social- and democratic-minded Christians.[173] From the beginning of the Council he saw the need to organize scattered forces for a "parliamentary" activity capable of resisting the conciliar majority. Consequently, in the second half of the first period[174] he set up a small committee as the regular body that, meeting weekly, would make decisions and take action, even though the name International Group of Fathers suggests rather a plenary assembly.[175] He dreamed, in fact, of a "mixed ideologico-national group after the manner of the International Committees of the majority and minority at Vatican I."[176] His plan, never realized, was to establish a "conference of episcopal conferences," the supreme authority of which would be a "conference of conference presidents."

[172] See Gómez de Arteche, Grupos "extra aulam," II/3, 241. The traits listed here can be seen, even during the second period, in interventions by fathers more or less close to the Group, as the reader has already been able to see in the preceding pages and as will be pointed out subsequently. A good presentation of the conciliar positions taken by the Group can also be found in Catholicus, Il Concilio e l'assalto del blocco Centro-Europeo (Rome, 1963).

[173] See History, 2:196.

[174] According to information given personally by Msgr. de Proença Sigaud to Gómes de Arteche (Grupos "extra aulam," II/3, 243 n.8), L. Perrin, in his address ("The International Group of Fathers and the Minority") at the Bologna Coloquium (December 1996), expressed doubts that a "small committee" existed as early as 1962: "I never saw the least sign of it." It is interesting that Msgr. Lefebvre's files on the Group contain no document prior to 1963. In addition, it was only in the summer of 1963 that Lefebvre asked Father Berto to assist him as his personal theologian. The same historian considers October 3, 1963, to be the date of the Group's birth (according to Berto's minutes) or October 2 (according to Dom Prou's agenda). According to the diary of G. Barabino, secretary of Cardinal Siri, the latter took part in an October 22 meeting of a group (about thirty fathers dissatisfied with the work in the hall) that was to take the name International Group of Fathers; at this meeting the fathers decided to meet every Tuesday (Siri continued to be informed but no longer took part in the meetings). See Lai, Il Papa non eletto, 210-11 n.10.

[175] During the fourth period, this name would cause the group difficulties even with Paul VI, who judged that an "international group of fathers sharing the same views on theological and pastoral matters" and set up within the Council was such as to prejudice free debate within the Council. As a result the Group became simply the Committee, but without changing its spirit. See Katholiek Archief 20, nos. 44-45 (10/29 and 11/5/65), cols. 1147-48; Wiltgen, 247-49.

[176] Gómez de Arteche, Grupos "extra aulam", II/3, 243.

From the outset the Brazilian prelate's chief collaborators were Msgr.
M. Lefebvre, French archbishop and Superior General of the Spiritans,[177] and Msgr. L. Carli, Bishop of Segni (Italy). It was during the
44th general congregation, October 7, 1963, that contact was established
between Carli and de Proença. The latter, in an address to the assembly,
had just spoken against the existence of an apostolic and episcopal college of divine right. Hardly had he returned to his place when he received a note from Carli, congratulating him on this intervention. A firm
friendship was thus born; de Proença introduced Carli to Lefebvre, and
the Bishop of Segni agreed to join their committee.[178]

The Group organized weekly lectures, given by fathers, sometimes by
cardinals, aimed at spreading its viewpoint on conciliar subjects. It distributed these talks to the fathers, initially by way of the presidents of the
episcopal conferences, then directly to the bishops. It incited interventions in the hall and sought support for them among the fathers.[179]

B. Numerous Ramifications

Without it being possible or right to connect them explicitly with the
International Group of Fathers,[180] numerous interventions in the hall

[177] Msgr. Lefebvre, who had been Archbishop of Dakar (Senegal) and had been transferred on January 23, 1962, with the personal title of archbishop, to the see of Tulle
(France), was at this time Titular Archbishop of Sinnada in Phrygia.

[178] For the story see Wiltgen, 89. In this context I note that Wiltgen, founder of the
Divine Word Press Service, was, like de Proença, a member of the Society of the Divine
Word and lived with him at the generalate of their congregation (via dei Verbiti). Still,
according to Wiltgen (149-50), on November 9, 1963 (which was the day after Lercaro's
notable intervention in the hall), Carli prepared for the pope's eyes a letter in which he
begged him "to ask the Cardinal Moderators to abstain completely from making public
interventions in their own name, both inside and outside the council hall," because they
gave the impression of being "interpreters of the mind of the Supreme Pontiff," while at
the same time being suspect of leaning "in a certain definite direction." It was supposedly
Cardinal Ruffini who dissuaded him from sending this letter.

[179] Its efforts would go so far as to compose counterschemas, e.g., on religious freedom. On the whole of the Group's activity, see Wiltgen, 148-50.

[180] While the Group was truly the catalyst for the conciliar minority, not all the fathers
of the latter belonged, in a strict sense, to the International Group, and some of them
expressly denied such membership. The Italian, Spanish, Philippine, Latin American, and
French episcopates were the ones most influenced by the Group's propaganda. There was
also a link with the group of missionary bishops (the *Vriendenclub*) through P. Schütte,
Superior General of the Society of the Divine Word and future reporter for the schema on
the Church's missionary activity. On these points see *History*, 2:199. Also, some conservative-minded Council fathers, while not formally allied to the Group, did organize meetings among themselves. Thus, for the period that concerns us, on November 14, 1963,

during the second period followed the line of the Group and, more generally, shared the convictions of the minority. Simply in the debate on the bishops, important examples include Carli's report and the speeches of Ruffini and Browne (November 6), of Florit, Batanian, Del Pino Gómez, and Mason (November 7), of Ottaviani, Browne, de Castro Mayer, Lefebvre, and Ruffini (November 8), and of Carli (November 13).[181] One is struck, first of all, by this "firing squad" that was at work during the first days of the debate on bishops and the government of dioceses.

As for the content of their speeches, we find the recurrence of some major characteristics of the minority outlook, which were mentioned above in the connection with the International Group: radical ultramontanism in response to everything that seemed to be a diminution of papal absolutism (Carli's report, Ruffini, Batanian, Ottaviani, Browne, Lefebvre); a quasi-identification of the Curia with the pope (Batanian, Del Pino Gómez, Mason, Ottaviani); stubborn resistance to the "new" doctrine of collegiality (Ruffini, Florit, Del Pino Gómez, Ottaviani, de Castro Mayer, Lefebvre, Carli); procedural opposition between the straw vote of October 30 and the Council's final decision, this even on the part of the Doctrinal Commission (Ruffini, Browne, Florit, Ottaviani, Carli).[182] Carli's intervention on November 13 was remarkable for having been made in the name of a number of other fathers; the nine signatures were all of formal members of the International Group of Fathers.

It is appropriate at this point to recall one of the ways in which this association acted. When it dealt with each individual father, as when it passed out its circulars, it presented itself expressly as a collective

Siri and Ruffini met with four foreign colleagues: Cardinals Caggiano of Buenos Aires, Santos of Manila, Garibi y Rivera of Guadalajara, and de Arriba y Castro of Tarragona. Cardinals Castaldo of Naples and Quiroga y Palacios of Santiago de Compostela were absent. Their purpose was to analyze the decree on ecumenism and come to an agreement in view of the next day's meeting of the directive bodies of the Council; see Lai, *Il Papa non eletto*, 214 ("Meeting of the Cardinals, Palazzo Pio, November 14, 1963," Siri Archive, Barabino Diary, second period). While Ruffini supported the action of the Group, Siri was hesitant (Berto notes, however, his siding with the Group on November 9, 1963). See Perrin, "Le Coetus internationalis Patrum et la minorité.".

[181] Note the largely "Latin" origin of these interveners: Italian, "Roman" (curial), Spanish, Brazilian, and French.

[182] There was evidently a complete acceptance of the declared purpose of the first meeting of the Group (minutes taken by V. Berto, October 3, 1963): "Opposition to the idea of collegiality in the schema on the Church, adopting as banner the defense of the rights of the Supreme Pontiff and, secondarily, those of each individual bishop" (Perrin, "Le Coetus internationalis Patrum et la minorité").

entity,[183] but when it addressed all the fathers, as in speeches in the hall, each intervener spoke in his own name or possibly, as Carli did, in the name of some other individual fathers, or with reference to previous speakers but not to the Group.

In addition to external support at the Lateran University, at the Roman Seminary, and in the French journal *La cité catholqiue*, this traditionalist organization could also count on the Divine Word News Service of Father Ralph Wiltgen, to say nothing of links with conservative political circles in Latin America and Spain.[184] It was Wiltgen who interviewed Ottaviani on November 13 concerning the Curia and collegiality; he was also to accept into his columns the report of Msgr. D. Romoli, O.P., Bishop of Pescia and former member of the Holy Office, on the procedure followed by that body in issuing a condemnation.[185]

The Group found support in the directive bodies of the Council: in the Council of Presidents, by way of Ruffini and Siri and in the General Secretariat and the Coordinating Commission, where Msgr. Felici, a native of Segni, was a valuable ally of Msgr. Carli and thus of the Committee. But it was only on September 29, 1964, that a cardinal would officially give his support to the organization. From then on, Cardinal R. Santos, Archbishop of Manila (Philippines), would serve as its spokesman in the Sacred College, while other cardinals (Ruffini, Siri, Larraona, and Browne[186]) would patronize the Tuesday evening meetings and lectures of the Group.[187] The audiences that could be counted on at

---

[183] This was the case, for example, with the circular of November 2, 1964 (addressed to "Venerable Father"). It dealt with the vote to be taken two days later on the new schema on the pastoral office of bishops in the church and urged a no vote; it was signed "Geraldo de Proença Sigaud in the name of the International Group of Fathers." The same flyer announced a public meeting of the Group to be held the next day at the Hotel Columbus (via della Conciliazione, 33) and a talk by Msgr. Franić (see Prignon Archive, no. 97).

[184] See *History,* 2:199-200.

[185] See Wiltgen, 118-19. Romoli's public explanations dated from November 22; see *ICI*, no. 206 (December 15, 1963), 17-18.

[186] Browne, we should recall, was vice-president of the Doctrinal Commission (the only one until December 1963), at the side of the president, Ottaviani; Santos too was a member of this commission, as were others of the same tendency (Florit and Franić). Larraona was the head of the Liturgical Commission until the end of the second period, and Dom Prou was a member. This information, which is only partial, helps in drawing a picture of the "antennae" that the Group had in various strategic spots in the meetings of the Council.

[187] Wiltgen, 149.

these meetings would enable the Group to collect as many as 450 signatures for some petitions.[188]

VIII. The Communications Media (November 14-25, 1963)

A. A "Forced March" Vote

During the first period the schema on the means of social communication had been treated somewhat casually. After the tense discussion of the schema on revelation and before the study of the schema on unity that had been prepared by the Commission for the Oriental Churches, the debate on the communications media had seemed like a kind of "break" or a moment for relaxation in the Council's work.[189] The examination had taken barely 360 minutes, divided among the general congregations of November 23, 24, and 26, 1962. Despite the report of Msgr. Stourm, who was convinced of the importance of the subject and of the very great possibilities that the media offered for evangelization, the schema had elicited neither serious fundamental criticisms nor really outstanding suggestions. In form, the schema was found to be too long and too repetitive; as for its substance, among the desires expressed was that the role of the laity be made more prominent and that more care be shown for youth. It was, then, with some eagerness that the fathers agreed to end this discussion. The following day, November 27, they voted on three points: (1) agreement on the substance of the schema; (2) the composition, after a careful study of the observations of the fathers, of a new text that would be shorter but substantially the same when it came to essential doctrinal principles and general pastoral orientations; (3) publication of a pastoral instruction containing practical guidelines.

---

[188] Ibid., 275-78. An example: the petition of the Group against the absence of an explicit condemnation of Marxist communism in schema XIII. Father Berto would say in 1964 that the tactic followed by the Group was to "make allies of the Romans" in order to prevent "a moral unanimity" on the schemas of the majority. He thought it realistic to say that the Group could rally a quarter of the fathers to their theses. The aim was almost realized on two occasions: in September 1964 the petition for the consecration of the world to the Immaculate Heart of Mary (510 signatures) and the already mentioned petition regarding communism in 1965 (454 signatures, according to Msgr. Carbone's count). Usually the number fluctuated between 100 and 250. See Perrin, "Le Groupe internationalis Patrum et la minorite".

[189] See M. Lamberigts, "The Discussion of the Modern Media," *History*, 2:267-79; "Décret sur les moyens de communication sociale," presented and translated by E. Gabel, in *Documents concili ares* 3 (Paris: Cerf, 1966), 375-408.

The vote was overwhelmingly in favor: out of 2160 fathers voting, 2138 were for, 15 against, and there were 7 invalid ballots.

The debate had been flat, then, and had found hardly any echo in the media. This lack of attention is only partly paradoxical, if we realize the deplorable state of conciliar information during the first session, when it was reduced to vague communiques from the Council press office on the progress of the general congregations. Apart from leaks and the press conferences given by some fathers, the English-speaking journalists in particular could count on only one source of useful information, the U.S. Bishops' Press Panel, at which, under the aegis of the bishops of the United States and in particular of Msgr. Wright (Pittsburgh), about a dozen American experts welcomed the journalists every afternoon in order to comment on recent events and above all on the general congregation that had just ended.[190]

After receiving overall approval on November 27, 1962, the schema was then returned to the Commission for the Lay Apostolate and Communications Media for revision.[191] During the intersession the competent subcommission had condensed and improved the text without changing its substance, as the reporter was to insist on November 14, 1963.[192]

---

[190] See *History*, 2, 552-58, especially 553 n.119; J. Grootaers, "L'information religieuse au début du concile: instances officielles et réseaux informels," in *Vatican II commence*, 211-34, especially 218-21.

[191] The 1962 schema had been composed during the preparatory period by the Secretariat for Communications Media, under the leadership of Msgr. M. O'Connor, who had since 1948 been president of the Pontifical Commission for Motion Pictures, Radio, and Television. A. Galletto was secretary of this commission and a member of the secretariat; see *Annuario Pontificio 1949*, 827, and *Annuario Pontificio 1961*, 1013-14 and 1126-26. When the Council began, this secretariat had been absorbed into and become one of the subcommissions within the Commission for the Lay Apostolate and Communications Media, chaired by Cardinal Cento. O'Connor remained its chair, serving also, with Cardinal Silva Henriquez, as vice-president of the entire commission; his secretary, Galletto, also served as secretary of the whole commission. See *Commissioni conciliari*, 53-55.

[192] During the second period the composition of the commission as a whole was as follows: Cardinal F. Cento (Curia), president; Cardinal R. Silva Henriquez (Santiago, Chile) and Msgr. M. O'Connor (Titular Archbishop of Laodicea in Syria; Curia), vice-presidents. Members: Bishops P. Yü-Pin (Nanking, China), A. Samorè (Titular Archbishop of Tirnovo, Italy), E. Colli (Parma, Italy), M. I. Castellano (Siena, Italy), W. Cousins (Milwaukee, USA), T. Morris (Cashel and Emly, Ireland), B. Kominek (Titular Archbishop of Eucaita, Poland), R. Stourm (Sens, France; reporter for the schema on the media), M. Larrain Errázuriz (Talca, Chile), E. Nécsey (Titular Bishop of Velicia; Apostolic Administrator of Nitra, Czechoslovakia), J. Blomjous (Mwanza, Tanganyika), J. Petit (Menevia, Great Britain), A. Herrera y Oria (Malaga, Spain), E. Bednorz (Titular Bishop of Bulla Regia; coadjutor with right of succession of Katowce, Poland), F. Hengsbach (Essen, Germany), J. Granier Gutiérrez (Titular Bishop of Pionia; auxiliary of La Paz, Bolivia), E. de Araujo Sales (Titular Bishop of Tibica; Apostolic Administrator *sede*

On November 11 the amended schema and the report on it were distributed to the conciliar assembly, which on that day was continuing its study of chapter II of the schema on bishops. The booklet contained the new schema, as well as the old one in an appendix.[193] At the request of the moderators, the vote was to be taken the following Thursday in two parts: a first vote on the introduction and chapter I, and a second on chapter II. The vote was to be *placet, non placet,* or *placet iuxta modum.*[194]

The shortened schema contained an introduction (nos. 1-2) on the meaning of the novel title, "Means of Social Communication," and on the "pastoral" purpose of the conciliar decree; the body of the schema was divided into two chapters. Chapter I set forth the teaching of the Church (nos. 3- 12) on several points: the Church's responsibility; safeguarding of the moral law; right to information; relationship between art and morality; public opinion; the duties respectively of "receivers" or users, young people and parents, media personnel, and authors; and, finally, civil authorities. Chapter II (nos. 13-22) spoke in detail of the pastoral activity of the Church: the responsibility of pastors and faithful; Catholic undertakings; the formation of media personnel, authors, and users; technical and economic support for the media; annual and world days; a special office of the Holy See; the competence of bishops; national offices and international associations. The conclusion (nos. 23-24) mentioned the future pastoral instruction and exhorted all persons of good will to make beneficial use of the communications media.

On Thursday, November 14, at the beginning of the 67th general congregation, devoted to the final interventions on episcopal conferences, the vote took place without any new debate and immediately after the report by Msgr. Stourm.[195] The latter said that the revision had followed the three requirements voted on by the fathers during the first

---

plena of Natal, Brazil), J. Ménager (Meaux, France), S. Valloppilly (Tellicherry, India), S. László (Eisenstadt, Austria), G. De Vet (Breda, Netherlands), E. Guano (Livorno, Italy), and L. Civardi (Titular Bishop of Tespia, Italy). Msgr. A. Glorieux and A. Galletto, secretaries; Father P. Dalos, Oratorian, taker of minutes. See *Commissioni Conciliari,* 77-79, and Indelicato, 208-13.

[193] *Schema emendatum Decreti de instrumentis communicationis socialis* (Vatican Polyglot Press, 1963 [58pp.: new schema, 5-13; old, 19-58]); *AS* II/5, 181-90. On the lot of the schema during the second period, see the almost exhaustive work of E. Baragli, *l'Inter Mirifica. Introduzione, Storia, Discussione, Commento, Documentazione,* Collana Magisterium 2 (Rome, 1969), 141-68.

[194] *AS* II/4, 707.

[195] *AS* II/5, 190-92.

period. First, the new revision was made up almost entirely from the substance of the preceding schema. Second, the revised schema was much shorter (9 pages instead of 40; 24 paragraphs instead of 114); the arrangement of the material had been simplified and divided into only two chapters; because of its brevity the text was now called a "decree" rather than a "constitution." Third, the reporter told how the commission had proceeded in its careful study of the observations of the fathers. Of these 82 remarks, a number were concerned with material that was left to a postconciliar instruction. The observations that referred to the shortened text were indicated in it by being put in upper-case letters.

The most important additions were these: (a) a larger place was given to the laity at three points (nos. 3, 13, and 19); (b) the dangers to which the press and spectacles expose the young were brought out better (no. 10 and no. 12 on the duty of parents and the civil authorities to be watchful); (c) Catholics were exhorted to read and spread Catholic newspapers (no. 14); (d) a reference was made to the theater (no. 14); (e) formal improvements were indicated in italics; (f) some emendations could not be introduced into the schema because they did not concern this directly. The emended text, Stourm concluded, was being presented to the assembly for two purposes: (a) to set forth, for the first time at an ecumenical council, the teaching of the Church on questions of the greatest seriousness for the people of today, such as the safeguarding of the moral law, the right to information, public opinion, and the formation of consciences; (b) to highlight the importance of the communications media for the pastoral activity of the Church, a more suitable spread of the gospel message to all human beings of good will, and the establishment of God's reign throughout the entire world.

The votes, separated by four interventions on the schema on the bishops, dealt successively with each of the two chapters of the document, these chapters having first been partially read by the Secretary General.[196] The latter made the results known at the ending of the session; meanwhile the fathers had agreed to end the study of chapter III on the bishops and had begun the discussion of chapter IV. The vote on the introduction and first chapter of the schema was 1832 yes, 92 no, 243 yes with reservations, and 1 void; on the second chapter, 1893 Yes, 103 No, 125 Yes with reservations, and 5 void. The two parts of the text thus received broad approval. By reason, however, of Article 61 §7 of the

[196] *AS* II/5, 192 and 198.

regulations,[197] the moderators decided that a new vote would be taken on the schema as a whole during the following week, the day to be decided; the vote would be either *placet* or *non placet*.

R. Laurentin, a contemporary commentator, gave the following interpretation of the moderators' decision. According to his information, readers of the schema were uneasy on the eve of the vote, for they saw that the shortened text had retained the defects of the old version: triteness, moralism, the trifling role given to the laity, etc.[198] Despite the shortness of time, contacts made in high places gave hope that the moderators would put off the vote in order to allow for further study. The moderators even met during the Mass before the general congregation on November 14. Their effort proved fruitless, but they succeeded at least, despite the much greater than two-thirds approval of the parts, in having a new vote taken some days later, this time on the schema in its entirety; the exact date was not determined at the time but was finally set for November 25.[199]

---

[197] "In particular cases, the moderator can ask for a new vote on the entire schema, in which case the fathers express their judgment on a ballot, saying either *placet* or *non placet*."

[198] See also the convergent testimony of Antoine Wenger, who reported that during a meeting of French bishops at Saint-Louis on Wednesday, November 13, Msgr. Schmitt, Bishop of Metz, had harshly criticized the schema which he found uninspired and lacking in doctrinal perspective. According to interviews conducted by Noel Copin, another newspaperman of *La Croix*, the criticisms of bishops publicly opposed to the schema took the same line: lack of theological perspective (nothing, for example, on the unity of the world that is willed by God and made possible by communication technology), lack of philosophical reflection (on the human significance of recourse to this technology in connection with the idea of dialogue), lack of a sociological basis (no analysis of the social phenomenon of "propaganda" or of the economic stakes in the media). In short, too much morality and too few dynamic ideas. See Wenger, 220-21; *La Croix*, November 24-25, 1963.

[199] See Laurentin, 166, and also the similar report made by Prignon, (typewritten text with "blank spots"): "The decision was made...on the previous evening [November 13] by telephone...at 10:00 p.m.; then Msgr. Villot, etc., and in agreement with Döpfner, the Cardinal [Suenens] promised to try to get the vote put off, because the schema is so impoverished. But unfortunately, before the meeting, the moderators conferred among themselves during Mass, and it happened that when Döpfner saw Cardinal Cento and one or two others passing by, he asked their opinion. And although they could have previously gotten Agagianian's agreement, when the others put their case, Cento reversed himself, and finally the majority of the cardinals present decided nevertheless to vote on the schema. In order to save the day, the Cardinal [Suenens] then proposed that a second vote be taken during the following week on the schema as a whole, allowing *iuxta modum* votes in order to try nevertheless to alleviate the poverty of the schema. Unfortunately, in the vote that day there were only 80 votes against, if my memory is accurate, and some 200 or 300 *iuxta modum* votes, far fewer than expected, which seemed to leave little room for hope. It seems to me that the fathers were weary and wanted at any cost to have this schema voted on" (Prignon Archive, no. 512bis; typewritten report on events from October 27, pp. 18-19).

B. A GROWING BUT BELATED OPPOSITION

Meanwhile, a more careful examination of the schema was causing an ever-growing number of fathers to want a revision. Various methods were then envisaged or undertaken. On the one hand, the chapter-by-chapter discussion provided for in the regulations had been omitted in the case of the schema on the media; it should normally have taken place before the promulgation in order to remedy the inadequacies of the text. On the other hand, since the Secretariat for Communications Media had been joined to the Commission for the Lay Apostolate, was not the examination of the schema the prerogative of the commission in its entirety, all the more so since this commission could now call upon lay people who were media professionals? Consequently, a "counter-expertise" could be suggested even before the presentation of the last *modi* to the assembly, or, again, the commission might be induced of its own accord to withdraw its text for revision.

These various efforts were to prove fruitless, The only solution left for those who wanted a revision was a negative vote. But how could they reverse themselves by rejecting the entire text by a 33 percent vote when each of its chapters had just been accepted by an almost 90 percent majority? Yet, for lack of any better course, an effort along these lines took shape.[200] As early as the afternoon of November 14, at the U.S. Bishops' Press Panel, some journalists concerned with their professional freedom asked for an explanation of Article 12 of the new schema on the special duties of civil authorities with regard to the defense and protection of "a true and just availability of information." They feared a possible governmental censorship of the press on the basis of the following passage, which stated that "the civil authorities, which are legitimately concerned with the well-being of its citizens, have the duty of promulgating laws and diligently enforcing them and thus seeing to it, in a just and vigilant manner, that serious danger to public morals and social progress do not result from a perverted use of these media."[201]

[200] On these several options, see Laurentin, 166-67. B. Olivier also notes that "as soon as the schema became known to competent persons," they disapproved it and that he himself did his duty as an expert "by letting the Congolese Episcopate know of the serious criticisms made of this schema." He adds: "Many bishops were hesitant to 'reverse' themselves by rejecting it, but the opposition to it was nevertheless strong. There was hope of at least a minority of votes against" (*Chronique*," no. 169, 30).

[201] See Wiltgen, 132; for the passage in the decree see *AS* II/5, 185-86. For other details on the activity of the U.S. News Service beginning on November 14, see Baragli, *L'Inter Mirifica* (note 197, above), 145ff.

Two days later, three American Catholic journalists decided to alert the Council fathers: they were John Cogley of *Commonweal*, Robert Kaiser of *Time*, and Michael Novak, correspondent for the *Catholic Reporter* of Kansas City, the *Pilot* of Boston, *Harper's*, and the *New Republic*. Their declaration was signed, as "worthy of consideration," by four well-known experts: J. Courtney Murray, S.J. (American), J. Daniélou, S.J. (French), B. Häring, C.SS.R. (German), and Father J. Mejia (Argentinean). It described the schema not as an *aggiornamento* but as a step backward, with its "hopelessly abstract" picture of relations between the Church and modern culture, its purely theoretical perception of the press, its moralistic emphasis and simplistic treatment of the difficult problem of art and prudence (see no. 6), its omission of the obligations of those who are the source of news (see no. 11), its attribution to the Catholic press of an "almost infallible" doctrinal authority such as does not belong to journalism and is not serviceable in the formation of a public opinion in the Church (see no. 14), its insertion of an ecclesiastical authority intermediate between individual workers in the media and their employers (see no. 21), and its granting to the state an authority over the mass media that is dangerous to political freedom and, in some countries, such as the United States, forbidden by the Constitution (see nos. 5 and 12). The declaration ends by saying that the decree might well be cited some day as a classic example of the inability of Vatican II to face up to the world around it.[202]

According to another witness, E. Gabel,[203] it was after being alerted by these journalists, among others, that the fathers tried to react. But they were paralyzed by the restrictive interpretation of the regulations regarding the vote on November 27, 1962, which had approved the schema "in substance"; it had, therefore, to be preserved. On November 18 a note signed by ninety-seven fathers, four of them cardinals (Alfrink, Frings, Gerlier, Lefebvre), reached Cento's Commission. It called for a new examination of the text, gave five reasons for not accepting it, and ended with the practical recommendation: "If a radical revision of the

---

[202] For the original French and English texts of the motion, which was distributed on St. Peter's Square on November 16, see Baragli, *L'Inter Mirifica,* 617-19. With the text in hand it is possible to show the basic reliability of the information given by Rynne, Wiltgen, and Wenger (Rynne, 257 and 260; Wiltgen, 133-34; Wenger, 221 n.3).

[203] See *Documents conciliaires* 3, 379-80; E. Gabel, A.A., had been a member of the Secretariat for Communications Media.

schema be no longer possible, it would be better to have no schema at the present time than to have this one."[204]

The step taken by the three journalists led in turn to a number of experts undertaking a campaign against the schema before the definitive vote. Through their efforts a Latin text was distributed, saying that the fathers ought to vote against the abridged schema, since it was no longer "in substance" the schema discussed during the first period but a new one; the fathers were therefore not obliged to reverse themselves on a schema they had already approved. The text suggested that instead the moderators pose the following question to the general assembly: "Does it please the Council fathers to have the Coordinating Commission incorporate this schema (the section on the theological foundations) into the schema on the lay apostolate and (for the section on the sociological foundations) into the schema on the Church in the modern world, in order better to bring out the connection between these two texts and the essential thrust of the schema on the media, which has been so carefully prepared by the commission?" A yes vote would be equivalent to a rejection of the schema of the decree on the media.[205]

Father Mejia, who had supported the declaration of the American journalists, himself launched another campaign. He sent the fathers a printed Latin circular marked "Urgent," with a large blank space for signatures.[206] Here is the text:

> Venerable fathers! After having reread the schema on the means of social communication in preparation for the definitive vote, many fathers think that the text of this schema is not at all suitable for a conciliar decree. The fathers are asked to consider whether to vote *non placet*. In point of fact, the schema does not at all meet the expectations of Christians and especially of experts in this area. If the decree were promulgated, it would endanger the authority of the Council.[207]

An accompanying letter urged the fathers, should they agree with the author, to collect as many signatures as possible and send them to him by the evening of the November 24 at the latest; Cardinal Silva Henriquez

---

[204] For the Latin original of the note, dated November 17, 1963, and the ninety-seven signatures (two of them illegible), see Baragli, *L'Inter Mirifica*, 620-21; on the incident, see 153ff.

[205] Wiltgen, 133.

[206] Ibid., 132-33.

[207] For the original Latin text see the copy (Philips Archive, P.049.14) of the circular distributed on the morning of November 25; it carries the signatures of twenty-five fathers. The text is also given in Rynne, 255. The ending repeats almost verbatim the final sentence of the petition of the ninety-seven (see above, note 205).

would carry them the next day to Cardinal Lercaro, who had promised to make good use of them. Wiltgen, from whom these details are taken, comments: "As was evident from the letter, Cardinal Lercaro, who was scheduled to direct that day's meeting, had a plan to block acceptance of the schema."[208] If this analysis of the Divine Word journalist is correct, it corresponds to Laurentin's interpretation and to Prignon's report, namely, that between November 11 and 25, in response to various requests, the moderators endeavored to postpone or even prevent the definitive vote on the schema.

In the face of these maneuvers and criticisms, what was the commission in charge of the revision to do? At most, it could emend the text along the lines of the *modi* submitted on November 14. There were 368 of these, but they had little to do with the substance, as Msgr. Stourm would explain in the report that he would give on November 25 (but which was distributed to the assembly on November 23).[209]

C. An Incident Showing the Council's Uneasiness

Such were the circumstances on Monday, November 25, the day of the final vote. Before the meeting, outside the hall, Mejia's petition was distributed to the fathers; it bore the names of twenty-five fathers (six archbishops, eighteen bishops, and one superior general, from fourteen countries; among them were such leading lights as Schäufele, Volk, and de Smedt).[210] When Secretary General Felici saw the petition being distributed, he tried personally to stop it. Being unsuccessful, he then sent

---

[208] Wiltgen, 134.

[209] *AS* II/6, 18.

[210] The order of the names in the document: H. Schäufele (Freiburg, Germany), A. Fernandez [for: Fernandes] (Titular Archbishop of Madras, India), M. Mihayo (Tabora, Tanganyika), C. Jurgens (Cuzco, Peru), M. Olcomendy [for: Olçomendy] (Malacca-Singapore, Malaysia), A. ven den Hurk (Medan, Indonesia), E. de Smedt (Bruges, Belgium), P. Schoenmaeckers (auxiliary of Malines-Brussels, Belgium) ["the only ones present in the Belgian College when the motion to be signed was brought there," says Olivier about the two Belgian bishops; see Olivier, *Chronique*, 30], J. M. Reuss (Auxiliary of Mainz, Germany), P. J. Schmidt [for: Schmitt] (Metz, France), M. Pourchet (Saint-Flour, France), H. Boyle (Johannesburg, South Africa), A. J. P. Fürstenberg (Abercorn, Rhodesia), J. Corboy (Monze, Rhodesia), F. X. Thomas (Geraldton, Australia), J. Cullinan [for: Cullinane] (auxiliary of Canberra Goulburn, Australia), R. Bogarin (S. Juan de las Mis., Paraguay), H. Maricevich Fleitas (coadjutor of Villarica, Paraguay), V. Zazpe (Rafaele, Argentina), E. Principe (auxiliary of Santa Fe, Argentina), M. Mendiharat (coadjutor of Salto, Uruguay), R. Caceres (Melo, Uruguay), L. Baccino (San José de Mayo, Uruguay), J. Schütte, Superior General of the Society of the Divine Word.

the papal guards. Furious, Felici rushed into the basilica and complained to Cardinal Tisserant, head of the Council of Presidents.[211]

During the 74th general congregation, which followed directly upon the incident in the square, after three addresses on the ecumenism schema then under discussion, moderator Lercaro announced the vote on the communications schema, but said that before that Tisserant would speak. The latter, as president of the Council, "strongly" deplored the distribution, "as did the moderators," because it disturbed the freedom and calm of the Council and was therefore unworthy of it. He first reminded the fathers that the conciliar text had already been accepted by more than the required majority and that each of its chapters was therefore approved.[212]

Next came Msgr. Stourm's report on the examination of the *modi*.[213] At first sight, these seemed to be very numerous, but their convergence allowed them to be reduced to a few; of all these *modi*, many, it seemed, should find a place rather in the postconciliar pastoral instruction. Of the few that remained, the commission thought it could keep only three, which improved the schema without altering its substance; they removed a needless note of severity or shed a better light on the "broad" role assigned to the laity in the schema.[214]

The Secretary General ordered two votes: the first immediately, to approve or not approve the commission's study of the *modi*; the second, later in the course of the same meeting, for a final vote on the schema in

---

[211] See Rynne, 256; but Laurentin, 168, and Wenger, 222, are more allusive. Wiltgen, 134, provides some further details but these disagree in part with Rynne and Laurentin. According to Wiltgen, Mejia himself was standing on the steps of St. Peter's with a stack of printed copies of his petition and distributing them to the fathers as they entered the basilica. A little later, Msgr. Reuss replaced him. When "the huge, angry figure" of Msgr. Felici appeared, he tried to take the papers from Msgr. Reuss's hands (see also Olivier, *Chronique,* 30); a scuffle ensued, and eventually Reuss yielded. According to Rynne, however, it was at the moment when Reuss was entering St. Peter's that Felici tried to take the papers from the hands of the priests who were distributing them; the Mainz auxiliary then protested that he was within his rights. When he failed to stop the distribution, the Secretary General called upon the Swiss guards (on this last point see the brief corroborative reference in Laurentin, and Olivier's *Chronicle,* 30). Baragli, *L'Inter Mirifica,* 161ff., has a slightly different version: one of the distributors, aided by Msgr. P. Nordhues, auxiliary of Paderborn, was in the atrium of the basilica; the other was with Msgr. Reuss on the steps of St. Peter's.

[212] *AS* II/6, 17. As Olivier noted, some persons chose to see in this intervention "an effort of the Council of Presidents to move out of its figurehead role" (ibid.).

[213] *AS* II/6, 18-20.

[214] Stourm seemed to be trying to defend his text against one of the most widespread complaints: the lack of scope left to the laity.

its entirety. Just before the second vote, Felici told the assembly that one of the fathers whose name was on the tract distributed that morning complained to the president that he had never signed it.[215] He also made known the result of the first vote: 1788 voted yes, 331 no, 1 (invalidly) yes with reservations, and 12 invalid ballots. For the definitive vote, 1598 voted yes, 503 no, and there were 11 invalid ballots. The schema was therefore approved.[216] But, says Laurentin, "the announcement of this definitive result elicited only some furtive and delayed applause, in contrast to the warm ovation that followed upon the definitive vote on the liturgical schema, three days before."[217]

The number of *non placet* voters had indeed grown during this second period, moving from 92 and 103 for the chapters on November 14 to 503

---

[215] The rumor went around that this was Msgr. Schäufele (see Caprile, III, 284); according to the archives it was Msgr. V. Zazpe (see Baragli, *L'Inter Mirifica*, 161-62 n.45). Others had supposedly signed thinking the document was meant solely for the directive bodies of the Council. According to the chroniclers, the two interventions of Tisserant and Felici sowed discord among the less convinced opponents of the schema (Laurentin, 168; Wenger, 222). According to Wiltgen and his theory of a plot, "In the face of this unfavorable publicity, the planned attempt at blocking the schema was dropped" (134). Rynne offered another view: "To some the whole incident was but another sign that the minority were prepared to infringe the Council's freedom of action when it suited their purposes" (257). This difference of interpretation doubtless says as much about the personal views of the commentators as about the obscurity of the incident and the closeness of the sources used to the reality. It must be added, however, that Tisserant's rebuke, uttered in his own name and that of the moderators (did he do it with their full consent? perhaps [see below]), could at least seem one-sided and was in fact met with "considerable murmuring" by a large number of fathers (Rynne, 256). They might well have asked why nothing similar had been done or said on October 29 during the vote on the insertion of the schema on the Blessed Virgin into the schema on the Church, when P. Balić's pamphlet had been surreptitiously circulated among the fathers or when the text of Msgr. D. Staffa against collegiality had been distributed in the council hall (Rynne, 256; see Laurentin, 169, who speaks of two papers against this insertion of the schema on the Blessed Virgin, these having been freely distributed at the entrance to St. Peter's). See the same reaction from Msgr. Schoemaeckers shortly after the vote: "I have voted against and I will vote against until the bitter end. This maneuver of Tisserant was unspeakable. Nothing was said when tracts on the subject of the schema on the Blessed Virgin were distributed, and on another occasion tracts of Msgr. Staffa were distributed within the very hall itself" (see Olivier, "Chronique"). Tisserant's argument that each chapter of the schema on the media had already been approved was hardly convincing, as we shall see.

[216] *AS* II/6, 20, 26, 35, 36-37, and 49.

[217] Laurentin, 168. In his diary Dupont likewise wrote: "Some scattered clapping greeted the event" right after citing the "prediction" of Belgian expert B. Rigaux that "this vote will cost the Church hundreds of millions, because it will meet with opposition from all the journalists" (Dupont Archive, "Rome-novembre 63," no. 1728, 164). The more we read the chronicles and especially the diaries, the more we are struck by the general disfavor for the decree among the experts of the majority.

for the entire schema on November 25.[218] It is true that a *placet iuxta modum* vote was possible the first time (there had been 243 and 125 respectively for the two chapters), but this ceases to be significant when one sees that the vote on the examination of the *modi* produced 331 *non placet* votes, which is a high number for a vote that was something of a formality. How was this rapid erosion to be explained?

The fathers who rejected the schema surely did so for varied motives: a minority because they did not find it strict enough at the level of morality, a majority because they found it too weak. As the text was studied, and despite the very short time of about ten days, criticisms continued to pile up. Some fathers had come to realize that the problems of the media had been completely evaded; the schema, introduced as an interlude during the first period, had been hastily voted on, without any new discussion, in order that the second period might end with the promulgation of at least one more decree along with the liturgical constitution.[219]

Even though these fathers were spurred on by journalists' criticisms of the shortened schema, relations between the Council and the press had nevertheless improved greatly and had done so, it must be emphasized, well before this November. Thus, during the intersession the different national press centers covering the Council had decided to coordinate their efforts; since the beginning of the second period a rather detailed account of each general congregation was given to the journalists by the Council press office (under the responsibility of the very recent Press Committee, headed by Msgr. M. O'Connor); furthermore, the fathers themselves were learning to face and use the media in interviews and press conferences.[220] Thus the data of the problem had changed somewhat, and many of the fathers were increasingly realizing the gap between reality and the text they had approved "in substance" the previous year.

The new text, which had hardly been altered between November 14 and 25, was nonetheless to be definitively accepted. The solemn vote and the promulgation by the pope took place on December 4 during the public session that marked the end of the second period. Even at this

---

[218] Rynne (254 and 256) reports a conviction widespread at the time that the negative vote would have been even larger, were it not for the fact that "many bishops had not even troubled to read the text, much less give it serious consideration."

[219] See Gabel, *Documents conciliaires* 3, 378-79. See section VI.C above, "The Conciliar Commissions," for the meeting of the Coordinating Commission on November 15, 1963.

[220] See R. Laurentin, "L'information au Concile," in *Deuxième*, 359-78.

point, part of the opposition would not surrender: there were 164 *non placet* votes against 1960 *placet* votes.[221] In fact, the number of negative votes on November 25 had revived the hopes of some of the fathers, who had even wondered if the pope might not decide to send the schema back to the commission, even at the risk of displeasing the majority in its favor.[222] On November 29, eighteen of the twenty-five fathers whose names appeared on the Mejia flyer addressed a letter of protest to Cardinal Tisserant. Here is the substance of it according to Wiltgen, who gives the text of the letter and the text of Tisserant's response.[223] The distribution of that flyer on St. Peter's Square, they wrote, was described as unworthy of the Council, even though no positive law of the Council forbade the action; "in fact, a short time earlier, a similar distribution took place without any mention of it being made by the President of the Sacred Council." In places where civil liberty reigns, it is not forbidden to draw the attention of the voters to the importance of their vote. This initiative had been taken in the absence of any other means. Thus the signers of the letter judged the Council President's statement to be offensive, and they expected "a rectification of the matter." In his personal answer to each signer, the Cardinal-president repeated the argument that "the schema had been properly prepared, properly presented, properly discussed, and properly approved," so that he regarded as unacceptable any action against it in the neighborhood of the council hall minutes before the vote. He stressed that "it was the Most Eminent moderators themselves who ordered me to deplore this affair, since complaints had been brought to them by Council fathers."

It is thus difficult to untangle the threads of this incident. Did the moderators, or at least "the three," quietly support the minority that was opposed to the schema on the media? This is more than likely, but at the same time (if we may trust Wiltgen's citation) they could not tolerate untimely actions, for they were the guardians of good order in the Council and, in addition, were being pressed by complaints. It would obviously be of very

---

[221] *AS* II/6, 409.

[222] See Wenger, 222-23; Caprile, III, 284 (statements of R. Trisco, B. Häring, and G. Higgins at the American bishops' press office on November 25); Baragli, *L'Inter Mirifica*, 164ff. These hopes, however, were disappointed as early as November 29, when, at the beginning of the 78th general congregation, the secretary of the Council announced the solemn vote and the papal promulgation of the "purely disciplinary" decree at the closing session on December 4; see *AS* II/6, 305. According to another interpretation, however, the pope was letting events take their course, for "it would be a good way to get rid of the measure and remove it from the Council's agenda, allowing events and experience to determine whether it should be vigorously applied or not" (Rynne, 260).

[223] Wiltgen, 135; Rynne, 256-57.

great interest to know the origin of these complaints, for it is possible that the pressure came chiefly from the conservative part of the assembly and from the directing bodies, which did not want a recasting of the text, for reasons either of ideology or also of the Council's effectiveness during the last days of this period as well as in the coming period the next year.[224] But in this perspective, this effectiveness also had an ideological purpose: the content of the preparatory texts was to be changed as little as possible.

Despite all these episodes and all the defects of the conciliar decree on the media, we must also call attention to its merits and novelty.[225] Even if it did not live up to its announced purpose, the text did have a noble twofold purpose, as explained in Stourm's November 14 report: to formulate, for the first time at a council, the official teaching of the Church on questions of importance to contemporary humanity (public morality and public opinion, news, formation of consciences);[226] and to give a better understanding of the importance of the media for pastoral practice and the universal establishment of the reign of God. In the thinking of the reporter at any rate, the plan was a vast one and at the very heart of Christianity. The introduction to the report given on November 25 pointed in addition to "the positive and constructive spirit" that had governed the composition of the schema.[227] I may add to this the happy coining of the expression "means of social communication." This suggested the topicality and "apostolic" need of such a conciliar document or, more accurately, of what the document could have been. But other schemas were in the works that might perhaps take up this "cultural" question again on a broader and more fundamental basis.

---

[224] Moreover, it seems that the fathers were, on the whole, tired and wanted an end to the period; see Prignon's report (above, note 199).

[225] See the lecture of Msgr. J. Bernard, president of the O.C.I.C., given in Rome to a good many Council fathers on November 29 (there is an echo of it in *OssRom* for December 2-3, 1963, 7, cols. 1-2). The lecture was intended as an answer to the criticisms in *La Croix* for November 24-25; for example, the schema's lack of theological perspective, philosophical reflection, and sociological basis (see Caprile, III, 283 n.4).

[226] In justifying the right to information and in locating the role of the state in the area of freedom of the press, the Church was displaying a significant movement beyond its attitude in the nineteenth century and even in the first half of the twentieth. Furthermore, for the first time in so solemn a manner, it was stating its interest in and pastoral concern regarding the real manifestation of civilization represented by the new possibilities of global communication. J. Dupont offers a similar analysis in his reflection on the second session: "The decree at least draws attention to this area which has hitherto been overly neglected by pastors. From this point of view, it can be useful as a starting point, as a first testimony to a concern on the part of the bishops, although the latter are still rather poorly informed" (Dupont Archive, "A Look Back," no. 1759, 8 verso).

[227] See *AS* II/6, 19.

CHAPTER III

TOWARD THE REFORM OF THE LITURGY

REINER KACZYNSKI

After the discussion of the schema of the Constitution on the Sacred Liturgy during the first period of the Council, the amendments proposed orally or in writing by the conciliar fathers were examined by the Liturgical Commission and its subcommissions, with those accepted to be submitted to the fathers for their vote. During the first period, however, the only amendments voted on were those for the preface and for the four sections into which chapter I had been subdivided.[1]

The amendments to the original chapters II-VIII were to be submitted to the judgment of the fathers during the second period.[2] In preparation for these votes subcommissions I, II, and VII-XIII of the Liturgical Commission had examined the proposed amendments up to May 1963 and, as far as was possible and necessary, had integrated these into the text of the schema. The text was then presented to the entire Liturgical Commission at its meeting of April 23 to May 10, 1963. At this meeting chapters VI (sacred furnishings) and VIII (sacred art) were combined into a single chapter VII; chapter VII became chapter VI (sacred music). The schema now had only seven chapters. Toward the end of the meeting it was decided to have the amended text studied again for its Latinity.[3]

---

[1] The votes were taken on November 11 and 30, December 3, 5, and 6. On December 7 a vote was taken on the introduction and the whole of chapter I; see *AS* I/3, 114-21, 157f., 693-707, 739f.; I/4, 166-72, 213, 266-90, 315f., 319f., 360f., 322-27, 361. For the final vote see *AS* I/4, 361f., 384; the result: 1922 for, 11 against, 180 yes with reservations, 5 invalid. For the entire subject see the detailed presentation by M. Lamberigts in *History*, 2:158-66.

[2] See the text prepared by the secretary of the Liturgical Commission, *Ratio agendi in commissione conciliari de Sacra Liturgia congregationibus generalibus concilii oecumenici vacantibus, id est a die 8 dec. 1962 ad diem 8 sep. 1963*, in *Acta et Documenta ad expendendas animadversiones circa Caput I Schematis Constitutionis de sacra Liturgia* [hereinafter: *Acta et Documenta*] (Rome 1962) 118f.

[3] On this point see the general report (dated October 3, 1963) given by Cardinal Lercaro in the council hall on October 8; *AS*, II/2, 276-79. On May 11, 1963, Bishop O. Spülbeck of Meissen was able to report to Cardinal Döpfner: "We finished our work in the Liturgical Commission yesterday with a very positive result in the voting. Although our concerns were not successful across the board, yet the door has been opened or remained open *in every area*. More was hardly to be expected if we want to receive two-thirds of the vote in the hall next Fall. There was good cooperation, although the struggle was

This work was undertaken by a special commission established for the purpose. A. Dirks, C. Egger, N. Ferraro, A.-G. Martimort, and E. Mura were the experts, and the commission met July 2-4, 1963, with Bishop C. Rossi of Biella presiding.

On July 18-19, 1963, all the proposed stylistic improvements were accepted by the members of the Liturgical Commission who were in Rome. Present at this meeting of the commission were Cardinals Larraona, Lercaro, and Giobbe; Bishops E. Dante and C. D'Amato; and P. Schweiger, superior general of the Claretians.[4] In addition, the questions to be raised for discussion in the hall were selected at this meeting. Also invited to the meeting were the heads of the theological and juridical subcommissions, F. Gagnebet and E. Bonet, who gave their reports on chapters II-VIII.[5] In addition, chapters II and III were read out with the improvements made by the Latinists. The reading of the other chapters was dispensed with due to the intense summer heat gripping Rome. On August 1 "everything" was sent to the printery. "Everything" probably meant the remaining booklets, VI-X, of the *Emendationes a Patribus Conciliaribus postulatae, a Commissione Conciliari de sacra Liturgia examinatae et propositae* on chapters II-VIII of the original schema.[6]

In order to inform all the fathers who were members of the Liturgical Commission about the emendations by the Latinists, the president of the commission, Cardinal Larraona, invited them (in July 1963) to a meeting set for Friday, September 27, 1963.[7] The meeting was continued on September 30.[8] The concise notes in the official minutes of both meetings hardly allow one to draw any conclusions about the content of the discussions. All that we are told is that three pages of suggestions from

often a hard one. Cardinal Larraona was a very prudent and well-intentioned president. All of us thanked him sincerely; without his openness a good deal would have been left undone. It is now fundamentally a matter of the rights and functions of the episcopal conferences, which play an essential role in our draft" (Döpfner Archive, Akt 1 Conc VI SQ Nr. 1).

[4] But clearly it was not only with "stylistic improvements" that the meeting dealt; see what is said below about the meetings of the Liturgical Commission on September 28 and 30.

[5] See *Relationes Subcommissionum theologicae et iuridicae circa capita II-VIII Schematis Constitutionis de sacra Liturgia* (Rome, 1963).

[6] See the minutes taken by Antonelli, AV2.

[7] The letter of invitation carries protocol no. 225/CL/63. The meeting in question, the thirty- eighth of the commission, was held at S. Marta on the morning of September 27.

[8] According to the minutes, this thirty-ninth meeting was held in the afternoon of September 30. This is contradicted by the statement in Lercaro's general report (October 3, 1963), according to which there was also a meeting on September 28; *AS*, II/2, 279.

Archbishop P. Hallinan and one from Father Gagnebet were distributed, and that J. Wagner brought with him a page of remarks.[9]

The primary subject matter of these meetings is explained in the private notes of J. Wagner and J. A. Jungmann. On September 26, the day of his arrival in Rome, Wagner met F. Antonelli at the Congregation for Rites and was invited by him to a meeting of the Liturgical Commission on the following day. Originally, only the bishops were to take part in this meeting, but that same day Larraona had told A.-G. Martimort that the experts were also to attend. At a meeting that same evening of Wagner with Martimort and F. McManus an attempt was made to draw up a plan of action, but it did not get very far.[10]

Before their journey to Rome, Wagner and B. Fischer had met in Trier with Bishop A. Martin of Nicolet, Canada. In conversation with him they found that Larraona, acting on the basis of a meeting of commission members present in Rome on July 18-19, 1963, had made a series of "emendations," especially in the chapter on the sacraments.[11] The main purpose was once again to restrict the rights over the Ritual that the schema gave bishops; this was done by altering the formula in Article 63b (previously 47): "These actions having been approved or confirmed by the Apostolic See" (*actis a Sede Apostolica probatis seu confirmatis*) so as to replace the merely explanatory *seu* with *vel* and to have it read: *actis a Sede Apostolica confirmatis vel probatis*.

A printed sheet of these emendations provided the basis of discussion at the meeting on September 27. Chapters II and III were discussed, and especially the change in the text of Article 63b. Each of the five members could offer further amendments. The reporter on chapter III, Archbishop P. Hallinan of Atlanta, had prepared a written document for the meeting, with the help of which he wanted to reverse the change in Article 63b and a number of other changes in the schema.[12] He was supported in this endeavor by Martimort and Wagner.[13] Hallinan succeeded

[9] Antonelli, Minutes.

[10] See Wagner's notes for September 26, 1963 (Wagner Archive, Trier, vol. 39).

[11] See Wagner's notes, September 27.

[12] See *Commissio de sacra Liturgia. Documenta secundae sessionis* [hereinafter: DOC, II] (Rome, 1963), 1-3. On the entire episode see *TJungmann* for September 9, 1963.

[13] Martimort had composed a memorandum on these amendments; we have handwritten notes of B. Fischer about this document (B. Fischer Archive, Deutsches Liturgisches Institut, Trier). Among the notes of Jungmann in the archive of the ISR there are, under the date September 9, 1963, Wagner's handwritten "Deliberationes utrum in Article 63b Const. de s. Liturgia praeferenda sit formula 'probatis seu confirmatis' an 'confirmatis vel probatis' vel alia", where Wagner came out unequivocally for the first of these formulas.

at least in the case of Article 63b in having the formula changed, on September 30, to *actis a Sede Apostolica recognitis.*

The day before, September 29, in his address during the second public assembly (which opened the second period of the Council) Pope Paul VI had described the liturgy as a broad field of work for the Council. There had been detailed discussion of the liturgy during the first period; now there was hope that this work would come to a happy conclusion.[14]

I. THE VOTES DURING THE SECOND PERIOD

At the beginning of the second period the introduction and first chapter ("General Principles for the Restoration and Promotion of the Sacred Liturgy") of the schema on the liturgy were already available in what was essentially the definitive version of the text, what was to become the Constitution on the Sacred Liturgy at the third public assembly. The *modi* submitted by the fathers had not required any further changes in content. The Council had thereby taken the most important step in its work on liturgical theology and pastoral practice.

It had made a definitive pronouncement, "The Nature of the Sacred Liturgy and Its Importance in the Life of the Church" (Articles 5-13); had issued guidelines, "The Promotion of Liturgical Instruction and Active Participation" (Articles 14-20); and had pointed the way in its "The Reform of the Sacred Liturgy" (Articles 21-40) by giving "General Norms" (Articles 22-25), "Norms Drawn from the Hierarchic and Communal Nature of the Liturgy" (Articles 26-32), "Norms Based on the Educative and Pastoral Nature of the Liturgy" (Articles 33-36), and "Norms for Adapting the Liturgy to the Temperament and Traditions of Peoples" (Articles 37-40), as well as encouraging the "Promotion of Liturgical Life in Diocese and Parish" (Articles 41-42) and the "Promotion of Pastoral Liturgical Actions" (Articles 43-46). These general principles were to be given concrete application in the next seven chapters of the schema; while these had already been discussed, they were at this point only available to the fathers in the form they had had at the beginning of the first period and not yet in the amended text that resulted from the work of the Liturgical Commission during the intersession.

[14] See *AS* II/1, 193.

A. The Votes on the Amendments

1. Chapter II: The Eucharistic Mystery

At the end of the 40th general congregation (October 3) General Secretary Felici announced the distribution of the proposed amendments to chapter II of the liturgy schema, on the mass,[15] and this took place on the next day. At the same time the beginning of the voting was fixed for the following Thursday, October 8.[16]

The Liturgical Commission had met for its fortieth session on the afternoon of October 7.[17] The next day, Lercaro first gave his general report, in which he summarized the work accomplished by the Liturgical Commission.[18] He began by referring to "Procedures of the Conciliar Commission on the Liturgy," which contained twenty-six articles and had been composed by a special subcommission headed by Cardinal A. Jullien.[19] He then named the thirteen subcommissions and reported

[15] See *AS* II/2, 64.

[16] See ibid., 67. The texts contained in the booklet, *Emendationes a Patribus Conciliaribus postulatae, a Commissione Conciliari de sacra Liturgia examinatae et propositae. VI. Caput II Schematis. De sacrosancto Eucharistiae mysterio*, are printed in *AS* II/2, 280-82, 295-308, 283-89.

[17] At this meeting the text of the general report that Lercaro was to make the next day was distributed, as was a sheet containing two suggestions for improvement: the one from Hallinan dealt with the section of his report dealing with Article 63b; the other, from Jenny, dealt with the final sentence of the declaration of the Council on reform of the calendar, which was intended as an appendix to the Constitution on the Liturgy. Both suggestions were accepted.

Because of this meeting, the German-speaking bishops on the Liturgical Commission were unable to attend the simultaneous meeting of the German-speaking bishops at the Anima and to report on the coming votes. Döpfner therefore asked Wagner for a written document, to be given to Frings, that would possibly guide the German-speaking Council fathers. In this one-page document, Wagner explained, with regard to the content of the proposed nineteen amendments of chapter II of the liturgy schema, that with one exception they were real improvements and corresponded to what had been said by the German bishops. Only the sixth proposed amendment represented an unnecessary weakening of the original text. It should nevertheless be accepted in order not to cause any delay. Wagner advised the bishops to vote *placet* on all nineteen amendments but then, in the vote on the entire chapter, to try to improve the text by means of *placet iuxta modum* votes, insofar as this seemed opportune. This was an appropriate move for Article 55 §2, where, according to the wish of many bishops, wedding masses should be included as a fourth example of communion in the cup. See Wagner's letter of October 7 to Frings, which was brought to the attention also of Döpfner, and Wagner's one-page document "Constitutio de S. Liturgia, Bemerkungen zu den beiden Abstimmungsvorgänge über das Caput II De Ss. Eucharistiae mysterio" (Wagner Archive, vol. 39).

[18] See *AS* II/2, 276-79.

[19] See *Ratio procedendi commissionis conciliaris de sacra Liturgia*, in *Acta et documenta*, 6-10 (first draft) and 11-15 (definitive text).

on their activity during the first period of the Council and during the intersession. Finally, he explained the structure of the pamphlets that were to be distributed on the following days, containing the amendments being proposed by the entire commission for a vote. In accordance with Article 60 §3 of the Regulations for the Council, the vote on each individual emendation had to be either *placet* (yes) or *non placet* (no), whereas in the concluding vote on the text in its entirety there could be a *placet iuxta modum* (yes with reservations) vote as well. Lercaro concluded his remarks by citing some words of the pope in his opening address: everyone hoped "that the work done might now be brought to a happy conclusion."[20]

After Lercaro's report, Bishop I. Enciso Viana of Mallorca, reporter for chapter II of the schema, spoke, limiting himself to the part of the draft that had been distributed to the fathers.[21] After assuring them that efforts had been made to examine carefully all the observations of the fathers, both oral and written,[22] he spoke only on the most debated questions, the use of the vernacular, communion under two kinds, and concelebration.

With regard to the vernacular, the suggested changes were very diverse and even contradictory: some were general, some were concrete; some proposed rejection, some approval, some a middle way. In Article 54 (previously 41) the commission had sought formulations such that no school of thought could use them to impose its practice on any other. The only thing prescribed was that all the faithful should know the Latin ordinary of the mass. The "territorial authorities" (the later episcopal conferences) were to have jurisdiction in the use of the vernacular in the readings and intercessions. For the other parts of the celebration of mass a distinction was to be made depending on whether they were read or sung by the community or by the priest. In regard to the former, the "territorial authorities" again had jurisdiction. The use of the vernacular was not excluded in principle for any part of the mass, although some fathers wanted such an exclusion for the canon.

---

[20] *AS* II/1, 193. The text of the report was distributed to the fathers at the end of this general congregation.

[21] See *AS* II/2, 290-95.

[22] The *Animadversiones in Schema Constitutionis de Sacra Liturgia* fill 218 pages for chapter II, *De Sacrosancto Eucharistiae Mysterio*; in addition, in the appendix volume there are a further 20 pages (38-57). The comments, like those on the other chapters, are typewritten and were duplicated for the use of the fathers and experts of the Liturgical Commission; see *AS* II/2, 295 n.1.

In Article 55 (previously 42) there was a sentence at the beginning about the community receiving communion "after the communion of the priest...from the same sacrifice." With regard to communion under both kinds the commission had weighed the reasons given by the fathers for and against this practice and had come up with a formulation that recalled the teaching of the Council of Trent and said that the cases in which communion under both kinds is possible are to be outlined by the Apostolic See. To the example of the mass of Ordination were added the mass for religious profession and the mass following the baptism of an adult (some fathers regarded a wedding mass as not a proper occasion); there were thus occasions for priests, for religious, and for the laity.

In Article 57 (previously 44 and 45) further possible occasions for concelebration were accepted, in addition to the mass of chrism and at meetings of priests. It was stressed that the introduction of concelebration did not mean that individual celebration was not possible or appropriate.

While the commission did not present minor, primarily stylistic changes for a vote, it did present the fathers with nineteen proposed amendments on which they were to vote.[23] On this same morning a vote was taken on the first five. These had to do with the theological content, a statement about Sunday mass, more precise instructions for the revision of the order of mass, and the homily.[24]

During the 44th general congregation (October 9), the voting on the amendments of chapter II continued. Seven of them were presented, four of them having to do with the language of the liturgy, two with the reception of communion, and one with the participation of the faithful in the entire mass on Sundays and feastdays.[25]

[23] See AS II/2, 280-82.

[24] (1) Reformulation of the future Article 47 (previously the first paragraph of the introduction): 2278 for, 12 against, 8 invalid. (2) Insertion in Article 49 (previously the third paragraph of the introduction): 2264 for, 14 against, 12 invalid. (3) Addition to Article 50 (previously 37) on the revision of the order of mass: 2249 for, 31 against, 4 invalid. (4) Completion of Article 52 (previously 39) by a description of the homily: 2263 for, 15 against, 7 invalid. (5) Addition to Article 52 (previously 39) regarding the homily on Sundays and holidays of obligation: 2261 for, 18 against, 5 invalid. AS II/2, 329, 335, 338, 342.

[25] On Article 54 (previously 41) on the language of the liturgy: (6) Use of the vernacular as a possibility: 2215 for, 52 against, 8 invalid. (7) Use of the vernacular in the parts belonging to the people: 2212 for, 47 against, 19 invalid. (8) The ordinary of the mass should be familiar in Latin as well: 2193 for, 44 against, 14 invalid. (9) Extension of the use of the vernacular: 2139 for, 67 against, 13 invalid. (10) Reception of the host from the same sacrifice: 2159 for, 46 against, 13 invalid. (11) Communion from the cup: 2131 for, 96 against, 9 invalid. On Article 56 (previously 43) on the participation of the faithful in the entire mass: (12) 2232 for, 14 against, 8 invalid. AS II/2, 360-61, 384.

The seven suggested improvements on chapter II that were presented for a vote during the 45th general congregation (Thursday, October 10) had to do with concelebration: it was to be given a theological basis, the number of occasions was to be increased, and the possibility of individual celebration was to be left untouched.[26] At the end of the day Felici announced that all the improvements had been accepted by the fathers and that therefore a vote would be taken on the entire chapter II at the 47th general congregation (Monday, October 14); at that point, a vote *placet iuxta modum* was possible. But anyone so voting must hand in, along with his voting card, clearly written *modi* on separate sheets.[27]

Since 2242 fathers were present, the two-thirds majority required for approval was 1495. In fact, only 1417 voted *placet*. There were 36 *non placet*, and 781 *placet iuxta modum*, while 8 ballots were invalid.[28] As a result, chapter II was not rejected, since a *placet iuxta modum* was essentially a yes, but neither could the chapter be regarded as approved. Rather, in accordance with the regulations of the Council, it had to be sent back to the Liturgical Commission with the stipulation that the *modi* be examined and, if need be, incorporated.[29]

2. Chapter III: The Other Sacraments

After the amendments proposed for chapter III (on the other sacraments and the sacramentals) had been announced in advance on October 10 and distributed the next day,[30] Archbishop Hallinan gave his report as the first speaker at the general congregation on October 15.[31] After letting the fathers know that the commission had considered most of the

[26] Proposals all having to do with Article 57 (previously 44-46) on concelebration: (13) Unity of the priesthood as basis: 2166 for, 92 against, 5 invalid. (14) Evening mass on Holy Thursday: 2088 for, 168 against, 9 invalid. (15) Meetings of bishops: 2111 for, 142 against, 6 invalid (ibid.). (16) Consecration of an abbot: 2006 for, 142 against, 18 invalid. (17) Conventual mass when there is no need of individual celebrations: 1839 for, 315 against, 9 invalid. (18) Meetings of priests: 1975 for, 245 against, 4 invalid. (19) Individual celebration: 2159 for, 66 against, 6 invalid. *AS* II/2, 435-36.

[27] See ibid. The voting procedure would be explained again the next day; see ibid., 439f.

[28] See ibid., 520.

[29] See *Ordo Concilii Oecumenici Vaticani II celebrandi*, Article 36, in *ADP* I, 318 (2d rev. ed. in *AS* II/1, 36).

[30] See *AS* II/2, 436, 439, and 548-71 for the texts the fathers received for amending chapter III.

[31] See *AS* II/2, 560-71.

proposed amendments to be good and useful,[32] he explained that many of the proposals were not taken up because they were the concern of other commissions or dealt with details that were left to be settled by the postconciliar commission or by pastoral directories or specific rituals or because they had already been sufficiently taken into account at some other point in the schema. Of the proposed amendments the commission did consider, some were not offered for a vote because they had to do with style and Latinity and were of lesser importance. Hallinan's written report commented on all twenty-four Articles, from 59-82. Only ten amendments were to be submitted to the fathers for a vote. During this same morning a vote was taken on the first four proposals, which had to do with the sacramentals, the use of the vernacular, the rite of baptism, and the anointing of the sick.[33] On October 16 a vote was taken on four more proposed amendments in chapter III: two had to do with the appropriate time for the anointing of the sick and with its repetition, and one each with the laying on hands at the consecration of a bishop and with the nuptial blessing.[34] The following day the final two amendments in chapter III were brought to a vote, having to do with the administration of sacramentals by lay people and with religious profession and renewal of vows.[35] It was also announced that on the next day a vote would be taken on chapter III as a whole and, that a vote, *placet iuxta modum*, would again be permitted; the fathers should therefore have

[32] The *Animadversiones in schema Constitutionis de Sacra Liturgia* contain 110 pages for chapter III, "De Sacramentis et Sacramentalibus"; there are eleven more pages in the appendix volume (58-69).

[33] (1) Introduction of Article 60 (previously a preface) on the nature and effects of the sacramentals: 2224 for, 12 against, 3 invalid. (2) Amendment of Article 63 (previously 47) on the use of the vernacular, with regard to the "form of the sacraments": 2103 for, 49 against, 7 invalid. (3) Amendment of Article 68 (previously 52) on the adaptation of the baptismal rite to a large number of baptizands: 2058 for, 42 against. (4) Reformulation of the first sentence of Article 73 (previously 57) on the names and recipients of the sacrament of the sick: 2,143 for, 35 against. *AS* II/2, 598, 601.

[34] (5) Reformulation of the continuation of Article 73 (previously 57) on the proper moment for reception: 2219 for, 37 against, 3 invalid. (6) Removal of the originally planned Article 60 on the possibility of repeating the anointing of the sick: 1964 for, 247 against, 5 invalid. (7) Addition to Article 76 (previously 61) concerning the laying on hands at the consecration of a bishop: 2124 for, 50 against, 1 invalid. (8) Amendment of Article 78 (previously 63) on the blessing of a couple outside mass: 2194 for, 24 against, 2 invalid. *AS* II/2, 639.

[35] (9) Amendment of Article 79 (previously 64) on the possibility of allowing lay persons to administer certain sacramentals: 1637 for, 607 against, 5 invalid. (10) Amendment of Article 80 (previously 65) on the revision of the rites of religious profession and renewal of vows: 2207 for, 39 against, 2 invalid. *AS* II/3, 48-49.

their *modi* ready.[36] On October 18, Felici introduced the voting on the
chapter III in its entirety. Of the 2217 fathers who cast votes, 1130 voted
placet, 30 *non placet*, 1054 *placet iuxta modum*, and 3 ballots were
invalid. Consequently, chapter III was not yet approved and had to be
sent back to the Liturgical Commission with the request that it examine
the *modi* and, if need be, incorporate them.[37]

3. Chapter IV: The Divine Office

On October 18 the fathers received the proposed amendments to
chapter IV, on the liturgy of the hours.[38] The first speaker on October
21 was Bishop A. Martin, who gave his report.[39] He stated first that an
especially large number of improvements had been suggested by the
fathers and that all of them had been carefully studied.[40] Also considered was a 1957 report from a Commission for the Congregation for
Rites of which Father A. Bea, as he was then, was president. That
report was based on the petitions regarding a reform of the breviary,
which the metropolitans had sent to Rome at the request of the Apostolic See and after consulting the bishops and experts of their ecclesiastical provinces.

Martin's report was divided into five sections. After a theological
description of the liturgy of the hours, its reform was discussed in general, followed by the reform of individual elements, the obligation to read
the breviary, and the language to be used. Thirteen amendments were to
be presented for a vote. On this day there was to be a vote only on the
first four, all of them dealing with what had previously been the introduction.[41] On October 22 a vote was taken on five more emendations of
chapter IV: three of them had to do with concrete reforms, one with the
spiritual value of the liturgy of the hours and one with the revision of the

---

[36] See *AS* II/3, 9.
[37] See *AS* II/3, 53, 91.
[38] Ibid., 53 and 114-46 for the texts the fathers received for amending chapter IV.
[39] See *AS* II/3, 124-46.
[40] The *Animadversiones in Schema Constitutionis de Sacra Liturgia* for chapter IV ran
to 204 pages.
[41] (1) Reformulation of the Article 83 (previously the beginning of the second paragraph of the introduction) on the priestly activity of Christ in the liturgy of the hours:
2153 for, 8 against, 4 invalid. (2) Reformulation of Article 84 (previously the end of the
second paragraph of the introduction) on those praying the liturgy of the hours: 2009 for,
12 against, 1 invalid. (3) A new Article 86, on the necessity of the liturgy of the hours for
priests in the care of souls: 2130 for, 9 against, 2 invalid. *AS* II/3 168, 171.

psalter.[42] The last five amendments, one having to do with the reform and the rest with the fulfillment of the obligation, were put to a vote on October 23.[43] The vote on the entire chapter IV followed on the next day. Of the 2236 fathers, 1638 voted *placet*, 43 *non placet*, 552 *placet iuxta modum*, and 3 ballots were invalid. Since 1491 was the needed two-thirds majority, chapter IV was approved.[44]

4. Chapter V: The Liturgical Year

Since time was pressing, the suggested emendations for chapter V, on the liturgical year, had already been distributed to the fathers on October 22.[45] Two days later, Döpfner, the moderator, gave the floor to the first speaker, Bishop F. S. Zauner of Linz, for his report.[46] The bishop said first that all the addresses of the eighty-five fathers who had given their views on chapter V had been collected in a single volume;[47] some of the observations made by the fathers pertained, however, to other commissions; a number of them touched on details to be decided on by the post-conciliar commission; and others had been considered in other chapters of the schema. He then presented the changes that had been made in the schema, among them the ten amendments that the commission was proposing for a vote. At the end he gave the reasons that had motivated the commission to place the statements on calendar reform in an appendix to the schema, where they took the form of a Declaration. The Council

---

[42] (4) A more concrete version of Article 89c (previously 68c) on the reform of Matins: 2113 for, 118 against, 3 invalid. (5) Reformulation of Article 89d on the discontinuation of Prime: 1722 for, 509 against. (6) Reformulation of Article 89e (previously 68d) on the "little hours": 1840 for, 371 against, 5 invalid. (7). Reformulation of Article 90 on the spiritual significance of the liturgy of the hours, which is to be taken into consideration in the reform: 2111 for, 12 against. (8) Expansion of Article 91 (previously 69) by advice on the way of revising the psalms: 2088 for, 20 against, 2 invalid. *AS* II/3, 215-16.

[43] (9) Omission of previous Article 72, which contained some remarks on concrete reform measures: 2111 for, 118 against, 1 invalid. (10) Addition of the first paragraph of a new Article 97 on the possible substitution of another liturgical service for the Divine Office: 2200 for, 24 against, 1 invalid. (11) Addition of the second paragraph of a new Article 97 on dispensation from or commutation of the liturgy of the hours: 2125 for, 34 against, 1 invalid. (12) Expansion of Article 101 §1 (previously 77a) on dispensation from the reading of the liturgy of the hours in Latin: 1904 for, 131 against, 5 invalid. (13) Expansion of Article 99 (previously 78) on the communal celebration of the liturgy of the hours (1960 for, 219 against, 2 invalid. *AS* II/3, 259-60.

[44] See *AS* II/3, 290.

[45] Ibid., 171 and 264-77 for the texts the fathers received on amending chapter V.

[46] AS II/3, 272-77.

[47] For chapter V, the *Animadversiones in schema Constitutionis de Sacra Liturgia* occupy eighty-six pages.

was unable to come to any decisions on calendar reform; because of the international implications of the problem it could only voice its opinion. And in order not to cause offense to the separated brothers, the Council should only let it be known that it had no difficulty with a fixed date for the celebration of Easter.

In the course of this general congregation the first five amendments were put to a vote. These had to do with the veneration of Mary during the Church year, the education of the faithful during the liturgical year, possibilities of adaptation, the celebration of Sunday, and Lent.[48] On October 25 the last five emendations for chapter V of the liturgical schema were called up for a vote. Two of them had to do with Lent, one with the veneration of the saints, and two with the planned appendix on calendar reform.[49] On October 29 a vote was taken on the entire chapter V. Of the 2193 fathers present 2154 voted *placet*, 21 *non placet*, 16 *placet iuxta modum*, and 2 ballots were invalid. Chapter V was thereby approved.[50]

5. Chapter VI (formerly VII): Sacred Music

On October 26) the booklet containing the proposed emendations in chapter VI (previously VII), on sacred music, had been distributed. In addition, the general secretary had earlier announced that the emendations for the former chapters VI and VII, dealing with similar matters, would be distributed later.[51]

---

[48] 1) Extensive reformulation of Article 103 (previously the conclusion of the first paragraph of the introduction) on the veneration of Mary, since she is closely connected with the saving work of Christ: 2217 for, 15 against. (2) Addition to Article 105 (previously the third paragraph of the introduction) on the education of the faithful through instruction, prayer, and works of penance and mercy: 2148 for, 9 against, 1 invalid. (3) Addition to Article 107 (previously 79) on possibilities of adaptation according to local circumstances: 2071 for, 11 against, 3 invalid. (4) Reformulation of Article 106 (previously 80) on Sunday: 2049 for, 10 against, 1 invalid. (5) Reformulation of the introduction to Article 109 (previously 82) on the twofold purpose of Lent: 2146 for, 4 against, 1 invalid. *AS* II/3, 345-46.

[49] (6) Addition of indications on catechesis for the sacrament of penance in Article 109b (previously 82b): 2181 for, 10 against, 1 invalid. (7) Addition to Article 110 (previously 83) on encouragement of the practice of penance: 2171 for, 8 against, 1 invalid. (8) Addition to Article 111 (previously 84) on veneration of the saints and relics: 2057 for, 13, against, 1 invalid. (9) Determination of the title of the planned appendix (previously Articles 85-86): 2057 for, 4 against, 1 invalid. (10) Reformulation of the introduction to the appendix: 2058 for, 9 against, 1 invalid. *AS* II/3, 390.

[50] See *AS* II/3, 527.

[51] Ibid., 349-50 and 576-89 for the texts the fathers received for amending chapter VII.

The first speaker on October 29) was Bishop C. D'Amato, O.S.B., abbot of St. Paul's Outside the Walls, who gave the report.[52] He explained that the fathers had made only a few observations on the chapter on sacred music[53] and that, consequently, only a few changes had been made in the text. Only six of these were to be voted on by the fathers, three of them during the present general congregation; of these, two related to a liturgy celebrated with singing, and one to the establishment of institutes of music.[54] On October 30 the vote was taken on the last three proposed emendations, one having to do with the training of missionaries, another with the organ, and a third with composers of liturgical music.[55]

Since all the votes on chapter VI had positive results, the moderator, Cardinal Lercaro, had the vote on the entire chapter VI taken immediately. Of the 2096 fathers present 2080 voted *placet*, 6 *non placet*, and 9 *placet iuxta modum*; 1 ballot was invalid. Thus chapter VI was approved.[56] Even before the result of this vote was announced the moderator made it known that the fathers who had voted *placet iuxta modum* could hand in their *modi* to the General Secretariat on the following day.[57]

6. Chapter VII (former VI and VIII): Sacred Art and Furnishings

The suggested emendations for chapter VII, which was made up of the previous chapters VI and VIII and dealt with liturgical art and furnishings, were distributed on October 30, with the vote announced for the next day.[58] Bishop C. Rossi of Biella was the first speaker and gave

---

[52] Ibid., 583-89.

[53] Chapter VII, on sacred music, occupied 38 pages in the *Animadversiones in schema Constitutionis de Sacra Liturgia.*

[54] (1) Reformulation of Article 112 (previously the first paragraph of the introduction) on liturgical singing as an integral part of the liturgy: 2087 for, 5 against, 1 invalid. (2) Reformulation of Article 113 (previously 91) on a solemn service with singing: 2106 for, 13 against, 1 invalid. (3) In Article 115 (previously 93), addition of a recommendation that higher institutes of music be established: 2147 for, 9 against, 1 invalid. *AS* II/3, 627-28, 671.

[55] (4) Change in Article 119 (previously 97) on the musical training of missionaries: 1882 for, 39 against, 1 invalid. (5) More precise terminology in Article 120 (previously 98) on the organ: 1897 for, 41 against, 3 invalid. (6) Reformulation of Article 121 (previously the second paragraph of 94 and 96) on Church musicians: 1990 for, 7 against, 2 invalid. *AS* II/3, 671.

[56] See *AS* II/3, 671.

[57] Ibid., 669.

[58] *AS* II/3, 631 and *AS*, II/4 10-27 for the texts the fathers received for amending chapters VI and VI.

his short report on October 31.[59] In it, he justified the joining of what
had earlier been chapters VI and VIII and then reported that many of the
fathers had submitted observations on the material, all of which had
been carefully examined during the improvement of the text.[60] He next
spoke of the individual emendations but emphasized that three questions
in particular had drawn the fathers' attention. The first had to do with the
acceptance of modern works of art into churches; the second with the
installation and veneration of images; the third with expenditure on
things needed for worship. The commission had sought to strike a balance between contradictory views and to hold a middle ground in the
schema's statements. Almost everything on liturgical utensils in the former chapter VI had been omitted, but the article on the use of pontificals
(130, previously 89) had been kept. In addition, the commission did not
want to involve itself in questions of detail, since this could not be the
role of an ecumenical council but rather of postconciliar commissions.

After the report the moderator, Döpfner, with the agreement of the
Council of Presidents, suggested that, because this final chapter of the
schema raised no controversial questions, the votes on the individual
emendations be omitted and a vote be taken immediately on the chapter
as a whole. The fathers applauded and showed their agreement by rising
from their seats.[61] Of the 1941 fathers present, 1838 voted *placet*, 9 *non
placet*, 94 *placet iuxta modum*. Thus chapter VI was likewise
approved.[62]

B. The Activity of the Liturgical Commission

Joseph Schmitz van Vorst, Roman correspondent of the *Frankfurter
Allgemeine Zeitung*, was probably not wrong when he reported the following from Rome, after chapter II of the liturgical schema did not
receive the majority required for approval at the general congregation of
November 14: "This result initially produced a certain discouragement

---

[59] *AS*, II/3, 24-27.

[60] The *Animadversiones in schema Constitutionis de Sacra Liturgia* contain twenty-
nine pages on chapter VI (sacred furnishings) and forty-five on chapter VII (sacred art).

[61] After the general secretary had read the emendations as well as the beginning and
end of the new chapter VII, the moderator indicated that any *modi* could be handed in
during the following week; *AS* II/4, 27.

[62] Ibid., 77.

among the Council fathers."[63] Martimort spoke even more forthrightly, in a letter of November 15 to Lercaro, of a "very great confusion — and even a disappointment of the fathers, as well as of public opinion outside the Council."[64] The Liturgical Commission realized that more hard work still lay ahead in the examination of the 781 *placet iuxta modum* votes on chapter II. The amount of work was sizably increased when chapter III was also not approved at the general congregation of November 18 and was sent back to the commission along with the 1054 *placet iuxta modum* votes.

Some members of the Liturgical Commission were probably pleased that after the votes on the emendations, chapters II and III had not yet been approved by the Council; they now had time further to "correct" the schema with the help of the *modi* and to blunt the force of statements that sounded all too "progressive."[65] The large number of amendments proposed for a vote, especially for chapters II-IV, had given the fathers the opportunity to express their displeasure by means of a *non placet* vote, and then with the final votes on the chapters they had seized the opportunity to recommend changes in the text by means of *placet iuxta modum* votes. On the other hand, the majority of the commission, and especially of its advisers, regarded the entire voting process and the negative results of the final votes on chapters II and III as endangering the schema.

After 781 fathers had voted *placet iuxta modum* on chapter II and 1054 on chapter III, most of the members of the Liturgical Commission were evidently fearful of the final vote on chapter IV. For this reason, on October 19 some of the members and advisers wrote a letter to all the

---

[63] *Franfurter Algemeine Zeitung, Das Konzil, Zweite Session,* 31. The same correspondent, however, was wrong when he reported from Rome on October 10, 1963, that "the 180 *iuxta modum* votes that had been handed in the previous December for chapter I of the liturgical schema had, as reported, gone by the board" (ibid., 30). After the vote on December 7, 1962, the general secretary of the Council had indeed stated that since chapter I as a whole had been approved, there was no need to send in *modi* (see *AS* I/4, 384); on this subject see the *Relatio Subcommissionis iuridicae de modis expendendis,* in *Commissio de sacra liturgia. Documenta secundae Sessionis* (Rome, 1963) 5-8. Despite the general secretary's statement the commission did undertake an examination of the observations (*expensio modorum*), although it was not obligated to do so; it was able to present these for a vote only in November 1963, along with the *expensio modorum* for the other chapters.

[64] Lercaro Archives, XXII 518. Martimort therefore suggested that as soon as possible, perhaps as early as the following Friday (October18), the *expensio modorum* be presented in the hall in order to correct the bad impression.

[65] See the effort of E. Dante to delay the work on the schema described in the report of the 42nd meeting of the Liturgical Commission.

CHAPTER III

episcopal conferences in which they almost implored the bishops to vote *placet* on the remaining chapters of the liturgy schema, without handing in any *modi*. *Modi* could indeed contribute to the improvement of the conciliar text, but they could also endanger the entire schema, because the Liturgical Commission could hardly complete its work by the date the pope had in mind and because, especially in chapter IV, on the liturgy of the hours, everything was so closely interconnected that one could not alter a single passage without seriously endangering the entire chapter.

The letter was signed by the presidents of the subcommissions responsible for the remaining chapters of the schema: Bishops A. Martin (IV: Liturgy of the Hours); F. S. Zauner (V: Liturgical Year); C. D'Amato (VI: Sacred Music); C. Rossi (VII: Liturgical Art). The letter was also signed by Bishops O. Spülbeck, B. Fey Schneider, and G. Bekkers, by R. Gagnebet and E. Bonet, the presidents of the theological and juridical subcommissions, and by advisers J. Wagner, A.-G. Mortimort, C. Vagaggini, and A. Dirks, men whose voices carried weight.[66] The letter did not initially cause any change in the voting process (only in connection with chapter VII did the moderator, Cardinal Döpfner, abstain from a vote on the individual emendations), but all the same, in the concluding votes chapters IV-VII were approved by the majority.

After October 14 the Liturgical Commission had to resume its work on the *modi*. On October 17 F. Antonelli, secretary of the commission, asked that its forty-first meeting be held that very afternoon in the meeting

[66] The letter was signed in the order just indicated and read as follows: "The undersigned bishops and experts humbly and urgently ask and beseech that you approve chapters four and following of the schema on the liturgy with a simple '*placet*,' omitting if possible all *modi* except for those regarded as necessary for very serious reasons. For although the decision to hand in *modi* can by its nature, due to your wisdom and learning, bring completeness and beauty to the text, *it nevertheless greatly endangers the entire schema*, both because, overwhelmed as it is by work, the Commission for the Liturgy will only with extreme difficulty meet the date set by Pope Paul VI and yourselves for 'bringing the Constitution to a successful conclusion,' and especially because the subjects treated in chapter IV, on the divine office, are so closely interconnected that if one is removed all the others will be destroyed at the same time. We hope and trust that you will by your votes approve our efforts to find a middle way that is acceptable to all; if we are not mistaken, there will be great rejoicing if you reach the desired promulgation" (Döpfner Archive, Akt 1 Con VII, S.Q. Nr. 9).

According to Jungmann the letter originated with Bishop A. Martin and on October 19 Wagner made it known to a group called together by Lercaro to meet at Vagaggini's residence, S. Gregorio al Celio. Jungmann himself refused to sign the letter; this was certainly connected with his intention to submit a *modus* regarding the "spiritual reading" in chapter IV, the liturgy of the hours; see *TJungmann* for October 19 and the detailed discussion. below of the 45th meeting of the Liturgical Commission on October 30.

room of the Congregation for Rites. For this meeting a "representative sample of the *placet iuxta modum* votes on Articles 54 and 55 of the schema on the sacred liturgy" was prepared.[67]

The fathers had handed in 150 *modi* on Article 54 (use of the vernacular) and 242 on Article 55 (reception of communion). The survey made it clear that the *modi* were to some extent contradictory, or that several fathers had submitted the same *modi*. For example, 130 fathers had asked that the use of the vernacular be excluded at least from the canon, while 108 asked for the vernacular for those prayers of the priests to which the people give an answer. Also, 120 asked that the wedding mass be named a celebration at which communion might be received under both kinds, while 20 rejected communion under both kinds in principle.

The commission facilitated its work by forming four groups among which the task of judging the *modi* was divided. Each group was headed by a bishop, aided by two periti. The *modi* on Article 54 (vernacular in the mass) were to be processed by Enciso Viana, Wagner, and Bugnini; those on Article 55 (reception of communion) by A. Martin, Frutaz, and de Clerk; those on Article 57 concelebration) by Spülbeck, Fey Schneider, Bonet, and Dirks; the remaining *modi* by Zauner, Martimort, and Vagaggini. The groups were to submit their results to the subcommission and the latter in turn to the full commission.[68] The basic question of the meaning ("force and scope") of the *placet iuxta modum* votes was submitted for clarification to Bonet's juridical subcommission.[69]

On the morning of October 18, as the Council was voting on, and not approving, chapter III, the subcommission for juridical questions met to discuss the legal questions regarding the examination of the *modi*. The results of the rather lengthy discussion may be summarized as follows:

1. An examination must be undertaken in every case, regardless of the number of *iuxta modum* votes, even when there is a two-thirds majority of *placet* votes.

[67] See DOC, II, 38-40.

[68] See *TJungmann* for October 17 and 21, Jungmann's notes on the sheet, "Specimen...," which was distributed at the meeting of October 17 (Jungmann Archive, ISR); and the notes of Wagner on the meeting on October 27 [*sic*: 27 must be a slip of the pen; the date was surely October 17]. It is noteworthy that Wagner mentions only C. Rossi as bishop in the first group. In Jungmann's notes the name Rossi is crossed out and "Enc." is written over it, meaning Enciso Viana; this corresponds to his journal entry on October 21. The minutes taken by F. Antonelli, now in the official Council Archives, mention only Bishop C. Rossi.

[69] Antonelli, Minutes.

2. A *placet iuxta modum* vote is to be considered basically a positive vote. Therefore, all the parts of a text that have been put to a vote, for which no *modus* has been submitted, are to be regarded as having a *placet* vote. A section of a schema is therefore approved if the *placet* votes and the *placet iuxta modum* votes on the schema as a whole form a two-thirds majority, but no *iuxta modum* has been cast for that section. For the *placet iuxta modum* votes to have the effect of postponing approval, their number must form a simple majority of the votes cast.

3. The following criteria are to be followed in the examination of the *modi*: (a) *modi* that seek to reverse an improvement already passed by the Council are to be rejected; (b) *modi* submitted in large numbers (the subcommission suggests fifty) are to be presented to the Council for a vote, but the commission may make known its own judgment on whether they should be accepted or rejected; (c) in the case of *modi* submitted in smaller numbers, a distinction must be made between those that the commission judges should be accepted and those that should be rejected; about these latter, however, something was to be said in the report.

4. If the fathers reject a *modus*, it is invalidated. If they accept an emendation, the emended text must be submitted once again for a vote.

Bonet, head of the subcommission, added to the part of his report that was approved by the entire subcommission some words on the "psychology of the hall": The fathers should, as far as possible, gladly accept the decisions of the commission so that the final vote, taken in a public session and in the presence of the pope, may be a positive one. Fathers who have proposed *modi* supported by only a few votes will be satisfied if the report takes the form described. The Council must make its opinion known on *modi* submitted by a number of fathers. Finally, the Liturgical Commission should give thought to the procedure for the final vote.[70]

On October 21 and 22 the subcommission on the mass met with the bishops who had been in charge of the four groups for the examination of the *modi* and with Bonet, head of the subcommis sion for juridical questions. They discussed the examination of the *modi* that had been undertaken, and the report to be given by Enciso Viana was prepared.[71]

The secretary issued the invitation to the forty-second meeting of the Liturgical Commission for the afternoon of October 23. Bonet began the

---

[70] See the *Relatio Subcommissionis iuridicae de modis expendendis* (signed by Bonet on October 23), in DOC, II, 5-8.
[71] See the introduction to the bishop's report in DOC, II, 41.

meeting by reporting on and explaining the work of the juridical sub-commission on the examination of the *modi*.[72] To his report Bonet added a brief statement on the difficulty that Dante had raised at the meeting on October 17, which surely had to be regarded as an attempt to delay the work on the liturgical schema, namely, that a vote had been taken only on the proposed emendations but not on the new, emended text as such, a procedure, Dante said, that was not valid. He had submitted the issue to the conciliar tribunal and, if his request were granted, no further work should be done. He had also gotten other fathers to share his concern. From Bonet's statement, dated October 23, it emerges that the procedure followed was legal according to Article 61 §6 of the rules of the Council, since after an approval of all the individual parts of a schema the whole was to be considered approved.[73]

In view of the many *modi* submitted on concelebration, the subcommission on the mass presented a new text drafted by Rossi, Fey Schneider, and Zauner for Articles 57 §1, section 2, and §2, section 1, which dealt chiefly with the rules for concelebration in religious houses.[74] A report on the examination of the *modi* followed. Finally, three groups were again formed for the examination of the 1054 *modi* on chapter III: Rossi, Wagner, and Bugnini were to deal with the *modi* on art 63 (the vernacular in the Ritual); Grimshaw, Bonet, and Dirks with the *modi* on Article 79 (sacramentals); and a group consisting of Spülbeck, Martimort, and Frutaz with the remaining *modi*.[75]

Two days later, on the afternoon of October 25, the forty-third meeting of the Liturgical Commission was held. After the secretary, Antonelli, had reported on the votes on chapter IV and had referred the *modi* to the subcommission for examination, there was a discussion of Bonet's report and of his reply to Dante's delaying tactic. Next, there began a discussion of Enciso Viana's report on the *placet iuxta modum* votes on chapter II.[76] In the process, there was a discussion of the real

---

[72] *Relatio Subcommissionis iuridicae de modis, expendendis.*

[73] Ibid., 8. On the entire incident see Wagner notes. In the minutes taken by F. Antonelli, no mention is made of Dante's remarks.

[74] See "Art. 57. Nova formula proposita a Subcommissione de cap. II," in DOC, II, 52. The final version, in which only the words "according to the norm of art. 22 §1" were dropped, seems to have been decided on at the meeting of October 29; see Wagner's notes on this meeting.

[75] See Wagner's notes.

[76] "Relatio circa modos caput II respicientes," in DOC, II, 41-51. The report is not dated, but Jungmann marked his copy October 25, 1963.

number of *modi*;[77] 781 such votes had been cast, but many fathers had submitted more than one *modus*. The *modi* were distributed as follows: 681 on Article 57 (concelebration), 242 on Article 55 (reception of communion), 150 on Article 54 (the vernacular), and 45 on all the other articles.[78] Numerous fathers had submitted the same *modus*, however, so in fact there were only 105 distinct *modi*.[79] No consideration needed to be given to those that (1) were contrary to what had been expressly approved; (2) contradicted documents of the ecclesiastical magisterium; (3) went beyond the scope of this chapter or had nothing to do with this chapter or the liturgical schema; and (4) had already been considered. The remaining *modi* were to be satisfied either by brief clarifications or by more detailed explanations. Special attention needed to be given to the *modi* for Article 54 (vernacular), 55 (reception of communion), and 57 (concelebration). The discussion of the report was not finished on this day.

At the same meeting, Bonet and his subcommission were charged with the preparation of a new version of his report.[80] They produced a new and more clearly organized version of his report of October 23.[81] After a brief introduction, a shorter first part dealt with the course taken by the schema up to the approval of the amended text; a second part, with two sections, dealt with the approval of parts of the schema and with the examination of the *modi*.[82] Many of Bonet's explanations found their way into Lercaro's report to the general congregation on November 18.[83]

At the meeting of the Liturgical Commission on October 29, Larraona announced the public session planned for the end of the second period. Antonelli urged haste and set 3:00 p.m. as the time for beginning the next day's meeting. There was further discussion of Enciso Viana's report. This contained a rejection of the proposal to make a wedding mass another occasion for communion in both kinds. In addition, the amended text on concelebration in religious houses was proposed. Rossi spoke in vain against the length of Enciso Viana's report.[84] The report on the origin, approval, and examination of the *modi*, for which Bonet

---

[77] According to Wagner's notes, the members seem to have spoken on this day only of the number of *modi*.

[78] According to the inventory based on the report (see DOC, II, 41) there were 1118 *modi* in all. Enciso Viana, however, spoke of only 917.

[79] See the final text of the report in *AS* II/5, 580.

[80] According to Wagner's notes.

[81] *Relatio Subcommissionis iuridicae de modis expendendis.*

[82] This untitled document is in DOC, II, 9-14.

[83] See *AS* II/5, 406-9.

[84] See Wagner's note on the meetings of October 25 and October 29.

had been asked on October 23, was distributed at this meeting on October 29. Dante objected to the report Bonet had given at the previous meeting (October 25), and a lengthy discussion ensued. Finally, as proof that the process was legal, Antonelli read aloud a passage from Mansi that had to do with Vatican I.[85] Difficulties were raised by Larraona, who wanted only interpretations, not changes, of a previously approved text to be allowed.[86]

At the meeting of the Liturgical Commission, on October 30, the discussion of Bonet's report continued.[87] Afterward, A. Martin reported on the 552 *modi* submitted for chapter IV.[88]

At this point, mention must be made of an undertaking that began, in a sense, on April 10, 1960, and was to be shipwrecked during these days. On that early date Jungmann had addressed to the Antepreparatory Commission for Vatican II a one-page *votum* of the theological faculty of the University of Innsbruck; half of it consisted of a request that the breviary be reformed to require that the diocesan clergy be obliged to pray only those hours — Lauds and Vespers — that had been recited in cathedrals and parish churches prior to the Middle Ages, and that in addition they be under the obligation of a half-hour's spiritual reading or meditation. In the preparatory Liturgical Commission and then during the first period of the Council, Jungmann, aided by friends in the pertinent committees, had endeavored, without success, to gain a hearing for his request.

While Jungmann was convinced that the history of the liturgy fully justified his request, he did not realize that it was impossible, by means of a sentence in a document regulating the reform of the liturgy in the twentieth century, to reverse a development over almost a millennium and a half, particularly one that had decisively marked the spiritual life of the very persons who alone had the authority to reverse it. Jungmann met with bitter resistance from Franciscan liturgical scholars, not, of course, because they did not recognize his historical competence, but because they did not think one could expect the Church to make a leap from the twentieth century back to the fifth.

It is moving to learn from Jungmann's journal entries on the commission's work during the second period of the Council (1963) how

---

[85] See Wagner's notes on the October 29 meeting.
[86] See *TJungmann* for October 29, 1963.
[87] See Wagner's notes on the October 30 meeting.
[88] See "Elenchus modorum circa caput IV," in DOC, II, 66-72, and the "Relatio circa Modos caput IV respicientes," ibid., 73-102.

determinedly he fought to the end for a proposal that he thought justified. Yet the journal also shows how astonishingly naive he was when it came to tactics for getting his proposal approved, and how he refused to let anyone talk him out of his undertaking. Although on October 3, he writes of the outcome: "There is no point to continuing this action," still on November 9, 22, 24, 27, and 31, he tells of how he tried to advance his project through meetings with bishops (Zauner of Linz, Fernandes of New Delhi, Reuss of Mainz, König of Vienna, Meyer of Chicago, Nordhues of Paderborn) and experts (J. Neuner, S.J., and B. Häring, C.Ss.R.). He rejoices that according to Article 67 §3 of the conciliar rules five members of a commission can submit a minority *votum* (October 9); and he refuses to sign the letter, originating with A. Martin, already signed by Martimort and Wagner, and addressed to all the episcopal conferences, that asked them to cast no more *placet iuxta modum* votes, so as not to delay the work (October 19).[89] He is convinced that the large number of *placet iuxta modum* votes, 552, on chapter IV is due to the action taken, along his lines, by Reuss (October 24).

At the Liturgical Commission's meeting on October 30 Jungmann was somewhat disappointed to learn that "there were only 51 votes in favor" of his request. There was further discussion of the matter. Larraona expressed misgivings, because it would mean revising an article. Jungmann's answer was that the change would be only an interpretation. Martimort stressed the point that in the commission there had already been "a great deal of discussion and that it had finally been settled that a clear distinction should be made between the Office and personal prayer." To this Jungmann answered that during the preceding year voices had been heard in the hall, among them that of Cardinal Léger, that had spoken for a link between the Office and meditation. He once again repeated the historical basis of his proposal, which his hearers listened to calmly, and he was able to give A. Martin a copy of his explanation, asking him to present it at a meeting of the subcommission the next day.[90]

According to information given to Jungmann by Wagner, at the meeting of the subcommission for the liturgy of the hours on October 31 Jungmann's explanation was read out by Abbot P. Salmon. "There was no doubt about the facts, and people were open to the objective reality, but it was decided to submit only a very few *modi* to the Council, and

---

[89] See note 66, above.
[90] On this point see *TJungmann* for October 30, 1963.

this one was not to be presented." However, A. Martin, Wagner said, was ready, in his report on the text in the schema, to interpret it according to Jungmann's view. Frutaz was even of the opinion that the postconciliar commission might allow a rubric in favor of a substitution for readings. "The Council is certainly not to be looked to for a broader decision; the matter is simply not ripe enough."[91]

At the meeting of the Liturgical Commission on November 8, Jungmann's proposal was definitively rejected. In the report intended for the hall, A. Martin mentioned the request but explained the subcommission's view that the matter should be left to the postconciliar commission. When Article 83c came up for discussion, Jungmann asked that the request be passed on "to the postconciliar commission for its benevolent consideration." Larraona was of the opinion that the Council must make this request; Martimort was of the opinion that the commission had to reach a unanimous decision on the matter. Martin stressed the point that the subcommission had regarded it as hopeless to get Jungmann's proposal through the Council, since it amounted to a complete abolition of Matins, when so many voices had been already raised against the abolition of Prime. Jungmann, with the help of Wagner, was able, however, to have the sentence about the abolition of Matins removed, now that Martimort had already seen to the removal of the historical justification of the *modus*.[92]

Jungmann assessed the situation correctly. Even the *modus* that had 263 votes for it and for which F. McManus was fighting at the meeting, namely, that episcopal authority to allow the use of the vernacular in the liturgy of the hours should not be limited by the phrase "in individual cases," was no longer viable. The reason was the haste with which people wanted the discussion closed. Regarding his own defeat, Jungmann finally came to share Wagner's view: "Many things are not yet ripe."[93]

Many meetings probably ran a similar course in the other subcommissions. The final meetings shall be mentioned only briefly. On October 30 and 31, the subcommission for the sacraments and sacramentals gathered with the bishops who had chaired the three groups for the examination of the *modi*. The results of the examination of the *modi* were discussed, and the report to be given by Spülbeck was prepared.[94] This

---

[91] Ibid., for November 3, 1963.
[92] Ibid., for November 9, 1963.
[93] Ibid.
[94] "Relatio circa Modos caput III respicientes," in DOC, II, 53-65.

report was then discussed by the Liturgical Commission at its meeting on November 5. At its meeting on November 7, the report on the *modi* for the introduction and chapter I was distributed and discussed, and the report on the *modi* for chapter V was distributed.[95]

At the meeting on November 8 the reports on the *modi* for chapters IV, VI, and VII were distributed. It was announced that in the conciliar text only the scriptures, the Fathers, and the councils were to be cited and, in addition, that in the future the only votes would be on the question: "Do you accept the examination of the *iuxta modum* votes on chapter *n.* as carried out by the Commission for the Liturgy?" Regarding both communications, the general secretary of the Council and Lercaro, one of the moderators, had been previously contacted, and both had accepted the proposals.[96] At the commission's meeting on November 11, the reports of the subcommission on liturgical music and liturgical art were discussed by D'Amato and Rossi respectively.[97]

On November 13 the Liturgical Commission held its fiftieth meeting, at which the final version of the report on the Introduction and chapter I, now in printed form, was to be discussed. At its meeting on November 14, the printed report on chapter II was discussed, and another heated discussion took place on the *modus* for Article 54, which 108 fathers had supported and which had to do with the use of the vernacular in the parts of the mass that "belong to the people." But no more changes in the text were to be made.[98]

At the meeting on November 15, there was a final discussion of the now printed report on chapter III.[99] At the meeting on the next day 18, plans were made for the work still to be done before the final vote on November 22. But during this week the proposals made for the application of the constitution also had to be examined.

For this reason, at the meeting on November 19, the commission occupied itself first of all with the reports on the *modi* for chapters V, VI, and VII, regarding which a single general vote seemed to suffice. Thus all the preparations had now been made for the full Council to undertake the final votes. At this same meeting a text prepared by Rossi, "The Application of the Constitution," was distributed and probably

[95] Antonelli, Minutes.

[96] Ibid.

[97] "Relatio circa Modos Caput VI respicientes," in DOC, II, 108-9, and "Relatio circa Modos Caput VII respicientes," ibid., 110-12.

[98] See *TJungmann* for November 14, 1963.

[99] For details on this and the following meetings, see Antonelli, Minutes.

also discussed,[100] as was a paper of Martimort on "The Territorial Ecclesiastical Authority Competent to Apply the Constitution."[101] At the commission's meeting on November 21, the entire text of the future liturgical constitution was distributed. Frutaz was assigned to complete the citations and Egger to make final slight improvements in the Latin.[102]

The fifty-sixth and final meeting of the Liturgical Commission took place on November 28. The application of the liturgical constitution was discussed. The text that Rossi and some experts had presented at the meeting on November 19 had obviously not satisfied the president of the Liturgical Commission, who therefore appointed Bonet, Martimort, and Wagner to work up a new text, which was presented at this meeting.[103]

C. THE VOTES ON THE EXAMINATION OF THE *MODI* AND THE FINAL VOTE

In an announcement introduced with some solemnity ("Let the fathers now pay attention to a very important communication") the Secretary General of the Council told the fathers at the general congregation on November 15 that the final votes on the liturgical schema would take place on Monday, November 18. With the exception of chapters II and III, he said, the schema had already been approved by the necessary majority. Having examined and responded to all the *modi,* the Liturgical Commission would present the result of this study to the fathers. While a vote had to be taken on some *modi* for chapters II and III, the only question regarding the other chapters would be a general one: Did the fathers agree with the examination of the *modi* by the Liturgical Commission? For this reason, a booklet containing the *modi* for the Introduction and chapter I was distributed on that day.[104]

The general congregation on November 18 began with Lercaro's report on the work of the Liturgical Commission.[105] He first made it

---

[100] See DOC, II, 113-18.

[101] Ibid., 119.

[102] See Antonelli, Minutes.

[103] Ibid. This was the text in DOC, II, 120-25.

[104] See *AS* II/5, 245f. The texts contained in the booklet, *Modi a Patribus conciliaribus propositi, a Commissione Conciliari de sacra Liturgia examinati. I. Prooemium — Caput I. De Principiis generalibus ad Sacram Liturgiam instaurandam atque fovendam,* are printed in *AS* II/5, 496, 510-26, and 497-509.

[105] See *AS* II/5, 406-9. The report was prepared with the help of at least Wagner and Jungmann (see *TJungmann* for November 16, 1963) and included Bonet's explanations.

clear that even in chapters II and III of the schema not a single article had been rejected by the voting fathers. Rather, all the articles, taken individually, had received the necessary two-thirds majority. He then explained the carefully conducted examination of the *modi* that was to be put to a vote on this and the following days.

1. Chapter I

In his oral statement Bishop A. Martin limited himself to a report on the twenty-fifth of the fifty-two *modi* for the Introduction and chapter I which the fathers had before them in writing. In connection with this *modus*, which had to do with the discussion of the presence of Christ in the celebration of the Eucharist (article 7), he explained why a change in the citation of the Council of Trent had been necessary.[106] No vote was taken on these two points or on a stylistic change (Article 6 was now to begin with *ideoque* instead of *nam*). Instead, the general secretary asked the question of principle: Were the fathers in agreement with the Liturgical Commission's examination of the *modi* for the Introduction and chapter I? The result was clear: 2066 for, 20 against, 4 invalid.[107]

2. Chapter II

The printing of the booklet with the *modi* for chapter II had been delayed so that it did not reach the fathers on November 18, as originally announced, but only the day after; this required a postponement of the vote for one day.[108] On November 20 Enciso Viana delivered only the second half of his report.[109] In it he explained that the commission did not regard it necessary to accept the *modus* submitted by 108 fathers, namely, to add at the end of Article 54, §1, that it is permissible to use the vernacular also in those prayers of the priest, outside the canon, to which the people are to reply. In addition, there was agreement in the commission not to make the wedding mass a further instance of communion in both kinds in Article 55, as 120 fathers desired, since it is not possible to introduce into a short conciliar text all the precautions regarded as necessary. With regard to the *modi* handed in by 563 bishops, all of which sought to

---

[106] See *AS* II/5, 510 and 518.

[107] See *AS* II/5, 545.

[108] See *AS* II/5, 405, 545, and 549. The texts in the booklet *Modi a Patribus Conciliaribus propositi, a Commissione Conciliari de sacra Liturgia examinati. II. Caput II. De sacrosancto Eucharistiae mysterio* are printed in *AS* II/5, 575-96.

[109] See *AS* II/5, 580.

safeguard better the right of the bishop to regulate concelebrations, the commission suggested having Article 57 §2 begin with this sentence: "It belongs to the bishop to regulate the discipline of concelebration in his diocese."[110] Next, three *modi* were put to a vote: one on the proposed change of the text in Article 57 §2 (concelebration), the other two on leaving unchanged the text of Article 54 (the vernacular) and Article 55 (reception of communion). Finally, a fourth question concerned agreement in general with the examination of the other *modi* by the Liturgical Commission.[111]

It seems at first sight striking that while the commission's explanations for leaving unchanged the text of Article 54 and Article 55 referred to *modi* that had been submitted by 108 and 120 fathers respectively, the vote resulted in 131 and 128 fathers respectively voting *non placet*. This may be due to the fact that the *modi* submitted for both articles were in fact a good deal more numerous: 150 for Article 54 and 242 for Article 55, as can be seen from the report given in the commission on October 25.[112]

The concluding vote on chapter II in its entirety was as follows: 2112 for, and 40 against. The vote was followed by applause in the hall.[113]

3. Chapter III

The booklet containing the *modi* was given to the fathers on November 20,[114] and the vote took place the next day. The reporter, Spülbeck, read only the first part of his report.[115] In it he dealt with the *modi* for Articles 63 (vernacular) and 79 (sacramentals), which the commission thought deserved special attention. Article 63 in its amended form had indeed received a two-thirds majority on October 17, but in view of the fact that 640 fathers wanted the use of the vernacular to be expanded in the celebration of the sacraments and sacramentals, the commission

---

[110] Ibid., 593-96.

[111] Results of the votes: *Modus* for Article 57 §2: 2057 for, 123 against, 2 invalid; *modus* for Article 54: 2047 for, 131 against, 4 invalid; *modus* for Article 55: 2014 for, 128 against, 1 invalid; fourth question: 2056 for, 32 against, 4 invalid. See *AS* II/5, 621. There was no need to vote on the commission's stylistic change in the introduction to Article 57 §1.

[112] See DOC, II, 41.

[113] *AS* II/5, 631.

[114] Ibid., 573. The texts in the booklet *Modi a Patribus Conciliaribus propositi, a Commissione Conciliari de sacra liturgia examinati. III. Caput III. De ceteris Sacramentis et de Sacramentalibus* are printed in *AS* II/5, 637-50.

[115] *AS* II/5, 643 n.1, and 646.

decided to accept the change in the text that was proposed by 601 fathers: "In the administration of the sacraments and sacramentals the vernacular can be used, provided the prescriptions of Article 36 are safeguarded."[116]

A vote was taken on this change in the text of Article 63 on use of the vernacular, and the result was 1848 for, 335 against, 2 invalid.[117] The high number of negative votes on this *modus* was to be expected, there being a large number of fathers who wanted to keep Latin in the words required for the validity of the individual sacraments. It was particularly providential that this group was unable to have its way, since its defeat avoided encouragement of a magical view of the celebration of the sacraments. The concluding vote on chapter III as a whole was 2107 for, 35 against, 1 invalid.[118]

4. Chapters IV-VII

On November 20 the booklet containing the *modi* for chapter IV was placed in the hands of the fathers,[119] while the one with the *modi* for chapters V, VI, and VII was given to them the day after.[120] At the general congregation on November 22 the first speaker was A. Martin, who reported on the chapter on the liturgy of the hours. He limited himself to the *modi* that had been submitted by a relatively large number of

[116] The commission explained its thinking in regard to Article 79, §§2 and 3: It is not necessary to add "of the place" to the words "ordinaries" or "ordinary," because in the first case it is obviously a question of the reservation of blessings, not in relation to all the faithful, but in relation to the ordinary's own subjects; in the second case, only the ordinary of the place can be meant, since there is question here of the administration of sacramentals by lay people, who can only have an ordinary of the place. Since the first *modus* was supported by 121 fathers and the second by 175, the commission asked for a declaration of agreement with its response; see ibid., 543-46.

[117] Ibid., 686. Further votes had to do with leaving unchanged the texts of Article 79, section 2, on the reservation of blessings (result of the vote: 2084 for, 96 against, 2 invalid), and of Article 79, section 3, on the administration of sacramentals by lay persons (result of the vote: 1972 for, 132 against, 2 invalid). A fourth question asked for agreement with the examination of the other *modi* as done by the Liturgical Commission (result: 1999 for, 29 against, 3 invalid).

[118] Ibid., 696.

[119] Ibid., 573. The texts contained in the booklet *Modi a Patribus conciliaribus propositi, a Commissione Conciliari de sacra Liturgia examinati. IV. Caput IV. De Officio divino* are printed in *AS* II/5, 701-24.

[120] Ibid., 636. The texts in the booklet *Modi a Patribus conciliaribus propositi, a Commissione Conciliari de sacra Liturgia examinati. V. Capita V — VI — VII. De Anno liturgico, de Musica sacra, de Arte sacra deque sacra Supellectile* are printed in *AS* II/5, 725-43.

fathers.[121] He began with the emendation of Article 89c, which originated with Jungmann and was supported by 53 fathers, to the effect that outside of choir, and apart from major feast days, Matins should be replaceable by a spiritual reading from the scriptures. The bishop also reported the various *modi* having to do with Prime (Article 89d), which were supported by 118 fathers. In both cases he referred the matter to the postconciliar commission.

He then gave the reasons for one of the three proposed purely linguistic changes (replacement of *curandum est* by *suadetur* in Article 99); this was wanted by 194 fathers. Finally, he mentioned the *modi* that had to do with language; the most important of these was one supported by 263 fathers, who wanted the removal from Article 101 §1 of the phrase "in individual cases" (in which the ordinary could allow his clerics to use the vernacular in the liturgy of the hours). But the commission wanted to stay with the universal law of praying the Office in Latin and to prevent the bishops from dispensing their clerics indiscriminately.[122]

Since no vote on the three stylistic changes was necessary, the question was immediately asked whether the fathers agreed with the examination of the *modi*. The result of the vote was: 2131 for, 50 against, 2 invalid.[123]

The next reporter, Zauner, spoke on the *modi* for the chapter on the liturgical year. He too limited himself to a few important *modi* for Articles 102, 106, 107, 110, and 111, as well as for the appendix. No changes in the text were thought necessary.[124] The reporter for the chapter on liturgical music, D'Amato, was able to present the whole of his short report,[125] while Rossi, reporter for the chapter on liturgical art and liturgical furnishings, presented only the *modi* for Article 130, on the use of pontificals. He closed his report by making his own the desire of Lercaro that the work might come to a conclusion on this sixtieth anniversary of the publication of Pius X's Motu Proprio *Tra le sollecitudini*, which had opened the way to the liturgical renewal.[126] The fathers were asked for their judgment on the treatment of the *modi* for all three chapters at once. Result of the vote: 2149 for, 5 against, 2 invalid.[127]

---

[121] Ibid., 706, 714, 721, and 724.
[122] Ibid. 712-14, 720, 721-23.
[123] Ibid., 757.
[124] Ibid., 733-39.
[125] Ibid., 739-41.
[126] Ibid., 741f. Also 742, and 743 n.1.
[127] Ibid., 757.

The fact that in the entire liturgical schema only two *modi* brought changes in content, and not simply stylistic improvements (the *modus* on concelebration [Article 57], supported by 563 fathers, and the *modus* on the vernacular in the Ritual [Article 63], submitted by 640 fathers) throws a peculiar light on the procedure for dealing with the *placet iuxta modum* votes of individual fathers. The freedom given to each father to express his opinion was commendable, but without the building of coalitions this freedom did not do much good. There were more than 2000 Council fathers. To submit each *modum* (and there were hundreds) to the fathers for a vote would have meant an irresponsible burdening and slowing of the Council's work. However reasonable, this procedure would have seemed unsatisfactory to the fathers involved.

This is what opened the way to the adoption of a method by which general questions would be presented to the fathers, analogous to those used when the moderators sought the will of the assembly in regard to important steps in future work; for example, whether the schema on Mary should form part of the schema on the Church, or whether it should be said in the schema on the Church that episcopal consecration is the highest degree of the sacrament of orders.[128] Jungmann reports that the idea of the question method surfaced in the commission one day and gives it as his opinion that Wagner was probably the first to suggest that this method be used also for inquiring into the agreement of the fathers with the examination of the *modi*.[129] In its written explanation of how it had dealt with the *modi*, the Liturgical Commission justified its attitude toward individual *modi* and did so in greater detail depending on the number of fathers who supported a *modus*; it was then able to ask the Council whether it agreed with the handling of the examination. In all these cases the Council expressed its agreement.

5. The Concluding Vote and Public Session

After the assembled fathers had accepted the examination of the *modi* and had approved all the chapters, a vote on the entire liturgical schema could take place. The result of the vote was: 2158 for, 19 against, 1 invalid. Applause was followed by words of thanks from the first of the Council presidents, Cardinal E. Tisserant.[130] Thus the path

---

[128] *AS* II/3, 345, 574f.
[129] See *TJungmann* for 11/22, 1963. It cannot be ascertained whether there was any connection with the letter sent on October 19; see note 66 above.
[130] *AS* II/5, 767f.

was cleared for a solemn vote on the liturgical constitution at a public session.

On November 25, the secretary general announced a public meeting for December 4,[131] and four days later he made known the pope's decision that the public meeting should deal with both the Constitution on the Sacred Liturgy and the Decree on the Means of Social Communication. In voting, the fathers were to bear in mind that this Council, which had a primarily pastoral orientation, would define something as infallible only if it made this intention explicitly clear. This would not be the case in the two documents that would be voted on in the coming public meeting. The pope nonetheless asked the fathers to meditate on and pray about the contents of the two documents, in order that the Spirit of God might enlighten them and inspire them to do what would contribute to the greater glory of God and the salvation of souls. The final text of the liturgical constitution was distributed during this same general congregation.[132]

During the public session on Wednesday, December 4, on the four hundredth anniversary of the closing of the Council of Trent, 2147 fathers voted for and 4 against the Constitution on the Sacred Liturgy. After this result had been made known and been greeted with great applause, the pope read the formula of approval. In it he made it clear that he was acting along with the fathers ("*una cum...Patribus*"), and that the decisions, which he was confirming, had been made in a conciliar and thus synodal manner.

> In the name of the Most Holy and undivided Trinity, of the Father and the Son and the Holy Spirit. The fathers have expressed their agreement with the decrees just read out in the presence of this legitimately assembled Sacred and Ecumenical Second Vatican Council. And We, in virtue of the apostolic authority given to Us by Christ, and in union with the reverend fathers, approve, establish, and ordain them in the Holy Spirit, and We order that what the Council has so ordained be published for the glory of God.

After renewed applause, the general secretary of the Council announced that the period before the decrees went into effect would last until the first Sunday of Lent, February 16, 1964.[133]

---

[131] *AS* II/6, 9.
[132] Ibid., 305f.
[133] Ibid., 407f.

II. THE SIGNIFICANCE OF THE LITURGICAL CONSTITUTION

Almost a quarter of the proposals for the Second Vatican Council that were sent to Rome from around the world in 1959 and 1960 had to do with the liturgy.[134] This was not surprising. The majority of the persons queried belonged to the Latin Church and celebrated the liturgy in the Roman rite. But in broad areas of this Church, especially in Europe, beginning with the so-called Mechlin Event[135] and continuing throughout the next five decades until the announcement of the Council, the liturgical movement had been increasingly influencing the internal life of the Church.[136] While this movement had at first developed independently in individual countries, collaboration across national boundaries began and increased after World War II.

One of the factors that conditioned this was certainly Pius XII's encyclical *Mediator Dei* on the liturgy, issued on November 20, 1947, which awakened the interest of the worldwide episcopate in the liturgical movement.[137] The Centre de Pastorale Liturgique (CPL; since 1965, CNPL) was founded in France in 1943. It was followed, in the year the encyclical appeared, by the establishment of the Centro di Azione Liturgica (CAL) in Italy and of the Liturgisches Institut (since 1989, Deutsches Liturgisches Institut) in Trier, Germany.

In Rome, soon after the publication of *Mediator Dei*, A. Bugnini, editor of the periodical *Ephemerides Liturgicae*, sent a questionnaire to about a hundred liturgical scholars and pastoral liturgists regarding a reform of the Missal and the Breviary, the liturgical calendar and the martyrology, and other liturgical books. While the reform commission (F. Antonelli, G. Löw, A. Albareda, A. Bea, A. Bugnini) appointed by Pius XII on May 28, 1948, was attending to the renewal of the Easter Vigil (1951) and Holy Week (1955), the editing of the Code of Rubrics (1960) and the new typical edition of the Breviary and the Pontifical (1962),[138] the directors of the Centre de Pastorale Liturgique (A.-G. Martimort) and of the Liturgisches Institut in Trier (J. Wagner) were

---

[134] See E. J. Lengeling, *Die Konstitution des Zweiten Vatikanischen Konzils über die heilige Liturgie. Lateinish-deutscher Text mit einem Kommentar* (Münster, 1965²) 47.

[135] See B. Fischer, "Das 'Mechelner Ereignis' vom 23. September 1909," *Liturgische Jahrbuch* 9 (1959), 203-19.

[136] On the liturgical movement see R. Kaczynski, "La liturgia come vissuto religioso," in *Storia della Chiesa*, ed. E. Guerriero, 23 (Cinisello-Balsamo, 1991), 395-420.

[137] *AAS* 39 (1947), 521-600.

[138] A. Bugnini, *The Reform of the Liturgy 1948-1975*, trans. M. J. O'Connell (Collegeville, Minn.: Liturgical Press, 1990), 7-10.

organizing seven International Liturgical Study Meetings. These took place in 1951 at Maria Laach, on the Roman Missal; in 1952 at Odilien-berg in Alsace, on the subject of "Modern Man and the Mass"; in 1953 in Lugano, on "Active Participation of the Faithful in the Liturgy"; in 1954 at Louvain, on the scriptural passages for the mass and concele-bration; in 1956 at Assisi, on the liturgy of the hours; in 1958 at Montserrat, on baptism and confirmation; and in 1960 at Munich, on the celebration of the Eucharist in East and West.[139]

Together especially with the International Pastoral Liturgical Congress in Assisi in 1956[140] and the International Study Week "Mission and Liturgy" in Nijmegen in 1959, these study meetings — which dealt with the most important liturgical celebrations and in which reflections on their renewal were by no means excluded — were essentially responsible for the fact that after the announcement of the Second Vatican Council by John XXIII requests for liturgical reform reached Rome from around the world. As a result, it was possible for the experts from various countries, who had long since become well acquainted with one another, to combine their forces and prepare the way for the document that on December 4, 1963, became the foundation of the liturgical reform.

This very briefly sketched background to the liturgical reform explains why the liturgical requests brought to Rome before the Council were all concerned with the Roman rite, that is, the rite most widely followed in the Latin Church, even though the Council was announced as "ecumenical." The problem implicit here was discussed from the outset and was also raised in the hall, especially by the Oriental bishops: could an ecumenical council limit itself to dealing with a single rite?[141] It was decided, in this context, not to ignore the expectations of so many Council fathers. As a result, this Council was the first in the history of the Church to compose a document on liturgical questions for a single rite, although such an activity would properly have been the task of a regional synod with the bishop of Rome presiding.

---

[139] See S. Schmidt, *Die internationalen liturgischen Studientreffen 1951-1960. Zur Vorgeschichte der Liturgiekonstitution,* Trierer Theologische Studien 55 (Trier, 1992). The concept of "active participation," which Pius X coined, is in the apostolic letter *Tra le sollecitudini* of November 22, 1903, which may be found in A. Bugnini, ed., *Documenta pontificia ad instaurationem liturgicam spectantia [I] (1903-1953),* Bibliotheca Ephemerides Liturgicae. Sectio practica 6 (Rome, 1953), 13.

[140] Bugnini, *The Reform of the Liturgy,* 11-13.

[141] See J. A. Jungmann, "Commentary on the Liturgical Constitution," in *Commentary,* 1:9-10.

Precisely because the Roman rite was so dominant, it was particularly important that each day, before their discussions began, the fathers should participate in the celebration of a Eucharist that was not always of the Roman rite but frequently of some other Western or Eastern rite.[142] Many of these non-Roman eucharistic celebrations met with rather close attention.[143] The celebrations made the breadth of Catholicism clear to the Council fathers, so that it became easier for them to approve Article 4 of the liturgical constitution, according to which the Church "holds all lawfully recognized rites to be of equal right and dignity." The formula "all lawfully recognized rites" was chosen instead of the one originally used in the schema, "all lawfully practiced (*vigentes*) rites," because what was meant here was not simply those rites existing at the time when the constitution was approved; rather, the thought was that further rites might come into existence later on. Since the reference could not be to new Eastern rites or to the rites of the separated Western Churches, the intention could only have been to raise no obstacle to the development of new rites within the much too broad realm of the Roman rite.[144]

Many had awaited the publication of the liturgical constitution with great anticipation, but they reacted with disappointment when, on

[142] It was clear that reflection on the liturgy and talk of it during the conciliar debates had an influence on the celebration of mass in the Roman rite. Writing of the opening of the second period Jungmann recounts: "Some progress, from the liturgical viewpoint (the bishops sang the Gloria and Creed together)" (*TJungmann*, September 30, 1963). See also, B. Fischer, "Konziliare Reform und kuriale Politik. Zum Umfeld der Liturgiekonstitution," in *Gottesdienst — Kirche — Gesellschaft. Interdisziplinäre und ökumenische Standortbestimmung nach 25 Jahre Liturgiereform*, ed. H. Becker, B. J. Hilberath, and U. Willers, Pietas liturgica 5 (St. Ottilien, 1991), 23-27, at 25. After Article 54, §2, had been approved, Bishop A. M. Cavagna expressed a wish that the fathers might give a good example by reciting or singing the Latin ordinary of the mass together; see his letter to Lercaro, October 11, 1963; Lercaro Archive, XXIII, 516. On that same date Bishop G. van Velsen of Kroonstad offered even more far-reaching suggestions: see the document addressed to the general secretary of the Council: Lercaro Archive, XXIII, 517.

[143] One might note one of the curious incidents still possible at that time. The press office invited some journalists to attend the mass celebrated by Archbishop J. Slipyi before the general congregation on October 29, 1963. Tickets of admission were also allocated to some women journalists, but initially they were barred from entering St. Peter's Basilica with the remark that the tickets probably had been given to them by mistake, since women were denied entrance to the Council hall. At last they were told that an exception would be made this time, but they were also told that there were not enough hosts for them to receive communion. This must be interpreted as an attempt to keep the women present from approaching the altar. See Lercaro Archive, XXIII, 565.

[144] See R. Kaczynski, "20 Jahre Liturgiekonstitution: Eine Bestandsaufnahme," in *Costituzionne liturgica "Sacrosanctum Concilium." Studi*, ed. Congregation for Divine Worship, Bibliotheca Ephemerides Liturgicae 38 (Rome, 1986), 491-506, at 498-506.

December 4, 1963, they saw that many of their hopes had not been ful-filled: concelebration was to be allowed in only a few cases (Article 57), communion from the cup was to be given only on rare occasions (Article 55), the vernacular in the mass was limited to the liturgy of the word (Article 54) and was to be an exception in the liturgy of the hours. The document had to be read carefully in order to see that it was opening and not shutting doors. Various possibilities, for example, were given for concelebration. Before the occasions on which the eucharistic wine could be given were listed, the word *veluti* ("for example") appeared. The use of the vernacular in the celebration of mass was indicated "especially" for the readings and prayer of the faithful, which did not mean that it could not also be used at other points, namely, "in those parts which pertain to the people" (Article 54). But in the final analysis, this meant all parts; therefore even the canon was not explicitly excluded. Care had been taken, again and again, not to burden the conciliar document with details. It was rightly thought that the important thing was the fundamental decisions regard-ing liturgical practice.

Even more important, of course, was the theological discussion of the principles that "can and should be applied both to the Roman rite and also to all the other rites" (Article 3).[145] Jungmann reports that Eastern bishops acknowledged "how significant the principles developed here were for their own liturgies."[146] In the following necessarily brief pre-sentation of the significance of the liturgical constitution for the Church, I shall first of all go into some of these principles of liturgical theology that lay the basis of a new understanding of the liturgy, then turn to those that concern the celebration of the liturgy, and end with some remarks on liturgical law.

A. Description of the Nature of the Liturgy

What is probably the most important statement in the constitution and the key to a rethinking of the liturgy is to be found in Article 7: "The liturgy, then, is rightly seen as an exercise of the priestly office of Jesus Christ. It involves the presentation of man's sanctification under the

---

[145] See C. Vagaggini's commentary on Article 3 for a list of the articles that are valid for all rites: *Ephemerides Liturgicae* 78 (1964), 231.

[146] Jungmann, "Commentary on the Liturgical Constitution," 9.

guise of signs perceptible by the senses and its accomplishment in ways appropriate to each of these signs. In it public worship is performed by the Mystical Body of Jesus Christ, that is, by the Head and his members." In this statement the Council did not indeed intend to give a definition of the liturgy but to describe what is to be understood by *liturgy*, or, in other words, to describe the nature or essence of the liturgy. Liturgy is not simply rites and ceremonies regulated by rubrics; that is, it is not the totality of external forms, however important these may be, but it is also and primarily their inner content, what is being accomplished under these external forms. This includes three things.

1. Liturgy as the Exercise of the Priestly Office of Christ

The primary celebrant is Jesus Christ, who in the liturgy exercises his priestly office and continues his redemptive work of salvation by making it present to the ends of the earth and to the end of time. The principal actor in the liturgy is thus Jesus Christ the priest. Priestly activity is mediatory, and this mediation is both descending, that is, from above downward, from God to humanity, and ascending, from below upward, from human beings to God. No human being can assume this mediatorial role; instead, the Son of God had to become human in order as "the man Christ Jesus" to act as sole "mediator between God and humankind" (1 Tm 2:5) and to restore the bond between God and humanity. Acting as this priestly mediator, Jesus concluded a new and everlasting covenant between God and mankind. In the celebration of the liturgy this new covenant is actualized, over and over again, by Jesus Christ himself. But in this exercise of his priestly office Jesus does not act alone but rather as head together with his body, the Church, which joins with him in his action. He is present, moreover, in every liturgical action of his Church.

In this same Article 7, just before giving this description of the nature of the liturgy, the Council speaks in detail about the presence of Christ in the liturgy. Christ is present, above all, in the celebration of the Eucharist: present both in the person of the human presider, whom we also call *priest,* and in the eucharistic species. He is also present by his power in the sacraments, so that, as Augustine says, when anyone baptizes, it is Christ himself who baptizes. This presence of Christ is of course not limited to the ordinary minister of baptism but extends also to any lay people who baptize. And, of course, it holds for all the sacraments.[147] Christ is also present in his word; he himself speaks when the sacred scriptures are read and interpreted in the Church.[148] Finally, he is present when the Church prays and sings, because he has promised to be in the midst of two or three who are gathered in his name (Mt 18:20).

2. Liturgy Is the Sanctification of Human Beings and the Worship of God

The Council's description of the nature of the liturgy makes it clear that liturgical action is not exclusively an action rising from human beings to God, not something human beings offer to God, but that it is also, and first of all, an action descending from God to humanity, as a result of which something happens in human beings. In the end, the description of the nature of the liturgy no longer accepts the distinction between sacraments (*sacramenta*) and worship (*cultus divinus*) that occurs repeatedly in official ecclesial documents. Along with its cultic or latreutic (from Greek *latreia*) aspect, that is, the aspect of adoration and veneration of God, the liturgy also has a salvific or soteriological aspect.

Article 7 of the constitution thus makes it clear that the worship of God, like the other saving actions of Jesus, has a dialogical structure. Liturgy is performed for the sanctification of human beings and the salvation of the world as well as for the glorification of God. In the liturgy God speaks to human beings and gives himself to them, and human beings answer and give themselves to God. Moreover, every turning of a human being to God results in a new turning of God to that person, which in turn effects a new turning of the person to God.[149]

The ultimate end of all human activity is the honoring of God. But the basis for this is God's gift of salvation. This is true also of the liturgy.

[147] If, as a result of the presence and action of Christ, any human being can bestow salvation on another in baptism and use the indicative form ("I baptize you"), so too an official empowered by ordination to do so can bestow salvation on another in the sacrament of reconciliation and use the indicative form ("I absolve you"). Yet it remains true that no one can forgive sins except God alone (see Mk 2:7).

[148] At the beginning of the Council the statement that Christ is also present when the scriptures are explained had not yet won the agreement of the majority of fathers. But in the Decree on the Missionary Activity of the Church an equivalent formula no longer caused the fathers any difficulty: The Church makes the author of salvation present "through the preached word" (Article 9).

[149] The pattern (word of God/answer of human beings) is especially clear in the liturgy of the word, especially on Sundays and solemnities: God's word comes forth in the first reading, and the human answer is given in the responsorial psalm; God's word comes forth in the second reading, and the human answer is given in the Hallelujah acclamation; God's word to human beings is proclaimed in the gospel and the homily, and the human answer is given in the profession of faith and the intercessions.

The ultimate end of every liturgical celebration remains the honoring of God. The ascending, cultic, worshipping aspect of a liturgical celebration takes precedence over the descending, soteriological, salvific aspect. But there is another order at work in the history of salvation as a whole and therefore also in the concrete performance of the liturgy: The descent of God in the incarnation was a presupposition of the paschal mystery, that is, the ascent in sacrifice and the exaltation on the cross. So, too, human beings can turn to God, pray, and offer themselves in sacrifice only if God has first turned to them: "He first loved us" (Jn 4:19). "We thank you for calling us to stand in your presence and serve you" (second eucharistic prayer). Human beings can glorify God only if God has first graced them. The initiative must come from God. The sanctification of human beings precedes their glorification of God. That is why, in its description of the nature of the liturgy, the Council puts in first place the sanctification of human beings and only then the glorification of God, which in the final analysis the sanctification of human beings promotes.

Both aspects, the latreutic and the saving, are present in every liturgical action, even if the emphasis is distributed differently. When, for example, people are baptized and God turns to them in the sacrament, this event is also an act of honoring God on the part of the Church, but the saving aspect obviously is more emphasized. When a priest utters the eucharistic prayer, his action is also for the salvation of human beings, but the latreutic aspect takes precedence.

The word *cult,* which is much used in connection with the history of religions, does not express the outward course of a liturgical action but is meant to describe the interior content. It is limited, however, to only one aspect of this content. *Cult* (*cultus*, from *colere,* "cultivate, worship") refers only to what human beings do in regard to God, not, conversely, what God does for human beings. Scripture uses the term only for the worship seen in the Old Testament (Nm 3:10; Jdt 5:17) and for the worship of idols (1 Pt 4:3). The word *cult* was unsuitable as a description of Christian worship and was therefore to be avoided when the reference was to the Christian liturgy. It is especially clear that the preconciliar concept of liturgy set down in the 1917 Code of Canon Law, canon 1256, was misleading because it did not include the sacraments; it was also narrow in that it stressed only the juridical aspect.[150]

---

[150] The name Sacred Congregation for Divine Worship (distinct from the Sacred Congregation for the Discipline of the Sacraments) for the Roman office that succeeded the Consilium for the implementation of the liturgical reforms on May 8, 1969, was unfortunate; even more so was the name of the office that combined the two on July 11, 1975:

The conciliar description of the nature of the liturgy correctly uses the word *cultus* ("worship") only of the human activity that ascends to God, but to avoid ambiguity the word should not be rendered by the misleading term *cult*. The conciliar description of the nature of the liturgy makes it clear that in a liturgical celebration and in every liturgical action not only does God receive worship ("cult"), but salvation is also offered to human beings. The term *liturgy,* which is borrowed from the Greek language (from *laos* and *ergon*), is considerably better suited than *cult,* because it can mean both "work for the people" and "work of the people," like the concept *opus Dei* or the German word *Gottesdienst*.

3. Liturgy Is Performed by Means of Sensible Signs

While the description of the nature of the liturgy emphasizes the interior content of the liturgical celebration, we must not forget that the liturgy also has an outward form and characteristic shape. Vatican II's description of the nature of the liturgy speaks of this aspect as well. The exercise of the priestly office of Christ, which includes the sanctification of human beings and the worship of God (and not only the sanctification of human beings as the 1983 Code of Canon Law, canon 834 §1 asserts[151]), is accomplished through sensible signs. Liturgical activity is carried out by using signs perceptible by the senses; these signs make up the external aspect of the liturgy, its form and characteristic shape. Liturgical activity includes more than is perceptible by the senses, but it is impossible without signs perceptible by the five senses.

Sensible signs are a necessity for the liturgy (a) for anthropological reasons: because as "inspirited" beings made up of body and soul, it is by way of the body that men and women enter into relations with the world around them, and it is through the body that knowledge of the environment is communicated to their spirits; (b)for christological reasons: because Christ, the incarnate Word of God (see Jn 1:14) and image of the invisible God (see Col 1:15), is the one who acts in the

---

Sacred Congregation for the Sacraments and Divine Worship. The same can be said of the Congregation for Divine Worship and the Discipline of the Sacraments, which has existed since March 1, 1989. The same judgment holds for the successive sets of decrees issued by the Joint Synod of the Sees in the Federal Republic of Germany (1971-75): "Worship" and "Main Emphases in Contemporary Pastoral Practice of the Sacraments."

[151] Even the title of Book IV of the new code is too narrow. Instead of speaking of "The Priestly Office of the Church," which would have signified both sanctification and worship, the title given, "The Office of Sanctifying in the Church," expresses only the first, whereas the book in fact deals with both.

liturgy; and (c) for ecclesiological reasons: because the Church is the root sacrament, that is, in it are rooted the sacraments instituted by Christ, the primary sacrament, those actions using signs that communicate God's invisible salvation and thus effect the salvation of human beings. Liturgy without signs that can be seen and heard, smelled, tasted, and felt, would therefore be not only unhuman but also non-Christian and nonecclesial.

It is important here to observe that the signs we can see, smell, taste, and touch, on the one hand, and hear, on the other, complement one another.[152] For a visible or tangible action (e.g., the laying on of hands) can have several meanings if its meaning is not specified by words. Words alone, however, can misrepresent the reality or at least express it less clearly (e.g., a sermon on Christ the Light during the Easter Vigil), if they are not further explained by visible signs (lighting of the Easter candle and the candles of the congregation). For this reason the liturgical constitution uses paired concepts: "rite and words" (Article 35) or "rites and prayers" (Article 48).

If sensible signs are essential to the liturgy, they must be understandable, so that the liturgy can be celebrated meaningfully. Unintelligibility turns the liturgy into something close to magic. The use of the vernacular in the liturgy (see Articles 36, 54, 63a, 101) is a primary requirement in light of the newly recognized importance of sensible signs. In view of its importance, the reading and explanation of God's word is to be given greater space than previously (Articles 35, 51, 52, 92a). In order, however, to avoid the danger of turning the liturgy into nothing but talk, care must be taken to provide proper room for "reverent silence" (Article 30); this does not mean the silence that descends when part of the liturgy is being carried out in a low voice by the presider, but the silence of all who are celebrating the liturgy.

No less important is it to use the other signs, not in the minimal form required for validity, but in an immediately understandable form that does not need a great deal of explanation (Article 34). It is difficult to see "the bath of rebirth" (Ti 3:5) in the pouring of a few drops of water on the head of an infant. Justice is not done to the Lord's command, "Take and eat of this, all of you," when the eucharistic bread kept in the tabernacle is regularly distributed (Article 55, 1). The regular refusal to

---

[152] It is reasonable to distinguish words from the other signs and the treat them separately, because they are the signs most frequently used in the liturgy, both in the form of God's word and in the form of human words in prayer and song.

extend the cup to the congregation amounts to disobedience to the Lord's words, "Take and drink of this, all of you" (Article 55, 2).

Attention must be called to one weakness in Vatican II's description of the nature of the liturgy: Western theology's forgetfulness of the Spirit, something often and rightly lamented. The covenant between God and humanity is actualized not only through Christ but also in the Holy Spirit, who is present both in the priestly activity of Jesus and in that of the Church. In celebrating the liturgy the Church turns to the Father through Christ, in the Holy Spirit.

B. THE COMMUNITY AS ACTIVE SUBJECT OF THE LITURGY

The Church is of its nature *ekklesia*, "assembly." It lives in and by its liturgical gatherings.[153] For "the Church of Christ is really present in all legitimately organized local groups of the faithful, which, insofar as they are united to their pastors, are also quite appropriately called Churches in the New Testament" (*LG*, 26). It is true, of course, that in the New Testament the term *ekklesia* is applied not only to individual communities (e.g., Acts 8:1; 14:23) but also to the totality of communities in a broader region (e.g., Acts 9:31) and in the entire world (e.g., Mt 16:18; 1 Cor 12:28; Eph 1:22; Col 1:18). Accordingly, the liturgical gathering is so characteristic of Christianity that even when the reference is to Christians of several communities (a "local Church," a "confession") or to all Christians living anywhere in the world, they are described as an "assembly" (*ekklesia*).

Although it is never the universal Church nor the entire local Church that celebrates a particular liturgy, still when a community celebrates the liturgy, it is a celebration of the local Church *and* of the whole Church. For "every legitimate celebration of the Eucharist is regulated by the bishop" (*LG*, 26), who in turn is a member of the college of bishops, in which the bishop of Rome has first place. Consequently, every community celebrating the liturgy is united to its bishop and to the bishop of Rome, the pope. For this reason the pope and the bishop are mentioned by name in the climactic part of every eucharistic celebration, the eucharistic prayer, and again in the intercessions at

---

[153] On this point see R. Kaczynski, "Erneuerung der Kirche durch den Gottesdienst," in *Lebt unser Gottesdienst? Die bleibende Ausgabe der Liturgiereform*, ed. Th. Maas-Ewerd (Freiburg- Basel-Vienna, 1988), 15-37, at 16-19.

Vespers. For every liturgy is celebrated "in union with the whole Church" (*communicantes*).

The activity of the Church does not, of course, consist solely of liturgical action (see Article 9), but the celebration of the liturgy is indeed the summit and source of that activity (Article 10). Therefore the Church must manifest itself in the liturgy and in everything that leads to it and springs from it, and the faithful must be able to experience it therein.

1. Liturgy as Celebration of the Entire Community

Among the norms that the liturgical constitution sets down as "drawn from the hierarchical and communal nature of the liturgy" (Articles 26-32), the first one affirms the basic right of the community gathered for liturgy (insofar as this community represents the Church of the locality; see Article 42), by assigning it the function of active subject of the liturgy: "Liturgical services are not private functions but are celebrations of the Church which is 'the sacrament of unity,' namely, 'the holy people united and arranged under their bishops.' Therefore liturgical services pertain to the whole Body of the Church. They manifest it and have effects upon it. But they also touch individual members of the Church in different ways, depending on their orders, their role in liturgical services, and their actual participation in them" (Article 26). This statement was a rejection in principle of the clericalized liturgy that had developed since the early Middle Ages. It is not only the clerical leader of the community, usually an ordained priest, who celebrates the liturgy; rather, the entire community gathered for worship has the "right and obligation" to celebrate the liturgy with "full, conscious, and active participation" (Article 14).[154]

Nor should all liturgical functions not belonging to holders of office be understood simply negatively, as functions not included in the sacrament of orders. Rather, they are to be seen as responsibilities that belong in principle to every Christian by reason of his or her baptism and confirmation, even if for certain services a formal commission must be given by the bishop or a priest. Altar servers are therefore not "substi-

---

[154] The 1983 Code is at least misleading when it states that official worship takes place "when it is carried out in the name of the Church *by persons lawfully deputed* and through acts approved by the authority of the Church" (canon 834 §2). If "lawful deputation" refers to baptism and confirmation, then the statement is of course correct; but then this should have been made explicit. The formulation suggests a special commissioning, but this is not required for the celebration of the liturgy in general, but only for special tasks.

tutes for the clergy," as the Italian name for them would suggest (*chierichetti* or "little clerics"); lectors and acolytes are not holders of "minor orders," who belong to the clergy; the church choir is not a replacement for a choir of monks or clerics, but is part of the community.

Pius X said that "the singers in the church have an authentically liturgical office," but he added that "therefore women, who are incapable of holding such an office, cannot be admitted to a church choir."[155] The participation of women in church choirs was indeed permitted in 1958,[156] but not until the liturgical constitution was it said that members of the choir, which includes women, "exercise a genuine liturgical function" (Article 29). There is no theological basis for a distinction between male and female lay people when lay people may undertake special ministries, such as those of lector and acolyte.

2. Liturgy as Celebration of a Structured Community

Since the community gathered for worship is the Church and one can say of it everything that one can say of the Church (it is the people of God, the body of Christ, the temple of the Holy Spirit), it is an image of the whole Church, heavenly and earthly. It is also an image of the Church inasmuch as it is a structured assembly. It is led by the bishop or by a priest as representative of the bishop and authorized by him. This ministerial priesthood that is communicated through ordination is distinct, in essence and not only in degree, from the common priesthood in which all believers share by virtue of baptism and confirmation. But the ministerial priesthood and the common priesthood are interrelated, since both share, each in a particular way, in one and the same priesthood of Christ (see *LG,* 10). The deacon assists the priestly presider at the liturgy.

Lay people, too, exercise special ministries when they read, sing, help with the distribution of communion, and serve at the presidential chair and the altar. In contrast to the preconciliar custom that the priestly presider at a liturgy had to read everything that others were reading and singing at that liturgy, as though these parts of the liturgy acquired their validity thereby, the liturgical constitution decrees that each person "who has an office to perform, should carry out all and only those parts

---

[155] Apostolic letter *Tra le sollecitudini* (November 22, 1903), in Bugnini, *Documenta,* 21.

[156] See the Instruction of the Congregation for Rites on Church Music and the Liturgy (September 3, 1958), 100, in Bugnini, *Documenta,* 98.

which pertain to his office by the nature of the rite and the norms of the liturgy" (Article 28). When priest and congregation, deacon and servers, cantors and lectors work together and each contributes to the sanctification of his or her fellow Christians and the glorification of God, the result is the authentic worship of the Church.[157] Because those celebrating the liturgy show themselves to be a structured assembly, they become an image of the Church.

3. Active Participation in the Liturgy

The newly recognized importance of the community clarifies what the liturgical constitution says about liturgical celebrations in general: "It must be emphasized that rites which are meant to be celebrated in common, with the faithful present and actively participating, should as far as possible be celebrated in that way rather than by an individual and quasi-privately" (Article 27). The document here takes up the idea of active participation (*participatio actuosa*), which Pius X gave to the liturgical movement at the beginning of the twentieth century[158] and which is a leitmotif running through the liturgical constitution and recurs in later documents as well. With this phrase is connected a series of other adjectives that describe, first, the ideal manner of celebrating the liturgy together (communal, true, authentic, appropriate, with understanding, conscious, internal and external, in a vital way, devout, full, complete), second, its necessity and frequency (obligatory and frequent), and, third, its result (effective, fruitful).[159]

Mere presence at the liturgy would not be "participation" as understood by the liturgical constitution. It is possible that for this reason the number of those "attending" the liturgy dropped after publication of the liturgical constitution, because not everyone wanted anything to do with a participation that meant involvement and a real communal celebration.

C. THE JURIDICAL ORGANIZATION OF THE LITURGY

The right of the bishops to establish liturgical law was excluded from the legal system of the Latin Church in the 1917 Code of Canon Law,

---

[157] See Jungmann, "Commentary on the Liturgical Constitution," 22.

[158] See note 139.

[159] See F. Kohlschein, "Bewusste, tätige und fruchtbringende Teilnahme," in *Lebt unser Gottesdienst? Die bleibende Ausgabe der Liturgiereform*, ed. Th. Maas-Ewerd (Freiburg-Basel- Vienna, 1988), 38-62.

for which liturgical legislation belonged exclusively to the pope; all that bishops had responsibility for was the sphere of popular devotion. They could no longer publish liturgical formularies or liturgical books, as they still could in the nineteenth century. Ecclesiastical authority in this area was synonymous with papal authority. In addition, no heed was paid to the different value or status of the various texts and rubrics; all liturgical texts and all details of the rubrics were assigned the same degree of obligation.

During the period of the liturgical movement and increasingly so during the preparatory phase of Vatican II, people began to desire also a decentralization of liturgical legislation. In the preparatory liturgical commission Jungmann was already arguing that bishops too should be entitled to organize the liturgy, or, to put it differently, that religious celebrations organized by the bishops (for example, the Corpus Christi procession) should be recognized as liturgy. His efforts were defeated by resistance within the commission.[160]

Unfortunately, the liturgical constitution itself did not take a fully clear position. On the one hand, it does say in Article 22 §1 that regulation of the liturgy belongs to the authority of the Church and specifically to the Apostolic See or, as the law permits, to the diocesan bishop. But when it describes celebrations organized by the bishop (Article 13), it does not apply the term *liturgy* to them but calls them "devotions proper to particular churches" (*sacra particularis ecclesiae exercitia*). These are activities that are only in harmony with the liturgy and are located, as it were, between the liturgy and the "pious practices" or "exercises of devotion" (*pia exercitia*) that can also be done privately. Thus the bishops are denied the right to organize the liturgy proper.

One certain reason for this exclusion of forms of worship organized by the bishops from the realm of the liturgy is that the liturgical constitution was discussed at the beginning of the Council and was published before the Church itself became the subject of concentrated reflection. When the liturgical constitution was being discussed, the focus was only on the universal Church and not yet on the local Churches. As a result, in the plenary meetings of the Council no one was ready to describe every form of public worship as truly "the worship of the Church," that is, as liturgy, but all were still subscribing to the idea that if liturgy were to be celebrated, the Apostolic See must necessarily intervene to organize it and approve the books for it. On this point the Code of 1983 at

---

[160] Jungmann, "Commentary," 16-17.

least went beyond the liturgical constitution and asserted, with an eye on
the fact, clearly set down in *Lumen gentium,* that the local Church led by
the bishop is also "Church": "It pertains to the diocesan bishop in the
church entrusted to him, within the limits of his competence, to issue
liturgical norms by which all are bound" (c. 838 §4)

With regard to the meaning of the liturgical constitution it may be
said, in conclusion, that it made this much clear: the liturgy is the most
important self-representation and the central vital activity of the Church,
though of course not the only one. It is, however, "the source from
which all the vigor of the Church flows" and "the summit toward which
all of its activity is directed" (Article 10).

III. THE BEGINNING OF THE POSTCONCILIAR LITURGICAL REFORM

Many in the Church had waited impatiently for the adoption of the
liturgical constitution, especially since some had hoped that it would
have been reached at the end of the first period of the Council. Not a few
thought that with its publication on December 4, 1963, every priest was
now able to make changes, "according to the spirit of the Council," in
the liturgy celebrated with him presiding. To many, the *vacatio legis*
also seemed too long.

Years later, however, the opinion was heard that the liturgical reform
had come about "much too quickly" and, in addition, that as a result of
its step-by-step implementation, it had demanded too frequent changes
in the communities; that it would have been much better to revise all the
liturgical books and then publish them all at once. But this view shows
ignorance of the expectations and hopes cherished at the time.

It was the wish of Pope Paul VI that, as far as possible, the first
reform measures should be published on the very day when the liturgical constitution was approved and promulgated;[161] but for whatever reasons this wish of the pope was not fulfilled, and in his address on the day
the liturgical constitution was approved, after he had given effusive
expression to his joy at the event, he warned:

[161] See Lercaro, *Lettere,* 177f.; Bugnini, *The Reform of the Liturgy,* 54; J. Wagner,
Mein Weg zur Liturgiereform 1936-1986. Erinnerungen (Freiburg-Basel-Vienna, 1993),
78; P. Marini, "Le premesse della grande riforma liturgica (ottobre-dicembre 1963)," in
Costituzione liturgica "Sacrosanctum Concilium," ed. Congregation for Divine Worship
(Rome, 1986), 78.

In order that all this [the reform of the liturgy] may be successfully carried out, no one is to act against the regulation of the Church's official worship by introducing private changes or particular rites. No one is to dare apply the constitution on the sacred liturgy, which we publish today, as he thinks fit and before relevant and clear instructions follow and the changes, to be prepared after the Council by special commissions to be appointed, have been legitimately approved. The sublime prayer of the Church must ring out over the entire world in peaceful harmony; no one may disturb it, no one may offend against it.[162]

The bishops shared the same concern. Thus the German-speaking bishops warned their clergy on December 4, 1963, "to practice restraint in matters liturgical.... 'Nothing apart from the bishop!' (Nihil sine episcopo!). We have waited a long time; now we must be patient a short time longer and give the bishops time for peaceful consultation."[163] In order to understand the situation that gave rise to such utterances, as well as the subsequent relatively slow-moving and initially disappointing beginning of the liturgical reform, it is necessary to speak of events taking place on the periphery of the conciliar event.

A. Activities Having to Do with the Postconciliar Liturgical Reform

During the first meeting of the conciliar Liturgical Commission, on October 21, 1962, the appointment of F. Antonelli as secretary of this commission was announced. In addition, Cardinal Larraona, president of the commission, appointed as his own substitutes Cardinals P. Giobbe and A. Jullien, whom the pope had called to be on the commission. Not only was there general surprise that A. Bugnini was the only secretary of a preparatory commission not to be appointed secretary of the corresponding conciliar commission (at the same period, the chair of liturgical studies at the Lateran University was taken from him), but it was no less astounding that Cardinal Lercaro was passed over in the appointment of the vice-presidents, even though he was the oldest cardinal on the commission, the only one elected by the Council fathers, and in addition, a recognized expert on liturgical questions. Curial forces were rightly seen at work behind these personnel

---

[162] AS II/6, 565f.

[163] "Pastoral Letter of the German-speaking Bishops to Their Clergy," in Lengeling, Die Konstitution, 11*.

decisions.[164] Steps were taken in good time to ensure that similar decisions were not made for the period after the promulgation of the liturgical constitution.

In view of the fact that the schema on the liturgy had been so carefully
prepared, people were of the opinion that it could be definitively adopted
at the end of this second period of the Council. For this reason, some
individuals who had little to do apparently began to think about the
course the liturgical renewal might take after the promulgation of the
constitution. There is an undated and unsigned memorandum intended
for Cardinal Lercaro entitled "Note on a Postconciliar 'Pontifical Liturgical Commission." In the index to the material in the Lercaro Archive,
the date of composition is given as "October 31, 1962 (afternoon)" and
Bugnini is identified as its author, something confirmed by its content.

The author first describes the work done in 1948 by the reform commission appointed by Pius XII, and then explains his ideas on a postconciliar reform commission. This must be autonomous, as the preparatory commissions had been; that is, it must be able to work quickly,
have no officials of the Curia as members, and be international in its
composition. He explains in detail how the work is to be done and suggests at least five years but preferably eight for the reform.[165]

On November 9, 1962, experts on the Liturgical Commission sent a
letter to Cardinal Cicognani, secretary of state. The author, writing in the
name of the "group of experts," complains bitterly of the ineffective
way in which the commission is going about its work. He asks, therefore, to set a deadline for Larraona by assigning the days on which the
suggestions for the improvement of the individual chapters are to be discussed in the hall. He also suggests that the direction of the commission's work be entrusted to Lercaro, with Larraona remaining as the official president of the commission. Finally, when it becomes possible to
foresee the date of the approval of the constitution, a postconciliar commission should be appointed for its implementation and be able to begin

[164] See Bugnini, *The Reform of the Liturgy*, 30. That similar problems were to be seen
in other conciliar commissions is shown by two letters, apparently dependent on each
other, that were sent to the pope during the last days of October 1963. One was in French
(October 25, 1963), from French-speaking Council fathers; the other was in English (no
date), and from English-speaking fathers. These letters asked, among other things, that the
president of a conciliar commission should not be the prefect or secretary of a Roman
congregation, and that vice presidents and secretaries be appointed only with the agreement of the entire commission. See Lercaro Archive, XXIII, 541 and 540.

[165] See Lercaro Archive, I, 24. For the reasons the memorandum can have been written as early as 1962, see notes 184 and 185, below.

its work immediately; this commission should consist of a president (the author, evidently thinking only of curial cardinals, suggests Bea or Confalonieri) and about twenty bishops and fifty experts. At the end he answers a question that he had apparently been asked, namely, whether at least some general norms for the reform should be approved by the Council in case the entire constitution were not approved; the author of the letter advises against this.[166]

That Bugnini was the author of this letter is suggested not only by reasons of content and style but by the fact that he enjoyed to some degree the confidence of the cardinal secretary of state, who was the brother of Cardinal G. Cicognani (d. February 5, 1962), who had been president of the preparatory liturgical commission.[167] A comparison of the content of this letter with the memorandum of Lercaro (November 11, 1962) to Archbishop A. Dell'Acqua, substitute at the Secretariat of State, shows Lercaro to have been clearly influenced by the letter or at least by its writer.[168]

On November 10, 1963, a meeting was held at a place Bishop Jenny called the "international liturgical workshop"; here there was discussion of the appointment of a postconciliar commission. Those present wanted to approach the moderators and possibly the pope with the request that this commission be appointed before the fathers went their several ways. It should not be left to the Congregation for Rites. Not only experts but bishops should belong to the commission. Its president should not be Larraona, who could not carry through a reform of the liturgy. Since there was no other suitable cardinal in the Curia, it would be best to assign the task to Lercaro.[169]

At an audience on that same day, November 10, 1963, Paul VI told the moderators of his desire that at the end of the second period of the Council the first regulations for the implementation of the liturgical constitution should be issued, and he commissioned Lercaro to prepare a document to this effect.[170] The next day Lercaro discussed the pope's

[166] See Lercaro Archive, I, 5.

[167] The author of the present chapter knows, from five years of collaboration, Bugnini's way of drawing up plans and his feel for their feasibility. The final sentence of the letter is entirely characteristic of the man: he excuses himself for the frankness of the letter and expresses his conviction "that frankness and a right intention have never worked against the solution of problems but make this easier."

[168] See Lercaro Archive, I, 6c.

[169] See the handwritten notes of Jenny in the archives at the ISR. Jenny addressed the subject in a letter of November 15, 1962, to Lercaro.

[170] On what follows see Bugnini, *The Reform of the Liturgy*, 54ff., and Marini, "Le premesse," 78-101.

plan with Bugnini and asked him to name a group of experts who could work together on the project. Thus Lercaro received a commission adapted to his personality and abilities, and Bugnini was to an extent rehabilitated.

As early as October 12, 1963, the experts named by Bugnini met with him at Lercaro's residence in S. Priscilla for a first conversation on the subject and for a distribution of tasks. Those present were E. Bonet, A. Dirks, J. A. Jungmann, A.-G. Martimort, F. McManus, H. Schmidt, C. Vagaggini, and J. Wagner. The first working sessions of the experts were held on October 19 and 20 at Vagaggini's home base in S. Gregorio al Celio. At these meetings the experts were obliged, first of all, to accept the fact that their overly extensive presentations for the first steps of the reform had to be shortened.[171] Further meetings were set for October 25 and 26, and a final meeting for October 30.

According to the original plan the document was to be ready on November 1, 1963. The first draft must have already existed as early as October 20. During the following day Bonet had to revise this draft in keeping with the observations of the experts. The second draft, of October 22, must have envisaged a papal document in two parts: a *motu proprio*, which should take up juridical questions (the first word was already decided on: *Primitiae*), and an istruction with practical directives. The work of the group concluded with the draft of November 1. The intention was clear to involve in the work a close confidant of the pope, G. Bevilacqua, who examined the draft at length.

The final versions of a *motu proprio*, which began with the word *Primitiae* ("Apostolic Letter Published Motu Proprio, in Which Some Norms and Regulations Are Given for Immediately Implementing the Conciliar Constitution on the Sacred Liturgy") and of an accompanying instruction ("Instruction on the Parts of the Liturgical Renewal to Be Immediately Put into Effect") were supposed to be ready on November 21.[172] According to Bugnini, the document was given to the pope on

---

[171] The names of the experts, given by Marini ("Le premesse," 79), are confirmed by *TJungmann* for October 12, 13, 19, and 20, 1963). On October 19 Jungmann was forced to accept, with a rather heavy heart, Bugnini's considerable shortening of his plan for a first reform of the mass, which he had discussed in advance with Wagner on October 13. But he also saw that the next day the plan of McManus and Vagaggini for the first reforms of the sacraments and sacramentals was "picked to pieces in a similar way."

[172] See the texts published by Marini, "Le premesse," 97-101. According to a different source Lercaro was to have gotten at least the proposed instruction to the pope by November 7; see Döpfner Archive, Akt 1 Conc VII SQ Nr. 17. It is known that Lercaro was with the pope on that day; see *Lettere*, 208.

November 21. While this is likely, since the moderators had an audience with the pope on that day, Lercaro reported that on November 24 he was working with Bugnini "to prepare for the Holy Father a list of the liturgical innovations that could be introduced immediately."[173]

The *motu proprio* contained six provisions:

1. The basic principles of the constitution were to be impressed on the faithful immediately.
2. The first concrete steps in the reform were to be taken from the Instruction.
3. The liturgical books were to remain valid until further notice.
4. Articles 22 §§1 and 3 were to be cited verbatim.
5. There was to be a clarification regarding which groups of bishops were meant in Article 22 §2.
6. The coming feast of Christmas was to be the first day on which the new provisions were to take effect.[174]

The Instruction went into some articles of the constitution: for the mass, Articles 50, 53, 54, and 57; for the celebration of the other sacraments and the sacramentals, Articles 63b, 66, 69, 71, 74, 76, 78, and 79; for the liturgy of the hours, Article 89.[175]

The document was supposed to be published at the beginning of December, but this did not happen. The background of the failure of the project is not known and not pertinent. Bugnini remarks that it was too late (although everything was in the pope's hands before the final vote on the liturgy schema!) for final approval to be given to the necessary changes before the end of the second period. It is possible that the "definitive version" of November 21 came into the possession of too many persons who found some fault with it, or of others who sought deliberately to delay or even prevent its publication.

Marini asks whether the entire *Primitiae* project thus proved to be a failure, and he denies this for three reasons.[176] First, the whole incident made clear the necessity of a broadly conceived reform. The publication of these two hastily prepared documents would possibly have caused more problems than it would have solved; the many who were

---

[173] *Lettere*, 234. It is possible, however, that Lercaro was referring to changes in the version given to the pope, due to interventions from individuals who took up the matter only after November 21 or deliberately wanted to keep the document from being published. On the entire incident see Bugnini, *The Reform of the Liturgy*, 54ff., as well as Marini, "Le premesse," 79f. and 97, who dates the final version to November 24.

[174] See Marini, "Le premesse," 98f.

[175] Ibid., 99-101.

[176] Ibid., 80-89.

expecting a more radical reform would have been disappointed.[177] Second, it became clearly necessary to set up a numerically larger commission and to entrust it with the organization of the work. The experts at the meetings on the Motu Proprio *Primitiae* were already maintaining the need of such an international commission that would be independent of the curial offices.[178] Third, the process brought to light the intellectual abilities and organizational talents of a few men such as Lercaro and Bugnini, to whom an implementation of the reform could be entrusted with promise of success. Most important, during these weeks there developed between Lercaro and Bugnini an amity and mutual confidence that lasted through the following years of the reform and proved advantageous to it. Furthermore, as one of the moderators of the Council, Lercaro met often with Pope Paul VI and had the opportunity to discuss with him the current problems of the liturgical reform. The work on *Primitiae* certainly contributed in a decisive way to the perfect harmony among the pope, Lercaro, and Bugnini. Finally, on the occasion of this work, the vigor and organizational ability of Bugnini must have been so striking as to give rise to confidence in him for the subsequent work of liturgical reform.[179]

At that time there were probably many who had long since thought that the postconciliar liturgical reform would be put in Bugnini's hands. As early as October 29, 1963, Jungmann told Bugnini of what "he had some time ago decided and what was the case with him"; namely, that he did not want to play a part in the postconciliar commission. But Bugnini answered that he and Lercaro had already decided that Jungmann should participate.[180]

When the draft of the Motu Proprio *Primitiae* was rejected, things had not advanced to the point at which Lercaro and Bugnini could have gone on with the project. For this, both had to receive a new commission, but at this point it was unfortunately too late for them to continue and complete work on the document along the lines intended by them and their collaborators.

---

[177] Ibid., 84.
[178] Ibid.
[179] Ibid., 88.
[180] See *TJungmann* for October 29, 1963.

B. The Establishment of the Commission for
Implementing the Constitution on the Sacred Liturgy

It has been thought likely that Paul VI had already decided to whom he would entrust the postconciliar liturgical reform[181] at the time when, after the publication of the liturgical constitution in December 1963, he asked both the secretary of the conciliar Liturgical Commission and Cardinal Lercaro for a proposal for the organization of the postconciliar commission on the implementation of the constitution. Lercaro, therefore, asked Bugnini to draft a plan.[182]

The proposal of Antonelli, the secretary of the Liturgical Commission had three parts. The first listed fourteen study groups to be established. The second set out a plan for the organization of the work. The work of the study groups was to be directed by a small commission consisting of five bishops (Larraona and Lercaro and three diocesan bishops, F. Grimshaw, A. Martin, and F. S. Zauner) and eight experts (F. Antonelli. P. Borella, A. Bugnini, A. Dirks, P. Frutaz, A.-G. Martimort, C. Vagaggini, and J. Wagner). It was thought that the functions of a secretariat could be taken over by the secretary of the Liturgical Commission. The third part of the proposal dealt with the composition of the study groups listed in the first part. The proposal was presented to the pope on December 19, 1963.

Bugnini's plan was described differently by himself and by P. Marini. Bugnini gives a brief description of what he had written to Lercaro in the memorandum he had composed earlier, possibly in 1962.[183] The commission had to be autonomous, active, and international. It had to consist of a secretariat supported by experts, a commission of from twenty to thirty bishops with a cardinal as president, and, over that, a commission of cardinals. The work was to be done by study groups to which would be assigned the reform of the individual liturgical books or the revision of the resultant schemata from a variety of viewpoints. The work was to be coordinated by a special commission of experts (*commissio executiva*). The latter would present the work done, first to the commission of bishops and then to the commission of cardinals; it would then send it to the episcopal conferences for their assessment; and finally it would be presented to the pope. If the work were done with determination and

[181] See Marini, "Le premesse," 89.
[182] On what follows see Bugnini, *The Reform of the Liturgy*, 60ff., and Marini, "Le premesse," 89-94.
[183] Bugnini, *The Reform of the Liturgy*, 60-68.

energy and were properly organized, it could be finished in five years.[184] A schematic description of the various groups involved in the reform was attached to the proposal.[185]

Marini stresses that Bugnini in his proposal limited himself to a plan of work. Marini likewise mentions a schematic presentation. The work of the commission was to be in two phases: in the first, the Breviary, Missal, Pontifical, and Ritual were to be revised; in the second, the ceremonial of bishops and the martyrology were to be revised and a Code of Liturgical Law composed.[186]

Bugnini infers the effect that the two proposals had on the pope from the fact that on January 3, 1964, he himself was called to see Cicognani, the secretary of state, and informed that he had been appointed secretary of the commission for the implementation of the liturgical constitution. This oral communication was followed on January 13 by the official announcement of the appointment by the Secretariat of State. It was in this document that the new name of the commission appeared for the first time: Council [*Consilium*] for the Implementation of the Constitution on the Sacred Liturgy. The document also named the three cardinals appointed as members: Lercaro, Giobbe, and Larraona. These three, together with the secretary, formed the "constituent assembly" of the Consilium.[187]

The Motu Proprio *Sacram Liturgiam*, dated on January 25, 1964, gave the first regulations for the implementation of the liturgical constitution

[184] At this point in the description of his plan Bugnini directly cites part of a sentence that does not occur in this form in his memorandum to Lercaro (Lercaro Archive, I, 24): "The time required for the reform: five years, 'on the assumption that the executive commission set to work in a decisive, active, and completely organized way.'" This suggests that the memorandum had been composed earlier, perhaps in 1962, and only found its way into the proposal that Lercaro asked for in December 1963. There are no indications that make it necessary to locate the origin of the memorandum in the period of work on the draft of the Motu Proprio *Primitiae*.

[185] Such a schematic description is to be found in Lercaro Archive, I, 25 and is dated to December 1963. But since it does not correspond to the one described by Marini ("Le Premesse," 92), it seems to reflect an earlier study. The appended two pages list the names of the bishops who would form the Liturgical Commission, and of the experts who were to be on the executive commission. Since the list has Cardinal Confalonieri as president and the name of the secretary is not filled in, the list is probably to be dated to 1962 (see Bugnini's letter of November 9, 1962, in Lercaro Archive, I, 5, to which reference has already been made), as is the schematic description attached to the list of names. But then it can also be assumed that the memorandum for Cardinal Lercaro (Lercaro Archive, I, 24) also belongs to 1962.

[186] See Marini, "Le premesse," 91-94.

[187] Bugnini, *The Reform of the Liturgy*, 49f.

and mentioned the fact that the Consilium had been established (but did not yet use the name; it spoke instead of a "commission with the principal task of seeing that the prescriptions of the Constitution are put into effect)."[188] This may be interpreted as a sign that the new Consilium had little or nothing to do with the document, which also had nothing more precise to say about its competence. On January 31, the *Osservatore Romano* published the names of the three members and secretary appointed by the pope.

Bugnini says that he set to work immediately after Cicognani entrusted the organization of the Consilium to him. The constituent assembly of the Consilium held its first meeting, chaired by Lercaro, on January 15; an important item on the agenda was the assessment of the draft for the Motu Proprio *Sacram Liturgiam*, which had been forwarded to the assembly.[189] But Bugnini had already sketched out a program of work for the Consilium, and he presented it for discussion at this first meeting.

Everything in Rome was still marked by secrecy, but on the very day of the public session at which the liturgical constitution was promulgated, Bugnini, in his capacity as editor of the *Ephemerides Liturgicae*, had already asked some of his friends to collaborate on a commentary on the constitution. J. Wagner was asked to comment on Articles 77 and 78 (marriage) and Article 128 (revision of the regulations for the ordering of sacred spaces) and to submit his contribution by January 15, 1964. On this latter date Wagner wrote to excuse himself for having been unable, for reasons of health, to meet the deadline. At the same time, he asked for information, especially about the Instruction on the implementation of the liturgical constitution.[190]

Even before Bugnini could answer this letter, the news of his appointment as secretary of the Consilium had reached Trier, and, while still in the hospital, Wagner telegraphed his congratulations on January 21. On January 24 Bugnini wrote to thank him for the telegram and, after consultation with Lercaro, invited him to Rome "around February 10" to exchange ideas and to plan the study groups. At the same time, Bugnini

---

[188] Paul VI, Motu Proprio *Sacram Liturgiam*, January 25, 1964; *AAS* 56 (1964), 139-44, at 140; translation in *Documents on the Liturgy, 1963-1979: Conciliar, Papal, and Curial Texts* (Collegeville, 1982), 84.

[189] Bugnini, *The Reform of the Liturgy*, 50.

[190] Letter of January 15, 1964, in the Wagner Archive. Wagner often said that because of the taxing work in Rome during the Council he was completely exhausted for weeks after his return home.

also invited Martimort to Rome, telling him that if February 10 were not open for him, the meeting could take place even earlier.[191] Since Lercaro had to postpone his journey to Rome, the meeting of Wagner, Martimort, and Bugnini did not take place until February 13; the three then met with Lercaro on the afternoon of February 14.[192]

Bugnini's method of proceeding during these weeks, even before the Consilium could begin its work of reform, was typical of his activity in the service of liturgical reform, an activity that continued until July 11, 1975. As soon as he received a new commission, he was on the lookout for advisers and collaborators, and he usually found suitable ones. He was aided in all this by a high degree of prudence and knowledge of people. Thus he took it for granted, at this moment when the course had to be set for the work of the Consilium, that he should consult the two spokesmen for the German and French language areas: Wagner, the director of the Liturgisches Institut, and Martimort, the director of the Centre de Pastorale Liturgique.[193] Both had worked very well with him in the preparatory commission for the Council and had shown themselves publicly to be his friends when the direction of the conciliar Liturgical Commission was denied him and the chair at the Lateran University was taken from him.

On February 15, the day after the conversation with Martimort and Wagner, the "constituent assembly" of the Consilium held its second meeting, at which it completed its activity. At this meeting a first study group was appointed for the revision of the Psalter, which was regarded as an especially lengthy task. Most important of all, however, the list of

---

[191] The text of Wagner's telegram of congratulations and Bugnini's answering letter are in the Wagner Archive. The letter of January 24 (Prot. N. 21/64) is on stationary that already has the letterhead "Consilium ad exsequendam...," with its office address in Palazzo S. Marta. In this connection note Cicognani's order to Bugnini: "Wherever you wish, but not at the Congregation of Rites" (*The Reform of the Liturgy*, 52).

[192] See Bugnini's letter to Wagner, February 3, 1964 (Prot. N. 56/64) and his postcard of Februry 11, 1964, in which he says that because of another meeting he must delay the meeting on February 13, 1964, from 9:00 a.m. to 11:00 a.m.; the reference to 9:00 a.m. may be to the meeting at the Congregation for Rites in which Wagner took part (see Martimort's letters of February 21, 1964, to Lercaro [Lercaro Archive, XXV, 715] and Wagner [Wagner Archive, vol. 37]).

[193] Bugnini did not repeat the mistake he had made in the appointment of advisers to the preparatory commission, namely, of initially passing over Martimort and Wagner. At that earlier time he had feared that these two might exert too strong an influence on the discussions of the commission (see Wagner, 52). At that time, in fact, as editor of the *Ephemerides Liturgicae*, he was more familiar with the representatives of liturgical scholarship than with those of pastoral liturgical work; he probably thought himself still inferior to the latter.

persons to be proposed to the pope as members of the Consilium was discussed and finally accepted unanimously. The list was submitted to the pope, who issued the appointments. The names of the forty-two members — ten cardinals, twenty-eight bishops, one abbot, and three priests — were published in *Osservatore Romano* for March 5, which now for the first time stated that Lercaro was president of the Consilium. A first meeting of the Consilium took place as early as March 11, at which Cardinal Confalonieri was appointed vice-president.[194]

Also belonging to the Consilium, in addition to these members, were two groups of experts, the "consultors" (*consultores*) and the "advisers" (*consiliarii*). Consultors were given a permanent appointment, while the advisers were to be asked to collaborate case by case. From the beginning of March, consultors were being appointed by the president of the Consilium, Lercaro. They received their appointments along with a letter of the secretary inviting them to their first meeting, March 14-18. The *litterae testimoniales* from the Secretariat of State followed later.[195]

Following the model of the Roman congregations, the plan was to have two kinds of meetings of the members: ordinary meetings, to be held once or twice a month, and plenary meetings, to be held three or four times a year. Only those members present in Rome would take part in the ordinary meetings. In addition, there would be meetings of the consultors (the *Consulta*). The consultors were usually present at the plenary meetings of the members, though they did not have a vote. The consultors formed the study groups, which usually would be made up of five to seven persons and directed by a reporter, who was assisted by a secretary. There was, of course, to be complete freedom of discussion.[196] In contrast to the practice of the Roman congregations, the members at their meetings were not simply to follow rank in giving their opinion on a problem; they were to have real discussions, during which at a certain point the consultors present were to be asked for their views and were to answer.

[194] According to a letter from Lercaro to Larraona, a discussion between these two cardinals of the Consilium's program of work must have taken place that same day; Lercaro Archive, XXV, 719.

[195] Thus B. Fischer of Trier was asked to come to Rome in a letter of March 24, 1964 (Prot. N. 317/64); on May 23, 1964, he received the *litterae testimoniales* from the Secretariat of State, forwarded to him by Bugnini (Prot. N. 979/64). Jungmann received his appointment as consultor as early as March 3, 1964 (see *TJungmann* for that day).

[196] See the secretary's report on the first meeting of (at that time only) seventeen consultors on April 14, 1964; Fischer Archive.

Before the Consilium could begin its work, its tasks had to be determined and its competence defined. In a letter to the president of the Consilium on February 29, 1964, Cicognani assigned it the following tasks:

a. to suggest the names of persons charged with forming study groups for the revision of rites and liturgical books;
b. to oversee and coordinate the work of the study groups;
c. to prepare carefully an instruction explaining the practical application of the Motu Proprio *Sacram Liturgiam* and clearly outlining the competence of territorial ecclesiastical authorities, pending the reform of the rites and liturgical books;
d. to apply, according to the letter and spirit of the Council, the Constitution it had approved, by responding to the proposals of the conferences of bishops and to questions that arise concerning the correct application of the Constitution.

Appeals of decisions of the Consilium as well as the solution of particularly sensitive and grave or completely new problems would be referred by the Consilium to the pope.[197]

The tasks were thus made clear, but the areas of competence were far from being clear. In particular, there was no unambiguous explanation of the relationship of the Consilium to the Congregation for Rites, whose area of competence remained untouched. The following incident was significant. Cardinal Larraona had arranged for a meeting on February 13 "of the members of the Liturgical Commission who were present in Rome" and had invited Martimort and Wagner (present in Rome at Bugnini's invitation) to attend. Those invited discovered that this was not a meeting of the commission but of officials of the Congregation for Rites. Those present were Larraona, E. Dante, G. Sormanti, F. Antonelli, N. Ferraro, and P. Frutaz. The second point on the agenda was the answer that the Cardinal was to give to the episcopal conferences, which had already submitted the records of their decrees to the Apostolic See in accordance with Article 36 §3 of the liturgical constitution. The Cardinal was of the opinion that the Congregation could "grant" what the bishops were "asking." He seemed not to understand Article 36 and to interpret the bishops' decisions as a simple request for an indult.[198]

In letters sent on February 21 Martimort informed both Lercaro and Wagner of a document sent to the French episcopate on February 14.[199]

---

[197] Letter of the Cardinal Secretary of State, A. Cicognani, to the President of the Consilium, Cardinal G. Lercaro, February 29, 1964, in *Documents on the Liturgy*, 214.

[198] See A.-G. Martimort, "Note confidentiel sur le Motu proprio du 25 janvier 1964 et ses suites," Wagner Archive, vol. 37.

[199] See the letter of Cardinal Larraona to Archbishop P. Bertoli, Apostolic Nuncio in France (Lercaro Archive, XXIV, 576).

From the latter we learn that the Congregation for Rites had established a special section to "be in charge of the postconciliar liturgical movement" (a section made up solely of officials of the congregation, that is, those who had opposed the liturgical constitution). The claim was made that the congregation had discussed the matter with the Consilium (perhaps inasmuch as Bugnini was present at the meeting although not allowed to speak) and had heard a deputation from the conciliar Liturgical Commission (this deputation must have consisted of Wagner and Martimort himself).[200]

The following months saw a gradual clarification of the relationship between the Congregation for Rites and the Consilium. Bugnini has documented the individual steps,[201] which can only be summarized here:

1. On April 22, 1964, it was determined that the Congregation for Rites and the Consilium were to appear together in the promulgation of decrees issued as a result of the Council. After a lengthy back and forth the two reached agreement on the formula, first used in the publication of the first Instruction on the implementation of the liturgical constitution:

> This Instruction was prepared by the Consilium by mandate of Pope Paul VI, and presented to the pope by Cardinal Giacomo Lercaro, President of the Consilium. After having carefully considered the Instruction, in consultation with the Consilium and the Congregation of Rites, Pope Paul in an audience granted to Cardinal Arcadio Maria Larraona, Prefect of the Congregation of Rites, gave it specific approval as a whole and in its parts, confirmed it by his authority, and ordered it to be published and faithfully observed by all concerned, beginning on the first Sunday of Lent, 7 March 1965.[202]

2. After numerous disputes over experimentation with the rite of concelebration and over the confirmation of vernacular liturgical texts that had been approved by the episcopal conferences, Cardinal Cicognani, secretary of state, finally wrote a letter to Cardinal Larraona, prefect of the Congregation for Rites, on January 7, 1965. In it he determined that

---

[200] See Lercaro Archive, XXV, 715, and Wagner Archive, vol. 37. Bugnini, too, was informed (obviously by Wagner) of the letter of the Congregation for Rites to the Apostolic Nuncio in France, and on February 25, from his private address, he wrote Wagner a letter in which he bitterly complained of the step taken by the Congregation for Rites. He thinks that if Wagner and he were to take part in the Congregation's commission, they would be traitors (Wagner Archive, vol. 37).

[201] Bugnini, *The Reform of the Liturgy*, 71-73.

[202] Congregation for Rites, Instruction (first) *Inter Oecumenici*, on the orderly carrying out of the Constitution on the Liturgy, September 26, 1964: *AAS* 56 (1964), 900; *Documents on the Liturgy*, 110.

the study of questions and liturgical texts as required by the implementation of the liturgical constitution as well as the supervision of experiments
that seemed necessary were matters for the Consilium. The publication of
documents was up to the Congregation for Rites, but such publications
were to be signed by the president of the Consilium as well.[203]

From his own experience as an episcopal participant in the Council
during the first period and from the information that reached him during
the second period — particularly from Lercaro, who was both a moderator and a member of the Liturgical Commission and whom the pope
had commissioned in October 1963 to draft a document on the postconciliar liturgical reform — Paul VI knew that no liturgical reform could
be implemented using the existing departments of the Curia. Yet a
restructuring of the departments or the appointment of new personnel
would have taken so much time that the reform would have been significantly delayed. The pope had no other choice, therefore, than to establish a new body made up of persons from the universal Church and
responsible, in the final analysis, to himself personally. This was a
somewhat risky move that roused not a little indignation in the Curia but
that was ultimately for the good of the Church.

C. THE DISAPPOINTING MOTU PROPRIO *SACRAM LITURGIAM*

We do not know what the reasons may have been for not publishing
the Motu Proprio *Primitiae* and the Instruction giving it concrete application. In any case, some regulations for carrying out the liturgical constitution had to appear during the interim period (*vacatio legis*) that
would end on February 16, 1964. And, of course, others beside the little
group of experts brought together around Lercaro by Bugnini had been
endeavoring to advance their own ideas on the postconciliar liturgical
renewal. The conciliar Liturgical Commission had done preliminary
work on the subject. We have three documents that were composed during the final weeks before the close of the second period of the Council.

1. The Application of the Liturgical Constitution

The first is a text composed by C. Rossi and presented at the meeting
of the Liturgical Commission, on November 19, 1963. In it, the articles

---

[203] Letter of January 7, 1965. Text in *Enchiridion documentorum instaurationis liturgicae*, ed. R. Kaczynski, I (Turin, 1976), 379.

of the constitution are divided into four groups: those that have a didactic character or contain general principles and are therefore to be accepted immediately; others that can be put into practice without the territorial ecclesiastical authorities (the episcopal conferences) or the Apostolic See having to play an active role; still others that are to be put into practice by the territorial ecclesiastical authorities; and finally, those to be implemented through the Apostolic See.[204]

2. The Territorial Ecclesiastical Authority Competent to Apply the Liturgical Constitution

A short text, composed by Martimort, was also presented at the same meeting of the Liturgical Commission (November 19, 1963). According to it, the territorial ecclesiastical authority consists either of all the bishops of a country, including coadjutors and suffragan bishops, or of the bishops who gather together from a region or from several countries. A two-thirds majority is required for all decisions.[205]

3. The Suspension of the Law and the Application of the Liturgical Constitution

The introduction to a third document makes it clear that it was composed by Bonet, Martimort, and Wagner during the period between the approval of the liturgical schema on November 22 and the promulgation of the constitution on December 4, 1963.[206] The first part of this document proposes that the suspension of the constitution end on the first Sunday of Lent 1964. In addition, until the formation of the postconciliar commission for the liturgical reform, the conciliar Liturgical Commission should give practical interpretations of the liturgical constitution, resolve difficulties that may arise, and give the required approval, that is, confirmation or approbation.

The second part of this document, which includes the two previously discussed documents, divides the directives of the liturgical constitution into three groups: (1) those that are to be translated into practice in the

[204] See "De Constitutionis applicatione," in *Commissio de sacra liturgia,* 113-18 (Lercaro Archive, I, 39). Note that the location of this and the following document in the index of Lercaro Archive, in the period after December 4, 1963, is erroneous.

[205] "De auctoritate ecclesiastica territoriali competente ad Constitutionem applicandam," ibid., 119 (Lercaro Archive, I, 40). The caution in the previous note applies here also.

[206] It was discussed at the meeting of the Liturgical Commission on November 28, 1963.

future liturgical reform; (2) those that concern territorial assemblies of bishops (a statement follows concerning those who belong to such assemblies, pending an as yet to be issued determination by the Council); and (3) those that do not require a special intervention of an authority and acquire the force of law after the period of suspension of the law.

If it seems good to the pope, the document says, even now to allow something which of itself would be made possible only through the future liturgical reform, it would be good if this were to be put into practice at the end of the *vacatio legis*. Suggestions for such papal action would include Article 89d, which decrees that Prime is to be suppressed, and Article 89e, which permits the recitation of only one of the three "little hours." At the end of the document there is a list of ten decrees that will go into effect at the end of the *vacatio legis*.[207]

It may at first seem surprising that Bonet, Martimort, and Wagner, members of Lercaro's group that had drafted the Motu Proprio *Primitiae* and the accompanying Instruction, should have accepted Larraona's commission to compose this document, which was so very different from their earlier project. But the authors must have already surmised or even been told that the Motu Proprio and Instruction had no chance of succeeding. Therefore they supported a new document that would rescue the most important points.

Bugnini writes that at the beginning of January 1964 — that is, at a time when he had already been chosen as secretary of the Consilium — the secretariat of the Council, "which was in charge," and the secretariat of the Congregation for Rites took up the matter of a *motu proprio*. They decided to settle for a single document that would be juridical in character. Immediately after their appointment as members of the Consilium, the three cardinals, Lercaro, Giobbe, and Larraona, received a draft from Archbishop Felici. After an examination of this text at the meeting on January 15, 1964, they decided that it had to be rewritten. They retained the beginning and conclusion of Felici's draft, but in the section containing the regulations they made fuller use of the draft composed by the experts back in October.[208] These changes were unavailing. Later on, in a confidential memorandum, Martimort excused Larraona and the Congregation for Rites, on the grounds that the text prepared by the conciliar Liturgical Commission had been completely revised when it reached

---

[207] "De vacatione et exsecutione Constitutionis conciliaris de sacra liturgia," ibid., 120-25 (Lercaro Archive, I, 77). The location of this document in the period 1963-64 in the index of Lercaro Archive, is inaccurate.

[208] Bugnini, *The Reform of the Liturgy*, 55.

the hands of Archbishop Felici (January 15, 1964).[209] This statement corresponds essentially to the story of the origin of the *motu proprio* as given later by Wagner.[210] It seems very improbable, however, that Felici did not receive the draft until January 15.

The apostolic letter issued *motu proprio* by Paul VI was dated January 25, 1964, the fifth anniversary of the announcement of the Council, and was published in *Osservatore Romano* for January 29. It was concerned with "putting into effect some prescriptions of the Constitution on the Liturgy."[211] The individual regulations cited therein, which were to go into effect on February 16, 1964, corresponded, with a few exceptions, to the ten points listed at the end of the last document of the conciliar Liturgical Commission; they also included the two decisions regarding the liturgy of the hours, which, it had been suggested to the pope, he could best put into effect at the end of the *vacatio legis*.[212]

1. What is said in the constitution about formation in liturgical science and pastoral liturgy in theological faculties, seminaries, and religious houses is to be put into effect beginning in the next academic year.

2. The anticipated diocesan commissions for liturgy, church music, and church art are to be established.

3. The obligation to give a homily on Sundays and feast days goes into effect.

4. Confirmation may be administered during mass, after the gospel and homily.

5. Weddings are normally to be celebrated during mass after the gospel and homily. At a marriage apart from mass the epistles and gospel of the wedding mass are to be proclaimed. In any event, after the marriage rite the bridal couple is to be given the blessing provided in the Ritual.

6. Outside of choir Prime can be omitted; of the three "little hours" the person praying may choose the one best suited to the time of day.

7. Ordinaries may use their authority to dispense from or commute the prayer of the hours in accordance with Article 97.

---

[209] See A.-G. Martimort, "Note confidentiel sur le Motu proprio du 25 janvier 1964 et ses suites," Wagner Archive, vol. 37.

[210] See the "confidential memorandum" mentioned below in note 214.

[211] The document is translated in *Documents on the Liturgy*, 84-87, where the changes in the text as published in *OssRom* are noted.

[212] See "De vacatione," 124f. Only the point about confirmation during mass was not to be found there. Also expressly excluded there was the idea that those praying a "little office" were engaged in the public prayer of the Church.

8. It is determined that members of religious orders who, in keeping with their laws, recite individual parts of the liturgy of the hours or a "little office," are praying publicly with the Church.

9. Regulations are given for the use of the vernacular in the liturgy of the hours and other liturgical celebrations.

10. The phrase "assemblies of bishops with competence in given territories" is to be understood as meaning the national episcopal conferences, to which coadjutors and auxiliary bishops may be invited.

11. Finally, the provisions of Articles 22 §§1 and 3 are emphasized.

The publication of this papal document stirred widespread disillusionment and anger and elicited criticism and protest. It became clear that the bishops, who had been receiving an education throughout the two periods of the Council, would no longer stand for just anything that came from the Roman Curia. There was general disappointment that more extensive steps toward reform had not been taken. Cardinal Döpfner said as much in a letter to Lercaro: after what the pope had said at the public session, more reforms were expected.[213]

It was not surprising that the few things the *Motu Proprio* did say were viewed all the more critically. Let me indicate only the most important points. There was disappointment at the unnuanced language, for example, in nos. IV and V where "eucharistic sacrifice" was wrongly used instead of "mass;" that in weddings apart from mass there was no provision for using the vernacular in the scripture readings (no. 5); and that the hard-won conciliar formulation was tightened and ordinaries were told that only for just "and well-considered" reasons could they use their authority to dispense from or commute the liturgy of the hours.

The worst thing, however, was what had been done in no. 9. There the provision in the liturgical constitution, Article 36 §4, was changed, and it was decreed that the vernacular translations of the liturgy of the hours, which were proposed by the competent territorial ecclesiastical authorities, must be examined and approved by the Apostolic See. And this was always the course to be followed when Latin texts were translated by the competent authority. But Article 36 §4 of the constitution reads: "Translations from the Latin for use in the liturgy must be approved by the competent territorial ecclesiastical authority already mentioned."

---

[213] See letter of February 7, 1964 (Lercaro Archive, XXIV, 575).

A first critical discussion of the *Motu Proprio* came in S. Marsili's commentary in *Osservatore Romano* for January 30, 1964.[214] The first one to protest effectively against the changing of the conciliar decree in no. 9 of the *Motu Proprio* was Cardinal Lercaro. On February 2, 1964, after having evidently had a conversation the day before with the professors at the regional seminary, he wrote to Archbishop dell'Acqua, the substitute at the Secretariat of State. In his letter Lercaro explained the genesis of Article 36 §4. The commission had deliberately not accepted the originally proposed addition that stated that the Apostolic See must review translations approved by the territorial authority. The Council, he said, wanted translations to be approved by the territorial authority, without having to submit them to the Apostolic See.

He regarded it as a dangerous act that, even before being in force, the constitution should be modified, and this in a passage that touched on two themes close to the heart of the fathers: decentralization in favor of the bishops, and the vernacular in the liturgy. Lercaro feared that this alteration could be exploited as an argument for the weakening of the teaching and decrees of the constitution. The authority of the Council would thus be undermined; it was easy to imagine the disillusionment of the bishops on seeing the results of their work destroyed. Finally, Lercaro suggested that in the official version of the *Motu Proprio*, which would appear in the *Acta Apostolicae Sedis*, the text of this document be made to agree with the constitution.[215] This proposal was accepted in principle, although the restoration of the conciliar text in the *Motu Proprio* was not complete.[216] In the process many other passages in the text were corrected.[217]

In view of this letter of Lercaro, we can only agree with the already mentioned letter of Döpfner to him. In it Döpfner congratulated Lercaro on his being appointed president of the Consilium and (without knowing of the latter's letter to Archbishop dell'Acqua) explained that this appointment would be a consolation to him [Döpfner] amid the distress that the *Motu Proprio* had caused him.[218]

---

[214] See "I primi passi della riforma liturgica" (signed "s. m."), *OssRom*, January 30, 1964, 2. Wagner tells of the agitation "in Curial Rome and in clerical Rome generally" that was caused by this article and by the reactions in the Italian press: "The pope's mouthpiece criticizes the pope." See Wagner, "Vertrauliches Pro memoria vom 8.2.1964," in the Wagner Archive, vol. 37.

[215] See Lercaro Archive, XXV, 714.

[216] For the official version of *Sacram Liturgiam*, see *Documents on the Liturgy*, 84-87.

[217] See Bugnini, *The Reform of the Liturgy*, 59.

[218] "Your appointment is a consolation for me in the distress caused me by the Motu Proprio *Sacram Liturgiam*" (letter of February 7, 1964; Lercaro Archive, XXIV, 575).

After a meeting in Puchberg bei Weis of the liturgical and breviary commissions of the episcopal conferences of the German-speaking countries and after a conversation with Döpfner on February 2 in Munich, Wagner flew to Rome with the commission to obtain clarifications of the *Motu Proprio*. On February 7, Larraona, in the presence of F. Antonelli, explained to Wagner the genesis of the *Motu Proprio* and authorized him to report back on this to those who had commissioned him. Larraona had taken the preliminary draft of the conciliar Liturgical Commission and had sent it "upstairs" via Archbishop Felici (in the argot of the Curia, "upstairs" referred to the secretary of state or the pope, as the case might be). It had come back to him through the same channels, but greatly abbreviated and changed in its tenor. At this stage the "territorial groups of bishops" were already defined as "national, for the time being," a formulation that, because of its political implications, had been strictly avoided by the Liturgical Commission. But the present version of no. 9 of the *Motu Proprio* had not yet been drafted.

According to Felici it was the desire of Paul VI himself to have a stipulation regarding Roman approval of all translations. The text, he says, was then formulated in collaboration with the Latinists, who were unaware of the difficulties attendant on terminological choices; in any case, the Congregation for Rites had no part in the redaction of the *Motu Proprio*. Felici and P. Antonelli made an effort to carry out the will of the Council to the letter. Both of them hoped for a change of formulation in the officially published text. Admittedly, the text would not fully reflect the will of the Council, since it did not completely eliminate the need of Roman approbation, but it did turn this into a "confirmation."[219]

At the meeting of the Congregation for Rites that Martimort and Wagner attended, Article 9 of the *Motu Proprio* also came up for discussion, and Larraona explained why neither he nor the Congregation could be blamed for its present form. There was no real discussion of the matter at this meeting, but the two guests were given an opportunity to express their views. While Antonelli and F. Frutaz showed a

[219] See the "confidential memorandum" cited above in note 213. The wish of the pope can be readily imagined if one reads the circular letter sent by the Congregation for Rites on October 25, 1973, according to which, by order to Paul VI, the texts required for the validity of the sacraments had not only to be confirmed by the Congregation for Rites but had to be approved by the pope personally; see *AAS* 66 (1974), 98f.; *Documents on the Liturgy*, 298-99. This approval was, however, very soon left to the Congregation for the Doctrine of the Faith.

complete understanding of the difficulties raised, Dante would have none of it; he could only exclaim, "If the pope changes a law passed by a council, it is his right to do so."[220]

On February 27 Lercaro sent letters to Cardinal Frings, president of the German Episcopal Conference and to Martimort. In the letter to Frings he expressed his delight that the German Episcopal Conference had immediately introduced the use of the vernacular into the celebration of the mass and the liturgy of the hours; at the same time, he lamented the fact that this had required an indult from Larraona. With regard to the *Motu Proprio*, he himself had immediately written to the pope and had also paid him a personal visit; perhaps the text would be corrected in the official version.[221]

In the other letter Lercaro told Martimort of his audience with the pope on February 2; since there was not much time in the morning, he was allowed to come again in the evening of that same day and was able to talk with the pope for an hour and a quarter. The two together went through the *Motu Proprio*, as well as the observations of Bugnini and the responses of Felici. The latter wanted the text to remain unchanged in the official publication. The pope was afraid that a change in the text would set a dangerous precedent. The only hope, said Lercaro, was that the pope would allow the text to be changed in accordance with Martimort's proposal: the acceptance in Article 36 §4 of the rule set down in Article 36 §3.[222]

Once the *Motu Proprio Sacram Liturgiam* was published in the *Acta Apostolicae Sedis*,[223] the anger aroused by the Roman action slowly died

---

[220] See Wagner, *Mein Weg zur Liturgiereform,* 79, as well as Martimort, "Note confidentiel," and the confidential notes Wagner presented at this meeting: Wagner Archive, vol. 37.

[221] See Lercaro Archive, XXV, 718.

[222] See Lercaro Archive, XXV, 716.

[223] For the official version, see *Documents on the Liturgy*, 84-87. It is very regrettable that a similar indignation was not felt later on. When the 1983 Code of Canon Law, in canon 838 §3, granted the episcopal conferences the right only to see to the translation of the liturgical books into the vernacular and to adapt this translation, and then to publish it after prior scrutiny by the Holy See ("praevia *recognitione* Sanctae Sedis"), there was not a word heard about letters of protest from cardinals and bishops. And yet in setting up this provision the code clearly deprived the will of the Council of its force. In the letter cited in Lercaro Archive, XXV, 714, Lercaro wrote that the fathers had deliberately omitted this "scrutiny" of vernacular translations by the Holy See and that the text "was approved by a very large majority of the Council." Also accepted without resistance was canon 838 §§2 and 3, which imply that the vernacular books used in the liturgy are not "liturgical books."

down. After February 29, 1964, the task of the Consilium was clearly
defined. The struggle of the Consilium with the Congregation for Rites
regarding competence still caused annoyance in Rome, but outside
Rome people knew that the liturgical reform decided by the Council was
in the very good hands of Lercaro and Bugnini. The study groups set to
work with great enthusiasm and carried out, as best they could, the commission given them by the fathers of the Second Vatican Council, the
renewal of the liturgy, in order thereby to make an important contribution to the renewal of the Church.

CHAPTER IV

THE ECUMENICAL COMMITMENT
OF THE CATHOLIC CHURCH

CLAUDE SOETENS

I. FROM PROGRAM TO REALITY

A. AN OFFICIAL DOCUMENT ON CHRISTIAN UNITY

This is not the place to review all the signs and decisions that from 1959 to 1962 showed the intention of Pope John XXIII and then of the Council itself to commit the assembly of Catholic bishops to advancing the cause of the unity of the Christian Churches.[1] Pope Paul VI made this commitment his own. As early as June 25, 1963, he had Cardinal Bea send news of his election to His Beatitude Athenagoras, Ecumenical Patriarch of Constantinople,[2] and, shortly afterward, invite the patriarch to send representatives to the Council.[3]

Following upon the letter of congratulations that Metropolitan Maximos of Sardes sent to Paul VI in the patriarch's name on September 9, 1963,[4] the pope undertook to write personally to Athenagoras. This letter, dated September 20, was an important act, the first message in many centuries that a pope addressed to Constantinople.[5] In it Paul said that he was "solicitous for all that concerns the unity of Christians and all that can help to restore perfect harmony among them." He urged that the past be forgotten and prayed that the Lord would inspire both of them to actions which would bring fulfillment of the prayer "that they may be one."

---

[1] See M. Velati, "La proposta ecumenica del segretariato per l'unità dei christiani," in *Verso il Concilio*, 274-350; *History*, 1:263-71; M. Velati, *Una difficile transizione, Il cattolicesimo tra unionismo ed ecumenismo (1952-1964)* (Bologna, 1996).

[2] Letter of Cardinal Bea to Patriarch Athenagoras, in *Towards the Healing of Schism: The Sees of Rome and Constantinople*, ed. and trans. E. J. Storman, S.J., Ecumenical Documents III (New York: Paulist Press, 1987), 49.

[3] Bea to Athenagoras, July 8, 1963; ibid., 49-50.

[4] Ibid., 51-52. The delay in this reply was explained in the letter by the long absence of the patriarch because of his participation in the millennium of Mount Athos.

[5] Ibid., 52-53.

Seen in the light of his letter of September 20 to Athenagoras, the passages in Paul VI's opening address to the second conciliar period gave the impression more of a personal desire for ecumenical commitment than of an impulse being given to the Council along that line.[6] The most striking thing said was the prayer for the forgiveness of God and of the Christian brethren for the part played by the Catholic Church among the causes of the separation. The important point, in any case, was the clear determination not to neglect the ecumenical part of Roncalli's heritage.

During the audience for the delegated observers on October 17, the pope reasserted his good intentions in a more familiar tone, while also stressing the immensity of the task. He added that instead of turning to the past, except when it came to asking for forgiveness, the important thing was to look ahead to the new reality to be brought into being; as in his letter to Athenagoras, he cited the Letter to the Philippians (3:13-14), where the Apostle says that he is straining forward to what is ahead.[7] Christian unity thus provided a good opportunity to exercise the virtues of patience and hope!

It is not an exaggeration to see a strong contrast between the declared intentions of John XXIII and Paul VI and the long and chancy road traveled by the text on unity that was to be presented to the Council for its study beginning on the following November 18. Not only had it taken all the "pugnacity" of Cardinal Bea and Msgr. Willebrands, the leaders of the Secretariat for Christian Unity, to have their organization become a full conciliar commission (October 1962). In addition, the redaction of the text on unity ran into many obstacles between February and the final tuning of the document in May 1963.[8] This text, radically different from that proposed to the Council by the Commission for the Oriental Churches in November 1962,[9] "took as its starting point the real ecumenical movement as it had developed over the previous quarter-century."[10] It consisted of three chapters: I. on the principles of Catholic ecumenism; II: on the practice of ecumenism; III: on Christians separated from the Catholic

[6] *The Pope Speaks* 9 (1963-64), 125-41, Section III: "The Restoration of Unity among All Christians."

[7] Text of the allocution, delivered in French, in *Istina* 10 (1964), 519-22; Italian translation in Caprile III, 148-50; see *The Pope Speaks* 9 (1963-64), 239-33.

[8] On the obstacles met and on the preparation of the schema during the first intersession see *History*, 2:535-46.

[9] On this schema, which was devoted entirely to unity with the Orientals, see *History*, 1:203-4; 2:429-35.

[10] Ibid., 2:434.

Church, that is, both the Oriental "Churches" and the "communities that appeared in the sixteenth century."

As was true of other schemas, such as those on the liturgy and on bishops and the government of dioceses, the way in which the schema on unity was developed depended to a great extent on the theology of the Church and therefore on choices yet to be made in the future constitution on the Church. Even though all the important elements that would go into the latter, especially collegiality and the treatment of the people of God before the hierarchy, did not yet inspire the schema on unity,[11] it could be regarded as real progress that the unity of the Church was described no longer as an abstract concept but as a mystery and that the division was no longer looked at from a purely juridical point of view.[12] If, on the one hand, the final decree promulgated on November 21, 1964, would, because of last-minute papal amendments, fall somewhat short from the viewpoint of this new perspective, on the other hand, it would more successfully integrate the ecclesiological gains of *Lumen Gentium*, which was adopted on that same day.

The text completed in May 1963 was sent to the fathers, and the secretariat awaited their observations, which arrived in rather large numbers during the summer.[13] The secretariat organized six subcommissions for systematic analysis of the observations.[14] These were then synthesized into 192 amendments, which were presented to the fathers in a booklet at the beginning of the debate,[15] some of them being kept for presentation in

---

[11] This was noted by many fathers, especially the French, in the remarks they sent in during the summer.

[12] Quite conscious of the connections between the schema on unity and the schema on the Church, J. Martin, the first to give a report at the general congregation of November 18, would say that the decrees supposed the teaching given in the constitution (*AS* II/5, 473). A question that would come up several times during the debate and that had already been studied by the first of the secretariat's subcommissions was whether or not the communities emerging from the Reformation should be called "Churches." The bishops of the Piedmont had asked the question in writing: "Are these 'Churches' the Church?" The subcommission answered that the problem involved the schema on the Church and that it thought it necessary to keep the term "Churches" for the East and the term "ecclesial communities" for the groups that had emerged from the Reformation (Report of subcommission 1, meeting of November 20, 1963; *AS* II/5, 874-923).

[13] There were observations from forty-seven individual fathers and from eight groups of bishops (Piedmont; Argentina; South Africa; East Central Africa; the Melkite Synod; southern, western, and southwestern France; Indonesia; and an unidentified episcopal conference); see *AS* II/5, 874-923.

[14] On September 24, Chr. J. Dumont, an expert, had made an initial synthesis of the observations; see CLG, Thils Archive, 589. The reports of the subcommissions are given at the beginning of the collection of observations; Thils Archive, 1317.

[15] *AS* II/5, 442-67.

the reports given in the hall. During the debate the same subcommissions continued to work on a study of the oral and written observations offered by the fathers beginning on November 18.

During the first half of November informal groups of bishops met to study the schema and prepare their interventions. A working group of seven French bishops met on November 7 and 12, with three Dominican experts, Congar, Dupuy, and Le Guillou, in attendance.[16] Msgr. J. Martin, Archbishop of Rouen and a member of the Secretariat for Christian Unity, took part at least in the meeting of November 7. He drew upon these exchanges for the report on the first three chapters that he gave in the hall on November 18. Congar said that he was "very impressed by the seriousness and genuineness of the demanding ecumenical commitment" shown by the bishops present at the second meeting.[17] On November 7 some Spanish bishops also met to discuss the subject of ecumenism. "It is quite interesting," wrote Congar, who was present and observed that the positions of the Spaniards were "very diverse." A few days later he noted that a "real Spanish openness to ecumenism" was a matter of "great interest."[18]

We will have to come back to the reactions to the schema among the observers at the Council. Let me mention here that on November 12, at the weekly meeting of the observers held at the secretariat, four of these representatives of the other Churches gave their views on the text.[19] They judged the text to be much superior to the texts presented to the Council in December 1962, but they also made several radical criticisms: doubts about the ability of the Catholic Church to think of union as other than a return to itself, and about its ability to recognize the ecclesial character of the communities that emerged from the Reformation; the need, not mentioned in the text, to focus the ecumenical dialogue on the tension between the assertion of a full catholicity, to which all Churches aspire or which they claim, and the fact that this catholicity has not been realized.[20] On the

[16] *JCongar*, typescript, 360 and 364.

[17] Ibid., 364.

[18] Ibid., 360 and 369.

[19] See the report on this meeting in CLG, Moeller Archive, 431. The four speakers were O. Cullmann, H. Roux, C. P. Matthew, and L. Vischer.

[20] The conclusion of Pastor Roux, one of the observers from the Alliance of Reformed Churches, seems to sum up the thought of the speakers: "Granted the generosity which it shows toward the Christian confessions separated from Rome, the decree *De ecumenismo* should also make clear that the Roman Catholic Church is aware of the real and profound causes of separations that are not due simply to faults or deficiencies on the part of the '*disjuncti*' but have to do with fundamental points of the faith, which an ecumenical spirit and a willingness to dialogue should make it possible to address in a new way" (ibid., 4).

afternoon of November 18, the bishops of the Congo (Zaire) discussed planned interventions on ecumenism.[21]

By decision of the Coordinating Commission (CC) on August 31, the debate on the schema was to be the fifth of the texts to be discussed during the coming period.[22] In fact, it was moved to third place, partly because on October 29 the fathers voted to include the schema on the Virgin in the schema on the Church, partly because the moderators judged that the text on unity was more closely related to the fundamental elements of the schema on the Church than to the schema on the laity; in addition, they judged that it involved principles that were of greater concern to the Council because of the subtlety and permanence of the problems it raised.[23] Thus it was as part of "an equable plan of work" that the draft schema on unity arrived in the hall on November 18.

B. The Debate on Ecumenism[24]

"An historic day" — "a great day for the Council and for the Church" — "the hour of truth."[25] Such were the solemn expressions used by commentators to describe the important moment when, in concrete response to the impulse given by John XXIII, the assembly of Catholic bishops was called upon to take a stand on the drama of Christian division, on its meaning, and on the best means of bringing it to an end in answer to Christ's prayer for the unity of his followers. They had to do this by addressing a text that certainly had a pastoral purpose (how is the Church to act today in this area?), but which also, as Cardinal Lercaro

---

[21] See CLG, Olivier Archive, 169, "Chronique 2e session," 26. The intervention on the local Churches that was then decided on by Msgr. Cornelis, Archbishop of Lubumbashi, would in the end not be delivered.

[22] That is, after the first four chapters of the schema on the Church, and the schemas on the Blessed Virgin, the bishops, and the lay apostolate. As we shall see, the discussion of the last mentioned schema was left out and deferred to a later point.

[23] Cardinal Lercaro gave these reasons in his report on the work of the Council, which was presented to the pope at the meeting of the directing bodies on November 15, 1963 (AS V/2, 30).

[24] For the debate as a whole see the official acts: AS II/5, 405-95, 527-74; 661-700, 744-833; AS II/6, 9-91, 97-267, 375-401. Summary in Italian: Caprile III, passim; summary in French: DC (January 5, 1964), 33-81; (January 19, 1964), 115-62. In addition to the reports, there were 153 oral interventions and 141 observations submitted in writing by the fathers individually or in groups.

[25] Respectively, JCongar, 371; Wenger, 172; the title of Wenger's article in La Croix, November 20, 1963, p. 4

had said a few days earlier,[26] necessarily brought into play basic choices and, above all, the way in which the Church understood itself.

The text, which had been sent to the fathers in May, did not contain the complete schema but only the first three of the five chapters it was intended to have. The fourth chapter, on the attitude of the Church toward the non-Christian religions, especially the Jews, had been distributed on November 8. The fifth, on religious freedom, would be given to the fathers on the 19th. In the next section of this chapter I shall discuss the complicated journey of these two chapters, the origin of which was independent of that of the first three.

On November 18 the fathers received a booklet containing the 192 amendments the Secretariat for Christian Unity had accepted.[27] Many of the observations sent in by the fathers referred to particular points, but some dealt with the schema as a whole, either with its structure and organization or with some important themes. With regard to the structure, some wanted a section of the schema on the Oriental Churches to be combined with the schema on ecumenism; others asked for the insertion of a preface that would contain, in particular, a definition of Catholic ecumenism, or for a division of the document into two parts (the common faith of Christians, and the Catholic faith), or for a special mention of the Anglicans.

As for the content, we find in these observations almost all the subjects that would surface again in the oral interventions. Should the text speak of the principles of Catholic ecumenism (the title of the first chapter) or the Catholic principles of ecumenism (a definition of the Catholic position on the subject)?[28] In promoting ecumenism, was not the Church opening the way to indifferentism, and was it not forgetting the obligation to convert others? Should the communities that had emerged from the Reformation be called "Churches"? Should not the positive elements of Protestantism receive greater emphasis? Since not all the truths of the faith occupy an equal place in Christian life, was it not appropriate to introduce a passage on respect for the hierarchy of

---

[26] See note 23.

[27] See the synthesis of these observations at the beginning of the booklet of amendments, in *AS* II/5, 442-45.

[28] As some would stress in the course of the debate, the second formula (which would finally be kept) emphasized, above all, the point that the ecumenical movement is one and that it began well before any Catholic involvement, which simply made its own contribution. In his commentary on the decree, C. J. Dumont is not convinced that there is any real difference between the two formulas (*Istina* 10 [1964], 362-63).

truths?[29] One father remarked — and a number of others would repeat it orally — that the true Church is founded on Peter and his successors, and that it was necessary to stir doubts of conscience in other Christians regarding the legitimacy of their communities.

With regard to the practice of ecumenism, general rules should be set down in a directory, while leaving to the bishops the main responsibility for the application of these rules to local situations. Some fathers wanted a confession of Catholic faults against unity, echoing the reference to this by Paul VI in his allocution of September 29. Still others asked for a discussion of *communicatio in sacris* (shared worship). Finally, two fathers called for statements on religious freedom and on the relations of Catholics with other religions, especially Judaism. The twofold question of whether these two texts were opportune and whether they should be introduced into the schema on ecumenism would return in the debate in the hall.

As could be foreseen, two mentalities came to light during the twelve days of the debate. On the one side, there was the mentality shared by the wholehearted defenders of the Counter-Reformation position, who regarded Christian unity as meaning nothing more than the return of the "others" to the Catholic Church. On the other side, there was the mentality, whose extent among the bishops was not known, that, without neglecting the Church's consciousness of itself, understood that all truths do not stand on the same level, and that saw in the gospel message itself and in the cries of the contemporary world the need of a common witness to the Christian faith.[30]

It was difficult, however, for the bishops not to declare themselves as favoring, in principle, a "pastoral" decree on unity, since the search for unity had been included by papal will among the goals of the Council and since during the first period it had been clearly said that the ecumenical perspective should inspire the whole of the Council's work.[31] At

---

[29] In the synthesis he made of the document in September, C. J. Dumont asked that this point be more explicitly emphasized, and he added a suggested text, the substance of which did become part of the Decree (no. 11 §3).

[30] After the first morning of debate, Ch. Moeller, a Belgian expert, observed in his personal notes for November 18: "Two worlds: one prudential, abstract, juridical, moved by fear of relativism; the other evangelical, concrete, open. The first will turn to dust"; Moeller Archive, carnet X.

[31] See especially the address on November 19, 1962, of Msgr. De Smedt (Bruges), who spoke in the name of the Secretariat for Christian Unity (*AS* I/3, 184-87); this address was, significantly, the only one Msgr. Dumont included, in a French translation, in his dossier on the genesis of the schema on unity (*Istina* 10 [1964], 507-10).

the press conference on November 30, the spokesman said that such ample praise of a schema had rarely been heard in the hall.[32] This optimism, which was fairly well justified,[33] did not, however, take into account the fact, pointed out on December 2 by the auxiliary bishop of Sydney, that "a great deal has been said in the hall by people who do not know much about the subject!"[34]

In fact, the two mentalities did not express themselves in the same way. The advocates of a positive and open ecumenism were not afraid to say that the schema did not sufficiently commit itself to encounter with other Christians, while those unfavorable to it often clothed their criticism in reasons that might seem valid: the schema was too general, too superficial; insufficiently grounded theologically; not practical enough to act upon; or else, like Msgr. Carli of Segni, they offered corrections on a great many points of detail. Some of these same arguments were indeed offered by dedicated defenders of the schema, but for different reasons; in this case they were inspired by a concern to take into account the reactions of the other Churches.[35]

In an overview of the debate it would be arbitrary to isolate this or that intervention or part of an intervention. I shall therefore limit myself to describing the various reports that introduced the schema and to illustrating the interventions by analyzing some of the most important ones.

Out of respect for the Commission for the Oriental Churches, whose schema on unity had for practical purposes been rejected during the first

---

[32] A. Pangrazio, Archbishop of Gorizia, Italy. See Caprile III, 410 n.18.

[33] B. Olivier confirms the fact in his personal notes: "One would normally have expected a violent counterattack....It is surprising to see that, all in all, the criticisms are very moderate and that the very great majority of the addresses show an effective desire to iron out all difficulties"; "Chronique," 30. L. Vischer, the principal observer from the World Council of Churches, voiced a similar opinion on November 22: the debate was encouraging; there were few addresses against the text; the great majority of the bishops recognized the importance of the text (letter to W. Visser't Hooft, November 22, 1963, copy at the ISR, WCC archive, ACO 6).

[34] Th. Muldoon: AS II/6, 343-44. As R. Aubert observes in Storia della Chiesa XXV/1, 267: "Many of the fathers showed their complete failure to grasp 'the signs of the times' when they expressed utterly anachronistic judgments on the Orthodox and the Protestants — an obvious sign of their complete lack of experience in this area."

[35] For example, M. Hermaniuk (Archbishop of Winnepeg for the Ukrainians) said that instead of stopping at a declaration of intentions, the schema should have taken a concrete stand on the importance of the patriarchates and of the synodal system of government in the East as a ground on which union was possible; AS II/6, 350-54. On the same day, C. Butler, president of the English Benedictine Congregation, asked for the elimination of summary statements that linked the origin of the Protestant Churches to events of the sixteenth century, when in fact many of the Churches explicitly linked themselves to the early tradition; AS II/6, 358-60.

period, it was Cardinal Cicognani, Secretary of State but also president of that commission, and not Cardinal Bea, the president of the Secretariat for Christian Unity, who was given the honor of introducing the schema as a whole, that is, with its five chapters (of which the fathers had by then received only the first four).[36] After speaking of the "fusion" of the three texts on unity that had been made at the request of the fathers — "fusion" was, to say the least, a diplomatic word[37] — and after historical references focused on Catholic efforts in behalf of union, the speaker said that ecumenism was a method by which the Church endeavored to carry out more effectively its mission toward the separated Christians and toward the nonbaptized (an odd addition that was doubtless meant to justify the presence of the schema's final two chapters).

He then went on to explain how the schema had been developed. The first chapter gave principles, among which the Cardinal emphasized only the necessity of belonging to the one true Church, while passing over what the chapter also said about the values present in the other Churches and communities, about the necessary contribution of the latter to full catholicity, about legitimate diversity, and about the internal renewal of Catholicism. On chapter II, which contained eight numbers, the speaker contented himself with saying that in it the composers wanted to explain what a "good" ecumenism is. He then noted that chapter III, devoted to Christians separated from the Catholic Church, dealt first of all with the Orientals, since they were closest to us and were present, in a way, in the persons of the fathers from the Oriental Catholic rites. As for the Protestants, who were the subject of the second part of the chapter, the Cardinal simply mentioned the presence of their representatives in the hall.[38]

---

[36] See *AS* II/5, 468-72.

[37] The preparatory Commission for the Oriental Churches had developed a schema that was focused on reconciliation with the Orthodox Churches. The preparatory Theological Commission had included a chapter on ecumenism in its schema on the Church, while the Secretariat for Christian Unity had prepared a "pastoral decree" on Catholic ecumenism, which was not printed; see *History*, 1:266. During the first period of the Council it was the text of the Commission for the Oriental Churches that was submitted to the assembly of fathers, the end result being that this text, which was praised but was in fact quite unecumenical, was to be fused with the other two texts, under the joint responsibility of the Commission for the Oriental Churches and the secretariat; see *History*, 2:429-35. In fact, the delegates of the Commission for the Oriental Churches refrained from taking part in this work during the intersession.

[38] It must be said that many members of the secretariat were not satisfied with this part of the chapter, which had been very hastily composed following upon a directive from the CC at the end of the previous March (see *History*, 2:429-35).

In discussing chapter IV the speaker stressed that the concern for non-Christians and especially for the Jews had a purely religious reason.[39] The final chapter, on religious freedom, was justified in view of the growing number of individuals who were seeking information about the Church. In conclusion, the speaker noted that the draft of the decree had an especially pastoral character that corresponded to the nature of the Council. While this address had necessarily to stick to very general explanations, we must nonetheless recognize that it notably limited the significance of the decree and was not of a nature to enliven the debate now beginning.

The report on the first three chapters, which was now given by J. Martin (Rouen), a member of the secretariat, was quite different in tone and very clear.[40] The reporter began by saying that the schema was not a manual of theology, nor part of a code of law, nor a historical treatise. It was intended to be a temperate, irenic, pastoral decree which presupposed the teaching set forth in the schema on the Church; it also was new — new, that is. for the Catholic Church, no council of which had ever specifically taken up the subject. The Council was tackling it because the division among Christians was today seen as a scandal in the light of Christ's express will and it was paralyzing evangelization.

After giving the titles of the sections of chapter I ("Principles of Catholic Ecumenism"), Martin stated that chapter II ("The Exercise of Ecumenism") was not a bow to a fad but meant to offer practical means of action, which he listed (spiritual renewal, common prayer, mutual knowledge, cooperation in works of charity). Regarding chapter III, the speaker said that he expected criticisms of the positive way in which the other Churches were presented. He then gave some explanations. First, the drafters were not looking for compromises; the causes of the division were real, but they were also well enough known that they did not have to be summarized again. Second, dialogue does not proceed from indifferentism and does not lead to it; but if the truth is to be heard, it excludes all inflexibility in its explanation; besides, final unity is in God's hands. Third, the decree did not take up all questions but only the major principles; a directory now being prepared would issue more

[39] This statement echoed the two communiqués issued on October 18 and November 8 by the Secretariat for Christian Unity (Caprile III, 420-41) in response to rumors about the political character of the text, rumors that were abroad not only in the Arab world but also in newspapers that saw the text as an answer to Hochhuth's recent play, *The Deputy*, which had sharply criticized the silences of Pius XII on the persecution of the Jews during the war and had been staged almost everywhere during the last months of 1963.

[40] See *AS* II/5, 472-79.

precise norms, and the bishops of each region of the world would then have to set down rules adapted to each local situation.

By way of conclusion Martin emphasized the great diversity among the members of the secretariat who had prepared the text, their fraternal collaboration, and the contribution of the observers both delegated and invited. Some fundamental questions had not been answered, but a new spirit of collaboration was being established among Christians. In emphasizing the novelty of the decree Martin certainly did not want to leave the impression that ecumenism had its beginnings in the interest that the Catholic Church was taking in it. The purpose was rather to make it understood that all the efforts for the sake of unity should be looked at in a different perspective than unionism (return of others to the body), as this had been defined and practiced since Leo XIII. What was, however, only too real was the complete novelty of ecumenism for the majority of the bishops, who were little prepared to grasp its originality and to accept the fact that the movement as such had a Christian origin outside of Catholicism.

Many observers from the other Churches gently pointed out that the Church of Rome was only beginning its apprenticeship in ecumenism and doing so with the somewhat excessive enthusiasm of a neophyte. But while the debate showed this enthusiasm in the praises given the decree, it was also true that some of the interveners could have spared some of their remarks and objections if they had more carefully attended to the reporter's explanation with regard to the causes of division, the danger of indifferentism, and the need of a directory and of directives adapted to each region. The loss of time thus caused revealed, among other things, the lack of coordination between the assembly and the commissions, something which many at the time felt to be a handicap in the organization of the Council.

The reporter on the first three chapters had not given precise information about the content of chapter III. In fact, in order to allay tensions between the Commission for the Oriental Churches and the secretariat, Cardinal Cicognani wanted at least the first section of this chapter, on the Oriental Churches, to be presented by a bishop of his commission.[41] G. Bukatko (coadjutor of Belgrade) read his short report on November 19.[42] In it he pointed out that the subject of the section was different from that of the schema on the Oriental Churches, which dealt with the

---

[41] *History*, 2:435 n.177.
[42] *AS* II/5, 480-81.

Churches united with Rome. While acknowledging that the text of the section had been written by the secretariat, he said that his commission had made its contribution to it and that a certain number of points had been taken over from the schema presented in December 1962.[43] He concluded by mentioning the opportunity the fathers had of asking for improvements in the text. This first section of chapter III acknowledged the originality of the entire patrimony of the Eastern Churches and its value to the Catholic Church. As a result of the observations of the fathers, especially those of the Oriental rites, the section would later be partially reorganized.

A good picture of the debate is given by the nine interventions on Monday, November 18.[44] While all but one of the speakers were in favor of the schema, all also voiced criticisms, but along quite different lines. The first speaker, Syrian Patriarch Tappouni, chiefly emphasized the inopportuneness of the chapter on the Jews and said he was surprised by the announced chapter on religious freedom. I shall speak in the next section of the reservations expressed by a number of the fathers on these two points.

Two interventions were emblematic, those of Cardinals Ruffini and Ritter. Ruffini, the most prolix speaker at the Council, fired the first shot,[45] and he would also be one of the interveners on the final day of the debate, December 2. As his vast audience listened attentively,[46] he began by expressing his admiration for the very great industriousness with which the special conciliar commission, with its burning desire for the spread of Catholic truth and the reign of Christ, had prepared the schema. He then asked pardon for setting forth his concerns and hesitations. There were six of them. First, the term *ecumenism* did not seem to him fully the same in meaning as the word *ecumenical* that was used in naming the Council. The Council is rightly described as "ecumenical" because it is universal, whereas *ecumenism* designates a particular kind of apostolate. Moreover, this noun was introduced into theology forty

[43] See *History*, 2:429 n.163. It seems that Cicognani had handed over responsibility for the section to the secretariat, while inserting a series of alterations in keeping with the schema *Ut unum sint* of the Commission for the Oriental Churches. See *History*, 2:432 n.168.

[44] The successive speakers were Cardinals Tappouni (Syrian patriarch), Ruffini (Palermo; former teacher of Tappouni), de Arriba y Castro (Tarragona, Spain), Bueno y Monreal (Seville), Ritter (Saint Louis), Quintero (Caracas), and Doi (Tokyo), and Patriarchs Stephen I Sidarouss (Coptic) and Maximos IV Saigh (Melkite). See *AS* II/5, 527-45.

[45] *AS* II/5, 527-45.

[46] *JCongar*, 372: "You could hear a fly on the wing."

years ago by the Protestants, and the latter gave it an entirely different meaning than we do. They see the ecumenical movement as effecting a shift from the Church as human beings have shaped it to the Church that God wants; therefore, the existing Churches are all human institutions. If the term *ecumenism* is kept, it must be defined clearly and briefly at the beginning of the decree in order to avoid all equivocation; it would be better, however, to replace the term with a description of the reality and add: "Many today call this 'ecumenism.'"

Second, our oldest desire is for the return of the separated brethren to the one fold of which Christ is the supreme invisible shepherd and the pope is his visible vicar. There is still a certain closeness between them and us, but the schema should show much more clearly that the closeness is far greater with the Orientals than with the brethren who called themselves "reformers" and today go by the name of Protestants, Evangelicals, or other terms.[47] The speaker mentioned the many things common to Catholics and Orientals and stressed the point that among the Protestants and especially in the sects that differ more or less seriously from one another, very little has been retained of the ancient Catholic faith, except for the scriptures and baptism.

Third, the Italian Cardinal asked for a better order among the questions treated in the schema, especially by suppressing what was said at the beginning about the unity and uniqueness of the Church, these being points already discussed in the schema on the Church.

Fourth, if a special chapter is added on the Jews, why not speak in it of the very numerous adherents of the other religions? The latter are sometimes not further removed from Catholics than Jews and Protestants and, according to missionaries, quite often they open their hearts more readily to our faith.

Fifth, it might also be asked why ecumenism neglects the countless Catholics who are concerned about communism and, more specifically, about Marxism, which is spreading atheism throughout the world.

Sixth, the schema should set down specific rules in order that the so-called dialogue with the "non-Catholics" may be prudent and truly effective. Those who hold meetings with "non-Catholics" should be distinguished by holiness of life, fervent in prayer, and well-versed in Catholic theology, and must have the prior permission of ecclesiastical authority.

---

[47] According to Congar, these words were uttered "in a harsh tone" (*JCongar*, 372).

Two Spanish cardinals then addressed the hall. The Archbishop of Tarragona stressed the serious dangers of ecumenism, given the unpreparedness of the ordinary Catholic people and the increasing proselytism of Protestants. The Archbishop of Seville was less worried but regretted nonetheless that the schema did not include the precautions needed to avoid exposing the faithful to indifferentism; he suggested that all the religions be included in the search for unity.

These three addresses were a perfect example of the Catholic position current in recent centuries and undoubtedly still held, even with nuances inspired by good will and the climate of the age, by a large number of the Council fathers, especially those from regions with a large majority of Catholics. This position had a juridical and ecclesiocentric basis that could not be attacked at the level of the principles of Roman theology and at the level of pastoral defense of the Catholic flock, this being regarded as threatened by aggressors. The schema, on the other hand, bore witness, even if in a still limited way, to a real understanding of the contemporary ecumenical movement, which indeed had not arisen within Catholicism but which Catholicism could not ignore. This movement had specific characteristics. Were all the members of the Council, or at least a majority, capable, in the rather short time available, of grasping the novelty of the movement and taking it into account? This was the difficulty.

American Cardinal J. Ritter was the fifth speaker on the first day.[48] He was speaking in the name of some other bishops of the United States; in addition, his intervention had been approved by 91 of the 120 American bishops who had met the previous evening. His talk, which was heard with the same attention and the same silence as those that preceded,[49] was devoted in good part to religious freedom, which he placed at the heart of the ecumenical problem. Religious freedom, he said, is the foundation and prerequisite of relations with the other Christian "bodies"; it was therefore indispensable to deal with it in the schema on ecumenism and before approaching the exercise of ecumenism. By way of preface, the speaker expressed his deep satisfaction with the schema generally, because it was a response to the need to bring to light the practical consequences of *aggiornamento* in the Church. From the viewpoint both of theology and of history, the document marked the end of the Counter-Reformation with its unfortunate polemics. At the spiritual level, it compelled

[48] *AS* II/5, 536-38.
[49] See *JCongar*, 373.

us to examine our way of evaluating our brothers and sisters in Christ. From the pastoral viewpoint it urged us to hasten, "by prayer, study, dialogue, and action," the day when all will be one in Christ.

After calling attention to the reason for placing religious freedom among the principles of ecumenism, Ritter made the point that another foundational principle needed to appear more clearly in the schema, the Eucharist as sign and cause of the Church's unity.[50] At the same time, he said, we must affirm the validity of the orders and sacraments of the Oriental Churches. He then asked that in the amendments that would be introduced, the fathers avoid a perhaps offensive terminology. Without judging the validity of the orders and eucharistic celebrations of others, they should not hesitate to give the name "Churches" to the Christian bodies that the text called "communities." Next, Ritter was not reluctant to give his full approval to the chapter on the Jews as clearly relevant to the goal the Council had set for itself. Finally, he acknowledged that ecumenism is open to the dangers common to all living movements. It can be confused with a gentle rigidity; it can become sterile through excessive intellectualism; it can turn into indifferentism. He ended by announcing that he had handed in practical suggestions for the directory on the exercise of ecumenism, a document much to be desired.

By proposing that the search for unity be founded on the Eucharist and religious freedom, the American Cardinal gave the debate a quite different turn from that of the speakers who had preceded him. The interventions of the next two weeks would swing back and forth between this openness and the line taken by the defensive, ecclesiocentric tradition.[51]

In the last four addresses of November 18 we may note especially the very positive assessment of the schema by Melkite Patriarch Maximos IV, who took the same approach as Ritter; the urgent call of Cardinal Doi (Tokyo) for soliciting the necessary cultural and social collaboration of all Christians in countries still largely non-Christian[52]; the criticism of

---

[50] In his intervention on November 25, Ritter would return to the Eucharist as true center of unity and the one that is the source of the other spiritual steps to be taken.

[51] Congar summed up his impressions of this meeting as follows: "It is clear that two mentalities or, better, two worlds came to light: what an abyss between the evangelism of Msgr. Martin's report and those who, like Ruffini and the two Spanish cardinals, are wholly attached to a past that is *obsolete*!!" (*JCongar*, 375).

[52] This theme would be repeated several times in the days that followed, especially the next day by African Cardinal L. Rugambwa, then by A. Jacq (November 20), G. Huyghe (November 22), V. Gracia and F. Hengsbach (November 26), S. Baldassari (November 27), and A. Pildáin (November 28).

the Coptic and Melkite Patriarchs of the presence of a chapter on the Jews (these criticisms would be regularly repeated from various sides). Finally, another theme voiced was often to be repeated: the Church should ask forgiveness of the separated brethren (this was proposed on this first day by Cardinal Quintero of Caracas, in the spirit of Paul VI's address on September 29).[53]

Interventions were made on the following mornings at the rate of about ten a day, interrupted by votes on the amendments and chapters of the schemas on the liturgy and social communications. On November 19 the session opened with the report, already mentioned, by G. Bukatko on the first section of chapter III. This was followed by the important reports of Bea and De Smedt on chapters IV and V, of which we will speak below.

During this meeting Cardinals Léger (Montreal) and König (Vienna) gave their full support to the schema.[54] The latter also stressed the point that the rapprochement between the Churches could only be a lengthy process and that, while not rejecting the ecumenical movement that was going on in the other Churches, it was necessary to continue speaking of the Catholic idea of ecumenism, in order to avoid all ambiguity.[55]

The most noteworthy intervention on November 19 was that of A. Elchinger (coadjutor of Strasbourg), who fearlessly called for a radical revision of Catholic attitudes toward revealed truth.[56] Ecumenism, he said, is possible only under four conditions: (1) Acknowledgment of historical facts; giving examples, the speaker showed that divisions had arisen from a desire to assert truths that the Church had neglected. (2) Acknowledgment of truth, even if partial, in the teaching of the others, and giving a common witness in these areas. (3) Seeing the deeper study of the truth on both sides as an act of charity. (4) Not confusing unity in faith, charity, and worship with uniformity in rites and theological doctrines. It is necessary to have regard for legitimate differences and be

---

[53] This request for forgiveness would be favored especially by Elchinger of France (November 19), Czech Bishop Tomás (November 27), Malanchuk, the Ukrainian Exarch in France (November 28), and Dom Butler, president of the English Benedictine Congregation (December 2). Among the opponents of such a request: another Czech, Nécsey (November 27) and Muldoon of Australia (December 2), who would say, "If someone is guilty, let him go find a good confessor!"

[54] *AS* II/5, 550-54.

[55] The next day C. Morcillo (Saragossa) stressed once again the need to set forth the "Catholic principles of ecumenism," and not the "principles of Catholic ecumenism," since Catholicism should not give the impression of offering a completely new kind of ecumenism; rather, it must collaborate with the existing movement (*AS* II/5, 606-8).

[56] *AS* II/5, 562-65.

able to relativize, not the truth, which transcends the powers of the human mind, but our discourse and our ideas.

In the principal interventions at the two general congregations of November 18 and 19, the two choices — retention of the traditional Catholic position, focused on the "return" of the others; and revision of the Church's attitude — had found clear expression. However, neither on those two days nor subsequently was the schema itself called into question, at least for its first three chapters. The debate on the text as a whole lasted for four days, with a continuation on November 22. At the end of the morning of the 21st, a vote was taken on the acceptance or rejection of the first three chapters as a basis for discussion. Of 2,052 votes, 1966 were for, 86 against. Beginning on that day, and until Monday the 25th, the subject was chapter I ("Principles of Catholic Ecumenism"); part of the morning of the 25th was given over to the first interventions on chapter II ("The Exercise of Ecumenism").

It was also at this time that Bea answered various points made in the preceding interventions in order to bring clarity into the debate and doubtless also with the intention of shortening it.[57] The president of the secretariat promised, first, that the title "On Ecumenism" would be re-examined with a view to dissipating the doubts of some regarding whether the Catholic viewpoint was being adopted in the content of the text. Second, the speaker acknowledged that the various dangers mentioned (indifferentism, interconfessionalism, false irenicism) were real, but, he said, the remedy was not to do nothing; the directory in preparation would set down rules, and it would be up to the bishops to apply these to local situations. In addition, the dialogue would have to be conducted by specialists, and it would be necessary to give better ecumenical and catechetical training to the ordinary faithful.

To accusations that the schema did not give a good exposition of Catholic teaching and that it excessively praised the values of other Christians, Bea answered that, on the one hand, the text was addressed to Catholics, who were assumed to know their religion, and that, on the other, ever since Leo XIII, the popes had acknowledged these values and that knowledge of these by the faithful was the first condition for all ecumenical action.[58] He ended by stressing how important it was for all

---

[57] AS II/6, 14-17.

[58] The speaker responded, finally, to those who found common prayer for unity to be inappropriate, by referring to the 1949 Instruction of the Holy Office and by stressing the need of preparing the faithful for such a step.

Catholics to have accurate ideas about the ecumenical movement, which was being increasingly encouraged by the popes and was to be led and promoted by the bishops, for ecumenical action helps to the renewal of the Christian life of all.

The discussion of chapter II was broken off on November 27,[59] in order to make room for the first ten interventions on chapter III. It was becoming clear that despite the efforts of the moderators and doubtless also of the secretariat to limit the number of speakers, who largely repeated each other and sometimes strayed from the subject under discussion, it would not be possible to finish the debate on the five chapters by the appointed date, December 2. In fact, twelve speakers took the floor on this last date,[60] without counting Bea's concluding remarks and the brief report that Msgr. Hengsbach gave on the state of the schema on the laity, which could not be discussed during this second period.

The first of the speakers on December 2 was once again Ruffini, who said he was troubled. Priests and faithful, who were poorly informed by the press, would be disconcerted by the very serious questions the Council was in process of studying.[61] He felt bound, therefore, to emphasize five points: (1) Christ founded only one Church, the Catholic Church, which is infallible and indefectible and has the pope as its foundation and head. (2) Possible faults cannot be attributed to the Church as such but only to some of its children. (3) Those who have left the Church because of these faults are not innocent. (4) The true Church ardently desires the return of the separated brethren. (5) Conversations and dialogues are good if conducted "wisely and prudently" in accordance with norms set by the Holy See and if they conform strictly to the directory that was to be published. This energetic, last-minute appeal from a person

---

[59] But it was continued the next day in fourteen supplementary interventions.

[60] Still on chapter III and its description of the non-Catholic Churches and communities. Among the points taken up in these addresses I may single out these: the plea for recognition of a hierarchy among Christian truths (J. Rupp, November 29, and, earlier, A. Pangrazio, November 25); a greater emphasis on the plurality of ecclesial traditions, which does not detract from unity but makes it fruitful (especially G. Thangalathil and I. Ziadé, December 2); the need to restore *communicatio in sacris* with the Orthodox (Chopard-Lallier, November 20; Farah, November 26; Capucci, November 28; Hage, November 29; Layek, December 2); fear of yielding to some Orthodox demands for the abolition of the Uniate communities (Malanchuk, November 28), whereas the role of these communities in achieving union should in fact be expressly mentioned (Hermaniuk and Layek, December 2); a call for the recognition of Anglican orders (Goody, November 29; Green, December 2); revision of legislation on mixed marriages (Farah and Hengsbach, November 26; Ghattas, November 27; Frings, November 28).

[61] *AS* II/6, 339-40.

who was clinging to a model of the Church that was centered in the papal monarchy and anxious to preserve an uncompromising juridical rigor was apparently intended to make an impression on the fathers by gathering up into a few well-coined phrases what a certain number of bishops, mainly Spanish and Italian, had said in the hall, but also to draw the attention of Pope Paul VI to the perceived dangers of ecumenical openness.

In his conclusions,[62] Bea gave it as his judgment that the debate of the past two weeks had been fruitful, but he also acknowledged the need for numerous improvements in the schema; his secretariat was working on these. He promised that proposals not taken into the text would find a place in the directory, adding that it was not possible to descend to excessively inflexible and detailed applications, given the great variety of situations. This amounted to suggesting that the essential thing was the new attitude of ecumenical openness to which the future decree would commit the Church.[63]

A particularly felicitous way of ending the debate was suggested by the next-to-last speaker. Indian Bishop L. D'Mello proposed that the fathers, observers, and auditors join in saying the prayer of Jesus for unity and the Our Father. "Normally," Congar noted, "there should have been widespread applause, but half of the fathers were gossiping in the aisles. The suggestion failed."[64]

Thus the fated day, December 2, was reached without it having been possible to tackle the chapters on the Jews and on religious freedom. This was one symptom among others that the course of the Council was not failing to pose serious problems.

C. Two Sensitive Issues: The Jews and Religious Freedom

During the period of preparation for the Council two basic questions were raised regarding the composition of texts on religious freedom and on the attitude of the Church toward Judaism. Were these texts necessary, timely? Which body should prepare them? The "Decree on the Jews" of the preparatory period, a draft of seven pages composed by

---

[62] *AS* II/6, 364-67.
[63] A large part of Bea's address was an explanation of why chapters IV and V of the schema had been passed over in silence. I shall be speaking of this later.
[64] *JCongar*, 400.

Cardinal Bea at the request of John XXIII, had been set aside in June 1962, mainly because of Arab political reactions, which the Secretariat of State feared and which indeed had already been manifested.[65] In December of that same year Bea had returned to the subject in a memorandum addressed to the pope, who immediately approved the resumption of work on a document.[66] The old text was revised, approved at a plenary meeting of the secretariat in February 1963, and with the approval of the CC inserted into the schema on ecumenism.[67]

At the time this was the only way of ensuring the survival of the text, while avoiding the obligation of submitting it to the judgment of the Doctrinal Commission. Tenaciously faithful to the wishes of Pope John XXIII,[68] but also encouraged by his contacts with Jewish individuals between June 1962 and February 1963,[69] Bea thought it necessary to take account of the memory of the extermination of the Jewish people, which demanded an acknowledgment of the sins of Christian anti-semitism and, consequently, a purification of mentalities.[70] The Council needed to place itself on the strictly religious level by rejecting the serious error of making Jews collectively responsible for the death of Christ.

The status of the text on religious freedom was even more complicated than that of the document on the Jews. In the case of the former, two texts had been competing during the preparatory phase. In March 1962, the Theological Commission had approved the chapter of its schema on the Church entitled "Relations between Church and State and Religious Tolerance," which had for its focus the duties of the Catholic state in regard to religion. Meanwhile, beginning in December 1960, a

---

[65] See *History*, 1:270-71. Some details are given by T. F. Stransky in his chapter in *Vatican II by Those Who Were There*, ed. A. Stacpoole (London, 1986), 72-73.

[66] See Velati, *Una difficile transizione*, 380-81. Bea received a handwritten answer from the pope, which read: "I have carefully read this report of Cardinal Bea and I agree fully that the matter is serious and that we have a responsibility to take it up" (see Caprile III, 424 n.20).

[67] Although the new text bore the title "On the Attitude of Catholics toward Non-Christians and Especially Jews," in fact it dealt exclusively, after a short paragraph of transition from the preceding chapters, with the attitude toward the Jews. The choice of title reflected the desire of members of the secretariat not to focus too much on Judaism. The text takes up a little more than a page in *AS* II/5, 431-32.

[68] As Bea emphasized in his report of November 19, 1963. This does not exclude that Bea's will was strengthened by the publication at that time of R. Hochhuth's play *The Deputy*. Olivier notes in his chronicle for November 19: "It is said that Bea is holding fast to this chapter out of reverence for the memory of Pius XII, who has been challenged in the well-known German play" (Olivier Archive, 169, Chronicle, 26).

[69] See Caprile III, 416-17.

[70] In the memorandum to John XXIII, cited by Velati, *Una difficile transizione*, 380-81.

subcommission of the Secretariat for Christian Unity had worked on a text that focused on religious freedom, a subject on which the World Council of Churches was urging Rome to take a clear stand as a condition for serious dialogue. The definitive text, composed by Msgr. De Smedt, had been approved by the secretariat in August 1961 in the form of a draft of a constitution "On Religious Freedom"; this was sent directly to the Central Preparatory Commission. In June 1962 the two documents were the subject of a harsh confrontation in that commission between Ottaviani and Bea, which ended with the papal decision to set up a mixed commission for deciding between the two texts. This commission never met.[71]

During the first period the Council fathers received a collection of some preparatory schemas, which it was already known would not be discussed; the text on religious freedom was among them, with a note that spoke of the need to harmonize the text with the section on tolerance in the schema of the Theological Commission. Things were still blocked, then. The result was that in February 1963 the secretariat decided to compose a new, shorter text (six pages) that left aside the question of Church-State relations. At the meeting of the CC on March 29 Cardinal Suenens, reporter for the schema on the Church in the world, insisted that the new text of the secretariat be made part of this latter schema.[72] After discussion in May, this text was definitively approved by the fathers belonging to the secretariat.[73]

The perspective adopted in the new text is freedom of conscience based on the dignity of the human person; religious intolerance is unacceptable; a religious assent cannot be won by coercion; an individual with an erroneous conscience has a right to respect; he has a right to

[71] On these preliminaries see *History*, 1:296-300; Velati, *Una difficile transizione*, 240-41, 381- 82; idem, in *Verso il Concilio*, 326-31. See also J. Hamer, "Histoire du texte de la déclaration," in *La liberté religieuse. Déclaration "Dignitatis humanae personae*," Unam Sanctam 60 (Paris, 1967), 53-60. A significant fact should be noted: A note of the secretariat, composed by its secretary, J. Willebrands, dated September 26, 1963 (ISR, Dossetti Archive I, 33b), reviews the situation of the schema at a time when it had not yet been printed. A month later another note was written giving further details of the steps that Willebrands took in July-August 1962 in order to settle matters — a state that had still not been reached on October 30, 1963 (2d note at CCV, De Smedt Archive, 17/3).

[72] See *History*, 2:415, n.110.

[73] Note of the secretariat, October 30, 1963. The text was duplicated on May 30 (copy at the Moeller Archive, 1999). Among De Smedt's papers at Leuven (CCV, De Smedt Archive, 17/3) there is a copy supplemented with notes and revised as a result of the observations of the Doctrinal Commission at the beginning of November 1963.

honor God according to his conscience *and* to profess his religion. In
addition, the social aspects of this freedom are the object of a special,
expanded number (no. 5), which for the first time appeals to the common good and stresses in particular the lack of competence of the public
authorities in matters of religion and their duty to treat the followers of
all religions equitably.[74]

On April 4, Father John Courtney Murray, an American Jesuit who
had been prohibited from publishing writings on religious freedom since
1955, was appointed a conciliar expert. He did not take part in the writing of the text, which was completed on April 11 and which he judged
to be "not particularly good,"[75] but which he did provide with notes
"added as a kind of commentary on a text already composed."[76] In these
notes there are abundant references to the recent popes, but above all to
the encyclical *Pacem in terris*, which John XXIII had published in mid-
April.[77] From the end of 1963 on, Murray was to make a notable contribution to the renewed development of the future Declaration on Religious Freedom.

For the moment there still remained the twofold question of the
opportuneness of a such a declaration and its inclusion in a broader
schema, either the one on the Church in the world or the one on ecumenism. Behind this second question there was another: to whom was
the Church chiefly intending to explain its position, to other Christians
or to all human beings? A more serious matter was that at the beginning
of July the secretariat learned that the question of religious freedom had
been purely and simply suppressed from the agenda by the authorities of
the Doctrinal Commission.[78] Willebrands then asked Suenens to make

---

[74] For a comparison between the original text of December 1960, the schema of the
constitution (1962), and the text at the beginning of 1963, see Hamer, "Histoire du texte."

[75] Letter to M. F. Maher, rector of Woodstock College, November 22, 1963, cited in
D. E. Pelotte, *John Courtney Murray, Theologian in Conflict* (New York, 1976), 84. On
Murray's role at the Council see also R. Regan, "John Courtney Murray, the American
Bishops and the Declaration on Religious Liberty," in *Religious Liberty: Paul VI and
Dignitatis Humanae* (Brescia, 1995), 51-66.

[76] See D. Gonnet, *La liberté religieuse à Vatican II. La contribution de John Courtney Murray* (Paris, 1994), 108-9.

[77] The first of these notes was a statement of more than a printed page in length (in the
printed schema: *AS* II/5, 437-38), in which Murray emphasized the doctrinal progress
represented by a twofold distinction, first between false ideologies and civil institutions,
insofar as the latter follow sound reason, and second, between religious errors and the
person who is mistaken in good faith. At the end of the note the author cites, among the
principal human rights listed by recent popes, the free exercise of religion in society; this
point would later become the center of the Declaration *Dignitatis Humanae*.

[78] J. Willebrands to E. J. De Smedt, November 7, 1963, in De Smedt Archive, 17/3.

the text part of the schema on the Church in the world or to turn it into an autonomous schema that would have a place on the conciliar agenda. The agreement of three cardinals on the CC, Suenens, Döpfner, and Liénart, was won for the second solution.[79] But when Suenens told Willebrands of the meeting of the CC on July 4, he assured him that at his own suggestion the decision was made to add the text on religious freedom to the schema on ecumenism.

In fact, what Suenens said during that meeting in his report on the state of the schema on the Church in the world was that the question of religious freedom was to be developed "by a mixed commission in collaboration with the Secretariat for Christian Unity."[80] He must have known, however, that the mixed commission decided on in June 1962 had never been able to meet. The debate that followed the report showed Suenens trying to prevent the question of religious freedom from being condemned to oblivion, while Father Tromp objected that the subject had been eliminated by the Doctrinal Commission, which regarded it as insufficiently mature.[81]

The president of the CC, Cicognani, settled the matter by saying that the secretariat could prepare the text, which would then be submitted to the Doctrinal Commission, and that when the fathers had made their observations on the already printed schema on ecumenism (first three chapters), the secretariat would be able to rework the text and introduce into it the part on religious freedom.[82] This was a graceful way of putting the question off until later. On July 9, Cicognani promised Bea that the two chapters on the Jews and on religious freedom would be quickly printed for sending to the bishops. Bea therefore sent him the text two days later,[83] but after that nothing happened.

At the moment when the second period of the Council began, the authorities of the secretariat went back on the offensive. The already cited note of Willebrands, dated September 26, ended with the following remark and wish: "The text has not yet been printed, despite the decisions I have mentioned. It is to be desired that it be printed as quickly as possible, so that the fathers may consider it along with the entire schema 'On Ecumenism.'" The note was addressed to the four moderators on October 9, along with the text on religious freedom. The two documents

[79] Ibid.
[80] *AS* V/1, 633.
[81] Ibid., 636.
[82] Ibid.
[83] Letter of Willebrands to De Smedt, November 7, 1963.

served to support the urgent request that Bea was addressing at the same time to those who were then regarded as the real directors of the Council, that they would see to the carrying out of what he, Bea, thought in good faith had been decided the previous July, namely, that the text, which dealt with a subject "of the greatest importance in the area of ecumenism," should be submitted to the fathers of the Council.[84] A memorandum reviewing the essential events to this point was sent by the secretariat to the Secretary of State on October 15.[85]

It was clear that the Doctrinal Commission had not been moved to address the problem either by Cicognani or by the commission's authorities, and that the insistence of the secretariat was not enough to set things in motion. The intervention of the United States episcopate seems to have been decisive in having the text placed in the hands of the Council fathers.[86] In September, in the name of almost all his colleagues, Cardinal Spellman, who had already supported the request that J. C. Murray be appointed an expert, sent a strong letter to all those in charge of the Council asking that the subject of religious freedom be reintroduced into the agenda with the secretariat's text as the basis of discussion. It seems that in addition to this request Spellman also approached Paul VI personally and that it was as a result of this that the pope ordered Ottaviani to convene his Doctrinal Commission and issue the awaited opinion.[87] It is certain that Spellman's intervention, whatever form it took, was decisive.[88]

But there was more. The moderators had complained to the pope about the slowness and ineffectiveness of the Doctrinal Commission. This led to a handwritten *monitum* of Paul VI to Felici, dated October 24 and communicated to Ottaviani on October 26, demanding that his commission speed up its work, since, the pope said, it would be a serious matter if during this period the Council could not reach conclusions on important points of the schema on the Church.[89] On October 28

---

[84] Copy sent to Cardinal Lercaro (ISR, Lercaro Archive, XVI/28). A copy of this was sent to Cardinal Agagianian (ISR, Dossetti Archive, I/33a). As I mentioned earlier, a new version of this note, with further information (for July-December 1963) was dated October 30, 1963.

[85] Copy in ISR, Dossetti Archive, I/40.

[86] See Pelotte, *John Courtney Murray*, 81-82; Gonnet, *La liberté religieuse*, 125-26.

[87] According to Rynne, 191-92.

[88] At the meeting of the Doctrinal Commission on November 5, Ottaviani said that the pope and Spellman had insisted that the text be studied (*JPrignon*, 481: notes taken at the meeting).

[89] The text of the *monitum* is in *AS* V/2, 12-13.

Ottaviani told the commission that the text on religious freedom was to be submitted to it.[90] At the same time, he asked that, if need be, the commission should work every day, including Saturdays. The answer was: *Non placet!*[91]

The procedural debate on religious freedom took place during the plenary meeting of the Doctrinal Commission on November 5.[92] Ottaviani offered three possibilities: set up either a mixed commission with the secretariat, or a subcommission within the Doctrinal Commission, or debate the subject in the Doctrinal Commission itself. The decision was for the second method. A subcommission, with Cardinal Léger as president and comprising four members,[93] was not to prepare a new text but was to pass judgment on that of the secretariat. This subcommission met on November 7 and then reported back to the plenary commission on the 11th. The majority of the subcommission praised the text because it made an appropriate distinction between truth and the way in which persons gain access to it and because it took into account the de facto pluralism of modern society.[94] While giving a list of thirteen observations "that could profitably be passed on to the Secretariat for Christian Unity,"[95] the subcommission recommended that its report, showing a

[90] *JPrignon*, 479 (notes taken at the meeting of October 28, 1963).

[91] For the context, see below, the section entitled on "The Doctrinal Commission at the Center of the Dispute."

[92] I am using notes taken at this meeting by an expert, A. Prignon (*JPrignon*, 481) and Congar's journal.

[93] According to Congar, Ottaviani spoke of a mixed commission that would meet later. Of the six names suggested, in addition to Léger, at the meeting on November 5, Ottaviani chose four: J. Wright (Pittsburgh), chosen as reporter; F. Spanedda (Bosa); B. Gut (primate of the Benedictines); and A. Fernandez, master general of the Dominicans. Congar remarks that two of these (Fernandez and Spanedda) were "Ottaviani's men" (*JCongar*, 357). The two not chosen were M. McGrath and F. Šeper. The experts on the subcommission, who were present at the meeting on November 7, were seven: J. Ramirez, H. de Lubac, B. Häring, B. Kloppenburg, A. Naud, J. Medina, and P. Lafortune. See the report of this meeting, Moeller Archive, 1998.

[94] Report, 2. Others asked that an introduction explain more clearly how so great a leap was being made in the progress of doctrine; that the text be clearer so as to avoid any approval of subjectivism and indifferentism; that account be taken of papal documents on the subject. The next day de Lubac and Naud told Congar that Fernandez had criticized the text in the name of the Syllabus and other documents of Pius IX and Leo XIII, and that Spanedda, without offering specific criticisms, expressed general disagreement on grounds of the danger of indifferentism (*JCongar*, 362).

[95] Most of these had to do with form. See the Report, 3. The secretariat would accept ten of them (especially by adding, in the notes, references to documents of Pius XII, as a way of better describing "the common patrimony"). It did not accept the suggestions to revise its formulation of the "progressive and human" way in which God draws human beings to himself, to omit the two lines rebuking the various kinds of discrimination practiced by human beings, or to eliminate the last two numbers (6 and 7) as being redundant.

unanimous agreement on the printing of the secretariat's text, should be accepted by the plenary commission as the answer to be sent to the secretariat.[96]

The matter was discussed at a plenary meeting of the commission on November 11. It is not possible here to review the debate in detail.[97] Three leading lights of the commission expressed clear disagreement with the text — M. Browne, P. Parente, and F. Franić — followed by Ottaviani and then four others.[98] In contrast, A. Charue, H. Volk, B. Häring, J. C. Murray, G. Philips, and K. Rahner defended the substance of it and, in particular, maintained that there was question only of giving a general *nihil obstat*, since it was for the assembled fathers to debate it. Supported by some others, G. Garrone asked for a vote of general approval; the vote showed 18 in favor of the text, 5 against, 1 abstaining. Congar commented: "It is a fact: every time a vote is taken, it is favorable!"[99] In a broader perspective, it is certain that the pressure brought by the American bishops was extended into the meeting of the subcommission on November 7 by the determined action of Léger and of the reporter, Msgr. Wright; this was the decisive factor. Furthermore, egged on by the pressure exerted by the pope, the commission as a whole showed, in this case, a swiftness that was not habitual with it.

At a meeting on the eve of the opening of the debate on ecumenism in the hall, 110 of the 120 United States bishops declared themselves in favor of including chapters IV and V in the schema.[100] In their view this was doubtless the best possible way, at that moment, of saving the text on religious freedom, whose inadequacies, however, Murray had already shown them. The next day Cardinal Ritter told the fathers that without a clear acknowledgment of religious freedom any ecumenical dialogue would be seriously compromised, for it was a basis of relationships that should have a place among the principles of ecumenism (chapter I). But,

[96] Report, 2.

[97] *JPrignon,* 482. Congar, who was not present at the meeting, summed it up on the basis of hearsay (*JCongar,* 364-65). Murray, who was invited to the meeting by Léger, spoke of it in the already mentioned letter of November 22, which is cited in Pelotte, *John Courtney Murray,* 82.

[98] Among them was expert R. Gagnebet, "who violently attacked the arguments given in the text, while also expressing in very strong words his acceptance of its conclusions" (G. Garrone to E. De Smedt, November 12, 1963, in De Smedt Archive, 17/4).

[99] *JCongar,* 365. In his already cited letter to the Bishop of Bruges, chief author of the text, Garrone said he shared the latter's joy over the result of the vote, while at the same time asking him to take into account the remarks made at the meeting of the subcommission by Fernandez and Spanedda.

[100] Gonnet, *La liberté religieuse,* 120.

he went on to say, it was necessary to provide solid theological foundations for this freedom: the absolute freedom of the act of faith, the dignity of the person and the inviolability of the person's conscience, and the lack of authority by any civil power to pass judgment on the gospel and its interpretation.[101]

The addresses given on the following days showed, however, that for various reasons chapter IV (on the Jews) in particular but also the chapter on religious freedom were regarded as out of place in the schema on ecumenism.[102] The strongest advocates of the two chapters were, evidently, the two reporters, Bea and De Smedt, who by decision of the moderators spoke on November 19, the day on which the text of chapter V was at last distributed.[103]

Even the length of the reports, the presentation of which occupied a good part of the 70th general congregation, was unusual. The two reporters were aware that, after the difficulties repeatedly raised during the preceding months, the novelty of the two subjects in a conciliar debate required a careful explanation of their significance. In public opinion, too, this was a much awaited moment. In *Le Figaro*, for example, R. Laurentin entitled his article of the following day, "A Major Moment at the Council," and spoke of "two outstanding talks" that the members of the Council did not want to miss — the bars were almost deserted.[104] "With the serenity, modesty, and honesty that radiate from his person,"[105] Bea began by reviewing the history of the text and was anxious to make it clear from the very beginning that the text was not concerned with a national or a political problem but solely with a religious problem.[106]

After calling to mind all that the Church had received from the Israelite people, Bea gave a short course in Pauline theology in order to show from the Letter to the Romans that God did not reject that people, despite the condemnation of Jesus to death. He then reminded his audience of the

---

[101] *AS* II/5, 537. The speaker asked as a corollary of this final point that the text should affirm once again the complete independence of the Church from the civil power. These were points judged essential by Murray, who was the adviser to the American bishops on this entire matter.

[102] For chapter IV, the Oriental Catholic patriarchs in particular, as well as the Latin patriarch of Jerusalem, came out in favor of its suppression or its relocation.

[103] In order to obtain the distribution of chapter IV, Cardinal Bea had to write a short, curt letter to the Secretary General of the Council on November 6 (published in *AS* V/2, 18-19). The text was distributed on November 8.

[104] *Le Figaro*, November 20, 1963, p. 10.

[105] Ibid.

[106] *AS* II/5, 481-85.

antisemitism that had been widespread in various countries, especially Nazi Germany, and had contaminated Catholics. As the Church was endeavoring to renew itself at the Council, it had to face up to the question and show itself capable of imitating the charity of Christ and his apostles, who forgave their persecutors. To this end, it was necessary to get rid of prejudices inspired by propaganda: the Jewish people of today cannot, any more than this people in its entirety in the first century, be accused of responsibility for the death of Christ. The roots of antisemitism are indeed religious, but also political, psychological, social, and economic. The important point is that Catholics must use the weapons of truth, charity, and patience. In closing, the speaker made use, not unfittingly, of the "full approval" of John XXIII in December 1962 (cited earlier): his words bore witness to an utterly clear personal commitment, but they left the Council free to decide, as was typically the way of the deceased pope.

Both in the Council itself and outside, especially in the Arab countries, voices were raised against consideration of the text on the Jews. But G. Caprile's survey of the reactions expressed during subsequent weeks and months in the Catholic and non-Catholic press, among the bishops after their return home, and on the part of leading Jews, gives the overall impression of a positive acceptance.[107]

"With a more brilliant and no less effective eloquence,"[108] Msgr. De Smedt immediately followed Bea with his own report on chapter V, which had shortly before been endorsed by the Doctrinal Commission.[109] The main points of the report had been drawn up by Murray in a document entitled *Ratio schematis*; the main concern of this was with the development over time of teaching on religious freedom, which led in a coherent way to the emphasis on the dignity of the human person.[110] What was at stake in the debate was to show the permanence of principles beneath the variations in behavior, but also the priority of one principle (the dignity of the person) over the others; the question, then, was

[107] Caprile III, 425-30.

[108] *Le Figaro*, November 20, 1963. Congar wrote: "with power and fire, but in a somewhat theatrical manner" (*JCongar*, 376).

[109] *AS* II/5, 485-95. There is a rough copy of the report in De Smedt's hand, with notations by A. Prignon, in De Smedt Archive, 17/4.

[110] See the analysis of the document in Gonnet, *La liberté religieuse*, 109-14. In Murray's letter to Maher (November 22, 1963), the Jesuit said that the claim, spread by the press, that he had written the report was "substantially true" (see Pelotte, *John Courtney Murray*, 84).

to know how to interpret the tradition. De Smedt's lengthy statement was based on this formulation of the question by Murray.[111]

It is impossible for lack of space to summarize here all the nuances of a report that, according to the speaker, dealt with a question that was "very difficult and extremely important for modern life." De Smedt described in order the schema's five parts: (1) the behavior of Catholics toward others (especially respect for the right and duty that non-Catholics have of obeying their consciences); (2) the right to religious freedom for the entire human family (against every form of coercion, and this even if the conscience is upright but in error); (3) the right to the free external exercise of religion (a right limited by the common good that is based on justice and right reason). Parts 4 and 5 were historical in character and explained what was in the notes added to chapter V by Murray: there is a "rule of continuity" between doctrine and pastoral practice in regard to the liberty of the human being, who is created in the image of God, but there is also a "rule of progress" and deeper understanding depending on circumstances (reminder of the twofold distinction made in *Pacem in terris*, first between false ideologies and the institutions based on them, and second, between error and the erring person); these two rules were immediately applied to the teaching of the popes from Pius IX to John XXIII.

While expecting that the fathers would contribute improvements of the text, De Smedt had said in his introduction that the freedom in question was not indifferentism or laicism or doctrinal relativism. In his conclusion he anticipated another difficulty: a battle over conflicting interpretations of the pontifical documents. The texts must not be understood apart from their historical and doctrinal context. Referring to the pastoral character of the decree to be adopted, he reminded his hearers that the problem was one of real human beings in their real relations with others in today's society, and that the world was earnestly waiting for the voice of the Church on religious freedom; this was a clear allusion to the kind of Council Pope John wanted. Finally, the reporter expressed his hope that the text would be approved by the end of the present period, and he promised that the

---

[111] Two analyses of the report: (1) In Gonnet, *La liberté religieuse*, 114-19, who emphasizes in particular that De Smedt's analysis, from Murray, of the teaching of the popes from Pius IX to John XXIII was not accepted by the body of the fathers (there was a conflict of interpretation between, on the one hand, the primarily philosophical argument of the popes on the freedom of the relationship between the conscience and God and, on the other, the confused facts of history, some of them favorable, other opposed, to the free exercise of religion); (2) in Hamer, "Histoire du texte," 63-69.

Secretariat for Christian Unity would work "day and night" to finish the definitive text. He had no idea how lengthy a course would have to be traveled before the promulgation of a document so dear to his heart.

"The high quality of the report, and Msgr. De Smedt's fervor in defending it, elicited great applause."[112] Even if this response had been unanimous, which is hardly likely, it did not prevent some convinced defenders of religious freedom, such as B. Olivier, a moralist and the expert of the Zairean bishops, from putting a damper on things. This Belgian Dominican thought that the historical part of the schema "arranged the facts somewhat"; for example, how was it possible to claim that, even when restored to its context, namely, the danger of laicism, the Syllabus was a positive assertion of freedom?[113] In an article that appeared in *America* magazine on November 30 and caused a great stir, Murray expressed the opinion that the report did not go far enough in asserting the lack of competence of political authorities in religious matters and, more broadly, that the schema did not situate the problem on its proper terrain, that is, the constitutional and not simply the ethical terrain, especially by not setting forth the principles that limit the social exercise of religious freedom in the name of the common good.[114]

The bishops of the United States, for their part, fervently defended the text; after Cardinal Ritter on November 18, another leader, Cardinal Meyer (Chicago), made this clear on the 20th at the 71st general congregation. Some non-American bishops did the same. To cite only one, on the 27th[115] Msgr. P. Schmitt (Metz) developed the thought that religious

---

[112] Wenger, 183.

[113] Olivier Archive, 129 ("Chronque," 28). The same witness noted the negative reaction of Swiss Dominican H. de Riedmatten, representative of the Holy See at the United Nations in Geneva, who "strongly attacked" the report in regard to the complete freedom of the act of faith and to the rights of an erroneous conscience. According to a conversation Congar had had with de Riedmatten ten days earlier, the latter rejected the idea that religious freedom is based solely on the right of the person; he wanted to base it on the independence of religions vis-à-vis the state (*JCongar*, 363).

[114] See Gonnet, *La liberté religieuse*, 117-18 and 122-25; Hamer, "Histoire du texte," 72-73.

[115] *AS* II/6, 162-63. Wenger, 183-86, gives a summary of the interventions for and against. It is to be noted that a workshop on religious freedom was organized at the French seminary for the afternoon of November 22. Six experts took part, three of them, Daniélou, Martelet, and Cottier, being invited by the bishops. The meeting resulted in three proposals: the text should make clear that it does not treat the whole problem of religious freedom; it should concentrate on freedom as rejecting all physical and moral coercion; it would be better not to connect this freedom solely with the dignity of the person but rather to formulate its objective foundations in the transcendence of faith in relation to temporal structures and in the nature of the religious reality and of religion (*JCongar*, 388).

freedom is an indispensable condition for ecumenical activity and should therefore be brought in earlier, at the beginning of chapter II of the schema. If religious freedom is thwarted, he said, no dialogue is possible; the civil authorities will profit by it to take advantage of divisions among Christians; the transcendence of the Christian religion will be obscured; even the assent of faith and interpersonal relations will be disrupted.

Less positive views were also heard, especially from the Spanish bishops, who stressed the need to protect the Catholic people from Protestant proselytism and who feared that a hasty approval might be wrested from the Council. The same was true of the Latin American fathers, who were being faced with an offensive by the sects, and of the Italian bishops, who were troubled by the Christian Democratic Party's opening to the Left.

By a vote on November 21 the first three chapters of the schema on ecumenism were accepted as a basis for discussion. This dissociation of these chapters from the two on the Jews and on religious freedom caused some anxiety. There was talk of "very powerful pressures" brought to bear on the pope by the authorities directing the Council to have the two last chapters not brought to a vote and even to be set aside.[116] On the other hand, there was a request for such a vote, especially from C. Helmsing (Kansas City), because, he said, everyone was expecting it, even though the lack of time would prevent the beginning of the discussion.[117]

In his conclusions on December 2,[118] Bea expressed regret at not having been able to discuss these two chapters. The hitch, he insisted, was due "to the lack of time and to no other reason, no other reason." But could not the fathers have proceeded at least to a vote to consider the chapters? The cardinal answered that there would have been many favorable responses, but the moderators preferred to leave more time for discussing the first three chapters and so to avoid the risk of being reproached for hastiness in voting on the three chapters and then on the other two, which deal with questions so serious, so new, and so important in our age. There was need of reflecting at leisure and deciding during the next period, when the questions would be ripe for discussion.[119]

---

[116] *JCongar*, 390-91. Congar got this rumor from P. Haubtmann and Ch. Moeller. Caprile mentions it in III, 563.

[117] *AS* II/6, 313.

[118] *AS* II/6, 364-67.

[119] In an interview given to G. Caprile in January 1964, Bea explained at greater length the postponement of the vote and the discussion; he rejected the existence of pressures and ulterior motives aimed at setting aside the two chapters; Caprile, III, 563-65.

When the study of a question of first importance was put off (and religious freedom as a test and symbol of the reconciliation of the Church with the modern conscience was certainly one such question), the commentators automatically attributed the postponement to hidden maneuvering by those opposed to it. Was the reason given by Bea, the lack of time, entirely convincing? Two points must be raised here for consideration. The conciliar assembly undoubtedly did not know all about the energetic steps taken during the preceding months and weeks by the president and secretary of the Secretariat for Christian Unity, and by the American bishops, to get these texts finally into the hands of the fathers. But the assembly did know enough about them for Bea's change of position to cause surprise and, for a good many, disillusionment. The argument that the question needed to mature did not explain the absence of a vote simply to consider the text. All this makes it necessary to locate the problem in a much broader context, that of the organization and effective direction of the Council. I shall discuss this in detail further on.

When the moderators were appointed at the beginning of this period, it was generally thought that they would become the directors of the Council. But during November their position was seriously compromised for reasons already mentioned above in Chapter II. Whether this was due to the challenge to their authority in the form of a curial counteroffensive led by certain fathers in the hall, within the CC, within the General Secretariat, or even in the Doctrinal Commission, or whether it was due to the moderators' lack of cohesiveness and effectiveness, they seemed paralyzed when it came to taking the initiative. They could no longer put questions about future direction before the assembly (Cardinal Liénart's proposal for such a procedure in connection with the schema on the bishops was blocked); they were unsuccessful in cutting back on repetitions and irrelevant digressions in the speeches of the fathers and in avoiding other loss of time because of the lengthy ceremonies that were part of the daily general congregations.[120]

Under these conditions it could be asked whether the manner in which Bea sought to justify the lack of initiative of the moderators in connection with chapters IV and V was not a way of hiding their indecisiveness so as not to place them in an even more difficult position.

---

[120] Laurentin adds: "Questions put to them often met with evasions, and problems of which they were made aware often remained unresolved" (214).

D. The Voices of the Non-Catholic Observers

As M. Velati observes, the beginning of the discussion of the schema on ecumenism was inevitably the moment most keenly awaited by the observers, since here the Council was getting to the heart of the debate on the role Catholicism would play in the ecumenical movement.[121]

We know how important a place the observers had at the Council, especially from the beginning of the second period onward.[122] At the Tuesday meetings of the Secretariat for Christian Unity, they had been able to express their views on the schema on the Church, which was then being discussed in the hall.[123] They had had a papal audience on October 17, during which Paul VI had said that the Catholic Church "at the highest level of the highest responsibility" (that of the pope and the Council) wanted to enter into "the great dialogue" with the other Christian confessions.

These remarks had elicited a lively response from the secretary general of the World Council of Churches (WCC).[124] At that moment, in fact, the prospect was emerging of a direct Catholic-Orthodox dialogue, the most recent signs of which were the contact established between Paul VI and Athenagoras, and, likewise in September, the decision of the second Pan-Orthodox Conference of Rhodes to accept the principles governing an official dialogue with the Roman Church. On a broader scale, even if, as Dr. Visser't Hooft says in his memoirs, his principal fear was not a shift in the center of ecumenical initiative from Geneva to Rome,[125] there were certainly bad feelings (not to put it more srtongly)

---

[121] Velati, *Una difficile transizione*, 395.

[122] In comparison with the first period, the number of observers and guests had increased from forty-nine to sixty-six; the communities represented now numbered twenty-two instead of seventeen. Four of the new communities were Oriental Churches, the fifth was the United Church of South India.

[123] The reference is to the six meetings held between October 1 and November 5, 1963.

[124] On October 29, W. A. Visser't Hooft had composed a note entitled "Has the Dialogue between the Roman Catholic Church and the Other Churches Begun?" (copy at the ISR, WCC Archive, ACO 7), in which he meant to stress that fact that an official dialogue had not yet begun: "The very worthwhile contacts which the observers have with the fathers of the council must in no way be confused with a real dialogue of Churches."

[125] W. A. Visser't Hooft, *Le temps du rassemblement. Mémoires* (Paris, 1975), 411. As we shall see further on, the reservations of the WCC would become even stronger at the announcement of the meeting of Paul VI and Athenagoras in Jerusalem. On the feelings of Visser't Hooft at the time of these events and, more generally, on the attitude of the WCC and the great confessional families to the Council until September 1963, see *History*, 2:535-46.

at the WCC on seeing that in the Catholic Church there was a tendency to see the Council as the real starting point of the journey toward unity.

Despite the fact that the words of the pope and some addresses of the Council fathers were to some degree ecclesiocentric, as well as emotional, it is certain that the presence of the sixty-six Christian observers in Rome and in the hall exercised, by way of personal contacts with the bishops and in the tone of the interventions, a by-no-means-negligible influence on the ecumenical awareness of the Catholic authorities.[126]

At the meetings of the secretariat on November 12 and 19, the observers had an opportunity to exchange points of view on the schema on ecumenism. The delegates of the WCC tended to take a degree of leadership among the observers,[127] but without putting themselves forward at the meetings. During these meetings fourteen observers (among them only two Orientals, both Coptic Orthodox) spoke in order to share their views.[128] But at this same period, memoranda were submitted by at least six individual observers, by the group of Anglican observers, and by L. Vischer, the principal delegate of the WCC, whose text was prepared in collaboration with the other German observers.[129] Most of the interventions of the observers dealt with the chapters of the schema on the Jews and on religious freedom.

Since the schema was offered as an internal matter for the Catholic Church, the main problem for the observers was to know from what point of view they were to evaluate and possibly suggest revisions, at a stage when the Catholic Church had not yet officially begun a dialogue with the other Churches. While for some of the observers, it was a matter simply

---

[126] On this influence during the first period, see *History*, 2:521-23. At the time of the debate on ecumenism in November 1963, expert B. Olivier wrote: "It is undeniable that the presence in the hall of the non-Catholic observers, a silent but close presence, is exercising a great influence on the debates. Each father who speaks is conscious of speaking in their presence, and many speak for them" (Chronicle, 30).

[127] Velati, *Una difficile transizione*, 395. In summing up the positions of the observers, I rely not only on the archival documents cited in the following notes but also on Velati (395-400).

[128] Mimeographed reports in CLG, Moeller Archive, 431 and 1944.

[129] Mimeographed copies, ibid., 1946-1953. In its original German form Vischer's memorandum did not carry his signature. ("Bemerkungen zum Schema 'De ecumenismo'"; ibid., 440). The English version (ibid., 1946), however, was signed by E. Schlink, R. Skydsgaard, W. Küppers, G. A. Lindbeck, N. A. Nissiotis (another delegate from the WCC), and J. Miguez Bonino. This important memorandum is undated. We know from a letter of Vischer to Visser't Hooft (November 8, 1963; ISR, WCC Archive, ACO 6) that Vischer had composed his remarks before that date and that he had done so at the request of the German-speaking group of observers, with whom he then discussed them. In his letter he asks the secretary general of the WCC whether he agrees with the text.

of suggesting clarifications, Vischer thought the observers should be raising basic questions, as, for example, how the Catholic Church visualized itself in itself and in relation to the other Churches? How did it understand Christian unity? G. A. Lindbeck, delegate of the Lutheran World Federation, went further with a radical criticism of the presuppositions of the schema; that is, that the Catholic Church regarded itself as "the exclusive possessor of the fullness of unity," and, H. Roux of the Reformed World Alliance added, of the totality of the means of grace. Fr. Thijssen, spokesman for the secretariat, replied at the meeting on November 19 that it did not seem anti-ecumenical that a Church "through reflection on itself should determine its own outlook on the basis of its own vision of what the Church is"; it could not be asked to pass over some points fundamental for its own faith.

For the rest, the judgment of the observers on the schema was in general positive: the schema attested to a basic change in the Catholic attitude; and it set forth many of the values of the Orthodox and Evangelical Churches,[130] and this would make it especially enlightening to many Catholics.[131] Finally, the problem of the starting point was elucidated in a fundamental challenge to chapter III of the schema, which described the non-Catholic Churches. Not only was the description of these Churches and of the WCC inaccurate,[132] but also, and above all, the text judged the other Churches according to a quantitative norm, that is, according to their more or less full (or deficient) possession of the ecclesial elements and means of salvation found in the Catholic Church. The Christian Churches are thus not considered and evaluated in themselves but according to the measure of their agreement with the Catholic Church.

In his memorandum L. Vischer even suggested omitting the third chapter, and he based his request on a series of arguments, the main one being that "the communion established by dialogues between the Orthodox and Evangelical Churches is ignored." Many people will take it that

---

[130] According to L. Vischer ("Bemerkungen"), it was even too irenic by comparison with other conciliar texts, to the point of minimizing disputed doctrines, such as papal primacy.

[131] Professor O. Cullmann, a guest of the secretariat, opened the conversation at the meeting on November 12 by saying: "The publication of the schema on ecumenism will be an important event in the life of the Roman Catholic Church, and as Protestants we are grateful for the new attitude and the wish to understand the faith outside the Roman Church" (Moeller Archives, 431).

[132] This was a point made especially by the Anglican Observers in "Notes on *De ecumenismo* from the Anglican Observers" (Moeller Archive, 1952, pp. 3-4).

the Catholic Church is trying to start an anti-ecumenical movement. It would be better to take the ecumenical situation as it actually is, that is, as consisting in a global movement and in multilateral relationships. Vischer's point of view was, of course, that of the WCC, which wanted to avoid the development of chiefly bilateral relations between the Churches. Other observers gave a less critical assessment of the chapter III, asking only that it be revised.[133]

The views expressed by the observers, while respectful, were very frank and clear. They would not conceal differences in the name of good will. Paul VI's plea for forgiveness could not allow them to forget that along with faults on both sides the very idea of unity differed from Church to Church.[134] The schema, somewhat to the contrary, sought to be irenic, but interpreted differences chiefly on the basis of the Catholic understanding of the Church and of unity; the text was not entirely freed of the unionist premise, long established in Catholicism, according to which, as "the others" had separated themselves, so it was up to them to return.[135]

Among the observers who voiced their opinion of the schema, most also had reactions to the chapter on the Jews, and some to the chapter on religious freedom.[136] Of the fourteen interveners at the two meetings on November 12 and 19, eight spoke of these, sometimes at length; seven alluded to them, either in written observations or in letters; six said they were satisfied with the chapter on the Jews; four insisted especially on the need to incorporate the text into the schema.[137] While the Anglican

[133] For example, at the meeting on November 19, E. J. F. Arndt, an American Congregationalist, suggested changing the title of the chapter ("The Communities That Arose in the Sixteenth Century"); the non-Catholic Churches do not acknowledge this description of them, because they are apostolic and care about being evangelical and catholic (Moeller Archive, 1944, p. 9). The Anglican group made the same point in their "Notes" (ibid., 1952, p. 3).

[134] For example, O. Cullmann in his "Remarques sur le schéma" (Moeller Archive, 1951, p. 3): "The two conceptions of unity have deep roots in the *faith* of Catholics and of Protestants."

[135] A criticism made especially by L. Vischer in his "Bemerkungen." See also the "Notes" of the Anglicans (p. 4): "One notices with regret the assumption throughout that the Roman faith itself stands in no need of modification."

[136] Three documents say nothing of chapters IV and V: the "Bemerkungen" of L. Vischer, the "Remarks on *De ecumenismo*" of D. Horton, and the "Some Comments" of A. Morrison. Regarding religious freedom, R. McAfee Brown, an American Presbyterian, responded to the text in his "Comments," which were dated November 18 (as indicated in the secretariat's copy). Are we to infer from this that the observers already had chapter V before its distribution to the Council fathers, which took place only on the following day?

[137] The four were L. J. Van Holk, D. V. Steere, G. H. Williams, and R. McAfee Brown; the extra two were O. Cullmann and R. E. Cushman.

group and L. Vischer approved of the letter and spirit of the chapter, they eventually joined five other observers who thought that its proper place was not in a decree on ecumenism.[138] It is striking that the Anglicans and the Old Catholics gave the same reason for non-incorporation: to include the Jews in the schema would give the impression that the Catholic idea of ecumenism was limited to an attitude of benevolence toward all men and women of good will.[139] The two Coptic Orthodox observers respectively gave their view that as children of Abraham the Muslims have as great a right to be mentioned in a conciliar text and that relations with the entire body of non-Christians should be the object of a separate and much more developed schema.[140]

There were fewer opinions expressed regarding religious freedom. These were also equally divided: three for the inclusion, three against.[141] But it is worth noting that the only detailed commentary was that of the American, Robert McAfee Brown, who emphasized especially the principle at stake in the chapter, which "will be the most important *immediate* creative step the Council will take."[142]

The secretariat undoubtedly took these observations into account in its revision of the text at the beginning of 1964, although it did not regard all of them as valid. It is to be observed, in any case, that the opinions of the observers regarding the timeliness of the last two chapters and their incorporation into the decree on ecumenism corresponded pretty well to trends in the Council hall — a fact that could not have failed to catch the attention of those in charge of these texts.

The silent but influential presence of the observers at the general congregations and their important interventions by way of the Secretariat for Christian Unity belong to the internal activity of the Council. The importance of their participation in Vatican II loomed still larger when we consider other circumstances in which these delegates of other Christian Churches had occasion to get across their viewpoints. It is obviously not

---

[138] W. Küppers (Old Catholic), G. A. Lindbeck (Lutheran World Federation), C. P. Matthew (Syrian Church of Mar Thomas of Malabar), and P. El-Moharraky and F. El-Pharaony (Coptic Orthodox). For Vischer, see his letter of November 8, 1963, and his report of November 16, 1963, both addressed to Visser't Hooft (copies at ISR, Moeller Archive).

[139] Moeller Archive, 1944 and 1952.

[140] Ibid., 1944.

[141] For: L. J. Van Holk, G. H. Williams, and R. McAfee Brown. Against: W. Küppers, G. A. Lindbeck, and C. P. Matthew. Matthew suggested a special schema on the Jews and religious freedom.

[142] Moeller Archive, 1944.

possible to mention all the opportunities that they took to make their opinions heard by the bishops and experts who asked for them. There were individual or small group contacts throughout the time of the Council; in the second period, these intensified especially in regard to the key schema: the schema on the Church.[143]

However, some attitudes underwent a change during the final days of this period. On the afternoon of November 25, in St. Peter's Basilica and in the presence of the pope, there was a ceremonial transfer of the relics of St. Josaphat Kuncewicz, a great promotor of the union of the Ukrainians with Rome at the end of the sixteenth century. It was unfortunate that this ceremony coincided with the debate on the schema on ecumenism, because the Orthodox Church held Josaphat responsible for the martyrdom of Orthodox saints. The principal observer from the Patriarchate of Moscow, Archpriest V. Borovoy, received an order to leave Rome.[144]

On November 30, O. Cullmann, professor at the Protestant Faculties of Basel and Paris and a guest of the secretariat, gave a lecture at the Centre St-Louis-des-Français on the subject of the history of salvation in the New Testament. During the preceding weeks, the plan to hold this lecture at a pontifical university had caused agitation in the Secretariat of State, the Holy Office, and the Congregation for Seminaries, and authorization had finally been refused.[145]

The morning of Tuesday, December 3, was devoted to a commemoration in St. Peter's of the fourth centenary of the Council of Trent. Cardinal G. Urbani, Patriarch of Venice and a member of the CC, delivered an address entitled "I Believe in the Church," some strains of which called to mind the non-ecumenical period of the Counter-Reformation.

---

[143] For the second period see some general surveys, especially in Velati, *Un difficile transizione*, 395; Wenger, 270-81; and Wiltgen, 119-27. Vischer remarked: "There is also a great eagerness with many bishops to hear about the World Council and the experience made at ecumenical gatherings" (letter to Visser 't Hooft, November 22, 1963, copy in ISR, WCC Archive, AC0 6). More generally, see the report sent to Geneva at the beginning of November by another WCC observer, Masatoshi Doi of Japan, and several reports of observers to the WCC (ibid.).

[144] The order did not have to be carried out, because Borovoy turned to good account the fact that on November 25 there was also a Requiem Mass in Rome for President Kennedy, who had been assassinated three days earlier: thus the press would have been able to interpret Borovoy's absence from Rome as a political gesture. See Wiltgen, 125, and Wenger, 233-34.

[145] On the lecture, attended by the ambassador of France, four French cardinals, and 150 bishops, see *Le Monde*, December 3, 1963, p. 9. Congar speaks of the affair several times in his journal and concludes bitterly: "And this happened at the very time when they were discussing ecumenism in the hall!" (*JCongar*, 386).

Understandably, a number of the observers, among them the most important, judged it better not to attend this commemoration.[146]

The mention of these several situations is enough to show that, apart from debates on a text, the Roman "conversion" to concrete ecumenical relationships still had a way to travel.

II. A WORRYING PROBLEM: THE ORGANIZATION OF THE COUNCIL

A. WHO WAS DIRECTING THE COUNCIL?

The month of November 1963 was an especially uncertain time for the fate of Vatican II. The lack of precise definition of the respective roles of the directive bodies, together with the requests of the Council fathers that had accumulated during the preceding month, were in danger of bringing the Council to an impasse. It would be overly simplistic to reduce the crisis to poor administration or to a failure to apply the regulations, for these phenomena pointed in fact to a deeper problem. That problem was "political" and institutional; it consisted in a struggle for influence among various individuals and bodies. This struggle was in turn to be explained by different ways of understanding the reality and functioning of the Catholic Church as such. From this point of view, the vote in favor of episcopal collegiality on October 30 seems to have triggered the crisis in November.

The question of the distributions of powers involved the Council of Presidents, the Coordinating Commission, the moderators, and the General Secretariat. These bodies had to face, first of all, complaints about the functioning of the general congregations and the commissions, and

---

[146] In his *Evangelischer Bericht vom Konzil Zweite Session* (Göttingen, 1964), 58, G. Maron mentions L. Vischer, N. Nissiotis, O. Cullmann, E. Schlink, and K. Skydsgaard. Some observers gave lectures in Rome during this period, and outside of Rome after it. It was undoubtedly not by chance that in Rome, toward the end of the period, Schlink, a German Lutheran, gave a lecture in which he claimed the title of Church for the Protestant communities and refused to think of ecumenism as meaning a return pure and simple to the Roman Church (see *Le Monde*, December 3, 1963, p. 9). In January 1964 Vischer would give talks in various cities (Lyons, Fribourg, and Geneva among them) on the Church and unity, in which he returned to the ideas of his memorandum, "Bemerkungen": remarkable progress of Catholicism in the direction of dialogue; its positive view of the other Churches (he insisted that the schema on unity should speak at least of "ecclesial communities," which it subsequently did); the question of the ability of the Catholic Church to acknowledge the specific character of the other Churches; and the fear of seeing Roman Catholicism consider itself the new center of the ecumenical movement. See Wenger, 274-79.

then the broader problem of the conciliar agenda and the length of the
Council; in the background was the possibility of the establishment of a
permanent council of bishops around the pope. In connection with all
these questions, which weighed upon the Council itself and did not
escape observers at the time, it is of course necessary to try to understand the attitude of Paul VI, since the pontiff was the supreme directing
authority, on whom the several influences worked in different ways.

The revised version of the conciliar Regulations that had been
approved by the pope on September 13, 1963, did not establish any more
clearly than the Regulations of 1962 the prerogatives of the several bodies in charge of the Council. According to chapter II of the revised Regulations, which had to do with the general congregations, the Council of
Presidents was to see to it that the Regulations were followed, and the
four cardinals newly appointed as "delegates or moderators" were to
direct the work of the Council, taking turns in "ordering the debates at
the general congregations."[147] As for the CC, set up "to arrange or coordinate the business of the Council," which had for president the Secretary of State and for secretary the Secretary General of the Council, it
was simply mentioned in the Regulations after the ten conciliar commissions.[148] The first difficulty, then, was the exact definition of the role of
the moderators in relation to the CC, of which they were a part.

The main problem that had appeared during October concerned the
very functioning of the Council, that is, the relationship between the
general congregations and the commissions. The Council seemed to be
getting bogged down, and the malaise was increasing. This was brought
out very clearly in two meetings at the end of October, one of bishops
acting on their own, and the other a very official one of all the directive
bodies of the Council. First, there was the weekly meeting of the Conference of the Twenty-two held on October 25. The Twenty-two were a
group of bishops, delegates, whether official or not, of the episcopal
conferences of the five continents, who had come together on their own
during the first period.[149] At this meeting on October 25, according to a
memorandum addressed to the pope three days later,

---

[147] *Ordo Concilii Oecumenici Vaticani II celebrandi* (Editio altera recognita, 1963),
Article 45 §§1-2. The question was whether the direction of the work was limited to seeing to the order of the debates at the general congregations. The ambiguity came to light
as early as September 1963; see Alberigo, "Dinamiche," especially 140-48.

[148] Ibid., Article 7 §2.

[149] On this group, see J. Grootaers, "Une forme de concertation épiscopale au concile
Vatican II: La 'Conférence des Vingt-deux' (1962-1963)," *RHE* 91 (1996), 66-112.

there was quick agreement about the weariness and even anxiety of a great many fathers. It must be acknowledged, not with pessimism but with due seriousness, that the often confused slowness of the conciliar debates, the powerlessness of several commissions, and a number of other difficulties of which they hear rumors have frustrated many bishops, who are asking for the causes of this uneasiness.[150]

While this memorandum for the pope was directly connected with obtaining a straw vote on the five questions, the one granted on October 29, its perspective was much broader. Following as it did upon the meeting of the delegated bishops, who in view of the urgency had made it the subject of their dialogue on October 25, the memorandum analyzed successively the function of the general congregations and that of the conciliar commissions. First of all, it asked that the debates at general assemblies be "really guided" and that the moderators be given the powers needed for this purpose. Second, the assembly should concentrate its efforts on the major points of each schema. It was also necessary that each conciliar commission carry on a dialogue with the assembly in the form of answers to the questions and objections of the fathers.[151] The second part of the memorandum of the Twenty-two dealt with the defective functioning of the commissions, of which I shall speak later. In this area, too, the group called for reinforcing the authority of the moderators.

At their meeting on October 29, the directing bodies of the Council — the Council of Presidents and the CC — authorized the vote on the five questions about the episcopate and the diaconate. But the seventeen cardinals and the six bishops of the General Secretariat who were present

---

[150] Ibid., 107. The complete text of this memorandum of October 28, 1963, is printed as an appendix to Grootaers's article, 107-9.

[151] Ibid., 108. The Twenty-two also proposed that through free discussion the episcopal conferences should work up the questions to be submitted to the assembly; in this way the debates would be decentralized and the number of general congregations could be reduced. They also suggested varying the kinds of interventions in the hall: those aimed at clarifying the fundamental data of the question under study; those making known the judgment of a group of fathers; those, finally, having to do with particular points (it would be enough if these last were submitted in writing and briefly called to the attention of the fathers). Another anonymous document from this period suggested reducing the number of general congregations to one or two a week, in order to give the fathers time to study the questions for discussion. According to this note, the time of the assemblies should be limited to hearing (1) the reporters from the commissions, who would explain how the amendments proposed by the fathers had been studied; (2) the fathers whose views differed from those of the commission; (3) the fathers who wanted to ask for an explanation or the solution of a difficulty ("Observationes circa Ordinem Concilii Vaticano II celebrandi," Moeller Archive, 2893). In a critical summary of the proposals for altering the Regulations (see below), G. Dossetti, an expert for Cardinal Lercaro, cited notes handed in by four bishops or experts.

also heard Cardinal Frings, a member of the Council of Presidents, explain the proposals aimed at accelerating the pace of the Council.[152] He asked that the general congregations be prepared and organized; that the moderators divide the chapters of the schemas to be discussed into a few main points; that the speeches be classified according to these points, while also taking into account the position pro or con taken by the interveners; and that the platform be given only to speakers more representative of the two tendencies. Immediately after the debate on a point there should be a provisional vote, and the competent commission could then immediately begin to prepare the amendments on this point. Furthermore, given the vast amount of work required of the moderators, the General Secretariat, and the commissions, the congregations should be reduced to three or at most four a week.

This rhythm and reorganization of the work would, Frings hoped, reawaken the interest of the fathers and of everyone else present, all of whom were tired of having to listen to speeches that followed no order. In concluding, the German cardinal thought it indispensable that the present period of the Council should end with the adoption of at least one constitution, or even two — those on the liturgy and on the Church. He also suggested asking the pope to reduce the number of schemas from seventeen to five or six, since, for all kinds of reasons,[153] there should be no thought of prolonging the Council beyond a third period.

Frings's proposals were then the subject of an exchange of views during which the desire to accelerate the debates found acceptance, but with two different ideas about how to achieve this. For one, the only solution was to limit the right of Council fathers to speak; the other defended the current Regulations[154] and opposed Frings's proposals. This second group included Suenens and above all Cicognani, the latter especially with regard to reducing the frequency of the general congregations, since, he said, the pope, on the contrary, wanted to increase their number.[155] Frings's proposals for the reform of the debates were not accepted.

---

[152] Text of the explanation: *AS* V/2, 17-18; minutes of the meeting: ibid., 14-17.

[153] He cited "the needs of diocesan government, economic and psychological reasons."

[154] Agagianian: the fathers should speak according to the order of their requests (according to Article 57 §1); Suenens and Felici: the possibility that the fathers could express their views at meetings of the commissions (according to Article 65 §4).

[155] *AS* V/2, 16.

We may ask, however, whether in regard to the two points with which he ended his presentation, Frings was reflecting the pope's position or instead was trying to influence it. With regard to the adoption of one or two texts by the end of the present period, we know that five days earlier Paul VI had sent the president of the Doctrinal Commission a handwritten *monitum* in which he stressed what a serious matter it would be if the period ended without the Council having taken a stance on some of the principal deliberations about the schema on the Church.[156] As for the reduction in the number of schemas, we can see in the background of Frings's proposals the future Döpfner Plan; the two German cardinals must have taken counsel together on this matter,[157] but were they at this stage the sole initiators of the idea that the pope was to make his own publicly at the end of the period?

Thus, at the end of October a whole series of questions had already been raised about the progress of the Council. We have still to add questions about the functioning of the commissions. It was, however, characteristic that anxiety focused on the weariness of the fathers and that those who offered suggestions saw the remedy in better organization of the debates, while hoping that the moderators would manage to get the Council out of its rut. G. Dossetti, Cardinal Lercaro's expert, did not see the situation in that way. The team from Bologna, which during the previous summer had played an important role in the revision of the rules for the Council,[158] was concerned primarily with seeing to it that the work of the Council advanced along the line that had emerged during the first period. This team had played a decisive role in bringing about the establishment of the group of moderators, an action which, in its eyes, was to give the Council an effective and efficacious direction.

In a note of October 28 on the then numerous proposals for changing the Council Regulations, G. Dossetti took up the question of the general congregations.[159] He showed that the fault criticized by many, namely, the excessive number of interventions in the hall, did not correspond to the facts. If the discussion on chapter III of the schema on the Church lasted seven days when three would have been enough, the fault lay in

---

[156] *Monitum* of October 24, 1963, in *AS* V/2, 12-13.

[157] It was doubtless no accident that Döpfner abstained from speaking at the meeting of October 29 on Frings's proposals.

[158] See Alberigo, "Dinamiche," 115-64. At the end of October, Dossetti retired from his job as secretary to the group of moderators. In 1964 he became an official expert of the Council.

[159] "Proposte di modifiche all'ordo Concilii," a note of 6 pp., at ISR, Dossetti Archive, II/127.

the confusion about the respective competencies of the bodies in charge. Moreover, the moderators had made successful use of Article 57 §6 of the Regulations, which allowed them to propose the ending of debate, except in particular for still allowing three fathers on the "minority side" (that is, opposed to cloture of the debate) to speak, if necessary. Let the moderators continue to use this regulation prudently, and that would be enough. Dossetti then gave seven objections to a limitation on interventions by applying procedures not foreseen in the Regulations but called for by some.

Dossetti found the "main reason for the slow pace of the Council's work" in the persistence of serious defects in the structure of the directive bodies and of the commissions. A striking example: it took fifteen days for these bodies to decide whether the straw vote on the episcopate and diaconate, which the moderators had approved, was to be submitted to the assembly.[160] Dossetti did not ask for a change in the Regulations, because, he wrote, it was not appropriate to change the rules every month. He made it clear in his note, which was obviously intended for Lercaro and through him for the other moderators, that it was the direction of the Council that needed to be consolidated if it was to be effective.

But at the beginning of November, during the debate on the schema on the bishops, there was a minority movement which claimed that the five questions adopted by a very large majority on October 30 were invalid. This amounted to saying that the moderators had exceeded their competence, which this group thought was strictly limited to directing the debates in the hall, without any authority over the work of the commissions, which alone were to be considered qualified to place questions before the assembly. In the face of such a challenge, which was in a quite different way complicated by the attack on the methods of the Holy Office, and this at a time when he was convinced of the need to accelerate the work, the pope alone could take measures to resolve the crisis.

B. The Doctrinal Commission at the Center of the Disputes

At the institutional level the main issue was the running of the Council; the moderators were opposed to the position of the Secretary of

---

[160] In fact, the decision to submit the vote to the assembly was taken on October 29, the day after Dossetti's note.

State, who was president of the CC and had more daily contact with the pope, and that of the Secretary General of the Council, who wanted to control the work.[161] But in their concern to shorten the Council, Cicognani and Felici did not appreciate the work of the commissions, judging it ineffective. We know that this work had advanced only with difficulty during the intersession, due in large measure to the fact that these bodies remained dependent on direction by the Curia and wanted to win acceptance for the schemas prepared before the beginning of the Council.[162] The revision of the Regulations during the summer of 1963 had concerned primarily the conciliar commissions; through limitations placed on the discretionary power of their presidents, the commissions had been made more flexible in their interrelationships (possibility of mixed commissions) and brought into greater conformity with the directions taken by the majority in the assembly.[163] But the powers of the commissions still remained too extensive: they could put an end to inconclusive debates, make choices involving the life of the Church, and even eliminate essential problems by not keeping certain amendments requested by the fathers.

The experience of October 1963, a month devoted entirely to the debate on the Church, was not decisive as far as the work of the Doctrinal Commission, put on display at that time, was concerned. The leaders of that commission did not accept the renewal in ecclesiology on which the first two chapters of the new De ecclesia were based. They used procedural means to slow the progress of the work. The "obstructionism"[164] of the commission was undoubtedly the main reason for the wave of petitions that poured in during the second half of October. The multiplication of votes on the liturgical schema is another reason.

---

[161] In his Bilan de la deuxième session, 217, R. Laurentin summed up this situation thus: "The three bodies combined (council of presidents, Coordinating Commission, Secretariat) tended, by a kind of inherent determinism, to paralyze the initiatives of the moderators and to restrict the latter to the most limited prerogatives." This was a substantially accurate point of view, but needs to be qualified in at least two respects: the Council of Presidents did not always take the side of the CC (see the attitude of Cardinal Tisserant, president of the former group, at the meeting of the guiding bodies on October 29, 1963); and, while the term determinism rightly stresses the sociological mechanism at work in the functioning of every institution with several heads, it neglects two other dimensions: the complex interplay both of theological choices and of objective alliances that could, as we shall see, move in other directions.

[162] See History, 2:489-92.

[163] Alberigo, "Dinamiche," 145.

[164] Term used by Dossetti in a memorandum composed, probably on October 30, 1963, in view of an audience of Lercaro with Paul VI (ISR, Dossetti Archive, III/277c).

On the 14th, the presidents of all the episcopal conferences of Africa and Madagascar asked the Council of Presidents and the moderators to proceed to a new election that would revitalize the members of the commissions.[165] A week later, four archbishops from French-speaking Africa and nine archbishops and bishops of English-speaking Africa separately addressed more detailed and urgent petitions,[166] the former to the same addressees (Council of Presidents and moderators), the latter to the pope. In addition to revitalizing the members of the commissions, they asked that the presidents of these no longer be the prefects of the congregations; that the vice-presidents and secretaries be elected by the members; that new experts be called upon to help; and that the commissions meet "regularly and frequently."

In their already cited memorandum of October 28 the delegates of the episcopal conferences of various regions formulated requests concerning the commissions that were very close, even in their language, to those of the African bishops. It seems clear that the two parties consulted with each other with regard to replacing the commission presidents, the revitalizing of the membership, the election of vice-presidents and secretaries, the possibility of having some fathers intervening at the meetings, and the need for "regular and frequent" meetings.[167] But two points were added by the Conference of Twenty-two: that the commissions should do their work "with greater methodical strictness and effectiveness... with the aid of a better equipped secretariat and a more equitable division of tasks," and that they be placed "under the more direct authority of the moderators."[168]

---

[165] Petition in ISR, Lercaro Archive, XXIII/527d. During the preceding days, several African bishops or episcopates had given written support to Lercaro's *votum*, asking that the fathers who had made constructive suggestions in the debate on the Church should play a part in the work of the Doctrinal Commission (thirty individual or collective pages from Rwanda-Borundi, Congo-Zaire, and elsewhere, in ISR, Lercaro Archive, XXIII/524)

[166] The originals of the two documents, of which only the first is dated (October 22, 1963), are in ISR, Lercaro Archive, XXIII/521 and XXIII/540. Both say that the request "reflects the concerns of all the bishops of Africa and Madagascar." The signers of the first were the "presidents of the episcopal conferences or group of episcopal conferences" (B. Gantin, F. Scalais, J. Wolff, and J. Zoa). On October 25, seven French-speaking bishops of Africa sent the pope a request that was almost identical with the other two (ISR, Lercaro Archive, XXIII/541). It is possible that other documents of the same kind have been preserved, for example, in the papers of the other moderators.

[167] See the memorandum published in an appendix to Grootaers's article, "Une forme de concertation épiscopale," 109. The two secretaries of the two wings, French-speaking and English-speaking, of the Pan-African assembly of bishops, namely, J. Zoa and J. Blomjous, represented Africa at the meetings of the Twenty-two.

[168] Ibid.

The pope had thought it would be enough to issue the president of the Doctrinal Commission a call to order on October 24. But Ottaviani's reaction at the meeting of his commission on October 28 hardly augured well for a noticeable improvement,[169] and the proposal of Frings at the meeting of the guiding bodies on October 29, which did not even touch on the reform of the commissions, had been amicably set aside.

In view of a papal audience for Lercaro, Dossetti drew up on October 30 a memorandum that synthesized the petitions sent in on the previous days.[170] He thought it opportune to emphasize to Paul VI that the requests of the African episcopate were symptomatic of "an increasingly widespread sense of urgency." The revitalizing of the commissions had become the "crucial problem" that the expert from Bologna thought would have to be dealt with during the coming period of the Council, but an improvement in their functioning could be achieved immediately by using the possibilities of the Regulations, which provided for interventions at commission meetings by fathers who have important theses or amendments to assert. Now that the delegates of the episcopal conferences had submitted their memorandum, Dossetti added, the movement was spreading. He stressed the point that the solid favorable vote that very day on the five questions was also intended as the Council's vote of confidence in the moderators and a demonstration against the "obstructionism" of the CC and the Doctrinal Commission during the preceding two weeks.

During the first days after All Saints' Day, in face of the offensive aimed at obviating the effect of the success gained in the hall on October 30 and of the contrasting call for a reform of the Curia,[171] the pope did not think he should specify the extent of the moderators' powers; on the contrary, he seemed to be distancing himself from them.[172] The press

---

[169] As I noted in the previous section, at that moment Ottaviani tendentiously asked whether the commission ought to meet every day, including Saturdays. The answer was no, because the members wanted Saturdays free. It was, in fact, decided to hold meetings on the other five days of the week.

[170] The document is in ISR, Dossetti Archive, III/277c; two copies in the Lercaro Archive, XXIII/558.

[171] To which must be added the prospect, to which Paul VI himself alluded in his address to the Curia on September 21, of an association of some bishops with the pope in responsibility for the government of the Church.

[172] After a conversation with Suenens, Ch. Moeller noted in his journal for November 19: "He confirmed the fact that since All Saints the pope had been somewhat distant from the moderators of the Suenens-type" (Moeller Archive, carnet XVII). "Suenens-type" meant marked by prestige, effectiveness — and individual rather than collegial action. This may explain the greater prominence of Lercaro and then of Döpfner beginning in November 1963.

began to echo the serious difficulties that had appeared in the management of the Council.[173] In particular, the memorandum of the Twenty-
two was then beginning to become known.[174]

It was in this setting that a new and extremely sharp attack on the Doctrinal Commission was launched, coinciding with the challenge to the
Holy Office in the hall (November 8). The attack came in a memorandum
of apparently Chilean origin and meant for the pope.[175] The text began on
a solemn note: "We take the liberty of setting before Your Holiness a
question which, it seems to us and to a very large majority at the Council, must decide the success or failure of the Second Council of the Vatican." The text then pointed out that the previous work of the Doctrinal
Commission "has not led to any positive result." It was especially critical of the position of Ottaviani, president of the commission. His skills, it
said, are those of a canonist; nothing had prepared him to understand
either contemporary thought or the positions of the other Christian
Churches; his poor health makes him very dependent on his entourage,
which is "not necessarily attuned to the Council;" on collegiality and the
diaconate he has taken a position opposed to the text approved by his
own commission. "Allow us to say even that an increasingly large number of fathers think that if he were able to, the president of the Theological Commission would suppress the Council."[176]

After pointing out that several other commissions were running into
difficulties that were hindering the Council's work, the authors of the

[173] It was the Italian press that raised the subject. On October 23 the *Corriere della
Sera* ran a lead article on the atmosphere of tension at the Council, which had reached a
critical point. For the broader scene see Laurentin, 203-20. In an article entitled "Désir
accentué d'une intervention de Paul VI," Laurentin himself spoke "of present difficulties
in the Council," specifying that many questions "remained bogged down" and that "the
authority of the moderators is not sufficiently well established for them to able to act
effectively." As a result, "many bishops have for a long time, and increasingly, been
desirous of an intervention of the pope. This would be the only way of pulling through"
(*Le Figaro*, November 21, 1963, p. 10).

[174] Grootaers, (note 152, above), 90.

[175] A copy of this three-page, unsigned, and undated "Memorandum on the Conciliar
Commissions" is in the papers of Msgr. Philips, who added to it: "Manuscript: Chile"
(Philips Archive, P. 049.01). On the basis of internal criticism the document can be dated
to between November 9 and November 20. Note that on November 14, Chilean Cardinal
Silva Henriquez sent the pope a letter signed by 500 bishops; this was the best known
step taken to encourage the pope to reform the Curia and to associate the episcopate with
himself in the government of the Church (see especially Grootaers, "Une form de concertation," note 59). It is not surprising, then, that the memorandum was also of Chilean
origin.

[176] Ibid., 2. At the end of this passage the authors give it as their opinion that Cardinal
Ottaviani "no longer seems really qualified to preside over this commission."

document thought it "absolutely necessary that Your Holiness tell the Council to proceed to new elections for the conciliar commissions, before the end of this second session."[177] They thought it "likewise very important" that in each commission those newly elected should be able to choose their president, vice-president, and secretary. These measures were judged "an indispensable condition if the Council is to emerge from the impasses that threaten its success."[178]

C. REORGANIZE THE COMMISSIONS OR EXPAND THEM?

The most widespread view was that the commissions, and the Doctrinal Commission in particular, did not reflect the spirit and needs of the Council; the solid vote of October 30 on the five questions had showed that it was not representative of the majority of the fathers. In Dossetti's view, the "original sin" of Vatican II was the parallelism between the commissions and the Roman congregations;[179] never before in the history of councils had the presidents of the commissions been the heads of the dicasteries. As for how to reform the working of the commissions, the proposals set forth from mid-October on varied according to the degree in which their authors connected the problem with the very management of the Council (powers of the moderators over the commissions); made it a matter of individuals;[180] or connected the problem with broader issues, such as the duration of the Council, whether it should continue or not, or the creation of an episcopal senate and the reform of the Curia.

In addition, the petitions of the fathers, who had little appreciation of questions of procedure, spoke of "reorganizing," "renewing," "expanding," or "completing" the commissions, or even of "re-electing" their members. "Reorganizing" could imply a replacement of the leaders of the commissions and/or a redistribution of the competencies assigned to each of them.[181] "Renewing" could mean a complete replacing of the

---

[177] Ibid., 3.

[178] Ibid.

[179] In his "Proposte di modifiche."

[180] On November 14, Congar noted in his journal that the current idea was that "the Theological Commission will accomplish nothing with the president and secretary it now has" (*JCongar*, 368).

[181] The president of the Doctrinal Commission thought that all schemas should be submitted to his commission to the extent that they deal with doctrinal matters. Dossetti thought that there would then have to be as many commissions as there were major themes in the dogmatic constitutions ("Proposte di modifiche"). The report on the activ-

members.[182] The most frequent petitions called for increasing the number of members and replacing the presidents who belonged to the Curia; their clear intention was to get the commissions to act more effectively and more in harmony with the trends expressed by the majority of the assembly of fathers.

At the general congregation of November 8, Frings intervened not only to criticize the methods of the Roman Curia but also to assert, in connection with collegiality, that a commission could not pass a new judgment on a schema after the discussion in the hall but could only interpret the will of the fathers, since it was only an instrument of the general congregation.[183] To this Ottaviani gave a very sharp reply, saying in particular that the Doctrinal Commission was not bound by the vote of October 30 and that the five questions worked up by the moderators should have been submitted to that commission for study.[184] Shortly afterward, O. Rousseau, a Benedictine of Chevetogne, wrote that the incident had created "an atmosphere of very great discontent and even of anxiety." He added that the pope would undoubtedly be led to intervene, "either to guarantee the prestige of the moderators whom Cardinal Ottaviani had attacked or to give directives for the debate," since it was necessary "to get out of this oppressive situation."[185]

On the evening of November 15 a summit meeting of the directive authorities was held in the presence of the pope to assess the progress of the Council and to consider making some decisions to get the Council back on track.[186] The pope immediately gave the floor to Lercaro, who

ity of the Doctrinal Commission (seven printed pages), dated November 5 and distributed to the fathers on the 22nd, which was obviously intended to show the importance of the work already accomplished, showed the very broad range of competencies that the commission claimed for itself (CLG, Prignon Archive, 348).

[182] For example, in August 1963 Suenens insisted on the need to elect new commissions (interview given to the *Catholic Messenger*, U.S.A., cited by J. Grootaers, "Een sessie met gemengde gevoelens," *De Maand* 6 [1963], 599).

[183] Caprile III, 212.

[184] Ibid., 214-15.

[185] Article in the Belgian Catholic weekly *La Relève* for November 16, 1963, p. 13, cited by J. Grootaers, "L'opinion publique en Belgique et aux Pays-Bas face aux événements conciliaires de 1963 et 1964," in *Paolo VI e i problemi ecclesiologici al Concilio* (Brescia, 1989), 433.

[186] Minutes in *AS* V/2, 25-29. Since Cardinal Siri did not take part in the discussion, an indication that he was not present, there were twenty-eight at the meeting, nineteen of them cardinals. There were four items on the agenda: (1) report on the activity of the second period; (2) directives for a public session during the present period; (3) proposals for the work of the coming intersession; and (4) suggestions for the third period of the Council.

presented a report on the activity of the preceding weeks.[187] The Archbishop of Bologna made two points in particular about the functioning of the Council: the multiplicity of reports and votes on the liturgical schema was the result of excessive freedom of action granted to the competent commission; the slowness of the Council's work was due not to the debates at the general congregations but to the pace of the commissions' activity.

During the exchange of views that followed Lercaro's report, twelve cardinals and the Secretary General gave it as their opinion that, with regard to the future program of the Council, the subject matter still to be discussed had to be reduced, in one way or another, from the seventeen schemas planned at the beginning of 1963,[188] either by limiting their number or by trimming the content of some schemas. Thus one of the proposals along this line, the one made by Frings at the October 29 meeting of the directive bodies, was advancing, all the more so since the first one to opt for this way at the November 15 meeting was Cicognani, Secretary of State.[189]

Connected with the question of the program were two others: the fixing of the date for the third period and, more broadly, the duration of the Council. Of the seven cardinals who spoke on this subject, five thought that the Council should end after the completion of a third period.[190] One of them was Döpfner who also proposed a sizeable reduction in the number of schemas and to whom in the following month the pope was to entrust the working out of a plan for this reduction. At the end of the meeting, having heard all the opinions, the pope reached a decision on two points: the right time for a public session for promulgation, and the assurance that there would be a third period. On the other matters he said he wanted some time to think about them before deciding.[191]

---

[187] See *AS* V/2, 29-33. The report drew extensively on Dossetti's "Proposte" and on his memorandum at the end of October. For a detailed analysis of this report, see chapter II of the present volume.

[188] Three cardinals (Meyer, Alfrink, and Suenens) insisted that there be no neglecting of schema XVII on the Church in the world.

[189] He said that "rather than think of limiting discussion of the schemas, it is better to reduce the material in the schemas themselves" (*AS* V/2, 25).

[190] Alfrink specified that this third period should take place in 1965, in order to allow time to prepare properly for it. Meyer threw out an idea that, if we bear in mind Paul VI's hesitation until the first months of 1964, seems to have attracted him: "As for the duration of the Council, I do not think it opportune to prolong it beyond 1964, but without saying that the third session will necessarily be the last" (*AS* V/2, 28).

[191] A more penetrating analysis, which cannot be undertaken here, ought to be made of the positions taken and the silences observed at this November 15 meeting.

Thus the burning question of the functioning of the commissions was not tackled, except in Lercaro's report, and then only in passing.[192] Since the other questions — program of the third period, duration — will arise again later on, I limit myself here to what the directors of the Council were to decide about the commissions.

Paul VI very quickly decided on compromise measures: an increase in the number of commission members, "in order to accelerate the progress of the work and make it more efficient," and the election of a second vice-president and an assistant secretary. At its meeting on November 20 the CC decided on the measures to be taken for carrying out the pope's orders.[193] Here again, it wanted to act quickly. At the general congregation on the next day, Felici announced the steps taken, asking that the episcopal conferences hand in their lists of new candidates for the commissions by November 26.[194] Despite the short time limit, the assembly proved its effectiveness, especially by being able to draw up an international list of competent individuals, although there some procedural errors: incomplete lists; sometimes no indication of the commission for which the candidates were being proposed; repetition of names, both on the list of a given conference and on lists common to several conferences.[195]

---

[192] The day after the meeting some observers noted the lack of decisions, especially on the commissions: Moeller ("abandonment of the plan to re-elect the commissions": carnet XVII); Olivier (the pope "did not decide" about a renewal, because he judged a complete renewal to be neither "really possible nor opportune": "Chronique," 27); Dupont (from the November 15 meeting "nothing emerged....The pope did not dare to meet his responsibilities": notes on November 18, at CLG, Dupont Archive, 1728); Y. Congar (on November 18 J. Prignon told him the pope would not be "very favorable" to a reform of the commissions: *JCongar*, 374).

[193] Conclusions of the meeting, in *AS* V/2, 43-44: (1) four members were to be elected by the fathers and one appointed by the pope; (2) the election was to take place in the following week; (3) the episcopal conferences were to present four candidates for each commission; (4) the various episcopal conferences were invited to present joint candidates; (5) the members themselves were to elect an extra vice-president and an assistant secretary. Since the Commission for the Liturgy had completed its work, there was to be no election for it. The Commission for the Oriental Churches was to have only three new members, all of them to be elected. Since the Secretariat for Christian Unity had only eighteen members, it was to add twelve more, eight to be elected, four to be appointed.

[194] *AS* II/5, 635-36.

[195] Making use only of lists signed by the presidents of the episcopal conferences, the General Secretariat compiled the final list, which was distributed on November 27, along with the ballot papers. The list of proposed names formed a printed pamphlet of fifteen pages (see, e.g., in Moeller Archive, 2882), containing: (1) the list of 65 conferences from the five continents, with 67 names; (2) that of Switzerland (1 name); (3) Ireland (3 names); (4) Poland and Czechoslovakia (7 names); (5) Scotland (5 names); (6) China (10 names); (7) Korea (4 names); (8) Indonesia (38 names); (9) a single list for the Oriental Churches (18 names); (10) a list from the Ukrainian conference (3 names); (11) a list

The vote took place on November 28, and the forty-three newly elected were made known the next day.[196] No candidate was elected who was not on the international list. In relation to this list, the results brought only minor changes in the order of names, and this in seven of the ten commissions.[197] Among those elected were nineteen Europeans,[198] eight North Americans,[199] five bishops from Africa and Madagascar and from Latin America, four from Asia,[200] and two from Australia-New Guinea.

The pope completed the list by making twelve appointments, doing so only on January 8, 1964.[201] We may wonder about this delay. Did Paul want first to establish new norms for the Council's work? These norms, "to be studied" by the CC, were drawn up in his own hand on December 7, 1963.[202] They provided, in particular, strict rules for the experts but nothing for members of the commissions. But it is not impossible that at this time, when his dominant concern was to have the Council end quickly, the pope had tried to find a more effective way for the commissions to work before announcing the appointments that were his prerogative.

Contrary to the rules providing for enlarging the commissions, some of the latter did not wait for the pope's appointment of a supplementary member before moving to choose a second vice-president and an assistant secretary. For example, at the fourteenth plenary meeting of the Doctrinal Commission, on December 2, 1963, Msgr. Charue (Namur) was elected vice-president and G. Philips assistant secretary.[203]

---

from the conference of Latin bishops in the Arab countries (25 names); (12) a list from the Union of Superiors General (12 names). After having drawn up their own separate list, the Italians incorporated it into the international list, under the influence of the Conference of the Twenty-two (according to Laurentin, 174). But of the three Italians on the international list, only one was elected (L. Borromeo, to the Commission for Religious).

[196] There were 2227 ballot papers (9 of them invalid). The official list of results was published on January 11, 1964, in *OssRom*, after the pope had completed the list by adding his appointments. See Caprile III, 318-19.

[197] See Laurentin, 175-77.

[198] The two countries that came out first were Spain and Great Britain, with three elected, followed by Germany and France, with two each.

[199] Six from the United States, two from Canada.

[200] Among them the Maronite Archbishop of Beirut, I. Ziadé, for the Commission for the Oriental Churches.

[201] He appointed two Italians and one each for Germany, Belgium, United States, France, Great Britain (Scotland), Greece, Iraq, Kenya, Lebanon, and Mexico.

[202] *AS* V/2, 69.

[203] After the commission decided that an absolute majority was required, Msgr. Charue was elected on the second ballot by 12 votes out of 22 (Cardinal Santos received 5 votes, Msgr. Garrone 3, and Msgr. Florit 2), and G. Philips received 16 votes compared to 6 for Father Gagnebet (*JPrignon*, 488; notes taken at the meeting). Commenting on these choices in his diary, U. Betti remarked: "A hard knock for Father Tromp" ("Pagine di diario," *Lat-*

The "commission reform" operation was carried out in Roman fashion, that is, without removing anyone but by increasing the number of those involved. No consideration was given to the many requests for the replacement of the commission presidents and for a more effective influence by the assembly of fathers, in particular by way of the moderators, on the activities of the commissions. As "a half-measure,"[204] "a compromise solution,"[205] the affair left a large number dissatisfied. Laurentin's summation was moderate: "It remains to be seen whether this will be enough."[206]

III. A SUBDUED ENDING OF THE PERIOD

The month of November 1963 was a dangerous time for the fate of the Second Vatican Council. Problems raised by the organization of the Council were crisscrossed by questions regarding individuals and by the challenge to the curial system. One of the solutions considered by the majority current, especially in the Conference of the Twenty-two, was to support the idea of a representative episcopal council that would assist the pope. For the time being, Paul VI did not accept this request. On the other hand, the reform of the commissions was a timid affair. Meanwhile, although the assembly of fathers had taken up a much awaited subject, ecumenism, it continued to operate daily with the method of simply juxtaposed speeches, a method that made it impossible to take up the chapters on the Jews and on religious freedom.

Was the second conciliar period going to end in disillusionment and in uncertainty about the future? There was no lack of manifestations of both feelings at the time. There were some actions, however, that were enough to counteract a negative impression and to enable the fathers to depart without being completely disappointed. Among these, in addition to the untroubled revival of the draft text on the Church in the world,

---

eranum 61 [1995], 578). Philips, for his part, noted that the minority had not trusted him, and he added: "They prefer a fight; too bad" (CCV, Philips Archive, carnet XII, 4).

[204] H. Fesquet observed on November 23: "Like all half-measures, this will satisfy no one, but will give everyone the impression he has been partially understood" (*Le Monde*, November 23, 1963, p. 16).

[205] B. Olivier noted: "Here, then, is the result of the many petitions for a reform of the commissions! By and large, there is disappointment....The pope has thus chosen a compromise solution that will bring hardly any change" (Olivier Archive, 169; Chronicle of the second session, 28).

[206] Laurentin, 220. See also Grootaers, "Une forme de concertation," 99.

there was the adoption of the Constitution on the Sacred Liturgy, the pope's restoration of episcopal faculties, the grand ceremony commemorating the Council of Trent, and the announcement of the papal pilgrimage to the Holy Land.

A. Some Situations at the End of the Period

In August 1963 study of the schema on the Church in the world had been excluded from the agenda for the second period.[207] This need not, in principle, have prevented the mixed commission (composed of members of the Doctrinal Commission and the Commission for the Lay Apostolate) from emending the text, if those responsible had at least been willing to submit to the Council a text on this theme, which was so widely acknowledged as important. But there were two undeniable difficulties: Who was responsible for the text? Which basic text was to be chosen? At the end of May the mixed commission had, with many reservations, accepted a first text of about sixty pages, but at the beginning of July the CC decided to entrust the preparation of a new document to Suenens, reporter on the first text, which he judged inadequate; this new document was to be given to the competent commission for study. The result was the so-called "Malines text," which had been composed by a small international team that had gathered at Malines in September.[208] From this point on, then, there were two texts, each composed under the responsibility of a different authority. This situation, which was to say the least uncomfortable, was due to the failure to communicate to the mixed commission the decision made in July and to the lack of agreement between Suenens and the mixed commission, which saw its work being completely ignored.[209]

These circumstances by and large explain the fact that there was no movement until November 9, 1963.[210] On that day the moderators, who

[207] G. Turbanti, "La commissione mista per lo schema XVII-XIII," in *Commissions*, 228.

[208] On the prehistory of this schema during the first intersession, see J. Grootaers in *History*, 2:412-26.

[209] Ibid., 426-29.

[210] In October, however, a "high-ranking person" did intervene with the pope, asking that the mixed commission resume its work. On this subject and, more generally, on the subject of the Church in the world during the second conciliar period, G. Turbanti gives a detailed analysis in *La chiesa nel mondo*, a doctoral dissertation, University of Turin, 1996/97, chap. 5.

now knew that there would be a third conciliar period, decided to ask the Commission for the Lay Apostolate to intensify its preparation of schema XVII, on the Church in the modern world.[211] Cardinal Cento, president of that commission, by taking the initiative and asking the leaders of the Doctrinal Commission to resume the meetings of the mixed commission, made possible the start of the decisive process that would lead to the constitution *Gaudium et spes*. Initially set for November 26, the first meeting was actually held on the 29th, a day when Suenens was in Florence to give a lecture scheduled long before![212]

It was necessary, therefore, to study two texts, the draft from May and the Malines schema, the latter being in fact only a doctrinal exposition, which, in Suenens's thinking, was to be completed by concrete applications in the form of Instructions not submitted to the Council. During the meeting, the responses, especially that of Msgr. Garrone, focused on this distinction between a doctrinal section and a pastoral section; the Council should concern itself with responding to the concrete needs of people and to the problems of modern society.[213] This was a challenge to the Malines schema, but G. Philips and K. Rahner emphasized the point that a council should give a doctrinal basis for the role of the Church and Christians in the world. Behind the critique of the Malines schema there was another consideration: Suenens had played too great a part in the management of the schema, and this stirred distrust.[214]

Despite the interventions of Cento, who wanted to have the Malines schema accepted as the basis of the work, as well as of Charue and König, who asked that Suenens's point of view be heard, it became rather clear that the mixed commission meant to resume the initiative in preparing the schema. The texts of May and September were regarded as bases for a schema that would have to be rewritten. As for the concrete questions that Suenens wanted to see treated in the form of nonconciliar Instructions, it was accepted as a principle that these be composed as

[211] Turbanti, "La commissione mista," 229. For the development of this schema readers are referred to the work of A. Glorieux (secretary of the Commission for the Lay Apostolate), *Historia praesertim Sessionum schematis XVII seu XIII De Ecclesia in mundo huius temporis* (mimeographed, 122 pp., composed around 1966; copy at the ISR, Bologna). On the meeting of November 29, 1963, see 33-39. See also Ph. Delhaye, "Histoire des textes de la constitution pastorale," in *L'Eglise dans le monde de ce temps*, Unam Sanctam 65 (Paris, 1967) 1:227-28.

[212] See the text of the lecture, which was composed by Dossetti, at the ISR, Dossetti Archive, II/214a.

[213] Turbanti, "La commissione mista," and *JCongar*, 396.

[214] Turbanti, "La commissione mista," 230, and *JCongar*, 396.

"annexes," but without deciding on the problem of their relationship with the doctrinal part of the schema or on the question of whether these "annexes" would be true conciliar documents and submitted to the fathers for discussion.

In regard to procedure, the mixed commission accepted the proposal of Canadian Bishop G. Pelletier that a central subcommission be set up to coordinate the work of the individual subcommissions, which, established in May 1963, had been reconstituted, five in number, at the suggestion of Cardinal Browne; a central subcommission would ensure the overall preparation of a completely new schema.[215]

At its first meeting, held immediately after the plenary session on November 29, the central subcommission chose its experts. Some preference was given to those who had composed the schema at the beginning of 1963; Karl Rahner was not kept, but Pietro Pavan, principal editor of *Pacem in terris* and a strong advocate of attention to the problems of the world, was retained.[216] Bernhard Häring was an entirely new participant. With the new organization in place and with the decision having been made to compose an entirely new text,[217] it was clear that now, at the end of the second period, the development of a document on the Church in the modern world was entering an entirely new phase that would be controlled by the influence of a French theology concerned especially to take as its starting point questions raised by the contemporary world.[218]

---

[215] The central subcommission consisted of six elected members: three from the Doctrinal Commission (Ancel, McGrath, and Schröffer) and three from the Commission on the Lay Apostolate (Hengsbach, Ménager, and Guano). It chose E. Guano as its president and at the beginning selected ten experts: Pavan, Hirschmann, Tucci, Häring, Sigmond, Moeller, Philips, de Riedmatten, Congar, and Daniélou. Perhaps because Häring had offered a solution reconciling the positions of Rahner-Philips and Garrone, he was chosen secretary, while R. Sigmond became assistant secretary. In addition, A. Glorieux was invited to join the central subcommission. The five special subcommissions, each having five to seven fathers, dealt with (1) the human person in society; (2) marriage and family; (3) culture; (4) the economic order and social justice; and (5) the community of nations and peace.

[216] During the plenary session; see Glorieux, *Historia*, 37-37. Pavan was the first expert chosen for the subcommission. It seems that at that point he was offered the position of secretary but refused it.

[217] The central subcommission intended to operate as a limited working group and, at its meeting on November 29, decided to poll bishops from various regions of the world, as well as Father Lebret, and some lay people.

[218] This was true even though, by authorization from Cardinal Cento, the central subcommission, whose members were almost all Europeans, expanded its makeup at the first session by electing two non-European members, J. Blomjous (for Africa) and J. Wright (for the United States).

At the second meeting, on December 4, Glorieux and Sigmond were assigned the task of organizing the work. At the meeting on December 30, Sigmond was given the responsibility of composing the new text, which he did in January 1964, along with Häring and Tucci and probably with the help of Belgian Dominican L. Dingemans. This text, entitled "The Active Participation of the Church in the Building of the World," was to be studied by the central subcommission at its meeting in Zurich in February.[219]

While the preparation of a schema on the Church in the world got back on course during the final days of the second period, the discussion of the schema on the lay apostolate, originally on the agenda for this period, did not take place. As a result of the movement of lay revival and of the organization of the laity, first in Catholic Action and then on the occasion of the two world congresses held in the 1950s, and as a result also of the express wish of John XXIII that the status of the laity be part of the conciliar program, there was, of course, great expectation in the Catholic world regarding this question. Between January and March 1963 an important revision of the preparatory schema on the laity had been accomplished by the relevant commission.[220] A document of forty-eight pages, dealing first with the lay apostolate in general and then with particular aspects, had then been sent to the bishops for their opinion; the bishops were free to consult lay people, a freedom all the more useful in that there was no lay person on the commission, even though there had been unobtrusive consultations with lay people in Rome in February.

In addition, the CC had asked at the beginning of July that the Commission for the Lay Apostolate suggest points intended for the revision of the Code of Canon Law and for an Instruction on the apostolic formation of the laity.[221]

By the beginning of September the commission had received only a limited number of episcopal responses to the schema.[222] Initially, Cento

[219] See Glorieux, *Historia*, 40-41, and Turbanti, "La commissione mista," 231-32. It is to be noted that during December small working groups gathered in Germany, France, and Brazil.

[220] See Grootaers, *History*, 2:435-46.

[221] On July 10 four experts of the commission (Klostermann, Papali, Sabattini, and Tucci) prepared "some points" for the revision of the code (ten pages, in Prignon Archive, 155), and the secretary, Glorieux, informed the members and experts that the commission would meet right after the beginning of the second period or during its early days in case the replies of the bishops required a reworking of the schema (circular of July 10, 1963; ibid.).

[222] Circular from Glorieux dated September 4, 1963 (Prignon Archive, 156). On September 17 there had been forty-two replies from individuals, along with replies from two national episcopal conferences, three regional conferences, and two groups of African bishops; in all, there were replies from fewer than 300 bishops (Prignon Archive, 159).

thought that there was no reason for the commission to meet before the beginning of the second period;[223] but later he changed his mind. A first meeting, originally set for September 21, was held two days later to hear the remarks and amendments of the bishops.[224] A second meeting, which undoubtedly concerned itself with the two appended documents on points for the code and for apostolic formation, was held on October 3,[225] after which the activity of the commission seems to have broken off.

In any case, the schema had not been revised when, on November 20, Glorieux, encouraged by Cento, wrote to Lercaro, and perhaps also to the other three moderators, to express the intense concerns of the members of the commission: Will our schema, which is responding to a strong expectation among the faithful as a whole, soon be presented and discussed at the Council?[226] If it is not, Glorieux pointed out emphatically, "this will cause deep disappointment among the laity" and "will result in serious difficulty for the future work of the commission," since the small number of members does not permit a serious revision. How, then, is this revision to be directed during the intersession if we do not know, from at least two or three days of debate, the general opinion of the conciliar assembly?

This intervention was not successful in unblocking the situation. The commission had to be content — and this as a result of steps taken by Cento[227] — with having a brief report given to the fathers by Msgr. Hengsbach, a member of the commission, on December 2 at the final general congregation of this period.[228] The Bishop of Essen brought the assembly up to date on the genesis and state of the schema and asked that the fathers let their remarks be known as soon as possible (by January 15) for the purpose of making the schema clearer, simpler, and more coherent.

---

[223] Circular from Glorieux, September 4, 1963.

[224] Circulars from Glorieux, September 12 and September 17 (Prignon Archive, 157 and 158). To the first of these Glorieux appended the "first outline" of an "Instructio de laicorum formatione ad apostolatum" (5 pp.; ibid.). The responses of the fathers were favorable on the whole, any criticisms being directed at the length and sometimes verbose character of the draft ("Animadversiones et emendationes propositae a patribus concilii"; Prignon Archive, 159).

[225] According to the circular of September 28, 1963 (ibid., 510).

[226] Glorieux to Lercaro, November 20, 1963, with a memorandum dated the day before (ISR, Lercaro Archive, XV/253).

[227] Letter of November 27, 1963, to Cardinal Agagianian, AS V/2, 44-45.

[228] AS II/6, 367-71.

The next day the commission met in order to welcome the newly elected members and in order to settle the agenda for the intersession.[229] At this meeting Cento made known the directives given by Cicognani, who asked mainly that the schema on the laity be shortened and that the new text be ready by the end of March 1964. In order to save what the revised and shortened text would not be able to say, several members proposed that a directory be compiled, which would not be discussed at a general congregation. Glorieux pointed out the difficulties of scheduling during the intersession, due to the fact that the commission, or at least those of its members and experts who were involved with schema XIII, was henceforth dependent on the agenda of the Doctrinal Commission, to say nothing of the fact that the latter had still to revise the part of the schema on the Church that dealt with the laity and that the Commission for the Lay Apostolate would have to take into account.[230] After lengthy discussions, two dates were more or less set: January 15 was confirmed as the final day for receiving the observations of the fathers, and February 10 or 24 for the next meeting of the commission. Meanwhile, the experts present in Rome were to compose the revised and shortened schema.[231]

At the Council, the place of the laity in the Church was not solely, or even principally, the object of a text on their "apostolate," a text that was caught in a pincer movement between the text on the Church and the document on the Church in the world. Representative lay people had been consulted and some were being increasingly associated, unofficially, in the preparation of various conciliar schemas.[232] In this connection the dominant fact at the second period was the participation of thirteen lay auditors in the meetings of the Council; this had been decided on by Paul VI, who was used to collaboration with lay people, having himself been ecclesiastical assistant to the Italian Catholic University

[229] Report of this meeting in Prignon Archive, 751. The commission was of the opinion at this time that there was no need of choosing an extra vice-president (it already had two) and that an assistant secretary would be elected later on only if the work demanded one.

[230] It was decided that Cento should write to Cicognani proposing that the secretaries of the two commissions consult with each other on the schedule and that a mixed commission (lay apostolate and doctrinal) be once again started for working on the chapter on the laity in the schema on the Church.

[231] On December 6 Hengsbach submitted a proposal containing the norms to be followed in working up the new text (Prignon Archive, 760). He suggested a three-part plan: (1) vocation, obligation, and formation for the apostolate; (2) forms of the apostolate; (3) place of this apostolate in the Church's mission as a whole.

[232] On this collaboration during the first intersession see *History,* 2:440-43.

Association.[233] The group of auditors met regularly to study the subjects being debated at the Council. They had an acknowledged role as experts, which was exercised mainly in the Commission for the Lay Apostolate, but was expanded later on, especially with the arrival of women auditors in the third period.

The wish expressed by some fathers to hear the laity give their views in the Council hall was granted only in the very official setting of the addresses given on December 3, 1963, during the commemoration of the Council of Trent. On this occasion Jean Guitton testified to his ecumenical experience, and V. Veronese told the pope of the gratitude of the lay auditors.[234]

Around November 20 the lay auditors made public a joint declaration that was addressed primarily to the members of the international Catholic organizations that they represented, but also to "the laity who have placed their trust in us."[235] The document mentioned, first of all, the power of renewal at work in the assembly and the great variety of positions that found free expression but also the impatience of some at the slowness of the work. Referring then to the method of back-and-forth between assembly and commissions, it emphasized the place occupied in the commissions by a number of lay people, whose interventions were taken into account.

After paying tribute to the "courage" of the Council, which was not afraid to let its inquiries and disagreements be displayed to the observers from the other Churches, the document raised the question of the laity. The Council had raised this question "in its full extent" and was trying to give a place to the laity, whose participation in the life of the Church

---

[233] Initially ten in number, the auditors became thirteen in October 1963: S. Golzio, J. Guitton, M. de Habicht, E. Inglessis, J. Larnaud, R. Manzini, J. Norris, H. Rollet, R. Sugranyes de Franch, A. Vanistendael, J. Vazquez, V. Veronese, and F. Vito. Most of these belonged to the boards either of the standing Committee of the International Congresses for the Apostolate of the Laity (COPECIAL) or of the Conference of International Catholic Organizations (C.O.I.C.), which had conducted a number of studies on such subjects as social justice, education, freedom of scientific research, and the collaboration of the laity in pastoral activity. See especially the two articles of R. Goldie, "La participation des laïcs aux travaux du Concile Vatican II," *RSR* 62 (1988), 54-73, and "L'avant-Concile des *Christifideles laici* (1945-1959)," *RHE* 88 (1993), 131-72.

[234] French text of Guitton's address in *DC*, no. 1415 (January 5, 1964), 81-84. Commenting on the address, Congar noted in his diary: "A rather fine address, although too academic, too optimistic, and even too complacent about ecumenism. It is not very realistic. But I am glad that a layman has spoken at the Council and that he spoke of ecumenism. It is the first time and very important" (*JCongar*, December 3, 404). The text of Veronese's address is in Caprile III, 447.

[235] Text in *La Croix*, November 28-29, 1963, p. 8.

would be "gradually transformed." After welcoming the decree on liturgical reform, the auditors said: "As we can bear witness, the Council is
thinking of the world" and sees the signs of the times, a list of which
follows. Finally, the auditors mentioned their own regular meetings at
which they sought "the greatest possible unanimity" on problems that
affected them and on which they were being consulted; they mentioned
also the appointment of Italian bishop E. Guano, a member of the Commission for the Lay Apostolate, as official intermediary between their
group and the assembly. The entire statement was prudent and moderate,
emphasizing the positive aspects of this first experience of lay people at
a council, but witnessing also to the road that had already been traveled
for some decades now by an organized laity more conscious of its place
and mission in the Church.

During the discussion of the schema on the Church, a number of bishops noted that the Council was saying a great deal about bishops, deacons, and the laity, but practically nothing about priests. This was not
entirely correct. But since the four preparatory schemas dealing with
special and disciplinary questions regarding the clergy had been reduced
to one, which was approved by the CC on March 25, 1963, and since
this one schema did not come up for discussion during the second
period, it could be asked whether the conciliar authorities were aware of
the doctrinal and pastoral implications of the ministerial priesthood,
especially in the perspective of the Council's work. In this respect, the
plan for a message to priests during the second period marked a stage in
the development of outlooks, perhaps all the more so because the plan
was unsuccessful.

At their audience with the pope of November 7, the moderators were
assigned, among other things, the task of preparing such a message; it
was Suenens who solicited drafts from Msgr. Conway (Armagh), Msgr.
De Smedt (Bruges), and Msgr. Renard (Versailles).[236] At the meeting of
the moderators on November 19, Suenens presented a text composed by
Msgr. De Smedt.[237] But, oddly enough, Döpfner then offered to prepare
the document before it was printed, and the offer was accepted. Yet the
draft submitted to the Council fathers on November 29 was the text

---

[236] According to a conversation between Suenens and Prignon on November 10, 1963
(Prignon Archive, 512bis). Two points remain obscure: Did the initiative come from Paul
VI or from the moderators, with the subsequent approval of the pope? Did the other moderators give Suenens an explicit mandate to deal with the matter, or did he do it on his
own?

[237] AS V/3, 712. I was unable to find De Smedt's draft; that asked of W. Conway does
not seem to have seen the light of day.

asked of Msgr. Renard and prepared by some French bishops.[238] It was divided into three parts and emphasized the deep union of bishops with priests in the one priesthood of Christ, in one and the same mission, and in an identical path of holiness. The Council fathers were given twenty-four hours to introduce possible observations, so that the text might be officially approved on December 2, the last working day of the period. The observations were over sixty in number and came in even after the deadline. As a result, by decision of the moderators, Secretary General Felici announced on December 2 that the text would have to be revised and its publication put off to another time.[239]

In his address two days later, at the end of the period, Paul VI urged the bishops to send their priests "a message of fervor and love"; this was done, in particular, by the bishops of the apostolic region of Paris and by the bishops of Coutances (L. Guyot) and Livorno (E. Guano).[240] The idea of a message to priests was not taken up again later, due to the fact that, after receiving an order at the beginning of 1964 to reduce its schema to a few propositions, the Commission for the Clergy was authorized in October of that year, under pressure from the fathers, to work up a genuine schema on the life and ministry of priests.

B. FACULTIES ACKNOWLEDGED AS BELONGING TO THE BISHOPS

At the audience granted the moderators on November 7, the pope also asked that a list of faculties be drawn up which could be immediately acknowledged as belonging to the bishops and no longer as given to them for a certain period by the Bishop of Rome.[241] It is not possible to determine with certainty the real source of this initiative: the pope, the

---

[238] *AS* II/6, 306. The draft, in French, is found, among other places, in ISR, Lercaro Archive, XXXI/1097. The Cardinal of Bologna marked it: "Well done." To explain the abandonment of De Smedt's draft it has been suggested that he planned to refer to priests who had left the priesthood (according to his conversation with Prignon on November 10) and that this aspect of it was not approved by the moderators.

[239] *AS* II/6, 338. Laurentin alludes to a possible opposition of the Holy Office to some erroneous propositions (180). The French Dominican Féret thought the message was "somewhat paternalistic" (*JCongar*. November 19, 395).

[240] Paul VI: "Cannot you yourselves send your clergy a message of more ardent charity?" (*AS* II/6, 569). The message of the bishops of the Paris region repeated the substance of what the Council was asked to send to priests; it was published in the *Semaine religieuse de Versailles* for December 13, 1963, and reprinted in *DC*, no. 1416 (January 19, 1964), 153-56. For the messages of I. Guyot and E. Guano, see Caprile III, 399 n.4.

[241] Conversation of Suenens and Prignon on November 10, 1963 (*JPrignon*, 512bis).

Council, or the moderators themselves. The idea certainly arose against the background of the bishops' challenge to the course of the Council and was directly connected not only with the discussion then going on of the schema on bishops and the government of dioceses but also with the plan to associate the bishops with the government of the Church. Why was it necessary that a pontifical Motu Proprio anticipate the adoption of the schema?[242] Was it a question simply of granting some desires of the bishops, as the introduction to the document claims? Or was it a reflection of Paul VI's concern not to end the period without concrete results? Or, again, was it a way of preventing Rome from being overwhelmed by calls coming from the Council and of showing that the pope retained the initiative?

At their meeting on November 9 the moderators "suggested" creating a technical commission to prepare the papal document, and four names were put forward.[243] Was this commission actually set up? At the meeting of the directive bodies with the pope on November 15, Cicognani spoke on the need to reduce the material in the schemas and used the case of episcopal faculties, with which the Holy See was dealing, as an example of lightening the Council's work.[244] And, on the same occasion, Secretary General Felici declared: "The material is ready for publishing a pontifical document on the faculties of the bishops."[245] Was this a maneuver aimed at ruling out the suggestions of the moderators? Or, on perhaps a broader scale, was the intention to short-circuit properly conciliar activity?[246]

Whatever the answer, the Curia seemed fully prepared at this moment to meet the pope's wishes. The Motu Proprio *Pastorale munus* was

[242] In his notes (transcription of the conversation recorded on November 9), Prignon points out that this "acknowledgment" of powers was to precede the promulgation of the decree on the bishops. And, according to the published minutes of the moderators' meeting on November 9, it was "suggested" that before the end of the current period the pope should give the faculties listed in the schema on bishops (which were twenty-nine in number, along with four privileges) and others as well, if there was reason for doing so (*AS* V/3, 709).

[243] *AS* V/3, 709. The names: E. Cibardi, an assessor of the Congregation of the Consistory; C. Colombo, a Council expert (and, be it noted, an adviser of the pope); F. Antonelli, secretary of the Commission for the Liturgy; and C. Berutti, assistant secretary of the Commission for Bishops. Although on the following day Suenens told Prignon that the pope gave him the task of preparing the list of powers, there is nothing in the minutes of the moderators' meeting to suggest that this responsibility was given to the Belgian cardinal.

[244] *AS* V/2, 25.

[245] Ibid., 29.

[246] On November 14 Congar noted in his diary: "People in the Curia (Ottaviani, Browne, Staffa, Carli...) are doing everything to keep the episcopate from regaining the rights that have been stolen from it" (*Jcongar*, 14 November, 369).

signed on November 30 and read to the Council fathers at the — non-conciliar — ceremony on December 3 that commemorated the fourth centenary of the end of the Council of Trent.[247] Forty "powers" were listed as belonging by right to residential bishops and to others who were assimilated to them (vicars, prefects, apostolic administrators, abbots, and prelates *nullius*). To these were added eight "privileges" belonging to residential and titular bishops.[248]

Some commentators have focused on the way in which the powers were granted: was it a concession? an acknowledgment? a restitution? Previously, at the audience on November 7, Suenens supposedly insisted that the document not speak of a concession of powers but that the formula "granted by the law itself" (*ipso iure recognoscendi*) be used.[249] In fact, the introduction of the document begins by saying that historically the Holy See "has given powers," a statement that falsifies the perspective; it then shifts back and forth between "concession" and "belonging by law," without speaking of "acknowledgment," but in the title of the document "concession" alone is used: "Apostolic letter...by which faculties and certain privileges are granted to the bishops."[250] Did this represent a concern not to decide matters before the adoption of the schemas on the Church and on the bishops, or a difficulty in acknowledging longstanding mistakes as well as rights that do not emanate from the Roman See? In Congar's opinion, the pope was making a "concession" to the bishops "when in fact he was only restoring — and with ill grace — a part of what he had robbed from them for centuries!!!"[251]

---

[247] Official text: *AAS* 56 (1964), 5-12; in French, in *DC*, no. 1415 (January 5, 1964), 9-14.

[248] These powers that were granted or given back were generally of minor interest; for example, to allow priests to celebrate two masses on weekdays and three on Sundays; to grant the sons of non-Catholics a dispensation from the impediment to ordination that arose when their parents "persisted in their error"; to dispense from minor impediments to matrimony; to allow priests to erect stations of the cross; to permit religious men and women to transfer from one diocesan congregation to another; to authorize certain individuals to read and keep forbidden books.

[249] According to what Suenens said to Prignon on November 10.

[250] In his closing address on December 4 the pope spoke of "several faculties which...We have declared to belong to the office of bishops" (*AS* II/6, 566). But in the French translation based on the Latin text published in *OssRom* (December 5, 1963) this appears as a power that "We desired should be included in the competence of bishops" (*DC*, no. 1415 [January 5, 1964], 5), while in the French translation distributed to the experts before the papal address it speaks of "powers which We desired to declare to be part of the competence of bishops" (Thils Archive, 1762).

[251] *JCongar*, 405.

C. The Close of the Conciliar Period

I have already referred to the ceremony on December 3 to commemorate the fourth centenary of the end of the Council of Trent. This celebration, initially intended to be part of the next day's celebration, was a kind of interruption of the Council, of which it was not directly a part.[252] Some regretted this doubling of ceremonies at a time when so much work remained to be done.[253] In addition, as the absence of many non-Catholic observers from the celebration made clear, it was not a happy thought, right after the discussion of ecumenism, to highlight the sixteenth-century council that had hallowed the break between Catholicism and the Reformation.[254] After the mass celebrated by Secretary of State Cicognani, the morning of Tuesday, December 3, was divided into three parts. The Patriarch of Venice, Cardinal Urbani, gave an address in Latin that lasted a little over an hour, in which he described on a broad canvas the fruits of the Council of Trent and the lessons to be drawn from that council for Vatican II.[255] Next came the addresses of two laymen, J. Guitton and V. Veronese, of which I spoke earlier. Finally, Secretary General Felici read the Motu Proprio *Pastorale munus*, the text of which was distributed to the bishops.

Since October, Paul VI had been urging the Council to produce some concrete results by the end of the current period. He was thinking chiefly of the main schema, the schema on the Church. If it proved impossible to offer at least a part of this key document, it was important to attach the greatest solemnity to the promulgation of the two documents adopted during the preceding weeks: the Constitution on the Sacred Liturgy and the Decree on the Media. This act was the focus of the concluding public session on Wednesday, December 4.[256]

---

[252] The acts of this celebration are not included in the *Acta Synodalia*.

[253] Laurentin, 182-83.

[254] *La Croix*, December 4, 1963; and Wenger, 235.

[255] Summary of the address in Caprile III, 442-44; complete French translation in the Moeller Archive, 1891; Italian translation in *OssRom* for December 4, 1963.

[256] On this public session, see *AS* II/6, 405-70. All the published chronicles of the Council give more or less extensive accounts of it.

D. Two Documents Are Promulgated

The voting on the schema on the liturgy required eighty-five ballots taken from October 8 to November 22;[257] the voting on the Decree on the Means of Social Communication took place over two days (November 14 and 25).[258] We may ask why there was this multiplication of almost microscopic votes. In fact, it was not simply a matter of voting on amendments to each article,[259] but, in the case of the liturgy, of pushing subtlety to the point even of presenting the fathers, from November 18 on, with five booklets (158 pages in all) that contained reports on the evaluation of the final *modi*, so that they might vote on whether in each case the commission's examination of the *modi* had been correct.[260]

The weariness of the fathers had found expression especially on October 31, when they were to vote on seven points of detail having to do with art and sacred furnishings. When the moderator, Döpfner, proposed a single vote, the assembly responded with applause and stood up spontaneously to show its approval.[261] In his report to the summit meeting on November 15, Lercaro had put his finger on the important aspects of the problem. The Commission for the Liturgy, he said, was trying to win approval for the amendments it thought should be accepted while neglecting others of great importance instead of allowing the fathers the opportunity to choose.[262] In other words, it was always the excessive

---

[257] These included, first, the votes on the amendments introduced by the Commission for the Liturgy, those on chapter I of the schema ("Principles") had already been the subject of limited votes, then of two votes on the whole chapter at the end of the first conciliar period. Then, beginning on November 18, there were the votes on the final *modi*. On November 22 the vote on the entire schema yielded 2,158 favorable votes, 19 negative, and 1 void ballot. On these votes see Caprile III, 100-104, 140-45, 322-24; for a chart of all the votes see Laurentin, 306-11. For details, see Chapter III of the present volume.

[258] The vote on the schema as a whole: 1598 for, 503 against, and 11 invalid ballots.

[259] For the text on the liturgy this meant: (1) for chapter II (the Eucharist) 20 ballots (October 8-14); (2) for chapter III (sacraments and sacramentals), 11 ballots (October 15-18); (3) for chapter IV (Divine Office) 14 ballots (October 21-23); (4) for chapter V (liturgical year) 11 ballots (October 24-29); (5) for chapter VI (sacred music) 7 ballots (October 29-30); and (6) for chapter VII (art and furnishings) 8 ballots (October 31).

[260] Caprile III, 422.

[261] Ibid., 145. See also the letter addressed to the fathers on October 19 by seven members and six experts of the Commission for the Liturgy, in which they urgently begged the bishops to avoid as far as possible any *iuxta modum* votes on chapters 4 and following (still to be adopted) of the schema. Otherwise there was great danger of compromising the adoption of the schema as a whole and of not achieving the promulgation that the pope and the assembly desired (copy of the letter at the ISR, Bettazi Archive).

[262] *AS* V/2, 30.

power of the commissions that was the issue, with the corollary of their tendency by various maneuvers to postpone the adoption of texts or even to block them. It is thus that on November 9 the moderators had decided to order the Commission for the Liturgy to present the definitive text "as quickly as possible."[263]

Before the beginning of the second period two other questions had been raised: the precise scope of the conciliar documents, commonly called their "theological qualification"; and the formula the pope would use when the time came to promulgate the definitively approved documents, either by himself or acting collegially with the fathers. The first question, which was studied in October by a subcommission of the Doctrinal Commission, has been dealt with earlier in this volume. The point at issue was an important one. Aside from the criteria of theological interpretation the question was what was to be the significance of the positions taken by Vatican II. John XXIII had not wanted the Council to issue either dogmatic definitions or anathemas. But those who wanted to limit the importance of the conciliar decisions as much as possible interpreted John's choice as militating against any irreformable commitment.

Was it possible, then, to find a formula that would do justice to the fully coherent positions the Church was going to adopt at the Council? On November 29 the fathers were presented with an amended formula[264] that was not fully satisfactory.[265] While reading the text, the Secretary General showed that the principal distinction, namely, between doctrine and discipline, continued to prevail in dealing with a pastoral approach that included both terms; he stated, in fact, that the liturgical constitution and the decree on the media dealt "solely with

---

[263] *AS* V/3, 709.

[264] C. Colombo insisted on adding two points: (1) The manner of defining must take into account not only earlier councils but the *particular purpose* of the present council, *which is chiefly pastoral*; (2) what the Council did not explicitly define as *irreformable* (the final official text would say "as infallible") belonged simply to the authentic magisterium, thus establishing a clear distinction between two forms of teaching (ISR, Dossetti Archive II/142b and III/277c).

[265] *AS* II/6, 305. "Account being taken both of the custom of councils and of the special purpose of this council, which is chiefly pastoral, this Sacred Synod defines infallibly as to be held by the universal Church in matters of faith and morals only those points which the Synod itself clearly says are such. Therefore, other points of which the council does not clearly say this are not infallibly defined by it but are set forth by the authoritative teaching office as the doctrine of the Church. Therefore, should there be a definition of the faith, the fathers of the Council are forewarned and will be forewarned to use in the text expressions that make explicitly clear the intention of thus defining something."

disciplinary matters."[266] The question of the exact significance of the Council's choices was going to come up again later, without its being able to move beyond the classic juridical distinctions: faith — morals; definition — decree — canon; infallibility — authoritative magisterium.

Like the theological qualification of the Council's decisions, the question of the papal formula for the promulgation of documents had been submitted by the moderators to Paul VI as early as September 30. The formula envisaged in the conciliar Regulations was identical with one of those used at Vatican I: the pope gives his approval and alone promulgates.[267] But after the straw vote in favor of collegiality on October 30, it was difficult to maintain this idea. How, then, to express in a single formula the combined authority of the Council and the pope, on the assumption that the latter accepted the principle of collegiality? On November 7, Paul VI gave the moderators the responsibility of supplying him with such a formula, and two days later they discussed it at their meeting.[268] It seems, however, that a small group with Colombo and Dossetti as its nucleus, but with several other experts contributing, had already studied the matter.[269] In any case, exhaustive discussions of the formula were held during the first two weeks of November, a time when the "Colombo-Dossetti" formula already existed and when the pope had rejected a formula by which he alone would give sanction to the document that had been approved by vote.[270]

A historical note composed at this point explained that beginning with Lateran IV (1215) the pope promulgated documents with the *approval*

---

[266] On the other hand, when, on November 9, 1963, the moderators approved the formula brought in by the Doctrinal Commission, they admired the phrase on the pastoral nature of the Council but made it clear that this indicated only the spirit in which the texts would be promulgated (*AS* V/3, 709). The intention in this reservation was probably to ensure that the doctrinal character of the documents would not be underestimated.

[267] *Ordo* (1963 ed.), p. 43, Article 49 §2: "The decrees and canons just read were accepted by the fathers with no one dissenting (or, if some have perhaps dissented: with the exception of [the appropriate number]). We, with the approval of the sacred Council, decree, establish, and ordain them as read." The formula is the same in the first edition of the Council's rules (*Ordo Concilii*, 1962 ed., p. 41). On the formulas of Vatican I, see G. Alberigo, "Una cum patribus," in *Ecclesia a Spiritu Sancto edocta. Mélanges théologiques. Hommage à Mgr Gèrard Philips* (Gembloux, 1970), 292-94. In promulgating the two constitutions *Dei Filius* and *Pastor aeternus*, Pius IX replaced "decree, establish, and ordain" with "define and confirm."

[268] *AS* V/3, 708.

[269] Three documents from the Dossetti Archive attest to a thorough study of the formula to be proposed, but the documents are not dated. Among others who gave an opinion I have found Cerfaux, Jedin, Martimort, Mörsdorf, Philips, Prignon, Rahner, Thils, and Vagaggini. M. Maccarrone also made his contribution.

[270] Notes of the Prignon-Suenens conversation of November 10 (*JPrignon*, 512bis).

of the council, this approval having a strong sense.[271] It concluded that to replace this with "the pope, together with the council," as had been done at the Council of Florence (session IX, 1440), would be neither an innovation nor a substantial change. This note and another historical study by the Benedictine C. Vagaggini showed that formulas had in fact varied over time depending on historical, theological, and juridical factors, and that each formula had its value.[272] On the other hand, account had to be taken of the fact that Trent and Vatican I did not have the ecumenical concerns that this Council now had in 1963; from this point of view it was important that the conciliar documents be clearly shown to be collegial acts.

At the meeting of the moderators on November 9 two formulas were submitted.[273] One, the result of an exchange of ideas between Colombo and Dossetti, said, in substance, that, the decrees having been acceptable to the fathers, the pope *confirms* and orders them to be promulgated.[274] The other had been composed by the Munich canonist Klaus Mörsdorf and was introduced in slightly different form by Döpfner.[275] By saying that the pope was acting within the Council as its head and by replacing "we decree" and "we establish" with "we confirm," these two proposals departed from the formula contained in the Council Regulations, but they retained the clear distinction between the decision of the fathers and the action by which the pope alone gives his *consent* and/or *confirms* and finally promulgates what the assembly of bishops has voted.

At the November 9 meeting Lercaro approved the Döpfner-Mörsdorf text, while Secretary General Felici, followed by Agagianian, thought

---

[271] *Nota sulle formule conciliari*, November 6, 1963, 3pp., doubtless by Dossetti (in ISR, Lercaro Archive, XXIII/542). The first use of the formula "with the approval of the council" (*approbante concilio*) was, in fact, at Lateran III (1179). And, according to Alberigo's study "Una cum patribus," the formula served primarily to support an approval that the pope gave on his own authority.

[272] Dossetti summed up the point of view given in Vagaggini in his own text, *Documenti annessi alla nota sulla conferma pontificia* (Dossetti Archive, VII/531, annex 1, p. 2).

[273] *AS* V/3, 708.

[274] I do not have the text of this first formula. It can be inferred from what Dossetti later suggested (see below). Since Dossetti would then insist on removing the word "confirm," we may assume that it had been introduced at the request of Colombo.

[275] "The decrees and canons just read were accepted by the fathers with no one dissenting (or, if some have perhaps dissented: with the exception of [the appropriate number]). We give our assent and by the apostolic authority of the head of this sacred Council we confirm and ordain those things have been thus synodally decided, and we order their promulgation" (Dossetti Archive, II/138). The formula Döpfner proposed at the meeting was a little different: "...by the apostolic authority...we give our assent and we confirm those things that have been thus synodally decided" (Prignon Archive, 543).

that the idea of consent was not consonant with the pontifical authority: the pope should give his positive and personal approval to the Council's decisions, just as each father had done. And if there was a desire to replace the words "with the approval of the sacred Council" given in the Regulations, Felici proposed saying "together with the fathers of the Council we decree, establish, and ordain..." Along with this new formula, the one that would be retained, the retention of the three verbs made it possible to give full force to a pontifical approval that was thought of as a primatial act. Suenens, for his part, was content with proposing that the decision on the choice of formula be left to the pope himself.

In the days that followed some experts held discussions aimed at reaching a consensus. Suggestions made by K. Rahner, G. Thils, and C. Vagaggini had in common an open acceptance of collegiality; in the decision, pope and council were closely linked, and the juridical formula of promulgation (a heritage from a time when the authority of pope or council was challenged by institutions such as the universities) was entirely omitted.[276] In his memoirs H. Jedin speaks of his participation in a meeting on November 14 at Döpfner's residence during which Mörsdorf and Rahner could not reach agreement.[277] He was also present at the larger meeting the next day at the Camposanto, where the formula proposed by the experts was adopted.[278]

This formula read as follows: "In the name of the Most Holy and Undivided Trinity. We, Paul VI, by our apostolic authority as head of this sacred Council, give our full consent to the decree (or: decrees) which, just now read, commended themselves, without dissent (or: with [so many] dissenting) to the fathers of this sacred and universal Second Vatican Synod, legitimately gathered in the Holy Spirit, and We order

[276] Rahner: "We, Paul VI, and the bishops of the Church...decree, establish, and ordain"; Thils: "The Second Vatican Synod, legitimately gathered in the Holy Spirit, convoked by pope John XXIII, with Pope Paul VI presiding and confirming, has unanimously established and decreed"; Vagaggini: "Vatican II, with its head, the Roman Pontiff, and under his supreme authority, legitimately gathered in the Holy Spirit" (Dossetti Archive, VII/531 annex 2, pp. 1-2). See the explanation justifying Rahner's formula in Dossetti Archive, II/137. Thils's formula, with the justification for it, is in the Thils Archive, 347bis. Thils believed that the formula "We...with the approval of the Council...establish" should be avoided, because it does not take account of collegiality, is "anti-ecumenical in the highest degree," and is of rather recent origin (i.e., Lateran IV). In an appendix he gives the text of the formulas used at eight councils since Chalcedon.

[277] H. Jedin, *Lebensbericht,* ed. K. Repgen (Mainz, 1984), 213-14.

[278] Jedin mentions the presence of Colombo at this meeting (ibid.). We must add Dossetti, who wrote on the adopted text "Committee of Jedin, Rahner, Colombo, Mörsdorf" (Dossetti Archive, II/139). See also *JCongar,* 392.

the promulgation of the decrees thus issued by the synod."[279] On the one hand, then, the formula preserved the principle of pontifical consent, not confirmation, while abandoning the separate decision and sanction that Felici had tried to retain; on the other, it preserved the juridical act of promulgation. Since the pope as head of the Council was a member of it, he simply cast his indispensable vote by giving his consent, without having to confirm himself.[280]

At the meeting of the directive bodies in the presence of the pope on November 15, Döpfner asked the Holy Father to give his opinion on the formula chosen, and Paul VI answered that he was hoping to see developed a formula that was "more felicitous and more in keeping with the reality being celebrated,"[281] having in mind, no doubt, the formula provided in the Regulations. But it was not exactly the formula suggested by the experts that the pope used on December 4. In the printed booklet *Methodus servanda et preces recitandae* ("Procedure to Be Followed and Prayers to Be Said"), which the Secretariat of the Council prepared for this public session, the place for the text of the formula had been left blank (on p. 8). After the Secretary General had read part of the Constitution on the Sacred Liturgy, a yes or no vote was taken that yielded 2,147 votes in favor and 4 against.[282] Paul VI then uttered the following formula:

> In the name of the most holy and undivided Trinity, the Father and the Son and the Holy Spirit. The decrees just now read at this legitimately assembled sacred and universal Second Synod of the Vatican were acceptable to the fathers. We too, by the apostolic power (*potestas*) handed down to us from Christ, approve, decree, and establish them in the Holy Spirit, in

[279] Dossetti Archive, II/139. In Alberigo, "Una cum patribus," 299, this formula is set side by side with the formula provided in the Regulations, with that adopted by the pope on December 4, and finally, with that which would appear later in the official editions. The invocation noting the subordination of the entire ecclesial magisterium to the Trinity and to the "holy and universal synod lawfully gathered in the Holy Spirit" was taken from Thils's suggested formula, and in part also ("sacred council...legitimately gathered in the Holy Spirit") from Father Vagaggini.

[280] In his note "Sulla formula dell'approvazione finale nelle sessioni publiche," Dossetti opined that a papal confirmation was justifiable only if a council were held at a distance from the pope and without him presiding (Dossetti Archive, II/141). On November 14 Dossetti presented the new formula to Prignon, who approved the replacement of "we confirm" by "we consent," and he insisted that the fathers adopt "consent" rather than "assent," since the former more clearly suggested a collective act (*JPrignon*, 512bis).

[281] *AS* V/2, 27 and 29.

[282] Recall that the vote of November 22 on the schema as a whole had yielded 19 against.

union with the venerable fathers, and we order that what has thus been established in synodal fashion be promulgated to the glory of God.[283]

The mention of the individual persons of the Trinity gave the formula a more religious tone.[284] Mention of the number opposed to the decree had disappeared.[285] But the essential point, from the viewpoint of ecclesiology, was to be seen in the very carefully composed third sentence. On the one hand, the pope's "authority" (*auctoritas*) was replaced by "power" (*potestas*), and his full consent by three verbs pointing to the special character of this power received directly from Christ; on the other hand, the pope was no longer called head of the Council but said that he was acting in union with the fathers.[286]

The same procedure was followed for the Decree on the Means of Social Communication. To the very end, as we saw earlier, this had been strongly criticized. The vote taken on November 25 on the schema in its entirety had yielded 1598 votes for and 503 against.[287] On December 4 there were 1,960 votes in favor but still 164 against, by far the highest number of negative votes for any of the sixteen conciliar documents.

Specialists waited anxiously for the formula of promulgation used by Paul VI. Father Congar wrote: "I am relieved. The formula is a good one."[288] The principal commentators called attention to the novelty of "together with the fathers." Laurentin, for example, remarked that the text "makes clear that the Council is legislator together with the pope. A

---

[283] *AS* II/6, 407.

[284] The entire trinitarian formula was already in Thils's suggested formula. The second mention of the Holy Spirit was shifted from the Council to the action of the pope.

[285] It is quite unlikely that this almost liturgical manner of indicating unanimity was inspired by the manner of expression proper to the Oriental Churches. We should think rather of Paul VI's constant concern to achieve a real agreement among all the fathers on the documents adopted or to be adopted.

[286] On the eve of the public session, Congar noted that he had been told by Dossetti and Alberigo that the pope had not accepted the formula of the experts but had "entrusted the matter to Felici" (*JCongar*, 403). Felici's influence is clear in the formula used, since the latter tends to make pontifical approval a primatial act. But the work of the experts was not entirely in vain: it made possible an improvement in composition as compared with the formula in the Regulations; it led to the omission of the pontifical *sanction* and the replacement of "with the approval of the Council," which in the past had served rather to reinforce the pope's isolated decision, with "together with the fathers," which can be understood as giving a degree of emphasis to collegiality.

[287] In order to satisfy the pope's desire to promulgate more than one document at the end of the period, the moderators had decided to get the decree on the means of social communication passed by having a vote taken on it on November 14. But that vote still had to allow *modi* (*AS* V/3, 709), of which there were 368. The strong movement of opposition to the mediocre text on November 25 was not enough to prevent its immediate definitive adoption.

[288] *JCongar*, 406.

step forward for collegiality."[289] In his 1970 study of the subject, Professor Alberigo gave it as his opinion that the formula chosen "represented a substantial step forward in comparison with earlier formulas," even though it gave only imperfect expression to the new ecclesiological consciousness on the part of the bishops and the Church. It was to be hoped, he said, that in the future there might be a "less mechanical and merely juxtaposed" combining of the pope's will with that of the episcopal college.[290]

Of the two documents promulgated, the one whose implementation was most anticipated was the liturgical constitution. As we know, this did not happen without difficulty. To say nothing of the lasting resistance of certain strata of Catholicism, the Roman braking system showed itself at work as early as January 1964 in a Motu Proprio that tried to stall implementation, but this did not prevent the setting up in March of the commission (Consilium) for the implementation of the constitution.

E. THE POPE'S ADDRESS

It was late morning by the time the pope began his address marking the end of the period.[291] He began by mentioning the need for the bishops to return home after a lengthy absence and thanking the various categories of persons who had contributed to the happy progress of the Council. He cited the Council of Presidents, the moderators, "in a special way" the secretariat, the commissions, the experts, and the press and television services, and he gave particular thanks to the bishops who had contributed to the financing of the conciliar undertaking.[292]

---

[289] Laurentin, 188. See also Wenger, 260, and other references given in Alberigo, "Una cum patribus," 298 n.14. It is to be observed, however, that Caprile (III, 448) reproduces the formula used without explaining the fact that it had been changed.

[290] Alberigo, "Una cum patribus," 314. The same author points out that although Paul VI was to use the same formula for all the occasions of promulgation up to December 1965, the official editions of the conciliar documents would, as early as 1963, attribute to the pope a formula appreciably different (no trinitarian profession; no "Council legitimately assembled"). See ibid., 295 and 299.

[291] Latin text in AS II/6, 561-70. The text, translated into various languages, had been distributed by the conciliar press bureau before it was delivered. The Italian manuscript of the discourse, in the pope's hand, was placed in the archive of the Istituto Paolo VI in Brescia. According to G. Colombo, it contains very few corrections as compared with the address delivered; see "I discorsi di Paolo VI in apertura e chiusura dei periodi conciliari," in Paolo VI e il rapporto chiesa-mondo al Concilio (Brescia, 1991), 248.

[292] Also cited were the technical services and the residences that had received the members. But the thanks to the fathers and to the CC seem to have been added for the

Repeating in a minor key the thoughts on the sense and consciousness of the Church that had been dominant in his address at the opening of the period on September 29, the pope acknowledged that the Church's reflection on its own mystery was calling for a new effort to plumb this mystery more deeply, but also that this reflection had been fostered by the acquisition of mutual understanding among its pastors. He also foresaw a development of canon law through the clearer recognition of functions and the strengthening of hierarchic authority through growth in agreement and mutual respect.

After greeting the observers, briefly this time, along with the lay auditors, and expressing his pleasure at the complete freedom of expression that had allowed the most varied opinions to find a voice, Paul VI turned to what had been accomplished. He cited, first of all, the adoption of the liturgical constitution, which deals with a subject that is the loftiest possible from the viewpoint of spiritual values but which had been approved only at the end of difficult and complicated discussion. In passing, the pope issued a warning against those who wanted to begin to implement the constitution immediately without waiting for the instructions that were to appear during the appointed *vacatio legis* (until February 16, 1964). He then turned to the fruit "of no small value," which was represented by the Decree on the Means of Social Communication as well as by "the many faculties which, in order to promote the pastoral ends of the Council itself, We have declared to be within the competence (*pertinere ad*) of the bishops."[293]

Next came a sentence that seemed to allude vaguely to the straw vote of October 30 on the five ecclesiological questions, but perhaps also to the plan for a council of bishops around the pope and to the acceptance of the first three chapters of the ecumenism schema as a basis of discussion. The pope said that "tentative solutions [of many questions] are already partly formulated in authoritative decrees. These will be published in time, once they have been submitted to definitive resolutions and work is completed on the topics to which they belong."[294] If this

official publication; they are not in the French and Italian texts that were distributed (see, e.g., Moeller Archive, 2868, 2869), but are in the Latin text published in *OssRom* for December 5, 1963, p. 1.

[293] Translation of this and the following passages is from *The Pope Speaks* 9 (1963-64), 221-29. According to the French text distributed: "which we willed to declare as belonging to their competence"; the same in the Italian text.

[294] Latin: "enodationes in gravibus sententiis penitus contineri dicendae sunt, quae post argumenti, ad quod attinent, tractationem, suo tempore definite proponentur ac legitime promulgabuntur" (*AS* II/6, 566).

obscure statement was aimed chiefly at collegiality, it must be said that the pope committed himself to this only with great care.

How did Paul VI envisage the continuation of the Council? In dealing with the "other questions" still to be discussed and which the pope hoped to see brought to a profitable conclusion during the third period (a statement suggesting rather clearly that the third period would also be the last), the commissions were to do their work while taking into account the opinions expressed by the fathers and would thus prepare condensed and shortened texts that would make the debates easier and speedier.[295] Is it only in the light of papal positions taken in the coming weeks that we are inclined today to see in this passage of the address the intention of shortening the Council?[296] Be that as it may, at this moment the commentators did not show any concern.

What were the questions still to be dealt with? "To give an example," Paul VI mentioned, but briefly and in general terms, the question of revelation; then, by way of completing Vatican I, the question of the nature and function of the episcopate, to be resolved in such a way that the hierarchic structure of the Church would not be weakened but strengthened.[297] Another question was that of the schema on the Virgin Mary, which the vote on October 29 had attached to the schema on the Church; without confirming that action, the pope chose to emphasize the position, "privileged above all others," of the Virgin in the Church, a position so exceptional, he went on to say, that she could be honored with the title "Mother of the Church."[298] It was to these three questions, currently being studied but also more or less in abeyance, that Paul VI limited his

---

[295] "...their [the commissions'] proposals for future meetings...will be profoundly studied, accurately formulated, and suitably condensed and abbreviated so that the discussions, while remaining always free, may be rendered easier and more brief" (ibid.). Two important ideas were contained in this sentence: texts were to be shorter, and so were the debates. In this context the pope did not yet come down on the side of fewer schemas; he would do this shortly.

[296] The address is no less clear in another passage: the Council will have to take a position on the principal questions in shorter schemas, while leaving to postconciliar commissions the task of developing these schemas and casting them in the form of laws (ibid., 567).

[297] This, he made clear, was to be by strengthening the prerogatives of the pope, which contain all the authority needed for the government of the universal Church, and without thinking of the episcopal function as "independent of (*sui iuris*), or separated from, or, still less, antagonistic to the supreme pontificate of Peter; but with Peter and under him it strives for the common good and the supreme purpose of the Church" (ibid.).

[298] This statement paved the way for Paul VI's solemn proclamation of Mary as Mother of the Church on November 21, 1964.

list. These were for him fundamental theological themes. As for the "large number" of other questions still to be treated, these would, he said, be the subject of shorter schemas to be produced after the Council. This was an allusion to a new, unspecified form of collaboration of the episcopate in the service of the universal Church.

Finally, after pointing out the positive aspects of the period just ending, the pope said that the Council would have to deal with "current questions concerning the episcopate," but he did not speak of reviving the schema on the Church in the world. He simply suggested that the bishops speak encouragingly to their priests, the laity, youth, the world of thought, workers, and the poor.

At this point the address ended in the version distributed to the fathers. The pope had already spoken for thirty-five minutes, but he continued on and made known his intention of visiting the Holy Land during the coming January. He wanted, he said, to be a pilgrim in the land of Jesus and to pray there for the successful conclusion of the Council, as well as for the renewal of Church, for her call to the separated brethren, for world peace and the salvation of humanity. He asked that all go with him in their prayers.[299] This unexpected announcement was punctuated by hearty applause.

The final word was addressed to the bishops who were "absent and suffering." The reference was not specific, but the pope had in mind those who were prevented from attending the Council for political reasons, especially the bishops of mainland China.

In this lengthy pontifical allocution, which was "academic and wearisome,"[300] the burning subject of episcopal collegiality, which had been the focus of the upheaval back in October, was passed over in silence. Nor was anything said about ecumenism or about the reform of the Curia, which had been the subject of very lively exchanges during the debate on the episcopate. Only with a vague promise did the pope respond to the wishes given strong expression at the beginning of November for an episcopal council around the pope. The expectation of a radical reflection on relations of the Church with the modern world, especially in the area of religious freedom, was met only with an exhortation to a more efficacious love of humanity. The important questions

---

[299] Ibid., 569-70.

[300] *JCongar*, December 4, 406. In his analysis of the addresses of Paul VI to the Council, G. Colombo notes that the address of December 4 was "certainly subdued in tone" and "perhaps the least typical" of all those delivered by the pope during the Council; see "I discorsi di Paolo VI," 248.

debated or taken up during the two preceding months had thus been passed over. The pope had chosen to be silent on the serious problems raised by the organization of the Council; he doubtless knew that the option of simply enlarging the commissions had not met with much enthusiasm, and therefore contented himself with saying that the work must be speeded up both in the commissions and in the general congregations.

While the best informed commentators expressed their astonishment at the "kind of withdrawal" in relation to the Council that the pope's address seemed to represent,[301] the majority of them emphasized primarily the announced journey to the Holy Land, which alleviated the mixed, if not negative impression that public opinion was likely to have of the address. In any case, the papal journey very quickly came to attract wide attention in all the media. As early as the day after the address, reflections on the supposedly symbolic meaning of the plan did not fail to appear: "a mystical resolve,"[302] "the best commentary on ecumenism" and "rich in lessons,"[303] "sign of a return to the gospel sources" and "to the humble beginnings of the Church," "a step in the direction of the poor," "an ecumenical step toward the East, whence the light comes."[304]

F. GENERAL IMPRESSIONS

At the end of this period of the Council many among those "in the know" had the impression that Paul VI's commitment to the Council had weakened.[305] What did the "health bulletin" of Vatican II contain?[306] If we look beyond the impressions of the commentators of the

---

[301] In Father Rouquette's chronicle in *Etudes*, reprinted as *La fin d'une chrétienté* (Paris, 1968), 2:424, Congar is cited as saying that the address "is far removed from that of September 29" (*JCongar*, 406). The same impression was had on the Lutheran side in Maron, *Evangelischer Bericht vom Konzil. Zweite Session,* 59-50, who concludes: "If we compare the addresses of Paul VI during these last months, we can only speak of a falling off, if not of a discontinuity. In any case, Pope Montini has not yet acquired a clear image" (60). B. Lambert describes the address as "simple, modest, and almost subdued" (in his *De Rome à Jérusalem, Itinéraire spirituel de Vatican II* [Paris, 1964], 253).

[302] Congar, in *ICI*, no. 206 (December 15, 1963), 3.

[303] Wenger, 261.

[304] Laurentin, 194.

[305] During the public session on December 4, Msgr. Boillon, Bishop of Verdun, told Congar that he had told the pope's secretary of the widespread impression that the pope has "backed away" by comparison with September. Congar notes: "The secretary denies this utterly. It is nonetheless the impression of many" (*JCongar*, 406).

[306] "Health bulletin" ("Bulletin de santé") is the title of Laurentin's sixth chapter.

time and their attempts to analyze events,[307] what data must be taken into account in evaluating the situation of the Council at that moment?

In general, the press in 1963 presented the second period as a success for the new pope; only one English newspaper (*The Universe*) expressed a fear that he was putting a brake on the policy of his predecessor. An essential point to consider, however, is that the analyses offered at the time did not yet enter into the majority-minority dialectic but gave pride of place to the relationship between the Council, considered as a whole (with its work being regarded at the time as disappointing), and the pope, to whom the analysts tended to give credit.[308] In fact, matters were less simple. The majority mind of the Council had been made known on a series of fundamental questions: collegiality, a council of bishops, the rejection of curial influence in the commissions, and commitment to ecumenism. The influence exerted by an unofficial body such as the group of delegates from the episcopal conferences was a good witness to this conciliar mind. It is important, however, to point out that the minority of bishops who opposed these choices had begun to take organized form in October, making the subject of its first meeting its opposition to collegiality and, significantly, seeing reasons for hope in the pope's address on December 4.[309]

As for the pope, the thing that the best informed seemed to fear was a weakening of his conciliar consciousness. Some detected Paul VI being pulled in two directions: between conservatism and progress or, better, between preserving the essentials of the traditional heritage and adapting this heritage (which, in his mind, seemed to consist in presenting it in

---

[307] In addition to the commentators cited thus far, see the general report of P. Levillain, "L'opinion publique et Paul VI pendant la seconde et la troisième période de Vatican II," as well as the reports of J. Grootaers (for Belgium and the Netherlands), M. Barrois Valdès (Chile), Ph. Levillain and Fr.-Ch. Uginet (France), E. Fink (Germany), E. Yarnold (Great Britain and Ireland), G. M. Vian (Italy), T. Peronek and J. Turowicz (Poland), P. Busquets Sindreu (Spain), V. Conzemius (Switzerland), Fr. Skoda (Russia), and G. Fogarty (United States) — all in *Paolo VI e i problemi eccesiologici al Concilio,* 274-85 and 431-559.

[308] Levillain, "L'opinion publique," 283.

[309] See Luc Perrin, "Il 'Coetus internationalis Patrum e la minoranza conciliare," *Evento,* 173-87. The meeting on October 3, 1963, was attended by fifteen fathers from three groups: the French, the Italian, and the Brazilian. The principal personages at the beginning were G. de Proença Sigaud (Brazil) and M. Lefebvre (superior general of the Spiritans), who was elected president of the group. Moreover, Cardinal Siri (Genoa), a father who represented the same tendency and was to become one of the backers of the International Group, publicly stated after the period had closed that the vote of October 30 on collegiality was void (Caprile III, 412 n.20).

forms more adapted to modern culture).[310] Moreover, in his address to
the Roman Curia on December 24, 1963, Paul VI explained this "dialectic" that is at work in the Church on its "voyage," during which it is
constantly involved "in a twofold difficulty: to preserve the precious
and untouchable cargo of its religious patrimony, while also sailing forward on the rough sea of this world."[311] It is difficult to grasp the real
attitude of the pope toward the advances of the second period. Confronted by the movement toward a degree of decentralization, did he
want to restore the balance by emphasizing, as he did especially on
December 4, the Roman foundation of the Church? Or was he positively
favorable now to those who opposed collegiality?

Whatever his personal choice may have been regarding this aspect of
ecclesiology, which dominated the second period, it was evident that
Paul VI had multiplied his interventions in the course being taken by the
Council. It is true that beginning in the second half of October appeals,
individual and collective, from the bishops had nudged him into taking
positions. The pope had given varying responses to these manifestations
of uneasiness: by spurring on the work of the Doctrinal Commission
(especially on the subject of religious freedom), by calling for concrete
results by the end of the current period (he hoped that at least one chapter of the schema on the Church would be adopted), by presiding over a
meeting of the directive bodies, by telling the moderators of his wishes,
by timidly reforming the commissions, by granting some powers to bishops, and by taking two initiatives that had a lofty symbolic scope (the
choice of a rather collegial formula of promulgation and the decision to
journey to the Holy Land).

How were these interventions (I have mentioned only the principal
ones[312]) to be understood? It was certainly not accidental that on
December 4 the pope emphasized his concern for the freedom of the
Council fathers. Was he not afraid, however, of being overtaken by ideas
that were too advanced or, rather, by certain leaders (Cardinal Suenens,
for example) who were inclined to rely on a majority that was still forming? If Paul VI had such thoughts and if we add to them the dissatisfaction of a certain number of bishops and experts, we would have in hand

---

[310] Rouquette, *La fin d'une chrétienté*, 2:424-26; Lambert, *De Rome à Jérusalem*,
253.

[311] *Insegnamenti*, I, 427.

[312] When the archives are made accessible, one of the first researches should be into
the relations between Paul VI and Cardinal Cicognani, Secretary of State and president of
the CC.

factors that would suffice to explain the wish expressed by the pope in December for a limitation of the number and content of the schemas still to be discussed and, more generally, for a more rapid pace of Vatican Council II.

However, the uncertain state of the entire enterprise at this point should not make us forget that, at a loftier level, the assembled pastors of the Catholic Church had been confronted by considerable challenges. These were clearly pointed out by the future Cardinal Etchegaray, at that time secretary of the group of delegates from the episcopal conferences.[313] The principal questions debated during the period (he cites collegiality and ecumenism) were "almost completely *new*" and "exceptionally *serious*"; the discussion had come up against age-old situations of *fact*; and, due to the death of John XXIII, the assembly had had to meet the test of a formidable change, which, according to the author, it had done in an "exceptionally prudent" way.

G. THE CONTINUATION OF THE COUNCIL

At the general congregation of November 29 it was semi-officially announced that the third period of the Council would last from September 14 to November 20, 1964.[314] The pope reserved official confirmation of this to himself, and the confirmation was not given on December 4 — a sign that the Council's future calendar, which was of course linked to the determination of its program, was still uncertain. Program and calendar were also not unconnected with serious questions of procedure, which had been debated for some weeks.

The view that the Council should end without delay was becoming widespread.[315] At the important meeting on November 15, various cardinals spoke, in one way or another, to that effect.[316] But, wrote Charles

---

[313] In an assessment of the period that he presented to the members of this group on January 10, 1964 (ISR, Etchegaray Archive, copy).

[314] *AS* II/6, 305.

[315] *JCongar*, 368. Moeller wrote to his mother on November 20, 1963: "The majority is for having only one more session" (Moeller Archive, 2887).

[316] By approving the (already proposed?) dates of September 8–November 25 for the third period (N. Gilroy, *AS* V/2, 26), or by asking that the material to be discussed be pruned to the greatest possible extent (especially Cicognani, Lercaro, and Döpfner, ibid., 25-27), or by saying clearly that the Council should end in 1964 (especially Döpfner, ibid., 27). Lercaro asked that the fathers might be consulted on the future duration of the Council (ibid.).

Moeller, "a minority, though an active and well-advised one, is working to have a further session in 1965."[317] This was true at least of Suenens, who had a list of arguments drawn up in favor of "a reasonable prolongation of the Council."[318] The arguments: (1) The opportunity for a real examination of the Church's self-understanding in view of its *aggiornamento* is an extraordinary grace that is not to be neglected through haste. (2) The Council certainly ought to deal with such crucial problems as the missions, studies, seminaries, and the place of religious in the dioceses; the deletion of these schemas from the program in order to save time would lead to a much greater loss of time in the coming years. (3) The fact of being in daily contact enables the bishops to tackle their common problems; as a result, there is an incomparable opportunity for the exercise of collegiality, the necessity and importance of which have been solemnly affirmed. (4) It is true that given the present rhythm of work much time is being wasted, but this is a question of procedure, which ought to be handled by energetic measures, without adversely affecting the duration of the Council. The document concluded to the necessity of allowing for two more periods. We do not know what use Suenens made of this text.[319] It was probably distributed to the cardinals of the CC and perhaps to some other fathers.

At the end of the period the pope made no decisions. He was concerned, however, as we have seen, to speed up the work of the commissions and was inclined to lessen the number and content of the schemas. He also spoke of his journey to the Holy Land as a step taken in order to intensify prayer "for the successful conclusion of the Council."[320] He was thus seriously thinking of putting an end to the enterprise. At the meeting of the CC on December 28, 1963 (which will be fully discussed further on, in the chapter on the intersession), Döpfner gave a report on the future reduction of the Council's work.[321] In it the Cardinal used arguments close to those advanced by his German colleague, Cardinal Frings, on October 29. On the other hand, we must bear in mind that the leaders adopted different positions on the difficult question of the Council's

---

[317] Moeller to his mother, November 20, 1963.

[318] Document of two pages, undated, composed by A. Prignon (Prignon Archive, 547).

[319] At the meeting on November 15 Suenens appeared to be rather isolated. In opposition to many of his colleagues, he asked that the schemas not be reduced to skeletons. He stressed the need of dealing with the schema on the Church in the world during the third period (*AS* V/2, 28).

[320] *AS* II/6, 569.

[321] Report of the meeting, *AS* V/2, 95-96. Döpfner's report, ibid., 85-94.

future, doubtless under the influence of pressures that still await a thorough examination. At the moment, the choice had been made. The year 1963 ended with the prospect of a shortened Council.

IV. PAUL VI IN THE HOLY LAND

In his address on December 4, 1963, the pope had announced his intention of making a pilgrimage to the holy places of Palestine during the following January. My purpose here is not to comment on the course of this event or to examine its ins and outs, but simply to situate the event in relation to the progress of the Council.

Commentators of that period pointed out that in choosing his closing address as the occasion for announcing his pilgrimage, the pope doubtless had in mind to restore serenity to the atmosphere at a point when uncertainty and disillusionment had the upper hand. What the commentators did not know was that the decision to go to the Holy Land had been made much earlier.[322] Moreover, despite the pope's reference to the Council, for which he was going to pray, the best informed observers did not grasp the fact that the event was refocusing the attention of the entire Church on a step that was entirely papal and not conciliar. Was that also the intention of Paul VI, who by this extraordinary action would be saying that the phase of his pontificate's commitment to the Council was now past?

In the pope's mind, the journey was to have a strictly spiritual significance, even though he added to this a concern for the defense of the holy places, the hope of meeting with other local Christians, and the hope of a rapprochement with the Jews and the Muslims.[323] Are we to

---

[322] Three pieces of information make it possible to date the decision to right after the election of Paul VI. In January 1964 Msgr. Willebrands told the secretary general of the World Council of Churches that the pope had spoken of his plan to some of the cardinals in July 1963 (note of W. A. Visser't Hooft on his meeting of January 5, 1964, with J. Willebrands and P. Duprey, in ISR, WCC Archive, ACO 8). Father P. Gauthier said that "as early as July Paul VI had secretly made the decision to go as a pilgrim to the Holy Land" (in his *"Consolez mon peuple." Le Concile et "l'Eglise des pauvres"* [Paris, 1965], 258). In a note of September 21, as he set the plan in motion, Paul VI began by saying that he had devoted much thought to it (autograph note reproduced in its entirety in the official volume *Il pellegrinaggio di Paolo VI in Terra Santa, 4-6 gennaio 1964* [Vatican City, 1964], between pp. 10 and 11). In his preface to this work historian M. Maccarrone says that the idea of the pilgrimage went back to the first days of the pontificate.

[323] According to the pope's note of September 21, 1963, cited in the preceding note.

see a connection between the ecumenical purpose contained in this program, described in the note of September 21, 1963, and the first letter that
the pope addressed to Patriarch Athenagoras on September 20? In any
case, it is certain that it was during that same period that the pope spoke
of his plan to Cardinal Bea.[324] But then there was no question at that time
of a meeting with the Ecumenical Patriarch. The pope was thinking only
of meeting the Christian authorities in Palestine; only in December
would the thought arise of a summit meeting in Constantinople.

It was on the morrow of the papal address on December 4 that
Athenagoras proposed that on the occasion of the pope's pilgrimage "all
the heads of the holy Churches of Christ, of the East and the West" should
meet in Jerusalem in order to "open up...a new and blessed road...to the
restoration of all things."[325] The official Roman reaction was to make it
known that such a plan was not feasible.[326] Since the Secretariat of State
had already settled all the details,[327] it no doubt thought that it was important to preserve the autonomy of the papal journey and that there could be
no question of changing its organization at the last minute.

But Cardinal Bea and his Secretariat for Christian Unity saw things in
a different light. Was this not an unexpected occasion for promoting a
Catholic-Orthodox dialogue, which the Pan-Orthodox Conference of
Rhodes had accepted in principle during the previous September? The
pope agreed that P. Duprey, a delegate of the Secretariat for Christian
Unity, should go to the Phanar and explain the papal intentions and the
pope's readiness to meet Athenagoras in Jerusalem if he should be there
at the same time as the pope![328] It was in this way that the patriarch's
plan, reduced indeed in its scope but nonetheless meeting one of his
dearest and long cherished desires, became a reality. On December 28, a
delegate of Constantinople came to Rome to settle the program for the
reciprocal visits that the pope and the patriarch would pay in
Jerusalem.[329]

---

[324] See S. Schmidt, *Augustine Bea: The Cardinal of Unity*, trans. L. Wearne (New
Rochelle, NY: New City Press, 1992), 000-000.

[325] Communiqué of the Ecumenical Patriarch, December 6, 1963, in Storman,
Towards the Healing of Schism, 54-55.

[326] See O. Clément, *Dialogues avec le patriarche Athenagoras* (Paris, 1969), 361.

[327] In particular, J. Martin, a representative of the secretariat, and Msgr. Macchi, had
spent a week in the Holy Land to make preparations for the journey. See J. Martin, "Le
voyage de Paul VI en Terre sainte," in *Paul VI et la vie internationale* (Brescia, 1992), 173.

[328] I am relying here on the testimony of Msgr. Duprey (conversation on May 26, 1995).

[329] On the visit of Metropolitan Athenagoras of Thyateira to Rome see Storman,
Towards the Healing of Schism, 58-61.

The ecumenical aspect of the journey thus took on an unanticipated importance that the media around the world would magnify still further. Before the event, however, and even in the words that he addressed to the patriarch in Jerusalem, Paul VI seemed to want to make ecumenical advances secondary to his pilgrimage.[330] But the spiritual intensity and the very warm atmosphere would lead him to attribute to the two meetings in Jerusalem a decisive importance in the process of rapprochement.

The fact that an ecumenical dimension was added to the journey interfered with the planned organization. Moreover, the manner of proceeding could be understood as a way of taking the initiative in the rapprochement away from the Council. In addition, it was not without its dangers in terms of possible reactions from the other Churches, including the Orthodox.[331] In any case, ever since his note of September 1963 Paul VI did not cease emphasizing the purely religious purpose of his pilgrimage: a "very quick" journey that was to be marked by simplicity, devotion, penance, and charity, with few persons accompanying the pope (the entourage numbered twelve); and to consist chiefly of times of prayer and acts of worship at the principal places made holy by the mysteries of the gospel. The pope did not want to turn the pilgrimage into a political act.[332] In emphasizing this point, he had particularly in mind the idea, feared by the Arabs, that he might come out in favor of recognizing the state of Israel and that he might take a position on the Palestinian refugees, who included, in particular, some Christian Arabs. On the contrary, Paul VI, a man very sensitive to symbolic gestures, meant to make of his journey the act of the supreme pastor, who prays for Christian unity, world peace, and the successful conclusion of the Council,

---

[330] When the pope visited the patriarch on January 6, 1964, he twice said that it was Athenagoras who wanted the meeting; see Storman, *Towards the Healing of Schism*, 62-63. But Msgr. Duprey interpreted these remarks as a gesture of papal thoughtfulness (conversation with the author on May 26, 1995).

[331] The Orthodox Churches showed themselves, by and large, to be reserved toward the planned meeting; see Clément, *Dialogues*, 365-66, and V. Martano, *Athenagoras, il patriarca (1886-1972)* (Bologna, 1996), 468-69. People at the World Council of Churches were troubled at not having been officially informed about Athenagoras's first plan. They feared, above all, that the patriarch might cut himself loose from the ecumenical movement centered in Geneva and that the Catholic Church might keep to itself the entire initiative in the politics of interecclesial rapprochement. See two confidential notes of W. A. Visser't Hooft, general secretary of the WCC, dated January 3 and January 21, 1964 (photocopies in the ISR, WCC Archive, ACO 8).

[332] See the emphasis on this point in the pope's reply to the good wishes of the diplomatic corps on December 28, 1963. See *Il pellegrinaggio di Paolo VI*, 18.

and is keenly aware of having to steer the ship of Peter and even the entire world toward salvation and perhaps unity.[333]

The enthusiastic welcome of the largely Muslim crowds in Jerusalem and Nazareth could only strengthen these intentions of the pope, who showed himself impressed by his reception. As for Judaism, he understood it in its religious character and its biblical aspect, and it was at this level that he sought an opening to it and not to the state of Israel; his meetings with the Israeli authorities on January 5 remained simple acts of official courtesy. This did not keep the Israeli people from showing great interest in the papal journey.

If, then, we may set priorities in the program of the papal journey of January 4-6, 1964, we must give first place to the specifically religious step that Paul VI was taking as supreme pastor of the Catholic Church, and to his prayer intentions, which ranged from the prosperity of the Church to the welfare of the entire human race and included especially the responsibility of Peter's successor, Christian unity, the successful conclusion of the Council, and world peace.[334]

As far as their place in the program for the journey was concerned, the ecumenical meetings came second. Still, it was due to these — and to the fact that a pope left Italy for the first time since the beginning of the nineteenth century — that the event owed the worldwide stir it created. There were eight exchanges of visits with the Orthodox and Armenian patriarchs, then with representatives of other Christian communities.[335] But it was the two meetings on January 5 and 6 with the patriarch of Constantinople that were the most striking, not only in the eyes of pub-

---

[333] The pope developed these broad perspectives especially in his homily in Bethlehem on January 6; see *Il pellegrinaggio di Paolo VI*, 99-106. At the special audience granted to the diplomatic corps on January 25, 1964, the pope emphasized his universal fatherhood, going so far as to call himself, though in an analogous sense, "leader of the world" (ibid., 213-17).

[334] The pilgrim-pope visited thirteen holy places in three days: in Jerusalem and its environs, in Galilee. and in Bethlehem. There was a principal intention for each place, but others interacted with this. One might point out the most frequent themes and study the emphasis given to them. In the apostolic exhortation of January 15, 1964, the pope repeated the intentions that he considered to have priority and asked all the bishops of the world to share them with him: the Church, the human family, and Christian unity (*Il pellegrinaggio di Paolo VI*, 198-203).

[335] Reception of Benedictos, Orthodox Patriarch of Jerusalem; Athenagoras, the Ecumenical Patriarch; and Derderian, the Armenian Patriarch; then visits to the same. Reception of the Orthodox Syrian and Ethiopian bishops and of the Lutheran pastor, then of an Anglican delegation led by Archbishop A. C. McInnes. That the pope should pay a visit, in this case to the three patriarchs, was a novel gesture, but one Paul VI went along with without difficulty.

lic opinion but also in the mind of the pope, who seems to have become aware on this occasion of the full extent of his ecumenical vocation[336] and, to some extent, of the importance of these meetings for the future of rapprochement between the Churches.[337] The thoughts exchanged, especially in private on the evening of the 5th;[338] the gestures made, in particular the joint blessing on the 6th; the highly symbolic character of the gifts;[339] the repeated embraces, and the enthusiastic reactions of those present, both Catholic and Orthodox: all these created an atmosphere of great intensity and exceptional fervor.

The words that the pope spoke on the evening of January 4 to the Oriental Catholic hierarchy in the Basilica of St. Anne and then at the Latin patriarchate on the morning of the 6th adopted to a degree the same ecumenical perspective: respect for the variety of local Churches and an invitation, on the one hand, to a "collaboration without rivalries" among Catholics and, on the other, to collaboration and mutual esteem among the Catholic communities of the various rites.[340]

On a third level in the pope's intentions was his desired encounter with Islam and Judaism, to which his addresses made discreet allusions. The enthusiastic welcome by the Muslims, which followed the warm reception by King Hussein of Jordan (a happy surprise, it was said, to the pope), stood in contrast to the official courtesy shown by the Israeli authorities; this, it is true, was to be explained in good measure by the polite reserve of the head of the Papal State, which did not recognize the state of Israel.[341] If the pope had little awareness of the contemporary reality of Judaism, this did not prevent the populace and even the Israeli press from taking, on the whole, a rather favorable attitude toward him.

---

[336] On this subject see the remarks the pope addressed to the crowd in St. Peter's Square, and then to the cardinals, on the evening of his return to Rome; see *Il pellegrinaggio di Paolo VI*, 137-41.

[337] For the addresses at the two meetings, see Shorman, *Towards The Healing of Schism*, 61-63 (joint communiqué, 64; remarks to crowd in St. Peter's Square, 64-65). See also *Il pellegrinaggio di Paolo VI*, 87-90 and 107-11; Clément, *Dialogues*, 362-64; Martano, *Athenagoras*, 472-76.

[338] The text of the recorded remarks is published in A. Wenger, *Les trois Rome* (Paris, 1991), 145-47.

[339] The pope gave the patriarch a chalice as symbol of his desire for the restoration of eucharistic communion; the patriarch gave the Bishop of Rome an enkolpion (a pectoral chain with a medallion), a sign of the unity of the two Churches in one and the same episcopate.

[340] *Il pellegrinaggio di Paolo VI*, 56 and 118.

[341] In addition, the pope thought he had to respond to the accusations in Rolf Hochhuth's play, *The Deputy*, by defending Pius XII to the president of Israel for his attitude to the Jews during the Second World War.

Finally, while the world situation was not forgotten during the pil-grimage, this theme, viewed in some of its particular aspects, was clearly less developed, at least in the addresses and homilies delivered during the three days. At Nazareth the pope did emphasize in particular the importance of family life and of the world of work and urged love of the poor. In Bethlehem he greeted all human beings of good will, even those who denied God, and issued an urgent appeal for peace to those in authority over the various nations.[342]

The pilgrimage activities of Paul VI in the Holy Land suggest that we should place the entire event in the very broad perspective of his oft-repeated desire to return to the sources: return of a twentieth-cen-tury pope to the gospel sources, return of the contemporary Catholic Church to the community assembled around Peter the Apostle. To the crowd gathered in St. Peter's Square on the evening of January 6 the pope spoke of the direct line running from Christ to Peter and to Rome. Given this perspective, how was the journey to be understood in relation to the Council? Was the pope moving beyond the stage represented by Vatican II and preparing for the postconciliar period, or was he, on the contrary, stimulating the dynamic at work in the Council?[343]

It must be noted, first of all, that Paul VI had situated his plan directly in the framework of his primatial function and that as time went on he constantly saw it in that perspective. Thus the position recently taken by the Council on episcopal collegiality had no influ-ence on the way he acted. As for the ecumenical perspective to which the Council had begun to open itself, the pope gave the impression of taking it over, with, no doubt, the determination to give a decisive impulse to Catholic commitment in this area; in this respect his actions in Jerusalem were more eloquent than all the addresses. But the presi-dent of the Secretariat for Christian Unity displayed a certain embar-rassment in face of the apprehension felt in several quarters within Orthodoxy, as well as in the World Council of Chuches, at what seemed to them a monopolization of the ecumenical movement by

---

[342] *Il pellegrinaggio di Paolo VI*, 74-79 and 99-106.

[343] This question was raised at the time in an article of J. Grootaers that appeared in *De Maand* 7, no. 1 (January 1964), 33-30 (partial translation in the Belgian Catholic weekly, *La Relève*, February 8, 1964, p. 15).

Catholicism.[344] In any case, here again the primatial action took precedence over the action of the Council.

As for the admittedly very modest opening to relations with the other religions and to the problems of the world, the steps taken by the pope could again suggest both Rome's intention of moving further in these directions and of encouraging the Council to go more deeply into the question of relations between the Church and the non-Christian world.

To these signs of renewed focus on papal initiatives and of uncertainty regarding both the place of the Council and the pope's commitment to it were added the steps taken in December 1963 with a view to speeding up Vatican II and shortening its duration. These circumstances suggest that while the pilgrimage, by its spiritual and ecumenical intensity, may have encouraged the Council fathers to move forward, it did not seem to have given the conciliar undertaking the stimulus it needed, both institutionally and in the direction of its work.

---

[344] For Russian Orthodoxy, see the communiqué issued by the patriarchate of Moscow on January 21, 1964 (published in Wenger, *Les trois Rome*, 304); for Greek Orthodoxy, see Martano, *Athenagoras*, 466-47; for the WCC, see the already cited note of W. A. Visser't Hooft, dated January 21, 1964, and his report of a conversation with J. Willebrands and P. Duprey on January 27, 1964 (ISR, WCC Archive, ACO 8).

CHAPTER V

THE INTERSESSION (1963-1964)

EVANGELISTA VILANOVA

INTRODUCTION

While the first intersession could be thought of as a "second preparation," the second was marked by an effort to bring the Council to completion on the basis of a feasible plan of work, even if this meant a drastic reduction of the schemas. The complexity of the subjects being
discussed and the multiplicity of persons involved had placed a drag on
the proceedings, thus tending to hinder a smooth completion of the
Council within a reasonable time. This situation seemed clear not only
during the periods in which the fathers were assembled in their general
congregations but also, and above all, during the intersessions.[1]

In fact, some of the decisive moments of Vatican II occurred during
the periods between the four conciliar sessions, for it was then, in the
absence of the bishops, the majority of the experts, and the representatives of the press, that some members of the Curia and some Roman theologians who were opposed to tendencies favoring the *aggiornamento*
counted on regaining at least temporary control of the situation and correcting, by restricting, the texts approved by the majority.[2] In this

---

[1] Jan Grootaers has spoken of this second intersession as a "third preparation":
concerned by the progress made by the majority current in 1963, the leaders of the CC
expanded the so-called Döpfner Plan with the goal of ending the Council as quickly as
possible; as a means of achieving this goal they wanted to prune the schemas not yet
completed. This procedure was prepared during the 1963-64 intersession ("Sinergie e
conflitti al Vaticano II. Due versanti dell'azione degli avversari," in *Evento,* 404 n.57).

[2] In this context G. Alberigo has written: "Inquiry must be made into the relationship
between the phases of the plenary assembly's activity and the so-called 'intersessions.' It
is a fact that of the 38 months' total duration of Vatican II, general congregations were
held for 8 months, while the remaining 30 months were intervals, but intervals that were
far from idle. From the very first weeks there was a concern that the spirit and orientations brought to maturity in the assembly should be continued in the important work that
would go on during the intersessions. This was a problematic matter, analogous to the no
less thorny matter of the fidelity of the commissions to the full body of the Council. We
know the mechanisms that were put to work in order to avoid the perverse spiral by which
the conclusions that had emerged in a congregation were contradicted in the commissions
or lost from sight during the lengthy pauses that were the intersessions. But, looking

Roman atmosphere during the intersessions the representatives of this majority were often isolated. Cardinal Cicognani, who held the office both of Secretary of State and president of the Coordinating Commission (CC), exerted a considerable influence along those lines and did not avoid to some degree confusing his two different roles.[3] This mingling contributed to intensifying the difficulties that arose in relations between Paul VI and the Council. This was a situation that proved favorable to the minority group and constantly harmed the majority.

Cardinal Tisserant, dean of the Sacred College and of the Council of Presidents, and an especially authoritarian personality, joined Cicognani and the Secretary General, Msgr. Pericle Felici, in forming a triumvirate that exerted a preponderant influence during the second half of Vatican II. This influence could be seen in an obvious reserve toward the so-called Döpfner Plan. This explains how it is possible to distinguish, during the second intersession, a first phase that was initially open to the Döpfner Plan and dominated by the attitudes of the various commissions; a second phase focused on the "observations" made by Paul VI on chapter II (eventually III) of the schema on the Church and ending with the sending of the schemas by the CC (April 27, 1964); and a final phase, lasting until the opening of the third period (September 14), during which the fruit of the Döpfner Plan was examined and criticized.

The interval between the second period and the third, which was to begin on September 14, 1964,[4] saw an intensification of the study by the experts and in the meetings of the commissions devoted to correcting the schemas on the basis of observations from the fathers, as well as to determining in greater detail the working schedule for the coming period.[5] The program was determined by the Döpfner Plan. On the very day of his coronation Paul VI received Döpfner in an audience, and it seems that it was on this occasion that he asked him to develop a plan for improving the management of the Council.[6] In this plan, which was sent to the pope and perhaps approved by him, the fourth and final section

beyond these mechanisms and their greater or lesser effectiveness, we must inquire into the degree of influence which the main characteristics of the conciliar event had on the 'lesser' moments and phases, that is, on those not involving the assembly" ("Luci e ombre nel rapporto tra dinamica assembleare e conclusioni conciliari," in *Evento*, 513).

[3] See V. Fagiolo, "Il cardinale Amleto Cicognani e mons. Pericle Felici," in *Deuxième*, 229-42.

[4] See the official communiqué of the Secretary of State, July 3, 1964: *AS* III/1, 15.

[5] See the minutes of the meetings of the CC, in *AS* V/2.

[6] See Kl. Wittstadt, "Vorschläge von Julius Kardinal Döpfner an Papst Paul VI. zur Fortführung des Konzilsarbeiten (Juli 1963)," in *Fe i teologia en la historia. Estudi en honor d'E. Vilanova* (Montserrat, 1997).

included some concrete suggestions regarding the rhythm of the work to be done during the intersession between the second and third periods of the Council. As we shall see, the plan was presented to the CC on December 28, at its first meeting during the second intersession.

The energies released during this intersession were extraordinary. When the time came to resume the general assemblies of the Council, those present saw that there had been an awakening of the commission reporters and that the draft texts had recovered their vitality and had been expanded and clarified in the process of retrieving the emphases previously lost in the bosoms of the mysterious commissions. After this intersession and during the third period of the Council, the interventions in the hall by Cardinal Bea (on the question of the Jews), Msgr. Hengsbach (on the lay apostolate), and Msgr. De Smedt (on religious freedom) were revelatory of that change. In general terms, during the intersession the task of the competent bodies was to implement the main choices previously made: the CC was to follow the directives of the general assembly, the commissions the directives of the CC, and the working groups those of the conciliar commissions.

At such key moments it was necessary to be alert and to maintain control of the changes that were being made at various levels, and to see to it that these changes were consistent with the schema as a whole. This kind of vigilance was shown, for example, by Msgr. Philips, who was able at these key moments to demonstrate his "political" ability. In the case of the schema on the Church and of schema XVII this strategy was made possible by a combination of rather extraordinary circumstances, that is, by the collaboration of representatives of three different levels: (1) Cardinal Suenens, who was in charge of supervising both schemas in the CC; (2) Msgr. Charue, to whom a great deal of attention was paid in the Doctrinal Commission; and (3) Msgr. Philips himself, who was assistant secretary in that same commission and the writer of important texts. These three individuals, so different among themselves, acted as a team throughout these three years, thanks to the collaboration of a much larger group.[7]

Among the schemas to be studied were those that had already been discussed during the previous periods and that had therefore already received the needed corrections. These schemas, after various partial and comprehensive votes, would reach their goal in a final conciliar form.

[7] See J. Grootaers, "Le rôle de Mgr. G. Philips à Vatican II," in *Ecclesia a Spiritu Sancto edocta. Lumen Gentium, 53* (Gembloux, 1970), 353.

There were also those schemas that had not yet been discussed and had to be presented to the fathers for a first debate. This distinction, which was emphasized by E. Schillebeeckx,[8] made it possible to think of the former as different from "dry bones," since the spirit of the Council had given them life, whereas the second group had not advanced beyond the stage of simple working papers of the commissions and had not yet been drawn by the world episcopate into the dynamic movement of the Council. As a result, the state of the conciliar projects at the beginning of April 1964 was as follows:

Schemas already discussed, ready for changes and votes:

1. "On the Church" (except for the chapter on the Blessed Virgin, not yet discussed).
2. "On ecumenism" (except for the chapters on the Jews and on religious freedom, not yet discussed but presented in broad outline during the second period).
3. "On bishops."

Schemas completely rewritten, to be brought up again for discussion:

1. "On the missions" (printed and sent to the fathers; on the basis of the latter's observations it was to be emended in May).
2. "On the apostolate of the laity" (might be reduced to a number of short statements).
3. "Schema XVII" (still being developed at this time).

Schemas reduced to propositions:

1. "On priests."
2. "On the formation of seminarians."
3. "On Catholic schools."
4. "On the Oriental Churches."
5. "On religious."
6. "On the sacrament of matrimony."

To understand the work as a whole, it is necessary to go into the troubled history of each of the projects. The documentation is sufficient for us to grasp the underlying forces at work. The attempt to reduce or drastically simplify the texts to be discussed and voted on was not due solely to the desire to end the Council that was expressed by the pope and proposed by

---

[8] *L'Eglise du Christ et l'homme d'aujourd'hui selon Vatican II* (Le Puy, 1965), 139.

Döpfner; it was due also to the tendency, quite widespread in curial circles, to finish the Council in the shortest possible time, possibly in the third period, that is, 1964. But the debate on this subject did not prevent a laborious, intense — and sometimes tense — activity from being carried on during the second intersession and thus the taking of a decisive step toward the successful conclusion of the Council. Years later Cardinal König, who had played an outstanding part, would be quoted as saying:

> The second interval was therefore filled with hope and optimism. It was precisely during this period that the Council took the path leading to achievements which Oscar Cullmann, the theologian of the Swiss Reformed Church, said were "beyond all expectations." The great themes of the Church, ecumenism, and religious freedom, which were introduced after the election of Montini, were to find concrete shape and acceptance in the two subsequent sessions.[9]

To the work done on the texts during these intermediate periods we must add that from its very beginning, in January 1964, the second intersession was marked by two initiatives that were brought to maturity entirely by the pope. The first was the short pilgrimage to the Holy Land, which was discussed in the preceding chapter. The other papal initiative was the establishment of the Council for the Implementation of the Constitution on the Sacred Liturgy (Consilium), of which Cardinal Lercaro was appointed president, with Father Annibale Bugnini as secretary.

These were two extraconciliar initiatives of undeniable importance. While relations between episcopal collegiality and papal primacy were the focus of the conciliar debates, Paul VI made it clear that he was not losing his freedom of action. As a result, these initiatives were at once in line with the Council's work and in seeming tension with it. Paul VI was a pope of symbolic gestures. His pilgrimage to Jerusalem, where he embraced Patriarch Athenagoras, sharpened the picture of him as "messenger and explorer" of the Council, as Ph. Levillain put it. The Consilium carried a special significance, both because it was in fact the first postconciliar body and because the role of president was given to a residential cardinal and not to a representative of the Curia.

---

[9] Cardinal Franz König, interviewed by Gianni Licheri, *Where Is the Church Heading?* (Middlegreen, 1986), 34.

I. First Phase:
The Council's Work on the Basis of the Döpfner Plan

A. Continuation of the Many-Headed Structure of the Council[10]

After the experience of two preceding periods, the multiplicity of directing bodies provided for in the first edition of the Regulations was maintained. In this connection Paul VI always gave the impression of wanting not to obtrude himself but to show great respect for the freedom of the assembly, as he said on several occasions. During the second period this attitude had annoyed some fathers, for example, when the validity of the vote on October 30 and the authority of the moderators were challenged. In his encyclical *Ecclesiam Suam* (August 6, 1964) Paul VI gave solemn expression to these same sentiments of reserve and respect in relation to the work of the Council. But he clearly neither cut himself off from the Council nor allowed himself to be swept along in its course. In his address at the end of the second period he did not hesitate to give directions for the study of the different questions nor to set out the program for future work, for example, regarding the schema on revelation, the chapter on the Blessed Virgin, and "the great and complex question of the episcopate." The part played by the pope in directing the contents and method of the debates was clear and generally accepted, although some observers disagreed with the pope's thinking on the central subject of the episcopate.

This brief recall of the personal participation of Paul VI in the Council, which was to take concrete form in specific interventions during the second intersession, must be completed by noting its connection with a major concern of his which he emphasized patiently and insistently in, for example, his opening address of the second period, his pilgrimage to the Holy Land, and his encyclical *Ecclesiam Suam*, and allocutions. This obsession was with the "re-centering" in Christ, of which Father De Lubac spoke,[11] or the "re-forming" of the Church in light of its model, Jesus Christ, in order that it might bring his salvation to the world.

---

[10] The term "many-headed" (Laurentin) or "plurisynodal" (Rouquette) corresponds, paradoxically, to the term "headless" used by G. Alberigo; see his essay "Concilio acefalo? L'evoluzione degli organi direttivi del Vatican II," in *Attese*, 193-238.

[11] A "re-centering" in Christ supposes a "de-centering" of the Church that is infinitely more important than the "decentralization" of which so much has been said; see H. De Lubac, "Paul VI, pèlerin de Jérusalem," *Christus* 11, no. 41 (1964), 97-101.

The official activity of the members of the Council of Presidents[12] and of the moderators[13] was interrupted during the intersession, but this did not prevent them from having influence in specific cases, whether due to the prestige of their office or to them personally or at the request of other fathers. It should not be forgotten that the moderators were in fact members of the CC, the body that played a decisive role during the intersession. The work of the CC during such periods was fundamental both in planning the schemas and in examining and approving them.

Also evident was the influence of Felici, Secretary General of the Council,[14] and of his entire secretariat. The latter was a body intermediate between the pope and the assembly and had for its task the (nonmaterial) organization of the Council's work. John XXIII had appointed Felici secretary first of the Antepreparatory Commission (May 1959) and of the Central Preparatory Commission, and then successively of the Council, of the CC, and, finally, of the Central Postconciliar Commission. John XXIII had himself decided to appoint four subsecretaries "in order to bring out better the international character of the assembly"[15]: Msgr. Villot (France), Msgr. Kempf (Germany), Msgr. Krol (USA), and Msgr. Morcillo (Spain), to whom Msgr. Nabaa, Melkite Bishop of Beirut, was added a few days later. According to Msgr. Villot, the General Secretariat was closer to Tisserant than to the moderators.[16]

Felici showed great ability in exercising an undeniable authority at the Council, and his influence was almost unlimited. During the 1963-64 intersession with its atmosphere of uncertainty he reined in the Döpfner Plan, which in a veiled form was trying to secure a rapid end of the Council. In May 1964 Felici announced that votes would be taken without previous discussion on only a few schemas that had been reduced to "programmatic proposals," each of these being preceded by a report to

---

[12] According to M. Maccarrone, "the council of presidents had not really and truly directed the Council"; he goes so far as to speak of its having caused "the paralysis of John's Council." See "Paolo VI e il Concilio. Testimonianze," in *Paolo VI e i problemi ecclesiologici al Concilio* (Brescia, 1989), 409-10.

[13] The role of the moderators met with resistance and opposition, although the alterations in the Regulations, which Msgr. Felici communicated to the bishops on July 7, 1964, brought no real change in the moderators' powers but simply acknowledged their authority to regulate the general congregations. It is surprising that R. Wiltgen, who does not hide his sympathy for the minority, should give a positive assessment of the role of the moderators (Wiltgen, 285).

[14] See V. Carbone, "Il segretario generale del Concilio Ecumenico," in *Il Cardinale Pericle Felici* (Rome, 1992).

[15] L. J. Suenens, *Souvenirs et espérances* (Paris, 1991), 59.

[16] See A. Wenger, *Le cardinal Jean Villot* (Paris, 1989), 35.

be read in the hall. The seven proposals, a few pages in length, seemed intended for the use of future postconciliar commissions. These "short schemas" dealt with very important subjects, such as priestly ministry, the Oriental Churches, the missions, religious, seminaries, and Christian education.[17] This reductive plan, which in the view of the majority risked bringing the Council to a hasty end, was watered down by the moderators and by Döpfner himself, although it was to him that the effort at simplification continued to be attributed.

These facts show the structural impotence of this "many-headed" or "headless" or even "plurisynodal" arrangement. Since the norms governing the Council left open a margin for decision-making, it was natural the Secretary General would not hesitate to fill it, especially when the other directing bodies showed themselves incapable of decision.[18] This situation, according to an expert in things Roman, was the "original sin" of the Council.[19]

B. The Meetings of the Coordinating commission

The role of the CC as protector was exercised in a special way during the intersessions, when the Council fathers had left Rome and immersed themselves in the problems of their respective dioceses. The CC gave direction to the commissions charged with editing the schemas in view of the third period. Thanks to Msgr. V. Carbone's publication of the minutes of the CC's meetings,[20] the reconstruction of its work can be carried out today on the basis of a more detailed knowledge.

The CC met six times during the second intersession: December 28, 1963; January 15, March 10, April 16-17, June 26, and September 11, 1964. The meetings were always held in the apartment of Cicognani, Secretary of State, who presided. Not all the meetings were equally important. The first two represented a first phase, devoted to planning the work of preparation for the third period. The next two were devoted to a more careful examination of the Döpfner Plan. The fifth and sixth

---

[17] P. Felici, "Il concilio ecumenico: ora di Dio," *OssRom*, May 20, 1964. See the articles of F. Vallainc, "Come va il concilio?" *ibid.*, March 11, 1964, and "Le nuove stesure degli schemi e le aggiunte al regolamento," *ibid.*, July 18, 1964.

[18] See D. A. Seeber, *Das Zweite Vatikanum, Konzil des Überganges* (Freiburg, 1966), 328-29.

[19] R. Rouquette, *La fin d'une chrétienté* (Paris, 1968), 2:518-19.

[20] *AS* V/2, 61-694.

represented the final phase, during which the decisions taken were checked and the schemas that had been composed or reworked by the various commissions were examined. The meeting on the eve of the opening of the third period had a practical purpose, namely, to prepare the calendar for the work about to begin, as well as the order in which the schemas were to be discussed.

1. Prehistory and Context of the Döpfner Plan

Even before Paul VI commissioned the Döpfner Plan, which was to be presented to the CC at its first meeting of the second intersession, there had been numerous attempts to make the Council move along more quickly. Döpfner's attentiveness to the working of the Council was already to be seen in his relations with Jedin and Dossetti.[21] On December 3, 1962, after a meeting with Jedin, Dossetti drew up a proposal in which he asked that "the agenda of the Council be reduced to fewer subjects."[22] On December 21 Döpfner wrote along the same lines to John XXIII,[23] and on January 17 Jedin sent a memorandum to Dossetti. During that same month Dossetti sent Döpfner two sets of remarks, on the CC and on the work of the Council.[24] On January 21 Döpfner gave a report to the CC on "his" schemas, but the first three pages of it dealt with "General Principles for the Reviews of Schemas": shortening the schemas, emphasizing a few constitutions and decrees, and approving very brief conciliar resolutions or conclusions that would make it possible to finish the work in the second period.[25] Two days later Dossetti and Döpfner met and discussed the possibility and danger of the Council's limiting itself to "very general principles."[26]

After his election Paul VI received various cardinals and urged them to give their opinion on the continuation and rationalization of the Council. On the very day of his coronation, June 30, he gave an audience to Döpfner, asked his views on the best way to bring the Council to a conclusion, and perhaps charged him with drawing up a plan that could

[21] See Alberigo, "Dinamiche," 117, 120-21, 122-23.

[22] *Propositio*, in ISR, Dossetti Archive, II 123a.

[23] Wittstadt, "Vorschläge von Döpfner." Wittstadt also speaks of a "Memorandum zur Frage der Anderung und Neuaufnahne von Bestimmung über die Abstimmung zur generellen Annahme oder Ablehnung eines Schemas in Ordo Concilii Vaticani II celebrandi," composed by G. Gruber, Döpfner's secretary, and dated December 31, 1962.

[24] See Alberigo, "Dinamiche," 127, especially note 30.

[25] Lercaro Archive, 371, Latin typescript of three pages; not in *AS*.

[26] Dossetti Archive, 1/11.

attain this goal in a feasible way.[27] Paul VI received proposals from other cardinals as well, among them one from Lercaro, which Dossetti had drawn up.

Döpfner worked throughout July on the task given to him; bringing together the concerns and leading ideas of the preceding months, he composed *Reflections on the Continuation of the Council (Überlegungen zur Fortführung des Konzils)*. This work was dated July 20, 1963, and contained four chapters. Chapter I sought to ensure the continuity of the Council (1) by maintaining its principal purpose, the pastoral renewal of the Church; (2) by preserving its ecumenical character and its openness to all of humanity; (3) by guaranteeing a real freedom of debate, while reducing from five to four the morning general congregations so that the commissions and episcopal conferences might have more time; (4) by the pope's continuing the attitude taken by John XXIII to the Council by interpreting the Regulations in a liberating way and remaining in close communion with the episcopal college; (5) by renewing the direction of the conciliar commissions, not excluding the establishment of special new commissions to deal with particular problems.

Chapter II was devoted to improving the activities of the Council when it met again: (1) by strengthening the CC; (2) by reworking and completing the Regulations; (3) by improving relations with the press; (4) by including lay people among the experts; (5) by improving the Council's liturgical celebrations. Chapter III proposed making a selection of topics: (1) concentrating on the schemas on the Church and on ecumenism and revelation; (2) having the CC present a "report on the state of the work" at the beginning of the next period; (3, 4, 5, 6) providing directives for the remaining schemas. Chapter IV suggested lengthening the intersession so that the third and final period might be held in 1965.[28]

Still during the second period, the trend toward a drastic reduction of the conciliar agenda emerged at the meeting of the CC on November 20,

[27] This is what Döpfner himself said in a letter, some weeks later, to Paul VI; see Wittstadt, "Vorschläge von Döpfner."

[28] Lercaro Archive, XXXIV 1140, 109 typewritten pages, dated July 20, 1963; not in *AS*. In his *Julius Kardinal Döpfner 1913-1976* (Würzburg, 1996), 152-53, Kl. Wittstadt publishes a rough draft of a letter of Döpfner (June 30) to Paul VI that accompanied the *Reflections* for which the pope had asked, along with some "Thoughts on the Coronation." Also preserved is a preparatory draft (*Entwurf*) of the *Reflections*, consisting of fourteen double-spaced pages (perhaps composed by some of the cardinal's collaborators) with a great many corrections in Döpfner's hand. Wittstadt, "Vorschläge von Döpfner," gives a detailed summary of the *Reflections*.

in connection with the decision to expand the membership of the commissions. On that occasion both Cicognani and Döpfner expressed their conviction that new members ought to be elected only for those commissions dealing with schemas that would remain for the Council's study. Both men listed a series of subjects that ought to be eliminated and left for consideration after the Council. Although the formal decisions spoke only of expanding the membership of *all* the commissions, except for the liturgical, which had finished its work, not only had the problem of the reduction in the number of schemas been raised, but Cicognani considered it permissible to submit to Paul VI the text of his own letter to the presidents of the commissions. In this letter he referred to the recent meeting of the CC and urged them to work during the coming intersession for "a reduction of the material in their schemas... thus leaving aside for the coming revision of the Code of Canon Law such subjects as are mainly juridical in character."[29]

A month later Döpfner again presented his proposals to a meeting of the CC on December 28, in a text entitled "Topics to Be Brought before the Council in the Third Session."[30] But there were some considerable differences. First and foremost, the first point in the *Reflections* was replaced by a lengthy citation from the address of Paul VI at the close of the second period. Second, the emphasis in the proposals was entirely on the need to end the Council with the coming period, to achieve which very detailed and insistent suggestions were made, while nothing was said of the points made in the first section of the *Reflections* on the nature of the Council.

---

[29] Letter of November 29, 1963; *AS* V/2, 45-46. Paul VI gave Felici approval for sending the letter, as a N.B. tells us. Was this a sign that the Secretary of State knew that the letter went beyond the conclusions reached by the CC? Not long after, in an interview given to Caprile for *CivCatt* (Caprile III, 568-69), Bea took the occasion to express a cautious but explicit disagreement with the tendency to end Vatican II after the third period. While acknowledging the understandable impatience of the bishops to return to their dioceses, as well as the financial burdens that the prolongation of the Council entailed, the cardinal added that "we must also appreciate the great benefit which the pastors of souls are deriving from a serious and unhampered exchange of ideas on the very serious problems still to be dealt with," and he concluded that if the Council "is not to end in the third session, it can certainly do so in a further and final session."

[30] *AS* V/2, 85-94. The document was divided as follows: I/1. How many more sessions: Can we end with the third? I/2. Very serious reasons for ending with the third session. I/3. A fourth session only for very serious reasons and only for voting. II. Proposals for shortening the subject matter to be deal with by the Council. III. Keep the schemas on the Church, ecumenism, revelation, the presence of the Church in the world, and the lay apostolate; everything else to be cut down. IV. Overview of the tasks and the time allotted to each.

For the period from the development of the Döpfner Plan to its presentation on December 28, there is little information on how it was prepared, how its wording was decided, and how it was adapted. On September 2 Döpfner had an audience with Paul VI at Castelgandolfo, as we
know from a letter he wrote to the German bishops on the 7th of that
month. Were the differences between the two texts due to requests from
Paul VI or to Döpfner's own second thoughts? The problem being faced
was a complicated one, and opinions on it were numerous; many were
convinced that the preparatory material that had survived the thinning
out in the autumn of 1962 was still excessive and poor in quality. Nevertheless, was it wise to hasten the end of the Council? Did such a step
not favor those who were opposed to any conciliar deliberations on the
state of the Church in history and in the contemporary world?

On December 14, 1963, ten days after the close of the second period,
Felici wrote to Döpfner informing him that he had been appointed to
prepare the first subject on the agenda of the coming meeting of the CC,
which was set for the end of December. His task was to offer a plan for
reducing the number and content of the schemas, and this on the basis of
the points made by the pope in his address at the close of the second
period.[31] Thus the passage was made from the implicit phase to the
explicit phase of the project, and Felici's letter was, as it were, the "birth
certificate" of the Döpfner Plan. Finally, mention must be made of the
"Norms for the Council's Work," issued by Paul VI on December 27,[32]
to which were added "Norms for the Work to Be Done by the Experts,"
which was likewise sent on by the pope.[33]

When the Döpfner Plan was set forth at the meeting on December 28,
reactions were not slow in coming, and various interpretations were
given of this operation intended to accelerate the work of the Council
and to hasten its end. A very important interpretation was that of the
Cicognani-Felici axis and, in general, of the enemies of renewal. In their
eyes the plan had the advantage of being a plan turned to the future, that
is, of being a real alternative to the numerous and substantial projects
being presented by the majority current, and therefore of being a more
authoritative alternative to the preparatory schemas, which it was no
longer possible to defend. It could not go unnoticed that Paul VI himself,
convinced that the Council had already accomplished the essential part

[31] *AS* V/2, 53-54.
[32] *AS* V/2, 69.
[33] Lercaro Archive, XXIV 571.

of its task, wanted to speed up the Council's work.[34] According to Wenger, Paul VI thought that the Council had exhausted its possibilities; to press on further in the areas of ecclesiology or ecumenism would run the danger of deepening the division between the two sides. Wenger goes so far as to say that "the moment seemed to have come for the pope himself to act, and on his own initiative."[35] If this judgment is accurate, there is justification for distinguishing two stages in this intersession and for saying that the second was marked by a greater papal initiative.

2. Eleventh Meeting of the CC (December 28, 1963)

In a letter of December 15, 1963,[36] written in Cicognani's name, Felici summoned the members of the CC to meet on Saturday, December 28. Cardinals Spellman, Suenens, Roberti, Urbani, and Liénart were absent from the meeting, but the last two contributed to the discussion by sending in their views. Some handwritten remarks of Paul VI on the Regulations for the Council's work were presented to the members of the commission.[37] One important remark had to do with "reducing the length (and number) of the schemas and emphasizing the principal statements (the canons)."

With this in mind, Döpfner had drawn up a plan for reducing the conciliar schemas,[38] one that made it possible to set down a detailed schedule of work during the third period. As a way of trying to finish the work in the third period, the plan proposed taking up only the six most important schemas: on the Church, on bishops and the governnance of dioceses, on revelation (which would still cause many problems because the Doctrinal Commission intended to study it again), on the apostolate of the laity (the doctrinal bases of which had already been clarified in the second period during the discussion of the *De ecclesia*), on ecumenism, and on the effective presence of the Church in today's world. Other schemas, though being discussed, were to be reduced to a few proposals that would be the starting point for postconciliar institutions: the schemas on religious life, on the Oriental Churches, on the missions, on

[34] But this impression seemed paradoxical in light of the fact that in his address at the close of the second period Paul VI had also made an assessment of the road still to be traveled.

[35] Wenger, 322.

[36] *AS* V/2, 61.

[37] *AS* V/2, 69.

[38] For the text of the Döpfner Plan, see *AS* V/2, 85-94; for the minutes of the meeting, ibid., 95- 96 and 99.

seminaries and the care of souls, on Catholic education, and on the clergy. The schema on marriage was to be turned into a *votum* to be sent to the commission for the reform of Canon Law, while the question of mixed marriages would be taken up in the schema on ecumenism.

Döpfner's proposal was based on two fundamental and mutually enriching principles: flexibility in relation to life and firmness on the most fundamental questions. On this basis he described the general purposes of the Council and the improvement of the working method; out of these was born the proposal already described for choosing and organizing the themes of the Council. After remarking that "the arrangement of the seventeen subjects [originally] proposed had received little attention because of the disparities present in the preparatory period," Döpfner concluded his proposal with a detailed plan of work for the third period. If we compare the directives given by Paul VI on various occasions with the Döpfner Plan and note the similarities between them, we can see how the key points emerging from this meeting were determined: reduction of the Council's work, improvement of its method, greater participation by the laity,[39] and greater attention to ecumenism, in the broad sense of this word.

3. Twelfth Meeting of the CC (January 15, 1964)

On January 2 Felici called another meeting of the CC for January 15; attached to the letter of convocation was a note on the conclusions reached at the meeting on December 28, along with a list of the schemas to be discussed during the third period.[40] At the meeting, which was not attended by Spellman and Döpfner,[41] nor by Nabaa, Villot, Krol, and Kempf, Döpfner's plan was studied again. It was not easy to reach agreement, since this presupposed beginning with a tabula rasa as far as the agenda was concerned, and this in turn affected the major themes. The commission decided that since the schemas on the Church (except for chapter III on collegiality), revelation, and the bishops had already been reworked, they should not be further discussed in the hall but should immediately be put to a final vote.

[39] This intention was doubtless behind the letter of Msgr. Dell'Acqua, January 20, 1964, on increasing the number of lay auditors (see Caprile III, 326 n.3).

[40] *AS* V/2, 109-11.

[41] Döpfner was unable to reach Rome in time because a fog prevented his plane from taking off (*AS* V/2, 122).

Although the official minutes of the January 15 meeting speak of unanimous agreement that the Council should end in 1964, this presentation of the facts needs to be nuanced. Liénart protested against the minutes: neither the alleged necessity of ending the Council in the next period nor the refusal to study the schema on the lay apostolate reflected the positions he had taken at the meeting. Felici then tried to tone down the minutes, and so calm Liénart, by stating that the commission had not taken any definitive position on the ending of the Council; it had simply acknowledged the opportuneness of doing so, in line with the view expressed by the pope, although he too had not come to any decision.[42] The minutes of the meeting contain no trace of the text, critical of the Döpfner Plan, which Suenens had presented and Prignon had composed for the occasion.[43]

Following up what had been decided at the January 15 meeting, on January 23 Cicognani, in his capacity as president of the CC, wrote to Cardinals Pizzardo, Masella, Ciriaci, Marella, Antoniutti, and Cento, presidents respectively of the commissions for the schemas on clergy formation, on marriage, on the clergy, on the care of souls, on the states of perfection, and on the lay apostolate,[44] and to Msgr. Felici and Father Gregory Welykyj, secretary of the Commission for the Oriental Churches. His letter urged them to make the agreed-upon reduction in order to respect the suggestions given by the pope, and to proceed to the development of the texts that would be studied during the third period.

This second meeting of the intersession was thus intended as a continuation and at the same time a completion of the previous one in the perceptible effort to define the direction to be followed and to give the commissions the opportunity to pursue their activity, which would have to be intense during the intersession. In this connection it is worth recalling what Paul VI had said on December 4, 1963, as he brought the second period to a close:

> Other questions are still subject to further studies and discussions. We hope that the third session in the autumn of next year will bring them to completion. It is fitting that we should have more time to reflect on these difficult problems, and We place great hope during this recess period in the assistance of the competent commissions, trusting that their proposals for future meetings, prepared to reflect the mind of the Fathers particularly as

[42] See AS V/2, 133-34.
[43] Prignon Archive, 787b.
[44] AS V/2, 123-28.

expressed in the general congregations, will be profoundly studied, accurately formulated, and suitably condensed and abbreviated so that the discussions, while remaining always free, may be rendered easier and more brief.

The CC intensified its own work in order to translate these general directives of Paul VI into concrete action for each of the conciliar commissions.

C. THE ACTIVITY OF THE COMMISSIONS: NEW MEMBERS

1. Introduction

The general impression was that the majority of the commissions were very faithfully following the instructions given by the conciliar majority and, taking the Commission for the Liturgy as a model, should use the written *modi* of the fathers in order to compose texts to be presented to the Council. The members of the Doctrinal Commission, for example, were satisfied with the way it was doing its work during the second intersession. As we know, this commission had been enlarged after the additional votes taken at the end of the second period and as a result also of the papal appointments made later. As a result of these elections the commissions were more representative of the majority current. It was then that the CC paradoxically developed the Döpfner Plan, which presupposed a control of the commissions' work during the 1963-64 intersession.

It is also a fact that all who came in contact with the Doctrinal Commission agreed in saying that Cardinal Ottaviani presided over it with real impartiality; he is a "perfect chairman," said one American.[45] Similarly, it was said that very frequently the fathers of the commission achieved almost complete unanimity regarded the questions debated. But these statements, made as they were by persons outside the commission, did not accurately reflect the sometimes rather troubled reality of the search for an undoubtedly brittle unanimity. What might be said of one commission could probably not be generalized and applied to others; that possibility depended, naturally, on each commission, on each individual case, and on the subjects being debated. The restrictive nature of the Döpfner Plan caused many tensions, and there are numerous testimonies to the resistance it met from the presidents and members of the commissions.[46]

---

[45] See Rouquette, *La fin d'une chrétienté*, 2:438-39.

[46] See the critical reactions of Cento, Marella, Philips (in a memorandum), in *AS* V/2, 48-53; for Felici's response, ibid., 100-105.

From a doctrinal point of view, according to Laurentin, the commissions were threatened by two dangers: internal contradictions and powerlessness. The first was obvious: in what I have called the second phase, the conciliar minority was to take important initiatives in the Doctrinal Commission and, in the final meetings of the latter, was to launch counterattacks (for example, the one at the beginning of June) that left little time for reaction. Furthermore, feeling itself at a disadvantage in the commissions, the minority tried to influence the pope directly by letting him know its apprehensions on various debated matters: the role of the Virgin in the economy of salvation, the question of the "deicide" attributed to the Jews, religious freedom, the higher value set on scripture as compared with tradition, and, above all, the subject of episcopal collegiality, which could, it was thought, disturb the balance of the dogma approved at Vatican I. In regard to this last-named problem, Paul VI sent the commission thirteen "suggestions" to be studied at its meeting in June.

As for powerlessness, it is certain that the preponderant role of the Doctrinal Commission caused the failure of valid suggestions made by other commissions. In this case, however, the danger was due to the already described "structural impotence" of the Council which was caused by its "many-headed" character. The fact is that tensions between the representatives of the majority and those of the minority were found in all the commissions charged with the development of new texts to be presented to the Council fathers.

The guidelines followed in the unfolding work of the commissions were contained in the exhortation of Paul VI, guidelines "that enjoy the supreme support of the pope, together with that of the Council fathers."[47]

2. The Doctrinal Commission for the Schema on the Church

a. The Reworking of the Text

As we saw above, the subcommission for the revision of the schema on the Church, as well as its various subcommittees, had already studied the text before the intersession began and had to some extent put their seal on this work by appointing Charue and Philips as vice-president and

---

[47] Allocution on December 24, 1963, to the Sacred College and the Roman prelates, in *Insegnamenti*, II, 429.

assistant secretary of the Doctrinal Commission. In fact, however, the compromises reached between the theologians and fathers of these very small working groups were discussed again at various levels and by various jurisdictions during the months that followed. On two points, collegiality and religious, the first phase of the intersession brought important changes.

It quickly became clear, in fact, that the work on collegiality would be a very touchy business. The disagreement among the theologians of the fifth subcommittee, which had been charged with the revision of the articles having to do with the episcopal college and with the three episcopal functions of teaching, sanctifying, and governing, had been balanced out in two extensive competing memoranda of Rahner (32 pp.) and Tromp (10 pp.). Rahner had said he was inclined to accept the solution offered by Maccarrone, who wanted to avoid the word *college* (although even Salaverri's manual of 1962 asserted its existence!) and use the term *ordo* instead. On the other side, Tromp had limited himself to deploring the fact that there should be confused debates such as those on revelation and collegiality, which were harmful to the authority of the Council, "to say nothing of our faith."[48]

A text, however, did exist, even if one strongly marked by a universalist conception of the Church and of collegiality within it. There could be resistance to it, but it did not seem insuperable; an almost unnoticed sign of this was a letter that Cicognani sent to Ottaviani on January 23, 1964, in which he asked that "in particular, the text on the sacramentality and 'collegiality' of the episcopate be strongly emphasized, so that it may receive the most careful consideration of the Council fathers."[49]

But this emphasis was not followed by any direct and forceful actions in subsequent weeks. When the subcommission approved the substance of the text of the experts on the power of the college, Cardinal M. Browne (February 12, 1964)[50] and Tromp raised some objections. In their view the text suggested a right of the bishops to share in the government of the Church along with the pope, which meant a lessening of the fullness of the pope's personal powers. But their action did not raise an alarm or lead to disputes. Browne renewed his objection at the March meeting of the Doctrinal Commission,[51] at which, however, it was

[48] Report of subcommission V *De collegio*; mimeographed copies in Philips Archive.
[49] *AS* V/2, 129.
[50] Text in *Primauté*, 85-87.
[51] See U. Betti, *La dottrina sull'episcopato del Concilio Vaticano II. Il capitolo III della costituzione dommatica Lumen gentium* (Rome, 1984), 200.

decided to retain the text approved by the subcommission, except for a small change suggested by J. Heuschen, auxiliary bishop of Liège.[52]

By now even such men as Parente, the assessor of the Holy Office, had accepted the arguments in favor of collegiality.[53] Only a few fringe figures wanted to turn the question of collegiality into the banner of total opposition. This can be seen from the tone of articles against collegiality by D. Staffa in *Divinitas* and from the tenor of Father L. Ciappi's statement at the assembly of the Italian episcopate on April 16, 1964, in which he voiced his fear that Vatican II was amending *Pastor aeternus*. The pope, however, had no such fear at the end of the winter; the conclusions of the commission, which had met in plenary session on March 6, were communicated to him, and he implicitly approved them in his address on Holy Thursday, March 27, 1964. In this address he stated his determination to bring the ecumenical Council to a successful end "by giving episcopal collegiality the meaning and value which Christ intended to bestow on the apostles in their communion with and respect for the first among them, Peter, and by furthering every proposal aimed at increasing charity, collaboration, and trust within the Church of God."[54]

The second matter on which debate continued with some tremors was the subject of religious; proposals of the subcommittee on the topic were to be studied at the meetings of the commission on March 13 and 14. The main question raised was whether or not it was appropriate to divide the chapter into two parts: the first on the universal call to holiness, and the second on the profession of the evangelical counsels in the religious state. The collision of the two options saw Msgr. Charue and his supporters opposed to Father J. Daniélou. The latter regarded the division of the old chapter into two parts as a victory for clarity, since it recognized

---

[52] Heuschen had pointed out that by including the expression "*under* the head" the text once again proposed a subordination, which, to tell the truth, already appeared eight times in the same article and which, in addition, was already contained in the word "head." The commission agreed with the remark and returned to the formula of the previous text: "together with (*una cum*) its head."

[53] Parente was impressed by G. Alberigo's study *Lo sviluppo della dottrina dei poteri nella Chiesa universale tra il XVI e il XIX secolo*, which had appeared during these months. In light of this investigation (inspired and promoted by Dossetti), the abuses and excesses of the collegial theory of the Councils of Constance and Basel did not seem sufficient to reject an institution that had its origin in the apostolic college and whose existence and functioning were attested in the course of history. On P. Parente, see *Protagonisti*, 213-14.

[54] *OssRom*, March 28, 1964.

that religious are not part of the structure of the Church.[55] The chapter
thus became two: chapter V, which kept as its general title the call to
holiness in the Church, and chapter VI, devoted to religious. The original chapter thus was divided into two clearly distinct sections. Each contained new elements that brought out the suitableness of all the states of
life for reaching Christian perfection, as well as the special importance
of the religious state in the life of the Church. The most important
change introduced at the March meeting had to do with the sections on
the nature and importance of the religious state and on its relationship to
the authorities in the Church; both of these were placed in the second
section, that is, the one on religious. On the other hand, the decision on
whether this section should form an independent chapter was postponed
to the plenary session in June; but in fact it was not discussed even then,
the commission preferring to let the fathers decide this question in the
council hall.

On March 28, 1964, the periodical *Ecclesia* (Madrid) announced a
new chapter on the Church of the saints; the "text of this chapter was
worked out on the basis of a draft presented by Cardinal Larraona…who
had received from John XXIII the assignment of bringing up to date a
text on the eschatological aspects of the Church."[56] Pope John had been
thinking essentially of the veneration of the saints. Paul VI ordered that
the text be sent to the Doctrinal Commission so that it might be integrated into the schema on the Church. At its meeting on March 2 the
Doctrinal Commission created a subcommission with the task of composing a new text that could be a coherent part of the schema.[57] This text

---

[55] See J. Daniélou, "La place des religieux dans la structure de l'Eglise," *Etudes* 320
(January- June 1964), 147-55.

[56] C. Calderón, "Tareas de las Comisiones conciliares en orden a la tercera sesión del
Vaticano II," *Ecclesia* (Madrid), no. 1185 (March 28, 1964), 423.

[57] The Doctrinal Commission had received the text on February 5, 1964; on the 28th
of that month the pope expressed his wish that account be taken of this chapter in revising
the schema on the Church. At its meeting on March 2 the Doctrinal Commission was not
very enthusiastic about the idea of adding another chapter at this stage; in its view, a paragraph on the subject in the chapter on the Virgin would have sufficed. The problem was
discussed again at the meeting on March 14, but the resolution of it was postponed to the
June meeting. The commission regarded as unsatisfactory the revisions made in the text in
the interval, and on June 6 ordered a special subcommission to make further adaptations of
it, so that it might find a place between the chapter on the call to holiness and the chapter
on the Virgin. On June 8, therefore, everything was arranged in a more suitable way. The
members of the subcommission were R. Santos, F. König, and G. Garrone, assisted by
experts Molinari (who had helped Larraona), M. Labourdette, and C. Stano.

was sent to the fathers for their observations.[58] Later, in June, the text was studied once again under the direction of Cardinal Browne and then sent once more to the fathers; in the booklet it was presented as an "emended text," while the text approved between March and June was reproduced as the "previous text."[59] The text endeavored in a thorough way

> to analyze the eschatological fulfillment of the reign of God; it shows the bond uniting [the Church] with the saints already glorified, and it also justifies the veneration which the Church pays them. The veneration of the saints meets with a good deal of opposition in the modern world. It will find its full meaning only when expressly conceived in a Christological perspective and when it shows its fruitfulness, not by way of a superficial explanation of it but rather through a conscious penetration of the mystery of salvation as represented by the mystical body of Christ.[60]

This new and completely unanticipated chapter — "prepared at the last moment," as one expert said — was to be harmoniously introduced into the schema at a point and in a way that would enrich the latter. This would be done, first, by the chapter's title, "The Eschatological Nature of our Call and of Our Union with the Heavenly Church," and second, by its location, just before the final chapter on the Virgin,[61] thereby overcoming once and for all the doubts of those who saw the placement of the text on the Virgin "after those on the laity and religious" as a "way of banishing and destroying her." In fact, when the Virgin was located in the eschatological perspective of the glorious Church and at the same time united to the pilgrim Church, it became possible to bring out more easily her preeminent place in the Church, a question that had been the focus of difficult discussions from October 24 to October 29, 1963.

b. The Text on the Blessed Virgin

In his discourse at the end of the second period Paul VI had given rather explicit directives. These seemed even more important in light of

---

[58] The most radical criticisms came from the German bishops, who asked that the chapter be eliminated because it dealt with the Church triumphant and this in only an incidental way. The text should limit itself to considering the Church militant as such in its relations with the blessed.

[59] The experts were Congar, Moeller, Rahner, Gagnebet, Molinari, and Salaverri. They agreed with Browne that this chapter should be the next to last, before the chapter on the Virgin.

[60] G. Philips, "Le Schema sur l'Eglise," *De Maand* 7 (1964), 11.

[61] *DC*, no. 1428 (August 2, 1964), 980-81.

the great difficulties the Marian question had encountered during that
period. His remarks were compressed into a sentence that is difficult to
translate into modern languages:

> For the schema on the Blessed Virgin Mary, too, We hope
> for the solution most in keeping with the nature of this Coun-
> cil: that is, the unanimous and loving acknowledgment of the
> place, privileged above all others, which the Mother of God
> occupies in Holy Church — in that Church which is the prin-
> cipal subject matter of the present Council. After Christ, her
> place in the Church is the most exalted, and also the closest
> to us, so that we may honor her with the title "Mother of the
> Church" to her glory and our benefit.[62]

The address suggested a goal and two ways of reaching it. 1. The goal
was to restore unanimity, to gain a fervent consensus regarding the Virgin ("*ut uno consensu et summa pietate agnoscatur*"), by setting aside
irrelevant or impassioned arguments. In this connection the pope used
the expressive word *enodationem* rather than the current term, *solu-
tionem*. He proposed two essential means of reaching this goal:

2. The Virgin has her own place in the Church ("*locus...in sancta
ecclesia*"). On October 11, 1963, at the very time when the idea was
advanced that the introduction of the Marian text into the schema on the
Church was insulting to the Virgin, the pope clearly suggested that, on
the contrary, this introduction was appropriate; in the presence of the
Council fathers gathered in Santa Maria Maggiore he said: "Our Council...is learning to utter the name of the Madonna at part of the great
vision of the Church." And, further on, "O Mary! May the Church of
Christ, which is also your Church [*sua et tua Chiesa*], acknowledge you,
as it defines itself... "[63] These recommendations were then confirmed in
the closing address and above all in the vote by which on October 29 the
introduction of the text was approved by a slight majority.

3. Such an insertion into the text on the Church was not to mean a
reduction of the Virgin to the level of the other members of the Church.
The pope emphasized this point because the propaganda abroad in October had unfortunately persuaded some that this solution diminished the
privileges of the Madonna. To banish such fears, the pope made use of
several formulas: The Mother of God has the "highest" place and one
"peculiarly hers" (a phrase misinterpreted in many translations), "a

---

[62] *Insegnamenti,* 1:378; *The Pope Speaks* 9 (1963-64), 226.

[63] *Insegnamenti,* 1:207.

place so high that we may call her 'Mother of the Church.'" In this way he suggested "Mother of the Church" as a way of giving concrete form to his own thoughts about her.[64]

The atmosphere did not make it easy to draft a text that would satisfy all the fathers. Some accidental factors (difficulties of a psychological kind, in Laurentin's view[65]) accentuated oppositions that had no dogmatic basis. Differences of sensibility inhibited genuine dialogue on essentials.

The subcommission charged with reducing the former schema on the Virgin to a chapter in the schema on the Church moved very slowly. A preliminary meeting of ten experts at the Hospice of Saint Martha on November 25 still reflected the rather heated and far from merely academic atmosphere in which the vote of October 29 had been taken. The subcommission, made up of Cardinals Santos and König and Msgrs. P. Théas and M. Doumith, decided to entrust the composition of the text of the new chapter to Father Balić, president of the International Marian Academy and principal composer of the first schema, and to Msgr. Philips, who had just been elected as assistant secretary of the Doctrinal Commission.

The directives given to the two experts were to achieve harmony between the two tendencies that had come to light in the assembly and so provide a text as satisfying as possible to all the fathers. On the one side were those who wanted a solemn proclamation of the doctrine of Mary as Mother of the Church or the definition of the doctrine Mary as Mediatrix of all graces. On the other side were ecumenical circles that, observing the activity of what Congar called "galloping mariology," urged that the advance toward unity not be troubled by new dogmas. On this subject Bea had submitted a written intervention at the end of the second period,[66] and he now published a broad study entitled "Doctrine et piété mariales en accord avec l'esprit oecuménique" ("Marian Doctrine and Marian Devotion in Harmony with the Ecumenical Spirit"),[67] which influenced public opinion, especially that of the Council fathers. Given these circumstances, a new redaction of the schema on the Virgin became an urgent task.

The basis of the new redaction was a draft that Philips quickly composed in December. While taking into account the observations sent in,

[64] R. Laurentin, La Vierge au Concile (Paris, 1965), 18-21.
[65] Revue des Sciences Philosophiques et Théologiques 48 (1964), 45-46.
[66] AS II/3, 677-81.
[67] This appeared as a preface to volume VII of Marie, ed. H. Manoir (Paris, 1964), iii-xiii; it was reprinted in a number of languages in various journals.

he developed first and foremost the biblical basis of Marian doctrine, locating Mary in the history of salvation and giving greater space to the relationship between Mary and the Church. He did not emphasize the ideas of co-redemption and mediation but rather the role of faith in the life and activity of Mary.[68] There now began an irritating back-and-forth between Philips and Balić, which would end, provisionally, with a compromise, namely, with a redaction (the fifth) that was approved by the Doctrinal Commission in March 1964.[69] The commission accepted it as a basis of discussion despite stubborn opposition, notably in the form of motions offered by the Spanish bishops.[70]

On January 9, 1964, Balić had received the new version, the third, designated later as the "corrected text"; this was the text that Balić himself had composed on November 27 and that Philips had then corrected. In asking pardon for the delay in sending this corrected text, Philips explained that it was due to the fact that he had taken the liberty of submitting it to various experts and theologians with a view of reaching a common point of view. Following this example, Balić sent the corrected text, along with other documents, to the Spanish consultors, whose judgment was quite unfavorable.[71] It was in relation to this revision that Father Llamera wrote his "study of the corrections" and Father García Garcés wrote four pages of criticisms. But criticisms of the text did not come solely from the Spanish mariologists. The bishops of Germany and the Scandinavian countries were also critical, deploring the inadequate ecclesiological emphasis and asking that greater stress be placed on the relationship between Mary's privileges and the reality of the Church; they also asked that the "ecclesial" nature of Mary's mediation be asserted.[72]

[68] See *Caput VI seu epilogus de loco et munere B. V. Deiparae in mysterio Christi et ecclesiae*, C XIX 24.

[69] *Caput VI seu epilogus. De beata virgine Deipara in mysterio Christ et ecclesiae.* — *Textus a rev.mo D.no G. Philips et a p. C. Balić compositus*, C XIX 30. After approval by the Doctrinal Commission, the text was included in the booklet *De ecclesia: Textus propositus post discussiones martii 1964* (Vatican Polyglot Press, 1964), as chapter VII (or VI) or as an epilogue with the title "De beata Maria virgine deiparae in mysterio Christi et ecclesiae," on pp. 52-58. For the ups-and-downs of the text see G. N. Besutti, "Note di cronaca sul concilio Vaticano II e lo schema 'De beata Maria Virgine,'" *Marianum* 26 (1964), 1-42.

[70] On this subject a good source of information is A. Niño Picado, "La intervención española en la elaboración del cap. VIII de la Constitución 'Lumen gentium,'" *Ephemerides mariologicae* 18 (1968) 5-310, which supplies abundant documentation.

[71] See C. Balić, "El cap. VIII de la Constitución 'Lumen gentium' comparado con el primer esquema de la B. Virgen Madre de la Iglesia," *Estudios marianos* 27 (1966), 137-38 n.5.

[72] *AS* II/3, 837-49.

The Chilean bishops, for their part, asked in their observations for "an exposition of doctrine that will make it clearer how Mary is so intimately a part of the people of God that she is a synthesis of it," since in the text the person of Mary seemed still too isolated.[73] On the same lines as the Chilean bishops and Abbot Butler, the English Benedictine, Laurentin remarked that the text of the chapter was not sufficiently developed in relation to the communion of the saints in Christ.[74] In these circumstances Balić decided to compose a new version (the fourth) of the schema on the Virgin.[75] But in face of new difficulties and in view of the goal of presenting a common text as desired by the subcommission, he accepted the fifth (and final) version, written by Philips, which was presented to the subcommission on February 20, 1964, as a text agreed on by both.[76]

During the first week of June this text was the subject of new discussions, and new emendations were allowed. It was then that, by a surprise vote, the term *mediatrix* was introduced into the debate, an action that Philips judged contrary to the conciliatory approach taken by Msgr. Charue (president of the subcommission on the Blessed Virgin) and himself. The difficulty was to find a proper balance between those who wanted the title of mediatrix and those who did not. The "liturgical" solution that was offered found a place in the final text. After some finishing touches (as we shall see) the text was approved by the commission on June 6 and then definitively prepared for presentation in the hall. On July 3 Paul VI ordered the schema on the Church, in its complete version, to be passed on to the fathers. This text, circulated as an "emended text," was to serve as the basis for the debate. The Doctrinal Commission was unanimously of the opinion that the chapter on the Blessed Virgin should come in last place, "because it presents minds with a summary of the extensive material set forth in the schema."[77]

[73] *AS* II/3, 830-34.

[74] See *Animadversiones in cap. VII (seu epilogum) de B.V.M. (15 mars 1964)*, C XIX 32; *Le chapitre marial du Vatican II doit-il parler de médiation?*, C XIX 33; *Médiation, intercession, patronnage. Pour la solution d'un problème de vocabulaire*, C XIX 34.

[75] See Balić, "El cap. VIII."

[76] According to Laurentin, the subcommission now read the text for the first time; after some improvement it was printed at the end of March. After further correction during the discussions in March, the schema was emended once again in the discussion in June, where it became the "emended text." See R. Laurentin, "Genèse du texte conciliare," *Etudes mariales* 22 (1965), 11-12.

[77] See G. N. Besutti, *Lo schema mariano al Concilio Vaticano II* (Rome, 1966), 234-68.

In sending this volume to the fathers, Msgr. Felici attached a letter in which he reminded them of the new arrangements for an improved handling of the work: "Those who want to speak on the chapter on the Blessed Virgin must submit their request to the General Secretariat, along with a summary, before September 9."[78]

3. The Commission for the Schema on Revelation[79]

On December 4, in his address at the close of the second period, Pope Paul VI mentioned that the question of revelation was among those still waiting for an answer from the Council. New comments then began to come in from the fathers; avoiding the danger of remaining entangled in the now familiar discussions, they were increasingly marked by greater serenity and objectivity. They began in July 1963 and continued to come in until April 1964, although the final date for accepting them had been set as January 31. About 300 fathers sent in their comments; seventy-five of them sent them as individuals, while others did so as members of various episcopal conferences or groups. The numerically largest group was the sixty German-speaking bishops; the group marked by the greatest fervor for renewal was perhaps the twenty-eight Indonesian bishops.

There were not many completely negative criticisms of the schema, except for two groups of fathers who, though for different reasons, asked that the schema be abandoned: for the one group, the schema lacked any interest because it did not tackle the central themes; while for the other,

---

[78] As a result of this letter, the secretariat of the Spanish episcopate asked Father García Garcés, in a letter of August 22, to compose a report on chapters VII and VIII (the one on the Virgin) that would orient the fathers with a view to the third period. This report, translated into Latin, was widely circulated in Rome. During these same days there also appeared a letter from the Spanish mariologists, members of the Sociedad Mariológica Española, dated September 12 from Madrid and likewise circulated among the Spanish fathers. Both documents are very important for knowledge of the rigid demands made by the Spanish mariologists right up to the last moment.

[79] See especially J. Ratzinger, ""Dogmatic Constitution on Divine Revelation: Origin and Background," in *Commentary*, 3:155-66; B.-D. Dupuy, "Historique de la Constitution," in *Vatican II. La révélation divine* (Paris, 1968), 1:61-117; H. Sauer, *Erfahrung und Glaube. Die Begründung des pastoralen Prinzips durch die Offenbarungskonstitution des II. Vatikanischen Konzils* (Würzburg, 1993), and R. Burigana's review of this book in *CrSt* 16 (1995), 683-89; *Constitutio Dogmatica de divina revelatione "Dei Verbum,"* ed. F. G. Hellin (Rome, 1993); *La "Dei Verbum" trent'anni dopo: Miscellanea in onore del p. Umberto Betti*, ed. N. Ciola (Rome, 1995), which contains the conciliar diary of Father Betti, author of *La dottrina del Concilio Vaticano II sulla trasmissione della Rivelazione* (Rome, 1985); R. Burigana, *La Bibbia nel Concilio: La redazione della costituzione 'Dei verbum' del Vaticano II* (Bologna, 1998).

the schema should not advance because it should have confronted debatable questions in this or that manner. On the other hand, neither was there a great deal of unconditional praise; only about sixty fathers took that line.

The number of emendations proposed (2,481!) and their varied origins showed that not all the fathers were in agreement in their judgment and resolution of points that had remained unexpressed or were doubtful. Some found the language of the schema to be insufficiently precise, while others found it to be overly academic. While some praised the absence of condemnations, others saw the schema as anxious to find errors everywhere, and still others were disappointed at not finding a more extensive condemnation of errors.[80] There were those who expected that the exegetes would find in the document further encouragement for their work, but others feared that the document would encourage exegetes to even greater rashness in their studies. But these disagreements did not succeed in hiding a common concern to rework the schema and complete it on points that had been left undetermined.

All this made it clear that the intersession would be marked by zealous activity in composing a new text (which would now be the third, since the mixed commission had already proposed a "Text 2" on April 22, 1963) which would be offered for discussion in the hall during the third period. The petition that the schema on revelation be debated during the third period had been sent to Felici by Cardinal Liénart as early as December 19, 1963;[81] Cardinal Urbani sent in a similar request, due specifically to the words of Paul VI in his closing address for the second period on December 4.[82]

At the eleventh meeting of the CC on December 28, 1963, it was decided that the schema on revelation should be brought to the fathers after it had been restudied by the Doctrinal Commission in light of the comments received.[83] On January 2, 1964, Felici called the CC to meet on the 15th of that month for continued discussion of the conclusions reached at the December 28 meeting.[84] The next day he informed Ottaviani of the decisions taken on the schema on revelation and told him

---

[80] They appealed to, among other things, the papal address on December 4, at the end of the second period: "...the Council will give a reply [on revelation] which, while defending the sacred deposit of divine truth against the errors, abuses, and doubts that endanger its objective validity..." (*The Pope Speaks* 9, 225).

[81] *AS* V/2, 66-67.

[82] *AS* V/2, 67-69.

[83] *AS* V/2, 95-96.

[84] *AS* V/2, 109-11.

that the CC wanted to be kept informed about the revision of the schema.[85]

That same day there was a meeting of the mixed commission, whose members agreed on the feasibility of resuming their work, provided that the principles adopted in 1963 were not set aside. The commission recognized that even though "Text 2" had not been discussed in the hall, it had been the subject of numerous written emendations and that these were important enough to necessitate a revision of the text.[86] The mixed commission then left to the Doctrinal Commission the task of undertaking such a revision in accordance with its usual working methods. The result would then be submitted to Cardinal Bea. On January 13 Döpfner wrote to the Council fathers of Germany, Austria, Luxembourg, Switzerland, and Scandinavia, telling them about the present situation of the schemas and putting forward some concrete suggestions regarding the schema on revelation.[87] This action made evident the degree of excitement that surrounded the subject.

On January 15, at its twelfth meeting, the CC agreed with the need to revise the schema in light of the comments sent in by the fathers and approved by the Doctrinal Commission. There was to be added, in an appendix, a report explaining the changes made and the reasons for them. During this meeting Liénart read some remarks on procedure during the third period; his remarks also referred to the norms for revising the schema on revelation.[88]

It is not unimportant, in view of the activity of those days, that Garrone proposed including the schema on revelation in the schema on the Church. According to Philips, the proposal was submitted to the mixed commission, which rejected it on the grounds that the schema on revelation should remain autonomous.[89]

At a meeting of the Doctrinal Commission on March 3, Henríquez, auxiliary bishop of Caracas, asked for the creation of a subcommittee of bishops and experts that would assess the comments of the bishops on the schema. Father Tromp, secretary of the commission, answered that a

---

[85] *AS* V/2, 100.

[86] A few days later Ottaviani let Felici know that the Doctrinal Commission had received comments from about 300 bishops (*AS* V/2, 100-101).

[87] Brouwers Archive, 11.

[88] *AS* V/2, 116-22. A few days later, on January 23, Cicognani wrote to Ottaviani confirming that the schema should be reworked on the basis of the comments of the fathers that had been received by the mixed commission (*AS* III/3, 887).

[89] Philips Archive, 79, 3. Garrone's proposal echoed earlier French suggestions.

report on these comments had already been made.[90] However, on March 7 the Doctrinal Commission did in fact set up a subcommission with the task of developing the schema on the basis of the Council's comments. The subcommission comprised seven fathers (with Charue as president) and nineteen experts and was to have a crucial influence on the composition of the text of the constitution. The presence of some new theologians among the experts was decisive. The German theologians (Grillmeier, Rahner, Ratzinger, and Semmelroth), the French, Belgian, and Dutch theologians (Congar, Philips, Heuschen, Moeller, Prignon, Rigaux, and Smulders), and Betti, a Franciscan and Florit's trusted theologian, soon proved to be playing a key part in the work of the subcommission.

This subcommission met on March 11 to begin the work that was to lead to the composition of the constitution *Dei Verbum*; they broke up into two groups. The first, with Florit, Archbishop of Florence, presiding, was to deal with the first part of the text: the introduction and chapter I, "Revelation and Tradition" (the experts of this group were Schauf, Prignon, Moeller, K. Rahner, Smulders, Congar, Betti, Tromp, Ramírez, and, at Ottaviani's request, Van Den Eynde). The second, with Msgr. Charue and Msgr. van Dodewaard presiding, was to handle the second part, that is, the chapters on scripture; it relied on Cerfaux, Gagnebet, Garofalo, Turrado, Rigaux, Semmelroth, and Grillmeier as experts. Until mid-April the experts worked on classifying and assessing the comments of the fathers. The comments on the introduction were studied by Smulders, who was helped in preparing the text by Cerfaux, Colombo, Moeller, Prignon, and Msgr. Heuschen. Schauf and K. Rahner collected and assessed the comments on the first chapter. When it came to composing the next text, Rahner and Congar assumed the task of composing two partial texts on scripture and tradition. Two other texts, but dealing this time with the entire chapter, were composed by Betti and   Heuschen, the latter in collaboration with Cerfaux, Moeller, and Smulders.

The study of the comments on the second chapter fell to Semmelroth, Grillmeier, and Ratzinger. Rigaux and Turrado dealt with those on the fourth chapter, each making his own independent analysis. Finally, Semmelroth and Grillmeier composed the report on the comments on chapter V. On April 15, Betti, in his capacity as secretary of the subcommission, reminded its members of the time and place where they would

---

[90] *JCongar*, March 3, 1964.

gather to discuss the new schema; the meeting took place at 4 p.m. on April 20 at Santa Marta. From that time until April 25, in several group meetings and four plenary sessions, the subcommission discussed the changes studied by the periti. At the end it determined the text that was to replace the one developed a year earlier by the mixed commission.

The analysis of the introduction led to a lively discussion of two points. The first was the relation between deeds *(gesta)* and words *(verba)* in revelation. Tromp tenaciously defended the view that gave unqualified priority to words, on the grounds that faith comes "by hearing" and that all the texts of the scriptures and the tradition speak of the "word of God." The second point was the notion of primitive revelation, based on awareness that all human beings can be saved; according to Congar, this revelation began after Abraham, not after Adam. At Philips's suggestion the introduction was transformed into a first chapter, with the title "On Revelation Itself." Subsequently, in composing the third chapter ("On the Divine Inspiration and Interpretation of Scripture"), Grillmeier, Ratzinger, and Semmelroth would qualify some points under discussion. On the morning of April 23 the text on the Old and New Testaments was approved (easily, according to Grillmeier's diary). Prignon drew up the minutes of the subcommission's work, since there was to be a plenary session the next day.[91] At this session the second chapter was studied and approved;[92] a joint meeting of the two subcommissions was held, and they began to study the introduction and first two chapters, while in the afternoon they took up the remaining chapters.[93]

On the final day of meetings a new study of the last two chapters was made, and it was decided that all the comments be sent to Philips, who was asked to prepare a definitive version. At the same time, the group stressed the importance of the *Instruction on the Historicity of the Gospels*, which the Pontifical Biblical Commission had just published on April 21.[94]

On May 11 Felici sent the Council fathers the list of the schemas to be discussed during the third period; the schema on revelation came first on the list.[95] At the Doctrinal Commission's meeting on June 1, Tromp, who had assigned the discussion of revelation to the last place on the

[91] Prignon Archive, 823.
[92] Ibid., 743; *JCongar*, April 23, 1964.
[93] *TSemmelroth*, April 23, 1964.
[94] *AAS* 56 (1964), 712-18.
[95] *AS* V/2, 500-501.

agenda, made it known that Bea, in the name of his secretariat, had given his overall approval of the schema and therefore did not call for any further meetings of the mixed commission. In addition, the pope wanted the schemas on revelation and on the Church sent to the fathers as quickly as possible.[96] With Bea's *placet*,[97] the text went to the Doctrinal Commission for examination at four meetings held from June 3 to June 5 and was approved without any special difficulties, although the minority tried to block the first two chapters, and Ottaviani did his best to limit the interventions of the majority's theologians. Some differences arose only on the question of the greater objective content of tradition as compared with that scripture. When put to a vote, the proposed text, which did not take up that question, received the two-thirds needed for approval (17 votes to 7).

In order, however, that the positions taken by the minority might not remain buried forever in the debate within the commission, Franić, Bishop of Spalato, was appointed reporter for the minority, so that when the right moment came, he might present its views for the consideration of the fathers. At the same time, reporters for the majority were also appointed: Florit, for the first part, and van Dodewaard, Bishop of Haarlem, for the second.

4. The Secretariat for Christian Unity

a. The Schema on Ecumenism

Toward the end of the second period, on November 21, 1963, it was announced that the membership of the commissions and of the Secretariat for Christian Unity would be broadened.[98] Strengthened by this

---

[96] *JCongar*, June 1, 1964.

[97] When asked by Charue for an opinion, Bea had already received a positive opinion from De Smedt and some Louvain theologians.

[98] On November 29 the names of those elected to the secretariat were made known: M. Hermaniuk (Winnepeg, representing the Ukrainians), Ch. Helmsing (Kansas City, USA), J. W. Gran (coadjutor of Oslo, Norway), P. Cantero Cuadrado (Huelva, Spain), E. Primeau (Manchester, USA), L. Lorscheider (Santo Angelo, Brazil), G. Ramantonanina (Fianarantsoa, Madagascar), and D. Lamont (Umtali, Southern Rhodesia). On January 8, 1964 (*OssRom,* January 11, 1964) the pope appointed R. Rabban (a Chaldean of Kerkuk, Iraq), W. Hardt (Dunkeld, Scotland), Father B. Heiser, general of the Friars Minor (USA), and Father O. Degrijse, general of the Scheut Missionaries (Belgium). In February 1964 Paul VI sent further names to the secretariat: Cardinal Umberto Quintero, Archbishop of Caracas (Venezuela); G. Manek, Archbishop of Endeh (Indonesia); J. G. Raymond, Archbishop of Nagpur (India); and G. Stangi, Bishop of Würzburg (Germany).

new personnel, the secretariat would begin its work during the intersession. While the first three chapters of the decree on ecumenism had already been approved, the status of the remaining two, on religious freedom and on the Jews, had yet to be decided.[99]

After being carefully organized, the comments received were patiently studied by about twenty experts of the secretariat, among them G. Baum and J. M. Oesterreicher, both converts and of Jewish background, at a meeting which lasted from February 4 to 24.[100] The text that emerged from this study was reviewed at a plenary session of the secretariat (about fifty individuals), which was held at Ariccia on Lake Albano from February 24 to March 7.[101] In an interview published in *La Civiltà Cattolica*, Bea judged that the reworked text "was clearer, struck an even better balance between its several parts, and, in a way, was even more open."[102] But the group also had to decide where to place the last two chapters, which had not been discussed at the general congregations. After this plenary meeting the decree on ecumenism had for practical purposes reached its definitive form, despite some subsequent corrections.

To the three chapters of the original schema was added an introduction explaining the aims of the text; this in accord with requests expressed by some bishops[103] and in a document sent by the World Council of Churches (WCC) and signed by Vischer. This latter document had reached Bea at the beginning of February and contained a list of the WCC's "concerns and convictions." Some criticisms were voiced

---

[99] At the same time, however, countless comments were piling up that had to be integrated into the text. According to Cardinal Bea, "Problemi conciliari ed ecumenici. Intervista del card. Agostino Bea," *CivCatt*, no. 2732 (April 18, 1964), 105-13, by the end of January 1964, 471 statements, oral and written, had reached the secretariat; 75 of these had been sent by groups of bishops. These statements formed a volume of 226 pages of general comments on the schema, a volume of 340 pages of comments on the first and second chapters, a volume of 145 pages on chapter III, a volume of 72 pages on the question of the Jews, and finally, a volume of 280 pages on religious freedom, for a total of 6 volumes and 1,063 pages. For the activities of the cardinal and his secretariat during the second intersession see S. Schmidt, *Augustine Bea: The Cardinal of Unity* (New Rochelle, N.Y., 1992), 438-44.

[100] Not all the consultors who had worked on the schema were invited to this meeting (see J. M. Oesterreicher, "Decree on the Relationship of the Church to the Non-Christian Religions: History of the Text," in *Commentary*, 3:17-136; the writer does not explain the reason for this). See *AS* V/2, 165-66. There are also interesting details in M. Velati, *Una difficile transizione. Il cattolicesimo tra unionismo ed ecumenismo* (Bologna, 1996), 400-403.

[101] *AS* V/2, 151-52 and 166-69.

[102] Bea, "Problemi conciliari ed ecumenici," 106.

[103] For example, by Msgr. Carli; see *AS* V/2, 691-92.

regarding a conception of ecumenism that was essentially "Romanocentric," the failure to acknowledge the right of other Churches to be considered the true Church of Christ, and the silence concerning the bond of unity already existing within the ecumenical movement.[104] According to Vischer, the introduction should, in view of its programmatic nature, emphasize three aspects: acknowledgment of the presence of the Spirit in the beginnings of the ecumenical movement; the idea of ecumenism as a dynamic process; and finally, an explanation of the purpose of the entire document. There is no doubt that these very considerations were also present in the work of the secretariat's experts, as they were in the two drafts presented at the February meeting by Thils and Congar.

The conclusions reached and the general characteristics of the revision of the text on the Jews were these: (1) Although a few judged it inopportune to tackle this problem, the schema ought to be retained, both because of the intrinsic importance of the subject treated and because of the high expectations it had aroused throughout the world. (2) The schema had been reworked and shortened. (3) Given the special relationship between the Church and the chosen people of the Old Testament, the schema should remain connected with the schema on ecumenism, not however as a chapter but as an appendix. (4) In this same appendix, relations with the other religions, Islam in particular, were also to be taken up.[105]

In like manner, the chapter on religious freedom seemed to some fathers, among them Cardinal Léger, to be rather out of place in this schema, since it was concerned with principles for coexistence among the religions and not only among Christians. In this case, however, the members of the secretariat proved reluctant to separate this part of the schema from the rest, primarily for "tactical" reasons. The great fear of Bea and other members of the secretariat was of seeing the subject of religious freedom end up entirely in the hands of the Doctrinal Commission, which would have meant the reappearance of the conflict that had arisen two years earlier in the Central Preparatory Commission.

On March 9 Bea wrote to Cicognani and explained the results of the secretariat's meetings. In the CC, on May 16, Cardinal Confalonieri successfully proposed that the chapter on religious freedom be turned into a "First Declaration" and the chapter on the Jews into a "Second Declaration."[106]

---

[104] English version: *You Have Repeatedly Invited* (January 1964; 14 pp.); see WCC Archive 5.
[105] *AS* III/2, 334.
[106] *AS* V/2, 292-93.

b. The Question of the Jews

Some important information on the revision of the text on the Jews is to be found in the report with which Bea presented it in the hall on September 25, during the third period of the Council.[107] The attention that the CC had given the schema seems to have been significant, for the usual procedure, according to the Regulations, was for the CC to examine a schema before it was sent to the fathers, but in this case "the members of the CC know that this short text has cost them no little time." Descending to details, Bea explained that they had discussed at length the problem, which would remain crucial throughout the process of redaction, of whether and, if so, how to treat the question of "deicide". The reason behind this explanation had had consequences even for procedure. According to Bea.

> these deliberations took a great deal of time. Consequently it was no longer possible to submit this part of the declaration to the members of the Secretariat once again for their study. In fact, since the Secretariat had completed its analysis of all the other material for debate at the meeting in March, it did not seem suitable to call the members to Rome once again in order to discuss only this part.[108]

This fact required, in Bea's judgment, that the Council fathers examine this part of the problem more carefully.

One result of the situation was that the Oriental bishops aligned themselves with the minority in regard to the declaration. This seems to have been the only instance in which the Melkite fathers appreciably distanced themselves from the line taken by the renewal wing; on this point they gave priority to a concern to protect the Christian minorities in Muslim countries. Msgr. Edelby's diary, which is explicit on this point, does not fully examine these motivations, but it does reveal the uneasiness with which the Melkites confronted this subject at the Council. In any case, one fruit of the Melkite effort was the expansion of the conciliar document to include the non-Christian religions, including Islam and not excluding Judaism.[109]

---

[107] See *DC*, no. 1435 (November 1, 1964), 1421-28.

[108] *AS* III/2, 561. This fact explains the polemical intervention of some fathers who were members of the secretariat, of Heenan for example, according to whom the text had been composed not by the secretariat but by some "inexpert experts" (see Osterreicher, "Decree on the Relationship," in *Commentary*, 3:66).

[109] *JEdelby*, 213, 241-43.

c. Religious Freedom: From Simple Chapter to Declaration

The Declaration on Religious Freedom has been the subject of a number of well-documented studies.[110] In order to make clear the chronology of the course taken by this text we must start with the meeting of the CC on December 28, 1963. On that occasion Döpfner, reporter on the subject, said:

> Whether the chapter thus far numbered V (on religious freedom) remains in the old schema or is made a special decree or declaration, it can perhaps be even further shortened by omitting points that can give rise to rather bitter disagreements, without there being any need of dealing with them in the Council.

On January 3, 1964, Felici asked the secretariat for news on chapters IV and V of the schema on ecumenism. On January 14 Bea replied that, for the moment, he could not give a sure answer since a plenary meeting of the secretariat was to be held from February 24 to March 7. He did, however, give his personal opinion:

> Chapter V, on religious freedom, should be kept in the schema on ecumenism because of its importance among the problems of ecumenism and because of its connection with the thought of the schema. Furthermore, during these days the members of the Secretariat are studying the comments thus far received from the Council fathers and are looking for a formula that will make clearer the connection of the chapter with the question of ecumenism.

At its meeting on January 15, 1964, the CC abstained from making decisions on chapters IV (the Jews) and V (religious freedom) of the schema on ecumenism, because it was waiting for the proposals of the secretariat. Fearing that the Declaration on Religious Freedom might be rejected or substantially changed, Albert Meyer, Archbishop of Chicago,

---

[110] From the extensive bibliography: P. Pavan, "Declaration on Religious Freedom," in *Commentary*, 4:49-86; *Vatican II. La liberté religieuse*, ed. J. Hamer and Y. Congar (Paris, 1965), esp. 53-110; Ph. Delhaye, *DTC Tables*, col. 4323-24; J.C. Murray, "The Declaration on Religious Freedom," in *War, Poverty, Freedom: The Christian Response*, *Concilium* 15 (New York, 1966), 3-16; and D. Gonnet, *La liberté religieuse à Vatican II. La contribution de John Courtney Murray* (Paris, 1994). In following the concrete progress of the schema during the second intersession I have been helped especially by the studies of J. Grootaers and V. Carbone in *Paolo VI e il rapporto chiesa- mondo al Concilio* (Brescia, 1991), 85-176. The same volume contains the testimonies of three theologians who played a part in the development of the final text (J. Hamer, P. Pavan, and C. Colombo), but none of these provides information on what happened during the second intersession. For this one must consult P. Pavan, "Il cardinale Bea e la libertà religiosa," in *Simposio card. Agostino Bea*, ed. Secretariat for Christian Unity (Rome, 1983) 116-47.

wrote directly to the pope on January 28; on March 12, Cardinal Joseph Ritter, Archbishop of St. Louis, did the same.

The plenary meeting of the secretariat was held from February 24 to March 7 at the Casa di Gesù Divino Maestro in Ariccia. By that time the secretariat had received 380 written comments or suggested emendations, which were combined into a volume of 280 pages. The written report on this occasion listed five criteria: (1) Give clearer expression to the concept of religious freedom being used in the declaration, in order to avoid any erroneous or dubious interpretations. (2) Point out more explicitly the rights of religious communities. (3) Explain better the principle by which the rights of Catholics can be limited. (4) Emphasize the objective truth of the divine law with all its requirements, in order to exclude any danger of subjectivism or indifferentism. (5) Show how the present conditions of the human race confirm the need to assert the right to religious freedom.

On March 9 Bea told Cicognani that the text on religious freedom was to be chapter IV of the schema on ecumenism. This decision was approved by the CC on March 10. On March 23 Bea sent Felici the text composed and unanimously approved at the plenary meeting of the fathers of the secretariat.

Pietro Pavan sent the pope a long and informative note: "The right of persons — physical or moral — to freedom in the area of religion." This was accompanied by a letter in which it was said that "there is universal expectation that the Council will take a position on the subject; that position will surely have an immense and profound influence on the entire human family." On April 6 the pope had Msgr. Dell'Acqua pass this note on to Felici and Tromp. At its meeting on April 16 the CC studied the schema on ecumenism, which had the Declaration on Religious Freedom as an appendix. At Confalonieri's suggestion it was decided that the text should become a declaration. As a result, Felici told Bea on April 18: "To the first three chapters on ecumenism are added two Declarations: A Declaration on the Jews and non-Christian peoples... a Declaration on Religious Freedom."

5. The Commission on Bishops and the Government of Dioceses

This commission, which had Cardinal Paolo Marella as president and Msgr. L. Governatori as secretary, was expanded by decision of Paul VI toward the end of the second period.[111] At the beginning of the interses-

---

[111] The names of the four new elected members were made known on November 29: J. Carrol (auxiliary bishop of Sidney, Australia), E. Schick (auxiliary bishop of Fulda,

sion a study was made of the various projects that came together to form two schemas, "On Bishops and the Governance of Dioceses,"and "On the Care of Souls," which would have to be reworked. The former document, to which Louvain canonist W. Onclin had contributed to a special degree,[112] was divided into three parts. The first took up the theme of the bishop in the service of the universal Church (and not only on occasion of a synod of bishops[113]); the second had to do with the bishop in his diocese and with his threefold ministry of teaching, sanctifying, and governing; the third dealt with cooperation among the bishops, with a reference to the tradition of provincial councils and, above all, to episcopal conferences.

The commission decided to meet in Rome, December 27-30, together with the secretaries of the subcommissions, in order to settle its working method in the revision of the draft and in examining the possibility of consolidating the two decrees already drawn up. On December 18 Marella wrote a letter to the CC, asking for a decision on the suitability of combining the two decrees. On January 23, 1964, Cicognani, in his role as president of the CC, let Marella know the decision taken: the decree on bishops and the government of dioceses had to be reworked on the basis of the directives confirmed on November 26, 1963, which emphasized the pastoral character of the decree, while questions of a juridical kind were to be studied by the Commission for the Reform of the Code of Canon Law. As for the schema on the care of souls, this would no longer appear on the list of schemas with which the Council would deal.

At the meeting of the secretaries of the five subcommissions on January 27, 1964, the draft quickly prepared by Onclin and presented by representatives of the first subcommission was accepted. The entire formulation of the text, with its three parts — collegiality and relationship of periphery to center in the Church; the bishops in their dioceses; intermediate authorities (councils, synods, episcopal conferences) — was different from the preceding text. Not only was it less juridical, it also adopted theological foundations that the schema on bishops and the government

Germany), A. Viola (Salto, Uruguay), and O. McCann (Cape Town, South Africa). On January 8 the pope appointed B. Printesis (Athens, Greece).

[112] See J. S. Quinn, "Mgr. Onclin and the Second Vatican Council," in *Liber amicorum Mgr. Onclin* (Gembloux, 1976), 13-21. See especially the Onclin (Louvain) and Veuillot (Paris) Archives, which are valuable for details of the history of the schema during the second intersession (they can be consulted at the ISR).

[113] See J. I. Arrieta, *El sinodo de los obispos* (Pamplona, 1987).

of dioceses had lacked, except for the principle "the salvation of souls is the supreme law" and for the need to strengthen the jurisdiction of bishops.

But while such presuppositions were in line with the calls, frequent in the *vota* and in the debate, for the "liberation" of "monarchical diocesan power," the real innovation came in the prologue and first chapter of the new schema ("The Bishops in Relation to the Universal Church"), accepting as they did the dogmatic section on collegiality in the schema on the Church. The section on the "ordinary, special, and immediate power" of bishops was in fact inserted into chapter I (on their solicitude for the universal Church), after the description of a "central group or council" that would support the pope in caring for the business of the universal Church (the group had been suggested by many fathers during the debate in the hall), and before the proposal for renewing and internationalizing the Roman Curia. As for episcopal conferences, provision was made for giving juridical force to their decisions, but (as a result to some extent of Carli's report on chapter III of the earlier schema, on November 12, 1963) the text avoided discussing the theological foundation of the conferences, whose existence was instead justified on essentially historical and pastoral grounds.

This, then, would be the basis of the new schema, now titled "The Pastoral Office of Bishops in the Church." Starting with the tripartite structure just described, a limited commission composed a draft of a shortened decree, as requested by the CC. The Commission for Bishops met in Rome March 3-13, 1964, and after studying the text and making some changes in it, approved the version dated March 13. The text was then sent to the CC, which approved it at its meeting on April 16, after hearing Döpfner's report and despite the emendations sent by Carli to Cardinal Marella.[114] After a new meeting of the commission on April 27-28, limited this time to reporters and secretaries, the draft decree was printed and sent to the bishops on May 22, accompanied by a letter from Felici.[115]

6. The Commission for the Lay Apostolate

This commission, which had Cardinal Silva Henríquez and Msgr. O'Connor as presidents and A. Glorieux and A. Galletto as secretaries,

---

[114] *AS* V/2, 187-91.
[115] *AS* V/2, 500-501.

was expanded at the end of the second period. At the time J. da Silva (auxiliary bishop of Lisbon). M. Fernández Conde (Cordoba, Spain), A. Babcock (Grand Rapids, USA), Helder Câmara (auxiliary bishop of Rio de Janeiro, Brazil), and W. Möhler, general of the Pallottines (Germany) became new members.

The first months of 1964 were dominated not only by the need to produce a unitary schema, but also, like the other schemas under development, by a certain uneasiness owing to the need to end the Council as soon as possible. On December 13, 1963, the secretary sent Hengsbach's proposal to all the members and experts of the commission and asked for their comments on the text before January 6, in view of the plenary meeting planned for February. This phase of the work was important because it radically challenged the schema developed during the preparatory phase. This explains the surprise felt by various members of the commission, as can be seen from a letter that Cardijn sent to Glorieux with a request for precise details on the subject.

In January 1964 the Roman group summarized the responses of the commission members to Hengsbach's plan: "They are all quite favorable, even though many maintain that the plan is so schematic as not to allow a definitive judgment."[116] One French father added: "I see a serious defect: the absence of theological principles, which implies an excessive trust in the text of the schema on the Church, which will not provide everything we need"; he took the occasion to recall that toward the end of the second period of the Council a group of French fathers had sent in a more doctrinal text for the general section on the apostolate. Finally, a Roman expert worked out the Hengsbach proposal in greater detail. It was on these three bases that the definitive plan was developed and then presented in the form of three chapters at the meeting on January 25, 1964.

But on that very day the Commission for the Lay Apostolate received a letter from Cicognani, who in his capacity as president of the CC gave the following directives:

> The schema on the lay apostolate is to be reduced to its essential points and therefore presented in the form of propositions on which the fathers will vote after a short discussion; the entire remaining part of the present

---

[116] *Acta commissionis Conciliaris "De Fidelium Apostolatu,"* 77. The study meetings, open only to the Roman experts, were held on January 13, 16, 18. 22, 23, and 25, with Cento, Lentini, Quadri, Papali, Tucci, Bogliolo, and perhaps Ferrari-Toniolo and Pavan in attendance.

schema will be referred to the commission for the reform of the Code, or
will be used for special instructions from the Holy See.[117]

"The new situation in which our schema found itself displeased all a
great deal," but, unlike all the other conciliar commissions,[118] which
simply obeyed to the letter the orders of the CC, in this commission an
effort was made to save the text as much as possible by giving a broad
meaning to the expression "in the form of propositions." Accordingly,
the Secretary General of the Council was told that this was not simply a
matter of "drawing up a general index of subjects." Moreover, one of
the four moderators of the Council told one of the members of the commission that the norms formulated by the CC were to be understood in a
broad sense and that in practice a draft of ten or twelve pages would be
fair. Even the president of the CC said that the propositions could be
grouped so as to form chapters and that the whole which emerged from
them should not resemble a fleshless skeleton.[119]

From this the commission inferred that a list of propositions would
not be sufficient but that there ought to be some structure.[120] Buoyed by
these principles, the group of Roman experts who met on February 5,
1964, proceeded to the required reduction, even though they were in the
dark regarding the content both of the chapter on the laity in the constitution of the Church and the chapter in schema XVII, a circumstance
that prevented them from acting with complete assurance. The overall
schema was kept intact, but its content was reduced from seventeen
pages and forty-nine paragraphs to ten pages and twenty-four articles,
the only significant change being a new separation between the treatment of charitable action and the treatment of social action.[121] The document produced by the Roman group (known as *Propositum ulterius
abbreviatum*, that is "Draft Still Further Shortened") was accepted by
the full commission after a rather harsh discussion that carried over into
the meetings on March 2 and 3, 1964.[122]

As far as the schema as a whole was concerned, the most important
aspect of that plenary meeting was the fact that various individuals, especially Father Tucci, editor of *La Civiltà Cattolica*, asked for a revision of

---

[117] Ibid., 79.
[118] Ibid., 120.
[119] Ibid., 83.
[120] Ibid., 82.
[121] Ibid., 79-80. See F. Klostermann, "Decree on the Apostolate of the Laity," in
Commentary, 3:273-404.
[122] *Acta commissionis*, 80-85.

the three-chapter structure of the schema. It was obvious that the "propositions" could not exhaust a subject so important and so burdened with expectations; furthermore, since the schema had been presented in 1963, at the end of the second period, the commission was justified in ensuring that it had some continuity.

At Tucci's suggestion a study group was formed to examine the propositions; its work led to a new schema in five chapters, in addition to a prologue and a closing exhortation: I: The call of the laity to the apostolate (nos. 1, 3, 2); II: The communities and life-milieux, that is, the human situation in which all Christians should carry out what is said in chapter I (nos. 10, 11, 4, 12); III: The goals to be pursued according to the gospel: charity, social justice. 1. Human conversion and progress toward God (new no.); 2. Mercy and charity toward the poor (nos. 13, 14); 3. The Christian establishment of the temporal order (nos. 15, 16); IV: Forms of association: everything said in chapters I, II, II also holds for the forms of association (nos. 5, to be completed; 6 and 7 and the no. on Catholic Action); V: The order to be followed, as well as coordination and even cooperation with non-Catholics (nos. 17, 18, 19, 20, 21, 22, 23, 24).[123]

We possess a comprehensive report on the work of the commission and subcommissions from March 4 to 12, and particularly on a possible "directory" to be added to the schema.[124] On March 13 and 17 Glorieux received from the commission various comments to which he tried to respond on the basis of the majority of recurring views in the criticisms sent by the fathers. However, despite this procedure some questions were not settled, and Cento, Guano, Tucci, Glorieux, and Dalos met on the 18th in order to deal with them.[125] The results obtained were examined by the CC on April 16-17, 1964, after the report from Cardinal Urbani.[126]

---

[123] Ibid., 89-90. The structuring of the text in five chapters determined the formation of five subcommissions, each responsible for working up a chapter. The makeup of the subcommissions: Chapter I: Nécsey, Ménager, Fernández Conde, Guano, P. Moehler, Lentini, and Worlock, and Fathers Papali and Bogliolo; Chapter II: Morris, Yu Pin, Helder Cámara, Stourm, Gutiérrez, Ligutti, Ch. Boillat, Father Leethan; Chapter III: Castellano, Larraín, Babcock, De Aruajo Sales, Guadri, Ferrari-Toniolo, Rodhain, Tucci; Chapter IV: Herrera Oria, Petit, Laszlo, De Vet, Civardi, Cardijn, Klosterman, Piovesana, Steiff, Father Dalos; Chapter V: Cousins, O'Connor, Hengsbach, Da Silva, Ramselaar, Higgins, Géraud, Father Hirschmann.

[124] AS V/2, 164-65; A. Glorieux, in Vatican II, L'apostolat des laïcs (Paris, 1970), 170.

[125] Glorieux Archive, 21/378 and 379.

[126] AS V/2, 473.

The text presented to the CC in April consisted of some twenty propositions, divided into five chapters and fitted out with a prologue and concluding exhortation.[127] Despite the commission's critical reading, several times repeated, of the chapter "The People of God and the Laity in Particular" in the schema on the Church, the ecclesiological foundation of the schema on the lay apostolate remained the mystical body of Christ. The lay apostolate was thus understood as a response to the Christian requirement of obedience to the commandment of charity, an obedience to which all the members of the body are called. The lay apostolate, which is at once a right and duty, has its origin in the sacraments of baptism and confirmation and is nourished by the Eucharist.

A first chapter on the call of both the Church and in particular the laity to the apostolate was followed by a second on the areas in which this apostolate is to be exercised: the family, the Church, and society. The third chapter, on the aims of the apostolate, distinguished the goal of evangelization and the direct sanctification of human being and the goal of a Christian leavening of the temporal order, two goals that coexisted in the Christian consciousness of the lay person, who is at once a believer and a citizen.

The fourth chapter was devoted to apostolic associations; unlike the schema of 1963, it emphasized the freedom allowed bishops of choosing, on the basis of the local Church's needs, the form of association to be fostered. The privileged status of Catholic Action still remained but was extended potentially to other structures characterized by the "four notes."[128] Finally, the last chapter spelled out the principles regulating relations between laity and hierarchy; a careful distinction was made between canonical mission, "mandated" apostolate, free apostolate subject only to

---

[127] The proposed directory for the lay apostolate, planned by the commission on March 6, was to take into account two demands of a contrasting kind: on the one hand, to retrieve the material eliminated from the preparatory schema; and on the other, to involve the laity themselves in the composition of it, the entire task being referred either to a suitable postconciliar commission or to a possible third-world congress of the lay apostolate. This last hypothesis had the advantage of removing any static dogmatic cast to what the Council would say, and also of facilitating the reception of the Council. See *Acta commissionis conciliaris De fidelium apostolatu: Storia del testo (1962-1964)*, ed. A. Glorieux and P. Dalos, on the basis of extracts from the reports made to the member bishops of the commission (in the Caprile-Tucci Archive on the lay apostolate, 31/1, 923-94).

[128] The "four notes" that marked Catholic Action and other movements regarded as its equivalents had to do with the goal of its activity — a goal shared with the Church — namely, the sanctification of individuals and the building up of the body of Christ; the modalities of lay collaboration with the hierarchy; the action both individual and organized of the laity within the organization; and the supervision by the hierarchy of the laity's involvement, in the form of an explicit mandate (see *AS* V/2, 366).

a general ecclesiastical supervision, forms of cooperation between laity and pastors, and finally, "full-time" service of lay persons in the Church. There was a brief expression of desire for the constant fostering of cooperation of the laity with Christians and non-Christians, on the basis of a common evangelical patrimony and shared human values.

Continuity with the preparatory schema and with the revision made during the 1963 intersession seemed clear to the CC: the conceptual nucleus had remained unchanged.[129] In relation to the text of 1963, which had preserved the entire content of the preparatory schema, the version of March 1994 was only one-fourth as long. The initial idea of the commission that it was in its competence to think out the ecclesiastical status of the laity left room for assigning this function to the constitution on the Church,

The schema of 1964 was in fact a "practical guide" for the laity. Although an effort was made to emphasize the call of the laity to the apostolate, the intention of drawing up a detailed list of cases and situations showed through at various points in the new schema: particular areas and settings that justified the intervention of the laity were set down; reasons for today's call of the laity by the Church were offered; norms to be observed were given; and terms were defined that described the various conditions for the exercise of the apostolate. Moreover, the shortening of the schema, while fostering a selection of crucial themes, also brought out the limitations, already found in the preparatory text, of considering the subject apart from reflection on the Church. An exclusive concentration on this limited area meant remaining within the limits of a pastoral effort understood as a clarification and organization of what already existed.[130]

The most important change was in the way in which the material was organized. The schema of 1962-63, with its general and special parts, clearly distinguished the apostolate as direct advancement of the reign of

---

[129] In the *Relatio circa schema "de apostolatu laicorum"* Urbani emphasized that "it is not my task to judge the merits of the treatment but only to judge the extent to which the schema has succeeded in keeping the substance, the essence, of all the earlier numbers [of the preparatory schema]. The effort made reveals an exposition that is a little too generic, but in general the entire schema seems to me to be complete and to have the pastoral style proper to our Council" (*AS* V/2, 402-3).

[130] The decree on the lay apostolate was meant to be, and in fact was, a complete and pastoral exposition of "the substance, the gist" of the preparatory schema, that is, it was meant "to order systematically that which in one or other way already exists;" see Glorieux's intervention in the minutes of the commission: *Acta commissionis*, 35 (meeting of March 7, 1964).

God from charitable and social action, while the new schema moved beyond this distinction, adopting a less "academic" approach and eliminating numerous repetitions. The initial, doctrinal part of the earlier schema was also considerably shortened, on the grounds that "everything having to do with the place of lay people in the Church" had to depend on the constitution on the Church.[131] The introduction into schema XVII of the section on the social action of the laity had contributed to emptying the decree of some original contributions made in the preparatory texts. It was thought that the decision to give preeminence to disciplinary themes would get around the real difficulty, which was ecclesiological in nature.

The content of the text produced during the second conciliar intersession shows an inability to overcome the ambiguity that marked thinking about the laity. The schema remained imprisoned in the limits and by the conceptual difficulties of preconciliar thought on the so-called theology of the laity. On the one hand, it was henceforth impossible to avoid admitting the need of the collaboration of the laity in the Church and the assignment of responsibility to them; on the other, the composers of the schema wanted to direct this process of emancipation and subject it to the control and direction of an ecclesiastical hierarchy that was worried about losing its juridical and theological position as a "superior caste."

The approval of the CC, given on April 17, ensured that the schema would be taken off the blacklist of mini-schemas that had been drawn up in January; it ensured that this schema too could be extensively discussed in the hall. On April 27 the pope decided that the text, the third to have been developed, should be sent to all the fathers. Unlike those that had preceded, this third printed text staked out a line that the final text would follow, although profound changes would be made in it in response to the criticisms of the fathers that had either already arrived in writing during the summer of 1964 or would be expressed orally during the public debate, October 7-13, 1964.

7. The Commission for the Missions

The expansion of this commission by the entrance of four new elected members would have important consequences.[132] African, Asian, and North American participation was increased; the average age of members

---

[131] Urbani, *Relatio circa schema "de apostolatu laicorum (AS* V/2, 402-3).

[132] J. Schütte, S.V.D. (Germany), E. D'Souza (Bophal, India), J. Comber (titular bishop, superior general of the Maryknoll Society, USA), J. Dogget (apostolic vicar of Aitape, New Guinea), plus one appointed by the pope, C. Cavallera (Nyeri, Kenya).

was reduced to 57; and there joined the commission an individual who would play an important role in the future: the superior general of the Verbites, the tireless German, Johannes Schütte. On December 5, the first day of the intersession, Cardinal Agagianian, prefect of the Congregation of Propaganda Fide and president of the Commission for the Missions, sent Cicognani a new text[133] that had been worked up during the second period thanks to the hard work of four subcommissions, one for each chapter of the schema.[134] On December 17, after its approval by the CC, the pope ordered it sent to all the bishops who were to submit their comments by March 31.

However, as happened with the other schemas not yet discussed in the hall, this one, too, the CC decided at its meeting on January 15, was to be reduced to simple propositions. The members of the Commission for the Missions were called to be in Rome for May 4; the four subcommissions reworked the text in the form of propositions on May 8-9, and then met again from May 11 to May 13 to put the finishing touches on the text. Father Schütte explained how the approval had come about: "Not one of us on the Missions Commission was satisfied with the propositions. We voted unanimously in favor of them, however, because the Coordinating Commission had ordered drastic cuts, and we believed that the six pages were the best that could be produced in the circumstances."[135]

The schema, the former title of which was "On the Missions," became in its new form "Draft of Propositions on the Missionary Activity of the Church" and consisted of barely six pages: a prologue and

---

[133] The preceding text had been rejected by the CC on July 3, 1963: *History*, 2:455-60, 490 n.3, and 512. See S. Paventi, "Iter della schema 'De activitate missionali,'" in *Il destino delle missioni*, ed. J. Schütte (Brescia, 1968), 56-91; idem,"Etapes de l'élaboration du texte," in *Vatican II. L'activité missionaire de l'Eglise* (Paris, 1967), 149-81. See also S. Brechter, "Decree on the Church's Missionary Activity. Introduction and Commentary," in *Commentary*, 4:87-181; idem, "Das Missiondekret des Vatikan im Gesamtwerk des Konzils," *Zeitschrift für Missionswissenschaft* 22 (1966), 241-59; J. Glazick, "Die Mission in II. Vatikanischem Konzil," *Zeitschrift für Missionswissenschaft und Religionswissenschaft* 50 (1966), 3-10. For the contribution of Msgr. Paventi to missiology and to the work of the Council, see H. Rzepktowski, *Lexicon der Mission. Geschichte Theologie Ethnologie* (Cologne-Vienna, 1992), s.v. "Paventi." For a better grasp of his thought during the preparatory work for the Council, see S. Paventi, *Prospettive missionarie* (Rome, 1964).

[134] The membership of the subcommissions, along with the experts of each, is given in Paventi, *Prospettive missionarie*, 178.

[135] Wiltgen, 193.

thirteen propositions.[136] This skeletal schema was to be presented to the fathers for the first time in the third period. But before the period began, there was a strong reaction from a group of missionary bishops, especially the Dutch, who were concerned to defend the rights of the missions. Gathered around the charismatic figure of Tarcisius van Valenberg, they circulated a counter-schema, as well as two successive revisions of the official text. They gave it the name "Our Document" and sent it to the General Secretariat of the Council with the request that it be printed as an unofficial commentary on the schema of propositions. This suggestion was rejected by the secretariat.[137]

Along with a letter, the schema of fourteen propositions was then sent to Cicognani on May 25. Once it was approved, Felici sent it the Council fathers on July 7, along with other schemas to be discussed during the third period. The request of the Dutch that their report be placed before the schema did not resolve the problem of a dull and unsatisfactory text. They asked for the explicit recognition of missionary institutes and their special character; they also requested a reform of Propaganda Fide, which assigned the tasks of organizing missions and controlled the mission territories; they also asked that the problem of dialogue with the non-Christian religions be raised; and, finally that the missionary task be explained as the responsibility of the college of bishops under the direction of the pope.

But the schema was even more feeble from the standpoint of theology and as a reading of the historical moment: decolonization, the globalizing of problems, and poverty remained outside its scope, as did the ecclesiological criteria recognized in the schema on the Church. The schema planned a prologue that set down the "principles" of missionary activity that was (despite the acknowledged obsolescence of the distinction) being carried on in lands subject to Propaganda or where the implanting of the Church had not yet taken place.

The individual propositions established (no. 1) the necessity of missions, which were needed even today in order to show the Church to be "the universal means of salvation." Missionary activity is carried on, according to no. 2, by the authority of the bishops through the missionaries, who are guided by their religious orders, their institutes, or the example of the apostles. The stages of missionary work (no. 3) are

---

[136] On this change see J. B. Anderson, *A Pneumatology of the Paschal Mystery: Ad Gentes I* (Rome, 1988), 45.

[137] Wiltgen, 193; see E. Louchez, "La commission *De missionibus*," in *Commissions*, 251-75; Van Kerckhoven Archive 6. The schema is in *AS* III/6, 327-36.

divided into the acceptance of the poor, preaching as a call to faith in Christ, catechizing the converted through the sacraments of baptism, confirmation, and Eucharist, participation in the life of the Christian community with a view to forming indigenous vocations and hierarchies, and the ability of the Church to teach religious truth and a morality of the natural order governing society.

Missionary activity (no.4) is directed by a "Central Council for Evangelization" which is set up as a "secretariat of experts" from Propaganda, the latter's powers not being limited in any way by this group, to which residential bishops may belong. No. 5 considers the missionary task to be the duty of the entire episcopate, from which arises the "communion of Churches" (an expression that would become a theological theme reaching far beyond the passage in which it was uttered). Priests of "both clergies" owe the same kind of readiness, as do the institutes of perfection and the laity (nos. 6-8), who are the instrument of the "consecration of the world." No. 9 brought together in a very short section the principles governing "fraternal collaboration" with non-Catholics as set down in the schema on ecumenism.

As for relations with believers of other religions, reference was made to "legitimately established norms" — which in fact permitted no contact at all. Nos. 10-13 had to do with formation: development of a Christian culture in mission countries, technical scientific education to be given in missionary institutes for development, formation of catechists and missionaries of the various institutes so that they might familiarize themselves with the language, mentality, and psychology of the people. It is understandable that the style and contents of such an approach would be severely criticized in the hall when the schema arrived there in the fourth period.[138]

8. The Commission for the Discipline of the Clergy and the Christian People[139]

The impression of owing something to priests became so strong among the Council fathers that at the end of the second period they

---

[138] According to N. Valmels, *La vie du Concile* (Le Jas, 1966), 271: "This schema smacked too much of the stale air of the office and not the fresh air of the woods."

[139] See R. Wasselynck, *Les prêtres. Elaboration du décret "Presbyterorum Ordinis" de Vatican II. Synopse* (Paris, 1968); J. Frisque, "Le Décret 'Presbyteroum ordinis.' Histoire et commentaire," in *Vatican II. Les prêtres. Formation, ministére et vie* (Paris, 1968), 124-85; J. Lécuyer, "History of the Decree," in *Commentary*, 4:183-209.

decided to send a message to the priests of the world. On November 29 a draft was submitted, but the message remained on the back burner. The unofficial explanation was that the emendations submitted were so many as to make a definitive version almost impossible in the short time remaining.[140]

The preparatory commission[141] had composed three schemas entitled "The Holiness of Clerics," "Clerical Offices and Benefices," and "The Distribution of Priests," and another on "The Care of Souls." On the basis of these schemas, the conciliar Commission for the Discipline of the Clergy and the Christian People worked up a new text entitled "On Clerics," which was approved by the CC on March 25, 1963, and sent to the fathers shortly afterward.[142] The text was then finally reworked on the basis of comments received and acquired the title "On Priests."

On January 23, 1964, the CC let it be known that the schema had to be reduced to its essential points, in the form of propositions. The new text, emended accordingly, contained ten propositions, preceded by a prologue in which reference was made to what the constitution on the Church had said about the nature of the priesthood and the ministry of priests. From then on, the new schema on priests underwent further changes in accordance with the written comments sent to the commission by some fathers.

The changes in the corrected text as compared with the initial schema (these changes being the result of proposals put forth by the commission at its meeting on April 27, 1964) were evident in a shift in viewpoint perceptible in the explanations and directives provided by the commission. The schema on clerics had made no explicit reference to the people

[140] For further information on the subject consult, e.g., Wenger, 228-32. *ICI*, no. 206, p. 13 has this: "Was the extent of the comments from the fathers the only reason for the failure of the message? The next day, December 3, Cardinal Feltin told a reporter that in fact the text was held up by the Holy Office, which had decided that the proposal presented was marred by errors."

[141] After the beginning of the Council, Cardinal Pietro Ciriaci continued in the office of president of the Commission for the Discipline of the Clergy and the Christian People, the secretary being D. Alvaro del Portillo, of Opus Dei.

[142] The commission had distributed the work among four subcommissions that were appointed to develop the various chapters: Chapter I (On the perfection of priestly life); reporter, F. Marty, Archbishop of Rheims; secretary, J. Lécuyer, C.S.Sp. Chapter II (On the study and science of pastoral care): reporter, H. Janssen, Bishop of Hildesheim; secretary, S. Sigmond, O.P. Chapter III (On the proper use of ecclesiastical property): reporter, H. Mazerat, Bishop of Angers; secretary, Msgr. W. Onclin. Chapter IV (The distribution of clergy), which was more of an exhortation: reporter, V. Enrique y Tarancón, Bishop of Solsona; secretary, Msgr. G. Violardo.

of God but limited itself to an individualist perspective: priests were considered as Christians who, because they were priests, were obliged, more than other Christians, to seek holiness. It was possible to see in this viewpoint a certain affinity with the concept of "the priest-monk" who had chosen the "perfect life" or a "state of perfection"; this outlook reflected the most persistent aspect of a spirituality that had its roots in a priestly piety going back to the time of St. John Chrysostom. The text of April 27, on the other hand, began by looking at the life of priests in its essential connection with the apostolate, this last being described in a less atemporal way. The "pastoral" orientation made its appearance in the first four introductory lines in the form of a direct reference to the schema on the Church.

9. The Commission for Seminaries, Studies, and Catholic Education

The president of this commission was Cardinal Pizzardo, the vice-presidents were Cardinal De Barros Câmara and Dino Staffa (both appointed by the pope), and the secretary was German Benedictine A. Mayer, former rector of the Anselmianum in Rome. Of the elected members only five had belonged to the preparatory commission, among them Blanchet, titular archbishop and rector of the Institut Catholique of Paris. The preparatory commission had produced two schemas: one on priestly vocations and the other on the training of future priests. In January 1963 the CC decided to retain only the schema on the training of future priests. The competent commission then drew up the text entitled "On the Training of Candidates for Orders," which was sent to the Council fathers in May 1963.

But during the second intersession, on the basis of the directive sent by the CC on January 23, 1964, the schema was reduced to some simple propositions that were to be submitted to the Council for a vote without any preceding discussion. The commission in charge of the schema had these propositions ready by March 11, 1964, under the title "The Training of Priests." On April 27 the CC approved them and in May they were sent to the fathers.

The text reflected "a middle course for the reform of seminaries and a balanced outlook" (Carraro).[143] The problems of seminaries were not

---

[143] For an understanding of the precise intentions of the commission, see the analysis in J. Sauvage, "Orientations conciliaires pour la formation des prêtres," in Les prêtres dans la pensée de Vatican II, a special issue of the periodical Vocation (Paris), January 1966, 193-223; see also G. Lefeuvre, La vocation sacerdotale dans le IIe concile du Vatican (Paris 1968).

avoided, but neither were they tackled in the radical manner called for by some fathers in the hall (Döpfner, Léger, and Suenens, for example).[144] In regard to formation, the recommended study of the *philosophia perennis* (as well as of the teaching of St. Thomas Aquinas) would be challenged in the hall. When the schema came to the revision of studies (chapter V, nos. 13-18), it urged that the minds of the seminarians be opened to the mystery of Christ, which dominates the history of the Church and the world (no. 14, 1). It was therefore necessary that their studies begin with an introductory course centered on the mystery of salvation (no. 14, 2) and that there be a harmonious integration of the philosophical disciplines, on the one hand (*philosophia perennis* and recent philosophies, no. 15), and the theological disciplines, on the other (with sacred scripture being the soul of these, no. 16), the goal being a unification of philosophical and theological formation (no. 17).

In formulating this orientation the secretary of the commission had asked the help of Father B. Häring, especially in dealing with moral theology. In line with this, some bishops in their *iuxta modum* votes had asked that the Council explicitly condemn the legalist moral theology of recent centuries. Häring, realizing that this was impossible, proposed a text that could prevent a regression to the distortions of the past:

> Students should receive a most careful training in holy Scripture, which should be the soul, as it were, of all theology... In like manner the other theological subjects should be renewed through a more vivid contact with the Mystery of Christ and the history of salvation. Special care should be given to the perfecting of moral theology. Its scientific presentation should draw more fully on the teaching of holy Scripture and should throw light on the exalted vocation of the faithful in Christ and their obligation to bring forth fruit in charity for the life of the world. In the same way the teaching of canon law and Church history should take into account the mystery of the Church, as set forth in the Dogmatic Constitution *De Ecclesia* (*Optatam totius*, no. 16).

Since this meant an extensive change in the text, a special vote was required, which brought an almost unanimous approval.[145]

This document, like the one on the ministry and life of priests, did not elicit very many comments in the hall, but later it became the object of

---

[144] See R. Rouquette, *Une nouvelle chrétienté* (Paris, 1968), 137-53.

[145] B. Häring, "Testimonianze. La mia partecipazione al Concilio Vaticano II," *CrSt* 15/1 (1994), 174-75. On the subject of morality, Häring was behind an important section on the dignity of conscience in *Gaudium et spes*.

rather radical criticisms.[146] It seemed to ignore, so it was said, the crisis of priestly identity in the Western world that was visible at that time, in the light, for example, of the experience of the priest-workers in France, who were a symbol of the passage from a clerical Church to a Church conceived of as the people of God, as required by a more secular society and by the spirit of the Council itself.

This same commission (whose work had the same area of competence as the corresponding Roman tribunal, the Congregation for Seminaries and Universities) also handled the question of Catholic schools. During the second period of the Council the commission began to develop the fifth version of the schema; the text was ready at the beginning of the 1963-64 intersession. As in the case of the other schemas, so in this one the CC told the commission on January 23, 1964, that it must be shortened, and the commission was therefore asked to turn it into a *votum* that would bring out the importance of Catholic education and Catholic schools. But on March 3 the commission presented not the requested *votum* but a text of seventeen propositions (sixth version of the schema). The CC in fact preferred this text to the *votum* and accepted it on April 17.[147]

The successive reworkings of the text show the difficulties that cropped up in determining the direction to be taken; within the commission there were tensions that sometimes became quite strong. In the Council a movement of opposition to Christian institutions made its appearance: a secularizing current wanted to do away with Catholic schools. Some regarded these schools as an essential means of evangelization, others as a tool of privilege and power; according to some of the latter, the schools should never have existed at all. The Church was thus faced in a rather radical way with the problems of Christian education.[148]

For this reason it seemed timely to go beyond a specific consideration of Catholic schools and to publish a declaration on Christian education, of which Catholic schools continued to be one of the privileged vehicles. But even then it was not easy to decide concretely on the perspective to

---

[146] See, e.g., G. Alberigo, in *Storia dei concili ecumenici* (Brescia, 1990), 422 and 445-46; see also, from a different perspective, H. Legrand in *RSPT* 59 (1975), 688-93.

[147] On this entire evolution see especially J. Pohlschneider and P. Dezza, "Declaration on Christian Education," in *Commentary*, 4:1-48; Ph. Delhaye, *DTC. Tables*, cols. 4326-27; A. Greiler, "Erneuerung des Seminäre, Erneuerung der Kirche," in *Experience*.

[148] See the article of J. V. Daem, Bishop of Antwerp, a member of the commission and reporter for the declaration: "A propos de la Déclaration conciliaire sur l'éducation chrétienne," *OssRom* (French ed.), November 12, 1965, p. 8.

be adopted in such a declaration, for even when this orientation was understood and accepted as having "the advantage of not closing any doors and of offering suggestions that could be helpful in bringing renewal to this immense realm" (Laurentin), it was not clear how to create a message proper to a council on a terrain so rich in ambiguities. Some members maintained that it would be necessary to develop canonical legislation for Christian schools; others thought that the commission needed to work on a kind of proclamation or declaration on education and schools; then, too, there were those who thought the commission should list the difficulties in the area of education and find adequate solutions.

All this explains the troubled history of the redaction of a text on a set of problems that involved questions of great importance, inasmuch as they called for the collaboration of the family, the state (confessional or non-confessional?), and the Church. Furthermore, as would become clear in the conciliar debate during the third period, the question was also conditioned by various geographical and historical contexts. As a result, "at the end of the debate it was rather difficult to know the opinion of the Council on this declaration."[149]

10. The Commission for the Oriental Churches

If the valuable diary of Msgr. Edelby, Titular Archbishop of Edessa and a member of the Commission for the Oriental Churches,[150] contained information on the intersessions also, we would have a detailed knowledge of the fortunes of the text entrusted to this commission. Since it does not, we must be satisfied with the information which the same Msgr. Edelby, along with I. Dick, published in the commentary that appeared in 1970 in the Unam Sanctam series.

In the course of a week's work, March 10-16, during the second intersession, the Commission used the emendations and proposals submitted to correct and improve the text that had been sent to the Council fathers in May 1963, under the title "The Union of Oriental Christians."[151] The most active leaders of the commission — Patriarchs Maximos IV

---

[149] Wenger, *Vatican II. Chronique de la troisième session* (Paris, 1965), 219.

[150] *Il Vaticano II nel diario di un vescovo arabo*, ed. R. Cannelli (Cinisello Balsamo, 1996).

[151] See *Vatican II. Les Eglises Orientales catholiques. Décret "Orientalium Ecclesiarum,"* ed. N. Edelby and I. Dick (Paris, 1970). See also *Decreto sulle Chiese Orientali cattoliche*, ed. A. Favelle and I. Ortiz de Urbina (Turin, 1967), 435-60; J. M. Hoeck, "Decree on the Eastern Catholic Churches," in *Commentary*, 1:307-31.

(Melkite) and Paul-Pierre Méouchi (Maronite), Melkite Bishop N. Edelby and German Abbot Hoeck, as well as Msgr. Provenchéres (France) and Msgr. Baudoux (Canada) — complained that they had not been invited, as they should have been, for the work of the intersession; as a result this work was left in the hands of "the experts living in Rome" (Edelby). At the same time, however, in accordance with the requirement sent from the CC on January 23, 1964, the text was reduced to 29 articles (version C). After this new text had been emended by a subcommission presided over by Patriarch Batanian of the Armenians (Lebanon), it was approved almost unanimously by the commission at a plenary meeting in March.[152] Once it was accepted by the competent authority, the text was sent to the Council fathers on April 27, 1964.

11. The Commission for Religious[153]

At the beginning of the second intersession, the members and consultors of the commission appointed to study the problems of religious life had not changed in any important way by comparison with the commission established on June 5, 1960. The only exception was its president: Cardinal Antoniutti replaced Cardinal Valeri.

Intending to apply the Döpfner Plan, the CC told Antoniutti on January 23, 1964, to reduce the text of the document, which had a long history behind it,[154] to simple propositions. These would, in turn, have to be

[152] Edelby and Dick, *Vatican II. Les Eglises Orientales catholiques*, 78-81.

[153] See the classic studies by Fr. Wulf, S.J., "Decree on the Appropriate Renewal of the Religious Life," in *Commentary*, 2:301-22; and A. Le Bourgeois, "Historique du Décret," in *Vatican II, L'adaptation et la rénovation de la vie religieuse* (Paris, 1967), 51-72.

[154] In February 1962, during the preparation for the Council, the Commission for Religious, with Cardinal Valeri as president and Father Rousseau, O.M.I., as secretary, had worked up a first schema (see A. Indelicato, *Difendere la dottrina o annunciare l'evangelo* [Genoa, 1992], 161-65; L. C. Marques, "Per il rinnovamento della vita religiosa," in *Verso il concilio*, 442-44; for the background of the problems that arose during the first intersession see *History*, 2:473-79). The Council of Presidents (at the end of November 1962), Cicognani in the name of the pope (December 5, 1962), and the CC (in January 1963) successively asked that the schema be shortened. This was done on February 20, 1963, by the conciliar commission, whose president was Cardinal Antoniutti. After the arrival of the emendations suggested by Döpfner, this second version, entitled *Schema de Religiosis*, appeared on April 22, 1963, in the form of a booklet of thirty-five pages. It was less juridical in character than the preceding version and emphasized more the need of renewal. But the text was still too long and detailed. Cicognani therefore asked for a further version. For detailed information on the evolution of this commission's work, see L. Gutiérrez Martín, "Processus historico-doctrinalis decreti conciliaris: De accomodata renovatione vitae religiosae," *Commentarium pro religiosis* 45 (1966), 17-39.

approved without debate, after having been adapted in the light of written comments. As it began its work, the commission[155] was organized into three subcommissions,[156] which were directed by a coordinating subcommission that prepared the schema.[157] Laudable effort produced a text of four pages and nineteen articles, entitled *De religiosis*. The text was examined at a plenary meeting March 4-7 and bears the date April 20, 1964. This rather meager text was not well received by the Council fathers.[158] On the basis of the few written comments of the bishops the document was slightly modified, beginning with its title, which became "The Up-to-date Renewal of Religious Life."

---

[155] At this point the commission, which still had Father Rousseau as secretary and Father Le Bourgeois, superior general of the Eudists, as assistant secretary, was made up of twenty members elected by the Council and ten appointed by the pope. The representation of the various geographical areas was more balanced than in the first commission (see A. Indelicato, "Formazione e composizione delle commissioni preparatorie," in *Verso il Concilio*, 57). Here is the list of members: *Elected*: Msgrs. Huyghe (Arras, France); Leiprecht (Rottenburg, Germany); Tabera (Albacete, Spain); Bortignon (Padua, Italy); Cardinal Landázuri (Lima, Peru); Msgr. Beck (Salford, England); Retz, O.S.B. (Beuron, Germany); Msgrs. Echevarria (Ambato, Ecuador), Flahiff (Winnepeg, Canada), Daly (Des Moines, USA), Tomizawa (Sapporo, Japan), Urtasun (Avignon, France), Sépinski, O.F.M., Cahill (Cairus, Australia), McShea (Allentown, USA), Botto (Cagliari, Italy), McDevitt (auxiliary of Philadelphia, USA), Borromeo (Pesaro, Italy), Stein (auxiliary of Trier, Germany), Cordeiro (Karachi, Pakistan). *Appointed*: Jansens (general of the Society of Jesus), Ziggioti (general of the Salesians), Perantoni (Lanciano, Italy), Mels (Congo), Philippe, O.P. (Curia), Haller (primate of the Canons Regular), Compagnone (Anagni, Italy), Vendragon (Kuala Lampur, Malaysia), Sipovic (titular of Mariamma, Italy), Kleiner (general of the Cistercians).

[156] For chapters I, IV, V, VI: P. Botto (president), Cardinal Landázuri, L. Haller, B. Echevarria, C. Borromeo, P. Perantoni; experts: A. Combes, Tocanel, E. Gambari, S. Goyeneche. For chapters II and III: P. Philippe (president), J. Urtasun, A. Tabera, G. Beck, Th. Cahill, B. Reetz; experts: G. Thils, J. Fohl, Ch. Berutti, J. Sanchis, Zacaria of S. Mauro. For chapters VII, VIII, IX: C. Leiprecht (president), G. Flahiff, H. Bortignon, J. McShea, G. Huyghe, McDevitt; experts: Ch. Moeller, G. Van den Broek, E. Heston, A. Gutiérrez.

[157] Cardinal Antoniutti (president), C. Leiprecht, P. Botto, J. Urtasun, P. Philippe, B. Stein, H. R. Compagnone, G. Huyghe, S. Kleiner, A. Sépinski; experts: G. Thils, Th. Gascon, M. Abellán, E. Gambari.

[158] The text sent in the spring of 1964 was not regarded as very satisfactory, even though the commission had not received many written comments before the beginning of the third period, except for the sixty-six bishops of Germany and Scandinavia; see *Observationes Exc.morum ac Rev.morum Patrum Concilii Oecumenici Vaticani II circa schema "De religiosis," in Sessione generali Concilii approbandum* (Rome, September 9, 1964). A further schema had to be prepared, the fourth, which was distributed to the fathers on October 23, after the second had already been presented on October 10. Döpfner himself, who had closely followed the text on religious since its birth, was dissatisfied with schema II and gave a radical criticism of it. Religious institutes, he said, make a necessary contribution to the reform of the Church. Would this text be able to promote their renewal? In his judgment, no; it lacked any center of gravity, any *Schwerpünkte*.

12. The Commission for the Discipline of the Sacraments

At the beginning the preparatory commission had a broad task, which consisted in the composition of three schemas (*On the Sacrament of Confirmation*, *On the Sacrament of Penance*, and *On the Sacrament of Orders*) and dealing with other matters of ecclesiastical discipline. The tone taken was predominantly canonical, due perhaps to the personality of the commission's president, Cardinal Aloisi Masella, and even more to that of its secretary, Spanish Jesuit R. Bidagor, professor of canon law in the Gregorian University of Rome.

The CC reduced the ambitions of the conciliar commission to more modest proportions. All that was to be left of the planned schemas was a *votum* on the sacrament of matrimony, and this was to be passed on to the commission formed by Paul VI for the reform of the Code of Canon Law. Since there was question of practical measures rather than of doctrine and since the Council was not concerned with the reform of the Code, all that was left for the conciliar commission to do was to draft a *votum*. The first draft sent to the fathers in the spring of 1964 was already a third version, drafted between March 3 and March 7, 1964, according to the prescribed form. The Pope then gave permission for it to be sent to the Council fathers on April 27.[159] It was a short text of barely two pages that was mainly although not exclusively concerned with the problem of mixed marriages. Father Häring, who since the beginning of the Council had been writing on questions of pastoral practice in matters of matrimony, and especially on mixed marriages, was consulted, although he did not belong to the commission. Called upon by Franz von Streng, Bishop of Basel and a member of the commission, Häring collaborated effectively on the drafting of the text that was to be presented in the hall on November 20, 1964.[160]

The Congregation for the Sacraments, a branch of the Curia, had for its part already issued rules for mixed marriages; it came to rather detailed conclusions, even if these were not always consonant with the ecumenical spirit that marked the Council. It was easy for Cardinal Masella and P. Bidagor, prefect and secretary of the Congregation, who held the same posts on the conciliar commission, to transfer the conclusions reached by the Congregation to the conciliar commission. This explains the fact that during the debate a new text was distributed that

[159] See B. Häring, "Schema voti de matrimonii sacramento: Vorgeschichte und Kommentar," in *LThK. Das Zweite Vatikanische Konzil*, 3:595-606.
[160] Häring, "Testimonianze," 168-69.

was clearer and more complete than the preceding and contained details on impediments to marriage, mixed marriages, and the manner of celebrating these. The question was a *crux*, said Döpfner, in relations between Christians of different confessions.[161]

D. SCHEMA XVII (FEBRUARY 1-3 AND JUNE 4)

During the second intersession this schema passed through one of the most exciting phases in its evolution.[162] The schema, which Henri Fesquet described as the "star of the show" and which Father Yves Congar called "the promised land" of the Council, went through a dozen versions.[163]

1. The Schema at the Beginning of the Intersession

The first text, the "Roman" schema, had been worked up in the spring of 1963 by a mixed commission of members from the Doctrinal Commission and from the Commission for the Lay Apostolate. The publication of the encyclical *Pacem in terris* on April 11, 1963 set several things in motion. Dissatisfied with the first text, the CC entrusted to Suenens the preparation of a new draft of the schema, still known as schema XVII. The result was the so-called Malines Schema.

These efforts displayed a certain fluctuation reflecting different responses to the question whether to give primary importance to a statement of theological principles or to provide an empirical description of the reality of a world in process of transformation; from beginning to end this opposition between a "theological" and a "sociological" viewpoint was never clearly transcended. As a result, the text resembled a pendulum, being marked initially by a chiefly sociological approach (Pavan draft, May 1963), in a second moment by a theological approach

---

[161] See Rouquette, *Une nouvelle chrétienté*, 155-80.

[162] See Ch. Moeller, *L'élaboration du Schéma XIII. L'Eglise dans le monde de ce temps* (Tournai-Paris, 1968), which was the subject of a nuanced critique by J. Perarnau, "Lovaniense I o Vaticanum II?" *Analecta Sacra Tarraconensia* 41 (1968), 173-79; A. Glorieux, *Historia prasertim sessionum schematis XVII seu XIII. De ecclesia in mundo huius temporis* (mimeographed); Häring Archive (ISR).

[163] The history of the schema that would become the constitution *Gaudium et spes* has been the subject of numerous studies which have been brought together with scrupulous care by G. Turbanti, *La redazione della costituzione pastorale "Gaudium et spes"* (doctoral dissertation, University of Bologna, 1996).

(Malines Schema, October 1963), in a third more by the sociological (Zurich draft, February 1964), in the fourth and final, as a result of corrections by the doctrinal working group, by a juxtaposition rather than integration of the two perspectives (September 1964).

The intention of the working group during the second intersession was to integrate in a harmonious way the material on which it was working by limiting the abstract and deductive presentation of doctrine and expanding the concrete and inductive analysis. As could be expected, the multiplication of groups charged with developing schema XVII made it more difficult to produce a satisfactory version to presen to the fathers. As the third period began in the fall of 1964, it was clear that, despite all the efforts, an integration of the doctrinal, sociological, and pastoral aspects had not yet been achieved.

Shortly before the second period ended, Cento called for a meeting, which was held on November 29, 1963.[164] On December 4, at a meeting of the central subcommission held at Msgr. Hengsbach's residence, it was agreed that each of its members should offer an outline of what he thought the schema should be. On the basis of these suggestions and referring to the preceding texts, the new secretary and subsecretary of the central commission, Häring and Sigmond, were then to prepare a new text with the help of experts resident in Rome and under the direction of Guano.[165] The members were also asked to send in the outlines before Christmas so that the Roman experts, especially Sigmond and Tucci, might be able to study them and begin the work of producing a draft around January 10.[166]

2. The First Draft of the Schema during the Intersession

The writers worked on the principle that the CC was not expecting a corrected Roman text or Malines Schema nor simply a combination of the two but rather an entirely new text on the basis of a new consultation.[167] On December 15, Ménager offered some rather detailed ideas[168]

---

[164] See R. Tucci, "Introduction historique et doctrinale," in *L'Eglise dans le monde de ce temps* (Paris, 1967), 2:33-127; Ph. Levillain, *La mécanique politique de Vatican II* (Paris, 1975), 344-45; Häring, "Testimonianze," 169-71. On that same day, at Cardinal Florit's invitation, Suenens, using a text prepared by Dossetti, gave an important conference in Florence entitled "The Church of Today and the Plurality of Cultures" (Dossetti Archive II, 214a).

[165] Häring Archive, 2347.

[166] Ibid., 2441; see also Glorieux, *Historia*, 40.

[167] Häring Archive, 2441.

[168] Häring Archive, 2342; on December 22 he added "Nouvelles remarques" (Häring Archive, 2322).

in which he maintained that it was not enough to point out the concrete problems of humanity, but rather that with these as a point of departure the schema should speak of the mission entrusted by Christ to the Church and go on to provide concrete answers to the problems. His schema had three parts: (1) Questions raised by today's world (the problematic); (2) The theological principles that are the basis for a theological response to the questions; (3) The concrete application of these principles to the questions raised.[169]

This was doubtless intended as an alternative to the Malines Schema and was quite different from the Roman. Ménager's draft was sent to the episcopal consultants in order that they might take it into consideration as a point of reference. In Germany, Hengsbach gathered a small study group consisting of himself, Schröffer, Höffner, and Hirschmann.[170] In France, Ancel in Lyons[171] and Ménager in Meaux likewise organized study groups. Ménager consulted Renard, Bishop of Versailles, Jesuit J. Thomas, Canon Haubtmann, and a set of advisers connected with the Jocist group around Father Le Guillou of the Istina center and Father Maxime Hua of the Mission of Paris.[172] Ménager also sent his texts to bishops of other countries, for example to Vietnamese Bishop Hien, in order to obtain a more complete range of views. In Brazil, Msgr. Helder Câmara gathered a group of experts under the direction of Candido Antonio Mendes Almeida.

By December 18, Hirschmann sent in the proposals of the German group which looked to an integration of the Roman text with the Malines text and showed the group's concern to maintain the ecclesiological orientation and to emphasize the active presence of the Church in the building

---

[169] Ménager, "Note sur le schéma XVII," in Häring Archive, 2158.

[170] Häring Archive, 2350.

[171] On the overall contribution of Ancel to *Gaudium et spes,* see O. de Berranger, *Alfred Ancel. Un homme pour l'Evangile (1898-1984)* (Paris, 1988), 225-33.

[172] At the end of February 1964 Father Chenu sent Guano and Ancel "a compilation drawn up by a small group and based on the suggestions of Ménager (Bishop of Meaux) on the relation of Church to world"; this gave the impression of being a Le Guillou-Hua text. These same months saw the first meetings, at St. Louis des Français (Rome) and in Montreuil, of the working group on the "Significance of the Priest-Worker for the Church's Mission in the Industrial World"; the group consisted of bishops and theologians, among them Ancel, Chenu, Le Guillou, Martelet, and Laurentin. See G. Turbanti, "Le rôle de M-D. Chenu dans l'élaboration de 'Gaudium et spes,' in *M.-D. Chenu, Moyen Age et modernité* (Paris, 1997), 173-212; see J. Grootaers, "Marie Dominique Chenu, revisité," *Revue théologique de Louvain* 27 (1996/1), 78-84. Chenu's influence was to be seen in the improvement of the Zurich schema, although Haubtmann was the chief author (schema of Ariccia).

of the modern world.[173] Taking as his starting point the address with which Paul VI had opened the second period, Ancel offered a schema built on the idea of a dialogue with the modern world: "The Church and the Major Problems of Our Age."[174] With the idea of dialogue as a guide, this schema distanced itself from the ecclesiological perspective and looked for a way of responding that was based not on technical solutions to serious social questions but on the moral aspect always implicit in such questions.

Ménager then prepared a new "Draft of a Plan for Schema XVII." He suggested a first chapter on the attitude of ready listening which the Church needed to maintain toward the world and of attentiveness to "the signs of the times;" a second, more theological chapter, giving "God's answer" in light of creation-salvation; and a third and final chapter entitled "Consequences for the Church and Its Members," which pointed out three duties: presence, dialogue, and service. Consultation with Haubtmann and some lay people produced a somewhat different proposal which Ménager then brought to Rome. This schema was not theological and deductive but rather psychological and pedagogical "and endeavored to lead people in a concrete way toward a Christian outlook by working with them on a human level and acknowledging the value of such efforts to resolve the problems of human beings and so to bring them, at the end of this road travelled together, to a clear expression of Christian truth."[175]

Comments from the non-Latin world included those of Hien,[176] and of Blomjous, for whom the goal was "to show the people of our time what the meaning of this work is in God's sight and what the principles are which Christians and all human beings of good will must follow in carrying on this great work if they are to remain on the path traced out by God's plan."[177] On December 30 Blomjous was able to take part in a preliminary meeting in Rome with Guano, Sigmond, Tucci, and Häring, at which the bases of a new schema were laid down in reliance on these various contributions. The Roman group made its own Ancel's idea of dialogue with the world: the schema was to be "a proclamation of those truths that relate especially to the building of the world and that can promote or prepare for

---

[173] Häring Archive, 2350.
[174] *Project d'un schéma sur l'Eglise en face des problèmes du monde d'aujourd'hui*, in Häring Archive, 2332.
[175] Haubtmann Archive, 849.
[176] Häring Archive, 2349.
[177] Ibid., 2328-30.

a dialogue with today's world." Its theological foundation was to be christological, and the "presence of the Church" was to be interpreted as a continuation of the mission of Christ. This approach differed both from the anthropological approach of the Roman schema and from the ecclesiological approach of the Malines Schema. The decisions taken at the December 30 meeting were communicated to the members of the central subcommission, who sent in their own comments and clarifications.

Among the contributions received, it is worth singling out that of the Le Guillou-Hua group, a draft of an organized schema titled "Outline of Schema XVII: On the Active Presence of the Church, the Handmaid of the Lord, among Men of Good Will."[178] The radical nature of this document when it came to denouncing the injustices of the modern world showed that it was inspired in some degree by Chenu; no less clear was the influence of Congar's book *Pour une Église servante et pauvre*, which had appeared the year before. Many other suggestions came in from various groups that were encouraged to collaborate on and improve this very important schema.

The commission residing in Rome met at the Alfonsianum on January 7, 14, and 21 to study the material received, and it composed a text that would serve as a basis for the study meetings to be held in Zurich, February 1-3. The title given to this text was "The Active Participation of the Church in Building the World." Häring insisted on stressing the close connection between the lives of human beings and the "signs of the times." Every section ought to begin with a description of the signs of the times, move on to a description of the signs of God's presence, and finally take up those signs of the times that rouse concern, always in the spirit of availability to people and of the optimism of John XXIII.[179]

It was during this phase that the opening words of the document were already formulated: "The joys and sorrows, the hopes and anxieties of the people of our time."[180] In general, the introduction was chiefly descriptive and took as its starting point the recognition of the challenges with which progress was confronting humanity. It was addressed not solely to Catholics but also to the separated brethren, the members of

---

[178] *Adumbratio schematis XVII. De activa praesentia ecclesiae ancillae Domini in hominibus bonae voluntatis*: Häring Archive, 2323; Guano Archive, 57.

[179] Häring,"Testimonianze," 170.

[180] This *incipit* was probably meant to capture once again the spirit in which Chenu had sketched the first draft of the "Message to the World" as set forth in his article "Un Concile a la dimension du monde," *Témoignage Chrétien*, October 12, 1963; see A. Duval, "Le message au monde," in *Vatican II commence*, 104-18.

the Abrahamic religions, and all human beings of good will, "in order to suggest that they join us in reflecting on Christ's thinking about humanity (1 Cor 2:10ff.) and to offer them the sincere collaboration of Christians in the building of an earthly city." The introduction ended with a short section, "The Church, Servant of Humanity," which defined the areas in which the Church could intervene with its teaching; this teaching, in accordance with the direction taken by Ancel, remained outside the realm of technical problems.

Four chapters followed. The first was anthropological; it preferred a christological approach to a creationist and emphasized both spiritual and earthly values and the oneness of the human vocation. The second chapter related the mission of the Church to its relationship with the world. The third chapter was devoted to the principles governing the behavior of ordinary Christians in the world: active involvement, practice of the spirit of poverty, and dialogue. The fourth and final chapter of the schema dwelt on the most urgent tasks of the present time: hunger, war, the dignity of the person, and the family. In Häring's judgment the chapters had been worked out essentially on the basis of the text of May 1963, the Malines Schema, and the suggestions sent to Rome, especially those of Ancel and Ménager.

Even before the Zurich meeting the text was subjected to criticisms. Among the most important were those that Hua sent to Ménager, in which he criticized the schema's lack of attention to the signs of times, which thereby ceased to be a central category of the document.[181] We must recognize how difficult it was for the commission in charge of the redaction to work up a synthesis satisfactory to everyone. However, the one that had been done remained the text that the central subcommission would study at its meeting in Zurich.[182]

But before that meeting began, Guano, Moeller, and Tucci had a meeting with Vischer in his capacity as representative of the WCC; he already had the text of January 21. The point of that meeting was not simply to give him the new redaction of the schema but to face up to the critical problem of dialogue with the separated brethren. Vischer thought some expressions in the text to be rather inopportune, as was the lack of any reference to the separated brethren in no. 19. The conversation then moved on to the problem of the optimism underlying the text and of the christological meaning of the Church's mission.

---

[181] *Schema XVII. Réflexions sur le projet du 21 janvier 1964* (Häring Archive, 2366), and *Schéma XVII — Nouvelles observations, 30/1/64* (ibid., 2365).

[182] Glorieux sent it to the eight members of the central commission on January 23, 1964 (see Glorieux to Hengsbach: Hengsbach Archive, 123).

3. The Zurich Schema[183]

The Zurich meeting was held in the office of *Orientierung*, the periodical of the Swiss Jesuits. Tucci, Sigmond, and Hirschmann were present along with the eight members of the central subcommission. The anticipated meeting of the Doctrinal Commission and of the Commission on the Lay Apostolate created conflicts in scheduling for some of those invited. It was then decided to combine the two meetings: that of the subcommission on the Church and that of the central subcommission for schema XVII. Seventeen people attended the meeting, among them Glorieux, De Riedmatten, Moeller, Medina, and two lay men, Sugranyes de Franch and De Habitcht.[184]

With the text of the preceding January as basis, the foundations were laid in Zurich that would remain as the guidelines for the document until the very end of the redactional process. At that meeting some new points and principles emerged regarding the attitude of the Church toward the world, and these would be decisive in the final version of the text. (1) Emphasis on the importance of the idea of dialogue with the modern world (defended especially by Ancel). From this principle there followed: (2) The principle of the Church's solidarity with the entire human race; this was suggested especially by the French theologians and by Father Thomas in particular. (3) The principle of "the signs of the times," which was present in some French documents sent in to the subcommission, especially in that of LeGuillou and Maxime Hua, who adopted the line sketched out in *Pacem in terris*. In this perspective the point was not simply to encourage an optimistic vision of the Church in the modern world but also to give earthly realities as such the status of a *locus theologicus* or source of theology. The principle of "the signs of the times" meant a shift in theological method from the deductive approach that had been used to the inductive approach employed in the Zurich schema.[185] (4) Another central principle was both anthropological and christological: the central place of both the human person and Christ emphasized the unity of the human vocation and the importance of earthly values and activities.

---

[183] See Tucci, "Introduction," 60-66.

[184] Glorieux, *Historia*, 43.

[185] A special commission was set up, with McGrath as president, that would analyze the more important problems of the contemporary world. It began to meet in September 1964 in order to compose an "introductory statement" that would precede the schema and explain the concrete historical context in which the latter was to be placed and understood (*Document sur le schéma 13. Travaux*, in CLG, Moeller Archive, 1178). For the later participation of Father Chenu in the subcommission on "the signs of the times," see *Primauté*, 81 n.4.

At this meeting the members worked hard and in an atmosphere of cordiality. They studied the overall structure of the text and its various sections (twenty-three in all, in addition to the conclusion; all in twelve dense pages). Time was lacking to tackle the fourth chapter, but the first three were completely studied, and there was agreement on the main lines of the fourth and of the appendixes complementing the text.[186]

The introduction stated the intentions of the Council, which desired to experience, from within, the problems of people in today's world. Following a series of steps worked out during the writing, the text was addressed first to the sons and daughters of the Church, then to all Christians, and then to all those who admitted the existence of God and to all men and women of good will.

The first chapter, "The Integral Vocation of the Human Person," showed how the human person does not have solely a supernatural call from which the search for human values would be a kind of desertion. The point of the text was to locate the human vocation midway between two extremes, that is, simplifying somewhat, between atheism[187] and materialism, on the one side, and the medieval "contempt for the world" *(contemptus mundi)*, on the other. On this basis, the second chapter went on to analyze the service of "pastors" in relation to the world, and the third inquired into what the attitude of the "people of God," and the laity in particular, should be. It said that an emphasis on dialogue and on the passage from dialogue to collaboration, provided that this is possible in the light of Christian or rational principles of morality, would avoid the multiplication of "private institutions of a temporal kind" that were reserved solely to Catholics.

Chapter IV consisted of a rather wide-ranging bloc of material that was further expanded in the appendixes. In this chapter the editors had condensed chapters II-VI of the draft worked up in May 1963, which

---

[186] Thus in an interview in *Orientierung*, February 15, 1964, 25-27 (reprinted in *La Croix*, February 23-24, 1964. See R. Stalder, "Une commission conciliaire au travail," *Choisir* [March 1965], 3-4), Guano expressed the hope that the appendixes, which were not to be discussed in the hall, might nevertheless be promulgated at the same time as the constitution. These appendixes were contained in a booklet distributed to the fathers on September 30, 1964; there were five of them: I. The Human Person in Society; II. Marriage and Family; III. The Proper Advancement of Cultural Progress; IV. Economic and Social Life; V. The Community of Nations and Peace (see Ph. Delhaye, "Histoire des textes de la Constitution pastorale," in *L'Eglise dans le monde*, 1:244-46).

[187] See P. Ladrière, "L'athéisme au Concile Vatican II," *Archives de Sociologie des Religions* 32 (1971) 53-84.

took up various subjects: the dignity of the human person, marriage and family, education and its promotion, economic and social life, and solidarity among peoples. The text discussed in Zurich underwent a process of gradual maturation that lasted until June 1964.

On returning to Rome, Häring, acting in Guano's name, informed Ottaviani and Cento of the results of the Zurich meeting, while Guano informed Suenens. Meanwhile, the work of correcting the text on the basis of suggestions made in Zurich was accelerated in order to have it ready for the meeting of the members of the mixed commission at the beginning of March. The text was distributed in good time, in Latin and French versions, accompanied by a "Note of the Subcommission on the Nature of This Schema and the Norms Used in Developing It." This note, offered as an overall interpretation of the schema, is very important for grasping the intentions of the central subcommission. It called attention to the difficulty of clearly delimiting the object and meaning of the document and noted the need to enhance its theological status.

Another report, circulated, it seems, on the same occasion and probably written by Häring, "The History, Character, Method and Spirituality of Schema XVII," stressed the continuity of the document with previous versions. What it said about spirituality was important:

> The responses that came from the various continents required that the text set forth a spirituality and not arid doctrine. Such a spirituality should not be chosen in a unilateral fashion but should be in a way a "synthesis of opposites," in order to emerge with something acceptable in its entirety or at least something more balanced. Optimism toward the "world" (meaning by this word the creation which God made good but which groans beneath the weight of sin and yearns to share in the freedom of sons and daughters) is false and dangerous if not balanced by another focus, that is, without the spirit of poverty and self-denial.[188]

This was an effort to answer the criticisms of some theologians who thought questions of great importance were left unanswered in the Zurich schema. Of these it will be enough to mention the matter of an adequate distinction between the natural and supernatural dimensions of the human being and between the Church and the world. There was also criticism of the excessively optimistic spirit of the schema, which ended up obscuring the reality of evil in the contemporary world, as well as the reality of suffering and injustices, and in particular the problems of

---

[188] *De historia, stilo, methodo et spiritualitate schematis XVII*: Häring Archive, 1857-2446; Haubtmann Archive, 913.

poverty, concerning which the Council could not remain silent because the Church's credibility was at stake.

Such criticisms were voiced at the March 4 meeting of the mixed commission (which had not met since November 29, 1963). They came from men with divergent positions, among them Rahner, Florit, Civardi, Franić, and Laszlo. Congar said he was very disappointed by the meeting.[189] The commission met again on March 12, and this time it opened with the reading by Sugranyes de Franch, in the name of the lay auditors, of a document favorable to the schema.[190] An effort was made to focus the discussion on general themes: Doumith, for example (along with others, including Ancel himself), criticized the excessive and superficial humanism of the text. The difficulties being met by the commission also raised the question of the shortness of time still available for reworking the schema. Cento gave himself the assignment of speaking to Paul VI about the problem and pointing out the resultant need for a fourth period. At this point the text had to be corrected and a new version prepared for the next meeting of the mixed commission scheduled for the beginning of June. This job was given to Häring and Sigmond, who prepared a sketch of a new version; this was sent to the members of central subcommission on April 15, 1964.[191]

At the March meeting the subcommissions were assigned the task of writing the *Directory for Developing a Pastoral Instruction on the Church in the World*,[192] which was to be presented to the central subcommission at the end of April. Subcommissions were set up on the human person in society, marriage and the family, the proper advancement of cultural progress, and the community of nations and peace.[193]

4. The Maturation of the Schema

On June 3 the central subcommission met at the Alphonsianum in order to make final preparations for presenting the schema to the mixed commission,[194] which met, as scheduled, in plenary session on the next

---

[189] *JCongar*, 430-31 and 438.
[190] *Rémarques générales sur le schéma XVII*. Häring Archive, 2729.
[191] Häring Archive, 2221.
[192] Ibid., 1679.
[193] Glorieux, *Historia*, 62-64, 73.
[194] See the interview with Ancel in *La Croix*, June 3, 1964, in which he gave some details of the work of the central subcommission and said he was optimistic about the way the text was developing.

day.[195] The meeting began with Guano's report, which rather carefully described the limitations of the discussion and the criteria adopted in reworking the schema. Philips and Rahner once again criticized the confusion of the natural and supernatural orders in the text. Also heard was a request for greater care in use of the term *world;* this led Garrone to speak of the "consecration of the world" as something required by the faith.[196]

The reading of each chapter gave rise to new criticisms; for example, on the following day Parente proposed replacing *sensus fidei* with *sensus fidelium.* But the most controverted subject was the competence of the Church in specific matters. As Rahner put it: "If the Church is silent, what are individual consciences to do?" The discussion thus came up against the problem of the relationship between the magisterium and the individual conscience. The fourth chapter elicited an incisive criticism from Lebret regarding the section on the economy, which he considered weak in facing the worldwide problems of underdevelopment and unemployment.[197] At the meeting on June 6, at which Ottaviani presided, this chapter was also directly attacked by some members of the Doctrinal Commission with ties with the Holy Office who attacked Häring on marriage and specifically on the question of its ends.[198]

At the end of the meeting on June 4 a vote was taken on the schema as a whole, in order to decide whether or not to send it to the CC. After some hesitations, the schema was approved by a large majority[199] and then passed on to the CC, which studied it on June 26.[200] The CC then

[195] It should be mentioned that the contrast in the perspectives of the Doctrinal Commission and the Commission for the Lay Apostolate emerged anew at the meeting on June 3. The two secretaries, Tromp and Glorieux, were not in agreement on the thrust to be given to the text. Rahner, for his part, was critical of the text. See Glorieux, *Historia,* 65-81.

[196] See the summary of the debate in *JCongar,* 482-83.

[197] Although Paul VI especially esteemed and relied on Lebret's work, Rome's acknowledgment of Lebret still lay in the future; only in February 1964, after the Zurich meeting, was he moved from "unofficial expert" to "peritus." On Lebret's contribution to the Council and specifically to schema XIII, see D. Pelletier, *"Economie et humanisme." De l'utopie communautaire au combat pour le tiers-monde (1941-1966)* (Paris, 1966), 394-424.

[198] Members of the Holy Office subjected Häring to a real "public trial" before the commission on the basis of Denzinger and a decree of the Holy Office itself! The schema passed, but Häring had to be "sacrificed," as would become clear in the fall. According to Congar: "There is a great concerted attack: Franić, Lio, Tromp...in short, the Holy Office" (*JCongar,* 491).

[199] Glorieux, *Historia,* 77-79.

[200] The entire schema, adjusted on the basis of the comments and emendations suggested by the mixed commission, was sent to Cicognani by Ottaviani and Cento on June 15; see *AS* V/2, 602-27, 545-46.

changed the place of the schema on the conciliar agenda: it would now be no longer schema XVII, but schema XIII. It was at last decided to send it to the bishops at the beginning of July, along with all the necessary instructions and cautions and with a request that they send in their comments before October 1.[201]

In the history of the schema, the publication of Paul VI's first encyclical, *Ecclesiam suam*, which focused on the idea of dialogue,[202] played a key role. Such is the testimony of two privileged chroniclers, M. G. McGrath and R. Tucci. Häring, too, said that the encyclical "made a decisive contribution to schema XIII."[203]

During the summer of 1964 a body was set up, consisting of members of the central commission and the presidents of the subcommissions (thirteen persons in all), to correct and rework the text during its discussion by the fathers in the council hall. This commission began to meet in September in order to examine the comments that had come in during the summer. Among these were the comments of Philips and Congar, as well as those of Hengsbach, which were the result of a meeting of German bishops and theologians. At one meeting of this new body Guano suggested forming two subcommissions, one to go into the question of the "signs of the times," the other theological. Ferrari Toniolo insisted on the formation of a third subcommission whose task would be to clarify relations between Church and state,[204] a subject which in his judgment played a central role in the schema. When the two subcommissions were formed, with McGrath and Garrone as their respective presidents, individuals were invited to take part who had not shared in the writing of the Zurich schema. The subcommission on the signs of the times invited Daniélou, De Riedmatten, Ligutti, Gagnebet, Medina, Lebret, Putz, Greco, Martelet, Dingemans, Neuer, Caramuru, Gregory, Galilea, Moeller, Joblin, Delhaye, and Houtart (who became the secretary), as well as many bishops representing the real situation in various countries: Blomjous, Zoa, Câmara, Wojtyla, Wright, Ancel, Ménager, Nagae, and Ayoub.[205]

---

[201] *AS* V/2, 640-42.

[202] Two exhaustive studies of this theme are the one published by the Instituto Social León XIII, *El diálogo según la mente de Pablo VI* (Madrid, 1965, 1968²), with an extensive bibliography; and the *Comentario eclesial a la "Ecclesiam suam,"* ed. Francisco García-Salve (Bilbao, 1965).

[203] Häring, "Testimonianze," 171.

[204] See G.-H. Baudry, "L'Eglise et l'Etat à Vatican II," in *Kecharitômenê. Mélanges René Laurentin* (Paris, 1990), 537-48.

[205] The minutes of the subcommission on the signs of the times are collected in *Document sur le schéma 13. Travaux* (Moeller Archive, 1178).

On this occasion, Msgr. Wojtyla, Archbishop of Cracow, sent Häring a complete replacement for schema XIII. Known as "the proposal of the Polish bishops," it had been composed in Cracow under the direction of Wojtyla himself, who was also in contact with Msgr. Kominek and with a group in Warsaw. One of the leading ideas in the Polish schema could be formulated thus: "The presence of the Church depends not only on the will of God but also on the will of the human beings who freely manifest their agreement with the divine will." The Polish schema as a whole took up, in order: (1) The bases of the Church's presence in the world; (2) The goals of the Church in the world; (3) The main mission of the Church; (4) The means of carrying out this mission in the contemporary world, namely, the testimony of faith, the life of each person, associations, relations with non-Christians and relations with civil society. It is clear that these viewpoints were conditioned by the special situation of Poland.[206]

This substitute text could not, however, be taken into account as a whole because the so-called Zurich schema had already been put on the agenda of the CC.[207] In addition, difficulties were raised within the conciliar commission about taking the situation of the Polish Church as basis for analysis of a document to be discussed at a universal council. But the Polish text was included among the Ariccia documents (June 1965) and had some influence on the new version of schema XIII.[208]

The theological subcommission met on September 11 and 12, with Garrone, Philips, Congar, Rahner, Moeller, Ferrari Toniolo, Daniélou, Benoit, Rigaux, Glorieux, and Sugranyes de Franch taking part.[209] Rahner's criticism (insisting that a clear distinction be drawn between the natural dimension and the supernatural) was challenged by Congar and Daniélou. Philips offered a series of theological distinctions that clarified some of the points being discussed. The results reached by the theological subcommission were forwarded to the central subcommission, which was continuing its study of the comments that had come in during the summer. The conclusions reached in the debates of these September days were put together in a short programmatic document to be presented to

---

[206] See Ph. Levillain "Les épiscopats de l'Europe de l'Est à Vatican II," *Documentation sur l'Europe centrale* 11/2 (1973), 93.

[207] See Delhaye, "Histoire des textes," 254. In note 4 the author said: "But some points in the document were kept because of the clarifications it provided on the relations of the Church with an officially atheistic and communist society."

[208] J. Grootaers, *Dal Vaticano II a Giovanni Paolo II* (Casale M., 1982), 140-42.

[209] Glorieux, *Historia*, 83, 106.

the fathers along with the schema; its title was "Guidelines for the Future Development of the Text."[210]

In order to prepare the report that was to accompany the presentation of the text in the hall, Guano, who had been elected the official reporter on the schema, called several meetings of the central commission: on September 21 and 29, and again on October 6. At these meetings, the president of each subcommission was asked to draw up a report on the appendixes.

II. SECOND PHASE: THE DÖPFNER PLAN AND THE INITIATIVE OF PAUL VI

A. THIRTEENTH MEETING OF THE CC (MARCH 10)

On March 10 the thirteenth meeting of the CC took place, and it marked the beginning of a new phase of the intersession. All members were present except for assistant secretaries Nabaa and Krol. On the agenda were the study of some proposed changes in the Council Regulations[211] and the presentation of some revised schemas. Cardinal Roberti's report on the Regulations was also important for the theme of Döpfner's very concrete comments on a method for the third period.[212] Among the decisions taken on the Regulations the following may be noted: (a) the development of internal rules for the use of the moderators;[213] (b) raising the number of signatures needed for permission to speak from five to seventy fathers; and (c) merging the schemas to be discussed. It was also decided to hold more frequent meetings of the CC and the moderators during the Council's work, in order better to divide up their respective contributions.

The ambiguities of the Döpfner Plan emerged in his "Remarks on the More Expeditious Conduct of the Council's Business during the Third Period," which were dated March 3. In them he said: "Since it has been decided by the CC, with the approval of the Supreme Pontiff, that the Council should as far as possible *be concluded after the third period...*"[214] It is quite surprising that when Felici submitted a review of

---

[210] *AS* IV/2, 698-99.
[211] *Patrum sententiae et vota*, in *ADP* IV/1, 445-46, 455-59, 461-64, 468, 470-78, 504-13.
[212] *AS* V/2, 152-56.
[213] Lercaro Archive, XXIV 591.
[214] See *AS* V/2, 143 (emphasis added).

the CC's meetings during the intersession, some months later, in October 1964, he omitted any reference to the meeting on March 10.[215] The various interpretations of the plan, already mentioned, differed on the basis on the many changes in the texts that were to be shortened; this was one of the many reasons for the uncertainties that, as seen from outside, collected around a rather mysterious plan that was drawing the attention of some commentators although it seemed that no one had ever had it in his hands.[216]

Later in that same meeting approval was given to a letter by Cardinal Bea in which he said the section on religious freedom was to become chapter IV of the schema on ecumenism, while the section on the Jews would be an appendix to it. The meeting then moved on to the reports of some commissions that had already studied the directives from the CC on the schemas within their competence: the Commission for Bishops and the Governance of Dioceses; the Doctrinal Commission, which set forth the status of the studies commissioned for the schema; and the Commission for the Lay Apostolate. In addition, extensive information was given on the activity of the Secretariat for Christian Unity (meeting of the experts, February 3-24; plenary session, February 24-March 7; working methods). Finally, an explanation was given of the new shape of the texts composed by the Commissions for the Discipline of the Clergy and the Christian People, for the Discipline of the Sacraments, and for Seminaries, Studies, and Catholic Education. The contents of these new versions were not studied; rather, a check was made on whether the schemas were consistent with the guidelines given for their new versions.

B. FOURTEENTH MEETING OF THE CC (APRIL 16-17)

The agenda for this meeting was very full; it was devoted to approving the list of schemas to be discussed during the third period of the Council. Agagianian's report on the schema on the Church led to a lively discussion, especially of collegiality. In his intervention Urbani reported on the way in which that question had been tackled in

---

[215] See *AS* V/3, 28-30.

[216] See *ICI*, April 1, 1964, no. 213, pp. 5-6, and *Katholiek Archief* 19, no. 21 (July 17, 1964), 770-77. As we today read the reports published at the time by the better informed authors, e.g., G. Caprile or R. Laurentin, we observe that the list of schemas to be changed varied from author to author.

the Italian Episcopal Conference and on the opposition of Ottaviani and Florit to no. 22.[217] Nevertheless, it was decided that the schema should be sent to the fathers as the Doctrinal Commission had presented it.

Next on the agenda were the presentations of the schemas on the pastoral office of bishops in the Church, reported by Döpfner,[218] on the Oriental Churches, reported by Cicognani,[219] and on ecumenism, again with Cicognani reporting. At Confalonieri's suggestion it was decided that the schema on religious freedom and that on the Jews and non-Christians should take the form of independent Declarations. The study of the schemas continued on the 17th: Lercaro reported on the schema on priests/clerics, Döpfner on religious, Urbani on the lay apostolate, Roberti on the sacrament of matrimony, and Confalonieri on the training of priests[220] and on Catholic schools. The meeting ended with Döpfner's plan on the procedure to be followed in the third period, especially in what concerned the functions of the moderators.[221]

C. SENDING OF THE SCHEMAS TO THE FATHERS (MAY 11 AND JUNE 2)

When the CC sent the schemas to the Council fathers, it could be said that part of the Döpfner Plan had reached completion.[222] As was said earlier, this plan, drawn up at the request of Paul VI, aimed at improving the work of the Council, especially during the intersession; the pope and the cardinal wanted an effective Council, even if this meant excluding some subject matters or limiting the size of the documents. As could be foreseen, the plan excited the resistance of the commissions, and interventions with the pope in opposition to the cardinal's proposals were not lacking. But Döpfner's vision did prove

[217] *AS* V/2, 288-91.

[218] The schema was the subject of a broad range of comments from Carli, Bishop of Segni, which in his opinion were "theological in character." They had already been submitted without receiving an answer from the commission; see *AS* V/2, 187-91.

[219] The schema was followed by an interesting appendix entitled "Historical Report on the Preparation of the Schema" and by another on the emendations accepted or rejected; see *AS* V/2, 474.

[220] Liénart addressed an appeal to all, especially to the young, regarding the greatness of the ministerial vocation and on the role of priests; see *AS* V/2, 474.

[221] This was the plan presented at the meeting of the moderators on March 11; *AS* V/2, 143-49.

[222] It was on June 2 that Döpfner sent Cicognani a letter in which he said that a fourth period of conciliar work was needed, *AS* V/2, 528-33; see also *AD* 527-30, where there are negative comments from Cicognani.

effective at the level of working methods. His proposals to shorten
texts and debates went beyond specific cases or subjects, always in
light of the overall conciliar event.

After the plan had been explained to the CC on December 28, 1963,
steps were taken to bring it to a successful outcome. On March 3, 1964,
Döpfner added some "Remarks on the Business of the Third Period."[223]
The following May he emphasized the necessity of ending the Council
as quickly as possible, in view of the dangers that prolongation would
bring. It was in this context that he added "Remarks on the Order to Be
Followed during the Third Period of Vatican Council II."[224] The results
of the plan became visible when the schemas to be discussed during the
third period were sent out.

The pressures of time were obvious during the second intersession. It
was necessary to finish the reworking of the schemas, obtain approval of
them from the respective commissions, and send them to the fathers in
sufficient time for them to study them before September 14, when the
third session would open. Each schema had had its ups-and-downs in the
course of its composition and revision. In addition, the approval of the
pope was needed. This explains why some texts were not always ready
to be sent out by the anticipated dates, while in other cases they received
papal approval within a short time. This was the case, for example, with
the schema on the missions, the sending of which to the fathers had been
authorized as early as January 17.[225]

The hard work of the commissions bore fruit. At its fourteenth
meeting on April 16 and 17 the CC approved the list of schemas to be
studied during the third period; at the same time it ordered the following schemas to be printed and sent to the fathers on the basis of
Cicognani's "rescript" of April 27[226]: propositions on religious; the
votum on the sacrament of matrimony; propositions on the training of
priests; propositions on Catholic schools; the decree on ecumenism;
the decree on the lay apostolate; propositions on priests; the decree
on the pastoral office of bishops in the Church. It was to the sending
of these that Paul VI referred on April 30 in the apostolic letter Spir-
itus Paracliti.[227]

[223] AS V/2, 143-49.
[224] Ibid., 478-79.
[225] See Caprile III, 281.
[226] AS V/2, 517.
[227] AAS 56 (April 30, 1964), 355; French trans. in DC, no. 1424 (1964), 611-12.

In a letter of May 11 Felici informed the Council fathers that he was sending them the following schemas of constitutions, decrees, propositions, and a votum: On the pastoral office of bishops in the Church; On the Oriental Churches; On ecumenism; On religious; On priests; On the lay apostolate; On the sacrament of matrimony; On the training of priests; On Catholic schools.[228] Unfulfilled, on the other hand, was the intention of the CC at its meeting on April 16 that the fathers be sent the schema on the Church, even though the various points of view on the schema were still not completely clarified.[229]

It was, instead, at the meeting on June 26 that the CC approved the sending of the schema on the Church,[230] along with the schemas on revelation,[231] the missions,[232] and the Church in the modern world.[233] In a letter of July 7, therefore, Felici told the fathers that he was sending them the remaining schemas that they might study them before September 14.[234] These schemas were those on divine revelation, on the Church, on the missionary activity of the Church, and on the Church in the modern world, as well as the second declaration, in the schema on ecumenism, on Jews and Non-Christians.[235] In the same letter Felici also told the fathers of the order that would be followed in discussion of the principal schemas. In first place would be the schema on the Church and, in particular, its last two chapters (On the eschatological character of our call and our union with the heavenly Church; and On the Blessed Virgin Mary, Mother of God, in the mystery of Christ and the Church). If the fathers wanted to make comments, Felici asked that they send them to the General Secretariat before September 9.

---

[228] *AS* V/2, 500-501.
[229] Ibid., 291.
[230] Ibid., 638.
[231] Ibid., 640.
[232] Ibid.
[233] Ibid., 641.
[234] Ibid., 646-47.
[235] This declaration had received the approval of Paul VI on July 3: *AS* III/2, 327.

D. THE ACTIVITY OF SOME COMMISSIONS

1. The Schema on the Church

a. The Thirteen "Suggestions" of Paul VI on Chapter III[236]

On May 19, 1964, a letter of Felici informed the Doctrinal Commission of thirteen "suggestions" sent to him by the pope and having to do with collegiality, the subject of the new chapter III (formerly II). This initiative was unprecedented and marked by a certain ambiguity. On the one hand, the pope, who was himself a Council father, but also natural president of the Council, chose to intervene in the development of the key constitution of the entire Council by sending the Doctrinal Commission a request comparable to the *modi* of the bishops. On the other, he did so nearly at the last possible moment, after the schema had been developed by seven subcommittees, carefully scrutinized by the Commission for the Church, and approved almost unanimously at a plenary session of that commission. The Pope seemed, therefore, to be making himself sponsor of the concerns of the minority, which had been defeated both in the subcommissions and in the commission.

The suggestions had to do with the chapter on the hierarchy and above all with the relations between Pope and college, and they did so from a relatively new point of view. Instead of challenging the teaching set down in the chapter of episcopal collegiality, Paul VI was asking for a closer study of some expressions in order to avoid erroneous interpretations of them in light of the doubts expressed to him.[237] At the same time, as Ottaviani noted when telling the commission of the thirteen "suggestions": "When expressly asked by him, the pope answered that the commission was completely free to decide."[238]

Without going into details, I shall describe the thirteen papal "suggestions" according to their main tendencies. (1) Four suggestions referred to the description of the pope; in two of them the proposed

---

[236] *AS* V/2, 507-9. See *Primauté*, 125-32; Cl. Troisfontaines, "A propos de quelques interventions de Paul VI dans l'élaboration de 'Lumen gentium,'" in *Paolo VI e i problemi ecclesiologici al Concilio*, 104-14.

[237] Caprile lists the individuals consulted by the pope on chapter III in 1964 and the kind of communication: Tromp (remarks), Browne (correspondence), Ottaviani (oral), Parente (Biblical Commission), Colombo (consulted), Bertrams (asked for a special opinion), Philips (kept informed).

[238] See Betti, *La dottrina*, 203; also Troisfontaines, "A propos de quelques interventions," 105 n.14.

change would remove the description "head of the college," but the commission opposed such a change; in the other two instances, the suggestions looked to introduce the words "head of the college," but in both cases the commission offered an alternative: "pastor of the Church" in one case, and "supreme pastor" in the other. (2) Two suggestions asked for better biblical justification of the expressions used. (3) There was an effort to reduce collegiality to the case of an ecumenical council. (4) One suggestion was to remove a reference to the local Churches. (5) Two proposals had reference to the exercise of papal authority independently of the authority of the bishops.[239]

The discussion within the commission (June 5-6, 1964) began with a determination of the precise significance of the "suggestions." The members quickly saw that they were not emendations but suggestions offered for free discussion. For this reason the commission, in its official reply on June 7, began by thanking the pope for the freedom allowed to it.[240]

The Pope having asked that the Pontifical Biblical Commission also be consulted, on May 27 the questions were sent to its secretary, Father Wambacq. At a meeting on May 31 the latter studied them in the presence of the members resident in Rome: Msgr. Smit and Fathers Ciappi and Salmon, Msgr. Garofalo and Fathers Duncker, Penna, Kerrigan, Kearns, and Castellino. All agreed that according to the scriptures Peter and the apostles form an apostolic college, in the true and proper sense. "From sacred scripture alone it is not clear," the Biblical Commission said, that the pope and the bishops form a college that succeeds to the apostolic college. But it did offer a textual basis for such a teaching, which would have to be established from tradition: Mt 28:16-20; Mk 16:14-18; and Rv 21:14. The Pope also wanted to know whether the powers granted to Peter in Matthew 16:19 belonged at the same time to the apostles according to Matthew 18:18. The commission answered in the affirmative, but it was less decided on the nature of these powers. The answers of the commission were sent to the Secretary General of the Council on June 2. Philips, for his part, also asked for a report from L. Cerfaux, biblical scholar at Louvain.[241]

---

[239] Some analysts see here the influence of W. Bertrams, who later played an important part in the introduction of the "Preliminary Explanatory Note" (see *Primauté*, 41-48, 110-13).

[240] The account of the deliberations of June 5-6, written by Tromp, is in *Primauté*, 161-65.

[241] Answer in the Philips Archive, dossier P 39, under the title "De collegialitate — 13 suggestions, 5-6 iunii 1964."

The position that the Doctrinal Commission took on the papal suggestions was that there should be no yielding on the principles of sacramentality and collegiality asserted in the schema and accepted by the
majority in the straw vote of October 1963. On one particular point (no.
7) the commission proved cautious: the pope's suggestion tended to
limit the exercise of collegial power: it was "to be exercised according
to the prescription of the head."According to Philips's interpretation,
this restriction would have brought the danger of preventing the college
from acting in extraordinary circumstances in which the pope was not in
a condition to give his formal assent to a proposal. The commission preferred, therefore, to defend the negative formula already implicit in the
October vote in the hall, namely, "which power cannot be exercised
independently of the Roman Pontiff," in order to show the sufficiency of
a pontifical approval, even, possibly, after the fact.[242]

For all the emotions they aroused, the requests of Paul VI did not
change the shape of the schema on the Church nor were they intended to
do so; in September the pope himself, in rejecting the minority's accusations that he had accepted the "emptying" of the primacy, would
adduce the "suggestions" as evidence of his misgivings, to the point of
"requiring" the commission to look again at certain questions.[243] Paul
VI's wish was that the Council might approve the schema on the Church
with as much unanimity as possible. This he regarded as more important
than the consistency of the statements on collegiality. On the other hand,
his personal sensibilities and his cultural formation made him very sensitive to the accusation that he was failing to defend the papal prerogatives out of fear of the Council, even though he had difficulty in entering fully into the views of the majority on collegiality.[244]

The outlook, however, that took shape within the commission and
among the authors of the revised schema was different; they were concerned by the "objective alliance" that existed between the demands of

[242] The observations and Philips's report on the discussion of the suggestions are
published in *Primauté*, 133-39. On 140-45 there is the exegetical note that Philips had
asked of Cerfaux.

[243] Colombo had pointed out to Paul VI that Siri himself had written in his *Corso di
teologia dogmatica - La chiesa - La Rivelazione trasmessa* (Rome, 1950²) 279, that "the
fact that the college is a reality, the fact that in addition to the pope there are the bishops,
the fact that they are possessors of infallibility, all this shows that the bishops too are true
teachers of the faith, because the subjects who possess magisterial infallibility are two:
the college and the pope personally: the two subjects, however, are not fully distinct since
the pope is part of the college and also its head (inadequate distinction)."

[244] *Primauté*, 32-33.

the minority and the authoritative "suggestions," but they were also hopeful. On June 10, 1964, some days after the commission's discussion of the thirteen "suggestions," Charue, Bishop of Namur and vice-president of the Doctrinal Commission, had a forty-five minute audience with Paul VI. At that point the pope had not yet received the answers, which the commission had sent to Felici on the 7th. Charue therefore quickly explained the drift of those answers, and Paul VI replied: "Collegiality is beyond doubt, but what power *(potestas)* does it enjoy? I have read some studies on the problem and intend to read others. Then I shall decide before God."[245] This statement shows the kinds of difficulties the question of collegiality raised in the mind of Paul VI.

The Pope expressed interest in meeting Philips and received him on July 7. During the audience Philips endeavored to give a convincing explanation of the meaning of collegiality, the exercise of which could not threaten papal primacy but would complement it. When Philips returned to Louvain after the meetings in June and the audience in July, he was not completely at ease over the fate of the schema on the Church; he feared new attempts at reining it in.

What is certain is that the minority did not cease to play its own cards during the summer of 1964. Despite Parente's acceptance of positions favorable to collegiality, there was, as the result of a generational change, a rejuvenation of the minority's organization through meetings and the spread of ideas, above all by the efforts of Bishop Carli and Professor Dino Staffa, who were behind an intense effort at raising barriers. Clearly, those who disapproved of the entire direction taken by Vatican II had found their point of attack in chapter III of the schema on the Church. As it had during the preparation for the Council, the periodical *Divinitas* gathered up and urged the objections to the foundational theses of the chapter in an article by Staffa. Echoes were to be heard in a whole series of notes, appeals, and threats passed on to Paul VI during the summer, culminating in a lengthy confidential note conveyed to the pope in person by Cardinal Larraona and signed by about twenty cardinals, ten or so superiors of religious orders, and some bishops.[246]

---

[245] Troisfontaines, "A propos de quelques interventions," 112-13.

[246] The text of this note, which was sent on September 13, is published in M. Lefebvre, *J'accuse le Concile* (Martigny, 1976), 55-66. It reached Paul VI with a number of copies of the last page: each page bore the name of a "first signer" and the names of those whom this individual had asked to sign the appeal. The full dossier prompted by this note is available as edited by G. Caprile, "Contributo alla storia della 'Nota explicativa praevia,'" in *Paolo VI e i problemi ecclesiologici al Concilio*, 587- 697.

The note stated that the minority did not want the sacramentality of the episcopate confirmed, because this would be a way of canceling infallibility and the primacy, which do not have their origin in a sacrament. It also did not want recognition of the existence of the episcopal college as successor to the apostolic college, because this would change the view stated in the ordinary magisterium on the precedence and greater excellence of the Petrine office when it came to safeguarding and teaching the true faith. In addition, the minority maintained that the affirmation of a power by divine right for the college changed the "monarchic regime" of the Roman Church and opened the door to "foolish" demands of the bishops, with serious harm to the unity and cohesion of Catholicism. Finally, the minority challenged the "irregular" way in which the Doctrinal Commission had studied the *modi,* turning an opinion of the schools into a proposition in a dogmatic constitution.

The practical proposal made to Paul VI (not in these articles but in letters such as those of Larraona or in notes sent at the beginning of September by Cardinals Micara and Ruffini) was that everything having to do with collegiality be removed from chapter III as "immature" or that it at least be put off to a time distant from the Council or alternatively (Larraona) that it be assigned to a congregation of "impartial" theologians, which obviously would have to propose its suppression. In September 1964 Philips wrote a refutation of Staffa's article in *Divinitas,* while Colombo also prepared, for the pope's eye, lengthy responses to the attacks.

It is to be noted that during this intersession theological activity connected with the third chapter increased to a considerable degree. Conferences were given by cardinals, bishops,[247] and observers;[248] important works appeared on the history of collegiality in the early tradition[249] or in "Roman" ecclesiology from Trent to Vatican I.[250] The line taken by

[247] Guerry, in *DC,* no. 1419 (March 1, 1964), cols. 315-30; no. 1420 (March 15, 1964), cols. 367-85; Bea, ibid., no. 1423 (May 2, 1964), cols. 583-90, especially col. 587.

[248] *DC,* no. 1420 (March 15, 1964), cols. 393-410.

[249] J. Lécuyer, *Etudes sur la collégialité* (Le Puy-Lyons, 1964); G. D'Ercole, *Communio- Collegialità-Primato e sollicitudo omnium Ecclesiarum* (Rome, 1964); the entire second number of *Irénikon* for 1965, pp. 161-227 (D. W. Allen, A. M. Allchin, T. Strotmann, H. Marot); M.-J. Le Guillou, *Les structures sacramentelles et collégiales de la communion et de la mission de l'Eglise en marche* (Paris, 1964), 91-146. On the opposite side: D. Staffa, "De Episcoporum Collegio," *Divinitas* 8 (1964), 3-61; H. Lattanzi, "Quid de Episcoporum collegialitate ex N. T. sentiendum sit," ibid., 62-96.

[250] G. Alberigo, *Lo sviluppo della dottrina sui poteri nella chiesa universale. Momenti essenziali tra il XVI e il XIX secolo* (Rome, 1964). The papers sent in on this subject to the Colloquium of L'Ilafol, at Chevtogne, in April 1964, and at Constance, on Pentecost of the same year, were published as volume 52 of the Unam Sanctam collection (Paris, 1965).

the opponents found renewed expression in the two lengthy articles in *Divinitas*. At the end of these debates, if we judge by what Philips wrote in July 1964, it appeared that "the two terms are not pope and episcopate but pope and college of bishops, of which the pope is a part and which he directs. The powers of the one in no way lessen the powers of the other, and the assistance of the Holy Spirit guarantees a lasting understanding."[251]

The Pope, for his part, answered Larraona in a long handwritten letter, in which he lamented the way in which fathers who enjoyed so much authority had tried to cast a shadow over the Council's work just as it was about to reach its goal. He asserted the correctness, scrupulosity, and safety-mindedness of his own commitment to see to it that nothing unclear or open to misinterpretation should be approved.[252] Nothing was now left for the minority but to turn to the public debate in the hall. If the pope had not agreed to change the schema on the Church at their urging, they might be able to exploit his concern about a "correct interpretation" to attempt to boycott the Constitution on the Church.

b. The Chapter on the Blessed Virgin

Characteristic of the new text was its search for formulas to harmonize the opposing currents of thought. This effort showed through clearly right from the introduction: while the fundamental principle in the preparatory schema had been the single predestination of Christ and Mary, in the new text Mary was seen in relation to the mystery of Christ and the mystery of the Church.[253] Because the chapter did not attempt to set forth a complete teaching on Mary or to take a position in theological controversies,[254] when it asserted the dignity of Mary in relation to her Son, it made no reference to the single decree of predestination that Balić had wanted. The result was a compromise text (no. 53).

The faith of Mary during the hidden life of Jesus was made known by introducing one of the texts regarded as "anti-mariological." The Doctrinal Commission retrieved a formulation (which already had been present in Philips's first draft but had disappeared during the subsequent ups-and-downs of the text) on Mary's lack of understanding of the mystery of

---

[251] *DC* (October 18, 1964), col. 1340.
[252] Paul VI to Larraona, September 14, 1964 (ISR, Vatican II Archive); published in *Paolo VI e i problemi ecclesiologici al Concilio*, 632-35.
[253] See the preparatory schema in *AS* I/4, 92, and *textus emendatus*, no. 52, pp. 197-98.
[254] *Textus emendatus*, 198.

Christ and her meditation on it.[255] The same thought was repeated in the presentation of the public life of Jesus. So, too, nothing was said of the Virgin's state of holiness, which had been present in the *textus prior*, where Balić had spoken of her being "endowed with the splendors of the most perfect holiness," an expression that the commission replaced with "an altogether unique holiness." It was by faith and obedience that she collaborated in human salvation as servant of the Lord (and no longer as "associate of Christ"); it was in this sense that the Fathers had been able to draw the parallel between Eve and Mary.[256]

Following this same line, the amended text played down the participation of Mary in the passion of Christ and did not emphasize the self-offering of the Virgin. At Ancel's suggestion, it corrected the final phrase to read: "giving her loving assent to the sacrifice of the victim she had borne." Tromp was opposed to this and succeeded in winning at least a reference in the note to *Mystici Corporis*, which spoke of the analogy between the co-offering of Mary in the sacrifice of the cross and the co-offering of the faithful in the sacrifice of the mass.[257]

The section on relations of Mary with the Church was divided into three parts: on her cooperation with Christ in redemption; on Mary as exemplar of the Church; and on proposing Mary and her virtues for imitation by the Church. The first section, which referred more directly to the articles of the preparatory schema on the doctrine of co-redemption and mediation, was the one that gave rise to the great conflicts. Balić proposed the formula "mediatrix of grace," while Philips defended the idea that Mary "was for us the mother of grace" and that she continues to intercede for us in heaven. For this reason "her cooperation and mediation in the order of grace" (Balić) or "her motherhood in the order of grace" (Philips) lasts from the consent given at the annunciation to the final consummation.

The second section compared the mediation of Christ with the maternal role of Mary. Balić proposed speaking of her "mediation in Christ," but Philips won the phrase "maternal task." When the Doctrinal Commission acted to clarify the earlier text at its meeting in June 1964, it changed, first of all, the order followed in the exposition. The amended text began by speaking of the mediation of Christ, to which the maternal role of Mary was completely subordinate.

---

[255] Ibid., 200.

[256] In Philips's first draft he had emphasized the role of Mary in the incarnation; in Balić's view this aspect had not been given adequate treatment. In the end, however, Philips won the use of "serving" (*inserviens*) in place of "allied with" (*sociata*).

[257] *Relatio secretarii*, C II 5, pp. 5ff.

In the passage on the cooperation of Mary with Christ here on earth, the commission combined the two versions of Balić and Philips, that is, it included the titles "humble handmaid of the Lord" and "generous associate" (no. 61) but played down this last phrase by placing Mary on the same plane as other "associates," along with an assertion of her special but not exclusive role. On the other hand, this approach rejected a clause proposed by Volk, Bishop of Mainz (Germany), which emphasized the cooperation of Mary with Christ in the context of the mystical body. Accepted instead was a concrete description of the activity of Mary, who "in a wholly singular way cooperated by her obedience, faith, hope and burning charity in restoring supernatural life to souls" (no. 61).

In the third section, on the present influence of the Virgin, the commission asserted the motherhood of Mary in the order of grace: the definitive text read "the motherhood of Mary in the order of grace" (no. 62), instead of what Balić suggested: "her cooperation or mediation in the order of grace." Finally, the commission added a sentence in which the term *mediatrix* was used, but with great caution, as one title among others, which, while honoring the Virgin, added nothing to the efficacy and dignity of the sole mediation of Christ. Thus the text skillfully emphasized the role of Mary in relation to humanity without ever relating this role to the Church as such; on the other hand, it was never said that this role included a mission of *mediation*, much less of *co-redemption*.

The point about the Virgin as model of the Church in the order of faith and charity and as anticipatory and perfect embodiment of the Church — but as communion and not in its "hierarchic" character — had been defended with special zeal by Laurentin in support of Philips's first draft: while Mary surpasses the Church, the Church is not wholly included in Mary if we think of the Church as "sacrament of Christ the head." From this it followed that the Virgin, who "is resplendent as exemplar of the virtues," was one term in a relationship of moral exemplarity in which she continually advanced, like the Church, through faith, obedience, charity, patience, and fulfillment of the will of God. The fathers, then, with communion as their goal, successfully presented the relationship of Mary to the Church not only as one of precedence in glory but also of participation in the common Christian condition, that is, faith, obedience, and the search for the will of God.

At the same time, the fathers wanted to distinguish between the idea of human cooperation in the work of God, a cooperation in which Mary took first place, and the idea of mediation, which is the exclusive work of Christ; they thereby located the activity of Mary within the activity of the Church.[258] Thus they avoided giving Mary too exclusive a place on the same level as Christ as co- redemptrix and mediatrix (a help to this end was the return to the gospel sources in their entirety, as well as the debate on the predestination of Mary), and they were able to locate Mary at the heart of the people of God as it makes its pilgrimage in faith and patience. In contrast, concentration on the idea of mediation led to an emphasis on the motherhood of Mary, which helped determine a primarily ecclesiological approach.[259]

2. The Schema on Revelation

On June 26, after listening to Liénart's report, the CC approved the schema and also decided, with the pope's approval, to send it to all the Council fathers.[260] The schema was printed on July 3 in a format in which the new text stood beside the old, each page being divided into two columns. Each chapter was followed by a report from the experts in which the main comments were assembled and the changes made were pointed out. At the end was added a general report on the comments received and on the way in which the assigned subcommission had carried out its revision.[261] The text thus assembled was the one presented on September 30 during the third conciliar period.

It is worth pointing out, even in a summary way, the novelty of the text developed during the intersession as compared with the preparatory Theological Commission's initial schema on the two sources of revelation.[262] It also differed in both form and substance from the version that had been sent to the fathers in April 1963 but was never discussed in the hall.[263]

[258] This idea came up frequently in the comments of the German bishops. See *AS* II/3, 837-49.

[259] An example of the ecclesiological approach is seen in the second Chilean draft (*AS* II/3, 830- 34).

[260] *AS* V/2, 589-90, 634-1; see Caprile IV, 109.

[261] In order to reconstruct this whole enterprise see the accounts kept in AV2, the reports of Tromp on the activity of the Doctrinal Commission, and those of J. Willebrands on the work of the mixed commission. To this material can be added the diaries of some participants (Y. Congar, J. Dupont, Florit, Léger, O. Semmelroth, and R. Tucci, kept at the ISR; Betti's diary has been published in *La "Dei verbum" trent-anni dopo* [Rome, 1995]). See R. Burigana, "La commissione 'De divina revelatione,'" in *Les commissions à Vatican II*, 27-61, and idem, *La Bibbia nel Concilio: La redazione della costituzione "Dei verbum" del Vaticano II* (Bologna, 1998).

[262] See *History*, 2:249-66.

[263] On the new version, see H. Sauer, *Erfahrung und Glaube* (Frankfurt a. M., 1993), 310-13; Burigana, "La commissione 'De divina revelatione,'" 44-46. On the debate on revelation, see also the more general work of H. Waldenfels, *Das Zweite Vatikanische Konzil auf dem Hintergrund der neueren Theologie* (Munich, 1969).

The preface was shorter and completely new; the old preface had been transformed into the first chapter (on revelation itself), in which the nature and object of revelation were described. The historical process in which the plan of salvation had been revealed was revised; the words and actions of God made known the working of this plan, which was brought to full fruition in the incarnation of Jesus Christ. In the second chapter (on the transmission of divine revelation) the section on the relation between scripture and tradition (no. 9) had been reworked to omit any explicit reference to the theory of the two sources of revelation, which had drawn the largest number of criticisms during the first period of the Council. This decision had aroused strong resistance in the Doctrinal Commission, but in the end it prevailed over a statement of the constitutive value of tradition in the transmission of divine revelation. At the same time, the editors had avoided entering into the merits of the ongoing debate on the sufficiency of scripture and on the relationship between magisterial tradition and apostolic traditions.[264] Extensive use was made of citations from the Bible and of passages from conciliar documents and the papal magisterium in order to show the doctrinal continuity of the positions taken.[265]

In the fifth chapter, on the NT, a new section was introduced on the historicity of the gospels (no. 17) in order to take account of the Instruction *Sancta mater ecclesia,* which had been published by the Biblical Commission on May 14, 1964.[266] In the sixth and final chapter (scripture in the life of the Church), thanks to the interventions of A. Grillmeier and O. Semmelroth, emphasis was placed on the importance of recourse to the Bible as the focus of preaching, catechesis, and the liturgy — and of theological study as well, of which scripture should become the soul.

The new schema on revelation met with the approval of those who had been fighting for a return to the sources in the description of revelation

[264] For the state of the debate on the relationship between scripture and tradition, see J. Dupont, "Écriture et tradition," *Nouvelle Revue Théologique* 85 (1963), 337-56; K. Rahner, "Écriture et tradition. A propos du Schéma Conciliaire sur la Révélation divine," in *Mélanges H. de Lubac* (Paris, 1964), 3:209-21.

[265] The notes of the chapter contain citations from Pius XII (*Humani generis* and *Munificentissimus Deus*) and from the councils of Constantinople IV, Trent, and Vatican I. For an assessment of the chapters and their redactional fortunes see Betti, *La dottrina,* 119-25.

[266] See *AAS* 56 (1964), 712-18. Among the many commentaries on the Instruction, see A. Bea, "La storicità dei Vangeli sinottici," *CivCatt* 115/2 (1964), 417-36; idem, "Il carattere storico dei vangeli sinottici come opere ispirate," *CivCatt* 115/2 (1964), 526-43.

and for the renewal of Catholic exegesis.[267] The text ushered in a new era, rich in promise, which Father de Lubac summed up as follows:

> One [of its] principal merits is that it brings everything into unity. Unity of the revealer and the revealed, both being Jesus Christ, "author and finisher of our faith"; unity in him of the two Testaments, which bear witness to him; unity of scripture and tradition, which are never separable; unity, set forth in the final chapter, of the Word of God in the two forms in which he becomes present among us: scripture and the Eucharist.[268]

3. The Secretariat for Christian Unity

a. The Text on the Jews

As can be seen in Bea's report of September 25, 1964, the revision of the schema on the Jews was complicated and laborious.[269] Strong political pressures from the Arab states were accompanied, probably at the urging of the Secretariat of State, by direct interventions of the CC calling for changes in the text, an anomalous step from a procedural standpoint. Until all the documentation on the work of the commissions is available, it will not be possible to say with certainty which changes were made by the Secretariat for Christian Unity and which by the CC during the troubled redactional journey of the text. During the intersession there were four intermediate versions of it before the one sent to the fathers as a second appendix to the schema on ecumenism.[270] It is nonetheless possible to uncover some essential stages through a comparison of the versions.

During the lengthy plenary meeting of the secretariat in February-March 1964, and in the course of the examination of the text on the Jews, the wide spectrum of the fathers' opinions was displayed rather fully. Despite the deep differences that had emerged, the secretariat had decided to keep the chapter both because of the objective importance of what was said and because of the great expectations it had

---

[267] At the end of June the progress made in the new version of the schema on revelation was pointed out by Congar in a note for the French episcopate: "Le texte révisé du 'De Revelatione,'" *Études et Documents* 13 (June 30, 1964), 1-12 (Florit Archive, 322). Spanish Jesuit L. Alonso Schökel, professor at the Biblical Institute in Rome, likewise gave a favorable report in a letter to Bishop M. McGrath in July 1964; the letter is in VCND, McGrath Archive, 14, 4, 6.

[268] H. de Lubac, *La Révélation divine*, 3d ed., rev. and enl. (Paris, 1983), 174.

[269] See *AS* III/2, 558-64.

[270] See Felici's memorandum on the redactional fortunes of the decree, with the attached documentation, in *AS* V/2, 570-79.

aroused. At a plenary meeting it was then decided to make the chapter an appendix to the text, while maintaining its initial focus on the Jewish people and therefore rejecting the suggestion of some bishops that references be introduced to the other non-Christian religions and to Islam in particular.[271]

The line taken in the text, which had been developed and unanimously approved at the plenary meeting of the secretariat,[272] was nonetheless made the subject of discussion by the CC at its meeting in mid-April, during which the secretariat was asked to make some changes; in particular, to remove the explicit reference to the question of deicide and give some consideration to the other monotheistic religions.[273] By comparison with chapter IV of the schema on ecumenism, which had been presented to the fathers in November 1963, the text reworked by the secretariat (which had also involved two outside experts, Moeller and Congar[274]) and sent on to Felici on May 2, 1964, showed a substantial acceptance of the points made by the CC, which gave voice to the pressures coming from the Secretariat of State.

First, the text was a little longer than its predecessor and was divided into three sections: the first dealt with the heritage common to Jews and Christians; the second dealt with the universal fatherhood of God; the third introduced a new, summary rejection of every form of discrimination based on race, social condition, or religion.[275] The language and the tone seemed more nuanced on the whole. In the first section, after eliminating the explicit reference to deicide (which the secretariat had kept in the February-March version) and after encouraging theological studies and fraternal dialogue, the text went on to stress the point that as the Council "sternly rejects harm done to human beings everywhere, so too it deplores and condemns hatred and persecution of Jews, whether in the past or today." The conclusion of the first part read: "Therefore let all see to it that whether in catechetical instruction and preaching or in daily conversation there be no presenting the Jewish people as condemned and that nothing else be said or done which can give rise to hatred or contempt of Jews."[276]

---

[271] On this point see Velati, *Una difficile transizione*, 402, and G. M.-M. Cottier, "L'historique de la déclaration," in *Les relations de l'Eglise avec les religions non-chrétiennes*, Unam Sanctam 61 (Paris, 1966), 37-78, especially 48.

[272] See *AS* V/2, 283-84.

[273] Ibid., 287.

[274] See *JCongar*, 49-60

[275] See *AS* V/2, 571-72.

[276] Ibid., 571.

The other important novelty in the new version of the schema consisted of the introduction into the second section of an explicit reference to Muslims; this came after the assertion of the need of a fraternal attitude toward all human beings, which is the inevitable consequence of all having God as their one Father.

After having been submitted to the pope, who suggested some changes and additions,[277] and then having been sent back to Bea, the text continued to receive a series of retouches and corrections, especially in the last part of the first section. On this point the solution finally adopted, after news of the elimination of the deicide passage had elicited widespread negative reactions, was the addition of a clause that replaced the eliminated passage, namely, the specification "that what occurred in the passion of Christ is not to be imputed to the Jews of our time."[278]

The existence of such disagreements explains why the new text of the Declaration was approved by the pope only on July 3 and therefore could only then be sent to the fathers.[279] I may add that the encyclical *Ecclesiam Suam* gave support to the cause championed by the schema, as Cardinal Bea noted.[280] The reporter on the schema explicitly rejected any political background for the conciliar text. In doing so, he could rely on the tranquil words of Paul VI on May 30 at an audience for a group of directors of the American Jewish Committee, a group from the United States.[281] The conciliar text would be the conclusion of repeated efforts at mutual understanding between Catholics and Jews,[282] even though an official Jewish presence at the Council had not been possible for various reasons: strong opposition from some Orthodox Jewish groups; the reaction of the Arab countries; and the desire of the Vatican to avoid difficulty and touchy situations.[283]

---

[277] Ibid., 572-73

[278] See *AS* III/2, 328.

[279] Ibid., 327. See the lecture that Bea gave in Cologne (March 15, 1964) during Brotherhood Week; text in *Monumenta judaica, Fazit-2000 Jahre Geschichte und Kultur der Juden am Rhein* (Cologne, 1964), 169-75. Bea referred only briefly to the content of the schema; out of respect for the Council he did not go into details.

[280] See *AS* III/2, 564.

[281] *OssRom*, May 31, 1964.

[282] *Civcatt*, no. 2738 (July 18, 1964) 174.

[283] See P. Secco Suardo, "Gli Ebrei e il Concilio," *Humanitas*, April 1963, 340-45; A. Segre, "Gli Ebrei e il Concilio Ecumenico," *Il Mulino* 13 (1963), 82-92. The Spanish bishops were extremely alarmed by the schema and ordered their experts to make a thorough analysis of it; this process ended in October 1965 with an appeal to Paul VI.

b. The Text on Religious Freedom

This text was printed and sent to the fathers by a rescript from Secretary of State Cicognani, dated April 27, 1964.[284] On September 10, just before the third period began, a group of twelve bishops (some of them belonging to the International Group of Fathers) wrote to the pope expressing their uneasiness at the lack of theological and conceptual precision in some schemas. These bishops noted that the confusion in style and ideas lent itself to wrong interpretations and permitted developments alien to the thinking of the fathers. In their view some schemas, especially the schema on ecumenism and the declaration on religious freedom, were written using terms and with a meaning that were formally opposed, if not openly contradictory, to the ordinary magisterium and to the extraordinary declarations of the magisterium of the last century. Neither Catholic theology nor sound philosophy were recognizable in these schemas, which had been infiltrated by dangerous ideas and theories against which the Holy See had always warned. The letter ended with a request that the pope solemnly insist, at the imminent restart of work, on the fact that doctrine was to be expressed without ambiguity. Nonetheless, at the third session of the Council, on September 23, the declaration on religious freedom came up for debate.[285]

In order to grasp the essential chronology of the course taken by the text during the second intersession, and specifically its doctrinal maturation, we must trace the intellectual journey of North American theologian John Courtney Murray, a a specialist in this area who enjoyed the trust of the majority of the North American bishops. At the beginning of the Council, however, he was still in disfavor with the Holy Office[286] and with Vagnozzi, the apostolic delegate in Washington,[287] to the point where his appointment as an expert, which was due to the insistence of Cardinal Spellman, was delayed until April 4, 1963, hardly a week before the publication of *Pacem in terris*.

---

[284] *AS* V/2, 517.

[285] *AS* III/2, 354ff.

[286] See the biography by D. E. Pelotte, *John Courtney Murray: Theologian in Conflict* (New York, 1976); Gonnet, *La liberté religieuse*, 122-35; and J. A. Komonchak, "The Silencing of John Courtney Murray," in *Cristianesimo nella storia, Saggi in onore di G. Alberigo*, ed. A. Melloni, D. Menozzi, G. Ruggieri, and M. Toschi (Bologna, 1996), 657-702.

[287] See G. P. Fogarty, *The Vatican and the American Hierarchy from 1870 to 1969* (Stuttgart, 1982), 386-403.

During the first phase of his participation, Murray's remarks on the existing text were critical. He was able to take part in the meeting of the Doctrinal Commission on November 11-12, 1963, thanks to Léger's intercession. During that same period De Smedt asked him to collaborate on the drafting of the report on the *textus prior*.[288] After the schema on ecumenism had been presented in the hall, November 19-21, 1963, the secretariat asked the fathers to send in their remarks and reactions. The work of evaluating these suggestions (and not the drafting of the second schema) was assigned to Murray. A heart attack that struck him down on January 15, 1964, did not permit him to carry out this evaluation in a scrupulous manner, but it did not keep him from moving about much more than the doctors had recommended. We know that he was able to share in the work at the end of February. His main concern was to show that the schema discussed in November 1963 took an overly theological and abstract starting point and that, on the other hand, it neglected the juridical aspects of the question. For these reasons the draft of the declaration did not seem to him sufficiently clear in the way in which it dealt with the problem of the limitations placed by society and the law on the right to religious freedom. Another drawback that Murray pointed out was that the secretariat had drafted the document before the publication of John XXIII's encyclical *Pacem in terris*, which had put the seal of approval on a lengthy development of theological thought. This last objection coincided with Pavan's proposals.

In the spring of 1964, after analyzing the many written responses from the Council fathers, Murray composed a penetrating study with the twofold purpose of giving the most objective description possible of the two conflicting points of view and of opening a dialogue on the objections of both sides.[289] Murray's thinking prior to the Council had led him to a realization that the constitutional argument was decisive if religious freedom, which had emerged from the Church's experience of freedom, was to take on a theological dimension and be able to become part not only of the constitution of a state but also of the real life of a society.

---

[288] Hamer, "La liberté," 74, and Pelotte, *Murray*, 84.

[289] See Murray, "The Problem of Religious Liberty at the Council," *Theological Studies* 25 [1964], 507-75; it was also published by the Dutch Center in Rome [DO-C]). Earlier Murray had published an important article, "On Religious Liberty," *America* (November 30, 1963), 704-6 (French trans.: "Liberté religieuse: la position de l'épiscopat américain," *Choisir* [1964], 14-16; and in the series *Études et Documents*, 2 [February 4, 1964], which was distributed to the members of the Council. The text of the *America* article was later published in the volume *La liberté religieuse, exigence spirituelle et problème politique* (Paris, 1965), 9-12 (see Pelotte, *John Courtney Murray*, 90).

On reaching the Council, Murray was able to disentangle the muddle of varying positions on this subject. The distinction between *thesis* and *hypothesis,* which had prevailed in the nineteenth century, was characteristic of what he described as the "first conception": it relied on a principle (the *thesis*) that made the Catholic state the ideal, that is, a state in which Catholicism was the state religion. The *hypothesis,* on the other hand, consisted in the compromise under which Catholics lived in a non-Catholic state.[290]

Despite not having had a part in the preparatory work in the earlier phase of the Council, Murray ended up exerting a major influence on the composition of the text presented during the third period. It was a text that had undergone a process of revision and development as compared with previous drafts and would be the basis of subsequent drafts. As a matter of fact, on the eve of the opening of the third period in September 1964, Murray told the secretariat of his objections to the *declaratio prior* that was to be discussed in the hall. In this setting he ventured even further and presented what Grootaers has called "the Murray program,"[291] which was to have a great influence on the final form of the text.

4. The Decree on Religious Life

The part played by the seven general chapters of various religious orders and acknowledged throughout the debate in these months and in the address of Paul VI on May 23 appears to have been extremely important.[292] On that occasion the pope answered questions raised during the second period on the place of religious in the Church, on the nature of the vows, on the manner of practicing them in our time, and on the apostolate of religious under the guidance of the bishop. He formulated his vision in solemn fashion in the presence of Antoniutti and Philippe, who were respectively the prefect and the secretary of the Congregation for

[290] Murray was disposed to agree that the Spaniards might keep their special system of relations between Church and state to the extent that it fitted into their historical context. He rejected the idea, however, that the Spanish should regard this as the "Catholic ideal," that is, the *thesis*. He tried to show that the Spanish *theory* was insufficient, but without any intention of condemning Spanish policy, which, given the conditions in which the country was living, had to be regarded as valid (see Pelotte, *John Courtney Murray*, 91). The Spanish bishops had met with their experts from January 10 to January 24 in order to study the subject of religious freedom, and they submitted a lengthy, critical report to the secretariat.

[291] J. Grootaers, "Paul VI et la déclaration conciliaire sur la liberté religieuse *Dignitatis humanae,*" in *Paolo VI e il rapporto chiesa-mondo al Concilio,* 91-95.

[292] "Directrices para la vida religiosa," *DC* (June 7, 1964), 690-94.

Religious and were also responsible for the conciliar text on religious life that had been drafted less than a month before the papal address.

III. FINAL PHASE: FADING OF THE DÖPFNER PLAN

A. THE WORK OF THE COORDINATING COMMISSION

1. Fifteenth Meeting (June 26)

On June 26, in the absence of Cardinals Suenens and Spellman and undersecretaries Morcillo, Kempf, and Nabaa, the CC came to a decision on the second part of the schema on the Church and on the schemas on revelation, the missions, and the presence of the Church in the world. It also completed its study of some questions of procedure for the third period.

Agagianian reported on the two last chapters of the schema on the Church, that is, on the eschatological character of the Church and on the Virgin Mary. It was decided that the texts should not be changed, although Liénart expressed reservations on the use of the title mediatrix for the Virgin. More important was the discussion of the suggestions of Paul VI regarding the third chapter of the schema on the Church.[293] Although there was no unanimity on these suggestions, it was agreed to send the text to the fathers.

After the Declaration on Jews and Non-Christians was examined, Liénart reported on the schema on divine revelation.[294] Cicognani reported that Paul VI had been informed of the proposal, unsuccessful in the Doctrinal Commission, of expert H. Schauf;[295] namely, that the text should have expressly stated that tradition is a constitutive source of revelation. Although this question was not settled at the meeting, the schema was sent to the fathers.

Confalonieri then read the draft of the schema on the missions. Cicognani's suggestion that "activity" be substituted for "work" in the title was not accepted. Finally, Urbani read the report on the schema on the Church in the modern world.[296] Felici told of the *votum* sent in by Suenens and communicated the wish of Paul VI that something be said in

[293] *AS* V/2, 508-9; see *Primauté*, 690-94.
[294] *AS* V/2, 580-88 and 589-90.
[295] Ibid., 539-40.
[296] Ibid., 627-31.

the schema about the worlds of culture, art and science, and labor, and that some address to youth be included. The cardinals on the commissions discussed the direction of the schema. Urbani, for example, pointed out the danger of relativism that was inherent in speaking so much of the "signs of the times," while Liénart maintained that the distinction between the natural and the supernatural orders was not clear enough. Despite such disagreements, it was decided to send the text to the fathers. Felici ended the meeting by reporting on the calendar of work for the third period and told the commission that the pope wanted to know its opinion on the distribution of booklets and on other points raised in a memorandum we have already seen.[297]

2. Sixteenth Meeting (September 11)

The day after the meeting of the moderators the CC met for the last time in the second intersession, together with the Council of Presidents and the moderators. The questions to be studied "concerned the calendar of work during the third period of the Council, the order of the schemas to be discussed, and the procedure to be followed in voting."[298] With Tisserant presiding, this meeting began with an informative report by Agagianian on the status of the various works in progress. Thirteen schemas had been given a place on the Council's agenda; some of these were not to be further discussed but were to be simply voted on.

Felici described Philips's plan for voting on the schema on the Church;[299] this had already been studied and to some extent modified by the General Secretariat.[300] The plan, which provided for a larger number of votes on the third chapter because of its doctrinal importance, was to be presented to the assembly for a vote. Felici then read a letter from Frings on "complete secrecy" for some general congregations; many fathers had been afraid to express themselves freely because of leaks to the press. After a discussion in which Ruffini in particular insisted on making the violation of secrecy a reserved sin, the commission limited itself to a simple exhortation. At this point the work needed for the opening of the third period on September 14 had been completed.

[297] Ibid., 632-33. The reference was to the freedom the fathers had to distribute writings, notes, proposals, remarks, booklets, and so forth, and to the role of the General Secretariat in regulating the material exchanged.

[298] Ibid., 663.

[299] Ibid., 669-78.

[300] Ibid., 681-82.

B. TOWARD THE END OF THE COUNCIL?

1. The Question of the Council's Duration

A council that had begun without carefully deciding how long it was to last left open a major question.[301] While Pope John had hoped to end the Council on December 25, 1962, he came to realize that the complex body of subjects facing the Council would require at least two periods of work. He then expressed his desire to end the Council in 1963, the anniversary of the end of the Council of Trent.[302] But when doubt remained after the end of the second period in December 1963, the need of a third period was undeniable. And of a fourth?[303] Some worried that the third period might also be the last.[304] This seems to have been Paul VI's desire, expressed, although unobtrusively, in his address as the end of the second period (December 4, 1963), when he alluded to the possibility of a more expeditious procedure based on the shortening of the schemas and the delegation of some subjects to postconciliar commissions. It is true that in his text the pope made no explicit proposal, but it was clear that he preferred a quick conclusion. The context in which this entire question was located has already been described in connection with the prehistory of the Döpfner Plan.

Given this climate of uncertainty, the statements of Fausto Vaillanc, director of the press office of the Holy See, as reported in *L'Osservatore Romano*, seemed justified: "This address [of Paul VI] and hints given repeatedly on various occasions make clear the pope's hope that the coming third period of ten weeks, September 14 to November 20, 1964, will be the last of Vatican II, inasmuch as it will see brought to term the work already so thoroughly done and long matured."[305]

Journalists of all nations raised the same question,[306] and some bishops gave a negative answer, among them Cardinals Ritter, Suenens,

---

[301] See *History*, 1:336-39.

[302] V. Carbone, "La durata del Vaticano II: le previsioni e la realtà," *OssRom*, October 11, 1987, 2; see also M. Maccarrone, "Paolo VI e il Concilio: Testimonianza," *Rivista di Storia della chiesa in Italia* 43/1 (1989), 101-3.

[303] See Henri Cardinal de Lubac, *Entretien autour de Vatican II* (Paris, 1985), 33-36.

[304] See "Faut-il terminer le Concile?" *ICI*, April 1, 1964, pp. 5-7; ibid., April 15, 1964, 6; *HK* 18 (1964), 452-53.

[305] *OssRom*, March 11, 1964.

[306] See, e.g., C. Calderón, "Perspectivas conciliares tras el viaje del Papa a Palestina," *Ecclesia* (Madrid), no. 1177 (February 1, 1964), 23-26, especially the section, "Concilio, 1964, fase final?" (25); see also Calderón's chronicle in *Ecclesia*, no. 1183 (March 14, 1964), 25.

König, Cushing, Alfrink, and Tisserant; Msgr. Holland, auxiliary bishop of Portsmouth (who spoke of pressures brought to bear on the fathers); Msgr. Shehan, the Archbishop of Baltimore;[307] Bishop Zauner of Linz. According to Patriarch Maximos IV, further periods were needed in view of the large number of questions remaining to be answered. To facilitate the Council's work, it would have been fitting that the moderators be given authority to manage the Council freely without oversight from some other organism; in view of this it was not fitting that the moderators should be appointed and not elected. The result of that procedure was that the influence of the congregations of the Roman Curia was controlling the course of the Council.[308] Villot, adjunct secretary of the Council, voiced his concern in a letter of March 20:

> I cannot hide my uneasiness at seeing a faster pace imposed on the Council. There is certainly a need to improve procedures... But since at the present time no one doubts the fact that the Council would easily end with a fourth period, why butcher what remains to be done by making November 20 [1964] the date of the desired end? It is true that the pope is looking to a future different from the present, because there will be a council representative of the worldwide episcopate. But the grace of the Council is something quite different![309]

In the view of these bishops, then, a quick end of the Council would be inopportune and have a negative effect. As they looked at the work of the commissions during the second period and the intersession that followed, they claimed that the importance of the discussion and of the ongoing research required that opposing theses be absorbed and articulated and that issues raised in the debate be addressed. Time was required to make the formulas proposed more balanced and prudent, more vigorous and clear. The breadth and complexity of the problems

---

[307] Holland maintained that to end the Council after the third period "would be a sin, because there are subjects of great importance for the Church which we have hardly touched on... It takes time for ideas to mature, and the space from now to the next session is not enough to bring these ideas to an acceptable degree of maturity. Unfortunately, there is a financial burden that is leading the pope to end the Council after the next session... But it would be lamentable for the Council to end before it is ripe." Msgr. Shehan said: "It seems to me far too difficult to end with the third session. Everything depends on how the commissions work during this intersession" (*ICI*, April 15, 1964, p. 6; *CivCatt* [September 15, 1964], 595).

[308] Caprile III, 493.

[309] Wenger, "Mgr. Villot et le concile Vatican II," in *Le deuxième concile du Vatican*, 255.

needing to be faced and, above all, the fact that a council by its nature had to determine its own rhythms and seasons, recommended a continuation. The suggestion was also made of having a lengthy pause (even one of some years[310]), which would make room for a period of experimentation before the definitive formulation of the texts on reform.

On the opposite side, various considerations made some fathers favor the idea that the Council should end with the third period.[311] Various arguments of a practical kind seemed to support Paul VI's clear preference for the reduction proposed in the Döpfner Plan.. Some remarked that the Council as such, given the profound innovations it had in view, was also giving rise to a state of suspense, or even a kind of paralysis, in minds and structures; such a state ought not to be prolonged, since the spirit is subject to weakness and structures to

---

[310] Dossetti had already suggested this in a memorandum, "Supposizioni sull'agenda della seconda sessione," written in view of the meeting of the CC called for August 31, 1963, at which Lercaro was to make a statement. The first part of the memorandum points out the inadequacy of a Council that would continue on the pattern of the first period, which was marked by a lack of incisiveness and even by a "substantial paralysis" caused by the lack of "prior choices that would give direction and rise above the viewpoints of an unyielding bloc, such as the unqualified requirement that Latin be used, the absolute centralization of the power to issue norms in matters liturgical,...the still prevalent ignorance of the situation in civilizations outside Europe." On the basis of this analysis, and taking into account the recent election of the new pope, Dossetti maintained, "at the cost of seeming even absurd," that "the second session cannot open next September 29 without very serious detriment and dangers" and that it is desirable that there be "a postponement even of as much as an entire year" (Dossetti Archive, II, 106).

[311] This was the view expressed by Cardinal Siri in an interview given to the National Catholic Welfare Conference (*The Tablet*, April 11, 1964). The atmosphere reflected in the interview shows that one part of the Italian episcopate found it difficult to share the spirit desired by the majority. The same was shown in many interventions at the Council, e.g., those of Ruffini or Siri, especially in regard to ecumenism. So true was this that at the end of the second period, on November 26, an American bishop, Leven, auxiliary of San Antonio and a man with a great sense of humor, asked his venerable conciliar brothers to "put an end to the scandal of mutual recriminations"; he was referring explicitly to his Italian colleagues (the text of this intervention is in *DC* for January 5, 1964, cols. 66- 68; see also Caprile III, 352-54). All this led Paul VI on April 14 to exhort the Italian episcopate to look at the Council through impartial eyes and to participate in a way that was not "fearful or uncertain or carping or polemical." It is difficult not to see in these remarks an allusion to the reserve of one section of the episcopate, all the more since Paul VI added: "If this [participation] becomes more coordinated and desirous of opening a correct way to understanding the legitimate expressions of the other fathers, the Italian episcopate will better serve the pope and the Church." Finally, the pope exhorted the Italian episcopate to enter into dialogue with the "episcopal groups" of other countries. In fact, the Italian episcopate had been one of those least disposed to enter into relationships with other episcopal conferences during the first two periods, even if, to tell the truth, numerous individual contacts had been established during the second period (*OssRom*, April 15, 1964).

atrophy,[312] and since there is a tendency for these two factors to combine when directives are lacking that would guide the action of many Christians, who want these clear and precise directives. Others referred to humanity's state of expectation, which tended to slacken as the Council prolonged its work due to interruptions between the periods, the debates, the improvement of the schemas, and the delay in decisions; some feared that this uncertainty would prove scandalous and would beget a state of weariness and distrust that might affect the Council itself.[313]

Mention was also made of a more concrete argument: the state of inertia in which the periodic absence of the bishops left the dioceses, especially those of the more distant and poor continents and of countries passing through difficult political situations. In addition, there was the uneasiness of the Roman Congregations, whose life remained suspended, as it were, during the work of the Council; the formulation of this grievance emphasized the idea that a council represented a time of exceptional activity in the life of the Church, but that this should not hamper the governmental activity of the curial bodies, which wanted a "return to normality." Emphasis was also placed on the huge costs of a council: the infrastructures in St. Peter's, used for only a few months of the year; expenses for travel; and so on. On this point Cushing, Archbishop of Boston, had something to say; he was a man (it was claimed) more skilled in collecting contributions than in theological subtleties.[314] Another point made was the existence of a growing agitation within the Council.

From all this it was inferred that according to some fathers "less inclined to innovation" (C. Calderón) the prolongation of the Council had disadvantages for the overall progress of the Church; they made the point repeatedly that the period of transition necessarily associated with the duration of the Council would not be useful to the Church but on the contrary would promote the absence of a clear direction in many areas in which the conciliar debates were inducing crises. The result would be a certain lack of disciplines in some areas and a great deal of confusion in others.

---

[312] For the division of this intersession into periods and for the psychological reflexes of those taking part in it see J. Grootaers, "Le pape, le Concile et le renouveau de l'Eglise," publication no. 11 of the Centrum coordinationis Communicationum de Concilio, translated from *De Maand* (Brussels), VII/7 (August-September 1964), 434-48.

[313] R. Laurentin could write, with reference to this intersession: "A movement of discouragement never previously felt took hold of those who had devoted their activity to the conciliar reform": *L'enjeu du Concile. Bilan de la troisième session* (Paris, 1965), 11.

[314] De Lubac, *Entretien*, 34.

In an article entitled "Il Concilio ecumenico, ora di Dio," Felici
wrote:

> People often ask when the Council will end... [A council] is an undertaking
> in which the one who begins it cannot ensure that it will end after a specific
> period. Many factors come into play, above all the freedom left to the
> fathers. But in the end it is the Spirit of God who has to say "The End" to
> the great drama... It is understandable, however, that the one who is direct-
> ing the vast work is concerned to arrange things so that its completion may
> come as soon as possible.[315]

On June 2, 1964, after a meeting of the German and Scandinavian
bishops on the prospects for the third period, Döpfner addressed Cicognani and explained the need for a fourth period.[316] Cicognani did not
shrink from some negative remarks on the subject, these based on the
desire to adapt to the guidelines given by the pope on December 27 for
facilitating procedures and thereby reducing the length of public debates.
If this were done, a fourth period would perhaps be unnecessary.

2. The Attitude of Paul VI

The addresses of Paul VI kept referring to the question of the Council's duration with an insistence that could seem premeditated. In his
address at the opening of the second period he had expressed "fear" that
"the discussion of some questions might have to be put off to a later session." In view of the vast amount of work remaining and of the evidence
that the end of the Council was still distant, the pope's words suggested
a veiled reference to a prompt conclusion.[317] Later, in the address at the
end of that period, the pope expressed the hope that the questions still to
be debated "in the coming session... may reach a happy completion,"
and he suggested that the conciliar commissions formulate the schemas
so as to render the discussion "easy and rapid." He suggested, further,
that the conciliar periods be limited to discussing and reaching agreement on the "main subjects," while the explanation and definitive formulation of the documents might be left to ongoing conciliar commissions.[318] Especially important was the address that Paul VI delivered to
the Italian Episcopal Conference, in which he said:

---

[315] *OssRom*, May 20, 1964.
[316] *AS* V/2, 85-94.
[317] Address of September 29, 1963: *OssRom*, September 30, 1963, 2.
[318] Address of December 4, 1963: *OssRom*, December 5, 1963, 2.

It is Our intention not to intervene at this stage of the Council's work on the merits of doctrines and decrees which will be discussed at the Council's reopening... [319] Our only concern has been to see to it that the preparatory work of the commissions and the Secretariat proceeds with dispatch. In this interim between the second and third sessions the aim is twofold. First, to review the schemata in the light of observations made by Council Fathers at earlier sessions, and to resubmit them quickly to the Fathers. Secondly, to have the resulting suggestions and observations collected by the competent commissions so that the schemata can be properly redrafted for submission to the Council. The hope is that as a consequence thorough deliberation in the assembly will more rapidly yield some conclusive decisions, one way or the other. But this is not meant to prejudice the question of the Council's duration, about which one cannot say anything definite as yet. These measures are meant to expedite the efficiency and progress of the Council, not to force limits or decisions upon it.[320]

But the work still to be completed was enormous. By mid-April 1964 the CC had on its table about ten schemas already revised by the respective commissions and waiting to be sent to the fathers. Some in particular were of great interest to the assembly, and the world was awaiting the Council's position on them: the texts on the Church, revelation, and ecumenism, and the one, still not presented in the hall, on relations between Church and world. In addition, there were two schemas, those on religious freedom and on relations with the Jewish people, which had been given the form of independent declarations and no longer of chapters in the schema on ecumenism. Finally, there was a group of drafts that were of lesser interest to a broad public but were of great pastoral importance; these were dependent on the theological direction taken in the constitution on the Church. These were the schema on bishops and the government of dioceses and others, not yet even discussed in the assembly, on priests, the laity, religious, the missions, the Oriental Churches.[321]

---

[319] After this speech Paul VI maintained that it was his duty to intervene in the Council not only on questions of the rules but also on doctrinal matters, and he did this by way of the commissions, as in his "suggestions" for the revision of chapter III of the schema on the Church (May 19). For an overall view of the pope's interventions, especially with regard to the texts on ecumenism and on religious freedom, see V. Carbone, "L'azione direttiva di Paolo VI nei periodi II e III del concilio ecumenico Vaticano II," in *Paolo VI e i problemi ecclesiologici al Concilio*, 58-95, and P. Duprey, "Paul VI et le décret sur l'oecuménisme," ibid., 225-48; C. Soetens, "Interventions du pape Paul VI au concile Vatican II (Périodes II, III, IV: 1963-1965)," ibid., 561-83.

[320] Address of April 14, 1964: *OssRom*, April 15, 1964, 1; *The Pope Speaks* 9 (1963-64), 413- 14.

[321] "Chronique de l'intersession: Il reste six schémas," *ICI*, June 15, 1964, p. 5.

Despite the drastic reductions in the Döpfner Plan, the Council continued to suffer from the overabundance left to it from the preparatory
phase. After two periods scarcely a third of the program had been dealt
with: only one important schema out of seventeen presented had been
promulgated, and only four others had been even partially studied. Paul
VI spoke of all this in an address to the Sacred College on the vigil of
the Feast of John the Baptist when he described the "important and difficult" tasks that awaited them in the third period. While he was confident that there would be a "joint loving study" aimed at "summing up
and setting forth the teaching of the Church on subjects so varied and
important." he said nothing about the question of whether the third
period would be the final period of the Council.[322]

On August 26 Felici reported to the pope on the progress of the work.
When the Secretary General had finished, the pope said: "It would be good
if the Council could be ended with the third session." Echoing the concern
expressed by many bishops who had to be absent from their dioceses when
their nations were experiencing difficult times, he exhorted Felici to hasten
the pace of the work, both in the hall and in the commissions.[323]

3. The Uncertainty at the Beginning of the Third Period

On September 12 Msgr. O'Connor, president of the conciliar committee on the press, held a press conference in order to sketch out the main
lines of the work about to begin. That work would be organized by the
moderators, who had met on September 10 in the apartment of the Secretary of State, together with the Council of Presidents and the CC.[324]
Anticipating the question about the duration of the Council, O'Connor
said:

> Will this be the final phase of the Council? No certain answer can be given
> one way or the other. The Holy Father has repeatedly said that he does not
> intend to "impose limits and decisions" on the Council, thus lessening the
> freedom of the fathers. It is certain, however, that even if this turns out not
> to be the final period, it will nonetheless be a period of decisive importance
> and a sure advance toward the end.

In an interview on Vatican Radio, Felici also emphasized the special
importance of the third period both because of the very intense labor of

---

[322] *OssRom*, June 24, 1964.
[323] Carbone, "L'azione direttiva."
[324] The agenda was set down in Felici's letter (August 24, 1964) calling for the meeting. See Lercaro, *Lettere*, 251.

meditation on and polishing of schemas that preceded it and because of the subjects on the agenda.[325] In a second interview, this time on Italian television, he referred to the "varied and complex" subjects that were to be tackled, to the conclusions that might be reached, and to the "freedom of speech that is to be maintained in its entire substance," even while there was a concern to make procedures more supple. To the question whether the third period would be the last, Felici answered:

> I do not think it possible to give a definite answer at this moment. There are many factors at work in the Council that make it impossible to foresee with certainty when it will end. To be sure, everyone wants the Council to end as quickly as possible, in order, among other things, to begin the phase of application of the conciliar decrees, a phase that is perhaps more important than even the Council itself.[326]

C. New Changes in the Regulations (July 2, 1964)

1. The Conciliar Regulations at the Beginning of the Intersession

The first Regulations for the course of the Council had been published by John XXIII on August 6, 1962, in the Motu Proprio *Appropinquante concilio*.[327] Their preparation had not been easy,[328] and the results had proved unsatisfactory during the first period. Hardly had he been elected when Paul VI showed himself aware of the problems that had arisen and entrusted the revision of the Regulations to Cardinal Lercaro.[329] On September 3, 1963, Lercaro, with Dossetti's help,[330] presented a draft that

---

[325] *Radiogiornale vaticano*, Studio no. 77, September 14, 1964.

[326] *OssRom*, September 13, 1964.

[327] *History*, 1:326-35. See also Indelicato, *Difendere la dottrina*,17-54; Levillain, *La mécanique politique*, 107-70; H. Jedin, "Die Geschäftsordnung des Konzils," in *Lexikon für Theologie und Kirche: Das Zweite Vatikanische Konzil*, 3:610-23.

[328] See G. Alberigo, "La preparazione del regolamento del Concilio Vaticano II," *Vatican II commence*, 54-72.

[329] See Alberigo, "Dinamiche e procedure," 115-64, an article solidly based on the archives of Lercaro and Dossetti, which are kept at the ISR.

[330] Dossetti's role, according to G. Martina, V. Carbone, and M. Maccarrone (in *Paolo VI e i problemi ecclesiologici al Concilio*, 39 n.50; 61 n.10; 411), was exaggerated by Alberigo in his introduction to Giacomo Lercaro, *Per la forza dello Spirito* (Bologna, 1984), 23-24. In "Dinamiche e procedure," Alberigo replies to these criticisms and shows them to be unjustified.

was approved by the pope with some minor changes and then made public on September 13.[331]

During the second period, however, the need was felt of further changes having to do, first, with the composition of the commissions, in order to make them more reflective of the directions being taken by the majority,[332] and, second, with the need to speed up the pace of the work and the interventions. To satisfy this second concern, Lercaro, on November 15, with the advice as always of Dossetti, gave the pope some proposals that were subsequently explained to the CC and the Council of Presidents at a joint meeting.[333] Three months later Döpfner offered other suggestions leading in the same direction.[334] But after consulting Cardinal Roberti, the CC judged that the time had not come for introducing important changes.[335]

2. The Revision of the Regulations during the Intersession

Faced with this situation, on March 14 Liénart explained the thinking of those responsible for applying the Regulations: "It is not possible to change the Regulations of the Council, but if that cannot be done, we can in any case focus our efforts on the manner of applying them."[336] The Council fathers were dissatisfied with the pace of the congregations and with the way in which the debates were carried on, defects due in part to the fact that the functions of the moderators were not adequately defined. According to Laurentin, the difficulty was due to the fact that "the Regulations for Vatican II had been drawn up partly in the light of parliamentary practices and partly in the light of ecclesiastical traditions, which in turn derived from imperial (senatorial or other) practices;" the result was "if not a real paralysis, a certain degree of creakiness."[337]

---

[331] *Ordo Concilii Oecumenici Vaticani II celebrandi. Editio altera recognita.* The text is in *AS* II/1, 23-46; see Ph. Levillain's favorable judgment on the new Regulations in "Les choix de Paul VI," in *Deuxième*, 467-71. The new Regulations contained some changes in structures and others in procedures. The most important of the former was the introduction of the moderators, who were in charge of directing the general congregations. Procedural changes were aimed at rendering the work of the commissions and the debates in the hall more flexible.

[332] The pope accepted this suggestion and at the end of the second period, November 21, 1963, he made it known that each commission was to be expanded by the inclusion of five more members, four elected by the assembly, and that the commissions thus expanded were to elect a second vice-president and second secretary; see Laurentin, 171-78; *CivCatt*, no. 2732 (April 18, 1964), 182-84.

[333] *AS* II/5, 406-9. See Lercaro *Lettere*, 220-22.

[334] *AS* V/2, 142-49.

[335] Ibid., 153-56 and 158.

[336] Ibid., 159.

[337] *Bilan de la troisième session* (Paris, 1965), 300.

The nervousness that was spreading in conciliar circles explains the insistence, especially of Lercaro and Dossetti, the nucleus of the so-called Bologna group, that led to some changes in the Regulations for the sake of more effective work. The majority began to worry, as could be seen in the words of Liénart, especially when on February 2 Carli, Bishop of Segni and spokesman for the minority, sent the pope a series of polemical remarks on the Regulations then in force.[338] The remarks had to do with procedure and with the votes on October 30 and contained veiled references to Dossetti as author responsible for the Regulations in question, for the votes on October 30, and for the moderators. A month later, on March 3, Döpfner wrote to Felici,[339] explaining that if changes in Articles 33 and 57 were being proposed, it was in order to make the debates move more smoothly, while changes in Articles 60 and 61 were aimed at improving the process for altering texts.

The CC studied the concrete proposals for changing the Regulations and on March 10 approved a report of Roberti.[340] Later, on July 2, the pope approved five additions to the Regulations,[341] which were then sent to the fathers on July 7, with a letter from Felici.[342] There were five points: a request, even by cardinals, to make a statement in the hall would have to be presented five days in advance and not three as previously; in order to speak after the end of a debate it would be necessary to have the support of seventy fathers and no longer of only five; in addition, the distribution of mimeographed material in the hall or its vicinity was prohibited.[343] The moderators were given authority to have the fathers who had entered their names speak on only a single subject so as to avoid wearisome repetitions; at the same time, the role of the moderators was recalled, emphasized, and to some extent further clarified: their function would no longer be simply "to direct the work but also to decide on the order of the discussions at general congregations."

This confirmation of the contested authority of the moderators was to have good results. During the first weeks of the third period many of the

---

[338] *ADP* IV/1, 482-504.

[339] Ibid., 504-12.

[340] Ibid., 322-25.

[341] Ibid., 326.

[342] *AS* V/2, 646-47; see *DC* (August 2, 1964), 981-82, and (October 4, 1964), 1237; *ICI*, (September 15, 1964), 21-22.

[343] This prohibition seems to have been the result of the incident that took place at the close of the second period, when some fathers had had fliers distributed in which they asked for the rejection of the schema on the means of social communication, the text of which seemed to them insufficiently matured.

tensions caused by a many-headed leadership disappeared. Understanding was facilitated by the moderators deciding not to have their own secretary,[344] which was expected to improve collaboration with the General Secretariat of the Council. In any case, some fathers still complained of an inadequate division of competencies among the various directing bodies of the Council, as when Schmitt, Bishop of Metz, complained of "the absence of unchallenged authority." The fact is that the changes so greatly desired were reduced to a short note containing five (not very radical) points and filling a little less than a page. It is understandable, then, that Giuseppe Alberigo should write:

> The repeated changes in the Regulations, which were inspired by the search for a quantitative efficiency, did not manage always to take into account the need of a genuine dialogue within the Council. In fact, in the third period even more than in the first two, interventions would be made without regard to their usefulness to the commissions. In this situation, interventions that took a general approach and gave an overall assessment of problems instead of particular, concrete proposals ended up being the least utilized, because there was no discussion of them in the Council and because the commissions did not find in them concrete textual variants which they could index and use.[345]

D. THE IMPACT OF THE ENCYCLICAL *ECCLESIAM SUAM* ON THE COUNCIL

The encyclical was announced on June 24, 1964, and published on August 6. Since this was the first encyclical of Paul VI and since it was in addition a programmatic encyclical, it had historic value, for it represented both the end result of the pope's previous experiences and thinking and the moment in which he told the bishops and the entire Church his own conception of the pontifical ministry at this historic juncture. The Council fathers were thus brought to realize, if this was still necessary, that the Council would pivot on the problem of the Church, regarding which they had already expressed their own thinking in the vote of October 1963.

---

[344] Dossetti had acted as secretary of the moderators, thus carrying out a role not foreseen in the Regulations; his influence had been a matter of concern, especially to the Secretary General of the Council. As was his way, Dossetti quietly dropped this unofficial task, remaining the private adviser of Cardinal Lercaro; see Alberigo, "Dinamiche," 154.

[345] Alberigo, "Concilio Vaticano II," in *Storia dei concili ecumenici,* 424.

1. Significance of the Encyclical

Paul VI's original intention had been that the encyclical would appear just before September 29, 1963, the day of his address at the opening of the second period.[346] It was natural, then, that this address would be judged as if it were the first version of the encyclical. This shows that the encyclical cannot be looked upon as exclusively a preparation for the third period of the Council, which it was anticipated would be a rather troubled one, especially on the subjects of the episcopate and of collegiality in relation to papal primacy. A deeper understanding of the encyclical therefore requires a comparison of it with the teaching given in the inaugural address of 1963. In fact, the encyclical retains the main lines of that address and does not simplify its style, although some themes, concretely that of dialogue, are deliberately more developed.[347] The growing expectancy as publication drew near was due above all to the activity of Paul VI during the intersession in various areas within the competence of the conciliar commissions; this activity gave rise to various disagreements, as did the style of some of his ecumenical gestures, which did not draw universal applause.

It was in this climate, not free of tensions, that Paul VI in *Ecclesiam Suam* introduced a new style into papal literature. It was new, first of all, because the pope alone thought out, composed, and wrote this encyclical, something certainly rare.[348] New, above all, because Paul VI wanted his letter to be "simply a conversation by letter," he was telling the world his personal thinking in order to start a dialogue. In the encyclical the pope made known his major concerns and the main lines of his thought, while at the same time presenting a program, though not one determined a priori, as well as the course to be followed in a quest to which he was pledging himself.

---

[346] On the composition of that address see G. Martina, "Paolo VI e la ripresa del concilio," in *Paolo VI e i problemi ecclesiologici al Concilio*, 44-52, and G. Colombo, "I discorsi di Paolo VI in apertura e chiusura dei periodi conciliari," in *Paolo VI e il rapporto chiesa-mondo al Concilio*, 253- 63. See especially V. Peri, "Appunti per un'indagine sull'ecclesiologia di Paolo VI. Titoli di originalità dell'enciclica *Ecclesiam Suam*," *Rivista di storia e letteratura religiosa* 17 (1981), 409-60.

[347] See G. Colombo, "Genesi, storia e significato dell'Enciclica *Ecclesiam Suam*," in *"Ecclesiam suam." Première lettre encyclique de Paul VI. Colloque international, Rome 24-26 oct. 1980* (Brescia, 1982), 131-60.

[348] The absence of notes, rare in an encyclical, led some commentators to conclude that it was the work of the pope alone; see M. O'Carrol, "Pope Paul's First Encyclical," *Irish Ecclesiastical Record* 103 (1964), 14.

The encyclical, addressed primarily to bishops, was quite long. In his
concern for clarity, the pope began it with a spacious introduction in
which he pulled together all the many themes with which he would deal.
We must not forget that we have here a conversation by letter, in which
many subjects are barely touched on or are dealt with in programmatic
form. In a didactic treatise many points would have been placed in critical notes, but the encyclical repeatedly said that its intention was simply
to suggest a set of reflections without any effort to develop them.
Finally, the most direct section of the encyclical, and also the section
most accessible to a broader public, was the section on dialogue which
came only toward the end of the document and after a series of considerations not well adapted to rousing spontaneous interest. This explains
why from the time of its publication this document, which is so original
and personal, so carefully thought out and stimulating, did not receive
the response it deserved.[349]

Despite all this, there was a strong desire in ecclesiastical circles that
the encyclical should be published before the beginning of the third
period of the Council in the hope that it would express a sufficiently
clear papal orientation which would give a direction to the coming
debates. Churchmen wanted to know especially Paul VI's position on
the primacy, on which in fact he spoke in words that were thoughtful but
also unlikely to elicit understanding and acceptance from either the
Protestants or the Orthodox.[350] The pope repeated his desire that the
Council do its work with the greatest freedom, but he appeared at the
same time to distance himself and reserve for himself a role as "an outside judge, rather than as the supreme instance in Vatican II."[351] The following passage will serve as a sufficient illustration of this point:

> In this encyclical we are deliberately refraining from passing any judg-
> ment of our own on doctrinal points concerning the Church which are at
> present under examination by the Council itself over which we have been
> called to preside. It is our desire to leave full liberty of study and discus-
> sion to such an important and authoritative assembly. In virtue of our
> office of Teacher and Pastor, and placed at the head of the Church of God,

---

[349] In France, e.g., "the French theologians referred rather infrequently to the encyclical"; see J. Gritti, "L'image de Paul VI et son pontificat en France," in *Paul VI et la
modernité dans l'Eglise* (Rome, 1984) 190. G. de Rose and J. Prévotat have no hesitation
about saying that "Montini's theology in *Ecclesian suam* drew nourishment from Karl
Adam" by way of Romano Guardini, in ibid., 7 and 119.

[350] See Colombo, "Genesi," 151-54. See the article by P. Bourget in *Le Monde*,
August 28, 1964.

[351] Laurentin, *Bilan de la troisième session*, 15.

we reserve to ourself the choice of the proper moment and manner of expressing our judgment, and we will be most happy if we can present it in perfect accord with that of the conciliar Fathers.[352]

This passage and the perspective adopted in the encyclical justified Congar in saying that the document showed a "certain asymmetry and something a little Rome-, or pope-centered." The Protestants and the Orthodox likewise found fault with this aspect of the encyclical: "In my view, Paul VI came out of the age of Pius XII and his main reference for ecclesiology was Journet, who was surely a great thinker and very spiritual but also rather scholastic and Rome-centered. I think that Paul VI went through a major evolution and that in the document are his gestures as well as his words."[353] It is not surprising, then, that *La Civiltà Cattolica* came to the pope's defense, saying:

> In this way Paul VI responded to two kinds of fear...that have surfaced recently: the fear of those who were afraid that the pope would not intervene to correct the ugly turn taken, in their view, by the work of the Council... Paul VI has indeed intervened; but while on the one hand he wants the Council to carry on its work with full freedom, on the other he has reassured the faint-hearted that the Council is a gift of God to the Church, one of those moments when the Spirit of Pentecost breathes most vigorously within her.[354]

2. The Sources and Content of the Encyclical

Although the Istituto Paolo VI in Brescia contains a "file of notes gathered by Paul VI for use in the encyclical," it is not possible to find among these notes any verbatim passages from contemporary theologians (the only citations that appear are from earlier popes or the Fathers), despite the fact that the pope was in fact reworking what he had gotten from his reading. His handwritten notes are of little help in reconstructing the stages by which the document reached its final form; only a knowledge of concrete circumstances can shed light on that process.

The file for the encyclical is made up of seventy-four pieces and has for its title (written in the pope's own hand): "Notes for the Encyclical *Ecclesiam Suam* 6. VIII. 1964 (see the writings of Guitton, Bevilacqua,

---

[352] *AAS* 56 (1964), 622; Vatican translation, no. 33.

[353] Colombo, "Genesi," 114; see the remarks of E. Lanne on primacy in *"Ecclesiam suam":Première lettre encyclicque*, 126-27.

[354] "Un dialogo 'cordiale' con gli uomini d'oggi," *CivCatt* 115 (1964), 523-24.

and others)." From this it can be conjectured that "Guitton, Bevilacqua, and others" had prepared, at the pope's request, various notes for use in the encyclical, especially on the subject of dialogue.[355] The file is divided into four sections: the first is devoted to dialogue, the second to the consciousness of the Church, the third, which is very short, to reform or renewal, and the fourth to dialogue once again. In addition to keeping biblical categories in mind, Paul VI has recourse to Journet, de Lubac (*Méditation sur l'Eglise*), Congar, and the third volume of the well-known *Initiation théologique*. On the whole, however, Paul VI's ecclesiology is that of *Mystici corporis*, especially in regard to the aspect of renewal and mystery.[356] It was therefore natural that in his address at the beginning of the third period (in which he makes no direct reference to the encyclical *Ecclesiam Suam*) the pope should speak of the Church as "mystical body" and not use the expression "people of God."[357]

For the part on the "reform" of the Church (a word hardly used by John XXIII, probably because it seemed to refer to the great rupture in the sixteenth century), the sources of the pope's inspiration are more explicit. But according to Paul VI, there was no question of a revolution that would endanger the essential, divinely established structures of the Church in its fully authentic form. The aim of the reform was rather to make the Church more conformed to the divine plan, so that its essential structures would be able to carry out their essential mission, which is to communicate Christ. This was the idea put forth by Congar in his *Vraie et fausse réforme*. On May 23, 1964, at the offices of the Editions du Cerf, Cardinal Feltin publicly repeated the words of Paul VI in which the latter had said that Congar's work was one of those from which he drew his inspiration. The reader should bear in mind that cardinals have the great privilege of being able to cite in an authentic manner words spoken by the pope.[358]

---

[355] J. Guitton himself has told us this in his *Paul VI Secret* (Clamecy, 1979), 51-55. Note the reservations of H. Urs von Balthasar with regard to the panegyrical tone Guitton uses of Paul VI (see *The Office of Peter and the Structure of the Church* [San Francisco, 1986], 22 and 56).

[356] Colombo, "Genesi," 167-68; R. Aubert doubts that this theology reflected knowledge of the work of Mersch (ibid., 187). See, above all, Y. Congar, "Situation ecclésiologique au moment de la *Ecclesiam suam*," in *"Ecclesiam suam." Première lettre*, 79-102.

[357] *Insegnamenti*, 2:536-47. The expression "people of God" appears in the address at the beginning of the second period, but only as one biblical "image" among others (see ibid., 1:173).

[358] R. Rouquette, "L'encyclique *Ecclesiam suam*," *Etudes* (October 1964), 425. Congar admitted that on one occasion Cardinal Montini had written to ask for a copy of *Vraie et fausse réforme* (in *"Ecclesiam suam": Première lettre*, 179).

We may note that in the Italian text (which was said to be preferable to the Latin) the phrase "reform or renewal" appeared, whereas in the Latin text published in *Acta Apostolicae Sedis* the word "reform" is missing and is systematically replaced by *renovatio*. The important nuance of difference between *reform* and *renewal* is lost. Did "reform" perhaps disappear because of the purist mentality of the Latinists? It seems that Paul VI had chosen this bold word, with its undoubted ecumenical importance, just as John XXIII had popularized the word *aggiornamento* ("updating"). While deliberately using a word so freighted with history, Paul VI made clear the meaning he intended it to have, a meaning bound up with the idea of "conversion."[359]

Consistently with the duties of his office and with a scrupulous awareness of his historical responsibility, from the very outset of his pontificate he proclaimed without ceasing the necessity of a twofold reform, spiritual and intellectual, but in a manner that made it seem at times that he was afraid of the ideas he himself had promoted. The encyclical showed that this impression was mistaken. In words difficult to translate, he said that "we will be most happy if we can present it [our judgment] in perfect accord with that of the conciliar Fathers," thus supposing that the judgment of the pope could differ from that of the bishops.

But Paul VI rejected the temptation of exercising his role as teacher and pastor as if it were that of a spiritual and dogmatic dictator. In the encyclical he stressed his decision to leave the Council absolutely free, thereby avoiding the risk not only of taking up problems that the Council would have to debate, but also of giving the impression that he wanted the decisions of the fathers to move in a certain direction. In his encyclical he repeatedly asked the bishops, in an almost pleading tone, to advise the pope, to help him, to collaborate with him, to suggest to him the reforms that ought to be carried out, and, above all, to signal practical ways of living the way of poverty. Never before had a pope shown by his actions that his supreme function is not exercised "apart from the Church." I think that the reason why the word *collegiality* did not appear in the encyclical was that the Council had not yet voted on

---

[359] Neither did Paul VI have any hesitation about using, in the Italian version, a summary phrase referring to the mistakes of the Church: *i propri falli* ("its own faults"), something very rare until then in official documents. The translators from Italian thought themselves obliged to tone down the words and make them specific by using the Latin phrase *suorum membrorum errata* ("the mistakes of its members") rather than those of the Church itself. With regard to the term *reformatio*, the reader should bear in mind the great importance it has in the Decree on Ecumenism, 6.

the subject. The reality of collegiality, however, played an active part at every point in the text and was implicit in the very form taken by the encyclical: a monologue on trust.

3. The Connection between Ecclesiam Suam and the Council

Not only the history of the encyclical but also the spirit that animated it established a close link between it and the ecclesiology of Vatican II. Professor A. Grillmeier even wrote: "This encyclical can be regarded as an interpretation of the main goals of the Council and in particular of its Constitution on the Church."[360] Although this observation was correct, the encyclical was in fact not often cited in the conciliar documents, except by Paul VI himself in his opening and closing addresses when the subject suggested his doing so. But perhaps the scant use of the encyclical[361] can be explained by the fact that while the climate of dialogue with the world was notably present in the encyclical, as it was also in the Council, the document avoided concrete references to the problems taken up in the introductory part of Gaudium et spes and again in Unitatis redintegratio. On the whole, however, whatever these possible explanations, this scant use should not surprise us. According to Congar, it was due to the fact that the encyclical dealt with the spirit of the Council (the spirit of dialogue and openness to humanity) but did not outline its ecclesiology.[362]

It was undoubtedly Lumen Gentium that reveals above all the divergences from the encyclical, particularly with regard to the emphasis to be placed on the primacy of the pope or on the power of bishops.[363] In addition, the expression "People of God" occurs only once in the encyclical, and then in the citation from 1 Peter 2:9 on the royal priesthood; the pope's purpose in the citation is to point out that the hierarchy represents the people of God on its journey toward the grace of Christ. This led some critics to claim that Paul VI's intention in the encyclical was to satisfy the minority. Addressing the question, Congar raised the

---

[360] A. Grillmeier, "Esprit, position fondamentale et caractère propre de la Constitution," in L'Église de Vatican II, ed. G. Baraúna, II (Paris, 1966), 161n.

[361] In the four constitutions Ecclesiam Suam is cited only in Gaudium et spes (three times). Other scattered explicit citations are found in the decrees Optatam totius, Presbyterorum ordinis, and Christus Dominus, and in the declarations Dignitatis humanae and Gravissimum educationis momentum.

[362] Colombo, "Genesi," 104.

[363] See P. Granfield, "The Theological Context of Ecclesiam suam," American Ecclesiastical Review 151 (1964), 264; Primauté, 33.

problem of the relation between pope and council or, more accurately, between pope and assembly (since the council includes the pope) and made this distinction: the council includes the pope, but there is the assembly and there is the pope.[364] The pope is both within it and outside it at the same time; he is *intra Ecclesiam* and *supra Ecclesiam* (within the Church and above the Church). Consequently, rather than trying to satisfy the minority, Paul VI's intention had been to tone down the ongoing debates and pave the way for the unity of the Council fathers, who would have to approve the constitution *Lumen Gentium* during the coming session.

The absence of citations from or references to *Ecclesiam Suam* in the decree on ecumenism was due to timing. The decree, which would be promulgated, after some minor retouching, on November 21, 1964, had been approved by the pope on April 27, after it had been discussed in the hall but before the publication of the encyclical. It is to be noted that in the conciliar discussion before the final approval, some references were indeed made to the encyclical, although they played no determining role. Only D. Nezic, Bishop of Parenze and Pola, asked that the schema be rewritten because it had been superseded by *Ecclesiam Suam*,[365] but his request was neatly sidestepped by the reporter. In speaking of the influence of *Ecclesiam Suam* on the decree on ecumenism, we must recognize that the encyclical shows a certain advance over the conciliar decree. Lukas Vischer did not advert to this when he complained that "the Roman Church starts with the presupposition that it is the one Church of Jesus Christ." Vischer's article ended with a series of questions that were far from trivial:

> Does not the doctrine of primacy and universal jurisdiction lead inevitably to the position where the pope is obliged to regard himself as shepherd not only of the Roman Catholic Church, but of the whole of Christendom? True, the Council has made strenuous efforts to break out of the constricted and excessively juridical conception of primacy, and it is therefore very possible that the office of the pope will acquire a new look. The pope can meet in an entirely different spirit the churches separated from Rome. But does not the claim remain that he has been given jurisdiction over the whole of Christendom? Does not the conviction remain that the see occupied by the successor of Peter has a special function to be exercised with regard to all baptized Christians, i.e., that it is possessed of a function which elevates it above all other centres of Christendom? It is at all events a remarkable fact that Rome should be the only geographical centre which

---

[364] Colombo, "Genesi," 105.
[365] *AS* III/2, 909.

is mentioned in a dogmatic constitution. Is not the pope therefore bound to
meet the non-Roman churches in the consciousness that he has received a
commission to feed the whole flock in perfect unity? And is he not almost
inevitably bound in this consciousness to regard himself as the focal point
of the ecumenical movement, as the "father of the ecumenical movement,"
as it has already been put on occasion? Must he not be the voice of the
father calling divided Christendom to unity? These questions are not mere
inventions. Numerous pronouncements of the present pope appear to confirm that even today the Roman Catholic Church can hardly understand its
task otherwise. For the non-Roman churches, however, this claim represents a serious obstacle. Even if they differ from one another in their understanding of ecclesiology, they are agreed that this claim has to be rejected.
Therefore they can enter into a conversation only if it is not predetermined
by the claim. It must not become the framework of the conversation but
subordinated to it as a subject of conversation.[366]

Ecclesiam Suam had its most direct influence in the discussion of the
orientation that would be taken by *Gaudium et spes*. Two of the men
who played a role in the development of the schema have attested to
this.[367] During the discussions in the hall after the schema had been presented on October 20, 1964, Cardinal Léger made an explicit reference
to the encyclical. The subsequent repeated references were due to the
natural closeness of the encyclical to a document meant to introduce
clarity into the dialogue between the Church and the world. Despite this
fact, from as early as 1965 the encyclical received hardly any mention in
the immense bibliography on the ecclesiology of Vatican II.[368] This can
be explained by the fact that *Ecclesiam Suam* intended simply to offer a
direction, whereas *Gaudium et spes* gave concrete form to the dialogue.
In addition, the encyclical lacks the "optimism" characteristic of the
constitution and does not use the phrase "signs of the times," which had
been inherited from the *Pacem in terris* of John XXIII and symbolized
the theology of history that made it possible for *Gaudium et spes* to
move beyond the baroque and abstract post- Tridentine mentality.

On the other hand, *Gaudium et spes* is not only solid and concrete but
also without any kind of simplistic dogmatism; its teaching is sufficiently

---

[366] L. Vischer, "Roman Catholic Ecumenism and the World Council of Churches,"
Ecumenical Review 16 (1964), 384. For other reactions in the ecumenical world see
Velati, *Una difficile transizione*, 450-53.

[367] See M. G. McGrath, "Présentation de la Constitution 'L'Eglise dans le monde de
ce temps,'" in *Vatican II. L'Eglise dans le monde de ce temps*, 2:29; R. Tucci, "Introduction historique et doctrinale à la Constitution Pastorale," ibid., 2:72.

[368] An exception is Henri de Lubac's *Athéisme et sens de l'homme. Une double
requête de "Gaudium et Spes"* (Paris, 1968), in which the contribution and interpretation
of the pastoral constitution take *Ecclesiam Suam* as their explicit point of departure.

pluralistic but also firmly ethical and without any erroneous and amoral opportunism. In this respect it is in harmony with *Ecclesiam Suam*, which B. Häring, one of the drafters of *Gaudium et spes*, says was of fundamental significance for the pastoral constitution: "A new fact made its appearance with the publication of Paul VI's first encyclical on August 6, 1964, on the dialogue of the Church with the world. It made a decisive contribution to schema XIII."[369]

IV. THE ACTIVITY OF SOME EPISCOPAL CONFERENCES AND LOCAL CHURCHES

The return of the bishops to their dioceses during the intersessions not only brought a considerable change of rhythm as compared with their life in Rome; it also meant taking up once again a great many problems and pastoral activities that had been neglected in their absence. In addition to finding solutions for all these problems, which were exacerbated in some countries by political difficulties, the bishops still had to meet their conciliar obligations, that is, to inform their dioceses about the work done and their own experiences of conciliar life, while also getting to know, taking control of, and exercising discernment on undertakings that had started in the dioceses.

On the other hand, during the intersession the bishops were also required, both individually and in their episcopal conferences, not only to study the schemas to be discussed during the third period but also to deal with two very concrete matters: the application of the liturgical reform and the statutes of the episcopal conferences. All this explains why many bishops passed these phases of the Council at a frenetic pace, which they were able to endure only in the strength of the expectations and hopes raised by the conciliar event. On all the continents there were bishops who devoted themselves wholly to accomplishing the purposes set forth by John XXIII when he convoked the Council.

A. RELATIONS OF BISHOPS WITH THEIR PEOPLE: PASTORAL LETTERS

One of the concerns of the bishops was to inform their people about the work of the second period, and they did this principally by pastoral

[369] Häring, "Testimonianze," 171.

letters and conferences. The information given was, of course, not always the same. We need only think of the divergences among the bishops, even in one and the same country; in Brazil, for example, some bishops belonged to the group that met at the Belgian College to think out the problems of the Church of the Poor, while others were members of the International Group of Fathers.[370] In addition, the ability of the bishops to communicate differed, and so did the desire of the faithful to be informed. Then there were considerable differences among the various conciliar documents, which in turn were variously understood according to the preparation of the faithful and to specific situations. It was not always easy to convey a sense of the event.[371]

The faithful in all the dioceses were awaiting the return of their bishops. But to what extent did the bishops show the influence of their conciliar experience in the usual documents with which they commented on the liturgical year and communicated important ideas to their faithful? This, too, depended on their varying sensibilities, the situation in their countries, the preparation of the faithful, and the expectations they harbored. It is impossible to generalize here.

For example, we are surprised at the paucity of references to the Council in the documents written by the Uruguayan bishops during this intersession.[372] But the exact opposite was seen in Holland, where countless pastoral letters were the chief means of spreading the ideas and experience of the Council; the positions taken in these letters, the influences, the sources, and the situations call for analysis. An analytic study of these documents would require numerous distinctions to be made among the authors, the addressees, the general circumstances, the subjects taken up, the tone used (merely informative or concerned to suggest new horizons for the Church). These letters make known the stance taken by a given father, which ran the gamut from enthusiasm to reserve, excepting some that echoed ongoing controversies. Many bishops were

---

[370] *History*, 2:195-203; J. O. Beozzo, *A Igreja do Brasil. De João XXIII a João Paulo II. De Medellín a Santo Domingo* (Petrópolis, 1994), 88-90.

[371] It has been said of Brazil that "during the intersession the bishops on returning to their dioceses had understandable difficulty in communicating the full riches of their experience during the preceding sessions. The impact on them had been immense and required some time for its assimilation, before they could be in a position to communicate what the Council really meant for the Church": Servus Mariae (Raimundo Caramuru de Barros), *Para entender a Igreja do Brasil: a caminhada que culminou no Vaticano II (1930-1968)* (Petrópolis, 1994), 164.

[372] See P. Dabezies, "Condiciones de la recepción de la *Gaudium et Spes* en la Iglesia uruguaya," *Soleriana* 21 (1966/1), 13-39.

absorbed by diocesan questions that had come to a head in their absence and were unable to devote themselves with sufficient enthusiasm to this form of communication, so necessary for the cause of a council whose focus was precisely on the Church as a whole.

The authorship of the letters was also a weighty factor: the pastorals of Cardinal Alfrink, Döpfner, Frings, Gerlier, Léger, Lercaro, Liénart, Suenens, Wyszynski, and others, and the statement of Maximos IV, influenced the consciousness of Catholics living far from their dioceses.[373] The bishops of Central Europe were constantly publishing and acting. In Germany there were countless undertakings by individual bishops. In addition to the letters just mentioned of Döpfner and Frings, a lecture given by Rudolf Graber, Bishop of Regensburg, attracted great attention; entitled "Der Einbruch Gottes in unsere Zeit" ("The Irruption of God into Our Age"),[374] it showed how trust in the Council should be based first and foremost on the interventions of God in the history of the Church, while not excluding the necessary contribution of human factors. Another whose writings attracted great attention was Dutch Bishop Wilhelm Bekkers of 's-Hertogenbosch, who won the admiration of many Catholics sensitive to the conciliar *aggiornamento*.

Thanks to *La Croix* and *Documentation catholique* we are well informed regarding the pastoral letters published by French bishops in their diocesan newspapers. Of these particularly noteworthy were the two letters in which Émile Guerry, Archbishop of Cambrai, went into the doctrine of collegiality and the sacramentality of episcopal orders.[375]

The many pastoral letters written by Italian bishops for their own faithful were uneven in tone and value and reflected the plurality of views.[376] In view of the author's importance, mention must be made of the letter "Il Concilio in Cammino" ("The Council Moving Forward"), which Luigi M. Carli, Bishop of Segni, addressed to his clergy on February 16, 1964. The bishop took up very important subjects on which he had spoken in his statements in the hall; he analyzed the so-called tendencies among the fathers, relations between doctrine and pastoral practice, the problem of the sources of revelation, the principles and methods

---

[373] See *CivCatt*, no. 2740 (August 15, 1964), 403-5.

[374] Published in *Schweizerische Kirchenzeitung*, June 18, 1964, 321-24.

[375] *DC*, nos. 1419-20 (1964), cols. 315-30 and 367-84.

[376] *CivCatt*, no. 2740 (August 1964), 390-91, 393 (on the Church), 395 (the laity), 396 (the communications media). See *Lettere pastorali dei Vescovi dell'Emilia-Romagna*, ed. D. Menozzi (Rome, 1987), and *Lettere pastorali dei vescovi della Toscana*, ed. B. Bocchini Camaiani and D. Menozzi (Genoa, 1990).

of Catholic ecumenism, questions having to do with the nature of the
Church, relations between papacy and episcopate and between episcopal conferences and the Roman Curia. Also of great interest were the
pastoral letters on ecumenism from the pens of Nicodemo, Baldassari,
and Iannucci, which tackled the questions of the Jews and of religious
freedom.[377]

The majority of the Spanish bishops preferred to inform their people
by explaining the second period. The most polemical of these letters was
that of Msgr, Hervás y Benet, "Por la unión de los cristianos" ("Toward
the Union of Christians"), December 14, 1963, in which he approached
the sensitive matter of Protestants in Spain by complaining of the way in
which they "gave trouble" to Catholics.

Among the subjects that the North American bishops discussed, they
gave first place to religious freedom, but they also published many letters aimed at promoting a life based on the Council. In Latin America
there was a wide variety. It can be said that the National Conference of
Brazilian Bishops was the one that best grasped the meaning of the
Council and profited by a considerable renewal, the fruit of the contacts
and relationships that its members had had in Rome. It published, collegially, a "Joint Pastoral Letter of the Brazilian Episcopate" that focused
on renewal and gave hope to a country full of contrasts and quarrels at
every level.[378]

Many episcopates found themselves in a difficult situation. For example, the bishops of Peru had difficulty in dealing with the course of the
Council; they thought they were not personally prepared, since they
lacked any experience of episcopal assemblies (only six of them had
taken part in the first meeting of CELAM in Rio de Janeiro in 1955) and
did not think they had the qualifications for taking part in an ecumenical
gathering. As a result, "instead of bringing up their own problems they
simply followed the course of events,"[379] as indeed did other episcopates
of Latin America and the Third World. For this reason, it is an agreeable
surprise to come upon the document written by Viola, Bishop of Salto
(who had been elected a member of the Commission for Bishops and the
Governance of Dioceses) and signed also by his coadjutor, Marcelo
Mendihirat, which showed a new attitude toward the Council. The letter
was titled "A Call to Social Responsibility" and was published in May

[377] Ibid., 392.
[378] *Revista Ecclesiastica Brasileira* 23 (1963), 109ff.
[379] C. Romero and C. Tovar, in CEHILA, *Histora general de la Iglesia in América Latina* (Salamanca, 1987), 8:424.

1964. Taking as their starting point the parables of the Good Samaritan and of the judgment in Matthew 25, the two bishops reminded their readers that Jesus identified with the needy and the poor; on this basis they urged "a careful analysis of our reality as a nation" and ended with a call to set out on the way of justice and dignity. No less worthy of attention was the "Balance-sheet of the Second Session" that Mendihirat published in *Brújula* at the beginning of 1964. In addition to taking note of a positive evolution in the outlook of the bishops and of the raising of a series of subjects that "we did not take up in the seminary (at least in my time) and which are now part of ecclesiology," the coadjutor of Salto pointed out a novelty that would have been unimaginable four years earlier: the fact that poverty had become one of the essential elements in the credibility of the Church. Finally, he reminded his readers that one of the three goals set for the Council by John XXIII was an "openness to the world" (in addition to ecumenism and to the internal reform of the Church).

In speaking of Latin America I cannot omit mention of the pastoral plan of the Diocese of Riobamba. This had been developed in 1963 on the basis of guidelines from Msgr. Leónidas Proaño[380] and took on a completely conciliar character during the second intersession; it involved monthly meetings of all the clergy, religious men and women, and the laity. As part of the plan there was a socioreligious study made of the entire province, which French canon F. Boulard was invited to conduct. The result was the establishment of group pastoral care that was influential in changing the mentality of the people and thanks to which the poor ceased to be silent in the face of injustice.[381] This activity also led to a wealth of experiments in the areas of liturgy, catechesis, the missions, and so on. In this connection it should be mentioned that on July 11, 1964, the Ecuadorian government promulgated the first law for the agrarian reform of the country and that the bishops responded

---

[380] See J. Moreno Alvarez, "La Iglesia en Ecuador. Riobamba (desde 1962)," in *Historia general de la Iglesia en América latina*, 8:458-89.

[381] For Msgr. Proaño see his *Alocuciones semanales del programa radial "Hoy y mañana"*; his autobiography, *Creo en el hombre y en la comunidad* (Bilbao, 1977); *Concientización, evangelización y política* (Salamanca, 1987). Also Agustín B. Bravo (who was Proaño's vicar general), "La buena nueva de la revolución del Poncho," a report given at the II. Conferencia general, Historia da Igreja na América Latina no Caribe, Sao Paulo, 1995, and published in *CrSt* 18 (1997), 91-134. On the many activities and the stimuli given by Msgr. Proaño, as narrated in the above bibliography, it is difficult to say precisely which were located in the second intersession.

with a collective pastoral letter in which they were ready to give a good example by making available the lands belonging to the Church.[382]

The African bishops were also as active as was possible for them during the second intersession. Despite the undeniable energy that the Council brought to Christianity in Africa, the situation there appeared on the whole to be neither clear nor simple. Although some optimistic assessments were made, such as that of French Jesuit J. Y. Calvez,[383] we cannot forget the realism shown by Zoa, Archbishop of Yaoundé (Cameroon), who, in the framework of the work of the subcommission on the "signs of the times," was very emphatic on the ambiguity of the African presence at the Council: "They are participating intellectually in the settlement of European quarrels, but they have a sense that the real problems have not been raised."[384]

B. STUDY OF THE SCHEMAS

Despite the many pastoral duties that awaited them, the bishops, individually or collectively, were supposed to study the conciliar texts. Even though the final schemas did not reach them before May and June 1964, they did have drafts or provisional versions. The episcopal conferences sent materials to the bishops for their study and then organized meetings in order to establish guidelines on positions to be taken. Examples of such activity were seen in France, where the Conciliar Secretariat of the Episcopate used its bulletin *Études et documents* to give the bishops very valuable doctrinal information on the subjects taken up by the Council. During the period that concerns us here the bishops received twenty rather nuanced texts which helped them to understand the subjects on which they would be voting. The secretariat of the Spanish episcopate likewise reactivated its work of conveying information as soon as the second intersession began and sent material on the novelties introduced, more or less behind the scenes, by the second period on the Council: new plans for documents on the presence of the Church in the world and on religious freedom, as well as some studies of Spanish and foreign experts on this last subject.[385]

[382] "Pastorales y documentos colectivos del Episcopado Ecuatoriano, de 1939 a 1979," in *Iglesia-Ecuador, 1979* (Quito, 1979).

[383] "Présence du Tiers Monde à Vatican II," *Projet* (February 1966), 133-46.

[384] Session of September 12, 1964: report, 10.

[385] See M. García, "Concilio Vaticano II," in *Diccionario de Historia Eclesiástica de España* (Madrid, 1972), 1:533-35.

Other episcopates took advantage of their meetings to analyze the conciliar themes. Such was the case with the Italian Episcopal Conference, the plenary meeting of which on April 14-16 gave the bishops an opportunity to discuss the third chapter of the schema on the Church, which took up the main theme of the document "On the Hierarchical Constitution of the Church." The discussion focused chiefly on collegiality in relation to the primacy of the pope. Alongside the theological discussion a debate developed on the participation of the episcopate in the Council; the bishops gave discordant assessments, especially on the value of the interventions by individuals in the name of an episcopal conference.

Elsewhere a different procedure was tried that was more collegial and more effective: joint meetings of various episcopates. The bishops of Germany met for a working meeting in Innsbruck May 19-22, 1964, along with council fathers from Austria, Switzerland, the Netherlands, France (the French bishops were represented chiefly by Elchinger, Coadjutor Bishop of Strasbourg), and Scandinavia. On this occasion the bishops who were members of conciliar commissions presented their respective texts in a way calculated to promote a fruitful discussion.[386] The conclusions of the Innsbruck meeting were forwarded to Rome through Cardinal Döpfner.[387]

The same thing took place in Africa, where thirty-two archbishops, bishops, and apostolic prefects of French-speaking West Africa met in a plenary assembly in Dakar at the beginning of June, with Gantin, Archbishop of Cotonou, presiding. This assembly studied the schema on missionary activity and prepared about ten emendations aimed at emphasizing some needs specific to the African Church, in particular, the urgent need of evangelization, as well as the breadth and complexity of this work in view of the rapid transformation of social, political, economic, and demographic conditions on the continent. It did this in the spirit of safeguarding religious freedom, of ecumenical awareness, of dialogue with the non-Christian religions, and of the essentially spiritual nature of the Church. During the meeting a strong emphasis was placed on the

---

[386] See *KNA-Sonderdienst zum Zweiten Vatikanischen Konzil* 23/64, p. 2. Information was supplied regarding the texts on the lay apostolate (Lazlo of Eisenstadt), religious (Leiprecht of Rottenburg), clergy training and Catholic schools (Jachyn, coadjutor archbishop of Vienna, and Höffner of Münster), priests (Janssen of Hildesheim), marriage (Schneider of Bamberg), and Oriental Churches (Johannes Höck, Abbot of Scheyern).

[387] *AS* III/2, 876; III/4, 821-24, 955-58; III/5, 866; III/7, 789-92; III/8, 940-52 and 1172.

role of the bishop as the summit and center of the unity of the hierarchi-
cally organized apostolate, on the fundamental nature of the work of catechists, and on the opening of a dialogue among the episcopates of the
several continents in order that the help given to the most needy might
be better attuned to each specific pastoral work of evangelization.

On another level, the episcopate of West Africa decided to set up its
own conciliar episcopal committee that would organize and coordinate
work during the sessions of the Council. Van den Bronk, Yougbaré,
Maillat, and Henrion were elected to the committee.

In the Americas the episcopates worked in greater isolation from
one another. A significant example of this was Canada, where from
April 12 to 14 a working session was held during which the bishops
established a group of theologians charged with studying the
schemas.[388] In addition, an important office of the secretariat of the
episcopate was activated to supply the bishops with documentation,
including that produced by other episcopal conferences. Of special
interest was the partial report on the work done by the "Interconfer-
ence," of which Bishop Baudoux was in charge; among other things,
he had formed a group which made an in-depth study of all the
schemas that had been sent to the fathers.

In Latin America, despite the interest shown by the authorities of
CELAM, the study of the schemas was done in very different ways in
different countries. The difficult political situation in some of these did
not allow the bishops to devote much personnel to this study. A para-
digmatic case was Brazil where, despite the military coup in the first
week of April that had serious consequences for the activity of the
Church, the National Conference of Brazilian Bishops (CNBB) encouraged study of the conciliar schemas, which the bishops had received
through the conference. A theological commission (with Angelo Rossi
presiding and Dominican Romeu Dale as secretary) was to direct this
study and hold a meeting in Rio June 14-16.

In Chile Cardinal Silva Henríquez was quite active during these
months. The situation in that country required him to speak out on social
and political reforms, on a draft law on abortion, and also on the sensitive

---

[388] Paul-Emile Bolte, P.S.S., J. M. Tillard, O.P., Msgr. Lucien Beauregard, Msgr.
Elzéar Fortier, and Roger Cantin, S.J., spoke on the training of priests; Tillard again and
Jesuits Lucien Campeau, Richard Arès, Jacques Cousineau, and Jean Genest on schools
and educations. Abundant information was given on the schema on revelation and a
report was presented by the consultative committee on Schema XIII, which had been formed by Maurice Roy, Archbishop of Québec.

question of Christian instruction. He did not, however, neglect study of the schema on the Church; in fact, some proposals for its development had led him to compose a new version, known as the "Chilean draft." This was the fruit of the thorough work of a group of theologians: Jesuit J. Ochagavia, Salesian E. Viganó, and diocesan priest J. Medina. How important the work done was has been shown in the opening chapter of the present volume.

In Argentina the situation was different. While the assembly of bishops limited itself to distributing the schemas throughout the ecclesiastical provinces in the hope of eliciting some *vota,* the self-styled Argentinean Group, made up of eight Argentinean bishops and two Uruguayan, met at Villa Marista (Pilar, Buenos Aires) April 14 to 16, with the preparation for the third period as its agenda.[389] The debates on this occasion led, in subsequent work on the Council, to some "conclusions" on collegiality, the restructuring of seminaries, the participation of the laity in the general congregations of the Council, and concelebration.

In order to complete this section I must point out the divergent assessments given of the themes of Council by some episcopates. The Italian episcopate, for example, as already noted, focused much of its attention of the question of collegiality, while the African episcopate concerned itself mainly with the schema on missionary activity. An important example here is that of the Spanish episcopate, whose attention was preempted by two texts, that on religious freedom and that on the Blessed Virgin; on this last I refer the reader to the examination, in the present chapter, of its revision. As for religious freedom, a meeting the episcopate's experts from January 10-24, 1964 made a thorough study of the subject and drew up a sizable report. For the purpose the group investigated various studies both of Spanish theologians and of foreign experts. Afterward, on January 25, this material was studied in Seville at the second meeting of the episcopal committee on the Council.[390] The interest in this question becomes

---

[389] Reports were given by Alfredo Trusso, Carmelo Giaquinta, Miguez Bonino, a Methodist observer at the Council (reporting on ecumenism), Jorge Mejia, and Juan Vázquez (a lay auditor at the Council).

[390] Religious freedom was a burning topic. Hervás, Bishop of Ciudad Real, had published a pastoral letter, *Por la unión de los cristianos* (December 14, 1963), in which he had compared methods of ecumenism and brought up the subject of Protestants in Spain; he acknowledged the seriousness and uprightness of many among them but complained that others had been "upsetting" Catholics. The vast bibliography on the situation of Protestants in Spain was reviewed in *CivCatt,* no. 2739 (August 1, 1964), 294 n.4. On this subject, add the pastoral letter of Msgr. Pildain (April 11, 1964), who claimed that a law granting religious freedom to Protestants could unleash a "spiritual civil war" (see A. Chil Estévez, *Pildain, un obispo para una época* [Las Palmas de Gran Canaria, 1988], 129).

intelligible in the light of the implications that religious freedom would have for Catholic unity in Spain, a question debated by those, above all, who were caught by surprise by the new ideas gaining ascendancy at the Council.[391] For different reasons the text on religious freedom was also the subject of special study by the North American episcopate, which was quite aware of what it represented for civil society.[392]

C. THE STATUTES OF THE EPISCOPAL CONFERENCES

Episcopal conferences were already in existence before the Council — the *Annuario Pontificio* for 1962 already contained a list of them — and their prehistory and history are useful for understanding the organization and vitality of the Church.[393] A large number of these organizations were of a national kind, but others were wider in scope, as, for example, the episcopal conference of Central America and Panama, the plenary conference of Mission Ordinaries of French Africa, and the Conference of Ecclesiastical Authorities of South Africa. One organization, CELAM, established in 1955, covered the entire South American continent. These organizations were not always called episcopal conferences.[394]

The Constitution on the Sacred Liturgy, promulgated on December 4, 1963, made frequent reference to the important competence of episcopal conferences in matters liturgical. It presupposed their existence and implicitly alluded to the need for a link among episcopates.[395] When the schema on bishops and the government of the Churches was studied at the 65th and 66th general congregations (November 12 and 13, 1963), the problem of episcopal conferences became the main subject of the

[391] See, among numerous examples, the view of Temiño, in *El Concilio visto por los obispos españoles* (Madrid, 1964), 87-88. A more balanced position was taken in the Lenten pastoral instruction of Cardinal Bueno Montréal, in *Ecclesia* (Madrid), no. 1184 (March 21, 1964), 15-18; this was reported at length in *HK* 18 (1964), 367-69.

[392] See *American Participation in the Second Vatican Council*, ed. V. A. Yzermans (New York, 1967), 623-29. The problem, as defined and studied by the bishops with J. C. Murray as special adviser, is well explained by Gonnet in *La liberté religieuse*, 122-44.

[393] See K. Rahner, "Über Bischofskonferenzen," *Stimmen der Zeit* 172 (1962-63), 267-83; *The Nature and Function of Episcopal Conferences*, ed. H. Legrand, J. Manzonares, and A. Garcá y García (Washington, 1988).

[394] See *History*, 2:187-94.

[395] J. Manzanares Marijuan, *Liturgia y decentralización en el Concilio Vaticano II. Las conferencias episcopales, eje de la reforma litúrgica conciliar* (Rome, 1970); idem, "De Conferentiae Episcopalis competentia in re liturgica, in schemate codificationis emendata," *Periodica* 70 (1981), 496-97.

debate. Given the theological and juridical questions raised by the conferences,[396] it became obvious that conferences had to be established in countries in which they did not already exist. These conferences, the formation of which was a reflection of the evolving world, were not only a practical tool but also in fact a possible expression and appropriate manifestation of the solidarity of the body of bishops, that is, of collegiality,[397] and thereby introduced a degree of "decentering" into the government of the Church (Cardinal Alfrink).

Thus, without giving a theological definition of the conferences, the Council made them obligatory where they did not previously exist and recognized them as having the right to adopt, by a two-thirds majority, decisions binding their members, as can be seen from the decree *Christus Dominus* (nos. 37-38). It is therefore understandable that in this context the episcopal conferences (by whatever name they might be known) should almost everywhere want to draw up their own statutes,[398] conscious as they were of the "empirical nature and fragility (sociological and theological)"[399] of their identity. The first occasion for understanding the episcopal assemblies took place during the second intersession.

The German Episcopal Conference, which had its basis in a rich tradition dating from the nineteenth century, does not appear to have held any special meeting during the intersession for the purpose of defining its constitution.[400] It is worth emphasizing the fourth point in Ferdinand Oertel's report on ordinary meetings: since bishops living in the Soviet zone were not allowed to take part in the episcopal conference of Fulda, they should meet in Berlin under the name of Conference of Berlin Bishops.[401]

In Italy, an episcopal conference did exist (CEI), but its collegial activity was rather limited.[402] The plenary meeting of April 14-16,

---

[396] See Ch. Munier in *Vatican II. La charge épiscopale des évêques* (Paris, 1969), 334-52.

[397] See F. Houtart, "Les formes modernes de la collégialité épiscopale," in *L'Episcopat et l'Eglise universelle*, ed. Y. Congar and B.-D. Dupuy (Paris, 1962), 497-535.

[398] For more complete data, see R. Astorei, "Gli statuti delle conferenze episcopali," in *Europa* I (Padua, 1987).

[399] See J. Hamer, "Les conférences épiscopales, exercice de la collégialité," *Nouvelle Revue Théologique* 85 (1963), 969. See also H. Legrand, "Le développement d'Eglises-sujets, une requête de Vatican II," in *Les Eglises après Vatican II. Dynamismes et prospectives*, ed. G. Alberigo (Paris, 1981), 149-84.

[400] See W. Weiss, "Die deutsche Bischofskonferenz und das II. Vatikanum," in *Der Beitrag der deutschsprachigen und osteuropäischen Länder zum Zweiten Vatikanischen Konzil*, ed. K. Wittstadt and W. Verschooten (Leuven, 1996), 27-44.

[401] F. Oertel, "Die Zukunft der Bischofskonferenzen," *KNA-Sonderdienst zum Zweiten Vatikanischen Konzil* 30/64, 6-7.

[402] F. Sportelli, *La Conferenza Episcopale Italiana (1952-1972)* (Potenza, 1994). On the second intersession see 193ff.

1964,[403] was decisive in giving a dynamic impulse to the establishment of a conference conformed to the pope's and Council's idea of it. The meeting began with an address of Paul VI to the Italian bishops,[404] in which he emphasized their function: "It cannot be supposed that the Italian episcopate can henceforth do without this united expression of their thought, this means of union, coordination, mutual collaboration, and promotion, on the same level as that of the episcopates of other countries." This sentence makes it clear that the lack of a coordinating organization such as the majority of national Churches already possessed at that time represented a serious lacuna in the Church in Italy. The practical necessity of this relatively new institution was recognized. As has already been mentioned, the schema on the bishops and dioceses, which was debated during the second period, turned these national assemblies of bishops into a normal and obligatory canonical structure.

While asserting the vital need of episcopal conferences from the supernatural standpoint of the Church and expressing his wish for joint action, Paul VI also touched on some subjects discussed during the preceding period of the Council. We already know, in fact, that while, according to the discussions in the conciliar assembly, episcopal conferences were not strictly necessary manifestations of the power of the apostolic college over the universal Church, they nonetheless had a place in the logic of this collegiality. At the same time, various interventions had brought to light widespread reservations regarding the scope of the decisions of these conferences. In this context, was what the pope said simply a bit of advice suggesting a direction or was it a true and proper decision that required obedience? The pope, of course, did not resolve this dilemma, the solution of which was placed in the hands of the Council. But at that time it already seemed clear to all that mere advice would

---

[403] On February 17 Castelli, secretary of the CEI, sent a circular letter to the Italian bishops inviting them to the meeting. On the preparation for this meeting, see Archivio CEI: letter of Siri to Castelli (March 31, 1964), in which he referred to his precarious health and said that Ruffini should serve as president (Prot. CEI 5415); letter of Castelli to Dell'Acqua (April 3) and the reply in which the latter the next day approved Ruffini's presidency (Prot. N. 20590 of the Secretariat of State). In this connection interesting rumors circulated in Rome; Congar mentions them in his diary: "Cardinal Siri is ill. Cardinal Lercaro says that he, Siri, did not attend the meeting of the Italian bishops, of whom he is president. This gave rise to the rumor that he, Siri, and Msgr. Castelli were to be replaced by Cardinal Urbani and Msgr. Guano. But this is not what happened. In the place and position of Siri it was Ruffini who composed the text of a concluding message. But the text was so negative, so 'anti' and especially so anticommunist, that it was not accepted. The conference appointed a small committee (including Guano) to compose another" (*JCongar*, 452).

[404] Text in *IdP* (1964), II, 243-52.

not be enough to achieve unity of action, the absolute need of which Paul VI had called for on that occasion. The CEI did not fully grasp the meaning of the pope's programmatic address, and the pastoral themes he offered were not analyzed.[405]

In France the meeting of May 18-20, 1964, worked out a real and proper constitution for the future episcopal conference. First of all, what had until then been a de facto assembly meeting every three years became a permanent conference with the obligation of meeting annually for six days. As a result, the assembly of cardinals and archbishops disappeared. The conference was to be governed by a permanent commission consisting of a cardinal appointed by the cardinals, a bishop or archbishop elected by each apostolic region, the presidents of the episcopal commissions,[406] and, ex officio, the Archbishop of Paris. Thus it was election and not function that was to determine the makeup of the board of directors. The latter was to meet three times a year, and its council, made up of five members, was to meet every two months.

The cardinals in turn formed a council whose role as arbitrator, if needed, was poorly defined at the time but would be better determined through practice. In fact, because of their age the cardinals had a primarily honorific role; for example, the cardinal belonging to the permanent commission "presided" over it, but its real "director" was a vice-president elected by the plenary assembly. Similarly, the cardinals "presided" over the plenary meetings, but the permanent commission "directed" them. All functions had become elective and the mandate was a short one (three years, renewable no more than twice); this prevented the sclerosis caused by irremovability. "Decisions" were to be made by secret vote and required a two-thirds majority.

The approved statutes spoke of "decisions," but what did this mean? At the time there was an uncertainty that would be removed only by the voting at the Council and by the pope's approval of the schema on the bishops. Nevertheless, everything suggested that the national assemblies of bishops would be able to give the force of canon law to their decisions. People were increasingly realizing that diocesan autarchy, once regarded as a principle, no longer met the pastoral needs of a world so extensively socialized. The new value placed on episcopal collegiality by the ecumenical council made it possible to introduce a widespread

---

[405] See Sportelli, *La Conferenza*, 196.

[406] Two study centers were established: a "doctrinal" and a "pastoral." The number of commissions, based on anticipations at the time, was to be ten.

spirit of collaboration; at the same time, national assemblies of bishops seemed to be less a necessary consequence of episcopal collegiality than an organization consonant with this principle.[407]

In Spain the conference of metropolitans assigned the recently established commission for the Council the task of preparing a preliminary draft of statutes for the Spanish Episcopal Conference. After a good deal of time, this was completed on August 12; it consisted of seven chapters and thirty-six articles. Its sources of ideas were the address of Paul VI to the CEI, chapter III of the schema on the pastoral office of bishops, and a series of statutes from other episcopal conferences, in particular an extensive file of material sent by the secretariat of the French episcopate.[408]

The interest of the episcopates in defining their own collegial status was to be found on all the continents, as can be seen in the case of Africa, where it had a supranational character, and in two South American cases, where it had a national character but one that differed in the two instances. At the time when the national episcopal conferences were being organized, the African bishops decided by secret vote to keep alive the International Conference of French-speaking West Africa and to give a permanent institutional status to its statutes. These statutes, which were approved almost unanimously, provided, among other things, for election by a two-thirds majority and for a three-year term for the president of the conference (to be chosen from the metropolitan archbishops), as well as the establishment of pastoral commissions whose members were to be elected for a three-year term by a relative majority. The plenary assembly was to meet every third year, while a permanent committee, composed of the archbishops and the presidents of the commissions, was to meet annually.

Here are two Latin American examples, chosen from among many. In Brazil, under Don Hilario Pandolfo, who headed the general secretariat and signed letters in his capacity as general vice-secretary, the conference continued to take care of pastoral needs along the same lines followed by the preceding secretary, Don Helder Câmara. Don Hilario made special efforts to prepare for the sixth ordinary assembly of the CNBB, which was to be held in Rome at the end of the third period, and to win approval for new statutes and thus for a new organizational

---

[407] An excellent chronicle of the French assembly's meeting is given in *DC* (June 21, 1965), 757- 612; see also *HK* 18 (1964), 468-71.

[408] "Hacia la Conferencia episcopal española. Entrevista con Mons. Cirarda," *Ecclesia* (Madrid), no. 1217 (November 7, 1964), 9-10.

structure of the conference. In order to organize the coming assembly, the central commission held a fruitful meeting May 25-27 in the Convento do Cenaculo in Rio de Janeiro.[409]

The example of the Argentinean episcopate was not marked by the same extravagant hopes. During this intersession the episcopal assembly met twice (April 1-3 and May 5-9) with Cardinal Caggiano presiding and in the presence of the nuncio, Humberto Mozzoni. The assembly hardly concerned itself at all with the Council; the only communication from the latter was the document signed by Lercaro as president of the Council for the Implementation of the Constitution on the Sacred Liturgy, which contained detailed norms for the role of the episcopal conferences in liturgical matters. The question of revising the statutes of the conference brought up the subject, discussed by the Council but not yet finally adopted, of collegiality and episcopal conferences. But despite the insistence of Bishops Tato and Devoto (members of the Argentinean Group), questions raised by the Council found an echo only in the eighth resolution: "It is decided to entrust the study of the only new schema received for the third period to the ecclesiastical province of Bahía Blanca, and authorization is granted to the board of presidents to distribute to the other ecclesiastical provinces any schemas that may come in."

D. The Start of the Liturgical Reform

On the morning of December 4, 1963, when Paul VI gave an account of the second period, he presented the Church with some fully mature fruits. The first of these, not only in time but in importance for the life of the Church, was the Constitution on the Sacred Liturgy. In this constitution the Council had set as one of its goals to renew Christian life by means of the liturgy. To achieve this objective, it had also chosen the path of a general reform in which texts and rites would express more

---

[409] Due to this intense preparation it was possible to hold a satisfactory sixth ordinary meeting of the CNBB in Rome at the end of the third period. The meeting was enriched by the spirit of episcopal collegiality that was so strongly present in the climate of the Council. But a change also took place at the top and in a conservative direction; the internal structure of the CNBB was also modified, becoming more flexible, more efficient, and more representative through the creation of regional councils. At the same time, better links were inaugurated between the CNBB and the CRB (Conference of the Religious of Brazil), which in turn would be organized on a regional basis.

clearly the sacred realities they represented; in short, a reform that would bring the liturgy closer to the people and enable them to participate fully, actively, and as a community. The Council was fully aware that this goal would not be reached by a reform that was the same everywhere; a liturgy that is alive and easily understood and shared in would have to be adapted to the capacities of the faithful and to their unique mentalities and cultures. Therefore, according to the timely reminder by C. I. Calewaert, official reporter on the text, the Constitution as a whole had as its fundamental thrust the principle that reform would in good measure be carried out by the bishops themselves "in different ways according to different conditions."[410]

The post-Tridentine centralization, later sanctioned by the Code of Canon Law of 1917 (c. 1257 and its sources), was now being followed by an incipient decentralization that involved the episcopate of every nation or region in the important and delicate task of organizing the worship of the Church.[411] This was the first official step in a movement that Vatican II, with its sensitivity to the signs of the times and under the guidance of the Spirit, gladly accepted and fostered. It is easy to understand that so momentous a change could not be undertaken without adequate preparation; given the widespread conviction of the Holy See's sole competence in the matter, a process was started of promoting and developing the new discipline, a process rich in suggestions, plans, contrasts, and so on.[412] It was therefore natural that during this intersession the episcopal conferences should be much absorbed not only by study of the schemes of the coming period but also by the concrete problem of implementing the liturgical reform.

Some conferences had asked permission to introduce the language of their own countries in some parts of the liturgy; others girded themselves to make decisions on liturgical matters. The Consilium, by the act that established it on February 29, 1964, was to prepare an Instruction that would, among other things, "clearly outline the competence of territorial ecclesiastical authorities, pending the reform of the rites and liturgical books." Along with a letter of March 25, 1964, signed by

    [410] *AS*, I/4, 280.

    [411] See *Sacrosanctum Concilium*, 21.

    [412] See Manzanares Marijuan, *Liturgia y descentralización*. On the influence of the liturgical constitution on decisions made after the Council, see Cardinal G. Garrone, "Le rôle de la constitution de sacra liturgia sur l'évolution du Concile et l'orientation de la Pastorale," in *Miscellanea liturgica in onore di S. E. il Cardinale Giacomo Lercaro* II (Rome, 1967), 11-26.

Cardinal Lercaro, the Consilium sent this document to the presidents of the episcopal conferences. Conferences did not exist in all countries, and the Consilium was doubtless the first postconciliar body to highlight their value. In this context, then, the letter was a stimulus and a point of information, "a guide [that gave] assurance that pastors would be proceeding along the right lines," during the difficult time of transition to a new set of rules and a new spirit.[413]

1. The Reform in Central Europe

At their meeting at Hofheim in Taunus, February 17-19, 1964, the German bishops studied the Constitution on the Sacred Liturgy for the purpose of making it known and putting it into practice. The members of the episcopal conference of Fulda were thus acting, in accordance with Article 22 §2 of the constitution, as the "territorial authority" for Germany.[414] A very important congress entitled "The Liturgy at the Council" was celebrated in Mainz, April 20-24, under the auspices of the liturgical institutes of Trier (Germany), Salzburg (Austria), and Fribourg (Switzerland); the congress proved to be in harmony with the dynamics implicit in the Council. Priests were glad of the many possibilities opened up for them and, while full of hope, Cardinal Döpfner warned that the road to the reform of the mass would not be easy, adding that "an overhasty reform would be worse than a reform excessively delayed."[415]

---

[413] A. Bugnini, *The Reform of the Liturgy 1948-1975* (Collegeville, 1990), 99 (first quotation) and 207 (second quotation). See also Manzanares Marijuan, *Liturgia y descentralización.*

[414] It was decided that the biblical readings should be in the vernacular; the Schott and Bomm missals were authorized as provisional translations, and for the Breviary (in cases in which the vernacular was authorized) the translations of Schenk, Parsch, and Stephan; see *HK* 18 (1964), 317. After the plenary meeting of the conference a collective letter was published, dated February 18, which explained the scope and aims of the conciliar docu- ment in other areas besides language: *Erster Ausführungsbeschluss der deutschen Bischofskonferenze Zur Konstitution über Liturgie.* This document was preceded by a letter from all the German-speaking bishops to the clergy (text in *Schweizerische Kirchen- zeitung,* January 23, 1964); see A. Weitmann, "Der erste Schrift zur Liturgiereform," *Lebendige Seelsorge,* April 16, 1964, 134-39. The bulletin of the Archepiscopate of Munich and Freising (March 2, 1964) noted that the Sacred Congregation of Rites had replied to the questions asked it about the liturgy: "Use must be made in the biblical rea- dings and in the prayers of a German translation approved by the body of bishops...Car- dinal Larraona, Prefect."

[415] See *KNA-Sonderdienst zum Zweiten Vatikanischen Konzil* 19/64, 78; see also *HK* 18 (1964), 440-47.

In France, given the widespread desire of clergy and people to participate in the liturgical reform, many bishops sought to put the clergy on
guard against "local initiatives" that would try to anticipate guidelines
from the Holy See on areas of change. The plenary assembly of the
French episcopate met in Rome from November 30 to December 3,
1963, and gave the episcopal commission for the liturgy the task of
drafting a collective letter on the first applications of the constitution
Sacrosanctum Concilium.[416] The expected rulings appeared on February
1, 1964, and were to go into effect on the 16th of that month.[417] The
French episcopate later added two more regulations, which it published
in October and November of 1964.

All three regulations were the subject of study at the meeting of the
Centre de pastorale liturgique held in Versailles that same year. There
the report by Dominican François Louvel, titled "Qu'y a-t-il en de nou-
veau le 16 février 1964?"[418] described the direction being taken by the
activity of reform, especially as it concerned the controverted translations. This meeting, as a whole, directed and stimulated the greatly
desired liturgical renewal by facing not only the question of the translation of texts but also the rather complex problem of the translation of
liturgical songs into the vernacular. The episcopate was aware of the difficulty and in a unanimously approved note of May 20, asked, via its
committee on liturgical music, which had been set up for the purpose,
that in tackling this task account be taken of the conditions mentioned in
the note. There was, however, no intention of limiting "the creative freedom of the musicians called upon to compose a first-rate repertory."[419]

The implementation of the liturgical constitution in Switzerland found
some expert architects in Charrière, Bishop of Fribourg,[420] and Von
Streng, Bishop of Basel, who got the episcopal conference to act for the
purpose.[421] The situation was different in Holland. It was not easy for
the Dutch episcopate to implement the official instructions from Rome

---

[416] See *DC* (February 16, 1964), 253-59.

[417] A point of conflict, caused by the heedlessness of some journalists, had to do with
the translation of liturgical texts, which according to some reports were being used before
being approved by the Holy See. On this regrettable incident, see *Nouvelles de Chrétienté*, no. 428 (February 16, 1964), 9-14; see also *Kipa-Concile*, March 27, 1964. The
explanation given by the religion columnist in *Il Tempo* of Rome (February 28, 1964) was
not appropriate.

[418] Text in *La Maison-Dieu*, no. 80 (1964), 136-50.

[419] See *ICI*, August 1, 1964, no. 219, p. 12.

[420] See *Orientierung*, February 15, 1964.

[421] See *Die Bischöfe von Basel, 1794-1995*, ed. U. Fink, St. Leimgruber, and M. Ries
(Freiburg, 1996), 287-88.

on liturgical reform, because, in testimony of the undeniable vitality of the Catholic community in little Holland, it had produced a great abundance of texts, songs, and rites that were, in addition, quite different among themselves.[422] In Belgium two national commissions were established, one for the Flemish area and one for the French-speaking community, with L. De Kesel, auxiliary bishop of Ghent, as president of both and with two secretaries.[423] In January, Charue, Bishop of Namur, had already published a pastoral letter, *Mandement de Carême de l'an de grâce 1964 sur la restauration de la liturgie*. In February the episcopate gave the impulse for various projects while publishing practical guidelines for carrying out a balanced reform.

2. The English-speaking World

In England, a communication at the end of June from John Heenan, Archbishop of Westminster, announced that the episcopate of England and Wales, which was marked by the minority mentality peculiar to English Catholics, had decided to implement the liturgical reform. At its June meeting the episcopate decided on the dates on which the reform would go into effect, in two phases. Some commentators observed that these arrangements represented a happy compromise between the hopes of some and the fears of others, as well as the maximum that could be gotten "in a country seriously backward when it came to liturgical participation" (Desmond Fisher). J. D. Crichton, for his part, remarked: "We are at the beginning of a new era of great importance for Catholic life in this country."[424]

The collegial activities of the United States episcopate began with liturgical reform.[425] Meeting in Rome during the work of the Council, the bishops readied themselves for the use of English in the liturgy. On April 2, about 200 archbishops and bishops, along with four cardinals, gathered in Washington to take steps toward the concrete use of the vernacular. On May 15 Cardinal Spellman announced to the press that the

---

[422] See H. Oosterhuis, "La liturgie," in *Les catholiques hollandaises* (Paris, 1969), 83-105; above all, see J. A. Brouwers, *Vreygde en hoopvolle verwachting* (Baarn, 1989).

[423] See A. Haquin, "Le 'réception' de la liturgie de Vatican II en Belgique," *Belgique*, 251-68.

[424] *HK* 18 (1964), 283.

[425] See "Ist Amerika für liturgische Reform reif?" *KNS-Sonderdienst*, no. 96 (December 19, 1963), 14; F. McManus, "Changes in the Liturgy," *Commonweal* 79 (February 14, 1964), 594-98; C. J. McNaspy, "Liturgy: Barrier or Bond?" *America* (February 28, 1964), 278-80; *The Tablet*, May 3, 1964, 61; *KNA-Sonderdienst*, no. 24 (June 3, 1964), 1-2.

Holy See had ratified the decisions of the episcopate.[426] The Roman
decree specified that the chants had to be approved by the territorial
ecclesiastical authority and that two copies of the translated liturgical
books were to be sent to the secretariat of the Consilium.

At the end of April, 250 members of the diocesan liturgical commissions met in Kansas City and for three days studied the implementation
of the Constitution on the Sacred Liturgy. A national liturgical commission was set up; it was decided to establish a Higher Institute of Pastoral
Theology and to prepare a national directory that would bring together
all the norms governing the liturgy. In many dioceses lectures were
delivered and courses in liturgical updating were given. About 150 seminary rectors met in Detroit on June 18-19 to discuss the role of the
liturgy in the training of young clerics; instructions were also given for
minor seminaries.[427] E. D. Howard, Bishop of Portland, among others,
devoted his Lenten pastoral letter to the subject of liturgical reform.

In Canada the liturgical reform pushed the corresponding episcopal
commission into action beginning at the end of December 1963. Later,
at its Ottawa meeting on February 14, 1964, the first directives on translation into the vernacular were made known. At its important meeting on
April 14-16 the commission continued its study of the implementation of
the constitution, and various bishops, among them Cardinal Léger of
Montreal and Bishop Martin of Nicolet, established norms for their dioceses. In French-speaking Canada in particular the norms were greatly
appreciated.[428] At the beginning of September an important liturgical
congress was held at Chicoutimi for the purpose of stirring a deep interest in the reform, especially in regard to the liturgy of the Word.

In Australia the bishops met on March 3-5 with Cardinal Gilroy,
Archbishop of Sidney, as president. Their main work was to decide on
ways of introducing the liturgical reform. The cardinal was not very
optimistic that it would increase the participation of Catholics or help to
the unity of Christians.[429] G. Young, Archbishop of Hobart, did not
share that view; instead, he saw the reform as a positive liberation of the

---

[426] The text of the two decrees of the episcopate and that of the Roman approval were
published in *NCWC News Service*, May 26, 1964. The norms approved for Australia were
broader; see C. Howell, S.J., "The American Mass: Why Some Parts Are in English and
Others Not," *The Tablet*, June 13, 1964, 659-60.

[427] *NCWC News Service*, July 1, 1964.

[428] See W. J. Browne, S.J., "Canadian Renewal: A Report on the Progress of Liturgical Changes in French and English Canada," *America* (May 16, 1964), 675-76.

[429] See *NCWC News Service*, December 27, 1963, January 9-10, 1964, and June 1-6,
1964; *The Tablet*, June 13, 1964, 676.

Latin rites. In June, after receiving approval from Rome, the Australian bishops met to study concrete ways of implementing the reforms; they decided that these should take effect on July 1, depending on the judgment of each bishop. The reforms introduced presupposed a broad use of English in the liturgy.[430] In introducing these novelties, Gilroy expressed to his people his hope that they would facilitate understanding of the celebrations and that the introduction of English would also help non-Catholics to become interested in the teaching of the Catholic Church and to appreciate the beauty and richness of its liturgy.

In New Zealand, O. N. Snedden, auxiliary bishop of Wellington, was chosen to represent the local churches on the commission of ten members, delegated by the English-language episcopate, which was established to work up texts that would be as uniform as possible. The first question this commission faced was the immediate preparation of a text for the mass; later, the Missal, Ritual, and Breviary were revised.

3. The Mediterranean Churches

The program for the plenary meeting of the Italian Episcopal Conference (April 14-16, 1964) was focused on the implementation of the conciliar decisions, first the liturgical reform and second those having to do with the communications media.[431] Cardinal Lercaro, president of the CEI's commission on pastoral care and the liturgy, proposed "timely and feasible" reforms on which the assembly was to deliberate and offer *vota* in writing;[432] he also pointed out the need of gaining a thorough knowledge of the conciliar document. A discussion of specific questions followed, from the suppression of "classes" in liturgical services to the acceptance of Feder's "Little Missal," which Bugnini had translated into Italian.

In Spain the recently created episcopal commission on the Council met for the third time on February 17, 1964, and took up the implementation of the liturgical constitution.[433] On April 15 a plenary meeting of

---

[430] The directives on language went beyond those of the episcopates of England and Wales; see *The Catholic Herald*, June 26, 1964; *The Tablet*, June 27, 1964, 73.

[431] Sportelli, *La Conferenza*; for the conciliar period, see 171-224.

[432] On January 25, 1964, Paul VI signed the Motu Proprio *Sacram Liturgiam,* in which it was said that the national episcopal conferences were to implement the constitution *Sacrosanctum Concilium* (*AAS* 56 [1964], 139-44). See G. Alberigo, "Per una storia di Lercaro," *Il Regno*, November 15, 1976, 444-48.

[433] See E. Vilanova, "La aportación de la teología hispánica al Concilio Vaticano II," in *Zeugnis und Dialog. Die katholische Kirche in der neuzeitlichen Welt und das II. Vatikanische Konzil. Klaus Wittstadt zum 60. Geburtstag*, ed. W. Weiss (Würzburg, 1996), 138-63.

the episcopate was held in Madrid for the purpose of studying liturgical reforms in line with the conciliar constitution. The rules of the Spanish episcopate on the use of the vernacular in the mass and the sacraments were not published until November 12, 1964.[434] The climate was generally favorable to the renewal introduced by the Council, although not in all regions.[435]

4. The Liturgical Reform in Latin America

The situation was not the same in all the countries of this area, nor did the latter all experience the same disturbances when the time came to implement the liturgical reform, a remark that held not only for countries but for bishops as well. Some particularly alert bishops had anticipated the reform. This was the case with Méndez Arceo, Bishop of Cuernavaca (Mexico), a bishop open to the liturgical movement, who, beginning in 1956, had with evangelizing zeal started pastoral and even architectural reforms (the innovations he introduced into the cathedral won him the title "iconoclast bishop"). At the other end of the continent, in Chile, Larraín, Bishop of Talca and president of CELAM and an elitist by training,[436] was very open on the subject of liturgy as presented at the Council.[437] He was undoubtedly afraid that the renewal in a Church "confined sociologically to the neocolonial elites,"[438] would not involve a population largely belonging to the working classes.[439]

The creation of CELAM (1955), however, had become the basis of a shared ecclesial awareness that manifested itself during the second inter-session in the organization of some meetings on the implementation of

[434] *Ecclesia* (Madrid), no. 1219 (November 21, 1964), 7-9.

[435] J. M. Sustaeta, "La reforma litúrgica empieza," *Ecclesia* (Madrid), no. 1178 (February 8, 1964), 19-20.

[436] See M. Salinas, in CEHILA, *Historia general de la Iglesia en América latina* IX (Salamanca, 1994), 506-8. Larraín showed a striking dependence on French theological literature. For an understanding of Larraín, see M. Gallardo Mendoza, *Monseñor Manuel Larraín Errazuriz y el Concilio Ecuménico Vatican II desde la experiencia de la Iglesia chilena* (Valparaiso, 1995).

[437] Volume 2 of Manuel Larraín E., *Escritos completos*, ed. Pedro de la Noi (Santiago, 1977), is devoted to *La Iglesia en su liturgia*.

[438] Salinas, *Historia general*, 9:508.

[439] Workers and peasants, who comprised the great majority of the people of that country, contributed hardly five percent of priestly vocations. The clergy continued to come from the upper or upper-middle class sectors; see *La Iglesia en Chile. Estructuras eclesiásticas*, ed. I. Alonso, R. Poblete, and G. Garrido (Madrid, 1962), 118.

the liturgical reforms desired by the Council.[440] Under Larraín as president of CELAM, nine bishops of nine Latin American countries (only Colombia and Uruguay were not represented) and eight priests who were experts in liturgy met in Lima, April 22-24, 1964, to study the concrete forms of the renewal.[441] At that meeting some concrete decisions were made: (1) The training of professors of liturgy for seminarians, religious, and laity; the formation of mobile teams to help bishops who requested their collaboration; (2) The creation of a group of Latin American and Spanish specialists who would concern themselves with the translation of the liturgical books into Castilian, Portuguese, and even the various dialects.[442]

At that meeting Msgr, Leónidas Proaño remarked that the reform should be introduced in different ways depending on local conditions. It should begin with the translation of the epistles and gospels into Spanish; for the Missal as a whole some provisional translations already in use should be approved while awaiting an official edition of the Missal and the liturgical rituals. Also studied was the problem of translations into Quechuan, which was spoken by several million Indians in the Andean world (Ecuador, Peru, Bolivia).[443]

Another result of that same meeting was the assignment of a number of competent priests to the task of visiting various areas of the continent in order to make known the principles of the liturgical reform, this on the basis of a carefully coordinated operation. In July 1964 CELAM called about fifty theologians and liturgists to a meeting in Porto Alegre, Brazil. Among those giving reports were C. Colombo and Fathers Roguet and Daniélou. During the meeting there were two experimental eucharistic concelebrations according to the norms set down by the

---

[440] "Instructivo sobre la nueva disciplina litúrgica para uso del episcopado latino-americano," prepared by CELAM, in *Christus* (Mexico), 29 (1964), 304-8; see *Ecclesia* (Madrid), no. 1194 (May 30, 1964), 24; *ICI*, June 15, 1964, no. 218, pp. 8-9. Among other episcopal publications see Msgr. G. Kemerer (Posadas, Argentina), "Instrucción y exhortación sobre la Constitución Conciliar de Liturgia" (February 2, 1964), in *Criterio* 36 (1964), 107-9; Msgr. A. M. Aguirre (San Isidro, Argentina), "La Constitución sobre la Sagrada Liturgia" (February 12, 1964), in ibid., 176-77; "Carta del episcopado colombiano al clero," *Kipa-Concile*, May 18, 1964.

[441] See *CivCatt*, August 15, 1964, 400-401.

[442] Larraín, *Escritos*, 391: "El Concilio: las transformaciones en la Iglesia y relación con el mundo" (statements of Msgr. Larraín to the periodical *Incunable* of Salamanca).

[443] See M. Marzal, S.J., "La Liturgia en las zonas indígenas," *Christus* (Mexico) 29 (1964), 403- 11.

Consilium.[444] From that point on, episcopal commissions on the liturgy were established in the various countries, and at varying speeds, or at least the stimulus from Rome was accepted, as was the case in Argentina, Chile,[445] Uruguay,[446] Brazil,[447] and so on.

In Colombia the liturgy was the subject of a plenary meeting of the episcopate.[448] In other countries, such as Bolivia, Venezuela, and Ecuador, no great impetus was given to the reform, except for the activity of Msgr. Proaño, even though the very thing the renewal needed was strong stimuli from the ecclesiastical hierarchy. In Chile, for example, it was thanks to the hierarchy that the vernacular was introduced at the end of May in the liturgy of the Word and in most of the dialogues and prayers in which the participation of the people was

[444] The characteristics of the rite were described in *OssRom*, June 21, 1964, 6; see also the article of A. Baker in *The Tablet*, June 11, 1964, 771-72, and the study by T. Tihom, S.J., "De la concélébration eucharistique," *Nouvelle Revue Théologique* 86 (June 1964), 579-607.

[445] See L. Tolosa, "La reforma litúrgica: espiritu y proyecciones," *Mensaje* 129 (June 1964).

[446] The collective sensitizing of the Uruguayan episcopate in relation to the Council found at least formal expression in the liturgical reform. *Resoluciones del Episcopado Uruguayo*, on some aspects of the reform (vernacular, and so on), signed by Cardinal Barbieri and by Miguel Balaguer, his auxiliary and secretary of the episcopate, were published (April 20-24, 1964). Three further documents were published, two signed by Barbieri and one by Balaguer, all in April 1964, containing invitations to a Semana Arquidiocesana de Pastoral for the purpose of making uniform the regulations adopted in the liturgical reform (oddly enough, the letters made no reference to the Council). The episcopal conference likewise published two documents, signed by Barbieri and Balaguer, under the letterhead of Comisiones de Liturgia y Oficio Catequistico Nacional, which contained appointments to these commissions and made explicit reference to the conciliar Constitution on the Sacred Liturgy. *Vida litúrgica de los Fieles* by Msgr. Nuti, undated (June?), reported the results of a meeting of priests on the liturgy and several times cited the relevant parts of the conciliar document, On August 14 *Carta de los Prelados sobre el uso de la linguga vulgar en la liturgia* appeared; it was signed by all the bishops; Cardinal Barbieri had meanwhile been replaced in the government of the Diocese of Montevideo and for this reason did not sign the letter, which reported the approval by the Consilium of what the bishops had requested.

[447] See Servus Mariae, "Para entender a Igreja no Brasil," 158-79.

[448] The meeting's activities were summarized in three documents: I. *Instrucción pastoral del Episcopado Colombiano sobre la Sagrada Liturgia*; II. *Directivas pastorales del Episcopado Colombiano para la Santa Misa*; and III. *Ordinario de la misa en castellano, aprobado por el Episcopado Colombiano*, all from February 1865. The texts were published by the Permanent Secretariat of the Episcopate in *Conferencias episcopales de Colombia* III: 1962-1984 (Bogotá, 1984), 37-43. In 1965 the Instituto de liturgia pastoral de Medellín would be established as the organ for the theologico-pastoral training of the members of CELAM; see A. Botero Alvarez, "Institutos de liturgia en América latina: formación litúrgica del clero," in *Costituzione liturgica "Sacrosanctum Concilium,"* ed. Congregation for Divine Worship (Rome, 1986), 466-75.

anticipated.[449] In Brazil a national meeting of experts make clear the lines to be followed in the renewal, while at the same time a Higher Institute of Pastoral Liturgy was set up. In Lima the third week on pastoring was held, under the title "The Liturgy as Catechesis of the Church"; the session took its cue from the liturgical constitution. This was a week sponsored by the episcopate, during which about 120 priests studied both the changes involved in the liturgical reform and the spirit of the reform. In bringing the meeting to a close, Archbishop Landázuri of Lima said: "There is no reason why each country should do its own separate work when we can all profit from work done together."[450]

5. The Challenge of a Radical Inculturation

a. The Liturgy in Africa

As Father Chenu remarked,[451] the demands of the African Churches in the area of liturgy were adequately met because of the contribution they themselves made. The problem of a liturgy that would grasp and express the essential values of the African soul required of these churches a bolder and more penetrating investigation than was required of the Western churches with their spontaneous cultural affinity with the cultic expressions of the Latin Church. Nor was this a matter only of some marginal adjustments; it required an effective incarnation of the Christian "mystery" and, in the first place, of the word that conveys this mystery, even while respecting the substance of the Church's sacraments. This difficult undertaking required the exercise, when dealing with the innate resources of the African religious spirit, of a very sensitive effort at discernment based on the relationship between the transcendent mystery of Christ and the natural (or other) religions that spring from the human soul. It was therefore necessary to make these distinctions and establish this relationship with an optimism rooted in the understanding of nature and grace in an incarnational economy.

Memoranda were circulated among the fathers of the Council that made known actual experiences of integrating local ritual customs into the liturgical life of the community; the deviations, sometimes deserving condemnation, found in these customs could not hide the authentic

---

[449] See *The Tablet*, June 6, 1964, 648.

[450] *Ecclesia* (Madrid), no. 1179 (February 15, 1964), 29.

[451] M.-D. Chenu, "L'Afrique au Concile," *Parole et mission* 20 (January 15, 1963), 11-18, reprinted in his *L'Evangile dans le temps* (Paris, 1964), 647-53.

values they contained, not only in expression but also in religious content. It was only necessary to take into account the legitimate social desacralization being rapidly imported by industrial civilization, especially in the cities, in order not to make more or less romantic concessions to an archaic folklore that was in fact daily becoming ever more a thing of the past.

Not only individual rites capable of being christianized but also the characteristic traits of the African person can and must contribute to the Christians of that world riches which western culture, at least up to now, has not sufficiently put to good use: the sense human beings have of their place in the cosmic mechanism, their understanding of feasts as an expression of gifts freely given and a transcending of the monotony of daily life, the power of the word to Africans, the concrete aspect of praxis, and other typical characteristics. The well-known and important works of H. Gravrand adopted the perspective of a catechesis of initiation that invalidates the wretched African transcriptions of Western "instruction."[452]

In a pastoral letter of January 1964, Archbishop Ego of Abidjan (Ivory Coast), spoke of the liturgical reform as an enrichment of religious worship and exhorted the faithful to accept it generously and not be surprised by a certain "Africanization" of some ceremonies. He wrote:

> God asks us to sing his praises, to honor him and pray to him in harmony with our African soul. Until now we have done this on the basis of a Latin tradition, and the missionaries who proclaimed the good news to us were unable to convey it in any other way. Our gratitude to them is boundless, but an adult no longer speaks as he did when a child. The fact that we want to remain African in our relations with God does not signify ingratitude toward our fathers in the faith, since the Church itself asks us to combine the riches of our traditions with the praises that rise to our heavenly Father from all the countries of the world. I am sure that Europeans who will take part in our ceremonies will understand this and rejoice in them.[453]

It was a reason for great hope on the Ivory Coast that the superiors of the monasteries of Africa met at the Benedictine monastery of Bouaké, in the presence of the local bishop, Duirat, in order to make their contribution to the advancement of an authentically African liturgy. At the same time, the superiors took advantage of the meeting to discuss the

---

[452] H. Gravrand, *Visage africain de l'Eglise* (Paris, 1961).

[453] Text cited in *CivCatt*, no. 2740 (August 15, 1964), 397.

directions being taken by African monasticism, the conditions of recruitment, the intellectual and religious formation of postulants, the Divine
Office, and the economic problems of foundations in mission countries.
The final statement of the meeting showed a noteworthy knowledge of
and respect for African sensibilities; it expressed the members' "interest
in the spiritual attitudes seeking expression" and their determination
"once they had been initiated into the psychology of African prayer, to
help by their example as Christians in investigating more deeply its spiritual content."[454]

The episcopal conferences everywhere acted on the guidelines
received from the Roman Consilium. Thus in mid-May the bishops of
Ethiopia and Eritrea met in Addis Ababa to study liturgical reform.
From June 7 to 10, the regional conference of the bishops of Equatorial
Africa and Cameroon met at Yaoundé (Cameroon) to discuss the same
subject: a liturgical adaptation aimed at responding, in the translation of
texts and in chants and rites, to the requirements of the sacred on the
basis of the sensibilities of the African soul. At the end of the conference, basic guidelines were formulated in an interesting document.[455]

In the Congo the bishops of Katanga met in Stanleyville. The standing commission of the national episcopate drew up a list of points with
a view to the liturgical reform and the use of the vernacular. The
approval of the Holy See was accompanied by a pastoral letter to the
faithful and an instruction to priests. A national liturgical commission
was then established; Van Caulewaert (Inongo) was president, and the
body comprised representatives of all the ecclesiastical provinces. From
July 20 to 25 there were several days of theological reflection, devoted
mainly to study of the Bible and the liturgy in light of the guidelines set
down by Vatican II. Meanwhile, the priests of all the eight dioceses of
the Stanleyville district had met in May to study ways of carrying out
the reform and translating the liturgical texts into the languages of the
country.

In Tanganyka, too, an episcopal commission was formed with five
members (three of them Africans); it was assisted by a national commission of six priests (four of them African) in the work of ensuring a full
use of local usages and customs. In South Africa the episcopate decided

---

[454] *ICI*, July 1, 1964, no. 219, pp. 11-12.

[455] See *Kipa-Concile*, July 7, 1964, and *ICI*, July 1, 1964, no. 219, p. 10. These
themes were later studied in greater depth; there is a good explanation in J.-M. Ela,
"Symbolique africaine et mystère chrétien," *Les quatre fleuves* 10 (1979), 91-109.

to introduce the vernaculars in three stages. In this connection it is worth recalling the role played by Archbishop Hurley in the renewal.[456]

The enthusiasm of the African bishops in carrying out this reform was responsible for their full mobilization during the second intersession, but it did not achieve the result for which they hoped. The so-called "theodicy of domination" was one of the reasons why the critique of colonialism did not touch the system of truths associated with the Christian God. The result was that the upcoming African generations judged the dialogue which the Church tried to establish with the African world after Vatican II to lack credibility. The promising reform immediately ran into difficulties, in response to which Msgr. C. Guirma then complained:

> The Roman rite which we follow was not chosen by us and is deeply marked by western culture. Since the Council has recognized the dignity and personality of the local Churches, would it not be better for these Churches to be able to develop their own rite along lines more in keeping with the genius and culture of their peoples, instead of having a reformed rite that leaves them dissatisfied?[457]

This need of ritual pluralism made clear the difficulty of establishing a single rite, which could not be in harmony with the diversified African sensibilities. The Catholic Church of Egypt is a good example of such a diversity of ceremonies, since the Latin, Maronite, Coptic, Armenian, Greek, Syriac, and Chaldean rites, all of them Catholic, live side by side in the same territory.

b. India in Search of a New Liturgical Model

By means of meetings and preparatory studies the episcopate of India, with the dynamic Patrick D'Souza as its secretary, prepared for liturgical inculturation during the second intersession.[458] This was not a new problem for India; it had already been one of the concerns of seventeenth-century missionaries such as De Nobili and others.[459] After the approval of the constitution *Sacrosanctum Concilium*, however, the problem once

---

[456] See Ph. Denis, "Archbishop Hurley's Contribution to the Second Vatican Council," in *Experience*.

[457] *La Calao* 35, no. 3 (1976), 33. On this entire problem see R. Luneau, "Prendre la parole, être écoutés: une tâche difficile pour les Eglises d'Afrique," in P. Ladrière and R. Luneau, *Le retour des certitudes* (Paris, 1987), 103-21. For a comprehensive view of the problems of liturgical renewal in Africa, see M. Lamberigts, "Der Beitrag Afrikas während der Konzilsdebatte über die Liturgie," in Weiss, *Zeugnis und Dialog*, 186-207.

[458] See *ICI*, October 15, 1964, no. 226, pp. 17-18.

[459] See P. Puthanangady, "Inculturation of the Liturgy in India since Vatican II," in *Liturgy: A Creative Decision,* Concilium 16 (New York, 1983), 71-77.

again took center stage. The result was the start of a process that took into account the guidelines set down by Vatican II, the theological principles of inculturation, the cultural reality of the country, and the cultural situation in which Christian communities had not only to achieve the replacement of some rites by others, but also to distinguish among cultural elements within the act of worship, a very difficult task indeed. Careful preparation was made with all this in mind during the second intersession, although concrete results would be seen only in 1966.[460]

On the island of Ceylon the Church was passing through a difficult time, and its mission was being conditioned by rapid changes in political and social life. What the Church was being faced with during the Council, a time when signs of hope were not lacking, was the birth of a new world. As part of the journey to liturgical renewal, a commission of priests would establish who would collaborate with the Protestants on a translation of the Bible into Singalese. A Protestant minister of Ceylon, Archdeacon Harold de Soyza, had been one of the three Anglican observers during the first two periods of the Council, and on his return had expressed his fine impressions in lectures to Catholics. The attacks on the Catholic Church elicited, on the whole, clear sympathy for it in Protestant circles.

c. The Necessary Renewal of the Churches of the Far East

Two bishops of these Churches had been chosen as members of the Consilium for implementing the liturgical constitution: Willem van Bekkum (Ruteng, Indonesia) and Lorenzo Satoshi Nagae (Urawa, Japan).[461] Theirs was an important presence in view of the anticipated ritual inculturation. Episcopal meetings with steps to be taken in matters liturgical as their agenda were held in Japan and Korea, on Formosa, in Vietnam, and in other countries. The decisions taken were like those of other countries, especially as regards the vernacular. In Japan the episcopate decided to do away with the genuflection to bishops and the kissing of their rings (except when prescribed by the rubrics) and to replace the genuflection before the Blessed Sacrament with a profound bow, in accordance with the custom of the country.[462] During 1964 a study was made on Taiwan of the possibility of absorbing some Chinese feasts and

---

[460] *Report of the General Meeting of the Catholic Bishops' Conference of India*, held October 13-20, 1966, pp. 11-17; S. Rajamanickam, *The First Oriental Scholar* (Madras, 1967), 54ff.

[461] See "Die Liturgiereform nach der Konstitution *De Sacra Liturgia*," *HK* 18 (1964), 348-57.

[462] *Kipa-Concile*, July 3, 1964.

usages into the liturgical cycle, while in Hong Kong a group of priests and lay persons worked to prepare liturgical hymns based on traditional Chinese music.[463]

In January 1964 the bishops of Vietnam studied the possibility of adapting the instruction of Propaganda Fide on traditional rites in honor of heroes and ancestors to conditions in their country. On Formosa, too, a study was made of the possibility of introducing some Chinese feasts and popular customs into the Church's liturgical cycle.[464] In Indonesia the liturgical movement had laid a solid foundation, due above all, perhaps, to the reputation of van Bekkum, Bishop of Flores, who had attended the International Congress of Pastoral Liturgy in Assisi in 1956. In December 1963 the Indonesian episcopate was one of the first to publish a decree on the implementation of the liturgical constitution; the decree took effect on February 12, 1964. During Holy Week, the National Catechetical Center in Jakarta had ample freedom to try using the Indonesian language in the chants, readings, and prayers. In Java two missals in the native language were quickly printed, one for priests and one for the faithful. These were the fruit of a lengthy and persevering effort at adaptation of the liturgy and the introduction of local customs and modes of expression.

E. ECUMENICAL RELATIONS

1. A Privileged Contact with Orthodoxy

The Oriental fathers at the Council, with Patriarch Maximos IV as leader, were inspired by a great ecumenical longing. The group of Oriental bishops, who made up a real ritual mosaic, had seemed divided during the debates of the second period. The tensions between the Melkites (occasionally supported by the Maronites) and the Armenians and Chaldeans (supported by conservatives elements in Roman circles) were to be manifested openly at the very beginning of the third period.[465] Yet, despite these different views, there was in the attitude of the Orientals a common denominator in the form of attentiveness to a tradition

---

[463] See A. S. Lazzarotto, "I vescovi cinesi al Concilio," in *Experience*.

[464] *CivCatt*, no. 2740 (August 15, 1964), 396-97.

[465] See Edelby and Dick, *Vatican II. Les Eglises Orientales catholiques*, 76-77, 291-92, and 299- 300. See also J. Ancagne, "Oecuménisme et Orient chrétien," *Etudes* 322 (1965), 707-23.

often forgotten in Latin circles[466] and of an ecumenical sensibility that was fostered by their closeness to Orthodoxy.

This sensibility was strengthened during the second intersession when, in January 1964, during the pilgrimage of Paul VI, there was a fraternal meeting between Athenagoras and Maximos IV. On that occasion Athenagoras turned to Maximos and said: "You represent all of us. Thank you!" These were the most beautiful words the Melkite patriarch could have heard from the representative of Orthodoxy; in a sense, they also summed up the role of Maximos IV at the Council. After that pilgrimage the Melkite patriarch made a journey to Egypt (January 29 to April 13) in order to gain firsthand knowledge of the needs of the Melkite community that had Msgr. Zoghby as patriarchal vicar. On that occasion, Maximos, with the frankness typical of him, told President Nasser of the problems troubling the Melkite community. From May 30 to June 5 Maximos went to Turkey to visit Patriarch Athenagoras and make contact with the few Greek Melkite faithful living there (in Antioch, Alexandretta, Constantinople). During the meeting between Athenagoras and Maximos in Constantinople on June 2, the dialogue was marked by a friendly tone.[467]

As a result of the pope's visit, Hakim, Greek Catholic Archbishop of Galilee, circulated a note at the end of January that was published in the Italian weekly *Oggi* and became the object of attacks in the Jewish press. In the note Hakim showed himself concerned by the situation of Christians in Palestine, especially in Israel but also in Jordan, due to the growing phenomenon of Christian Palestinian emigration. With a clearly pastoral attitude, he had thus reasserted his position of solidarity with the poor, Christians first of all, but Muslims as well.[468]

In the area of ecumenism Elias Zoghby, Greek Melkite patriarchal vicar for Egypt, published important guidelines in the May-August issue of the bulletin of the Greek Orthodox patriarchate. Here he explained, in ten points, the conditions required, in light of the Council, for advancing

---

[466] The most representative spokesman for this position was Maximos IV, Melkite Patriarch of Antioch. See *L'Eglise melkite en Concile* (Beirut, 1967); E. Inglessis, *Maximos IV. L'Orient conteste l'Occident* (Paris, 1969); *Protagonisti*, 171-83.

[467] See Inglessis, *Maximos IV*, 72-73. When Maximos went to the Council, he was conscious of representing, along with his Church, the Christian East. He said as much in his "Mandement patriarcal à l'occasion de son départ pour le Concile oecuménique," *Proche-Orient chrétien* (October-December 1962), 348-51.

[468] See *ICI*, February 15, 1964, no. 210, pp. 11-12.

toward the union of the Latin Church and the Orthodox Churches.[469] The
Uniate Oriental Churches were in process of forming a profound ecumenical relationship with the delegates of other Churches, especially
within Orthodoxy.[470] The activities of I. Diadé, Maronite Archbishop of
Beirut; of N. Edelby, Melkite archbishop, titular of Edessa, and adviser
of Maximos IV; of Bidawin, Chaldean Archbishop of Amadiyah (Iraq);
of Scandar, Coptic Archbishop of Assiut (Egypt); and of Bayan, Armenian Bishop of Alexandria, to name only some of the protagonists,
showed their concern, which the Council had renewed, for the unity of
Christians, and also their desire for a better understanding of the liturgical rites (Clement Ignatius Mansourati, Titular Archbishop of Apamea in
Syria, had been appointed to the recently created Consilium).

In view of reaching this ultimate goal, there was great pastoral interest in Cardinal Lercaro's journey to the East[471] and more particularly to
Beirut, where he delivered an important lecture on the ecumenical value
of the liturgy.[472] His sensitivity and his office as president of the Consilium undoubtedly gave great weight to what he said.[473]

2. The World Council of Churches

It is well known how fruitful the presence of observers at the Council
sessions was and how great an interest the World Council of Churches
showed in Vatican II. Even during the second intersession the WCC did
not cease to voice a healthy disquiet over the development of the ecumenical dimension in the conciliar event. One need only skim through
the archive of the WCC to appreciate the tireless activity of Dr. Visser't
Hooft, who sent in texts, impressions, and so on. It is worthwhile to single out from among these his letters and report on the second period, his
general impression of future prospects, and the notes on the role of the
WCC in relation to Catholicism, which he sent on January 9, 1964, to
Anglican Bishop J. W. Sadiq of Naipur (India) and his sending of a

[469] Ibid., no. 224 (September 15, 1964) 16-17.
[470] See *HK* 18 (1964), 85-86, 392-93, 530-31.
[471] See G. Alberigo, "L'evento conciliare," in A. Alberigo, ed., *Giacomo Lercaro. Vescovo della chiesa di Dio (1891-1976)* (Genoa, 1991), 129-31.
[472] On April 11, 1964, at the University of St. Joseph in Beirut, before such persons as Armenian Patriarch Batanian and Nabaa, who was on the secretariat of the Council, Ler-caro spoke on "Ecumenism and Liturgy" (in *Per la forza*, 85-102).
[473] At the Greek College in Rome, on October 11, 1964, Cardinal Lercaro delivered another important lecture entitled "La signification du Décret *De oecumensimo* pour le dialogue avec les Eglises Orientales non catholiques," which was published in *Irénikon* 37, no. 4 (1964), 467-86.

schema on the Church in the modern world (dated April 2, 1964) to R. Niebuhr. Even during the summer the WCC engaged in intense activity that was concerned concretely with the encyclical *Ecclesiam Suam* of Paul VI.[474]

The interest shown in the meeting of Paul VI with Patriarch Athenagoras was another indication of how the WCC was following conciliar doings. Vischer's interpretation of the meeting, that it was "an attempt to draw attention away from the difficulties the Council was having in its work,"[475] was representative of the atmosphere of disappointment at the WCC after the end of the second period and as a result of Moscow's reactions.

We may not forget Cardinal Bea's correspondence with the WCC, which included the sending of a memorandum on the schema on ecumenism (February 3, 1964). Also important was the "Note préalable aux entretiens de Milan" (April 15, 1964), which was in preparation for the Milan meeting on Catholic ecclesiology and ecumenical dialogue; in it were raised the question of the central place of Rome in the ecumenical undertaking and the question of Rome and bilateral relations with the other Churches.[476] The *Conclusions des entretiens de Milan* proposed the establishment of three mixed working groups: on ways of collaborating, on "Faith and Order," and on practical problems. It was decided that the start of agreements would wait upon conciliar approval of the Decree on Ecumenism.

Lukas Vischer was the author of "Bases of Cooperation" (July 1964), a document on relations with Catholics that was presented to the executive council of the WCC. The themes that recurred in all this documentation and were to be studied were many, beginning with the key ideas of unity, communion, collegiality, the presbyterate, the Eucharist, and so on. In summary, it can be said that during the second intersession the WCC continued along the line it had adopted during the first, with no less interest and no less uneasiness. On the whole this revealed, in addition to an undeniable effervescence in doctrine, spirituality, and feeling, a "complex situation, but one full of hope."

---

[474] See Velati, *Una dificile transizione*, 450-53.
[475] Ibid., 433-39.
[476] Ibid., 439-45.

3. An Example of Ecumenical Collaboration in Africa

The African bishops who attended a council directed in a special way to the unity of Christ's followers were made even more appreciative of the subject by the presence of non-Catholic Christians in Africa. This fact was expressed rather clearly by Blomjous, Archbishop of Mwanza (Tanganyika), secretary of the English-speaking African episcopate and a member of the conciliar commission on the lay apostolate as well as of the mixed commission charged with preparing schema XVII. He published a very timely article, "Ecumenism and Conversions," in the January-February 1964 issue of *The Ecumenist* (Toronto),[477] in which he strongly urged thinking of the Church's "mission" not as a conquest of souls or territories but as a humble witness and service offered to society; this attitude would win trust and would prevent discouragement when the fruits of one's labors are not tangible. Collaboration with other Christians, the article said, was not a betrayal of the oneness of the Catholic Church but rather helped to a realistic understanding of the Church's function in an inevitably pluralistic Christianity. Friendship and help given to other Christians — something especially effective in the African world — was a contribution to the ecumenical movement that was to be blessed by Vatican II.

Blomjous understood ecumenism to be a quest of collaboration. The Catholic bishops were committed to this collaboration, chiefly in matters of the temporal order; but above and beyond these there were causes having to do directly with religion in which collaboration was possible and even imperative. He gave two typically African examples. First, there was the duty of exerting a common Christian influence on the Islamic cultures, not in order to convert Muslims to faith in Christ, but in order to help Islam open itself up and to undo the bonds that held it tied to national governments. Second, it would be necessary to undertake a joint Christian confrontation with the modern industrial world, in order to help people gain a deeper understanding of the meaning of our earthly life: work, diligence, unification, and socialization.

---

[477] The second part of this article was published in *ICI*, April 1, 1964, no. 213, pp. 3-4.

CONCLUSION

THE NEW SHAPE OF THE COUNCIL

GIUSEPPE ALBERIGO

On September 29, Vatican II began for the third time. This is not a paradoxical statement if we bear in mind that the Council's first began with Pope John XXIII's surprising announcement on January 25, 1959, and that a second beginning was solemnly made on October 11, 1962. Now, with the succession of Paul VI to John XXIII, and given the importance of the pope in the Catholic Church as natural presider over every council, the Council found itself beginning once again.

This did not mean, however, that the three years of preparation, the months of meetings in the first period in the fall of 1962, and, finally, the first intersession had been reduced to nothing. First as Cardinal and then as Pope, Montini had been explicit about his unequivocal determination to continue the Council. In the long history of the ecumenical councils interruptions had often had much more serious consequences. Vatican I, for example, had never been resumed; Trent had experienced interruptions of several years that had called into question whether the council should be continued. The suspension caused by the death of Pope John, then, could have had fatal consequences for the very survival of Vatican II, but the timely reconvocation for September 29, 1963, had given proof of its vitality.

Although the imposing mass of material produced by the complex machinery that had been charged with the preparation of Vatican II had been criticized, challenged, and rejected, it continued to burden the Council's work. Those who had produced that material continued to defend it and the image of the Council that had dominated it: one that would be short and sweet, approving the major teachings of the recent pontifical magisterium without prolonged discussion and, even better, without risking divisions. Almost all of the bishops had come to Rome in 1962 without a clear sense of direction and therefore inclined to go along with the scenario presented to them. During the first period, however, with the help of the lucid but unobtrusive direction of Pope John, these bishops had begun to develop a common consciousness focused on *aggiornamento* and a pastoral outlook. This was for them a new experience of active awareness and involvement, a wearying but also exciting experience.

Finally, the many theologians who, especially during the last period of Pacelli's pontificate, had felt marginalized and, often, suspect — from Chenu to K. Rahner, from Congar to de Lubac — had gradually realized that the Council brought a new climate of free confrontation and pluralism, not marked by prejudice toward "non-Romans." As had happened at major councils of the past, the actual experience of the conciliar assembly gave rise to a dynamic clash of ideas that was much more attractive than the dull debates of academia. It was much more interesting and gratifying to develop formulations for conciliar discussions than to produce books.

By contrast, the final week of work in December 1962 had been dominated by a fear that the directions which had surfaced in the debates first on the liturgical renewal and then on the so-called two sources of revelation might be ignored during the long months of the intersession. In addition, there was the shadow of an imminent change of pontificate, which many feared. Nor were these empty concerns, for, although this was not well known at the time because of lack of news, the 1962-63 intersession in fact was dominated by demanding and bitter clashes within the various commissions. Nevertheless, by the end of these months it had been possible to make a successful "second preparation," as described in the previous volume of this series. The Council seemed, once and for all, to have found its own way, but the lengthy journey still to come would show that even the apparently most solid gains could be subject to discussion once again.

It is therefore not inappropriate to think of the start of the second period of the Council at the end of September 1963 as a new beginning. Its key novel factors were the presence of a new Bishop of Rome and the effort made during the intersession to exorcize once and for all the limits imposed by the preparation. At the same time, however, there were impressive elements of continuity, not only because Paul VI wanted the slippage at the beginning of the second period to be limited as much as possible and because the great majority (over 80 percent) of the members of the assembly were the same as the year before, but also and above all because the impulse given by John, who had "invented" the Council, was still very alive and at work, all the more since it had now become part of the consciousness of the majority of the bishops. This was the clearest sign that the "institutional loneliness" that had isolated John XXIII had been completely transcended; "the pastoral" and "*aggiornamento*" were now the very platform of the Council. Finally, the key problems that the Council was facing were still those that had already come to light: the conception and structure of the Church, relations between Roman Catholics and the other Christian traditions, and the place of the faith and the Church in contemporary societies.

I. CONTINUITY AMID NOVELTY

How did the elements of novelty and continuity balance out in the second period? The play of influences on the pope could not but change in the transition from Roncalli to Montini. While Bea and Suenens saw their advice carrying less weight and Ottaviani was no longer the chief "policeman" of orthodoxy, Cardinals Döpfner and Ruffini and the Jesuit Bertrams gained in standing, along with Carlo Colombo, the Pope's trusted theologian. In the new parallelogram of forces, Secretary of State A. Cicognani, as president of the Coordinating Commission, acquired greater influence.

The novelty at the top of the conciliar structure was the creation, by the wish of Pope Paul, of a college of moderators; it implied the final marginalizing of the superfluous Council of Presidents, which had given a poor account of itself in 1962. The moderators gave the impression of swinging from one extreme to another: being a screen between Pope and the assembly and directing a council that often had given the impression of lacking a head. What guarantee was there that the crucial relationship between the express will of the assembly and the indispensable work of the commissions in composing the texts would be worked out in an above-board way that would not betray that will? As had already happened centuries before at Trent, the shaky unity of the four moderators, who differed both in tendency and in temperament, sometimes limited their effectiveness. The far-sighted effort to develop homogeneity and internal coherence in the group was frustrated by Felici's intransigent claims. Nor did the attitude of the Pope encourage the solidarity and incisive action of the moderators, for after creating them he was reticent about defining their responsibilities ("like prompters in their box"). It is, however, difficult to deny that they had a positive influence on the work of the Council and also on the maturation of the most important directions taken by the assembly.

The Secretariat for Extraordinary Affairs had been replaced by the Coordinating Commission (CC), which had been put in charge of the

1962-1963 intersession and which survived the reopening of the assembly and the creation of the college of moderators. In fact, Cicognani even made it the supreme source of direction for the Council.

The importance of the assembly's commissions grew gradually as the Council continued its own work and gave voice to tendencies that differed from those that had dominated the formulation of the drafts which it was now necessary to revise or redo. But the commissions suffered from the fact that they had been elected in the very first days of the Council, when the assembly was still shapeless, and because their presidents were the same people who were in charge of the corresponding curial congregations, men who by formation and for the sake of institutional solidarity supported the preparatory drafts. These various factors gave rise to a recurrent intractableness in the commissions and especially in the Doctrinal Commission, whose president was Cardinal Ottaviani, a man who balked at giving up an "autarchic" conception of his role. In this respect we must not underestimate the influence still exerted by the earlier preparatory commissions, which, with the same persons presiding, had worked with complete autonomy. At the end of the second period Father Congar could still say that "this council still bears the weight of John XXIII's original sin, that of thinking of the commissions as corresponding to the Roman congregations. Not only did he make the presidents of the congregations the presidents also of the commissions (first the preparatory, then the conciliar), but he conceived of the commissions on the model of the congregations, that is, as permanent committees dealing each with one area of business."[1] Thus the preparatory Theological Commission had claimed an exclusive doctrinal authority, analogous to that of the supreme congregation of the Holy Office.

Once the Council was in session, the system should have changed substantially. Instead, even the commissions elected as organs of the assembly continued to think of themselves and to act as relatively independent even of the assembly itself, the CC, and the moderators. This caused tensions that were not always fruitful and losses of time that were even more serious for a machinery that by its nature was already slow to act. As a result, gaps in coordination and direction naturally opened up that were quickly and effectively filled, *faute de mieux*, by the General Secretariat under the authoritative leadership of Msgr. Pericle Felici. The rejection of new elections of commission members, which had been desired in view of the new session of work, hindered the attunement of

---

[1] *JCongar*, December 3, 1963.

the commissions to the assembly. On the other hand, the supplementary elections of November 28, 1963, did have a modest effect, but only beginning with the intersession 1963-64.

At the vote in November 1962, which had "dared" to give minority status to one of the doctrinal drafts presented by the Theological Commission, many hundreds of bishops had discovered an unsuspected convergence of views, a convergence that during the second period was able to express itself on some critical points in the conception of the Church and thus became "the majority." In this way Vatican II acquired the structured physiognomy of an assembly, despite the pulverized condition of a great part of the Catholic episcopate and despite the bishops being so many and so varied. It must not be forgotten, moreover, that a body made up at different times of between 1500 and 2100 bishops (in addition to scores and scores of their theologians) was not only internally differentiated culturally, linguistically, and geographically, as well as by age and experience, but that it also inevitably had within it divisions and gradations that, initially or later, tended to show themselves, all the more so since it was only very recently that some bishops had accepted the prospects of renewal, an acceptance due in some degree to the attraction of the group that was winning. As a result, fissures and intolerances would soon come appear.

If during the second period the assembly had moved beyond the breaking-in phase, Paul VI was still experiencing the difficult novitiate of a new pope and one elected during a council. As a result, in many respects this period seemed still a part of "John's council." Vatican II was feeling the effects of impulses toward an active involvement of the bishops in the leadership of the Church, something the aged Pope John had fostered in the letter *Mirabilis ille,* which he had addressed to the entire episcopate on Epiphany 1963. But beginning with the 1963-64 intersession both pope and assembly were now "experts." Both were active agents in the conciliar dynamic but both were also obliged to take very much into account the Roman Curia, a kind of "guest of stone." There loomed, then, possibilities of clashes, whether when Paul VI intervened or when the assembly entered upon unforeseen or "dangerous" paths (such as the regulation of marriage, the creation of a permanent synod alongside the pope, or the possible revision of priestly celibacy). In December 1963 "Paul's council" began.

John XXIII had refrained from laying out a specific "plan" for the Council; he was utterly convinced that the Council had to enjoy the greatest possible freedom and see the light for itself. He placed his trust in an experience of the Spirit, confident that the "new Pentecost" would be able to forge its own way. Some saw in this attitude an unforgivable failure that left Vatican II at the mercy of circumstances; others, on the contrary, emphasized the unusual respect shown by Pope John to the universal episcopate, which was being asked to voice its views in a fully responsible way. Paul VI, for his part, had an education and instincts that were less pragmatic and tended to be "programmatic." This had already become clear in October 1962, when Cardinal Montini had sent the Secretary of State a letter with a plan that suggested some lines of direction for the course of the Council. When elected pope, the former Archbishop of Milan certainly did not drop this approach; indeed, it can be presumed that he felt he had been given the responsibility to supply Vatican II with the program his predecessor had failed to give it.

On the one hand, it might be thought that the conciliar assembly, now that the initial phase of its work was over, had matured and needed more explicit guidance than in the past; on the other, stronger initiatives on the Pope's part could risk rousing feelings of competition or even clashes. The third and fourth periods would show whether and how the Council's autonomy and the Pope's leadership responsibility would be reconciled.

2. CRUCIAL TRANSITIONS

In October and November 1963, Vatican II lived through some especially intense moments because of choices the assembly had to make and the tensions these choices generated. The wearying experience of the first session; the difficulty, even during the recently concluded intersession, of effectively dealing with and winnowing out the schemes still on the Council's agenda; and, at the same time, the original impulse to gear Vatican II toward the updating of the Church's image — all these things led many to propose the drastic step of including all the schemas in the schema on the Church (except for the liturgical schema, which was now almost ready). The result would have been a "maxi-schema" in which all major subjects, from the place of the Bible and tradition in the Christian economy to ecumenism, from devotion to the Virgin Mary to the problem of religious freedom, could be treated by reference to the ecclesiological nucleus. All the many other problems inventoried during the preparatory period would be referred to the revised Code of Canon Law, which had been planned by John XXIII and was thought to be imminent.

Another proposal was that the subjects on the agenda would have to be drastically reduced in number if the work was to be finished in the third period, set to begin in the fall of 1964. The Döpfner Plan, inspired (suggested? welcomed?) by Paul VI as early as the summer of 1963 and then worked out by the Cardinal of Munich, was probably meant to address a widespread concern to bring the Council to a close. In addition, the plan would have hastened the moment when the new Pope could act without the hindrances caused by the presence of the entire episcopal college in Rome.

Both of these plans, which were never submitted to the assembly, suffered shipwreck. They lacked sufficient agreement, due in part to the convergent resistance, on the one hand, of defenders of the preparatory work, who enjoyed the powerful support of Secretary of State Cicognani, and, on the other, of those who were convinced that the rhythm proper to the conciliar assembly should be respected, with allowance, if necessary, for a pause in the work but not for a shortening of it.

A. THE CHURCH

The Council's work resumed with the debate on the *De ecclesia* schema and with the votes on the liturgical schema. On both subjects there was an immediate manifestation of reluctance in sectors of the assembly that were hostile to the involvement of the bishops in the leadership of the universal Church (episcopal collegiality) and worried about the abandonment of Latin in the liturgy. Opposition to the renewal in ecclesiology found expression chiefly in the passive resistance of the competent and powerful Doctrinal Commission. Only when the entire assembly had been called upon to express clear doctrinal directions and had done so effectively, was it possible to overcome this resistance. The votes on October 30, after being held hostage for two whole weeks in a veiled struggle among the leaders of the Council and then being bitterly criticized by the conciliar minority, marked an undeniable and liberating turning point, similar in this respect to the vote in November 1962 on the two sources of revelation and to John XXIII's intervention that had reestablished the will of the majority.

This guidance in the direction of recognizing the sacramental value of episcopal consecration and the co-responsibility of each member of the college for the universal Church not only met the desire to restore balance to the image of the Church that had emerged from Vatican I, but also, when combined with the placing of the entire conception of the Church within the horizon of the Christian mystery, it opened perspectives of great relevance to *aggiornamento* and to the Council's pastoral character. According to Congar, this vote "was a definitive 'parting of the way.'"[2]

Even if with some uncertainty, the Council realized that an ecclesial renewal limited to the sphere of doctrine, however crucial and indispensable this is, would have remained without impact. Even the finest image of the Church would have been futile if it were not given an adequate and consistent institutional dimension. This insight reflected an elementary understanding of the order required by complex organizations, but it had an even greater importance for the Roman Catholic Church, since this Church, more than all the other Christian Churches, had over time gradually acquired a complex and carefully organized structure. It was not possible to ignore the danger that such a structure might now tend to live a life of its own, ignoring the norms and tendencies dictated by the general idea of the *status ecclesiae*.

These new ideas finally alarmed those circles that had banked on a council geared to conservative positions and drove them to get the Pope to share their anxieties, so that they might thus regain what they were losing in the conciliar assembly. Thus the second period and the second intersession were marked by increasing pressure on Paul VI to oppose or at least rein in the trends of the majority. Curial circles and the part of the episcopate that agreed with them seemed to enter, perhaps unconsciously, upon the very dangerous but well-known path of a clash between pope and council. The report on the Council's work that Cardinal Lercaro, in his position as senior moderator, presented to the Pope and directing bodies of the Council in November 1963 clearly grasped this danger and tried to neutralize it.[3] Yet numerous sources document an attempt to "demonize" the majority, which was described as hostile to the Pope and untrustworthy on matters of doctrine.

B. The Liturgy

After its first week of work Vatican II began an endless series of wearying votes on the liturgical schema. This was another attempt to

---

[2] Ibid.

[3] Text in *AS* II/1, 101-5, and in *Per la forza dello Spirito: Discorsi conciliari del card. Giacomo Lercaro* (Bologna, 1984), 265-75.

dampen the tendencies of the majority, using a device quite similar to parliamentary filibustering, namely, to impose two exhausting series of votes on the assembly as the price for approval of the liturgical reform, which the opponents had managed to slow down, but not stop, by means of annoying procedures in the Commission for the Liturgy. Thus, with the complacent agreement of the General Secretariat, the bishops were engaged throughout almost the entire month of October in a good eighty votes on emendations of chapters II-VII (not counting another six on each of the chapters in its entirety); to these were added another twenty in November, all of them, however, with a largely positive result.

C. BISHOPS

The schema on the bishops, which was directly related to the development of the document on the Church, occupied the assembly during the first half of November. Two subjects were especially important, in addition to those already discussed in the schema on the Church. For one thing, there were repeated proposals for the creation of a collegial body, comparable to the permanent synod of the Eastern Churches, which would regularly assist the pope in decisions of greater moment for the universal Church. Especially since the end of the World War II in 1945 and the resultant decolonization, the presence of Catholicism around the world had increased without interruption. Nor was this simply a quantitative increase; it also involved a structured contact with diverse cultures and social situations. There had begun an inexorable de-Europeanization and de-Westernization of the Roman Church, which was entering on a an entirely new state of "catholicity." In light of all this, the concentration in the person of the pope and in the curial bodies of decisions having to do with *causae maiores*, a term which had been given an increasingly comprehensive meaning, seemed excessive, intolerably burdensome, and prejudicial to the identity of the particular Churches. A second omission in the schema on the bishops was of a new set of regulations regarding the jurisdiction over the choice of new bishops, a choice that in the modern age had been increasingly centralized in Rome, with a corresponding marginalization of the communities concerned.

On both of these points hopes had been disappointed by a series of causes ranging from resistance by supporters of the status quo to the lack of maturity in the proposals for innovation and even to the reluctance of Paul VI to cede to the Council such specific areas of decision. In fact, although any thought of a possible conflict between assembly and Pope was utterly alien to the mind of the fathers generally (it would, in any case, have been catastrophic for the success of Vatican II), reports (or should we rather say "denunciations"?) were made to the Pope about the supposed heterodoxy of the conciliar majority.

Such a supposition, even were it only implicit, was calculated to ignite a conflict. The result was an atmosphere of uneasiness and concern among the bishops. A desire to avoid any hint of the sort explains why they did not take more decisive positions on some of these matters; this was an act of responsibility, not of timidity. The ambiguous "restoration" of some faculties to the bishops by the Holy See, at the end of the period, was a poor and almost derisive consolation.

D. UNION

The final subject tackled before the adjournment of the session was the elaboration of a text on the Catholic attitude to the other Christian confessions and to the ecumenical process that had been going on for decades. The subject was troublesome because of the entrenched Roman expectation of a "return" of "heretics" and "schismatics" and because of its habitual distrust of any emphasis on ecumenism. In addition, there were three different preparatory texts on the subject, developed respectively by Ottaviani's Theological Commission, Cicognani's Commission for the Oriental Churches, and Bea's Secretariat for Christian Unity; the three texts provoked jealousies and clashes over competence. Despite all this, the Council set out on the path of a profound renewal of the Catholic attitude, moving toward a pluralist vision of Christianity and the possibilities of overcoming divisions on the basis of "what unites," in the perspective of a convergence of all "so that they may be one."

This was the direction in which John XXIII had pointed the Council and which had then found expression in the invitation to the other Churches to send observers. The presence of the latter had become considerably more representative (despite the fact that observers from Constantinople remained only a hope); even more importantly, and unexpectedly, this presence became a factor in the maturation of the bishops' awareness and even a source of significant contributions in the development of the conciliar texts. The Tuesday meetings of the observers with the Secretariat for Christian Unity were faithfully kept up again in the second period, to the satisfaction of both sides. It is a satisfaction that was documented in the reports the observers sent back to the several Churches and to the World Council of Churches in Geneva, in their private correspondence, and in the daily journals that some of them kept. In addition, outside the weekly meetings there were exchanges through personal contacts, lectures, and the countless occasions provided by living together in the same city for many weeks.

The approach taken by the secretariat to the schema on ecumenism had also drawn attention because of the two problems raised by the need to revise Catholic attitudes toward religious freedom and toward the Jewish people. The schema marked the beginning of a fruitful journey, wearisome and full of surprises. A greater number of bishops than ever would become acquainted with hitherto unknown, or feared, perspectives that could prove rich in evangelical significance; other bishops, however, especially the Spaniards and Italians, would find reasons for uneasiness or even alarm.

III. The Council Begins to End

At the end of the second period Vatican II formally completed, with some difficulty, a lengthy gestation that had at times threatened to be barren: it definitively approved two texts, the constitution *Sacrosanctum Concilium* on the liturgical renewal and the decree *Inter Mirifica* on the communications media. While both subjects were of universal interest, the Council had devoted dramatically different amounts of time and attention to them. To the liturgy the Council had devoted generous attention and time, both in the assembly and in the commission, from the preparation through the first period to the solemn session on December 4, 1963. On the contrary, the development of the schema on the communications media had always been of marginal interest, so much so that at the end the lively dissatisfaction with a text that was at best inadequate had not been given sufficient room to voice itself.

The Constitution on the Sacred Liturgy, planned as a framework decree, issued in a renewal inspired by the idea of the active participation of the community of the faithful in the liturgical celebrations, described as the high point of the Church's life. Yet other important doctrinal perspectives, as, for example, a eucharistic ecclesiology, would be left in the background. Profiting by the development and experience of the liturgical movement, the Council had been able to traverse ground already sown, although difficult to plow because an omnivorous "rubricism" had controlled practice. This rubricism clung fast to the Latin language as inalienable and turned liturgical occasions into incomprehensible actions performed in an authoritarian fashion by the clergy with only some isolated moments of involvement of the ordinary faithful. As a result in their spirituality and piety Catholics had carved out for themselves alternative devotional spaces.

During the development of *Sacrosanctum Concilium* the bishops had often been torn between fear and boldness, as is attested by the references in the notes of the text that Paul VI had demanded and that were intended to emphasize a continuity that was in fact often rather weak. It may be added that first the Commission for the Liturgy and then the assembly had been able to shape the liturgical reform "chorally"; that is, without a leadership comparable to that which Bea, for example, was to exercise in the area of ecumenical problems. Not only, then, had the fact of starting the work with a study of the liturgical schema ensured a "soft" beginning, but in addition the entire work on the schema had helped the assembly to develop a balanced way of working that would hold up on more stormy occasions.

The impact of the constitution *Sacrosanctum Concilium* on the Church around the world was direct and rapid. It became immediately clear that the liturgical renewal was eagerly and widely awaited. The cautions included in the conciliar text itself were unable to restrain many ecclesial communities from taking the conciliar decree and putting it into practice without delay. Beyond all expectation, the innovations that could immediately be enjoyed, especially the transition to the vernaculars and the facing of the celebrant toward the people, went into effect almost everywhere, rekindling enthusiasm and also arousing some alarm. Popular enthusiasm ignored the delays set by the establishment of a special international body for implementing the liturgical reform and by the waiting period *(vacatio legis)* before the Constitution was to take effect in mid-February.

On the other hand, the reception of the scope and ecclesiological options of *Sacrosanctum Concilium* into the subsequent work of the Council was difficult, slow, and in the end unsatisfactory. The isolation from each other of the various thematic groups that Vatican II had inherited from the preparatory period did not allow for a quick osmosis among the various subjects. It is surprising to see how, apart from exceptional cases, the texts approved by the Council remained independent of one another, with hardly any reception in one area of conciliar work of conclusions gradually ratified elsewhere. Relevant ecclesiological implications of the liturgical constitution — centrality of the Eucharist in relation to institutions; importance of the local Church and territorial episcopal conferences; relationship of communion among the Churches and its ecumenical repercussions — had received greater thought in the liturgical movement than in the debate on the Church before Vatican II.[4]

The insight that had led to putting the development of a proper attitude to the media on the agenda of Vatican II was interesting inasmuch as it was based on the enormous impact of the media on contemporary societies. Yet it cannot be denied that the end result was a lost opportunity. The decree on the communications media was mainly held captive to the antiquated rhetoric of the "Catholic press." Until the very end there was hope that because of its evident immaturity the decree would not receive final approval. While the Central European bishops and theologians had made a decisive contribution to *Sacrosanctum Concilium*, the North American bishops and theologians unfortunately were unable to provide *Inter Mirifica* with a content matching the importance of the subject.

Despite the speeding up of the work as a result of the revision of the regulations and the direction given by the moderators, the Council was unable to avoid putting off the schema on the lay apostolate. The important place given to the people of God in the schema on the Church completely altered the controlling perspective of the schema on the laity, which had been mainly a captive of the "theology of the laity." In addition, the schema on the Church also planned a chapter on the laity. Less convincing was the silence on the poverty of the Church, even though the group inspired by Gauthier at the Belgian College had carried on its work vigorously and had sensitized very broad sectors of the assembly on the subject. Did the top-down management of the Council not permit informal "infiltrations" from below? Did the consensus of a large part of the many third-world episcopates (Latin American and African) not carry enough weight when not combined with Central European leadership?

It was with a view to these first solemn promulgations that two problems were settled: the formal nature of the conciliar decrees and the modalities of papal assent to the assembly's conclusions and of their canonical promulgation. *Sacrosanctum Concilium* is described as a "constitution," while *Inter Mirifica* is a "decree." The vocabulary of past councils had repeatedly shifted; at Trent the word *decree* was used

---

[4] See G. Lercaro at Beirut in April 1964, in *Per la forza*, 85-102.

consistently, while at Vatican I both *Dei Filius* and *Pastor aeternus* were labeled "dogmatic constitutions." The decision of the Theological Commission preparatory to Vatican II was to call its own drafts "dogmatic constitutions," while those of the other commissions were to be called (disciplinary) "decrees," a return to the late medieval distinction between "doctrine" and "discipline," even though this distinction had been disregarded in John XXIII's description of the new council as "pastoral."

It is quite clear that in the case of the two documents passed in 1963 the decision to call the text on the Church a "constitution" and the text on the media a "decree" did not renew that old distinction, since *Sacrosanctum Concilium* was not a "doctrinal" text and had not been the work of the Doctrinal Commission, the conciliar arm of the Holy Office. In subsequent periods approval would be given to "dogmatic constitutions" *(Lumen gentium* and *Dei verbum)*, a "pastoral constitution" *(Gaudium et spes)*, several "decrees," and some "declarations," all of which emphasized the move beyond the "doctrine/discipline" alternatives.

The happy formula of approval/promulgation that Paul VI chose on the basis of suggestions offered by the assembly had for its pivotal term the "agreement" *(una cum)* of the pope with the conclusions voted by the conciliar assembly. This marked the high point of convergence between Pope Montini and the conciliar majority. With this formulation the relationship between pope and council moved beyond the lengthy medieval and modern stage during which it had increasingly turned into a relationship of disjunction (the pope promulgated on his own authority, "with the approval of the sacred council," *sacro approbante concilio*), if not one of separation and disagreement (the pope reformulated the conclusions of the council after it had dispersed). It had been symptomatic that many doctrinal currents in the past had asserted the "superiority" of the council over the pope and, at the other extreme, that the primacy of the bishop of Rome had been seen as "superior" to a council and that after Vatican I that primacy was thought to render councils superfluous.

The satisfaction of finally reaching the first promulgations, after almost five years (three of preparation and fourteen months since the beginning of the work), did not hide, at least from the better informed, the extent to which the development of texts in the commissions and in the hall did not exhaust all the impulses and forces at work in the Council and perhaps not even its deepest dimension. Not only had the crucial document on the Church still to be concluded, but the treatment of

"Church-world" relations was still only beginning and for the moment was a matter more of expectations than of firm direction. On the other hand, the completion of the journey of the liturgical constitution opened up in an explicit way the problem of the Church's "reception" of the conciliar decrees. This was a process in which the approved texts, precisely because of their essentially pastoral nature, would need a vitality deriving from the "conciliar spirit," that is, from the set of urgencies, sensibilities, and proposals generated by the meeting of the universal episcopate and its common searching of the gospel. The centralized "implementation" (focused on norms and sanctions) that had followed the Council of Trent belonged to a type of council and a cultural stage now completely of the past.

IV. The Echo of Major "External" Events

The event of major international importance during the weeks of the second period was the assassination of J. F. Kennedy, president of the United States, on November 22, 1963, which was as intensely felt at Vatican II as elsewhere. But the stormy transition of Algeria in expectation of the final departure of the last French troops (completed on June 14, 1964) and the deterioration of the situation in Vietnam due to the increasing involvement of the United States, despite the growing resistance of public opinion in that country, also affected the atmosphere of the Council, which was not carrying on its work in an artificial isolation. Moreover, after the deaths of John XXIII and Kennedy, the political decline of Khrushchev in the USSR caused many to fear the end of the more relaxed international climate of the past year. In this respect it must be remembered how much the avoidance of a new inflexibility was due to the ongoing celebration of Vatican II and to the renewed boost given by Paul VI to the *Ostpolitik* started by his predecessor and being implemented with exceptional sensitivity by A. Casaroli and his younger collaborators who represented a new generation in comparison with the Secretariat of State under Tardini and Cicognani.

The growing political opposition of the Arab world to a possible conciliar study of the Jewish problem found a strong echo among the bishops from those countries who were backed by the Vatican Secretariat of State in their resistance to the document. Meanwhile, in another area, the Council saw the vast transformations going on in an entire continent. In fact, from Africa, represented initially by bishops who were in the majority "missionaries," the bishops now coming were increasingly "natives," men who were completely African. The echo of the problems created by decolonization and incipient independence thus reached Rome in the most authentic and direct way.

Add to this the fact that the Council was now proceeding in a situation of greater openness to the news media, which had moved beyond their marginalization of the preceding year. There was a new climate that not only facilitated news that was fuller and better reflective of public opinion, but also allowed calmer exchanges between journalists and members of the Council, even with regard to major international events.

As a result of all this, the original Eurocentric outlook, so deep-rooted in many, began to crack. A slow and difficult process began for which Catholicism was still largely unprepared, especially after the predominantly philo-occidental and philo-Atlantic orientation of Pacelli's long pontificate.

V. PAUL VI, PILGRIM TO JERUSALEM

The emotional announcement of the Pope's pilgrimage to Jerusalem surprised and elated the Council. It is difficult to deny that the announcement was the "child and fruit" of Vatican II, for it would be impossible to imagine such a decision were it not for the turnabout made by John XXIII and the meeting of the Council. It is certain, however, that at the time of his election Paul VI had thought of the journey and then planned it as a brilliant monarchical and primatial action. This is confirmed by the decision to entrust the preparation for it to a political body, the Secretariat of State, rather than to a conciliar body, such as the Secretariat for Christian Unity, which would have been a natural choice in view of the inevitable immense ecumenical implications of the venture. Looked at in retrospect, the pilgrimage seems to have been first and foremost a personal and autonomous decision of Paul VI, made independently of contacts with the Council going on in Rome. Was it an expression of an unconscious need of the Pope to perform at least one meaningful action all by himself, outside the pervasive shadow of the Council? Was he confident he could promote a detente between Arabs and Jews, thereby bringing serenity to the atmosphere that had just been created by the planned declaration on the Jews?

In any case, if it is true that the pilgrimage was made in the atmosphere of the rethinking of the entire Church that had been begun by Vatican II, then the meeting with Athenagoras, Patriarch of Constantinople, was the heart of the entire event, so that the original spiritual inspiration was transformed into an act of communion of the highest value, with uncontrollable ecumenical repercussions. From this point of view, its impact on the Council was exceptional and absorbed all the other aspects of the journey. It can be said, without partiality, that the journey achieved many different and fortunate goals insofar as it took on a primarily ecumenical connotation and led to the strengthening of Constantinople's position as a major pole ("second Rome") of the Christian world. Its consequences for Vatican II as well would be seen at the beginning of the third period in the fall of 1964, when, after being awaited in vain in 1962 and 1963, observers from that patriarchate at last arrived at the Council.

The very description of the Council as ecumenical was undeniably reinforced by the meeting between Paul VI and Athenagoras. The understandable uneasiness that the meeting caused in the World Council of Churches in Geneva, concerned that this might foreshadow a Roman-Orthodox domination of the ecumenical movement, was quickly dispelled by Cardinal Bea at a meeting with Visser't Hooft in Milan in mid-April of that same year, 1964.

VI. First Skirmishes of the Postconciliar Period

While plans for a quick and shortened conclusion of the Council had an uncertain fate and would in the end fail, the creation of the Commission (Consilium) for the Implementation of the Liturgical Constitution, which the Council wanted and on which Paul VI made a timely decision, represented a real anticipation of the postconciliar period. Vatican I had not been followed by any real period of reception so that the model which all now had in mind was the way in which the decrees of the Council of Trent had been implemented. At that time the Congregation of the Council had been "invented," to which the pope entrusted responsibility for seeing to the disciplinary aspect of an implementation, especially by means of a strict and effective centralization; supervision of the implementation of the doctrinal decrees was given to the Holy Inquisition.

After the approval of the liturgical constitution, there could be no putting off the appointment of a body that would orient its reception, conditioned as it was, for example, by the translation of the liturgical books into the vernaculars. The conciliar constitution had indeed given broad responsibility to individual bishops and episcopal conferences, but it seemed undeniable that both needed a body to refer to at the Holy See. It seemed impossible, however, to propose that this body be the Congregation of Rites, a part of the Roman Curia that had systematically resisted the development of *Sacrosanctum Concilium*. This explains the satisfaction with which Paul VI's courageous decision was received, all the more so since the Consilium was to be headed by two reputable liturgists, Cardinal Lercaro, Archbishop of Bologna, and Father Bugnini, who had both given repeated proofs of their commitment to the renewal. In addition, the Consilium was made up of a very large majority of bishops with care of souls on all continents, as well as of experts who had served in the liturgical movement.

In the spring of 1964 the Consilium seemed to be the "model" for the bodies that were to coordinate postconciliar activities. Perhaps the satisfaction and optimism that greeted it prevented people from perceiving the invisible but extensive deterrent effect that the decision had on the Roman Curia, which felt its own monopoly to be threatened. Even though the Council was moving toward its end and disappearance, the existence of bodies, such as the Consilium for implementing the liturgical reform, threatened to make the Council itself permanent in a different form and to interfere structurally with the Roman congregations. The Consilium was seen as the prototype of a shadow alternative to the congregations of the Roman Curia. Reactions were not slow to follow.

It is certain that the interest aroused by the approval of the liturgical constitution caused almost all the episcopal conferences of the various continents to undertake immediate initiatives. Almost everywhere translations of the liturgical books proceeded without any further decision being needed, confirming the unanimous expectations already triggered, in some cases, by the liturgical movement and roused, in others, by the Council itself.

VII. TOWARD THE THIRD PERIOD

The second period ended with some uncertainty about the further duration of the Council: would it end in 1964 or have a further period of work? It has already been shown how there were different and alternative perspectives. During the intersession the development of all the already existing drafts continued or was resumed. On the major subjects — the Church, ecumenism, religious freedom, the Jews, revelation — the firm opposition between the different orientations continued. For many other schemas — the bishops, the laity, the missions, religious, seminaries, the sacraments, priests — the respective commissions resisted the idea of concentrating the entire material into a few statements; they reasserted their "right," acquired, they thought, from the beginning of the preparatory period, to receive some place in the attention and decisions of the Council. As a result, the months, especially of the intersession, were filled with matters that were to a large extent repetitive or peripheral. The concentration of the assembly on a few major subjects was forgotten.

A case apart was Schema XVII, on the condition of the Church in societies, for this had no precedents in the preparatory period. Following a path through Europe that was odd but perhaps also significant, from Malines to Zurich and finally, in 1965, to Ariccia (Rome), there was a succession of versions that were very different because they had different authors and were composed in different languages. It was clear to everyone, however, that this project required a fourth period, since it certainly would not be ready for the third. Supporters and opponents of the schema desired or opposed the idea of a fourth period of work.

On the eve of the third period an encyclical letter was published that was especially important due to the diligence of Pope Montini in preparing it and because its very title, *Ecclesiam Suam*, showed it to cover the same ground as the principal subject of Vatican II. Here again the question arose of the delicate balance between pope and council. Some months before Paul VI had taken the initiative of submitting a volley of suggested changes to the Doctrinal Commission, which was engaged in reworking the chapter on the structure of the Church. His request, though troublesome in that it came when the commission had practically finished its work, was nevertheless handled by both sides with mutual respect and great freedom and was brought to a satisfactory conclusion, except in the eyes of the conciliar minority, which had been relying in vain on the Pope to reverse the situation.

VIII. The Journey of the Council

During the twelve months of the second period and the second intersession Vatican II had taken another step, beyond the one during which it had had to gain knowledge, make contacts, and find a direction. The Council's complex machinery set in motion all of its many bodies. The majority of the commissions emerged from their earlier torpor beneath which lay the illusion that the Council might simply surrender by rapid approval of the preparatory texts. The many beehives of experts went to work in full strength. Theologians, canonists, and historians acquired a new sense of responsibility as the passage was made from the clash of abstract principles that still dominated the first period to the assimilation by the fathers of the various options. The proximate preparation of final formulations on which the assembly would have to vote had a positive effect.

The clash of principles had brought into the open the differences that existed even within the conciliar majority, and, above all, the harsh stage in which many developments that had too long remained in a restricted academic setting. The pastoral nature of the Council also included the need to move beyond theoretical confrontations and to take account of the impact of teachings on the reality of faith and on the contexts in which it is lived out. All the more so since all this was coming under the attentive and interested observation of the Church as the *universitas fidelium* and of public opinion. Thus the Council took on meaning as a "sign of the times," as M.-D. Chenu had foretold; the conciliar event as such, even prior to the approval of documents by the assembly, acquired importance as a "source for theology" *(locus theologicus).*

An assessment of the second period also includes negative and positive aspects,[5] ranging from irritating wastes of time to uncertainties in the direction given by the moderators, from the improved pace of the debates to diligence in approving some first conclusions and to the development of the episcopal conferences and their coordination. The atmosphere had become more realistic and optimistic than at the end of the first period: Was the Council to give only a spur to renewal rather than the renewal itself?[6] The leadership of the Central Europeans had left room for a greater involvement of the United States bishops, while the pilgrimage to Jerusalem, interpreted as a return to the sources, gave an unexpected impulse to a more general *ressourcement* by theology and the Church.[7] Another thing that seemed very promising was the movement toward decentralization that had inspired the liturgical constitution and the decree on the bishops.[8]

---

[5] R. Laurentin, *L'Enjeu du Concile. Bilan de la deuxième session* (Paris, 1964).

[6] The question was posed by J. Ratzinger, *Theological Highlights of Vatican II* (New York, 1965).

[7] See Y. Congar, *Le Concile au jour le jour. Deuxième session* (Paris, 1964).

[8] This point is stressed by E. Schillebeeckx for this period in his *Die Signatur des Zweiten Vatikanums.Rückblick nach drei Sitzungsperioden* (Vienna, 1965).

After first contacts had been made during the summer of 1963, two preparatory meetings of the periodical *Concilium* took place in Rome in October and November, followed by other meetings in Trier, Hilversum, and Frankfurt in the spring and summer of 1964, with a view to public presentation of the undertaking in Rome during the third period (taking into account the uncertainty about a fourth period of work). European theologians, encouraged by the fruitful conciliar experience that was continued and advanced during the second period, were laying the foundations for continuing their collaboration after the celebration of Vatican II. The isolation and distrust that Congar and Rahner, De Lubac and Metz, Schillebeeckx and Chenu had suffered during the 1950s seemed light years away.

What, then, is the significance of this second period within the setting of Vatican II as a whole? The main characteristic that emerges and distinguishes this second period is the continuity of the Council. Despite the death of John XXIII and the change of pontificate, the resumption of Vatican II in September 1963 showed how strong the Council was and how it was able to surmount so traumatic an interruption. It is right to stress the importance of Paul VI's determination to continue the Council, but it also necessary to acknowledge that in these circumstances it was the general council that asserted its authority even over the Roman pontiff. The expectations aroused and the attention claimed around the world by the assembly of the Catholic episcopate in Rome left no alternative to its quick and faithful continuation. Even so authoritative and prestigious a pope as Montini, "politically" speaking, could only accept the Council and bring it to a happy end.

Something similar had happened before and during the Council of Trent, when the pressure of public opinion and then circumstances as well had "forced" the popes — Paul III, Julius III, and finally Pius IV — to convoke a council and, then after repeated suspensions, to reconvoke it. After the suspension of Vatican in 1870, however, nothing of that kind happened. In 1963, just four centuries after the conclusion of Trent, the punctual celebration of the second period of Vatican II showed that the idea of councils had an undeniable, even if unsuspected, vitality. This was a symptom of the renewed fortunes of conciliar awareness in contemporary Christianity. At its "third" beginning, Vatican II displayed a vitality capable of rising above the uneasiness caused the bishops by their repeated absence from their dioceses, the exasperation caused by the slow pace of the work, and the inertia with which the great majority of bishops were experiencing the Council itself.

From the doctrinal standpoint, the choices made in reworking the schema on the Church played a decisive part in ensuring that Vatican II would achieve its goal of completing and balancing the ecclesiology ratified by *Pastor aeternus* of Vatican I. These choices also went beyond a primarily institutional outlook by introducing premises that might inspire a clearly evangelical conception of the Church. The risk that the image of the Catholic Church might remain captive to the monopolistic "Roman" perspective set down in the encyclical *Mystici Corporis* ("Christ's Church, which is the holy, catholic, apostolic, *Roman* Church"), a risk present in the preparatory schema on the Church ("the *Roman* Church alone is rightly called the Catholic Church"), had been avoided.[9] This paved the way for a credible text on Catholic ecumenism and, to no less a degree, a non-hostile approach to modernity and therefore to the condition of the Church and Christians in contemporary societies. It is not rash to say that without the revolution in the way of conceiving the Church, Vatican II would not have been able to move beyond the obsolete, polemical, and Eurocentric approach to Church-state relations, and the question of a "friendly"presence in societies would likely have remained beyond the purview of the Council.

And yet we know that in the next period, 1964, on the very eve of the final approval of the Constitution *Lumen Gentium* on the Church, there was a new crisis, caused by Paul VI's demand for the addition of a *Nota explicativa praevia* to that constitution. At that moment it seemed that the votes on October 30, 1963, had been in vain or insufficient. That, however, would not be a convincing inference, because the maturation of both Council and Pope was in continual movement, and a historical reconstruction cannot prescind from this fact. So, too, it is not possible to neglect the shift in the strategy of the minority, which would focus less and less on the dialectics of the assembly and instead would increase pressures on the person of the Pope, even though this meant running the paradoxical risk of showing the weakness of an excessively personalized conception of the papal prerogatives.

Despite uncertainties and limitations, the second period and the second intersession marked a development of Vatican II and of the Catholic consciousness that would have been unimaginable only a few years earlier. At the beginning of the fall of 1964 the Council had run more than half of its course; in fact, five and a half years had passed since the

---

[9] See *Constitutionis dogmaticae Lumen gentium syopsis historica*, ed. G. Alberigo and F. Magistretti (Bologna, 1975), 38, lines 121-23, and 363, lines 112-13.

announcement in 1959. The idea of a "short" Council and the fears this had aroused were gone; the image of Vatican II as an opportunity for renewal had been reinforced, and yet there was also the impression that the results might not be entirely satisfactory. It was not by accident that people began to look with interest to the postconciliar period. The prospects of giving Catholicism a new, evangelical face were less persuasive than a year before. The Council itself was to be a stage on a journey.

INDEX OF NAMES

INDEX OF SUBJECTS